NICHOLAS & HELENA ROERICH

NICHOLAS & HELENA ROERICH

The Spiritual Journey *of*
Two Great Artists *and* Peacemakers

Ruth Abrams Drayer

Quest Books
Theosophical Publishing House

Wheaton, Illinois ♦ Chennai (Madras), India

First Quest edition, 2005

Quest Books
Theosophical Publishing House
PO Box 270
Wheaton, IL 60189-0270

www.questbooks.net

Photograph on page 11 courtesy of David Hopper. Other art images and photographs courtesy of the Nicholas Roerich Museum.
Cover images: Nicholas Roerich, *Pilgrim of the Radiant City*, 1933. Tempera on canvas, 61 x 96.5 cm. Nicholas Roerich Museum, New York. Photograph of Nicholas Roerich by E. O. Hoppe.

Cover design, book design, and typesetting by Kirsten Hansen Pott

Library of Congress Cataloging-in-Publication Data
Drayer, Ruth Abrams.
[Wayfarers]
Nicholas and Helena Roerich: the spiritual journey of two great artists and peacemakers / Ruth Abrams Drayer.—1st Quest Books ed.
        p. cm.
Previously published as: Wayfarers, 2004.
Includes bibliographical references and index.
ISBN-13: 978-0-8356-0843-5
ISBN-10: 0-8356-0843-3
1. Rerikh, Nikolai Konstantinovich, 1874–1947.   2. Rerikh, E. I. (Elena Ivanovna), 1879–1955.
3. Painters—Russia (Federation)—Biography.   4. Artist couples—Russia (Federation)—
Biography.   5. Philosophers—Russia (Federation)—Biography.   I. Title.

ND699.R42D73 2005
759.7—dc22
[B]   2005047542

5   4   3   2   *   15   16   17   18   19   20

Printed in the United States of America

Dedicated to Helena Ivanovna Roerich, Urusvati, the Light of the Star of the Morning, who foresaw the "Era of the Woman" as a time requiring great courage, cooperation, and compassion.

And to my friend and daughter Laurie Ann Brown, who is working to exemplify this era and who loves me.

CONTENTS

COLOR PLATES

FOREWORD

In 1961, after returning from the first trip into cosmic space, the Soviet cosmonaut Yuri Gagarin was asked to describe what our planet looked like from space. When he replied that it reminded him of a Nicholas Roerich painting, Roerich was a name familiar to only a smattering of people around the world. Few Russians recognized it because of the Soviet authorities' strict ban against Roerich, enforced by the KGB. Few Americans recognized it because former vice president Henry A. Wallace, at first a Roerich supporter, had denied him reentry into the United States in the mid-1930s. But for those who did recognize the painter's name, Gagarin's description was an eloquent statement, for Roerich's art portrayed a world of multidimensional beauty and lyric color.

How could a painter of such breadth and scope be so little recognized? Who was Nicholas Roerich? Why was it that Americans knew of the spiritual work of such Russian greats as Kandinsky and Chagall, but not Roerich? These questions plagued Ruth Abrams Drayer after she encountered his glorious artwork at the Roerich Museum in New York in 1982, beginning a chain of events that led her to move to India to work with the painter's son Svetoslav Roerich and to interview and correspond with an international assortment of people. She spent countless hours digging through crumbling scrapbooks and microfilm in many libraries and reading through old correspondence and files stored in the Library of Congress, the British secret files, and reports from various departments of the American government released through the Freedom of Information Act (although most lines were inked out to protect the informants).

Drayer's fourteen-year quest and hard work has resulted in the fascinating story of two truly great leaders of the twentieth century. Here is a rare look into the lives of two modern initiates—spiritually advanced souls who lit up the human world with sparks of divine color and imparted a fiery wisdom to all they met. Russian-born Nicholas Konstantinovich Roerich (1874–1947) was an internationally acclaimed artist, author, explorer, archaeologist, humanitarian, and peacemaker. His wife, Helena Ivanovna (1879–1955), was an inspired and influential writer and teacher. Partners in all things, they shared the belief that "knowledge and beauty are the real cornerstones of evolution, the gates to a world community." The Roerichs taught that a synthesis of knowledge from all fields of human endeavor was needed to form a fully developed being.

Nicholas Roerich wrote nearly thirty books and created over seven thousand paintings and theater designs, depicting scenes from ancient Slavic myths to the Himalayan Mountains to inspirational themes from the world's religions. People who see his art for the first time are often speechless at the inspirational use of color and the spiritual power it evokes—especially his later work, completed during and after their four-year Central Asian expedition. Roerich's paintings portray spiritual development, culture and its role in human evolution, and possibilities for peace in a troubled world. A broader and more metaphysical understanding is added to the paintings once the viewer penetrates Helena's deeply spiritual writings.

In 1923 the Roerichs founded the Master School of United Arts in New York to teach all the arts in one place, and the following year they started an international art center, Corona Mundi. They believed that "beauty is the force that can bring nations together.... Art and knowledge are the best international language.... They will unify all humanity." To reduce crime and illness—both mental and physical—Roerich promoted the benefits of hanging art in factories, hospitals, prisons, and city streets.

A daring explorer and archaeologist, Nicholas Roerich investigated remote and dangerous regions of China, Mongolia, and the Gobi Desert, where few Westerners had ventured before. In addition to seeking ancient manuscripts hidden in subterranean crypts and caves, their Asian explorations had deeper, hidden purposes. Following their Master's direction to establish a Buddhist spiritual country in Asia, the Roerichs were searching for the sacred site of Shambhala and for signs of the return of Maitreya (an Eastern name for the World Teacher, or Christ), whom they saw as a symbol of the future—the messenger for all humanity of the New World to come. They later established the Urusvati Himalayan Research Institute to study the discoveries made during their travels.

The Roerichs were Theosophists, studying the ageless wisdom of the East and West in depth and working inwardly with great spiritual Masters, sometimes called the "Hierarchy of Light." Roerich wrote, "We forged the tapestry of our spiritual armor with the same golden threads that weave throughout all the great religious principles." In the early 1920s they cofounded what became the Agni Yoga Society (*agni*, fire; *yoga*, union with God) to publish and promote the teaching of what they called "living ethics" and the wisdom they had received from the Masters.

While Helena preferred to stay quietly away from the spotlight, writing and doing her spiritual work, Nicholas went out into the public. In 1929 he was nominated for the Nobel Peace Prize for his work in creating the Roerich Peace Pact, signed by President Franklin Roosevelt and twenty-two other world leaders, to protect the art treasures of the world. Roerich was a friend and advisor to heads of state, scientists, artists, writers, and poets, and his work won the praise of Albert Einstein, Leo

Tolstoy, George Bernard Shaw, Jawaharlal Nehru, Rabindranath Tagore, and others.

Nicholas and Helena Roerich were spiritual pioneers, many years ahead of their time in promoting equality for women and brotherhood among races and nations. And like many pioneers, they saw their work attacked and sabotaged. Despite attacks and setbacks, the couple maintained a heroic serenity and dedication to their higher purpose and embodied the noblest of human qualities. Their greatest contributions to human evolution may never be known, for they are part of the sacred and mysterious work of all spiritually advanced people serving humanity.

Yet, nearly a century later, many of their key ideas have found a place in the human soul: the equality of the feminine and masculine principles, the wisdom of the heart, and striving for the common good and brotherhood. The eternal truths the Roerichs demonstrated on earth will echo through time, awakening humanity to beauty and unity: "Beneath the sign of beauty we walk joyfully," Nicholas wrote. "With beauty we conquer. Through beauty we pray. In beauty we are united."

Since 1961, despite all of the political upheaval in Russia and the present official Church condemnation of Roerich and other "new religious movements . . . incompatible with Christianity," Russians have "found" Roerich. In America, the book *Nicholas Roerich The Life and Art of a Russian Master* by Jacqueline Decter has done much to spread his fame, as have the Roerich Web site, www.roerich.org, and various articles, and a video available through the Theosophical Publishing House at www.theosophical.org.

However, of all the books and articles that have been written, Ruth Drayer's is the first to be written from a spiritual perspective, interweaving the heart and soul of the Roerichs' life journey. It also is the first work in English to introduce the Roerichs' plan to form a country where all Tibetan Buddhists could practice their beliefs in safety. Because Drayer's original research comes from an American perspective, it brings to light many unknown facts regarding the Roerichs' connection with America. This book is a valuable resource and contribution to the world knowledge of the Roerichs and the living flame of the ageless wisdom they worked so diligently to ignite around the world.

Corinne McLaughlin
The Center for Visionary Leadership
San Rafael, California

Acknowledgments

One fall day in 1982, Christie Mercer Platt, a friend since my Santa Fe days, met me in New York and introduced me to the Nicholas Roerich Museum. I was a professional numerologist, interested in art, and certainly had no plans to go to India or to write. But that day Roerich's glorious colors and images talked to me, and I left the museum curious to know more of this mystical painter.

Within days of returning home from New York, I was waiting for my friend Sandi Browne and there, on the very top shelf of her bookcase, was a book titled *Shambhala*. I stood on her sofa, pulled it down and opened it, and saw that it had been dedicated to Nicholas and Elena Roerich. From that day on, I was led, prodded, and propelled to continue researching them, and the rest is history. Over the next several years, I moved to Bangalore, India, returned to the United States, and wrote books. When people talk about my commitment to this endeavor, it always amuses me because it was truly something I could not have avoided doing.

What has been really incredible are the large number of interesting, kind, helpful people I have met and the many amazing experiences that have truly expanded and enriched my life. To have lived this closely with the Roerich family for all these years is something to be deeply thankful for, and I feel very blessed and humbled by the opportunity.

After fourteen years of work there are many people to thank, beginning with the two friends mentioned above and Sandra D'Emilio, former curator at the Museum of Fine Arts, Santa Fe. If Sandra had said, "Roerich? Never heard of him," there may not have been a book at all. Instead, she told me of his influence on the Santa Fe painters and showed me how to find all of the relevant files. The next thanks go to Daniel Entin, director of the Roerich Museum, who answered my endless questions, supported and encouraged me, and shared his knowledge, love, and consistency all these years. Thanks to all of the people who are associated in my mind with the Roerich Museum, officially or unofficially: Aida Tulskaya, Gvido Trepsa, Tamara Kachanov, Carl W. Ruppert, and most recently Vladimir Rosov, whose Russian book *Nicholas Roerich: The Messenger of Zvenigorod* (first volume) gave new meaning to mine.

Thanks also to Aditi Vasishtha for being my sister in Bangalore; Philip Holliday for a million telephone conversations; Russell Ian Cargill, Devon, England, for sending me copies of the British secret files and personal correspondence between George Roerich and his friends Robert Hornimann and Valentina Dutko, Madame Roerich's trusted translator; Robert C. Williams for magnanimously loaning me his Roerich research; and J. Samuel Walker for supplying me with his notes and articles. My friend the artist Robin Young "happened" to be teaching summers in Monhegan, Maine, where she was able to interview Eric Hudson's two elderly daughters, who recalled the summer the Roerichs came to Monhegan. David Hopper of supplying the photograph of the Tibetian temple in St. Petersburg.

To Tiska Blankenship, former director/curator, Jonson Gallery of the University Art Museum, Albuquerque, and David Witt, archivist, the Harwood Foundation, Taos, New Mexico, for access to priceless old diaries and boxes. Valentina P. Knyazeva, St. Petersburg, Russia, and Gunta Rudzite, Riga, Latvia, for their helpful letters and memories. Joyce

Lentz, for translating *Talashkino* from the French; Annie Cahn, Claude Benarroche, and Ives Chaumette for their help in Paris.

To Bonita Budd, for full access to her grandmother's library on Spiritualism, and Esther Roberts for loaning me Alice Bailey's *Autobiography*. My friend Pamela Smith for introducing me to her amazing mother, Mary Bailey. Bob Miner, Andy Mendoza, and Robert Buaas for their computer expertise and generous hearts. The unsung heroes in the lives of all researchers, the reference librarians, specifically at New Mexico State University and the Thomas Branigan Memorial Library: Nancy Callahan, Mark Pendleton, Alice Saenz, and Teddie Payne-Riehl.

To Earl M. Rogers, Special Collections Library, University of Iowa, Henry A. Wallace Papers; Dale Mayer, archivist, Herbert Hoover Library, West Branch Iowa; John Ferris, archivist, Franklin D. Roosevelt Library, Hyde Park, New York; and Myra Marsh, reference librarian, Rosicrucian Research Library, for the valuable photocopies they graciously supplied.

To my angels disguised as people skilled in various branches of the literary work unique unto themselves: Theresa Hocking, Allenda Dorrough, Jacquie Yost, Margaret Loring, Ann Sallemi, Amber Hittle; Ellen Lively Steele, agent and friend extraordinaire; Patricia and Brett Mitchell of Esoteric Publishing, Bette Waters, Bluwaters Press and the wonderful folks at Quest Books—all friends and sister/brother adventurers in the world of publishing.

To my health and well-being angels: Steven Walker, Andrea Pollock Davidson, Ellen O'Hara, Gail Butler, Elizabeth Moore, Donna Walton, Rosemary McLoughlin, Denise Flowers, Sam Siegel, Laurete Francescato, Carol Adrienne, William Kent Halla, Christine Carter Lynch, Marina Koval, and Rev. Martha Turner.

And the closest for last: my dear children and their life partners. And my six grandkids, who in their entire lives have never known me when I was not working on this project: Jordan, Kendyl, and Chase Drayer and Sarah, Hannah, and Aaron Brown.

To John-Roger and John Morton for being my guiding lights.

And in memoriam to five dear ones who died before they could see the culmination of my work: Dr. Svetoslav N. Roerich (who went to join his family in 1993) for all of the cups of tea and delicious conversation; Frances R. Grant, who openly shared her memories with me; Mary Bailey for good advice and much appreciated friendship; Sandra D'Emilio for her encouragement and enthusiasm; and my friend David Warrilow, who lured me to Paris and cheered me on.

The author wishes to extend special thanks to the people and organizations who provided financial support that helped make this book possible: Brian and Maggie Disbury; Joleen Du Bois, White Mountain Education Association; Linda Goldman; Celia Allen-Graham and Robin B. Graham; Regis Guest; Evelyn Hancock; Philip Holliday; Sarah McKechnie, Lucis Trust; Andres Mendoza; Brett and Patricia Mitchell, Esoteric Publishing; Elizabeth Moore; Sue Ruzicka and Elaine Paris; Kathy Vallenga; Dirk Wales.

While many people made it possible for me to write this book, any errors in my interpretation of information given to me are solely mine.

PROLOG

Any millennium can be said to be the best of times and the worst of times. Probably the desire for war and conquest has been with us as long as humans have inhabited the earth. What makes each millennium unique, therefore, are the people born during it and the accomplishments made. The nineteenth century abounded with wars and revolutions: mechanical revolutions, industrial revolutions, physical revolutions, moral revolutions, and spiritual revolutions. It seemed to be a time when people awoke and expanded.

The steam engine was invented, the telephone, the telegraph, electric lights, photography, and ironclad warships. Florence Nightingale revolutionized military medicine; Freud probed the unconscious; the First Church of Christ, Scientist, was organized to teach that illness, pain, and death are illusions. In 1893, in America, the first-ever Parliament of Religions was convened. Delegates came from throughout the world. The two from India were Vivekananda, representing the Hindu faith, "the Mother of all Religions," and Dharmapala, a Buddhist, who converted a number of Americans to Buddhism and founded the first Mahabodhi Society in America.

While serving in India, James Churchward discovered accounts of earth's first civilization, "Mu," believed to have been located somewhere in the great volcanic earthquake belt that encircles the Pacific basin. People who shared a conviction that death is not the end of the soul and that mediums can facilitate communication with the spirit world began the Spiritualist movement. They studied the laws of nature, received messages from beyond the grave, and observed phenomena on both the visible and invisible sides of life. The Society for Psychical Research was established to expand science and physics by investigating claims of unusual human powers.

An American Buddhist, Henry S. Olcott, and the courageous, fiery-spirited Russian Helena P. Blavatsky formed the Theosophical Society to conduct scientific research into unexplained aspects of nature. While traveling in Tibet, Blavatsky had learned of the *Stanzas of Dzyan*, which she believed were the essential teachings of a prehistoric, universal religion, the common ancestor of all the world's great religions. If all religions shared a common ancestor, then all religions were one—essentially teaching the same doctrines and inculcating the same ideals of conduct and life. External differences were necessary to attract dissimilar races and temperaments.

The research of the Theosophical Society demonstrated the character, presence, and diffusion of this universal religion in every land. Blavatsky disseminated these teachings through her books *Isis Unveiled* and *The Secret Doctrine*. The books, crammed with the most comprehensive overview of esoteric wisdom ever to appear in print, exposed Westerners to the Eastern beliefs of reincarnation, karma, and the Hierarchy of Masters of Wisdom and Compassion, who lovingly guide the development of humankind on earth.

Because Blavatsky's "Universal Fraternity and Brotherhood of Humanity" was open to people of all religions and its teachings encouraged investigation into the infinite, Theosophy attracted vast numbers throughout the world. Her books were hungrily digested by Nicholas and

Helena Roerich and other seekers, researchers, and people needing more than formal religion offered—many of whom would have been repelled if faith alone had been required.

One belief was that nothing is supernatural; rather, humans have inactive senses that, once stimulated, allow the perception of usually invisible realms. Blavatsky presented three basic teachings: (1) Human beings are immortal souls who mold and master their own destiny. (2) The evolution of the whole of humanity takes place with the help of a *Hierarchy of Light* that works from spiritual dimensions. (3) The Hierarchy is composed of people, called Masters, Mahatmas, Elder Brothers, or Arhats who have perfected themselves physically, mentally, and emotionally through many lifetimes and have dedicated themselves to working to uplift humanity while continuing their own evolution.

These teachings did not originate with Blavatsky. Down through the ages many secret societies and mystical teachings had spoken of the Hierarchy under many names, including the Great White Brotherhood, the Occult Hierarchy, the Great White Lodge, the Enlightened Ones, the Holy Assembly, and the Invisible Church. "White" referred to the light pouring through from the soul, symbolic of the Good. In early Egyptian tradition, these Elders were referred to as "the Immortals, full of Wisdom and Knowledge." In Persia they were called "the Magi," thought to be the kings who brought gifts to the baby Jesus. In the Chaldean tradition they were "the Great Ones," who knew the science of the stars and gave astrology to humanity. In 604 BC the Chinese philosopher Lao-tzu, author of Tao-te ching, spoke of them as "Ancient Masters." Many Tibetan monks believed that the Brotherhood began in Mu (the civilization of Churchward's discovery), then moved to Tibet until the city of Lhasa grew up around their retreat, after which they settled elsewhere, possibly in northwestern Tibet.

By whatever name, all teachings agreed that because the Masters had conquered death, fear, pain, suffering, and other human emotional and physical problems, they were no longer limited by the laws applicable to most humans. They were spiritually evolved enough to move about in their higher bodies or slow their vibrations into physical bodies. They had the wisdom necessary to know the will of God and what violated it, and they were said to hold the plan for the future of humanity. Their guidance would eventually lead humanity into a glorious future where people would live compassionately in gratitude, taking responsibility for themselves, one another, Mother Earth, and all of creation.

The ancient wisdom passes down the concept of the earth as a school, where the Elders or Masters choose to remain in total service rather than progressing on to other spiritual dimensions. Committing their lives to helping humanity evolve, they are the loving faculty who inspire, comfort, and teach but never force their ways upon us or interfere with free will, for that would dishonor the principle of karma.[1]

A widely held concept is that intermittently, when humanity is ready, the Masters initiate new ideals and aspirations by sending powerful waves of thought and feeling into the mental currents of the subtler worlds, which account for the important innovations and expanded perceptions that occur simultaneously in different parts of the world. The Hierarchy is credited with inspiring new goals, such as the intense desire for universal peace, the ideal of religious tolerance, and a society based on cooperation and responsibility for the welfare of others. These ideals are then picked up as inspiration or through meditation by more highly attuned people, who relay them throughout the flow of human consciousness. Helena and Nicholas Roerich were among those who received guidance from the spiritual Masters and shared their teachings through writing and art.

Only three copies of the *Stanzas* were said to remain in existence. One was believed to have been hidden in India during the reign of Emperor Akbar the Great. It, and many other exciting treasures, lay buried through time, perhaps awaiting discovery by some enterprising artist, archaeologist, and explorer and his courageous wife.

1

━◦◦◦━

AN INNER URGENCY FOR
ARTISTIC CREATION

What could prevent an adventuresome young Russian boy from dig-ging among the long-abandoned battlefields and ancient burial grounds scattered throughout the forest beyond his family's estate? By the summer the slim, blond, blue-eyed Nikolai Konstantinovich Roerich was ten years old, the answer was nothing. Early one morning, in 1884, when the lure of those mysterious moss-covered *kurgans*, or mounds, and intriguing piles of stones, called *tumuli*, became irresistible, he began exploring. Unearthing a tenth-century bronze ornament encouraged him to continue. Before long, he had a collection of burial urns, charred bones, double-headed axes, spears, bronze and iron swords, threadbare scraps of embroidered cloth woven from the hair of horses, reins, belts, brooches, and other relics that needed to be concealed from his parents.

On some days visions of campfire smoke seemed to float in the mists around him. He could almost hear horses neighing or glimpse young war-riors racing or brawling. Armed with short javelins, they were the dark-eyed Avars, who drank horse's milk and were buried beside their horses. They had traded with the Greeks on the shores of the Black Sea before being driven off by the fierce Iranian-Mongolians, who armored them-

1

selves and their horses in finely woven bronze chain mail. "With each swing of the shovel, each stroke of the spade, an alluring kingdom emerged," Nikolai later wrote.

As he dug, the ancient record that sifted through his hands gave life to the tribes he studied in school: the Scythians, who depicted animals in their art; the Sarmatians, who reigned supreme across southern Russia until about AD 150; the Celts; the Huns and Attila, who crossed Asia in AD 375 on the way into Europe. He also studied the Goths, whose tribes had dominated Russia's waterways long enough to multiply and divide into the Ostrogoths, the Visigoths, and the brutal Teutonic Goths, who clasped their tunics at the shoulder with the distinctive fibula. "My very first burial finds coincided not only with my beloved history lessons, but with my geography and Gogol's fantastic fiction as well," Nikolai wrote in his diary. At age eleven, he presented his school with a collection of his archaeological treasures.

History and tales of the olden days always fascinated him, especially the legend of Rurik, the Viking prince from Jutland whose blood was believed to run in Roerich veins. The story went back to AD 862, when the Varengians and the Pechenegs threatened to invade the settlements of Slavs from the Carpathian Mountains who were cultivating land and forming hill-fort communities. All along the Oka, the Don, and even the lower Volga River, Vikings were protecting villages in exchange for tribute. Prince Rurik had visited their land earlier, so the Slavs sent him a delegation requesting that he establish a dynasty and become their protector. Though he failed to stave off the waves of invasions, which continued long after his death, Rurik did succeed in fortifying the rivers and installing deputies in the outlying villages. As time went on, others of his line instituted Christianity, built churches and monasteries, opened the waterways for commerce, established trade routes, codified Russian law, and developed the alphabet. Since the Vikings had been called the "Russ," some believe Russia's name came from them.

Nikolai's mother, Maria Vasilevna Kalashnikova, traced her lineage back to the early Slavs who had invited Rurik and his tribe to rule. She was considered, therefore, to have an eastern, "Pure Russian" heritage. Since the Slavs belong to the vast family of Indo-Europeans, who entered European history in the sixth century, she could have been a mixture of many things, but her forefathers were known to have been merchants in Pskov, one of Russia's earliest cities, in the tenth century.

Wealthy and politically influential, Nikolai's father, Konstantin Fedorovitch Roerich, was a prominent notary and attorney born in Riga, Latvia. Throughout the centuries, many of the Roerich men had devoted their lives to service as political leaders, military figures, and members of secret societies like the Knights Templar and the Masons. Nikolai's parents were part of the intelligentsia, the class of educated and liberal thinkers who mingled with royalty and worked actively to improve conditions in their country. When they received guests on Wednesday nights, archaeologists and Orientalists were often among the group.

Nikolai Konstantinovich was born in St. Petersburg on October 9, 1874 (September 27 by the Old Russian Julian calendar). His birth coincided with the short epoch of reform that began in 1861 when the Tsar decided to abolish serfdom and liberate twenty-three million people. Young Roerich's colorful lineage gave him a love for beauty and music, an unquenchable desire to travel, and a fervor to preach, evident even when he was young.

The Roerich family occupied a gracious building on the Neva River across from the prestigious Admiralty. Konstantin Roerich's office was downstairs and the family lived in rooms above it. Much of their leisure time was spent watching ships coming up to St. Petersburg from the Gulf of Finland. The walls shook and the glassware rattled with each booming salute of an incoming military vessel. During the winter holidays, or when mosquitoes and cholera began to cloud the stifling hot, long "white nights" of summer, the family happily moved to their country estate,

3

fifty-five miles to the southwest. Its name, given by the previous owner, was Isvara, Sanskrit for "Lord" or "sacred spirit."

Prolonged bronchitis and weak lungs plagued Nikolai until about age eleven, when his doctor prescribed the fresh, cold air of the winter and spring to strengthen him. This radical treatment freed him to roam Isvara's three thousand acres, frequently accompanied by the estate manager, who imbued him with a love of the woods. It was here that young Roerich's happiest childhood memories were made. He loved being in nature and, as he learned to ride, trap, and shoot, he became a passionate hunter. Entire days were spent silently watching birds or tracking deer, bears, and tiny woodland animals. At twilight, he hunted the giant trolls and pixies hiding in the green and violet shadows of massive rocks and trees. The stones and clouds and the nature devas and spirits on other planes of reality seemed to speak to him. Once the snows fell, he strapped on skis and gulped great breaths of invigorating air while gliding down the sparkling white hills. His explorations eventually expanded to the serenity of the vast forests near the imperial hunting grounds and the neighboring villages.

The peasants greatly interested Nikolai, and they responded to his seriousness and curiosity by telling him stories and explaining their customs and traditions. Most Russians were devoutly Christian and belonged to the Russian Orthodox Church. Pilgrims and wise holy men of great spiritual authority, called *Startsy*, wandered the countryside. Many chose lives of poverty and asceticism so they could guide others through times of anguish and turmoil. Large monasteries were located everywhere. Hundreds of priests and monks staffed the plentiful churches filled with brilliantly colored, miracle-working icons that were looked to for healing, protection, and inspiration. Russia's immense landscape, with its dark forests and moonless nights, combined with the general lack of education to become a breeding ground for superstition, legend, and a rich tradition of the supernatural. Children's heads brimmed with stories of fairies, fire-breathing serpents, and dangerous water sprites, as well as the legends of Christ, the apostles, and the saints.

Nikolai was a serious, sensitive, highly creative, and imaginative child. He spent much of his time alone and was aware of otherworldly influences. People noticed that, despite his friendly smile, he remained aloof. He learned to read early and enjoyed stories of Russian heroes and historical events. The Vikings, Genghis Khan's army, and Marco Polo crossing the great unknown into China all marched through Isvara in the plays he created to be staged by his older sister, Lydia, and his two younger brothers, Boris and Vladimir. Drama, science, and geography were his favorite subjects. He collected plants, minerals, and ancient coins, and wrote poetry and essays on his views. Some of his hunting adventures were published while he was still in middle school. At age sixteen, he learned scientific procedures and methods of excavation by accompanying a noted archaeologist during the summer.

Nikolai's earliest drawings were efforts to illustrate things that could be explained better with pictures. When a family friend discovered he had received no formal drawing instruction, he gave young Nikolai lessons, and the top floor of Isvara was soon converted into a studio. Years later, Roerich confided to a reporter, "Between the time I began my first painting and completed it, an inner urgency for artistic creation took such complete possession of my entire being that it convinced me I would perish unless I devoted my life to art." However, obtaining his father's approval was another matter. Since Nikolai was the oldest son, he was expected either to serve in the military or to join his father in his law practice, but young Roerich believed he could help his country more with his art than with a sword or a degree in law.

This belief arose from his excavations, through which he discovered a richness of the Russian spirit too significant to be denied. From the time Peter the Great had first built St. Petersburg as "the window on the West" and demanded that people drop their traditional ways, Russians had been taught to look to Western Europe as the model of everything desirable.

Many regarded their ancient eastern heritage and bloodlines as savage, ignorant, and subhuman. Roerich wanted to give his countrymen national pride and believed his paintings could help them find the same dignity he had found in the legacy of their remarkable past.

He placated his father by attending both the Imperial University and the Imperial Academy of Art, holding himself rigidly to the following schedule: 9:00, rise; 10:00–1:00, Academy; 1:00–3:00, University; 3:00–5:00, work on sketches; 5:00–9:00, evening classes and practical training at the Academy; 9:00–midnight, reading literary works, meeting friends, and participating in student circles. Holidays and vacations were devoted to nature trips, archaeological excavations, and hunting. After his first year at the art academy, he wrote in his diary: "Still far from my goal, it is now time to begin preparation for it—the pouring out of light, illustrations of my own history. Why is it that our history is usually made to look coarse and violent? Why don't the paintings ever show any signs of joy in the eye? Isn't it possible that even emaciated peasants could have attractive qualities?"

Although the current artistic trend was toward realism, Roerich had no desire merely to illustrate actual historical events. He wanted to depict the ancient Slavs and Vikings colored with the feeling of the times in which they had lived. Using vivid primary colors, he began to portray them developing new lands, building towns, battling and hunting, giving his paintings titles such as *Guests from Foreign Lands*, *Building a Town*, and *The Slavs on the Dnieper*. Everything in his work was enormous: strong, sturdy ships with heavy sails; hills and mountains and humans that seemed carved from stone. The smooth, unbroken contours and calm rhythm of forms created an impression of clarity and monumentality. In his paintings, Nikolai transmitted the feeling of the harmony and beauty of the distant past that he had unearthed with the graves. "The whole district is akin to my soul," he wrote in his diary. "The horizons, hills, moss, lakes, rivers, and clouds—all of it is mine . . . all of it is me."

The financial burden of enrollment in two schools came at a time when the elder Roerich was having crippling financial misfortunes. To pay for art supplies, books, and acquisitions to his stamp, mineral, and archaeological collections and also to have money for the theater, concerts, and trips, Nikolai took an assortment of jobs, including painting icons for churches and writing short stories for magazines. Although his heart was at the art academy, he managed to complete both courses of study.

By the age of twenty-three, he had conducted archaeological expeditions throughout Russia and presented scientific papers discussing Slavic and Finnish archaeology from the eleventh through fourteenth centuries. After having several articles published in *Art and Archaeology* and other journals and receiving praise from the Archaeological Society of Prussia for his discovery of amber ornaments near the Baltic Sea, Roerich was elected to the prestigious Imperial Archaeological Society. He was the youngest member.

In 1899, when Roerich was twenty-four, the Imperial Archaeological Society sent him east to the provinces of Pskov, Tversk, and Novgorod to study Russia's oldest monuments. The home of Prince Putyatin, another archaeologist, was on his route; there Roerich found not only a night's accommodation, but his future wife as well. When he arrived, Elena Ivanovna Shaposhnikova and her mother were visiting her mother's sister, Prince Putyatin's wife, as they did most summers. Born on February 12, 1879 (January 31 in the old style), Elena was five years Nikolai's junior, extremely intelligent, beautiful, and gifted. Her family was distinguished and aristocratic—the composer Moussorgsky was her uncle, and Mikhail Kutusov, who had commanded the victorious Russian forces opposing Napoleon in the War of 1812 and been portrayed by Tolstoy in *War and Peace*, was her great-uncle.

Despite a protected childhood marked by frequent illness and delicacy, Elena was cultured, wise, mature, exceptionally sensitive, and an excellent pianist. She was a comfort and solace to all; even the birds and

Elena Ivanovna Roerich, ca. 1900

animals benefited from her healing skills. She had taught herself to read as soon as she could carry the family's two large volumes of the Bible illustrated by Doré, and by age seven she was able to read and write in French, German, and Russian. She was six years old when she first met the "tall figure, dressed in white" she came to know as a "Teacher of Light, who lived somewhere far away." Shortly afterward, she began having numerous dreams and visions that would allow her access to deeper realms of reality and gave her the ability to predict future events.

By the time she and Nikolai met, Elena had read the entire collection of books in her grandfather's library and had progressed to studying the philosophies and traditions of the East, such as the Hindu Bhagavad Gita, the Mahabharata, and the three Vedas, the oldest existing works of literature. The young couple quickly discovered that, except for Nikolai's love of hunting, they had much in common and shared all interests; before the end of the year they announced their desire to marry. Elena's family was at first opposed but relented after her third dream that the marriage was the wish of her deceased father. In December 1899, Roerich wrote in his diary: "The evening of the 30th I told E.I. all that was in my soul. Strange, when for the first time, you consider another person in addition to yourself. It is now a new year. In it I must be much newer."

Many other challenges also came with the new century. Roerich's father, disillusioned and depressed, died in the spring, leaving the family to face the debts left by his poor financial decisions. Isvara was sold, and

Roerich's share of the inheritance allowed him to study in Germany and France, as all rising artists were expected to do. The young couple thought of combining their honeymoon with Nikolai's year abroad, but it seemed wiser to postpone the wedding.

Finally, in the fall of 1901, they were married and moved in with Nikolai's mother. Roerich began working as secretary of the Society for the Encourage-

Nikolai Konstantinovich Roerich, ca. 1900

ment of the Arts, organizing exhibitions and lectures and appointing new, more broad-minded teachers. Shortly thereafter, he also became assistant editor of *Art & Artistic Industry*, a magazine for which he had been writing. Spiritual philosophy permeated their home and their hearts as the couple studied Vivekananda, Ramakrishna, Buddha, and the work of India's poet laureate, Rabindranath Tagore. Their two sons were born within the first three years of their marriage. Roerich continued his excavations and, becoming especially interested in the Stone Age, started a collection of relics that grew in time to seventy-five thousand, including one hundred pieces of amber ornaments accepted as being four thousand years old.

In 1891 delegates from China, Japan, Ceylon, Burma, and India had convened in India for the first International Buddhist Conference, where groups that had previously had little contact united in the common cause of restoring Bodh Gaya, the sacred place where Buddha had received enlightenment. This gathering began a Buddhist revival that rippled throughout the Orient, southeast and central Asia, Hawaii, America, and Russia.

In 1905, after mighty Russia was humiliated by tiny Japan in the Russo-Japanese War, Tsar Nicholas II saw the importance of courting the alliance of the Buriats, Kalmyks, and other Mongolian/Buddhist tribes in the eastern parts of Russia. In 1907 Kambo Laramba Agvan Dorzhiev, a Buriat from Siberia and an important figure in far eastern Russian politics, convinced the Tsar of the importance of having a Buddhist (or perhaps a Theosophist-Buddhist) temple in St. Petersburg. Dorzhiev raised most of the construction money, laid the cornerstone, and dedicated the temple to the thirteenth Dalai Lama, who blessed the undertaking. Fiercely loyal to St. Petersburg, Dorzhiev believed his purpose was to create a Tibetan-Mongolian federation with Russia, a spiritual empire led by the Dalai Lama but under the Tsar's protection.

Young Roerich, who enthusiastically supported the construction and designed the stained glass for the second story, had never met anyone with the charisma and authority of this lama-priest, diplomat, and trusted advisor of the Dalai Lama. Nikolai was captivated by Dorzhiev's ideas of peace, brotherhood, and enlightenment, and his prophecy of the dawn of Shambhala ignited a flame in the young man that never burned out. The prophecy involved the Panchen Lama,[1] the Second Coming of Christ, and the Maitreya, or Buddha to come; it predicted that if the Panchen Lama ever left Tibet, that would herald the final battle ushering in the new era. Dorzhiev, who saw himself as Tibet's emissary to the White Tsar (Nicholas II), spread the word that the mythical Shambhala was located in Russian territory, north of Tibet; therefore, its emperor was the White Tsar, the Bodhisattva Tsar.

Despite the Tsar's involvement and sanction, the building of the Buddhist temple caused great controversy, and feelings ran high among St. Petersburg's many Christians. By the time it was completed in 1915, some people were so disturbed by Roerich's active role in its construction that they called for an investigation into his racial background. The inference that Mongolian blood ran in his veins was intended to discredit him,

The Buddhist temple in St. Petersburg dedicated to the thirteenth Dalai Lama

for in the thirteenth century the Mongols (including the Tartars) had invaded Russia and controlled it for centuries. Had the charge been proven true, Nikolai would have been have been proud, for he later wrote: "The Mongol invasions have left such hatred behind them that their artistic elements are always neglected. It is forgotten that the mysterious Cradle of Asia has produced these people, and has wrapped them in the gorgeous veils of China, Tibet, and Hindustan.... The Mongol manuscripts and the annals of the foreign envoys of those days tell us unaccountable mixtures of both cruelty and refinement . . . yet the best artists and masters were found in the headquarters of the Tartar Khans."

With Roerich's work and travels, the couple's spiritual studies, and raising their sons, the first years of the new century passed quickly. Roerich was promoted to director of the Society for the Encouragement of the Arts, which, with sixty-three teachers and two thousand students,

was one of the largest art academies in Russia. He presided over a delegation authorized to establish a museum to display collections of art and
culture predating Peter the Great. He belonged to the Society for the
Protection and Preservation of Monuments of Art and Antiquity in
Russia, the Rheims Academy, the Vienna Secession, and the Paris Salon.
His frequently controversial style and technique could be recognized in
mosaics, murals, and monumental friezes scattered throughout Russia, as
well as in architecture, theatrical sets, and costume designs; he was gaining the reputation of being one of Russia's greatest contemporary artists.

Nikolai's extensive research, discoveries, and unique knowledge of
the restless, shifting natures of the tribal migrations over the centuries
gave him a rare understanding of the quantities of good and evil that all
humans possess. Had he been asked in those early years, like Dorzhiev he
would have said that brotherhood and unity were the hope for the world;
in time beauty was added to the list. In the years that followed, this philosophy would be severely tested.

*Members of the
Imperial Society for
the Encouragement
of the Arts,
St. Petersburg.
Third from
left, standing:
Nikolai Roerich*

2

MAGNETIC MYSTICISM

By the fall of 1916, widely recognized as an artist, archaeologist, historian, and anthropologist, Nikolai Roerich was painting, writing, teaching, traveling, excavating, and living in one of the most beautiful cities in the world, now named Petrograd. He and his family were prospering, and his future looked bright. But despite so much success, Roerich was suffering. His health was poor due to lingering lung problems after a serious bout of pneumonia, and he was worried about the revolutionary unrest in the streets that was causing widespread fear, anxiety, and alarm. Railway stations were crammed with soldiers, and millions of Russians were on the move.

Nikolai had been offered a position in the proposed Bolshevik government, and from an idealistic, theoretical perspective, he and many others could recognize much in Communism that was similar to Buddhism: both wanted to lift and better the lives of the masses. But more realistically, he feared that accepting would cost him his artistic freedom. Perhaps his question of what to do was solved by his doctors, who agreed that the city air was harmful for him; as in his childhood, he needed to breathe clear, frosty air. To get away from the city but still be close to it, he and Elena leased a house in a pine forest near the Finnish border in the vicinity of Lake Ladoga.

Elena saw great hardships ahead. Although their relatives thought that leaving Russia was madness, the couple gathered their sons and left for Finland on December 17, 1916, just as the fierceness of the revolution began erupting. It was twenty-five degrees below zero as they wrapped themselves in all of their blankets and rode the unheated late train up the Karelia Isthmus to Lake Ladoga, now controlled by Finland. Not wanting to give the impression they were leaving forever, they left behind their collections of archaeological relics and European masterpieces, their family heirlooms, and many other things. At first, traffic ran unimpeded between Lake Ladoga and Petrograd, and when affairs at the academy demanded Professor Roerich's attention he could be there quickly. Then, in May 1918, the frontier was tightly closed, but they were safely out.

Having abandoned everything, the couple had time to devote themselves to the arduous work necessary to prove the accuracy of their spiritual studies. Despite their pain and depression about the darkness rapidly covering their homeland, they started to work. Using themselves as instruments, exerting constant effort, and persevering through failure, they began to make important discoveries about the etheric part of the physical world, the subtle surrounding spheres normally invisible to the human eye. After experiences with the supernormal—with the nature and appearance of the emotional, mental, and soul bodies—they began to comprehend the purpose of existence and the laws of human growth and destiny.

Gradually a new understanding and truth began to emerge from the interweaving of their investigations into all spiritual teachings, including Buddhism and Theosophy. During what appeared to be the darkest time of the couple's life together, a spiritual peace began to ease their hearts. Many years later, remembering their pain and searching, Roerich wrote, "We forged the tapestry of our spiritual armor with the same golden threads that weave throughout all great religious principles." It was armor that would serve them well. Though people would later label Roerich a mystic, from his perspective, he was a scientist, studying, analyzing, and exploring life's mysteries.

The family could have remained safely in Finland, but when Nikolai regarded the surrounding snow-covered rocks, it was the magnificent Himalayas that filled his dreams. His true objective was India, the ancient land of spirituality and splendor, the home of the Masters and the Theosophical Society—India, the country so revered from their years of Eastern studies: the Vedas, the Upanishads, and the Bhagavad Gita had all been written there, and there the Buddha had received enlightenment. To the Roerichs, it was the "Abode of Light."

In the preface to *The Secret Doctrine*, Madame Blavatsky wrote that when the Library of Alexandria had been destroyed, seven hundred thousand books of ancient sacred knowledge were lost to the world. The Mahatmas had sought diligently to replace them and had hidden this treasure throughout Asia. During the reign of Akbar the Great, some of these priceless manuscripts had been stored in India. Others had been hidden in subterranean crypts and cave libraries cut into the mountains beyond the Karakorum Range west of Tibet and in solitary Kunlun passes. The Roerichs yearned to explore the region, and the idea of an expedition began to germinate. Moreover, since childhood, Nikolai had been waiting for the opportunity to see Mount Kanchenjunga, the Himilayan peak whose picture had graced the wall of his summer home.

Roerich mentioned mountains frequently in his diaries, seeing them as metaphors for life. "A magnificent environ is necessary for supreme achievements, and nothing is more majestic than the unconquered Himalayas, with all their inexpressible radiance and their exquisite variations of form. A pilgrim becomes stronger, purer, and more inspired toward good in the very striving to ascend." Without doubt, India was their destination. They would go to northern India and the Himalayas to search for hidden knowledge and, perhaps, find the home of the Masters.

However, large obstacles blocked their path. Considered "the jewel in the crown," opulent India was the imperial prize in the clandestine "Great Game" for mastery of Asia waged between Tsarist Russia and Victorian Britain. Although it had been played actively during the previous century, it began again concurrent with the Russian Revolution.[1] Colonial India was tightly controlled by the British, who feared the Bolsheviks would infiltrate their empire. Few Russians were allowed entry, and no recourse was available through diplomatic channels. Without the proper papers and with little financial resources, the Roerichs had little chance of reaching their dream.

Since leaving Russia, their days had been worrisome and lean. Because they had fled with only what they could carry and the rubles they could stuff into their belongings, they had little to barter or sell, and financial concerns quickly became a part of their life. But a recurrent pattern in their lives was that just when a miracle was most needed some person or event would intervene. So it was now. One day a man sought Elena out where she marketed and offered to loan them money. After the couple decided they would rather sell paintings than borrow, he accommodated them by arranging an exhibition in Stockholm. When the exhibition closed, an invitation reached them from Sir Thomas Beecham, who was devoting his own personal fortune to supporting English opera. Beecham wanted Roerich to design scenery at Covent Garden, and with the help of their friend Sergei Diaghilev, Nikolai was able to accept the commission. In 1919 the family crossed Scandinavia and reached London.

A year in London offered them a respite from worry. It also gave them new opportunities and temporarily altered their plans. Roerich's exhibition of paintings, Spells of Russia, was a tremendous success. The spectacle and color dazzled the crowds who flocked to see it. Several pages of the black scrapbooks Elena had begun keeping in Scandinavia were quickly filled with enthusiastic reviews, like this one from *The Arts Gazette*:

> The tender violet-like amethysts of his snows at dawn, the emerald-like grass of his prairies, the pale turquoise of his northern skies, the mother-of-pearl of his clouds, the jasper and malachite of his rocks, the amber and rubies of his sunsets. Roerich's genius armed with all the wisdom of artistic experience, his poetic inspiration, his mastery of color-harmonics, is continually rising towards new heights of achievement. His work is full of barbaric splendor in which primitive emotions are vehemently expressed in sweeping design and vivid colour. The delicate purpose of his genius, the magnetic mysticism which infuses his legendary or spiritual compositions—these are the things of which dreams are made, but of which the reality is seldom seen.

Their days in London contained many surprises, but nothing equaled the experience the couple had one day while passing a group of Indian men on Bond Street. Making eye contact with the tallest, they immediately recognized the piercing eyes of Master Morya, so well known to them from their daily meditations. Although bearded and wearing a turban, it was their Master, and their hearts must have paused at the sight of him. Later that night, he visited them in their studio flat at Queen's Gate Terrace. "Our meeting with the Great Teachers and their close approach," were the words Elena recorded in her diary. In her dreams she began to receive books to read, and two luminous silvery figures appeared at her bed with certain dates and glowing digits on their foreheads.

In March 1920, the thought transmissions, or communications, from Master Morya began. At first both of the Roerichs received messages; then, Elena carried on the work. The transmissions became their source

*Roerich's sketch of their
Tibetan Master*

of strength and brought a most precious solace into their lives. "Those who with a full heart fulfill our requests will attune their ears to the harmony of the Universe," said Master Morya. Reams of messages were transmitted throughout the rest of their lives, inspiring, educating, and counseling them and giving them knowledge almost impossible to attain in any other way.[2] Answers to their questions and encouragement for the future were often provided.

Over the next few decades, the transmissions were transcribed in books that sounded the call for a new time of "the power of thought." Given the name Agni Yoga, the teachings explained the creative relationship of human thought to the energy or fire of which the universe is made.[3] Master Morya said:

> I give you the Teaching, karmic messages, indications. The Teaching is intended for the whole world, for all beings. . . .
>
> The more broadly you comprehend, the more truly it is yours. My friends! Happiness lies in serving the salvation of Humanity. Put aside all prejudices and summoning thy spiritual forces, aid mankind. Turn the unsightly towards beauty. As the tree renews its leaves, so shall men flourish on the path of righteousness.

One day Nikolai, looking for a Russian transcriber, got into a conversation with Vladimir Shibayev. The men were surprised to discover that they both came from St. Petersburg and were members of the Theosophical Society; also Shibayev had been born in Riga, Latvia, as had Roerich's father. Shibayev became a regular visitor in the Roerich's home, and when they left England they entrusted him to take some of their notebooks and papers to Riga.

They made two other friendships in London. One afternoon, Rabindranath Tagore, the author of *Gitanjali*, the slim volume of beautiful poetry they treasured, appeared unannounced for tea in the company of a mutual friend. Nikolai was at his easel working on his Hindu series, *Dreams of the East*. The coincidence of Roerich's visualizing India when Tagore arrived struck them all, and they agreed that "life weaves the beautiful web as no human imagination can visualize it." Exchanging thoughts with like-minded friends was a rare treat for the couple, and they were pleased to find Tagore as inspiring as his poetry. When Tagore graciously invited them to visit him in India, it seemed the perfect solution to their entry problems, and they immediately began planning to go.

Robert Harshe, an American on holiday in London, extended a second invitation. Primarily a painter, Harshe was also an avid art collector, drawn especially to the forerunners of the Modern movement, the *peintres par excellence*. Deeply impressed by Nikolai's strong designs, use of color, and mystical symbolism, Harshe offered to arrange an invitation for Roerich to visit America under the auspices of the Art Institute of Chicago, of which Harshe was soon to become director. Going to the United States was not a new idea for Nikolai, who for years had been interested in furthering Russian-American friendship. Christian Brinton, an American art critic and great supporter of Russian émigré artists, had previously offered to arrange an exhibition and publicity. When Harshe assured the Roerichs that America was eager to see Nikolai's art and suggested a traveling exhibition, beginning in New York, they were greatly tempted. But they had already reserved passage to Bombay and applied for their Indian visas.

While awaiting permission to enter India, the couple were shocked to learn that Beecham's Opera Company had gone into receivership. Instead of declaring bankruptcy, Beecham had agreed to pay off his creditors at twenty shillings to the pound; therefore, even if the Roerichs were granted entry to India, they no longer had the money to travel throughout the country. So the Bombay tickets were exchanged for passage to America. Four hundred paintings were crated into eleven cases, and the family packed and departed. They were setting sail straight into a relationship with a country and some of her citizens that would completely alter their lives.

On Sunday, October 3, 1920, the SS *Zealand* steamed into New York. While the Statue of Liberty may hold a light and welcome weary travelers to America's shore, the Committee on Immigration and Naturalization was a different matter. Perhaps the Roerich family was not aware of it, but the circumstances of their arrival and their timing were very fortunate. By traveling first class, they had secured tickets immediately and avoided the year's wait encountered by passengers going steerage. If they had arrived a little earlier, they might have found themselves involved in the "Red scare" that swept through labor groups across America, resulting in thousands of Russian immigrants being arrested and deported. Had they arrived eight months later, the first quota law might have prevented them from landing altogether.

The Roerichs were joining forty thousand formerly rich or titled Russians seeking sanctuary from the Bolshevik regime. Just before they arrived, this article had appeared in the Sunday edition of the *New York Times*:

> Ellis Island is again a bedlam of strange tongues. Its momentarily
> lulled voices have gained in volume within the last year. There is

the old aura of nostalgia about it, mingled with a new and irresistibly flamboyant hope. For America is not merely the land of freedom now. It is the land of peace. Immigrants are coming in tens and hundreds and thousands . . . of a type, on the whole, better than in pre-war days. Mentally, morally, and physically they are in finer shape than we have ever found them—the highest type since the days of Columbus. They have better clothes, more luggage, and more money than ever before.

America had frequently been blessed and enriched by other countries' misfortunes. By 1910, over one million Russians had immigrated there to escape the tyranny of the tsars. But nothing before equaled the "Russian art movement." The wealth of culture, color, excitement, and artistry thrilled and overwhelmed New Yorkers and then filtered across the entire country. Great composers, painters, actors, dancers, singers, and musicians arrived alone or in troupes, some bringing their families. These included Stravinsky, Rachmaninoff, Prokofiev, Nijinsky, Pavlova, Chaliapin, Kreisler, Zimbalist, and members of the Moscow Art Theater, to mention just a few.

Many of the new arrivals had been involved in the Russian artistic revival that began in the late 1800s when Leon Bakst, Sergei Diaghilev, and several school chums started organizing exhibitions. Next, hoping to influence society's attitude toward art, they published a brilliant literary magazine, *Mir Iskusstva* (The World of Art), which announced itself as "the first voice of a generation thirsting for beauty." The magazine folded in 1904 but was reorganized in 1910 with Roerich as president. In 1911 Diaghilev, now more experienced, assembled Russia's finest collection of artistic talents and took them to Paris as the Ballets Russes. Their aim was to demonstrate Russia's brilliance in music, choreography, and painting to all of Europe. Within several seasons, their fresh, original, and sensually flamboyant productions accomplished their goal.

One of company's most outstanding ballets had been *Le Sacre du Printemps* (The Rite of Spring) composed by Igor Stravinsky and choreographed by Vaslav Nijinsky. Stravinsky and Nikolai had worked on the composition together at Talashkino, where the Roerichs had stayed for a while.⁴ Drawing on his unique knowledge of early Russia, Nikolai boldly designed the colorful costumes and intense scenery. When the score was completed, the two men enthusiastically inscribed excerpts of it on the living room beams. Although the production was expected to make an impact, no one anticipated the reception it did receive. When it premiered in Paris in 1913, some in the audience were so shocked that they screamed and shouted, drowning out the orchestra. The bewildered dancers, including Nijinsky, continued to perform, though fistfights erupted in the audience. A triumphant Diaghilev declared, "Let them hiss, let them cry! Inwardly they feel its value. It is their conventional mask that hisses. This is victory! And we will see great results from this." And it was true. The entire production made musical history. When Roerich wrote about it years later, he called it "the moment when modern art freed itself from conventionality and superficiality."

The Russian artistic infusion into New York completely changed the life of Frances R. Grant, the small, dark-eyed music critic for *Musical America*. A recent graduate from Columbia School of Journalism, she was enjoying the importance of her first job and the power and independence it brought. Raised in a home surrounded by culture, she was knowledgeable on many subjects, especially music, writing, and art; she was also quite bold, confident, and daring for a young woman of her time. She loved drama and spectacle, and the Russian whirlwind caught her up and impressed her deeply. While covering the Ballets Russes performances at the Metropolitan, Frances became acquainted with the premier danseur, Adolph Bolm, a graduate of the Russian Imperial School of Ballet and recent émigré. Bolm and his wife took such a fancy to Frances that before long she was visiting with them at the Hotel des Artistes, the residence hotel that served as home to many Russians. She began to share the anticipation of the Roerichs' arrival when Adolph insisted that she needed to meet the former head of *Mir Iskusstva* and join the group greeting the ship.

The Bolms had heard that Nikolai had not been well and had even heard rumors of his dying in Siberia, but during the revolution it was hard to know what to believe. When the Roerichs walked down the gangplank onto American soil, the Bolms saw a travel-weary family who had aged considerably since the last time they had all been together. At forty-seven, Nicholas,[5] always neat and well groomed, was a slight, small-boned man whose proud, erect carriage made him appear self-possessed and composed. There was a certain remoteness in his manner; even in a crowd, he seemed to be standing alone. Except for the lines across the bridge of his nose, his face was smooth and unwrinkled, his complexion fair. He had intense deep-set blue eyes, high Slavic cheekbones, and no trace of what had once been blond hair, for his scalp was completely shaven. Between his moustache and trim beard, his mouth was well chiseled and firm.

The reunion was emotional. As they embraced, Adolph Bolm could feel the warmth and vitality concealed by Roerich's delicacy, politeness, and good manners. Even though a mask of inscrutability seemed to hide his thoughts, his eyes often lit up with humor. Always a good listener, Roerich spoke with a trace of solemnity and formality, like a teacher or lecturer giving forth his opinions. His face looked grave, yet there was a gentle strength about him.

Standing to the side of the group, Frances Grant looked at Helena Ivanovna and was reminded of a cameo. Her creamy complexion, fine features, and sparkling brown eyes were crowned by wavy brown hair that had a startling streak of gray in the front. Despite the young critic's curiosity about meeting the Roerichs, her attention immediately went to their two handsome sons, who were more nearly her age: Svetoslav, sixteen, and George, eighteen, were both Nordic blonds, slightly taller than their father. Both spoke proper English; their father had a good command of the language but spoke with a heavy accent, and though Mme Roerich spoke good English, she was more comfortable with Russian or French.

When Bolm inquired if they were immigrating, Nicholas replied that they were merely pausing on their way to India. It was a reply Frances would hear many times over the next three years, but for now, she wondered how America could be on the route from London to India. She would find out the following Sunday, for Mme Roerich invited her to visit them at the Hotel des Artistes. Struck by Helena's warmth and graciousness, Frances agreed without any inkling of what lay in store.

October is one of New York's best months, and the Roerichs' first day in the city was fair and balmy, measuring up to all expectations. Walking out into the sunshine, leaving the security of the Hotel des Artistes behind, Nicholas must have been surprised by the action and noise. Cars and trucks honked horns of all timbres, and thunderous rumblings shook the pavement beneath his feet when the subway train rushed by. Crowds of people hurried somewhere, pausing only at street corners and to watch building construction. Noisy lifts and cranes seemed to be everywhere. No doubt Roerich could sense the "melting pot" at work assimilating everyone; the very air he breathed must have felt expansive and free, as if anything could be accomplished.

Robert Harshe, who had organized their trip to America, was on hand to greet them and help organize Roerich's first exhibition in the United States, due to open at the Kingore Gallery on Fifth Avenue in early December. Once the paintings had been uncrated, two hundred would be selected for the exhibition; the others would be stored at the Brooklyn Museum. In the month before the exhibit, canvases would need to be stretched, touched up, and framed. Time for sightseeing and for catching up with the many old friends now in New York would wait.

The pleasant visit Frances Grant had anticipated the next Sunday turned out to be one of the most incredible afternoons of her life. The conversation probably started casually enough, with Roerich explaining his plans to acquaint America with Russian art and culture and his visions of unity. After tea, however, the subjects deepened and turned to Madame Blavatsky, Theosophical teachings, karma, reincarnation, Frances's own past lives—and how they had all been together before. Frances was already familiar with Theosophy from her reading, and now, spellbound, she listened to their stories of the Mahatmas of the East. Just before leaving, she received a message from Helena's Master himself. Walking back out into the fall air, stunned, she was aware that she was no longer the same person who had entered hours earlier. In her later years, she reminisced: "It was all truly miraculous. . . . They spoke to me as if I were their daughter, and told me everything. . . . Perhaps if my family had been near, it wouldn't have happened so quickly . . . but from that time on, it all became a part of my life. It was just like a drama unfolding—and I became part of it."

When Frances mentioned that she would be going to New Mexico for the summer, she was surprised to hear them reply, "So are we! We hear it is very beautiful." Since New Mexico was one of the most recent states to join the union, Frances was more accustomed to people asking her where it was, rather than announcing they'd be going there, too. Excited, she volunteered that her sister lived in Santa Fe and, when they were ready, would be glad to find them a place to stay.

Roerich's European reputation had preceded him in New York, creating a great expectancy among cultured Easterners, the crème de la crème of society. The newspapers predicted thousands would be at the gala opening on December 18; it was later written ten thousand attended. Actually, two thousand were at the opening reception and several thousand more visited the show later. Although the gallery was unsuitably small, those attending seemed to step into another world.

Once, in Russia, a friend of Roerich's, the famous Russian writer Leonid Andreyev, had labeled the paintings "The Realm of Roerich."

That title was especially appropriate to the art now displayed. Roerich's "realms of singular harmonious peace and indescribable beauty" had been painted mostly in tempera, because he preferred that his works lighten with time, rather than darken as they would with oils. The realm was composed of vast, majestic mountains and great azure skies that glistened in the sunshine, while surreal images appeared in the clouds. Many viewers agreed that the lavish acclaim for the painter had been justly deserved. *Treasure of the Angels*, *Pagan Russia*, and *Ecstasy*, three huge pieces, stood out with "superhuman beauty and serenity." People said these could only have been conceived and colored by a mastermind akin to Leonardo da Vinci.

Milling among the crowd, Frances Grant recognized numerous brilliant artists and theater people whose work she had reviewed for *Musical America*, including Sina and Maurice Lichtmann, graduates of the Vienna Meisterschule. Although they had met only casually, Grant remembered the couple were the extremely talented Russian pianists who owned the Lichtmann Piano Institute. Sina Lichtmann later admitted that she had come to the opening wondering why she was there. Her original plan had been to avoid the crowds and attend the following day. Yet it had seemed as if "some powerful force" had pulled her to the opening. Once inside, the crowd seemed to recede until Sina was viewing Roerich's work alone, "face to face with *Infinity*." As she stood transfixed, she felt as if she were inside the painting "with the first man, building his dwellings, worshipping and communing with God, absorbed in the greatest glory" that she had ever seen. Tears welled up and overflowed her eyes while thoughts and emotions filled her. Eventually, she became dimly aware that someone was insisting on introducing her to the artist.

She later remembered:

There he stood, a man of medium height, with a beard shaped to a point; radiating some invisible benevolent force, with such a penetrating look in his luminous eyes that he appeared to be seeing into the very essence of my soul.... By his side stood his wife, Helena Roerich, so strikingly beautiful that I caught my breath. When we were introduced, I listened in amazement to the qualities in their voices as they spoke to me in my mother tongue, and realized they were smilingly inviting me to visit them that evening in the Hotel des Artistes. Surprised that I had been asked, I accepted the invitation, and then waited impatiently for evening to come.[6]

Profoundly stirred by the beauty of the paintings, Sina was also deeply touched by the Roerichs' warm and friendly attitude. "When we entered the big studio that evening," she remembered, "my husband Maurice and I felt that rather than meeting strangers, we were being received as old friends." The Lichtmanns' surprise increased as the Roerichs began explaining their mission in the United States and what was to follow. Expressing a deep interest in the Lichtmanns' music and teaching, the Roerichs offered plans that could converge their paths and let them work together to bring art and knowledge to the youth of America. "Art and knowledge are the best international language ... they will unify all humanity," stated Roerich firmly as he outlined plans of such vision and scope that the Lichtmanns were left breathless. The first step was to establish the Master School of United Arts, where music, painting, sculpture, architecture, opera, drama, and ballet would be taught under one roof and people would be encouraged to explore everything. Then would come cultural centers and international brotherhoods of artists—exciting places where artists could exchange ideas, encourage each other with new concepts, and hold unjuried exhibitions where everyone's work would be admitted.

Without doubt, the Lichtmanns went home with their heads spinning and stayed up talking until late into the night. Sina realized she had met her "Master" and recognized in Roerich "a noble messenger" sent to impel the hearts and souls of humankind steadfastly and fearlessly upward, seeking truth. She marked that evening as the beginning of her apprenticeship; it began an era of great cooperation and devotion to the Roerichs that ended only with her death—or perhaps not even then.

Recognizing that their teachers had appeared, teachers they were prepared to follow into the deepest understanding of art and the greater realities of Truth, the Lichtmanns joined Frances and the Roerichs in the unfolding drama. Another eighteen months would pass before the last two people appeared to complete the group that would oversee and execute all of the Roerichs' dreams.

3

Culture Is of the Spirit

When Roerich's art started to tour, Robert Harshe's prediction that Americans had not seen anything like it proved to be accurate. Critics were puzzled because it could not be classified. "School? It belongs to no school. It is just Roerich—and Russian. And the method and spirit are never twice the same." When asked about this by a newspaper reporter, Roerich replied, "Why should one do two paintings in the same way? Each subject requires a different approach and treatment. Each is painted as I feel."

Roerich's approach to painting was synthesized from several sources, including his own dreams and visions, his penetrating nature, and his accurate eye. From childhood, nature had taught him her secrets in the billow of clouds, the patterns in rivers, and the textures of the forest. And then there were the icons, which had embedded mysticism and symbolism deeply into his Russian soul. Painted in religious fervor or quiet meditation, they had communicated with him in a wordless language. Bright enough to be seen through wavering candlelight and the haze of incense, their blue horses, red mountains, and vigorous but tender pure hues had taught him that color could express profound emotion and triumphant joy.

The man Roerich considered his most influential teacher was Arkhip I. Kuindjy at the Imperial Academy of Art. He may have belonged to the mystical Order of Rosicrucians, which was tolerated by the Tsar and given unusual protection. On many levels, Kuindjy was the ideal teacher for Roerich, the perfect guru. Peerless in his treatment of contrasting color, sunlight, and moonlight, he discussed the deepest mysteries of life with the impressionable young man.[1]

Then, in Paris, Roerich had studied with Fernand Cormon, well known for his Stone Age themes. Cormon encouraged great individuality and freeness in his students, who included Toulouse-Lautrec and van Gogh. With only occasional supervision and individual talks, Roerich had been allowed to work alone in his own studio; under the different conditions and new influences, his compositions moved from realistic to stylistic. He adopted more mystical ideas, and his portrayals of Russian nationalism expanded to become more universal. Free to manage his own time, young Roerich spent much of it at the Louvre, where he was influenced by the simple, clean shapes of color and massive murals of Pierre Puvis de Chavannes, which encouraged him to paint on a large scale.

The massive social and cultural changes that had begun shortly before Roerich's birth had also contributed greatly to his approach to painting. America's Civil War had freed millions of Negroes from slavery. At nearly the same time, the Tsar had proclaimed an end to centuries of bondage for an even greater number of serfs. Liberation had stirred in every heart. Many artists and musicians felt they could no longer tolerate the traditional restrictions on their efforts. Demanding freedom to express themselves, some turned away from realism and explored their feelings and dreams. Since many of these people were also absorbed with the Theosophical belief that there is more to the world than what is seen with the eye, they tried to strip away the nonessentials and create a language of color through which to communicate. Simplicity was the key.

Roerich held himself to the firm discipline of painting almost every night from midnight until four, continually producing paintings no matter where else he was involved. He had developed a bold and uncomplicated style. Foremost for him was the freedom to discover original approaches to his subjects and techniques and new harmonies among color, line, and spirit. Even the way he applied paint was a continual discovery, from the lightest touch to the strongest, broadest, most palpable strokes, from translucent, moist, lovely, gentle caresses of color to startling ponderous effects with weight. His use of form as decoration often gave a charming vitality to his work.

Roerich seldom painted what he saw. Despite his boldness, many of his paintings were like dreams, filtered through his memory, imagination, and emotions. As time went by, he gave less prominence to humans, insisting that "man cannot be King of nature; he is her pupil, small in comparison to the forces of nature and nature herself. Man's place in the universe, that is what is important."

When lecturing or writing, he painted with words. Sometimes the words were heavy, cold, and harsh, reflecting the anguish and pain from which he had escaped; at other times, they were delicate and heartening, conjuring up poetic images and beauty. No matter which words he chose, he always stressed that the path of beauty was the divine path, that the struggle between the constructive and destructive principles of nature was the ultimate mystery of existence, and that humanity's goal—the Great Adventure of life—was to make the correct choices and evolve into independence, or self-completion.

Russians referred to "Roerich's clouds," "Roerich's rocks," and "Roerich's vistas," as if he had opened new windows in their minds and given them an additional viewpoint from which to discern more in nature than before. Soldiers in the First World War had written him from the front lines, telling him that the flames, the darkness, and the visions they saw around them during the fighting were exactly like those he painted.

The Russians considered Roerich a master "colorist," and his colors were spectacular; yet his early technique was crude and coarse compared to what it would eventually become.

The New York critics, however, saw his work differently than the Europeans:

> The touch is not only heavy; it seems at times fairly clumsy. His style has vigor that needs refinement; it arrests attention but exerts no charm.... Yet even while we are repelled by the crudities in Mr. Roerich's technique, we are won back to him by their indescribable Russian savor, their suggestion of an inborn and organically wholesome racial habit. His art, with all its limitations, remains profoundly genuine. There is personality and a rough native force in it. It is as though one traveled through Russia and suddenly came upon some romantic place marked by curious architecture, and peopled by picturesque figures flooded with reverberating color. The strangeness of fairyland descends upon the beholder and he feels it has come true.

After his show at the Kingore Gallery closed, Roerich accompanied his paintings to openings in Boston, Buffalo, and Chicago. Then they were to continue on alone, though this worried him greatly when he remembered the disastrous fate of his entire *Old Russia* series of church and monastery paintings fifteen years earlier. In 1904 about seventy-five of Roerich's paintings were included in a group of six hundred paintings sent to America for display at the Louisiana Purchase Exposition. It was the largest exhibit of Russian art ever to have left the country, and none returned. Seventy-some paintings had disappeared into thin air.[2] All were from sketches made during the first two years of his marriage when he and Helena had traveled to some forty Russian cities, investigating the vast assortment of ethnic groups.

It had been a unique time in their lives. While Nicholas had sketched the heavy towers, the wide churches with cupolas, the multicolored cathedrals, and the monasteries from Russia's rich past, Helena had taken many photographs. The couple had roamed the countryside, talking about the early legends and stories of the monks, the saints, Christ, the Eastern philosophies they were studying—and becoming acquainted with each other on a deeper level. The time also marked the birth of their sons, George and, two years later, Svetoslav. George carried the name of Russia's patron saint; Svetoslav was named after a grandson of Prince Rurik, whose mother is credited with bringing Christianity to Russia. Nicholas had wanted to impress upon his compatriots' minds and hearts the grandeur of soul and character of a long-forgotten Russia. The *Old Russia* paintings had been such a great success that the Tsar had intended to purchase the series.

However, if Roerich's plans to organize the Master School of United Arts were to materialize, he would have to trust Harshe's arrangements and permit his paintings to travel across America alone. As the exhibition went from city to city, Helena pasted more reviews into her black scrapbooks. The *Boston Globe* reported that between two hundred fifty and four hundred visitors viewed it daily at the Boston Art Club. Though many found the work difficult to understand, they nevertheless returned and eventually came to appreciate it. In Boston, several paintings were sold and a few friendships established. During a pre-opening night interview, Nicholas told the *Buffalo Express*:

> I am three years out of Russia, and of all countries where I have been, I am happiest here. To Russians, America is a sort of home country, a hope of what Russia herself may become. The freedom and big spaces of both countries must account for the similarities in the people. In London, I heard that Americans are only interested in business, with no tendency toward the spiritual. But in spite of the fact

that the streets are bustling with business, there are also many churches. I ask myself whether Emerson and Walt Whitman were materialistic? And of course you know that the first head of the Theosophical Society was an American, Olcott.

After the show opened, the *Buffalo Evening News* reported: "Roerich and his wonderful splashes of spiritual paint—he was too perturbed at the lack of understanding of his extraordinary canvases to more than clutch your hand gratefully, when you told him he made of *Solitude* a religion, and of religious fervor, a sacred safety valve for primitive emotion."

The *Chicago Tribune* reported:

Roerich brings a new sort of Russian propaganda to Chicago. The gospel he brings is not Bolshevist, though. It is the gospel of spirituality. Emphatically, Roerich insists, "Culture must conquer materialism. We often make the mistake of assuming that civilization is culture. The fact that a man dresses in modern fashion, utilizes modern conveniences, and goes forward with material progress, does not mean that he is cultured. Culture is of the spirit." Two hundred canvases illustrating the artist's versatility and almost barbaric boldness will be shown at the Art Institute for a month. Among the paintings is the model for one of the six settings Mr. Roerich is to execute for the Chicago Opera Company's fall production of Rimsky-Korsakoff's *Snegourotchka.*

Earlier, in Boston, Roerich responded to how he would portray the American girl: "I would paint a woman in whose face the struggle for spiritual culture over mechanical civilization had already gained victory. A woman who speaks and understands the cosmic language. She would realize that the true meaning of beauty and wisdom is not the superficial, artificial beauty, but the radiance which has its roots in the well-spring of the soul. . . . We should know, as we gazed upon her, that she had experienced the pain and joy of self-sacrifice."

At a society luncheon two months later, he gave the women more to think about than clothes when he spoke about the aura as a spiritual garment and colors that heal: "You know that these auras vary in accordance with our spiritual achievements. And every single thought is capable of either brightening or darkening it. . . . Man wears an eternal color dress around his spirit which he paints with his thoughts." Roerich thought the feminist movement in America one of the signs that America was "the land of the future." An ardent feminist, he appreciated the fact that women had won the right to vote and commented that his paintings *Song of the Waterfall, Language of the Birds,* and *Song of the Morning* were executed as "cosmic songs" for women.

With merely a glance at the daily paper, the Roerichs could see that all norms of conventional behavior were stretching beyond recognition. It was the beginning of the "anything goes" era. After winning the right to vote only a few months earlier, women were progressing on to bobbing their hair, shortening hemlines to several inches above their ankles, and smoking cigarettes. The first bathing beauty contest was held when thousands of soldiers were newly returned from war. When Prohibition was enacted, people were soon flouting the law, while gangsters and speakeasies made illegal fortunes. Everywhere Roerich went he heard talk of lawlessness, but he was looking for something better, and "in the shadow of elevators and steam shovels" he found it.

"The spiritual side is thriving . . . and a quieter movement is growing among people with higher ideals," he said of those he saw heeding the call of the soul. Christian Scientists, Unitarians, and Spiritualists were packing their churches, while many others turned to the wisdom teachings of Blavatsky, Vivekananda, Tagore, Alice Bailey, Rudolf Steiner, Gurdjieff, and others. Nicholas expressed some of his views in an article in *The Messenger*:

Only with a true eye and open heart can we grasp the miraculous things which surround us. In pointing out the spiritual issues of American life, I cannot ignore its cosmic nature. In America, in our very presence, by means of mixing the elements of the world in a quick experiment, a new nation is being composed. By synthesizing the qualities of ethnic importance, religions, and universal achievements, a new national soul is being formed. It will produce a future spiritual culture. Of all the world projects, this is the most marvelous experiment.... Beauty is the force that can bring nations together.... American art is more truly international because it is distilled from all countries.

That is why America will be one of the first to make art the universal language it is destined to become. Different races may not understand each other's spoken language, but all understand when the language is art.

Wherever Roerich traveled, he searched for like-minded people. In Chicago he found many colorful, exciting people who were Theosophists or were strongly influenced by Theosophical ideas. Many who recognized and embraced Roerich's visions were invited to become his colleagues, faculty members, and supporters once the Master School of United Arts opened. He gathered together businessmen, theater people, painters, musicians, composers, and writers whose names still have a familiar ring: Deems Taylor, Robert Sherwood, Rockwell Kent, Olin Downes, and Robert Edmund Jones. They recognized the necessity of bringing a greater appreciation of beauty to the world and knew it would take a tremendous collective effort.

With his rich imagination, Roerich had always loved theater. Between his Viking ancestors, the fairy tales his grandmother told, and the superstitious tales whispered by the servants, he sometimes had more trouble distinguishing reality than creating fantasy. While still in Russia, a new avenue of artistic expression had opened for him when he designed the costumes and scenery for theatrical productions recreated from the Middle Ages. Over the years, he had designed for several operas, dramas, and ballets and, finally, the Ballets Russes. His designs for Maeterlinck's *Princess Maleine* and *Sister Beatrice* were particularly outstanding. He thought the secret to his success and originality was the way he prepared for them. First, he steeped himself in the spirit of the composer and librettist and aligned with their thought patterns. Then, he chose "a color key," to write in, and based his entire composition upon it. His deep love was Wagnerian music, and his personal favorites were the designs he created for the mystical *Valkyrie*.

Roerich's arrival in America was, therefore, exciting news for the very competitive New York Metropolitan and Chicago Grand Opera Companies, who vied for his services. In February 1921, the Chicago company snapped him up because the director, the Scottish soprano Mary Garden, was a Theosophist and longtime friend from his Ballets Russes days. Unfortunately, she forgot to tell him that the company was in serious financial trouble and expecting to close. Two Russian operas premiered that season, Prokofiev's *Love for Three Oranges* and *Snegourotchka* (The Snow Maiden). The later based on an early Russian legend, filled with wolves, fairies, ghosts, beautiful water sprites, and goblins, Roerich loved it for successfully combining real life with the rich Old Russian world of enchantment, the best possible introduction to Russian nature and native costumes.

His designs were so superb that the production was called a "spectacle to dazzle the eye." *Snegourotchka* inspired Marshall Field's department store to come out with a line of high-fashion women's clothing. Unfortunately, none of Chicago's women wanted to look like they came out of a Russian enchanted forest. *Love for Three Oranges* had been involved in litigation for the entire previous year, but it, too, was a tremendous success, and played to sold-out houses.

The newspapers later reported the Chicago Grand Opera lost one million dollars that season, to which Garden remarked, "I don't know because I had nothing to do with the business end of it." All she knew was that they got the final blaze of glory she wanted, but Roerich thought he might end up with only smoke. In July 1922, the *New York Times* reported that Nicholas Roerich had been awarded a $3,500 judgment in an undefended suit against the Chicago Opera Association, yet it is questionable if he ever received anything. Despite the problems, Roerich was pleased because he was convinced that if Russia and the United States understood each other's cultural treasures, true understanding and real friendship would result.

While in Chicago, the Roerichs visited the Little Theater, a new concept in theater using exciting innovations with light and color vibrancy. Raymond Jonson, a scenic artist in the Little Theater, was one of their kindred spirits. He attended night classes at the Art Institute, taught at the Chicago Academy of Fine Arts, and was identified with the younger, radical painters in Chicago. After attending Roerich's exhibition, he confided to his diary:

> There has opened at the Institute the exhibition of the work of Nicholas Roerich. It is glorious. Would that I could express the wonder of it—I feel that at his best he has accomplished that which all artists hope to do. There are at least six paintings that I believe to be the most spiritual pieces of expression that I have ever seen.
>
> I feel here a great sympathy with my own feelings and desires. I feel very close to this art. . . . This art should be recognized as fundamental—should be thought of outside of all physical aspects—It is the great love, its only purpose is to feed the spirit. . . . *The Treasure, Ecstasy, The Call of the Sun* (second version) and some others of his best are great works of spiritual art. I feel very close and moved beyond by this man's spirit—his work. . . .

A few weeks later (June 14, 1921), he wrote: "Since my last entry I have been so busy that I've had neither time nor inclination to write—so great a deal has taken place. . . . A small group of artists have formed an organization which we are very much interested in. We finally decided on *Cor Ardens* as the name—meaning flaming heart. We have had many meetings, much discussion. . . . Roerich joined us with much enthusiasm. I feel it is a fine beginning and that much will come from it."[3]

When officers were elected, Jonson became secretary. So after only ten months in America, the first of Nicholas's dreams had taken form: the international society of Cor Ardens was born, a fiery, spiritual, radical group of young painters sharing Roerich's belief that "the only real fraternity among men is the fraternity of beauty as expressed in art." They founded it on the awareness that "art is the universal medium of expression, and an evidence of the dominant spirit in life." Roerich outlined its goals: a concrete step to bring together sympathetic isolated individuals, to walk the rising road of grandeur, enthusiasm, and achievement, free from commercial taint. Its aims were to form an international brotherhood of artists; to hold exhibitions without juries, prizes, or sales; to create contests open to art and artists of all countries; to work toward establishing universal museums that would permanently house works donated by the members.[4] Pure and idealistic, Cor Ardens' purpose was to encourage artists to artistic heights, not for the money, but simply for themselves; to hold exhibitions and contests so that their art could be shown but not bought; and to contribute their art to museums around the world so that more and more people could benefit from its beauty.

Roerich found it hard to understand that after centuries of bloodshed and war so few people were interested in world cooperation. The League of Nations had been formed without the support of popular opinion and was opposed by those wanting to "keep America free from foreign entanglements." But Roerich gathered nine painters, writers, musicians, composers, and sculptors from around the world who shared his vision of brotherhood to be honorary presidents of Cor Ardens with him: his old friend Tagore from India, Maurice Denis from France, Maurice Maeterlinck from Belgium, Ivan Mestrovic from Serbia, Ignacio Zuloaga from Spain, Asel Gallen from Finland, Augustus John from England, Ione Noguchi from Japan, and Richard Strauss from Germany. "Has chaos not opened the gates of unity?" Nicholas wondered. "Perhaps physically separated souls can begin to understand one another through Art, the language of the highest blessings."

One reporter succinctly summed it all up: "Roerich seeks to endorse art as a tongue to utter eloquent messages. You may find much with which you disagree . . . much that is mystic. But that is merely a question of subject matter. The important fact is that he is moving across the country, inspiring and invigorating every artist who is fortunate enough to see the exhibition . . . and exemplifying the possibilities of a vital and unfettered national art."

This story appeared in the *Denver Post*:

Elimination of racial animosities and prejudices—unity of Orient and Occident—that is the all-pervading philosophical passion of Nicholas Roerich, one of the greatest artists of our generation. How to attain this almost unbelievable Nirvana is the problem. Roerich, whose life is governed by the ebb and flow of beauty, believes with the true soul of an artist, that art and beauty will eventually work the miracle. Man, in common with all men, loves the thing beautiful. Beauty is the lifeblood—the goal. The doctrine of world unity, a common sympathy and understanding of philosophy and the love of art— therein lies the hope of mankind for a better world in which to live.

Wherever Roerich went, he spoke as a prophet of peace, and repeated the same messages: "Art and Knowledge, Beauty and Wisdom." He consistently told people: "Creation is the pure prayer of the spirit . . . art is the heart of the people . . . knowledge is the brain. . . . Only through the heart and through wisdom can mankind arrive at union and mutual understanding. To understand is to forgive."

A Kansas City woman was inspired with the idea of presenting her city's museum with the painting *Lord of the Night*, in the name of the children. The entire city and children of all ages enthusiastically adopted her plan. They made appeals through the news, held children's parades, and spontaneously raised one thousand dollars for the purchase. Roerich was delighted and wrote:

> If youth are taught to cooperate all the world over, this will link them with the future. While much is said about the differences and misunderstandings that separate members of different generations…small mention is made when they unite. Stress the sense of collaboration and responsibility and it will engender a healthy strain of thought; then people will be able to discover and rejoice in all that is beautiful. Encourage cooperation.
>
> Art and science, wisdom and beauty are the foundation stones upon which will rest the culture of the spirit.

One critic was touched deeply enough to observe, "Roerich is not only Russian—he is human." Another wrote, "Roerich is himself a seeker after hidden treasures, an idealist to whom reality is but a suggestion of that which lies beyond."

Nicholas felt his paintings would lead humanity to a future more magnificent than its past. "If the culture of spirit is to win, beauty must invade new regions—regions where now there is only ugliness." He preached that art should be hung in hospitals, asylums, factories, theaters, universities, public libraries, prisons, railway stations, city streets, and buildings as a means of reducing crime and illness—both mental and physical. His desire was to decorate everything. He wanted the world to blossom with art.

Roerich's few months in America had been full: painting, designing sets and costumes, crating and uncrating paintings, running for trains, traveling, attending openings, shaking hands, writing speeches, lecturing, and, in the midst of it all, completing his book of poetry, *Morya's Flowers*. Though the time had been stimulating, in many ways it was extremely difficult. He, Helena, and Svetoslav had moved many times, and money was a constant concern. They still did not have enough money for India, so their plans would have to be postponed again.

Russian men seldom spoke publicly about their wives; Roerich, however, was quick to acknowledge that life without Helena's strength and companionship would have been very different. During their years of travel and isolation, with only each other to turn to, their family closeness had deepened. Even having George away at school was hard for them, but his studies were preparing him for India. In London he had studied Sanskrit; now at Harvard, he was continuing to study Sanskrit while also learning Chinese and Pali, the language of early Buddhism. While George was the scientist and linguist, Svetoslav was the artist and a valuable assistant and apprentice to his father. The plan was that Svetoslav would join George at Harvard and begin architectural studies the next year. However, the school year was almost over, and then the reunited family would summer in Santa Fe.

A Pueblo Indian art exhibition had been at the Museum of Natural History when the Roerichs arrived in New York. It is doubtful whether many New Yorkers enjoyed it as much as Nicholas did, for he saw his own people of the steppes and the Asian desert reflected there. What he saw made him eager for more. The family's short time in Santa Fe would enable them to discover the culture of the New World, tour some excavations, and see more Pueblo art.

4

SANTA FE

Located high in the mountains, Santa Fe is a rare, spiritual place, unique in America. When the Roerichs arrived in August 1921, it was still adapted more to the pace of the sun than to that of the clock. The tiny adobe settlement was filled with mazes of narrow, crooked, dusty streets traversed by Mexicans, Indians, and burros loaded with firewood for cooking stoves and fireplaces. The sharp, sweet scent of piñon smoke gently drifted in the air. The beautiful, soft contours of adobe walls were accentuated by the intensity of the blue skies, fiery sunsets, gentle snowcaps, and vast vistas of serenity. Long the meeting places of trappers, traders, and Indians, Santa Fe, and Taos to the north, were rapidly becoming destinations for painters, musicians, and writers. Frances Grant had come earlier to visit her parents and found the Roerichs a house to rent on Galisteo Street.

With a population of 723, Santa Fe offered not only great beauty and charm, but also isolation and remoteness. The unavoidable influences and interferences of big cities and society's established traditions could be so completely forgotten that people were free to explore new ways. Founded in the 1600s by the Spanish, who conquered the Pueblo villages in an

attempt to force the Indians into Christianity, the town blended the richness of its earlier cultures with that of newcomers gravitating to the fresh
air and exotic beauty. Roerich was particularly interested in the ancient
cliff dwellings on Pajarito Plateau in the Jemez Mountains north of Santa
Fe. Excavations begun there in the early 1900s were continuing to uncover the remains of the life of America's prehistoric indigenous people of
the Southwest, revealing the existence of a civilization and culture long
before Europeans arrived.

Roerich lost no time in contacting Edgar Hewitt, who headed
the excavations and documented the discoveries.[1] Almost before the
Roerichs and the Lichtmanns could shake off the dust of their journey,
the newspaper was reporting that the Roerichs and Hewitt had just
returned from a few days in El Rito de los Frijoles, where they had toured
the two miles of village ruins along the base of a canyon wall.

Although Edgar Hewitt was an Illinois farm boy nine years Roerich's
senior, Nicholas had seldom met a person so similar to himself. Not only
did the two men share many of the same interests, but their personality
traits and life experiences were surprisingly similar. Hewitt had the same
zest for life and also stood firm in his sometimes unpopular and controversial convictions. Both men wrote poetry and articles of scientific
importance; both had law degrees, yet they had become educators rather
than lawyers. Hewitt had directed a large school and formulated an educational philosophy that credited students with innate knowledge waiting
to be developed, as had Roerich when he directed the School for the
Encouragement of the Arts in Russia.

In conversation, both tended to hold forth, as though unaccustomed
to interruption. Both continually sought the truth about humankind and
held firm principles of right and wrong, yet were broad-minded and convinced that one person's religion was no better than another's. Practical
men with high ideals, they desired to elevate humanity. Hewitt shared
Roerich's fascination with ancient sites and ruins and the importance of

preserving the past; both were absorbed in archaeology, ethnology, and anthropology and loved the actual digging and sifting involved. Each came from a well-to-do background and had experienced a life-changing upheaval resulting in comparative poverty. Both were deeply devoted to their wives. While Hewitt did not paint, he championed artists and encouraged them with free studio space. Both men held great hope for the future of humankind and deeply respected the tribes and ethnic groups being lost through the advances of civilization.

The first director of the Museum of Fine Arts and the School of American Research, both in Santa Fe, and the Museum of Man in San Diego, Hewitt still found time to visit with guests and people interested in his work. Both men must have enjoyed their days together. After showing the Roerichs Pajarito Plateau, Hewitt graciously continued to extend every courtesy. The group toured all the pueblos, saw the Hopi Snake Dance at Walpi and the cliff dwellings at Puyé, and visited Taos Pueblo, which Roerich later painted several times. Hewitt was one of the rare white men who had truly befriended the Indians, and so his guests were accorded special hospitality.

When Roerich presented Dr. Hewitt with a painting of ancient Russian dancers encircling idols in a sacred dance, everyone thought it was of Alaska or one of the Indian pueblos. Roerich later wrote:

> If you go through the fairyland of the Indian pueblos, listen to their wonderful songs and profound ceremonial dances, observe their feet bound in white linen, their unique headdresses, and ornamented shirts; after seeing the rich fantasy of their totem poles and examining their household utensils, you will then know the feeling of western Russia or Siberia. It all combines into evidence that strengthens the old legend that several Indian tribes migrated from Siberia and Alaska. Otherwise how could two groups on different continents, under vastly different circumstances, have such striking similarities?

As an artist, I can assert that rather than an invention of fantasy, the
pictorial and musical similarities are evidence that this old legend is
a fragment of truth.

Fourteen years later, when the University of New Mexico and the
School of American Research jointly sponsored a memorial volume to
commemorate Hewitt's seventieth birthday, Roerich, then in India, contributed the article "Mongolian Epic" as a tribute to his friend. "My
friendship with Dr. Edgar L. Hewitt will forever remain as one of the
most cherished remembrances of my work in the United States," he
wrote.

Santa Fe and the surrounding areas were more like remote Spanish
towns than anything Roerich expected to find in America. He delighted
in the variety of inspiring landscapes. "The beauty of Switzerland,
Norway, Central Asia, and the Caucasus . . . Africa, Spain, Italy—it is all
here and truly amazing," he told a reporter. Aware that Hewitt was meeting resistance from locals who did not want their sleepy town transformed
into a mecca for painters and tourists, he added, "I believe that in a short
time, Santa Fe will be a real art center with the greatest future."

Settled into Santa Fe life, the Roerich family began honoring the
tradition enjoyed by Nicholas's parents of "receiving" on Wednesday nights.
Hospitality and aesthetic discussions were offered to the freethinkers,
summer people, artists, musicians, writers, and town characters. Not only
were these gatherings a pleasant way to meet people, but they also gave
those who attended the opportunity to exchange ideas and opinions
without the superficiality encountered in most social situations. Although
Nicholas had a sense of humor and was known to joke on occasion
with those close to him, his time was too valuable to spend on pleasantries
and idle talk. Truth, beauty, and peace were his major topics of conversation. Though the Wednesday gatherings lasted for just a few short weeks,
their impact on some of those involved lingered for a lifetime.

On Thursday afternoons, members of the Santa Fe Arts Club gathered under the shade trees in their clubhouse garden to chat with their guests over drink. It was a delightful way for visitors, resident painters, and townspeople to meet, and those who did not attend could stay abreast by reading Inez Sizer Cassidy's chatty social column in the evening paper. When Nicholas attended with his two sons, Cassidy described him as "quite the most important guest" of the afternoon.

Once again, the Roerich family had timed their arrival perfectly. This time the planning was more intentional, for Santa Fe was on the verge of erupting with its annual Fiesta—four days of colorful pageantry, Indian dances, feasting, and gaiety celebrating several historical events. Roerich, along with sixty well-known artists from Santa Fe and Taos, was invited to display his work in the art exhibit at the Museum of Fine Arts. He was pleased to contribute *Pagan Russia* and *Oku, Sacred Mountain of the South* to the 106 paintings hanging in the show.

On the third day of Fiesta, Adolph Bolm and his family arrived, and the thousands of spectators were in for an unscheduled surprise. In full costume, Adolph performed the exciting war dance of an Armenian tribe, the Zeitoon, thrilling the crowd with his remarkable abilities. His "fearful leaps and bounds" suggested the mountainous country over which the Zeitoon traveled to war or to hunt. During the "thunderous applause" Bolm received, the Zunis, who had danced before his arrival, announced they would reciprocate. Then the stunned crowd enjoyed a rare treat, for the Zunis danced their magnificent "Yebechi" medicine dance for healing the sick, never before seen outside their pueblo. Bolm told reporters it was the most impressive Indian dance he had seen: "The tune, the form, the expression—were all strikingly beautiful, and full of meaning . . . we felt the confidence of the Red Man in the power of nature to heal by bringing the sick one back into harmony with nature's laws."

Roerich was invited to lecture several times, and these may well have been among the few occasions in the United States when he felt he was so completely among friends. Once, obviously relaxed, he revealed an unusual amount of himself as he spoke of the "new life that is rising amidst the ruins of human conventions." He reprimanded the "extremists who twist the concept of reality" and then excused them, saying it was not their fault for they had "forgotten that which rings in every atom of the starry sky... forgotten harmony... forgotten that the mysterious charm of art is in its origin... forgotten that art is not created by the brain, but by the heart and by the spirit." Perhaps he was exposing his own aloneness when he concluded: "I know how painfully difficult it is for you to walk past the gazes of those who have built life merely on the dark concept of money. I know you, the lonely ones, who sit alone in the light— remember there are many others sitting in this same light. And those who share this light cannot be lonely. Though your hand has not yet felt the pressure of another, your spirit will certainly receive this brotherly kiss."

Santa Fe was brilliant that fall, with the golden aspens and vivid red Virginia creeper against the azure sky. When the summer rains came to an end, the Fiesta guests and the summer people regretfully began to board the trains that would return them to their winter lives. The time had indeed been special for the Roerichs, whose group had expanded to include Natalie Curtis, an ethnologist, and her painter husband, Paul Burlin, the godfather of the Bolms' son. Frances Grant had included her sister and brothers, too. Now, however, they were scattering in different directions. George was going back to Harvard, soon to be joined by Svetoslav; Frances, the Bolms, and the Lichtmanns were heading to New York; and the Roerichs were continuing west to meet the exhibition in San Francisco.

As the train carried them toward California, September's intense, dry heat accentuated the monotony and flatness of the open land. After hundreds of miles of desert, they stopped at the Grand Canyon. Nicholas, who preferred the images he carried in his mind of the breathtaking wildness of India, the cloud-shrouded majesty of the Himalayan summits, and

Russia's vast charm, did not enjoy the stark beauty of the desert. Although *The Miracle* was painted as a radiant remembrance of the Grand Canyon, in *Himavat, Diary Leaves* he relates the story of a traveler so oppressed by the prospect of the endless descent necessary to reach the canyon bottom that even the expectation of seeing beautiful colors did not help. Whether that was Roerich's own sentiment or not, the paintings he completed at this time, other than *The Miracle*, were heavy, dark, and dull.

Traveling north through California, they stopped in some of the picturesque towns along the coast. Nicholas spoke on "Joy of Art" at the California Art School and the University of California, telling stories about the importance of his excavations and the beauty of Russian icons. A reviewer of his exhibition at the San Francisco Museum called Roerich "a Walt Whitman of painting" and wrote that only a master craftsman could handle tempera and pastel together in such a manner.

Traveling with his exhibition: Nicholas Roerich at the San Francisco Museum of Art

Within weeks, they were back in Santa Fe and once more among friends. On a warm Sunday afternoon in October, Nicholas spoke in the Women's Museum Room to an audience of Hewitt's invited guests. "New Beauty and Wisdom to Come From Present Era of Darkness, Says Roerich," read a headline the following day, and "Leader of Advanced School of Mysticism Makes Deeply Interesting Address."[2] Dr. Hewitt was quoted as saying in his introduction, "Other than what we read in the newspapers, we know so little of Russia...of the

Bolsheviki and the old-time anarchists and nihilists, that it is refreshing and enlightening to meet such representatives...as Professor and Madame Roerich, who have given us such a different idea of the Russian people."

In his talk the artist chose his words with as much exactness as he did his paints:

Like bees we gather knowledge, and like bees we pack it into odd honeycombs. But at the end of the year who has the real treasures? The things of yesterday are like the ashes of last night's fires, but even in the midst of accidents and destruction, evidence appears of that which is precious to our spirit. It is this that leads mankind through all circles of achievement. From the heavings and the conflicts of the old yesterdays, a new path of beauty and wisdom shall come. Great beauty eventually follows earthquakes, floods, and the greatest cataclysms; so will it follow this world conflict. Be of good cheer. Amidst the ruins of human conventions, a new life already rises...one in which art and knowledge will support the throne of Divine Love.

He went on to say that throughout his travels, although he had frequently visited a museum or gallery that had an entire room devoted to the art of a single country, he had never found an American room. And in the United States, he had found none devoted to Russia. Before concluding with praise for Santa Fe, its artists and writers, and everyone involved with the museum and the School of American Research, he said, "Here is a mission for America. Send your art to Europe. Show them what this young nation is doing, and bring the stimulation of Russian art to your museums and galleries. This is one of the things for which I will work because I believe in the great principles of America."

The next day's *Santa Fean* quoted his speech almost in its entirety, then concluded: "The fact that Professor Roerich is a well-known leader of the advanced school of mysticism as well as a leader in art, lent much significance to his address." Thus did Santa Fe bid farewell to someone they had taken into their hearts as the Roerichs started back to New York in October. The paintings were to tour until April, ending in Rochester after exhibitions in Madison, Omaha, Colorado Springs, Cleveland, Denver, Kansas City, Indianapolis, Columbus, Milwaukee, Minneapolis, Des Moines, Ann Arbor, Muskegon, Detroit, and a few other cities. Nicholas had fulfilled his lecture commitments, and Helena was back to her writing. Reunited with the Lichtmanns and the others, the "school of mysticism," the Agni Yoga group, reconvened for a period of intense study of Eastern philosophy under Helena's guidance, while Nicholas taught them a deeper understanding of art.

Since thousands were viewing his paintings, Roerich was quite disheartened that only a few had been sold. Although the United States was beginning to recover from a postwar recession, most Americans were provincially conservative in their artistic tastes. Most seemed to think that culture, refinement, and the ability to purchase art were only for the rich; many considered art a luxury and wouldn't think of spending their hard-earned dollars on anything so impractical. It would take another world war before middle-class Americans would be affluent enough to turn their attention to art. Furthermore, if Roerich's work was unclassifiable and confusing to the critics, it was even more difficult for the general public to understand. Exactly as Roerich himself had to search for that small segment of society that shared his views and beliefs, so did his art have to find its patrons. He observed there were far fewer people wanting to buy art than the great number of American artists struggling through great financial difficulties to continue creating it. He even heard that some people considered it bad taste to have too many art objects in one home. Wondering how one could be surrounded by too much beauty, he called this a "foolish prejudice." Accustomed to a different set of priorities, he distinguished between buyers of art and collectors, and lamented America's lack of the latter.

There had been more collectors than buyers in Russia. He remembered several who were "rich only in the brightness of their spirits" but neglected the more obvious necessities of life to collect art. In Russia, and throughout Europe, benefactors or patrons were a vital part of an artist's life. Roerich's *The Messenger: Tribe Has Risen Against Tribe*, from his first series *Slavic Symphony*, which incorporated his knowledge of Russian history and culture, had been purchased by Russia's famous patron, Pavel M. Tretyakov.[3] Nicholas had received his diploma from the Imperial Academy of Art with that painting, and its purchase established his artistic reputation. It also brought acceptance from his father, and recognition from Tolstoy.

Roerich had become accustomed to the large sums of money private collectors and the nobility were willing to pay to have one of his paintings in their personal collections or to donate to the famous treasuries such as the Louvre, the National Gallery of Rome, and the Victoria and Albert Museum in London. But in America, however, there was no royalty. American independence and private enterprise meant that people were expected to get ahead on their own; the "land of the free" was also the land of the "self-made" person. This expectation included artists. There were enough rags-to-riches stories to prove that all it took was initiative to become a success overnight.

If Roerich's sales were meager, his expenses were not. Living in New York was costly. With Svetoslav and George attending expensive schools, more money went out than came in. Nicholas, however, managed to look unruffled and seemed convinced that things would work out. Meanwhile, George wrote from Harvard that he had only one dollar to his name. In November, Henry L. Slobodin, Roerich's attorney, sent this note: "My dear Professor: I had a telephone conversation with Mr. Ross of the Hotel des Artistes. He says that you owe him up to October lst $500.00 rent, and $52.12 for some charges for September. In all, you owe him up to October 1st $552.12. Please send me a check for $500.00 and another check for $52.12 (if you owe it), and I will have the matter adjusted by securing from Mr. Ross a receipt in full for you." To settle the emergency temporarily, Roerich used his paintings as collateral for a loan from Fifth Avenue Bank. With these crises handled, it was easier to focus his attention on creating his vision, "the cornerstone" of his future endeavors and dreams: the Master School of United Arts.

Private experimental schools were springing up everywhere. The poet Tagore had opened one in northern India, and Theosophists had started educating their children privately. Roerich had molded his own philosophies of education while directing the art academy in St. Petersburg and working at Talashkino. Many of his ideas were so advanced they seemed revolutionary. The previous summer, in Santa Fe, he had boldly told a group:

> In the education of children we still forget the development of creative power. First, men seek to instill into the child a mass of conventional concepts, along with a full course in fear. Then the child is acquainted with all the family quarrels. Then he is shown films, those criminal films in which evil is so inventive and brilliant—and good so dull and unrewarded. Then the child is given teachers who have no love for their subject, and transmit that. Further, children see all the vulgar headlines in the news. Next, the child is plunged into the sphere of a so-called "sport" so he may grow accustomed to blows and broken limbs. And this is how the youth's time is occupied; he is given the most ignoble and perverted formulae; and after that, besmirched and rusted, he's expected to begin creative work. . . .
>
> We are often astonished by the unexpected character of a child's drawing, by the melody of a child's song, or by the wisdom of a child's reasoning. In the beginning, these things are always beautiful. But afterwards, when we notice that the child ceases singing or drawing, and that his reasoning starts to resemble that in so-called children's books, the infection of triviality has already sunk in. All the symptoms of this horrible disease become evident. . . . Boredom makes its

appearance, there is no lightness in the smile, the child becomes submissive and afraid of loneliness. Something near, some ever-present, guiding principle, has therefore withdrawn or receded.

But if even a machine suffers from dust and dirt, how destructive must spiritual grime be to the tender young soul? In mortal yearning the little head seeks for light. In mortal pain it feels all the offenses of its surroundings. It suffers, weakens, and sometimes lies in the dust forever. And the creative apparatus runs down and all its wires fall away. . . . Open the path to creative effort and the greatness of art in all schools. Preserve the child from the grimace of life. Give him a bold, happy life, full of activity and bright attainments. Develop the creative instinct from the earliest years of childhood. If the young soul creates, these scourges of humanity, triviality, loneliness, and weariness of life, will thus pass by.

A year later, in New York, he continued: "It is essential for young minds to search. If this is prohibited, it becomes necessary to destroy everything old, because in the young mind, everything old is connected with what has been prohibited. We must open the door to beauty not through denying and suppressing, but by demonstrating the real, practical way to search, we must impart a new feeling to the young soul: everything must be permitted. And only one certificate of honor should exist—the certificate of real culture."

Roerich knew that if a new era were to be achieved, it would be accomplished by the children, whose "young hearts search for something beautiful and true." He wanted to teach everyone that unity is achieved when all the arts fit together: "If we can see the beautiful evolution of civilization and culture, then we can understand that much more awaits us. It is near; it is vital; and it is practical for everybody. . . . Only the bridge of Beauty will be strong enough for crossing from the bank of darkness to the side of light."

5

THE MASTER SCHOOL OF UNITED ARTS

Roerich envisioned that the Master School of United Arts would offer the opportunity to put all of his theories about education into practice. Yet this endeavor was so large that he recognized the necessity of embarking slowly; little could be accomplished if the teachers did not all share his views. Nicholas compared the formation of the Master School to a tree, saying they were about to plant a seed that would grow into a sapling, blossom, and then bear fruit. At the same time, the family still cherished the dream of going to India.

As the Master School plans progressed in New York, the Cor Ardens painters in Chicago were having problems. Their work and that of scores of other American painters and sculptors had been rejected by Art Institute of Chicago officials from the 34th Annual Exhibition of American Art. Raymond Jonson, as official spokesman and chairman of the artists' delegation, told a reporter: "We are not exactly making a protest, we shall just ask the Institute what it all means. We shall ask for an exhibition of all rejected paintings—not only those of Chicago artists, but of painters and sculptors throughout the country—so that the public may judge for itself whether our works are inferior to those included in the show at

present. . . . We want to know why 90% of the work submitted was rejected. We think an explanation is due us."

Calling on Roerich's friend Robert C. Harshe, who by that time had
become director of the Art Institute of Chicago, the group requested a
special showing of the rejected works. Two days later, one thousand of the
rejected canvases were scheduled for exhibition at Rothschild's department store. Rudolph Weisenborn, vice-president of Cor Ardens International Art Society and "leader of the youthful insurgents," explained,
"Today we had a conference with Director R. C. Harshe. He was very
nice, but he couldn't promise us anything definite."

Roerich had grown up hearing stories of St. Petersburg painters who
had won artistic freedom by rebelling against the authorities. If America
was to have a unique art form, the contributing artists needed to be
encouraged in free expression. Whether he suggested this revolt to his
Cor Ardens group, or just enthusiastically spurred them on, the result was
the same: Nicholas's sponsor, Harshe, was caught in the middle with his
loyalties divided and his hands tied. Harshe's private taste may have run
to the forerunners of the modern art movement, but he was directing an
institute known for what one critic termed a "frozen Yukon" attitude
toward progressive art. Although the mutiny made the plight of the artists
more public, it did little to improve their situation. It went into artistic
history as "the bloodless Chicago art revolution."

Meanwhile, in New York the Roerichs and Lichtmanns were seeking
the best space for the Master School. One day, Nicholas and Maurice
Lichtmann saw a friend who could no longer pay the rent on his studio
on West Fifty-fourth Street. When Nicholas heard it was located above a
Greek Orthodox church, his interest heightened.

Few locations could have been more auspicious for the Master
School of United Arts than a church. The vibrations would be perfect.
After speaking with the priest in charge, seeing the beautiful wooden
floors, large airy windows and the lift, the Lichtmanns and Roerichs

The original Master School of United Arts, 312 West Fifty-fourth St.,
New York City, 1922–23

pooled their money and rented it. As Roerich signed the papers, he commented, "If the tree is vital, it will grow; if not, then only one room would be sufficient."

On November 17, 1921, the Master School of United Arts was officially chartered. They painted the large studio, rented two concert grand pianos from Steinway, hired a secretary, and organized classes. They bought some necessary furniture and equipment, printed the catalog, hung a magnificent collection of rare Italian and Dutch masterpieces loaned by a nearby gallery, and the Roerichs' school became a reality.

Chosen for having the best influences, January 22, 1922, was opening night. When the big night arrived, crowds of well-wishers swarmed onto the lift, bringing warmth and merriment up to the studio. The whole evening sparkled, and the Roerichs were gratified to see the large number of people eager to share this momentous occasion. Roerich's friend the

Russian composer Prokofiev was there; the Bolms attended and even friends from Chicago; Frances Grant joined the group later. Songs from *The Snow Maiden* filled the building with Russian melodies; music by Rachmaninoff followed, and then pieces by Lazare Saminsky and Deems Taylor, both members of the new music faculty.

Since the Master School of United Arts had actually merged with the Lichtmann Piano Institute, previously registered students were ready to continue their studies as soon as the new school opened. Their tuition immediately covered the rent and put the school on a self-sufficient basis. Many celebrated artists and teachers quickly volunteered their services, wanting to take part in this exciting endeavor. Besides piano, classes were conducted in violin, cello, painting, drawing, harmony and composition, music appreciation, and voice, and a guest-lecturer series was presented.

A series of concerts began in March to raise money for scholarships, which were given to forty-two gifted young people. With the credo Through Art to Light, classes were offered for the sightless. First-year enrollment surpassed all expectations. English, Russian, Swiss, French, Italian, American—at least a dozen nationalities were represented in the classes, and almost as many among the faculty. Everyone seemed amiable to demonstrating the same unifying spirit and sense of pride that was bonding America.

With the title of vice president, Maurice Lichtmann assumed responsibility for actually running the school, and he and Sina headed the music department. While Frances attempted to be involved in a general way, she was reluctant to participate more actively because her personal goal was Paris. She hoped to be a correspondent there and pursue a writing career. Although Professor Roerich was president, he felt confident enough of Maurice's abilities to plan on leaving for India and Central Asia in 1923.

In the spring, Frances's closest friends, Louis and Nettie Horch, returned to New York from California, where they lived most of the year. Nettie and Frances had begun a friendship as schoolgirls that continued despite Frances's career and Nettie's marriage and motherhood. Poor health had recently forced Louis to retire from the Wall Street firm of Horch and Rosenthal, where he was senior partner and foreign-exchange broker. The couple was searching for something to fill the void left by the tragic death of their little son the previous winter.

When they heard Frances's enthusiastic conversation about the Roerichs—the school, the paintings, their dreams for the future—the Horches wanted to see for themselves. The scope of Roerich's vision, his views, and his theories captivated them. Even though the couple was more at home on a golf course than in an art gallery and knew more about sports than cultural pursuits, Horch was too much of a businessman to fail to notice that all of the people involved in the school were artists. If the enterprise was really to flourish, someone practical with financial expertise would be needed for the business end. After buying some paintings, they implored Frances, "Let us be part of everything," and she agreed to discuss it with her colleagues.

Considering the financial problems the Roerichs had encountered, Louis Horch must have looked like a guardian angel; almost certainly, he looked like a patron. Over the next few weeks, Horch assured the group that though he knew little about art, he nevertheless had much to offer the school. Both Roerichs must have privately heaved deep sighs of relief when the couple was allowed to join. With Horch agreeable to exchanging paintings for money, Roerich's financial worries were eased for the first time in the five years since their departure from Russia. With that tremendous burden off his shoulders, everything seemed to have fallen into place.

Reflecting on the uncertainty of the troubled years now surmounted, Roerich might have thought about the many paintings he had created as a contribution to humanity. Beginning with his early rousing calls to Russians to take pride in their past, the paintings had ranged through many phases. As his own spiritual growth developed and deepened and his knowledge of the inner worlds strengthened, his paintings had progressed from grim warnings of the suffering and destruction of war to serene vistas of peace and hope. Although upon leaving Russia their days of alarm had been exchanged for days of uncertainty and unfamiliar problems, the work with their Master had put a fresh light on everything. Contact with the Hierarchy gave their lives true meaning and purpose.

The little circle of coworkers. Left to right: *Frances Grant, Sina and Maurice Lichtmann, Sina's mother Sophie Shafran, Louis and Nettie Horch, Esther Lichtmann, and Svetoslav Roerich, the Roerichs' younger son*

Now, with Horch part of the school, the uncertainty was behind. The Roerichs' sons were doing well. George had begun a young people's study group at Harvard. The Master School had opened, and the little circle of coworkers had been assembled and were meeting regularly. They would sit together as Nicholas, and later Helena, transmitted questions the students were allowed to ask Master Morya. The questions were on spiritual matters and issues related to developing the school; Nicholas wrote the Master's answers on big scrolls of sketching paper. Private guidance from the Master intended for the Roerichs alone was kept in Helena's journals.

The first book made from the scrolls was *Leaves of Morya's Garden: The Call.* In it, Master Morya said: "I disclose to thee the knowledge wherein is concealed Tibet's Wisdom. Friends, look forward, forget the past, think of the service of the future, and I shall come to give thee counsel. Exalt others in spirit, and look ahead." *Leaves of Morya's Garden* became the first of the Agni Yoga series—a record of telepathic transmissions from the Masters that the Roerichs continued to receive and record for the rest of their lives.

When summer arrives in New York, people are just as quick to abandon their city as the St. Petersburg aristocracy had been. Some head to the shore, while others retreat to the quiet setting of thick forests and gently rolling hills. The Roerichs had become intrigued by the stories told by Nicholas's artist friend Charles Hovey Pepper of giant rock formations and evenings spent gazing at the aurora borealis on a mystical island named Monhegan off the coast of Maine. A slower pace and cool air would be a welcome change from Manhattan. Reservations were made, the trip was organized, and Nicholas began planning the series of seascapes he would paint.

The ferry was Monhegan's link with the world. Everything arrived by ferry—mail, catalog orders, supplies, as well as summertime painters and guests. When the ferry was spotted offshore, all the residents would drop

Nicholas Roerich on the cliffs of Monhegan Island, Maine, summer 1922

what they were doing and scramble down to see who and what had arrived. Upon the Roerichs' arrival, everyone crowded the dock, curious to see the famous artist and other "refugees from Russia." Seventy years later, the two daughters of Pepper's friend Eric Hudson still remembered the event as the time "royalty" visited the island. The sisters liked to relate, "They arrived as a group, Roerich, two blond teenage sons, his wife, and several others, including a princess!"[1] The group stayed at one of the town's two hotels, Monhegan House, located in the north part of the village. And the aristocratic Roerichs gave the townspeople lots to watch. Mme Roerich walked off the ferry wearing red high-heeled slippers, and the islanders wondered how long it would be before she changed into something more sensible—but she never did. Soon it was common knowledge that the sons kissed their mother's hand upon coming down to breakfast, and some of the islanders were unsure whether to bow or nod in greeting.

Sina and Maurice closed the Master School for the summer and followed shortly. Once on the island, Sina appreciated the unique opportunity to spend private time with her teachers. Early mornings Helena devoted to recording meticulously her dreams, visions, and work with the

Masters, and Nicholas took the Lichtmanns out to where he was sketching. When Helena joined them, the young couple enjoyed listening while the Roerichs exchanged their thoughts about such things as the shoreline, the colors, and the clouds. It seemed to Sina that when Nicholas and Helena were together they were in complete harmony and agreement in all things and a bright aura of light surrounded them. She was continually impressed with their "unity of thinking," and felt that each word they uttered was a "pearl of wisdom." She would always remember how quickly the days sped by while the group was involved in their "joyous studies."

A lively correspondence began between Frances Grant and the Horches, still in New York, and the Roerichs and the Lichtmanns in Maine. Both for protection and to give the Master School better standing, Louis wanted to have the school incorporated, but they discovered it would not be possible unless the name was changed. That was completely out of the question for the Roerichs, who had picked the name with great consideration and purpose. So Horch was advised to fight for it. They exchanged several cables and finally reached a compromise: "Institute" would be substituted for "School." Thus it became the Master Institute of United Arts. With that settled, Frances and the Horches boarded the train for Maine, crossed over on the ferry, and joined the others on Monhegan.

Now that everyone was together, much needed to be accomplished, and less than two weeks remained. Since sharing the same vision and goals was essential, it was vital to bring everyone into a commonality of purpose. One principle of Agni Yoga is that all students develop at their own speed, building their own path and striving to surpass only themselves. Therefore, the Horches needed to be initiated into the wisdom teachings slowly so they would avoid "psychic indigestion."

Reincarnation and karma, difficult concepts for some, were accepted readily by the Horches because of the death of their son. To think that things worked according to a plan, with the Hierarchy, Mahatmas, or Masters guiding civilization, comforted them. The Horches were deeply touched and consoled when they received a "message" about their child who had passed over—and about the one to come, a daughter, who was born within the next few years. When Roerich revealed that he and Helena had actually met the Masters and worked in close cooperation with them, the little circle began to perceive that their work would have a greater depth and scope than they could have imagined.

The daily talks and conferences continued far into the night, as they laid plans for the future development and expansion of the institute. The Horches' backing made everything look different. They worked out an extensive advertising campaign, which Frances was appointed to handle; her first step was to contract for space in *Musical America*. With advertising, the school could become even more successful, and might need larger accommodations, but Roerich felt it was important to stay in the same location for another year, so they decided just to add a couple of partitions and create more classes for various teachers.

When the Master Institute matters were settled, the circle turned their attention to the next phase of Roerich's dreams: the creation of the Roerich Museum and Corona Mundi (Crown of the World), the international art center. The museum, intended to be the heart of the institutions, would coordinate and embrace all their activities. It would unify the arts with international cultures and all future artistic and scientific endeavors. The nucleus of the museum would be 350 of Roerich's paintings—the remainder of his traveling exhibition plus the unsold canvases painted in America.

Roerich believed that the entire fabric of contemporary life would broaden if people became more aware of the inspirational force permeating art, beauty, and culture. Corona Mundi's purpose, therefore, was to arrange exhibitions of Eastern and Western art. It would house an incomparable collection of the world's finest creative treasures so that all people could be elevated and influenced by the artistic accomplishments of other countries and other times.

Once they completed planning for the new institutions, India was next on the agenda. The greatly anticipated trip throughout Central Asia was finally to be scheduled. There were many versions of the purpose of this expedition. The public was told it was "to search the expanses of Asia, the cradle of mankind, for the origins of human culture, the earliest fruits of man's spiritual aspiration." The circle of coworkers was aware of additional purposes, such as being with the Masters and entering Shambhala—the spiritual center of the world. But the greatest secret, the one to which only a choice few had been initiated, was that since 1921–22, many messages had been received directing and explaining N. K. Roerich's destiny: He was to establish and lead the "New Country"—the "New Russia," a Buddhist spiritual state in the areas surrounding the Altai Mountains, Mongolia, and the Gobi.

Without even knowing the entire story, everyone was tremendously excited about the extent and possibilities of the undertaking. In addition to his artistic aims Roerich wanted to study the ancient monuments of Central Asia, observe the present conditions of religions and creeds, and note the traces of the great migrations of nations. Months earlier, the New York Museum of Natural History had sent an expedition led by Roy Chapman Andrews that left from Peking, crossed the Gobi, and traveled into Mongolia. The whole world had heard the thrilling news of the expedition's discovery of the first dinosaur eggs ever unearthed, for it substantiated the theory that Asia was the mother of life.[2] Now their own brave, fearless Roerichs were preparing to go off into the unknown, for perhaps four or five years, with the hope of bringing back "an immortal record of Asia's spiritual treasures and evolution." In preparation, George, who was to be the spokesman and interpreter, had become fluent in eight languages and fairly conversant in some twenty others. His parents would not have to rely on strangers for their translations.

No matter how much or little each of the group understood of the actual purpose, the opportunity to participate in one of the greatest adventures of all time was breathtaking. The five New Yorkers would be the expedition's lifeline. Roerich would be the first Western artist to return with paintings of the "Panorama of the East," the hidden, mysterious parts of Asia, and enough cultural and educational data for several publications. The Asian artifacts obtained would make Corona Mundi an international art center.

Each member of the group felt extremely privileged to be working with the Masters and with the Roerichs, whose mission was to better humanity, spiritually and culturally. For years thereafter, outsiders questioned the circle's intensity, commitment, and unwavering devotion. Newspaper reporters and others wondered what it was that kept them so connected. Were they a "cult"? The group, not wanting to give people any reason to discredit Roerich, kept their teachings secret. They kept Agni Yoga and their studies so well hidden and separate from the Master Institute that not even the teachers in the school detected a trace of the secrets binding them together.

Before leaving, Roerich pledged to contribute several hundred more paintings and agreed that all paintings resulting from the expedition would belong to the museum. He was not to receive any salary or financial compensation in exchange, but could use money raised by the Master Institute, the Roerich Museum, and Corona Mundi from various donors and sympathetic friends so that they could purchase artistic treasures for Corona Mundi during their travels. Louis Horch enthusiastically agreed to do his utmost to have all these plans realized and, when necessary, to contribute his own money to the institutions to enable them to finance the expedition.

Another item of great importance to Nicholas was the future of art in America. He stressed the necessity of encouraging the modernists to develop their own niche in the art world, perhaps by explaining that his benefactor Pavel Tretyakov had ultimately bettered the lives of both the painters, and all Russians, by contributing his vast collection of Russian art to Moscow. When Roerich recommended that the Horches become patrons and begin collecting the work of a few great American artists, they were so enthusiastic that they immediately ordered stationery and began planning for the first Museum of American Art.

Then the Monhegan respite was over. The group agreed with Sina, who remembered, "That lovely summer was forever ingrained in our hearts." On all levels, the things that transpired on that island completely changed the lives of every person there. Each member of the circle left committed to studying the Agni Yoga teachings and doing the work necessary to advance along the spiritual path. Nettie and Louis Horch now had a sense of purpose and the peace of knowing they had a new, firm direction. Ahead for the Lichtmanns were plans for a school with a far greater potential than anything they had imagined. Frances abandoned her dreams of Paris, resigned from *Musical America*, and took over the job of institute director. She would handle the publicity, advertising, secretarial work, and anything else needing attention.

The Roerichs could see many, many benefits from their time in America. Perhaps the path to and through India would now be cleared for them. Naively, they hoped that leaving from America with American financial backing and carrying the American flag would spare them from difficulties that could arise because they were Russian. Their Master advised, "Strive and thou wilt perceive the light. . . . Steadfastness is the requisite of those who strive for the path of ascension." Did that forewarn that problems awaited them?

Perhaps the Master's advice applied to Maurice Lichtmann's young sister, Esther J. Lichtmann, who joined the circle that summer. Years later, when Frances Grant remembered the whole affair, she would comment that Miss Lichtmann brought an "unfortunate note into the whole works." A recent émigré from Russia, Esther had escaped into Switzerland and had been staying with another of Maurice's sisters when Frances had visited earlier in the year. Seeing how poor their living conditions were, she arranged for them to get food and clothing and immediately informed Sina, who encouraged Maurice to bring Esther to America. Since someone was needed to teach children at the institute and Esther played piano, complying with the employment requirements for her immigration into the United States had been a simple matter. So it was that Esther appeared in New York one day. Before long, she had learned some English, joined their faculty, and was ready to take her perplexing part in one of the unfolding dramas.

6

India at Last

The Master Institute came to life with the beginning of fall. Throughout the days and evenings, the studio was filled with the pleasant hum of various lessons and the muted voices of people lecturing on architecture, drama, sculpture, or painting. Maurice experienced the biggest change, for he was able to leave the administrative work to Frances and focus on teaching.

Roerich conducted special art criticism classes for artists and took on the job of educating the Horches. Wanting to support innovative and experimental artists, he encouraged the Horches to purchase an abstract fantasy painted by Jerome Myers, a pencil-watercolor-pastel done by Maurice Prendergast, a landscape by Sidney Laufman, and a fine example of Ryder's work. Roerich's other favorites were George Bellows, Rockwell Kent, Marsden Hartley, and many of the artists he had met in Santa Fe and on Monhegan Island.

Louis Horch covered the business side of things, handling the bookkeeping and meeting with lawyers about planning and organizational needs. He gave much time and consideration to finding a future location that would easily accommodate the anticipated growth. As far as anyone knew, theirs would be the first school dedicated to teaching all the fine arts under one roof, and they shared the hope that it would be the fore-runner of many more. Interviewed in the *Musical Courier*, Maurice Lichtmann idealistically spoke of establishing similar art centers around the country to encourage artists to study both in their own fields of inter-est and in another of the arts. In *Art and Archaeology* he explained the Master Institute philosophy:

> From what we know of the Stone Age, we can state that at that time, art existed in practically every home. As a matter of fact, art was part of the daily work; every home had its own artist, who carved wood, chiseled stone figures, painted garments, pots, etc. And there was music, although since the instruments were made of wood, only rare traces remain. We are living at a time when it is of great importance to reawaken people to art. To do this, we need to give free art educa-tion to every child in public schools, or else to create special centers where every child could get instruction in music, graphic, plastic, and dramatic arts. . . .
>
> Art destroys hatred and creates beauty in our hearts. And if chil-dren are given spiritual beauty in harmony with physical beauty, then war, hatred, and sickness will disappear like darkness when the sun appears. We must start this great work at once. Many mistakes may occur, but it is a crime to delay. Thousands of dedicated artists will answer this call which is so near to their hearts.
>
> What true artist has not dreamed of imparting his knowledge to the masses, especially to children? The question of organization can eas-ily be solved, and a few community meetings will bring unheard-of results. Art centers can be temporarily established in public schools, churches, libraries, and museums. . . .
>
> If every child could spend only one hour every day studying all the arts, the results would be remarkable. Talent would be discovered,

almost daily. We would not have to wait almost two centuries for the birth of a genius. They would be found much more often than we think. . . .

When a call for instructors is issued, thousands will come. True artists will understand this spiritual message and give unselfishly. Each will become a spiritual educator and the centers of art will become the spiritual centers, where the children will show us the light.

Everyone agreed that the Roerichs should leave for Europe during late spring so they would have time to purchase all they needed for India. So the Horches could manage Corona Mundi competently, they would accompany the Roerichs to Europe and be instructed on European art. Several meetings were held with Horch's attorney, and an agreement was drawn up clearly stating that there were seven trustees of the institute, each a stockholder: the Roerichs, the Lichtmanns, the Horches, and Grant. No share of stock was to be sold or transferred to anyone outside the circle, even in the event of death. Louis Horch was elected president and treasurer of the Master Institute, and the others gave him their stock shares to be held in escrow. Knowing the Roerichs' had no need of their stock in India, Horch put their two shares and receipts in his safe.

Throughout the spring, Horch searched for the perfect house to display the Museum's large art collection and provide a comfortable environment for the classes and for Corona Mundi. Finally, 310 Riverside Drive in Manhattan was selected; after further consideration, the house next door was also purchased. The buildings were to be joined.

By the middle of May, all details were worked out. The new institutions would be ready to open soon after the Horches returned from Europe in the fall. The Roerichs were now free to leave. Helena assured the circle she would never leave them without spiritual guidance and would send whatever material she gathered and the writings she received from the Master back to them for safekeeping. All that was left were the packing

71

and the good-byes. Wishes for "safe journey" and "bon voyage" echoed throughout the building as friends stopped in for a last visit. And then they were gone.

Some of Roerich's influence in America remained behind with the five young Santa Fe painters who had decided to band together days after the Roerichs left Santa Fe. Wanting to be together, identified both personally and professionally, Willard Nash, Will Schuster, Fremont Ellis, J. G. Bakos, and W. E. Murk proudly announced themselves as "Los Cinco Pintores" (The Five Painters). United by the "bonds of youth, sincerity, and the strength of individualism," they saw banding together as the way to advance their shared goals of increasing popular interest in art, developing their individual expression, and protecting the integrity of art. The men restored five neglected old houses and converted them into studios.

Having taken a keen interest in them, Nicholas enthusiastically offered his influence and assistance to accomplish their purposes: "Friends, your idea of organizing a traveling exhibition pleased me indeed. You know my ideas of giving people true, honest art, and of introducing art in everyday life. Many cities are searching for art, and every opportunity to give it, is an honest necessity. . . . I'm glad to hear you are forming a brotherly group, and that this group is formed in Santa Fe, in the city with such a beautiful name, where the wonderful colored country and poetic background of old Indian culture give a real foundation for the next Master School. Good luck!"

Los Cinco Pintores did succeed in achieving mastery. Eighty years later, their spirit can still be recognized as the Canyon Road School of Artists. The streets surrounding their onetime studios continue to flourish as magnets for painters, photographers, sculptors, glassblowers, and tourists.

Roerich's influence was also acknowledged by the Transcendental Painting Group, formed in New Mexico in 1938 (and disbanded in 1942) by Raymond Jonson of Cor Ardens and Emil Bisttram, who taught painting at the Master Institute for several years. Their aim was to defend, validate, and promote abstract art, "to carry painting beyond the appearance of the physical world, through new concepts of space, color, light, and design." Other members were Ed Garman, Florence Miller Pierce, Horace Towner Pierce, Agnes Pelton, Stuart Walker, Dane Rudhyar, William Lumpkins, and Lawren Harris. Since Harris also belonged to the Canadian "Group of Seven," he introduced Roerich's ideas to that group.

While Roerich was in the United States, he kept in touch with Santa Fe through *El Palacio*, the semimonthly magazine of the Museum of Fine Arts and the School of American Research. Several issues mentioned him briefly, maybe a few lines on his travels or a review of an exhibition. *El Palacio's* last words about him were in August 1923, when it reprinted this item from *Art and Archaeology*: "Roerich leaves America at least assured that his visit has not been in vain, and that the institutions which he founded are already beginning to fulfill their purpose of spreading the international language of Beauty, which he proclaimed as man and artist, and which must open for all the Sacred Gates."

Then *El Palacio* summed up Roerich's time in America and added its own goodbye:

> It is difficult to realize that Nicholas Roerich . . . has only been in America since 1920. For in that short time Roerich's influence in our art life has been tremendous, one that has left a lasting and mature impression on artists throughout the country. . . . The result of his rotary exhibition of 200 paintings, which was seen in 28 cities in America, is felt in the great response from the people and younger artists, who have found in the work of this man a new goal towards which to strive. The personal honors and distinctions given to Roerich during his stay are too numerous to cite, but all attest a reciprocal tribute to the artist who, in Russia, first welcomed American art and showed belief in our artistic future.

It was roughly six and one-half years since the family had fled Russia. During that time, Nicholas had painted landscapes of Santa Fe, the Taos Pueblo, the Rio Grande, the Grand Canyon, and Arizona, produced hundreds of sketches and other paintings, and completed three series.

The *Sancta Series* depicted his Russian past: intense amber-yellow dawns, monks, hermits, bears, fishermen, churches, and candles, painted in crimsons, violet-purples, and sapphire blues. The names of the paintings seemed a message of hope: *And We Work*, *And We Do Not Fear*, *And We Open the Gates*, *And We Continue Fishing*, *And We Bring The Light*, *Saintly Guests*, *And We See*, and *The Messenger* (which he gave to the Theosophical Society in India).

The *Ocean Series* was clearly America, the result of his summer in Maine: Monhegan's coves, mists, and giant rocks were portrayed with spiritual power and infinite peace. The third series was *Messiah*, his finest work up to that point. The paintings seemed to integrate his past with the best of America: Russian legends burst into life, with the Grand Canyon and Monhegan's aurora borealis behind them. *Himself Came*, *Bridge of Glory*, and *Miracle* bore witness to the ripening of Roerich's true genius.

With his Russian perspective and his sublime handling of color, all the paintings were distinctively Roerich. People said that only he could combine the velvet blue of Monhegan's night and the glory of the northern lights with Saint Sergius reverently walking toward the spiritual bridge connecting heaven and earth, and the Grand Canyon with seven figures bowing to a golden, radiant light on the other side of the bridge. Perhaps he perceived in America the fulfillment of Russia's old prophecies.

All of his paintings seem to be leading the viewer somewhere, but where, he alone knew. Like the Theosophical teachings and Agni Yoga, they encourage greater striving toward the higher realms of beauty. Perhaps they are a monument of hope for the possibilities he felt for America. Or maybe they illustrate his optimism for the new era he saw approaching, or his expectations of India. But whatever their message,

India finally lay just beyond the bridge that Roerich and his family would shortly cross.

Nicholas, Helena, and George Roerich traveled to Europe with the Horches. Svetoslav needed to complete his studies before joining them in the fall. Once George was enrolled in the Sorbonne's School of Oriental Languages to finish his master's degree in Indian philosophy, the two couples set out to explore the world of art and antiques. As they studied the Dutch masters, the Rhineland painters, and the Italian masters in museums and galleries, they assembled a unique collection of art for shipment to New York. In September, the couples exchanged fond good-byes, and the Roerichs began preparing for India.

While staying on the Left Bank in Paris, the Roerichs were visited by a Siberian writer, George Grebentchikoff, and his wife, both devoted admirers. They wanted help organizing a publishing house, to be named Alatas, after a fairy rock often mentioned in old Russian tales. The name was chosen to symbolize their love for Siberia and to be the luminous, eternal, indestructible, and brilliantly flaming beacon for travelers that they hoped the business would become. Roerich was tremendously enthusiastic about the project, saying that since the

Helena Roerich, Nettie Horch, Nicholas and George Roerich, St. Moritz, Switzerland, 1923

letter *A* signified something primordial and life-bearing, three *A*'s in the name indicated good fortune, and therefore the business would burst with great vitality and potential. He not only agreed to help with the costs of forming the corporation, but went a step further and offered to help them reach New York. Alatas began operating in New York within several months.

For many years afterward, the Grebentchikoffs celebrated that meeting as a "glorious anniversary," and the grateful Siberian recalled in his introduction to Roerich's book *Himalayas* that both Roerichs radiated more light and unself-conscious joy than he had ever seen. Both Grebentchikoffs agreed that they felt the "very highest uplift of spirit in the Roerichs' company... and if so bidden, would have made any sacrifice, gladly." After completion of the Roerich Central Asian expedition, Alatas published the Russian editions of Roerich's books *Heart of Asia* and *Abode of Light*.

By November, the Roerichs felt they had anticipated and assembled everything they would need when Europe was a continent away. Stocking up on pigments, brushes, poster board, and canvas was an undertaking in itself. They purchased a shiny new Victrola and carefully selected records so they could hear the soothing sounds of Wagner, Beethoven, and their dear Boris Chaliapin whenever and wherever they desired. Endless rolls of film and a new motion-picture camera had also been securely waterproofed and crated.

On November 17, 1923, "All ashore who's going ashore" resounded through the Roerichs' ship in the harbor of Marseilles, signaling the family's imminent departure. Many people had come to see them off, including Charles Hovey Pepper from Monhegan. When the tugboats escorted the SS *Macedonia* out into the Mediterranean, excitement must have filled the Roerichs. They were about to close the gap that separated them from India.

Mahatma Morya told them: "Stretch thine arm across the abyss. Above the precipice there is no fear. More abhorrent to the spirit are the confines of room and rug."

Their long-dreamed-of journey had begun. They were sailing to Morya's land—Korya Morya—on the trail of the Mahatmas, and on their way to explore a vast unknown country. Soon they were sailing around the boot of Italy toward Greece, Crete, and Port Said. Most of the voyage the family spent in the lounge chairs, savoring the trip and enjoying the sea breezes. They watched the Muslims on board praying toward Mecca, aware that it lay somewhere ahead. Docking in Egypt, the passengers were allowed three days to view Cairo, the Sphinx, and the pyramids. Their joy at arrival quickly vanished when they found the mighty pyramids hidden behind a circus of gaudy curio shops. Camels for hire, peddlers, and beggars crowded around, holding out their hands for *baksheesh*. A disheartened Roerich saw the deteriorated condition of the pyramids and the mutilated Sphinx as a total lack of respect for Egypt's glorious past.

Back aboard the *Macedonia*, they passed through the Suez Canal and the Red Sea, gazing into the clear waters and imagining that they glimpsed wrecked vessels resting fathoms below. They were sailing southeast, crossing the Arabian Sea and approaching the lands immortalized by Ramakrishna, Vivekananda, and the ancient Bhagavad Gita. They scanned the shoreline expectantly, searching for the first signs of Buddhism and perhaps regaling each other with tales of the spiritual battles fought by Rama and his loyal monkey friend, Hanuman, in ancient Sri Lanka.

Since 1905, Nicholas had been dedicating paintings and essays to India. By creating the peace of India on his canvas, he had escaped thoughts of the bloodshed and violence of the thousands of Russian workers who had marched on St. Petersburg's Winter Palace and met bullets and death. The *Dreams of India* series he was working on when they first met the poet Tagore in England, *Song of the Waterfall*, *Song of the Morning*, and *Language of the Birds*, and several others were recognized as showing the influence of the Kangra style of painting, which flourished in the Kulu Valley of northern India in the eighteenth century.

Now the coast of India actually stretched before them. The family had been invited to stop in Adyar by Krishnamurti, the young man considered by many in the Theosophical Society to be the new Messiah. But the society had recently erupted with enough scandal and confusion to destroy it almost entirely, and Krishnamurti was questioning his own identity and duties, so now was not the time. Their plan was to sail to Bombay, cross India to Calcutta by rail, and be in Darjeeling by the end of the month.

Leaving Bombay, they decided to stop wherever they were drawn, for they were now in their Masters' country, and their journey was a pilgrimage. In Benares they stopped to pay their respects to the sacred Ganges, whose waters stay perfectly balanced and pure despite the hundreds of bodies and untreated sewage dumped into it daily. Roerich treasured the scenes he saw there, including a Sadhu sitting upon the water in meditation, as people on the banks watched. Ten years later, this event was immortalized in *The Lotus*, portraying the Sadhu in a river of aquamarine, holding a lotus and wearing little but the prayer beads around his neck, with the golden sky above him and the sun-drenched mauve ghats, catacombs, and caves behind.

Roerich also painted the gray-bearded man, his palms cupped like a chalice, offering himself to the rising sun, and the woman performing her morning pranayama on the shore. He speculated that she would return in the evening and send a garland of lights upon the river to pray for the welfare of her children. Her prayers would be as fireflies, traveling far upon the dark watery surface. When he thought of these offerings of the spirit or of the yogis who project their thoughts into space to construct the coming evolution, he could almost forget the fat, greedy priests he had watched in the golden temples.

Wandering among the thousands and thousands of bathing pilgrims and chanting crowds, the family felt at peace. As verses of Sanskrit scripture were being recited around them, the Roerichs were pleased to notice that the air smelled of incense, rosewater, and fragrant sandalwood rather than the burning bodies constantly being consumed in the purifying fires. The solemn cremations reminded Nicholas of tribal ceremonies performed in many other countries and times. Despite the accumulation of thousands of years of dust, the architecture of Benares charmed them. As they strolled through the streets, he identified the Hindu, Dravidian, and Muslim styles that contributed to the harmony.

Eventually they arrived in semi-European, semi-oriental Calcutta, which struck them as a fine mingling of East and West. Modern motorcars, horse carriages, rickshaws, cows, and a multicolored crowd of pedestrians streamed around them like a river. Calcutta was the poet Tagore's native city, and they had long envisioned being there with him. Although they had forgotten his address, they were unconcerned. Certainly if they had met Tagore in London and again in New York, finding him here would be a simple matter. So they flagged a taxi and requested to be taken straight to the poet Tagore.

Three hours later they were still driving around the streets. First they had been taken to the Maharajah Tagore; then, after asking many policemen, peddlers, and passing babus (old fathers), they were directed into a large variety of alleys. Eventually, they recalled he lived on Dwarka nath Tagore Street and arrived there only to learn he had left for China. Many of Tagore's relatives and friends, however, were ready to receive them graciously, including Kumar Haldar, director of the art school in Lucknow and a splendid artist himself. In Roerich's usual way, all were soon engrossed in the free exchange of ideas.

Afterward, Nicholas lamented to his diary the universally precarious condition of artists and scientists: "Why must the path of knowledge and beauty be so difficult?" He was pleased to hear that new schools and three new universities would soon decrease India's high rate of illiteracy and claim a victory for evolution: "Legions of newly enlightened workers for science and beauty were being prepared to serve mankind."

The Roerichs enjoyed discovering the monuments to the cherished teacher of Vivekananda, the great Ramakrishna, esteemed by Master Morya. Across the river from Ramakrishna's home, Vivekananda had established the Ramakrishna Mission and built a mausoleum to hold the revered ashes of Ramakrishna and his wife. Vivekananda had once dreamed of building a Hindu university that would integrate science with Vedanta, the synthesis of Hindu thought, and help create a unified world by teaching an amalgamation of East and West. Roerich regretted that the dream had not been fulfilled. If it were possible anywhere, he felt America would be the place.

The Roerichs were completely delighted to see the pilgrims and tourists as they jostled among the profusion of shrines lined with brightly colored gods, goddesses, animals, and mythical figures. Scents of jasmine, spices, and humans filled the air. Women silently flitted by, looking like butterflies in their brilliant saris. Smells, sights, and sounds jumbled together, defying description.

Wherever they went, they heard the Ramayana being spoken or sung, and four times each day all Muslims were summoned to prayer. They scarcely noticed the sacred cows and gentle-eyed dark water buffalo meandering serenely through the crowds, quite bland and colorless in comparison to the elephants, decorated in rich reds and mustard yellows, that paraded in religious spectacle.

While the Roerichs traveled through India, Helena Roerich and Master Morya were at work on the second book of *Leaves of Morya's Garden*, printed first in Paris. In it, Master Morya explained the quality and characteristics of the labor that expands consciousness, the universal functions, the cosmic laws, the commandments of Buddha and Christ, and infinitely more. These teachings of great delicacy and beauty would one day go around the world through Helena's books.

India surrounded them, adding great depth and dimension to their lives. Traveling gave the family wonderful opportunities for discussion, and they drew on the consistently encouraging messages from the Master.

I speak of alien bridges and gates. They must be spanned quickly without looking downward, and with only the wish to reach the other side. Since your way is determined, calmly demand your right of way and do not pause before foreign gates.

When times are difficult repeat: Nevertheless I am going into a Garden of Beauty. I fear not the predestined gates. Why is the shield above me? To safeguard me. If new dams arise I shall cross them because I do not fear!

When the raindrop taps upon the window—
    it is My sign!
When the bird flutters—
    it is My sign!
When the leaves are borne aloft by the whirlwind—
    it is My sign!
When the ice is melted by the sun—
    it is My sign!
When the waves wash away the sorrow of the soul—
    it is My sign!
When the wing of illumination touches the harried soul—
    it is My sign!

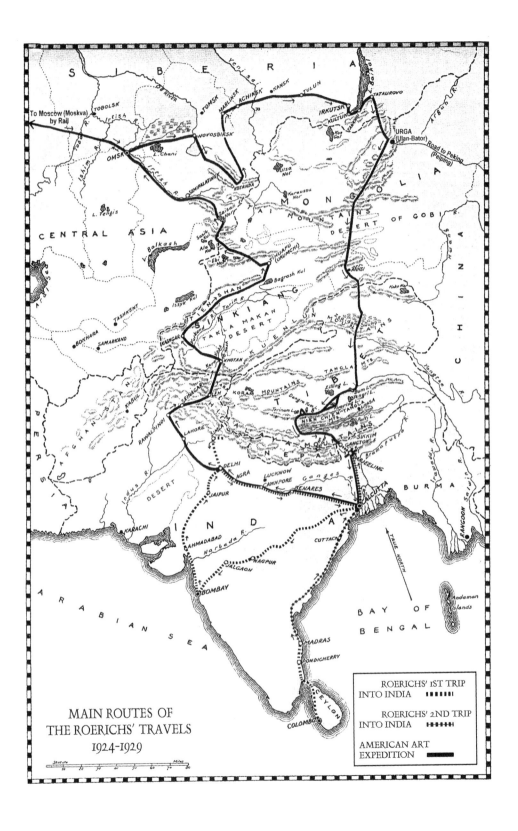

MAIN ROUTES OF
THE ROERICHS' TRAVELS
1924-1929

ROERICHS' 1ST TRIP INTO INDIA	
ROERICHS' 2ND TRIP INTO INDIA	
AMERICAN ART EXPEDITION	

7

WHERE CAN ONE HAVE SUCH JOY?

Five miles from Benares lies the Deer Park, where Siddhartha Gautama (the Buddha, or "Enlightened One") originally gathered his disciples and preached the Eightfold Path and the Four Noble Truths. Several gigantic stone stupas, believed to contain some of the Buddha's physical remains, flank the entrance.[1] In December 1923, the four Roerichs were standing on the very ground where the Buddha once stood, discussing the tremendous impact his forty-five years of public ministry had made on the world. They recalled the legend that the High Ones had been present for the Buddha's initiation "somewhere north of the Himalayas."

The exact location, however, was as much a mystery as the actual locations of Mount Meru, the mountain at the center of the world that connects heaven and earth, or the place where Jesus had spent his "lost years." Perhaps these places do not actually exist on the physical plane, but only in our consciousness, to be seen with the third eye.

When Padmasambhava brought Buddhism to Tibet in the eighth century, he also brought word of Shambhala, the mystical kingdom, hidden behind snow peaks somewhere north of Tibet. The capital, Kalapa, is located in the center of the kingdom. Most recently, Master Morya had spoken of it as "Our Abode": "Shambhala is the indispensable site where the spiritual world unites with the material world. As in a magnet there exists the point of utmost attraction, so the gates of the spiritual world open into the Mountain Dwelling. The manifested height of Mt. Guarisankar helps the magnetic current. Jacob's Ladder is the symbol of Our Abode."

The earliest references to Shambhala were found in the more than three hundred volumes of Kangyur and Tangyur, the sacred books of Tibetan Buddhism. They told that the hidden kingdom, an oasis completely ringed by high, snowy mountains glistening with ice, lay to the north of Bodh Gaya, the Buddhist shrine in northern India. The mountains, ice, and harsh weather prevent the unfit from entering. Some lamas thought the peaks were perpetually hidden in mist, while others believed they were visible, but too remote for anyone to get close enough to see. Many Tibetans regarded Shambhala as a heaven of the gods or a special kind of paradise, meant only for those on their way to Nirvana.

However, when Lama Dorzhiev had spoken of it during construction of the Buddhist temple in 1912, he was not speaking of it as a destination, but rather as a prophecy. Legend foretold the day when Rigden Jyepo, the king of Shambhala, would come with a great army to destroy the forces of evil and usher in a golden age: the Age of Maitreya. Shambhala, therefore, symbolized the great future, when the Panchen Lama would be reborn as Rigden Jyepo and the reign of Maitreya, the Coming One, would begin. Shambhala was not only the abode of mystical Buddhist learning, it was the guiding principle of the coming cosmic age. At the sound of that powerful name, "Shambhala," something surely awoke in the Roerichs, as it does in all mortals who yearn to live in peace and freedom.

But when Master Morya spoke to the couple of Shambhala as "the New Country" or the New Russia, that was another aspect of the meaning. In this context, they were to find the exiled Panchen Lama and take him with them into the Altai. There the New Country would be established, with Roerich ruling alongside him.

The study of *Kalachakra* (the Wheel of Time), the highest wisdom and most complex teachings of Tibetan Buddhism, would form the foundation of the New Country. The science of the mind, meditation, was at its heart. Kalachakra teaches people to use the material world, and its distractions, rather than renounce it as monks and hermits do. This attitude allowed the enlightened ones to develop an advanced science and technology, which they put to the service of spiritual ends. If Kalachakra were practiced correctly, eternity would be found in the passing moment—the indestructible in the midst of destruction. Enlightenment and extraordinary powers were gained through the practice. One reason George had learned Sanskrit, Mani, and various Tibetan dialects in his Oriental studies was so that his family could study Kalachakra from the original texts.

From their close contact with the Mahatmas, Nicholas and Helena knew that part of their mission was to find the abode of the Masters. Master Morya said:

> I have ordained for thee a great task . . . entrusted the success unto thee. The needed strength to follow Me is bestowed upon thee. Arrows, shields, and swords hast thou received, and I shall cover thy head with My Helmet. Fight in my name and I will dwell with thee. . . .
>
> Children, children, dear children. Do not think that our Community is hidden from humanity by impassable walls. The snows of Himalaya that hide Us are not obstacles for true seekers, but only for investigators. . . . Give thyself to thy work, and I will lead thee on the path of success in the yonder World.

Yet the discovery of the way would be a matter of utmost delicacy, requiring stillness and vigilance. Numerous hardships and great obstacles would have to be overcome to reach the goal. The entire expedition was to be a glorious test. As they traveled, Helena was to wear a fragment of the sacred Chintamani, a miraculous stone from the constellation Orion, through which the energies of the earth are tuned to the rhythm of the Heart of the Universe. The family had received it while they were in Paris. Before being passed to Helena, the Chintamani had passed from Atlantis, through the sacred temples of both the East and the West, and into the hands of King Solomon, Akbar, and other rulers. Now, because she had been selected by the Masters to symbolize the Mother of the World, the feminine principle in the new era, it had been bestowed upon Helena. She was to calibrate the stone's vibrations for the coming age. "And when they press around thee and cover thy garments with dust, then take in thy hand the chosen stone, and do not forget the Treasure of the World which I commanded thee to safeguard. Remember, remember, remember."

In her book *On Eastern Crossroads*, a collection of legends and prophecies of Asia written under the pseudonym Josephine Saint-Hilaire, Helena related the myth of the "Legend of the Stone," a mystical mission similar to the search for the Holy Grail:

> When the Son of the Sun descended upon earth to teach mankind, there fell from heaven a Shield which bore the power of the world. Between three distinct marks in the center of the Shield were signs in silver, that would predict events. . . . When the sun ominously darkened, the Son of the Sun was thrown into despair, and he dropped the shield and it shattered. But the power remained in the central fragment. "Verily, I myself have seen this fragment of the world—I recall its shape—the length of my little finger, shaped like an oblong flat fruit or human heart, with a grayish brilliance. Even with signs I remember but did not understand."

The stone had many rare qualities: when it darkened, clouds gathered; when it was heavy, blood was shed; when a star shone in it, success came; when it cracked, the enemy approached; when its bearer had a dream of fire, the world convulsed; and when it was tranquil, one walked courageously. It was to be carried in an ivory casket, no wine was to be poured over it, and only cedar and balsam could be burned near it. In *Himalayas, Abode of Light*, published in the year of his death, Roerich wrote: "The stone is usually brought by quite unexpected, unknown people. In the same way, in due time, it disappears again to be manifested some time after, in quite another country. The chief body of this stone is lying in Shambhala, and a small piece of it is given out and wanders all over the earth, keeping magnetic connection with the stone."

Like most travelers, the Roerichs were anxious to see the breathtakingly beautiful Taj Mahal, but it was Fatehpur Sikri, the long-abandoned city built by Akbar, the greatest of the Mughal emperors, that held the most interest for them. Descended from Tamerlane and Genghis Khan, Akbar was believed to have been an incarnation of Master Morya. When Akbar united India in the 1500s, he had been the richest and most powerful monarch on earth. Preaching the Spirit of One Temple, he had established the Temple of Universal Knowledge and attempted to create a new religion culled from the best of Hinduism, Islam, Zoroastrianism, Judaism, and Christianity. But opposition to his new faith was so tremendous that his teachings were abolished after his death. Akbar's hopes for a unified world lived on in people like the Roerichs. Thinking about the misunderstood ruler, the Roerich family studied the walls of the temple and discovered fragments of Buddhist, Hindu, and Christian symbols. After touring his tomb, the fort, and the long-abandoned city, they departed with heavy hearts. A veil of limitless sorrow seemed to hang over the remains.

In the wild mountainous country of the western Deccan, they visited the famous Ajanta caves, carved out of solid rock and concealed by jungle for two thousand years. They continued on to the splendid Ellora Caves, where they viewed Buddhist, Hindu, and Jain frescoes created over eight centuries. As they wandered among the thirty-four richly colored shrines strung along a cliff, Nicholas's first thoughts were for the preservation of the frescoes. Then he speculated about the possibility of hidden passages in the caves opening into extensive tunnels under Asia. According to ancient Brahmin tradition, when the Gobi was under the sea, the Nephilim who lived there dug tunnels and linked them to the outside world. It was even rumored that the tunnels were hundreds of miles long and connected with some in Tibet.

Before December was out, the family had seen roaring tigers; an arranged monkey battle; fakirs charming old, toothless cobras; pitiful yogis whirling in the bazaar; a fairyland astrological observatory; charming doors and balconies; and countless monuments. They had ridden through innumerable villages, observed superbly carved temples, strolled through marble palace halls inlaid with jewels, and toured places of artistic, historic, and religious significance. Continually astonished by India's striking beauty, they rejoiced to be in this land of endless wonder, and little escaped their attention.

To Nicholas's trained eye, everything seemed coordinated in tremendously lavish designs. He told his diary: "If in the crowd your next neighbor should be a skeleton, pale with leprosy, you are not frightened. Next to you will lean a sadhu, colored with blue stripes, with a headdress made of cow dung. You are not surprised. A fakir with toothless cobras will cheat you. You are smiling. The chariot of Jagernath crushes the crowd—you are not astonished. There is a procession of fearful Nagis of Rajputana, with blades like curved fangs. You are calm." Yet, compared with the real treasure of India, all of these things were as nothing: "Where are those for whose sake we have come to India? They do not sit in the bazaars and they do not walk in processions. And no one enters their dwellings without their consent. But do they really exist? Yes, yes, they exist, and so does their knowledge and skill. And all human substance is exalted because of them. Not even leprosy would turn me away from India."

The Roerich family in India, December 1923 (a rare shot of the entire family)

In Helena's messages, their teacher responded: "And when you ask yourself—where are They Who made promises?—We are standing behind you; and We rejoice, measuring the growth of the flower of your aura. We rejoice because this is Our Garden. Beyond bounded vistas the Light unites the hearts." The Master told them to ask not, "Where does He live? But rather, when can I be useful? When should I prepare myself for labor and when will the call come?"

They were told they could be useful from that hour unto eternity, to lose no time in preparation, to work by enhancing the quality of their labor, and even to sleep vigilantly. Roerich speculated that their friends in the West might think the wonders they saw were displays of a higher miraculous power: a man walking through fire, another sitting on water, a third suspended in air, a fourth lying on nails, a fifth swallowing poison without harm, while a sixth could kill with a glance, and a seventh was buried without harm. However, he did not believe he had witnessed any miracles, rather, displays of psychic energy obeying psychophysical laws. They were proof that obstacles of lower matter could be overcome. Anyone could learn to do them.

He pointed out that India had long been familiar with research presently taking place at the Metaphysical Institute in Paris into ectoplasm, the photography of auras, and attempts to transmit thought at a distance. Rather than unbelievable novelties, he saw these phenomena as the results of long-known laws—perhaps the consequences of the practical teaching of Buddhism, which developed indomitable determination and tremendous patience in the person attempting to achieve an independent consciousness.

Nicholas frequently corresponded with Tagore's friend Sir Jagadis Bose, the president of the Indian Science Congress and the first Indian scientist to receive international acclaim.[2] Bose postulated that the vegetable kingdom was the link between the worlds of animals and inorganic matter. His scientific experiments had validated the accuracy of Vedanta, the Mahabharata, and the poetry and legends of the Himalayas. Using ingenious and delicate instruments he had invented, Bose demonstrated that plants were sensitive enough to feel the formation of a cloud long before it was visible to the eye. These investigations delighted Roerich, who said that when the silvery tones of Sir Jagadis Bose's "electric apparatus" tinkled out the pulse of plants, they reopened long-sealed pages of the world's knowledge.

About this time, the Master began instructing them on the roles of flowers, herbs, and plants for the health and well-being of the planet and her people. Long interested in herbology, the Roerichs were instructed to study the structure of plants: "Plants are not only valuable when they are alive, but useful preparations can be made after they have been dried in the sun; however, since decomposing attracts imperfect spirits, care needs to be exercised to prevent this." Cut flowers were to be watched closely, for decomposition was subtle, and though it could be difficult to see, it could be smelled and sensed. Small pine trees were useful if flowers were out of season, for they are dynamos that accumulate more vitality than breathing correctly provides. Like a good rest, pine trees offer a most condensed supply of *prana*, the breath of life.

Their teacher explained that understanding the power of nature was better than magic and frequently provided a completely new set of possibilities. The Roerichs quickly set about using these messages about the medicinal uses of plants and herbs. The scientific possibilities excited Nicholas. "Since the acceptance of the theory of evolution," he told his diary, "the old forms of thought are crumbling everywhere. New ideas are arising to replace them and before us lies the marvel of the West moving toward parallel philosophies with the East."

In this country of extremes, the family found much to fascinate and charm them and much to horrify and repel them. As the days passed, they relaxed into the knowledge that they were at home. Things impossible elsewhere were possible in India. "The charm of India lies in the close interrelationship between the visible and the invisible," Nicholas wrote, "and the very thing

George and Nicholas in Darjeeling, 1924

which is unusual for a civilized European, will be an almost daily occurrence for the cultured Hindu, or Asiatic." It was remarkable to find so many people who shared their interests. India's very atmosphere seemed conducive to harmonizing and developing Nicholas's scientific, artistic, philosophical, and spiritual quests.

After crossing the endless miles of humid jungles surrounding the famous tea plantations of Darjeeling, the family finally saw the Himalayas, the Roof of the World, with Kanchenjunga rising above the deep valleys of Sikkim. In his *Treasure of the Snows*, Roerich rapturously wrote: "Legends of the heroes are dedicated not so much to the plains as to the mountains! All teachers journeyed there. The highest knowledge, the most inspired songs, the most superb sounds and colors, all are created there. The Supreme stands on the highest mountains, with the other peaks around as witnesses of the great reality. Even the spirit of prehistoric man enjoyed and understood their greatness."

Though it had been many years since Nicholas had last seen the treasured painting of sacred Kanchenjunga at sunrise, each line was etched into his memory and it was difficult for him to contain his excitement. Yet what he found in Darjeeling did not meet his expectations. British army barracks and plantation bungalows concealed the city's famous charms. Even the reportedly colorful bazaars were hidden. He grumbled in his diary: "Just as when nearing the Grand Canyon of Arizona, in approaching the foothills of the Himalayas, you go through the most boring landscape. Is it necessary to seek the Himalayas in order to find merely a corner of Switzerland?"

However, soon they would have time to investigate everything, for they planned to stay a while in Sikkim and collect everything into one place, and George could acquire a good speaking knowledge of the Tibetan language in preparation for the more extensive journey into inner Asia.

The tiny kingdom of Sikkim perches between the borders of India and Tibet; Bhutan lies to the east, Nepal to the west. The perpetually snow-covered Himalayas, the most majestic of all the world's ranges, occupy about two-thirds of the country. In 1924, perhaps some lesser peaks had been scaled, but no one had reached the top of Kanchenjunga ("Great Snow with Five Treasures"), which dominates the entire range despite being only the third highest. The third attempt on Mount Everest (Chomolungma, "Goddess Mother of the World" or "Goddess Mother of the Wind" or "the mountain so high no bird can fly over it") was being organized. Tibetan lamas retold ancient prophecies that the sacred summits would never be defiled and wondered why the strangers undertook such dangers to their physical bodies when there were simpler ways.

In *Altai-Himalaya* Roerich describes their arrival in Sikkim in December 1923: "We searched for a house, but the first information was not encouraging. . . . We want something further away, where the city orchestra does not play its conventional tunes—and all of the Himalayas can be seen. . . . We are persistent. We go ourselves, and we find an excellent house. And calmness and solitude and the entire chain of Himalayas lie before us."

A serene place of retreat, Talai-Pho-Brang was everything that they wanted. During his flight from the Chinese fourteen years earlier, the thirteenth Dalai Lama had maintained a three-year vigil and prayed for his country from one of its windows. In Buddhist tradition, anywhere the Dalai Lama stayed became a shrine, so no one had thought to show it to them. But if Roerich were to serve with the Panchen Lama in the New Country, it would be a fitting place for him to live. By a stroke of their guiding hand, the family was permitted to move in. Soon they became accustomed to being awakened at night by passing lamas bringing offerings and prayers. Bowing repeatedly to the sacred ground, they chanted, drummed, and marched around the house. The family was amused by tales that the house was haunted by a devil that appeared as a black pig. They were not amused, however, by the large number of servants required to run the house due to the strict Hindu caste system, which dictated the

Talai-Pho-Brang, Darjeeling. Svetoslav and Nicholas Roerich at far right

type of work each person could perform. Helena quickly learned to hire the good-natured Buddhists, who were fast, adaptable, and free to do anything.

Enthralled by the majesty and grandeur surrounding them, the artist was impatient to get the domestic details settled so he could devote his time to painting and exploring their teacher's land. The beauty of the glistening mountain peaks was enhanced by local legends that an ashram of the Mahatmas had once been located in Sikkim and that passersby had seen the Masters arrive on horseback. In June, midway into the rainy season, white spots of mold began to cover his tempera. Hoping heat would dry the mold so that it would flake off; they stoked up the fires. Yet, despite the roaring fires, the smoke-filled rooms, the heat and humidity, the couple was content. Helena knew this was the place for them to regroup and begin building for the new era.

She was involved in some very demanding and challenging work with the Masters and was being prepared to be able to discourse with them in the planetary center, called the Sacred Land. Searching for ways to better the earthly plane and improve utilization of their discoveries, the Masters wanted to establish new procedures through which distant worlds could communicate. Helena had been given the name "Urusvati" and told: "Today is the beginning of the feminine awakening. A new wave has reached Earth today—new Rays are arriving on Earth for the first time since its formation. Because the substance of the rays penetrates deeply, new hearths have been lit."

In the New Country, Helena's name was to be "She Who Inspires New Ways and Liberates from Prejudice." Roerich began work on a new series of paintings entitled *His Country*, dedicated to Master Morya. *His Country* was a turning point in the ripening of Roerich's art. The couple's work with the Masters and the wondrous experiences of India had deepened him to the point where his paintings expressed a new vitality. He was now able to portray the expansiveness of spirit, reveal uncharted dimensions, and bring the viewer into the sacred realms of color, strength, and beauty.

The series consisted of twelve paintings in tempera: *Book of Wisdom, Burning of Darkness, Fire Blossom, He Who Hastens, Higher Than the Mountains, Lower Than the Depths, Pearl of Searching, Remember, She Who Leads, Star of the Mother of the World, Treasure of the World—Chintamani,* and *White and Heavenly.*

Treasure of the World—Chintamani illustrates the Tibetan story from AD 331 about a chest that fell from the sky while being transported by a winged horse that flew throughout the universe—a messenger of the gods. One of the four sacred objects in the chest was the sacred Chintamani. Roerich painted the sure-footed steed carefully making its way among towering russet brown mountain peaks, the small, flaming casket upon its back emitting an inextinguishable, blue flame.

Burning of Darkness is one of the rare paintings in which Roerich portrays himself, Helena, and George. Several people are in a tunnel of midnight blues and purples. A woman and a white-bearded man stand to one side, a young man on the other, a few others clustered behind. In the foreground are three people with faint halos, robed in white. The leader holds a brilliantly illuminated box that lights up the two behind. This painting has given people much to speculate on.

The splendor of the Himalayas surpassed the couple's richest imaginings, and Roerich's fantasies soared there. He wrote in his diary:

> As you ascend the peaks of the Himalayas and look out over the cosmic ocean of clouds below, you see the ramparts of endless rocky chains and the pearly strings of clouds. Behind them march the gray elephants of heaven, the heavy monsoon clouds. Does this cosmic picture not fill you with understanding of the great creative manifestation?
>
> Before sunrise there comes a breeze, and the milky sea undulates. The shining Devas have approached the tail of the serpent and the great stirring has begun! The clouds collapse like the shattered walls of a prison. Verily, the luminous god approaches! But what has occurred? The snows are red as blood. But the clouds collect in an ominous mist and all around, the resplendent and beauteous becomes dense and dark, shrouding the gore of battle.
>
> Asuras and Devas struggle; the poisonous fumes creep everywhere. Creation must perish. But self-sacrificingly, the great blue-throated Shiva consumes the poison which threatens the world's destruction! All the evil spirits of the night disperse before Lakshmi's radiant beauty as she arises from darkness, bearing the chalice of nectar. A new cosmic energy is manifested into the world with the new day! . . .
>
> Where can one have such joy as when the sun is upon the Himalayas, when the blue is more intense than sapphires, when from

the far distance the glaciers glitter like incomprehensible gems. All religions, all teachings are synthesized here. . . .

Two worlds find expression in the Himalayas. The world of the soil—full of enchantment. Deep ravines and grotesque hills rear up to the cloud-line, into which melts the smoke of villages and monasteries. Upon the heights gleam banners, *suburgans*, or *stupas*. Sharp turns curve through the passes of the ascending mountain. Eagles in their flight vie with the colorful kites flown by villagers. In the bamboo stalks, amid the fern, the sleek leopard or tiger adds a glimmer of rich color. The dwarfed bears skulk on the branches and a horde of bearded monkeys often escort me.

A stately larch is all entangled with a blooming rhododendron and everything shades into the blue mist of the rolling distances crowned by a chain of clouds. I am startled to behold new ramparts mounting the clouds. Above the nebulous waves, above the twilight, erect and infinitely beauteous, stand the dazzling, impassable peaks, glimmering with sparkling snows. Two distinct worlds, intersected by a mist!

The fog seems to envelop the road to the side of the ascent, where the jagged, unending ridge of the Sacred Lizard merges the summits into one implacable wall. It is difficult for me to discern the points where the snowy summits of Jelep-la and Nathu-la are hidden. When the ragged, blue waves of fog crawled upward from Bhutan, they shrouded the snowy ridges and mountain paths in the deep mist and hid the glimmering Himalayas. Shall we deny the very existence of the Himalayas when they are invisible? How frequently when something is not visible to us, do we presume it does not exist?

Following the splendor of the sunset, a brilliantly gleaming night sky presented another world for his appreciation:

The stars are aglow here early and the triple constellation of Orion flames towards the east. This astonishing constellation has found its way into all the teachings. We once found a mosque called the Jawza Madjid. Since Jawza is a name of Orion, it means House of Orion. But only the sands of the great desert can identify which ancient cult was practiced there.

The wide-spread popularity of cults surrounding Ursa Major, Orion, and other constellations is amazing. The shamans worshipped them and Job pointed to them as the supreme act of achievement. The constellation of Orion contains the signs of the Three Magi, and in the ancient teachings it was as important as Atlas, who supported the weight of the world. Thus we see that Orion has unceasingly attracted the eye of man. Now the astronomy journals are telling of inexplicable pink rays suddenly flashing from Orion. Verily, it is the Star of the East! And only here in the East does one feel the vital sense and the scientific importance of astrology and astro-chemistry. The observatories in Jaipur and in Delhi overwhelmed me with their knowledge, and much remarkable data could undoubtedly be found in the old observatories.

Nicholas was continually aware of the diversity of mental powers displayed by the people; he recorded cases when people had been told, "Sahib will be sick," or "You will live only ten days," and because of the "evil eye" the persons named had, in fact, lost their energy, their resistance, and finally died as predicted. He speculated how psychologists and criminologists would handle patients with paralyzed nervous systems, incipient anemia, a stroke, or other visible effects caused by a dark command invading the will.

On the more positive side, he told of "attraction by thought," as when Helena received an old Buddha:

We had a great desire to find an antique Tibetan Buddha, but it seemed very difficult. We spoke and thought among ourselves, and in a few days a lama arrived with an excellent one, saying, "The lady wanted a Buddha, and I was told to give her the one from my house altar. I cannot sell this sacred image, please accept it as a gift."

"But how did you know of our desire to have a Buddha?" "The White Tara came in a dream and told me to bring it to you." And so it happens.

Comfortably settled in Talai-Pho-Brang, they hired a company of caravanners and servants and were joined by Laden-La, a general of the Tibetan army, and Lama M. Mingyur, a well-known scholar of Tibetan literature and teacher of most European Tibetologists. Soon they were out exploring the monasteries in Sikkim, Bhutan, and Tibet (but not Nepal, which was closed to foreigners until 1951). Roerich was constantly alert to designs or symbols that might offer a clue to Shambhala and the arrival of Lord Maitreya, or a sign from the Masters; no detail escaped his keen observation.

Nicholas's knowledge of historical legends and spiritual lore allowed him to derive meaning from things others might have overlooked. He recognized the power in simple patterns, formulas, gestures, and words, and enjoyed spotting similarities to things he

Svetoslav Roerich in Sikkim or India, 1924

had noted elsewhere. A person's facial structure, a head covering, the dances, jewelry, clothing ornaments, or the architecture could immediately remind him of Russian fairy tales, the American Indians, ancient periods of Italy or Spain, or perhaps the early Mongols.

He recognized in the Tibetan thankas the image of the same fish he had discovered on the walls of the Roman catacombs. In Buddha's Wheel of Life, he saw the circle of Christian mystical elements, united with the Wheel of Ezekiel. He searched through the great teachings of the world for material regarding pure fire, Agni, and found it everywhere. The cults of Zoroaster had been represented by a chalice and flame. In Solomon's time and in even older antiquity, a flame had been engraved upon the Hebrew silver shekels. Tibetan Bodhisattvas held chalices blazing with tongues of flame. The Holy Grail was shown afire, as was the Druid chalice of life. Nicholas observed the use of fire in ancient Hindu teachings and remembered that the enlightenment of Russia had been administered by St. Sergius of Radonega from a flaming chalice

An unprecedented event had occurred as the Roerichs arrived in Sikkim. Although the Dalai Lama had gone into exile previously, the Panchen Lama had never left Tibet. Now, following years of conflict between Tibet's two highest lamas, the Panchen Lama had fled to China. The government of Lhasa, in confusion, was searching everywhere. It was rumored that he had passed through Calcutta in disguise and was on his way to Mongolia via China.

With little way of receiving accurate information, the Roerichs could only wonder what military maneuvers were proceeding along the Chinese border and what was transpiring on the Mongolian side. Fulfilling the ancient prediction that "the time of Shambhala will occur after many ferocious wars have devastated countries, many thrones have fallen, many earthquakes have occurred, and the Panchen Lama has gone from his abode," this event was causing great speculation. Nicholas wrote in his diary: "Verily, a world-wide war has been fought, thrones have toppled around the world, earthquakes have destroyed the old temples of Japan, and now their revered ruler has left his country. The time of Shambhala is near."

Many special guests visited Talai-Pho-Brang, the Rimpoche of Chumbi (southern Tibet) chief among them. An exalted Buddhist lama, he was traveling throughout Sikkim, India, Nepal, and Ladakh attended by several lamas and lama artists, erecting new images of the Blessed Maitreya and teaching of Shambhala. He told Roerich: "I see you know the time of Shambhala has approached. If you know the Teaching of Shambhala—you know the future. . . . Evolution has been accelerated, and the enlightened rule of Maitreya will soon fulfill the prophecies. Then when the forces of evil have been defeated, peace and plenty will reign and the world will blossom with wisdom and compassion."

Nicholas enjoyed hearing the reverence and devotion with which the enlightened lamas spoke of Christ and was sure that if Christian priests valued Buddha in the same way, then benevolent understanding would surely be guaranteed for the future.

Lady Lytton, wife of the viceroy and acting governor general of India, was another honored guest. Other guests included the British political officer in Sikkim, Lieutenant Colonel F. M. Bailey, and the entire Everest expedition party, who arrived while Nicholas was painting *Burning of Darkness*. His portrayal of one of the glaciers their expedition had passed was so accurate they found it hard to believe he had not actually seen it.

Nicholas told his diary that on the trail one day their guide had turned to them and passionately said, "But men must finally realize that all are equal despite their possessions!" Remembering Vivekananda's teachings, Roerich realized that even among the blue hills of Sikkim, men were pondering when and how all people would finally be united in understanding. Roerich wholeheartedly shared the guide's opinion and expressed it so openly that Lieutenant Colonel Bailey eventually decided

Roerich must be a Communist. After conferring with the British Foreign Secretary, Bailey alerted the Tibetan government a few days before Roerich's fifty-third birthday.

Oblivious to the grave consequences that Nicholas's views would bring, and blissfully unaware of the letters being exchanged, the members of the Roerich expedition were preparing to continue their trip. Renewed by the quiet, gathering power, they began mapping their first two years, plotting a route from Kashmir to Ladakh, from Leh to Khotan, Khotan to Kashgar, and then up the Northern Highway into Urumchi. Although they had pored over Blavatsky's *Secret Doctrine* numerous times, they now were in the very regions she had described. On the verge of departure, they must have tingled with excitement as they reread of underground crypts and cave libraries cut in rock of large, wealthy lamaseries, monasteries, and temples in the mountains.

Blavatsky claimed that several such places were hidden in the solitary passes of Kunlun, beyond the Tsaidam. She described a certain hamlet lost in a deep gorge along the ridge of Altyn-Taga. Amid a small cluster of houses was a poor-looking temple, where an old lama guarded subterranean galleries containing a collection of books said to be too large to store even in the British Museum:

> The now desolate regions of the waterless land of Tarim were covered with flourishing and wealthy cities in days of old, though at present hardly a few verdant oases relieve its dead solitude. One such region is often visited by Mongolians and Buddhists who tell of immense deep abodes, and large corridors filled with tiles and cylinders.
>
> Traces are still to be found in Central Asia of an immense prehistoric civilization, and the gigantic, unbroken wall of mountains that hem the whole tableland of Tibet have strange secrets to tell mankind. The Eastern and Central portions—the Nan-Shan and the Altyn-Taga—were once covered with cities that could well vie

with Babylon. A whole geological period has swept over the land since those cities breathed their last, as mounds of shifting sands and now dead soil of the immense central plains of the basin of Tarim can testify.

Within those tablelands of sand there is water, and fresh oases are found blooming. Well-educated and learned natives of India and Mongolia speak of vast libraries reclaimed from the sand, together with various relics of ancient magic lore, which have all been safely stored away.

On the brink of one of the most formidable mountain systems of the world, the Roerichs intended to cross the upland plains, the dry deserts of sand and stone, and study the traces of cultures that once linked ancient China with the countries of the Mediterranean basin. However, entry into each country depended on securing the official documents and necessary visas. As Nicholas began applying for permission, everything bogged down and seemed complicated. He had no notion that his "Bolshevik views"—and Colonel Bailey's intervention—were causing it. Roerich fumed in his diary, "As for the English Major Hinde—he surpasses everything. He refuses us permits to enter Ladakh, saying 'no one can watch us there.' As far as he is concerned, 'expeditions of celebrated people with cultural goals are of no consequence; they do not exist.' All this trouble for Washington and London because of an insignificant Major. So much the worse for the government which retains such an uncultured agent."

Soon thousands of rupees had been spent on visits to the authorities and telegrams to contact Washington, London, and the viceroy of India. Finally, to expedite matters, Roerich and both of his sons sailed back to New York. It took them one month. Once things were straightened out, Professor Roerich and George sailed for Europe, leaving Svetoslav in New York to resume his schooling and keep an eye on things at the Master Institute and Corona Mundi.

Hoping to secure permission for the expedition to cross the Soviet borders so that they could go into the Altai Mountains, see the site of the New Country, and perhaps even enter Moscow, the two men stopped to see the Soviet consul in Germany. But again there was so much red tape that by the time permission was granted they had left for Saint Moritz, Switzerland. There they were scheduled to meet Vladimir Shibayev. The young Theosophist from Riga was to return to India with them to be Roerich's secretary and oversee affairs while they were on the expedition.

Accompanied by Shibayev, stopping a second time at the pyramids.
On seated camels: left, *Vladimir Shibayev;* right, *Nicholas Roerich*

Accompanied by Shibayev, Nicholas and George once more crossed the Suez and stopped in Egypt and Ceylon. This time they landed in Madras and visited the Theosophical Society in Adyar before continuing on to Darjeeling. Finally, back in Darjeeling, they were ready to depart on their Central Asian expedition.

8

THE CENTRAL ASIAN EXPEDITION BEGINS

On the morning of March 6, 1925, loaded down with luggage, the Roerich family climbed aboard the train for Calcutta. It was the official beginning of the Roerich Central Asian expedition. From Calcutta, their plan was to ride north on the Punjab Mail for two nights until the tracks ended, then continue by automobile to Srinagar, Kashmir, the major transfer point in the east. There they would outfit and staff the expedition.

Since in his writing, Roerich seldom mentioned his feelings or those of the others, one can only imagine the excitement the family surely felt on leaving Darjeeling and descending the eastern Himalayan slopes. Through the train's windows, they saw tropical jungles, fever-infected marshes, and rice fields slipping by, as an endless stream of hill people trod on dirt roads and cow paths beside the tracks. Finally, they arrived in the heat and dust of Calcutta. The railway station was filled with rushing people clad in saris, white turbans, or dhotis, pushing, shoving, and clamoring to board. Peddlers called out their wares above the high-pitched din. A peculiar and intense glare of the approaching hot season seemed to hang over the horizon.

Then, after the long rail journey across northern India, they motored along one of the most beautiful roads in the world, admiring the magnificent scenery and catching their breath as the road dipped and climbed to seven thousand feet in some places. Srinagar nestled in the Kashmir Valley, among towering snowy mountains, with majestic rows of elegant poplars lining the approach. Upon their arrival, the calm of the clear spring afternoon was quickly shattered by a shoving and yelling "motley crowd of Kashmiris" attempting to sell their wares or pitch the virtues of a houseboat for rent.

No more than two hundred years old, Srinagar held little interest for Nicholas. In his diary, he wrote: "Of the ancient 'City of the Sun' nothing remains. The world of Kashmir roses and shawls no longer exists. The old mosque is only a shell; traces of the reliefs in the excellent stones from the ninth and eleventh centuries can be spotted in the ugly rivets of the wharf." He speculated on the origin of Kashmir's canals and about who might have planted so many poplars. Perhaps it was "done by nomads from Central Asia, where winter necessitates the marking of the paths and canals needed for irrigating the sands." He wondered about the origin of the gondola-like boats being towed along the yellow banks of the Jhelum River, and remembered the Volga and the Mississippi.

Despite the trip to New York, the Roerichs had still not obtained travel permits. From their reading they were aware that until recently, European travelers had been allowed little freedom in Central Asia. Only a few years earlier, all foreign diplomatic envoys had been kept in confinement until it was time for them to conduct their business. They would then be led through the streets blindfolded. The explorers Colonel Przhevalsky, Sir Aurel Stein, and Sven Hedin had each mentioned the strict surveillance to which they had been subjected. However, since this expedition was traveling under an American banner, Nicholas expected better treatment. He gave little thought to the watchful eye of the British Colonial Office.

The Roerichs established headquarters in the Nedou Hotel and began hiring. Although George would be able to do much of their translating, they still needed to find other translators. They hired Lama Lobzang, a Kalmyk, and Tsai Han-chen, a Confucian in his eighties, who was an officer of the Chinese Army. They obtained a guide, drivers, porters, and pack animals, and stocked medical supplies, clothing, and food. Each small detail was considered. They would be crossing the highest mountain passes in the world, from Ladakh to the desert lands of Chinese Turkestan, and the well-being of the expedition would depend upon thorough preparation and forethought.

Upon leaving Sikkim, George began keeping an extremely detailed journal. His copious notes served as the trip logbook and later would be published as *Trails to Inmost Asia*. Nicholas started a new diary to sketch out images for paintings and jot down his thoughts. The two journals differ so vastly that comparing them allows tremendous insight into the personalities of father and son. For example, during their early days in Kashmir, Nicholas mused on the great Mongol hordes, the lost tribes of Israel, and others who had passed through the area: "All have passed by way of Kashmir, where lie the ancient ways of Asia, and each caravan is a connecting link in the great body of the East. . . . Beyond these sandy deserts awaits Peshawar, the blue peaks of Sonamarg, and the white slopes of Zoji La. To them we fly with the untiring spirit of eagles, maintaining a steady unalterable motion like the fleet steed."

George, on the other hand, was engrossed with keeping a watchful eye on their outfit orders and worrying about how things would be packed. He listed the number of animals required and his concerns about obtaining them. It becomes obvious in reading the journals that George, in addition to serving as spokesman for the expedition, was often the one who kept things functioning. He pragmatically listed the essentials needed for surviving the mountain passes and the winter in Chinese Turkestan: fur coats lined with soft Tibetan wool, fur-lined boots, caps, socks, and sleeping bags. Nicholas, however, was more interested in the special chants the Kashmiri weaver used while creating his designs.

Since Kashmiri artisans were famed for their excellent winter outfits and camping furniture, the family had waited to purchase what they needed. Now they ordered several waterproof canvas tents with warm pattoo lining, constructed especially to withstand rough traveling and mountain gales. Two flaps were added to keep strong winds from lifting the tent. Tent poles were made of thick bamboo with strong metal joints, the pegs galvanized iron. All supplies had to be packed in leather-covered wooden boxes.

In Srinagar it was possible to buy horses descended from the herds of Genghis Khan, famous throughout Central Asia for their quality and endurance. Deciding that having their own riding horses would allow them independence from the sometimes-unreliable rental horses, the Roerichs bought six fine mounts. They had occasion many times over to appreciate this wise investment. Pack ponies would be hired in relay along the route, as was customary.

While they were shopping, they began investigating a rumor they remembered from 1894 when Nicholas Notovitch returned to St. Petersburg from Tibet, claiming he had found a manuscript about Jesus in the monastery at Hemis. Subsequently published in French and English, it said that Jesus had spent his last years in Srinagar. The Roerichs spoke with some Muslims who agreed with that story and volunteered that, according to a local legend, the crucified Christ (or Issa, as they called him) had not died on the cross, but only lost consciousness. His disciples had hidden and cured him, and taken him to Srinagar, where he taught until his death. His tomb was located in the basement of a private house, which bore an inscription stating that the son of Joseph was buried there. Miraculous cures were known to occur near the tomb, where a pleasant fragrance filled the air. The Roerichs were excited by this information and continued to investigate it as their trip progressed. They found the story was widely accepted throughout India, Ladakh, and Central Asia, where it was also believed that Issa had been in those lands between the ages of thirteen and thirty.

Sikkim's solitude had left them unprepared for Srinagar's fast pace and bustle, so they quickly decided to rent a large houseboat on Lake Vulur, surrounded by great beauty and high mountains, while awaiting delivery of their supplies. On their first night, however, they learned that the houseboats were not actually seaworthy; the boatmen spent several anxious hours struggling against a violent storm that almost swept the entire entourage overboard.

Another day, six cooks arrived to prepare a Kashmiri feast for every-one. At 7:00 p.m., after an entire day with nothing but tea, the whole group was seated around a table strewn with blue irises, and served a mag-nificent twenty-seven-course dinner. Nicholas termed it "the apotheosis of mutton and spices," and lamented that the food was too foreign for them to appreciate fully. The singing, dancing, and good fellowship that followed, however, were easy for him to enjoy. The lyrics of the Urdu, Kashmiri, Persian, and Arabian songs touched him so deeply that he recorded many of them in his diary: "Thou walkest upon the road but art not visible to me. Thou gavest me the wine of life and walkest away from me. Everything depends on God." "If I see but one man or woman, I already behold the entire world." "They say their praises of Christ in all manner of words . . . better was He than sun and moon."

Relishing the evening, Roerich wrote: "And thus, eight Moslems on a red carpet, of their own accord, glorify Christ and creation until the hour of midnight. Next, the boatmen all moved and swayed together, wearing white turbans and chanting, while the saazes droned like the whispers of the forest and our Confucian Chinese murmured 'good' in Tibetan over and over."

In return, the Roerichs unpacked their Victrola and cranked the handle so that Chaliapin could serenade the group with the music of

Rimsky-Korsakov. While the "white turbans nodded understandingly," the program concluded with the locals singing the "Song of Akbar." Devoid of the slightest friction, the entire evening was completely pleasant. Roerich joyfully exclaimed: "We were one consciousness! And all was mutually understood and accepted with kindly smiles. Now in Kashmir as it was in Sikkim, I am amazed by the spiritual understanding. So much can be accomplished with intuition.... Before I hardly had time to crystallize my thoughts, my companion was already answering me."

About April 15, 1925, they moved to Kashmir's hill station, Gulmarg, in the foothills of the Pir Panjal. There they rented a sturdy yellow house, still covered with snow. Their preparations would be concluded in the coolness of the mountains as they studied the many challenges presented by their coming journey. George described their first week in his journal: "At night, the thunder rolled and crashed in the mountains and the lightning encircled us, making it bright as day. For several days we had to keep inside, completely cut off from the world. Never have we experienced electrical storms of such terrific violence."

Roerich wrote: "For three days it thundered and the glare of lightning blinded us cruelly at night. Rings of lightning! The gushing rains poured down and sudden hail blanched the green hills."

The Master explained: "In nature, ecstasies manifest as thunderstorms, earthquakes, eruptions of volcanoes and floods.... Hence, a similar laboratory of spirit begins to work. All are blessed sparks of ecstasy."

The blinding storms continued throughout May, June, and July, but nothing could dim the Roerichs' joy when permission to visit Tibet finally arrived from the British colonial administration. So, though there were earthquakes each week and rains that dropped hailstones as big as dove's eggs, when the stars were visible, bright as candles, everyone was very happy. The entire scene reminded them of Siberia, where towns are also "girdled by thundering storms, surrounded by cedar and pine groves and topped by the white caps of mountains, glimmering high above." Wood-peckers enhanced the picture, and turtledoves, orioles, musk deer, and mountain goats. All was fragrant with evergreen.

Amid this profound display of nature's powers, Nicholas completed more paintings to add to the *Banners of the East* series, following Master Morya's instruction to "think courageously about the Images of the Great Ones; thus you will follow their line of unity."

The series included *Buddha the Conqueror*; *Moses the Leader*; *Sergius the Builder*; *Confucius the Just*; *En-No-Gyoja*; *Milarepa, the One who Harkened*; *Dorje the Daring*; *Sarakha the Benevolent Arrow*; *Mohammed upon Mount Hira*; *Nagarjuna, Conqueror of the Serpent*; *Oirot, the Messenger of the White Burkhan*; *Watch on the Himalayas*; *Chalice of Christ*; and *Confucius*. Several composition sketches were also in this series.

Still thinking of "the Great Ones," Roerich also remembered Mani, the third-century founder of Manichaeism, who was crucified for his teaching of synthesis and belief in the commune, and Guru Kambala, who sacrificed his head as a symbol of devotion and service. About the woman Kali, the beautiful Kwan Yin, and the Mother of the World, he mused: "Who knows how ancient they are? Their light-bearing essences came down from incalculable antiquity, from continents gone long before the Bible or the Cabala. Future studies and investigation must be undertaken that will link the consciousness of the East and West without prejudice, with an eye for only truth and justice."

Nicholas wrote back to the New Yorkers: "You may wonder how we fare without theaters. We have plenty of drama daily. Without a stage, without frayed curtains or make-up—it is real life. . . . One day, it is a Chinese theater, with legends about unheard-of peoples; or perhaps the threatening monologue of the policeman; or perhaps the ill-omened bal-let of the Kashmiri merchants; or perhaps the drama of a boat beaten by the waves; or perhaps the procession of horses, or the peaceful evening songs, or a *furioso* of hail and earthquake. The whole world participates in the mystery of evolution and the creation of universal beauty when understanding triumphantly enters into life."

By the time the supplies from Srinagar were delivered, eighty-two pack ponies had been hired to haul everything up to Dras, on the Ladakh side of the Zoji La Pass. Because they had been told to expect poor forage along the way, George had hired extra ponies just to carry feed. This proved unnecessary and added considerably to their problems.

When their caravan was assembled on the evening of August 8, the scene must have been etched into their memories forever. As in the ancient nights of Genghis Khan, roaring campfires illuminated the velvet darkness surrounding the caravan, under a brilliant canopy of stars. Off to the side, eighty-two ponies and other animals moved restlessly in long rows, awaiting the morrow.

The supplies hauled up by boat from Srinagar were unloaded at daybreak. By late afternoon, amid shouting drivers and protesting animals, the expedition started to move. Helena, Nicholas, and George went by auto as far as Ganderbal, the land of Padmasambhava, and then mounted up. Astride Mastan, his Khotan horse with a star on its forehead, Nicholas quickly moved ahead to trot beside the guide. Step by step, hour by hour, they were leaving India behind, heading toward the land of the Buddha, following the thundering, yellow Indus up toward her snowy source.

Within days, a pace was established that allowed plenty of time for contemplation. Nicholas's thoughts centered on Buddha, Confucius, and Christ, "those teachers who carried the dream of a world united." In his diary he mused: "Is it not astonishing that the teachings of Christ and Buddha are leading all nations into one family? And the idea of the commune and communal welfare is also at the basis of Confucius' teachings? That the commandments of Christ and Buddha lie upon the same shelf, and that Pali and ancient Sanskrit unite the search for spirit?"

Roerich remembered Confucius's teaching, "If the hearts of mortals were kindled by love, then the whole world would be as one family—all men would be as one man and all things would appear to be the same element." Both Jesus and Confucius alike preached, "We must love others as ourselves and wish for them all that we wish for ourselves." Roerich asserted, "The time has come for the gilding to be removed, so that the image of Buddha can emerge as a great teacher, who preached against poverty, killing, intoxication, and excesses." In pondering the line of evolving humanity, he thought Buddha emerged with unquestioned beauty:

> Buddha had seen the true possibility of a "scientific approach to religion" and summoned all to reexamine their values, renounce their personal property, and labor for the general well-being. But Buddha, the Lion-conqueror, was not the only lawgiver of communal welfare. Throughout time many others had performed that service. There was Moses, the untiring leader; Amos, the austere; Confucius, justice of life, who also wandered from place to place, trudging the path of exile; Zoroaster, the flaming poet of the Sun; Plato, who transfigured and reflected by his shadows; the blessed Christ, great in the immortal sacrifice; solitary Origen, the wise commentator; Sergius, great ascetic. All had worked untiringly; all had fallen victim to persecution in their day; all had known that the teachings of good men would inevitably come to pass; all had understood that sacrifice for the sake of the general good was the only way.

The communistic concept of collective good for one and all seemed only logical and practical to Roerich. He saw it as the way to merge the earthly community with the greater community, composed of all galaxies. "Who could be opposed to this idea?" he innocently wondered, unaware that many people were waiting with an answer.

Fine weather accompanied the expedition as they crossed Kashmir, but they had their full share of other problems:

CHAPTER EIGHT

Flies, mosquitoes, fleas, earwigs! All possible gifts has Kashmir. . . .
Our departure was not without bloodshed. In Tangmarg, a band of
provocative rogues attacked our caravan and began to beat our men
with iron canes, hurting four. Order was only preserved with revolvers
and rifles.

Before we were allowed to leave Kashmir, it was necessary to
pay. We paid quickly and departed. In Ghund, our hostlers fed the
horses with poisoned grasses: four almost died the first night out.
They shivered and had to be walked throughout the entire night. No
local remedies helped, so we dosed them on bicarbonate of soda, and
it worked wonders. By the next morning, all were fine and the caravan proceeded.

New to caravan work, the drivers had to be directed in every detail.
One night they laid fires around the ammunition box, but the remarkably
efficient and cold-blooded headman kept them well in hand. A wildcat
crept into George's tent one night and was found lying in wait under the
cot. Nicholas wrote: "Wet, rainy Baltal. We had not yet succeeded in
spreading the wet tents when a new provocation arose. A policeman came
with a report that our people had just destroyed a medical post and had
seriously insulted the doctor. Fortunately, the guard at the railway station
did not confirm this evil accusation. We again bid our men not to answer
any insults. The caravanners insisted upon our waiting an extra day
because of their fear of avalanches on the Zoji."

Concerned that they would be robbed by wandering Afridi (from
Afghanistan), the caravan leader brought special guards out from the village. Though they looked to Roerich like "five ragamuffins," nobody came
to steal. Before the expedition could finally escape from Kashmir's poisonous herbs, cholera, and insects, they had to cross an icy bridge swing-
ing above a roaring river. The caravan made it intact and once they
crossed the 11,300-foot-high Zoji La, everything improved.

Zoji La Pass, one of the great Himalayan passes crossed by the Roerich Central Asian expedition. (Note expedition members in lower left corner)

As they descended, the landscape completely changed and appeared to be a different country. Typical Tibetan mountain country—boulders and barren mountain ridges—covered a broad upland plain lying between them and the scant grazing lands. The people seemed more honest, the streams healthier, the herbs more curative; the air was exhilarating, and even the rocks looked more lustrous.

They were now traveling along the ancient Kashmir-Ladakh road. Whenever possible, they took advantage of the dak bungalows, rest houses, and granaries provided for trading caravans and travelers. If these state-maintained accommodations were crowded, their men would set up camp and pitch tents. The brisk August mornings and afternoons of dry heat kept them aware that autumn was coming.

Casting shadows of purples and greens, impressive rocks surrounded them, and elegant carpets of golden grasses swayed with the breezes.

Roerich spied forms hiding in the crags and chasms, and expected Kwan Yin, or perhaps an enchanted stone knight, to emerge, liberated from the massive boulders. At sunset the rocks and shadows magically softened into endless varieties and subtleties of color.

They identified abundant varieties of aromatic healing herbs grow-ing from the recesses of the mountains down to the mud of the riverbed. Riding along the trail, Nicholas happily confided to his diary, "Although I know the beauties of Asia and am accustomed to their richness of colors, still nevertheless, I am astonished, and feel so elated that I could accom-plish the impossible." He breathed in the expansiveness around him, and speculated that original thought was possible only where conclusions do not depend upon any defined rules. "Verily," he said, "in this place, great decisions are possible."

Roerich often thought he could hear strains of Wagner's music coming from somewhere inside the rock formations. While it played, he reminisced about his friends in Russia, recalling the time when Igor Stravinsky had been ready to annihilate Wagner. Roerich, who loved Wagner, had de-clared, "No, Igor, this is heroic realism, these harmonies of achievement are not to be destroyed . . . ragtime and fox-trots will not supplant them."

Just before Dras, they encountered two stone steles, both etched with the image of a rider upon a white horse. Roerich happily recognized they were announcing Maitreya, the messenger of the new world to come for all humanity. From there on, he encountered countless statues of Maitreya—colossal ones and miniatures, seated or standing, Maitreyas from all centuries, each a reminder that the time of Maitreya was rapidly approaching. "Maitreya stands as the symbol of the future." Nicholas thought it was that belief alone, in reverence for the future, that bound all sects of Buddhism together.

Inspecting the rocks for signs from the past, he spotted drawings of deer, mountain goats with twisted horns, and horses. He remembered sim-ilar images in Siberia and on stones in North America—the same technique, the same stylization, the same reverence for animals. "On the wall of a semi-grotto where we paused for rest, the hands of some unknown travelers had left the figures of animals. Through these images, America and Asia stretch out their hands to each other." He found few human images, only an archer and several rows of people, perhaps representing some ritual.

Nicholas told his diary:

> Again a caravan. Again days and dates are readily forgotten. The character of the day becomes of more importance than its number or name. Like Egyptians who named the years according to their qualities—"year of battle," "year of lean crops"—one marks only the quality of the days. Perhaps the day of the horse—when the mount fell through the snowy bridge; the night of the wolf—when the packs stealthily approached the camps; the dawn of the eagle—when, with a whir of wings, the golden eagle sped upon the tent; the sunset of the castle, which arose so unexpectedly that it appeared to burst from the fiery copper peak.

An excellent relay service was operated for travelers on the Ladakh route. Therefore, at Dras, when their caravan animals returned to Srinagar carrying other cargo, the Roerichs expected to be provided with new teams. But the large number of animals they required put a heavy demand on the scant supply. Long negotiations were required with the local headman, but everything was settled by evening. At dawn, packhorses and dzo (a crossbreed of yak and cow) began pouring into the dak bungalow's compound. George began what he called "the ceremony of the distribution of the loads" as the headmen apportioned the caravan among the new drivers.

Among the crates loaded on the pack animals was the expedition library, including books by famous explorers who had traveled throughout northern China and Central Asia and two books by Rev. A. H. Francke, a missionary in the Moravian Mission Hospital in Ladakh. Much of the Roerichs' knowledge of the area came from Francke's *A History of Western Tibet* and *Antiquities of Indian Tibet*, which gave them an idea of what to see and where to stop. Francke wrote of being in exactly the same spot and hearing a tale told of "Ba-yul, the country of tall beings," said to lie nearby: "Only highly developed people could find anything about the life in this Ba-yul—and if a simple man approached the snowy boundaries, he might only hear babble."

Roerich loved these stories of hidden people and places; he collected and tried to investigate them. He remembered a well-known Central Asian legend of a mysterious nation of underground dwellers called the Agarti; anyone approaching the gates of this blessed underground kingdom would meet only silence. He had also heard a Russian tale of the "Tchud," who went underground to escape the persecution of evil forces, and a legend from the north about the subterranean city of Kitezh.

Listening around the campfires, Roerich felt that the whole world exchanged stories of underground cities, treasure troves, and temples. Russian and Norman peasants both spoke of these things with equal conviction, as did desert dwellers, who whispered of treasures that glow under the waves of sand and then disappear—until the ordained time for them to emerge. He remembered ancient stories that told of hideaways beneath the Potala Palace and subterranean dwellings near Lhasa and the Koko-Nor. A Mongolian lama had told them that when Tsong-kha-pa, the founder of the Yellow Hat sect of Tibetan Buddhism, had laid the foundations of the Ganden monastery in the fourteenth century, smoke of incense had been seen rising through gaps in the rocks. So a passage was cut and they discovered an old man seated, motionless, in a cave. When aroused from his ecstasy, he requested a cup of milk, asked what teaching now existed upon earth, and then disappeared.

After many failed attempts to gain more knowledge of things of this nature, Roerich speculated: "Since we are strangers, perhaps it is naive of me to expect people to trust us with more than a cautious response. One authoritative astrologer assured me he had only heard rumors—another who was versed in the ways of antiquity insisted he had not heard of any of what I inquired. And why should they do otherwise? They must not betray. I discern much of this hiding is done from true devotion.... If so much lies underground, how much more lies veiled by silence?"

Continuing at their leisurely pace from mountain passes to sandy plateaus, they passed castles built precariously atop craggy cliffs, half-ruined temples, old forts, palaces, and monasteries. After several days they arrived at Lamayuru, famous for having one of the oldest monasteries on the entire route. When they climbed to the summit, 14,000 feet above sea level, a view of unique grandeur spread before them: a vast amphitheater of rugged mountains and sharp rocks, with snowy peaks in the distance. It took them an hour to ride down.

At the entrance of a narrow gorge, they found stupas standing behind a low sandy spur. An amazing view of the picturesque lamasery of Lamayuru standing high atop craggy sandstone cliffs greeted them. The steep sides of the cliffs were honeycombed with

Ladakh, August 1925

numerous caves that the villagers used as storerooms and living quarters. Stupas and monastic cells were clustered in the narrow crevices. The village of Lamayuru was situated at the foot of the cliffs, a little above the rest house. Although the Roerichs had read that such caves existed throughout this area, the beauty of it was so great that they decided to spend an extra day and visit the monastery. Once there, Roerich noted: "All of the teachings of Tibetan Buddhism were practiced in Ladakh: *Gelugpa*, reformed in the fifteenth century by Tsong-kha-pa; *Sakyapa*, dating from the eleventh century; *Nyingmapa*, established by Padma Sambhava; and *Bon-po*, of pre-Buddhist origin, sometimes called the Black faith—worshippers of the gods of Svastika, whose ancient roots remain a mystery."

Since the Lamayuru monastery was considered a stronghold of Bon-po, they approached it with even more interest. Roerich wrote in his diary: "From one side they are sorcerers, shamans, perverters of Buddhism. But on the other, faint traces of Druid fire and nature worship can be found in their teachings." He felt the literature of Bon-po needed to be translated and thoroughly researched before it could be explained.

The location of the monastery, and the buildings themselves, had a unique fairyland beauty. If they encountered such beautiful sights in Ladakh, the Roerichs thought, what wonders could they expect to find in Tibet! After a complete tour, Roerich remarked, "Whoever built Lamayuru and Maulbeck knew true beauty and fearlessness. Italian cities pale before such expansiveness and adornment. These solemn rows of *stupas* stand like joyous torches upon the tourmaline sands. Where can one find such decorations as the castle of 'Tiger's Peak' or the endless ruins of the castles crowning all the slopes near the village of Kharbu? Where lies a country to equal these forsaken spots? Let us be just and bow before such true magnificence."

That night, a missionary from Yarkand rode into their camp. He had just crossed over the Khardong Pass by yak. His watch had stopped and he had lost all sense of days and dates. "It was a staggeringly hard journey," he kept repeating, while explaining that Khardong Pass and Sasser Pass were the worst spots to cross, though Karakorum, while higher, was easier. He praised the people of Turkestan highly and informed the Roerichs that the Amban (the governor) was already expecting their arrival and regarding them as his guests.

The next day's march was strenuous. In several places the caravan had to scale tremendous avalanche-swept slopes, struggle through huge accumulations of debris deposited by a recent avalanche, and wade across a stream of flowing sand and gravel. After three hours, they reached the open valley of the Indus, crossed the river on a suspension bridge, and stopped to rest in a pleasant apricot grove. Following the trail that led into the valley, they passed many interesting monasteries until they arrived in Basgo, famous for having both the ancient palace and one of the oldest monasteries of Ladakh. Nicholas wrote, "An impression of majesty was conveyed by Basgo. Ancient half-ruined towers and endlessly long walls sat atop the peaks of rocks, where they mingled with present day temples."

Kashmiri conquerors had invaded Ladakh and mercilessly destroyed all the Buddhist monasteries. What remained of their ancient glory and valiant spirit had been reduced to ruins. The name of the great hero of Asia, Genghis Khan (or Gessar Khan), rang throughout, for Ladakh is regarded as his birthplace. Inside the temple, a huge statue of Maitreya, erected about AD 1610, greeted them.

George also cherished the memory of Basgo. He wrote that it had the oldest convents of Ladakh and an ancient royal library possessing treasures never thoroughly investigated nor cataloged. It must have been difficult for them to leave these treasures. But Leh, the capital of Ladakh, was waiting.

9

LADAKH AND INTO CHINESE TURKESTAN

The following night they camped in tents at an altitude of 11,000 feet, only seventeen miles from Leh. Nicholas, who had gone to sleep early, was awakened by Helena shouting, "Fire! Fire!" Opening his eyes, he saw her silhouetted against an undulating violet-rose flame (the color of an intense electrical charge) that shot up like a bonfire. When she tried to extinguish the flame, it flashed through her fingers, escaped her hands, and burst into several smaller fires. Then they spread out, entirely illuminating the tent. The flames felt only slightly warm and there was no burning, no sound, and no odor. Helena explained that it had erupted when she had merely touched the blanket on her bed. The flames gradually diminished and finally disappeared, leaving them with the memory and a strong desire to know more of such a startling phenomenon.

Master Morya explained: "The entire being is shaken by the encounter with fires of different quality. But so important is the manifestation of fire, as a step in evolution, that I advise you to observe special caution at the time of mastering this element. This represents an essential part of the experiment of cosmic intercourse."

After the expedition was over and they were back in Darjeeling, Nicholas wrote in *Heart of Asia*, "We had many occasions to study electric phenomena, but I must say that we never experienced one of such proportions." Yet, later, in the Trans-Himalayas, they did have similar incidents: "We repeatedly experienced the effect of many different kinds of electric phenomena. I remember one night in Chunargen, at an altitude of 15,000 feet, when I awoke and, touching my bed rug, was surprised to see a blue light flashing from my fingertips, as though entrapping my hand." Thinking perhaps it was merely the result of contact with woolen material, he touched the linen pillowcase, then all kinds of objects—wood, paper, canvas—and each time, the blue light quietly flashed up, without warmth or odor. "Only in the heights do you come into contact with these inexpressible combinations of currents." Perhaps, as he wrote this, the idea of a research institute was beginning to form.

The greatly anticipated Leh gates now stood before them. In his journal George recorded: "As one approaches the town of Leh, the towering white mass of its great palace is seen from afar. Until conquered by Kashmir several centuries ago, it was the residence of the Maharajahs of Ladakh. Since about AD 1620 the eight-story palace has crowned and dominated the city, and the houses cluster around it like stone steps leading to an imposing altar. There is indeed a resemblance between it and the great Potala Palace of Lhasa after which it is said to have been modeled. Two impressive citadels."

Much about Leh was unique. Standing at the juncture of several important trade routes, it had the character of an ancient Asiatic caravan center. It also abounded with outstanding antiquities: palaces, stupas, and temples with carved stone images. Ancient graves, reminiscent of Druid graves, stood on a stony hill. At all times, a multicolored, motley crowd of shouting people seemed to jam the narrow streets.

A dak bungalow had been reserved for the family. They enjoyed sitting on the verandah, listening to the bells from the passing caravans and the singing of people harvesting grass. Caravans streamed by daily, transporting the products of India, China, Tibet, and Turkestan, or traders from Yarkand, Kashgar, and Khotan. The caravans from Turkestan usually arrived in July and August and began their return in October, or even November, before snow closed the passes for the winter. The Roerichs had intended to purchase their own caravan animals until they heard that hired ones were advisable, because the Karakorum trade route to Chinese Turkestan was so harsh.

After much consultation, they signed on Nazar Bey, a Karghalik who had thirty-six pack horses in good condition. Forty more were needed, so each day they went around to the rest houses, inquiring about new arrivals or planned caravans, until they located some new arrivals from the passes. After three weeks of feeding and resting, they would be fit to leave. Seventy-six rupees was agreed upon for each horse on the condition that the trip from Leh to Khotan would be made in twenty-four days. The family was now free to investigate Leh.

After all of their time in the saddle, they would have been perfectly content to spend the entire month waiting in Leh; however, the Hemis Monastery, where Notovitch had said he discovered the long-lost manuscripts about Jesus, was only a few days' journey, so they went. The trip revealed more than they had expected. They found and viewed the Notovitch manuscripts, but Roerich also wrote: "If one wants to see the reverse side of Buddhism—go to Hemis. On approaching, one already feels the strange atmosphere of darkness and dejection. The *stupas* have peculiar, fearful images—ugly faces. Dark banners. Black ravens fly above and black dogs are gnawing at bones. And the canyon encloses itself tightly. The temple and the houses are all huddled together. The objects of service are heaped in dark corners like pillaged loot."

The lamas he found there were half-literate; their guide laughed, saying, "Hemis, a big name, but a little monastery." Roerich perceived prejudice and greed. The only good things about Hemis were the Notovitch manuscripts and the stags he saw standing upon the sharp cliffs of the neighboring rocks, turning their heads to greet the morning sun.

Back in Leh, they continued to search for more information on Jesus, and were amazed to hear the legends denied by the circle of missionaries. Little by little, however, fragments and details were volunteered, until it appeared that, though reticent, the old people of Ladakh knew a great deal of Jesus' life: "Such legends about Jesus and the Book of Shambhala lie in the 'darkest' places. How many other relics have perished in those dusty corners because the Tantrik-lamas have no interest in them? This is the other side of Buddhism."

One afternoon, a slender man, dressed in Tibetan garb and with a fine, intellectual face, approached them and announced that he was the king of Ladakh, or rather the former king, now living with limited means in his summer palace. The Roerichs shared tea with him and spoke of their love for his country and the remarkably peaceful, honest people. Then Nicholas led the conversation onto Buddhism and the fine quality of the ancient places, and before long, the king offered to take them through his abandoned palace.

Entering through a fantastic network of walls, they were led to the famous Lion Gate. Then they climbed the steep uncertain staircases and passed along the dark crossings. "Then we paused upon the terraces and balconies, rapt in joy over the vista of mountains and sand-mounds spread before us. It was necessary to bend down to enter the low, tiny doors of the house temple, dedicated to Dukkar, the resplendent Mother of the World. She stood with Buddha on her right, fresh flowers before both images. The walls were hung with many fine colored banners and majestic paintings, startling in their richness of detail and depth finer than any we had seen in Sikkim."

In a separate temple stood a gigantic image of Maitreya—two stories high, feet to waist on the first floor, waist to head above. Nicholas, struck by the remarkable symbolism, compared it to life: "As though the common man should not perceive the grandeur all at once, but must ascend the upper way in order to reach the Image—as though of a higher world." The beauty of the temple and the surroundings touched him deeply. The lower floor was bathed in twilight, while rays of the bright, all-penetrating sun poured in through the narrow, glassless windows above. Outside stood many stupas, surrounded by glistening sands.

Nicholas began a new series of paintings based on many of the unique structures he had seen in Asia. He named it *Sanctuaries and Citadels*, saying, "I do not care to give them any ethnographical or geographical character. . . . By their general tone of heroism and attainment, the buildings will stand as banners that speak for this country."

The family attempted to rent a house from the Moravian Mission but was told they would have to sign an agreement "to do no religious, semi-religious, etc., propaganda." Roerich asked his diary, "Who could pledge himself not to exceed the incomprehensible limit of 'semi- and etc.'?" Perhaps shaking his head in disbelief, he wrote: "Only in the mountain does one feel safe. Only in the desert passes can one escape ignorance." They decided not to stay at the mission headquarters and accepted the king's invitation to the palace.

"So we live in a Ladakhi palace. The ruins of Italian castles pale in comparison with this picturesque pile, this mass which rises in the chalice of the many-colored mountains." Roerich tried to remember where he had seen such lofty roof terraces and previously walked upon such ruined alleys, and then it occurred to him—it was in a painting he had made in 1915, *Mehesky—The Moon People*. However, rather than the Mehesky he had painted, they were now walking among descendants of Gessar Khan.

Settling into the Ladakhi palace filled their days. They chose to occupy the top floor even though it trembled with each violent gust of wind. Upon the walls of the room they selected as the dining room, were paintings of brightly colored plants in vases. On the bedroom walls were symbols of Chintamani—the stone of the treasure of the world. For his studio, Nicholas chose the chamber with a door onto all of the roofs. The views from the roofs were compensation for everything. The studio, as George and Helena noted, looked as if it were straight out of his 1921 Chicago production of *The Snow Maiden*.

"Before nightfall, the wind blows freely through the passageways," wrote Nicholas, describing the little doors and narrow glassless windows above a high threshold. "Throughout the night, the wind whistles and the old walls shake." During their stay there, a door and a part of the wall collapsed. Every blast of wind was a reminder that each day was bringing autumn closer.

Tumbal, a fierce black dog, and Amdong, a gentle white one, joined the expedition here. The "two woolly travelers" soon became part of the family. Crowds of visitors arrived at the old palace: envoys from Lhasa, Tibetan merchants, Tashildar, and the district chief from Kashmir. "How wonderful that George knows all the necessary Tibetan dialects," Nicholas told his diary. "People here will not speak about spiritual things through a translator. And we must absorb all that we hear and try to gather knowledge from it."

Eventually the oldest, most revered lama came to visit them. Despite his poverty, he arrived with a retinue of about ten lamas and relatives. All of them knew of the Issa manuscripts and said many followers of Mohammed were also eager to see them. After speaking awhile of the Shambhala prophecies and plans to unite the Buddhists, the conversation continued to what Roerich termed "that which fills reality with beauty." When the visit was concluded, the entire retinue, dressed in their white caftans, surrounded the old king lama and bowed reverently. Roerich was impressed by the simplicity and beauty of it all.

Next, a Mongolian lama arrived. He had traveled from Urga to Ceylon to Ladakh bearing thrilling news about the Panchen Lama, whose heroic flight had succeeded. His capture had been thwarted by a miraculous snowstorm, which allowed the Panchen Lama's caravan to cross a lake thick in snow. But the ice had melted by the time their pursuers arrived, detaining them for several days. All monasteries now were discussing the ancient prophecies and the future, and raising and restoring images of the Maitreya! The prophecies and new commands quickly spread among the local inhabitants, who were excitedly comparing the dates of predictions that had already been fulfilled. Three years previously, the Panchen Lama had ordered frescoes to be painted on the walls of his inner chambers portraying him wandering through the exact countries where he now was. All were preparing for the coming of Shambhala.

Roerich wrote, "One must be here to understand the excitement that is occurring, and one must look into the eyes of these visitors, to realize how vitally important the meaning of Shambhala is for them. The importance of the Panchen Lama can be pieced out from fragments of the ancient prophecies. And though they are sometimes dust-ridden and perverted, the very structures of their future are connected with these dates and events, and this makes them vital and thought-provoking. We must understand that these dreams and hopes are the web of the new world for them!"

As the Mongolian lama's stay continued, the Roerichs' astonishment and pleasure increased. "He has seen so much and knows so much and has such keen insight." The Roerichs told him of a memorable experience they had near Darjeeling:

We were in an automobile, near the Ghum monastery, when a porte-chaise, carried by four servants in white garments, approached us. In it sat a lama dressed in a remarkably beautiful garment, with a crown upon his head. He had a bright, welcoming face with a small black beard. Our automobile had to slow down, and the lama smiled and joyously nodded his head. We thought that he was the important abbot of a large monastery. But afterwards, we discovered that lamas are not carried in porte-chaises, nor do they wear crowns when traveling or appear in such beautiful robes. No one had ever heard of this lama—and though we saw his face clearly when the driver slowed down, he resembled no one we have seen anywhere.

One evening, someone arrived who whispered exciting news to the Roerichs of a new manuscript about Shambhala. And on the same day, three items about the legends of Jesus reached them, though the missionaries quickly tried to discredit them. In his diary, Roerich wrote: "So Issa is being discussed, and thus slowly the news begins to leak out. The chief thing is the unusual depth of these legends and the wonderful meaning they have to all lamas throughout the entire east."

The old king had told them that Issa had preached from Leh's high terraces, and suggested that Nicholas paint a series of everything that could be seen from that point, for Buddha had been there also. A legend referred to a "great and very ancient structure" that had stood where now there were only cliffs and rugged stones. The original stones had been carted off to construct stupas, which in their turn had also crumbled. Nearby were a hoary village, a sharp-peaked heap of ruins, and the remains of an obsolete fortress. Nicholas mused that though much had changed, the same heavens were still crowning the earth with the same glowing stars, the tides of sand were still swirling around like a congealed sea, and the deafening winds persevered in sweeping the earth.

Roerich recorded in his diary a conversation with "a good and sensitive Hindu," who spoke about the meaning of the manuscript on the life of Issa while wondering, "Why does one always place Issa in Egypt during the time of his absence from Palestine? Of course His young years were passed in study, for the traces of His learning can be seen in His later sermons. And to where can those sources be traced? To Egypt and to India and Buddhism. It is more difficult to understand why the wandering of Issa by caravan path into India, and into the region now occupied by Tibet, should be so vehemently denied."

Roerich commented, "There are always those who love to scornfully deny when something difficult enters their consciousness."

Although the once lavish palace was ideal for visitors, it was not practical for the expedition's hundreds of cases and bales that needed to be packed and distributed into pony loads. Therefore, after several days, the family returned to the dak bungalow, where they had plenty of space to rearrange the loads and keep their horses stabled. The town was buzzing with reports that snowstorms had begun on the high passes, and the caravan men were anxious to get started. Once the northwest wind approached Karakorum, there would be only one more week to get through Shayok. If the passes closed, it would not be possible to proceed because people took the bridges apart and used them for fuel.

The party quickly had to prepare to march. If they were late, they would have to cross Khardong and Sasser, the very passes they had been warned to avoid. Short of men, they sent notice to the bazaars, and an assortment of Baltis, Ladakhis, Kashmiris, Arghuns, and Turkis appeared at the bungalow daily. Helena chose several promising ones, two of whom had served under Dr. Sven Hedin on his expedition of 1907–8, and several others who had worked on the Karakorum route before.

The family was pleased with the experienced men familiar with the difficulties and dangers. Most had been in Yarkand or Khotan before and spoke fluent eastern Turki. They were hired on as far as Khotan. Their return fare was paid, and each man was promised a warm fur coat and cap, a pair of soft boots, and felt socks. Though two tents were provided to shelter the men, many would choose to spend their nights sleeping in the open or under the flaps of the Roerichs' tents.

Nicholas was eager to get back on the trail and told his diary: "The sand is beckoning me . . . with desert nights and the glowing sunrises. And in this glimmer lies our whole dream and hope. Hence we start on the trail with suggestions of new possibilities, and walk up the mountains and then down to the deserts with our horses, with mules and yaks, with rams and with our dogs."

Few of the large isolated regions of the world are as rich in history as the Karakorum route—the gateway to Asia and turnpike of Eurasian history and religion. Whether on foot, mule, dzo, or yak, the only way to get from Leh to the oases of Chinese Turkestan or distant China is over the Kunlun Mountains and the Karakorum Range. Crossed by some of the mightiest tribes and clans of all time, this highest trade route in the world is crowned by the fearsome passes the expedition hoped to avoid. At 18,300 feet, Sanju Pass is the highest.

September 19, 1925, greeted the expedition with a brilliant morning and a wonderfully refreshing, cool mountain breeze. Surveying the scene of waiting yaks, horses, sheep, donkeys, mules, and dogs, the family thought they were seeing a scene from the Bible, or perhaps the ethnology display at the Field Museum in Chicago. Word had been passed that it was no longer possible for loaded horses to cross the first pass, so the caravan leaders unloaded the packhorses, mules, and donkeys and drove them on ahead to wait for the caravan on the far side. Although yaks had been reserved several days in advance, for some unknown reason only forty of the woolly beasts had appeared.

Much of the afternoon passed before they arrived, but finally, the noisy yaks were assembled, loaded, and moving. George wrote: "After we had passed the last Ladakhi village and barley fields, a group of Ladakhi women and girls approached our column with cups in their hands, brimming with yak milk. We were asked to bow low in our saddles, so that our foreheads, and those of our animals could be sprinkled with it. They were wishing us Godspeed and a safe journey amid the dangers of the forbidding Karakorum."

The group left Ladakh's lush gardens and verdant fields behind after only three hours. Already they could see the monumental mountains crested with glaciers and snow. As long as the sun was out, the approach to Khardong Pass was easy, but at dusk, a sharp, cold wind sprang up. Vast masses of debris swept down from the towering, rugged slopes waiting to be scaled. The expedition picked a promontory near a ruined stone hut to camp for the night. No sooner had they dismounted, however, than a piercing northwest wind started to blow, and they raced to shelter beside the neighboring cliffs. When the yaks caught up with them, looking like a large, dark moving mass and resounding with loud shouts and the drivers' whistles, they slowly filled the open space on the plateau around the camp. They were unloaded in complete darkness.

Unused to the specially constructed tents, the men had great difficulty erecting them in the blasting, bitter wind. The first night was spent in cold as fierce as the Arctic's, camped on a naked plain, listening to the cutting wind. Indescribable confusion reigned, for the Kashmiris refused to share their know-how with the Ladakhis.

Hemorrhages and headaches commonly attack animals and people on ascents higher than 16,000 feet. As soon as the Roerichs began the

Khardong Pass, Ladakh, September 1925.
Far right: *Nicholas Roerich*

early morning march, they spotted frozen blood in the snow and then passed the skeleton of a horse. "We ascended the pass on yaks at three o'clock in the morning. Because of their soft step and steadiness, those heavy animals were irreplaceable." From the top of Khardong the view was majestic. George thought the mountains looked like a giant sea crowned with sparkling, white foam. The entire northern portion was a powerful glacier, the descent so steep and slippery that they had to dismount and creep down. One loaded yak tripped and slipped down the smooth ribs of the glacier to the very edge of the precipice before it managed to right itself.

Ahead lay the Kunlun Mountains, which Chinese tradition called the "Abode of the Immortals." It was said that the Emperor of the Chou Dynasty (1001–946 BC) had journeyed there, to the bank of Jasper Lake, to have an audience with Kwan Yin, Goddess of Compassion. Lao-tzu had said the Kunluns were the location of *Hsi Wang Mu*, the headquarters of the Ancient Ones—the Great White Brotherhood.

Months earlier, the Master had told them of a friend of the Brotherhood who had gone hiking on a mountain path: "And being accustomed to long marches, he went beyond the protected boundary and fainted there. When the Masters found him with their telescopic apparatus, he was lying on the brink of a dangerous precipice while a man from a geological expedition, who also happened to be lost, was rushing to save him. Although hungry and weakened himself, he managed to lift 'Our Friend' (who was very tall) and carry him down the footpath." Since increased nerve tension accompanies that much effort, when "those sent by the Masters" arrived, the rescuer fell into a deep swoon. The Masters awarded him the honor of "co-worker" for his excessive efforts and reported, "He is presently engaged in historical research and is guardian of the paths, and is often heard to advise, 'Never fear an excessive load,' for he realized that the reason he had been lost from his own caravan, was so that he could be of service."

With this type of encouragement, the Roerichs blessed each obstacle and hardship. Although it was only autumn, as they crossed the pass, the family's fingers and toes were turning numb. One solicitous caravan man volunteered to rub them occasionally with snow. Nicholas, who found it impossible to sketch, wrote: "This threatening glacier is beautiful. Far below is a turquoise lake, which they say is very deep, and the entire path is strewn with gigantic boulders. I can well imagine how it looks during the winter."

Continuing by yak, they eventually descended. When they looked back, the pass appeared impenetrable. Once the caravan was reunited, they set up camp in a small, shady spot. For the next twenty-two days, the horses were able to carry the loads and still scale the forbidding heights of the mountain passes. After the party had left Khardong behind, they heard that a caravan of about one hundred horses and Balti men had frozen to death there with the men's hands cupped to their screaming mouths.

The expedition was now marching along the Shayok Valley. The country was gorgeous, with flaming yellow and red sandstone rocks, and flashes of green in the valley bottom. After the difficulties of the pass and the glacier, the granite boulders on the road seemed easy: "Following the piercing cold, we have heat and a vivid sun. The sands are hot; the mountains with their snowy rims, recede, and we have stream beds; sometimes a stream disappears into the stony mass and only the rumbling tumult remains to indicate the flow of the invisible water." Briar roses and tamarisks bloomed everywhere. The friendly natives told them the river was a ponderous torrent in the spring, but now, in autumn, it was divided into channels of unusually beautiful and intricate designs.

Since Helena had never ridden a horse before, her stamina and strength astonished her husband. "Mrs. Roerich has been on horseback all the ten days. She does not do things in a small way, here she suddenly goes on horseback through Karakorum, and is the first one ready and always valiant. Even the knee she injured in Kashmir has somehow ceased to trouble her." A few days later, he told his diary, "Helena was on horseback for more than thirteen hours without dismounting. It shows that the usual so-called fatigue may be conquered by something more powerful." When even the Chinese translator remarked about her endurance, Nicholas decided she must have been a rider in other lifetimes.

Three miles above Khalsar, they crossed a suspension bridge and rode as far as the picturesque village of Tirit, where their foreman owned an estate with a large, comfortable country house. He was anxious to offer his hospitality and made the family comfortable in the upper rooms of his clean, bright Tibetan home. The walls were gaily decorated with paintings, and in the middle of the room stood a heavy pillar on which, to their great pleasure, hung an image of Chintamani, the Treasure of the World.

The view from his roof was superb. Late into the night they enjoyed the magnificent moonlight that illumined the surrounding mountain country and the peaceful valley below. They spent the evening happily, with Buddhist psalms intermingling with the drawling, melancholy songs of Turkestan. Few of the caravan men singing around the campfire seemed to have any care about the hardship and privation to come.

The next morning dawned clear. They headed toward the golden sands on a road lined with hedges of briar roses. Behind lay the blue mountains, capped white with early snow. Soon they reached Sandoling Monastery, the final outpost of Buddhism before the desert, where they had arranged to meet the lama who would accompany them. At Sandoling, the Roerichs were surprised to discover a newly erected altar to Maitreya, the vibrant image glowing upon it. Nearby was an excellent statue of Dukkar, the Mother of the World. There was a good library, and a rich collection of various colorful banners vividly trimmed with silk, painted in Ladakh.

The family was told that their lama had stayed for the night, but had gotten an early start on the road to the frontier. They hastened to overtake him, but it was nighttime when a strange figure approached them from behind a stone in the moonlight. It was their lama, Lama Shak-Ju, dressed in a woolly cap and fur caftan like a Yarkandi. He proved to be a welcome addition to the expedition. Roerich later told his diary of an unexpected discovery: "It appears that the lama speaks Russian, and even knows many of our friends. All the while, no one would have suspected this. When we spoke Russian in his presence, not a muscle revealed that he understood. And his answers never once exposed that he knew what we had said. Once more, it is clear how difficult it is to appraise the measure of a lama's knowledge."

The following day the caravan reached the foot of the next pass and camped before beginning the ascent. The night was unexpectedly enlivened by a Muslim who came to share their fire and spoke to them of Mohammed and his reverence for woman. He knew the legends of Jesus' tomb in Srinagar and Mary's tomb in Kashgar. Roerich noted, "Again the legends of Issa . . . these are of especial interest to the Moslems too!"

Then the expedition started for Karaul Pass, which seemed more difficult than Khardong, despite being lower. Enormous masses of boulders lined the route; the path between them was so narrow that the caravan had to squeeze between rocks. As they filed past a trail of frozen animals' skeletons in all stages of decomposition, Roerich was glad that it was too cold to smell the decay. Congealed in a jumping position, they reminded him of the last leap of the Valkyrie.

Somewhere along the trail was the boundary line dividing Ladakh and Chinese Turkestan. No one seemed to know exactly where it was, which Roerich enjoyed, for that made it seem as if this beautiful land belonged to no country. An unknown land! They passed a few animals and an occasional caravan, and met some Muslim pilgrims bound for Mecca, hurrying southward before the snow blocked the passes.

When the expedition reached Karaul, the first Chinese outpost, they received a hearty reception from the Chinese frontier officer in charge.

Roerich told his diary: "Isolated in these far-off mountains, deprived of every means of communication, with his help and kindness this officer reminded me of those traits of the better China. This is so important to us—because we go to China with sincere friendship and an open heart!"

Touched by the officer's friendship, they set up their tents and spent the night in the dusty yard of the fort. While the Roerichs were waiting for their passports issued by the Chinese ambassador in Paris to be examined, they heard their elderly Chinese interpreter muttering "Chinese soil" thoughtfully to himself. Roerich was not sure whether the man was pleased or grieving. Before a few more of the passes had been crossed, there would no longer be any doubt.

Roerich, who had thoroughly loved the challenges of the passes, poignantly asked, "Crystals of the summits, can the lace of the desert sands replace you?" After a hard day's travel, the family loved the nightly campfires with their conversations, smiles, pipes, and rest. Fireflies of the desert, the campfires offered the opportunity to exchange stories with Ladakhis, Kashmiris, Afghans, Tibetans, Astoris, Baltis, Dards, Mongols, Sarts, and Chinese—each with his own astonishing tale. Nurtured by the silence of the desert, the Roerichs loved observing the people and watching their hand gestures as they spoke long into the night. And Nicholas's heart always lifted when he heard talk of Shambhala or the coming new era. Helena collected many of the campfire tales and parables, for she felt that they offered a glimpse into the souls of the peoples. They were published as *On Eastern Crossroads: Legends and Prophecies of Asia*.

From Karaul, two possible routes led to Khotan. The Roerichs thought it would save them six days and there would be fewer rivers to cross if they headed toward Yarkand, crossed over to Khotan, and continued straight. After Nazar Bey had strongly recommended this route, they headed toward Sasser Pass. Climbing in a dense whirl of snow, they had to stop and hastily pitch the tents for the night, a difficult task at an altitude of some 15,400 feet. They awoke to find the water frozen in the pitcher and everything deeply covered by snow, which had fallen throughout the night. The caravan leader, Omar Khan, had lost three of his best animals. The iron pegs were so frozen in the hard ground that it took almost two hours for the Ladakhis to pull them out.

The problems at the summit, however, proved the most challenging. A complete arctic stillness of glaciers and snow peaks greeted them as they approached 17,000 feet, and then a blizzard struck. While it intensified, the caravan men tried to shield the Roerichs from the sight of dead animals and human tombs scattered everywhere. Omar Khan lost two more horses. The numerous mummified carcasses of animals looked as if they had died in agony. Someone had stood several horses in upright positions, and with their heads thrown back, they appeared to be galloping on a ghostly track. George's horse went into a slide that almost carried him into a crevasse. One caravaneer suffered an attack of mountain sickness and, bleeding severely, fell off his horse. When the sun's rays pierced dense clouds for a brief moment, the whole snowy region sparkled with such unbearable intensity that it caused everyone's eyes to water. "The billowing clouds roll by and open up new, endlessly new combinations of the cosmic structure; we see only broad, flat lines, for everything is stripped clean of all ornaments and arabesques," wrote Roerich.

Finally they arrived at the northern edge of the glacier, and as they began the long descent, the weather suddenly brightened. When the rays of the setting sun hit the sand and rocks, the valley burst into flame. With the severity of the pass behind them, a tired George remarked, "A wonderful scene indeed!"

Continuing now toward the lowlands, they spotted Buddhist caves not mentioned in any of the travel books; the locals called them "Kirghiz dwellings." But landslides had obstructed the approach, so the Roerichs could only look up at the dark openings and imagine the frescoes and antiques that might be hidden there.

The gradual descent led them into a broad valley girded by grass-covered, rolling hills. It was a typical nomad highland, dotted with the light gray and white felt yurts of a Kirghiz encampment. The Kirghiz headman, a brave-looking man of about forty with a matchlock rifle and large fur cap, was waiting to accompany them. A picturesque crowd of nomads greeted them, and everyone enjoyed mingling once the camp was set up. Roerich noted: "They were extremely friendly, and offered us juicy melons—the first we had tasted for years. The women and children were neatly dressed, and the insides of the tents were artfully decorated with carpets and embroidery. These people seemed superior to their brothers of the Mongolian Altai and the mountain regions of Jungaria."

While horsemen shouted news of their arrival, a kindly crowd of Kirghiz women gathered around Helena and stared at her clothing. The women shook their high white headdresses in amazement over the camping equipment and everything else. Strings of camel caravans were slowly passing by on the way up the trail into the mountains the Roerichs had just left. Never having seen camels before, their Ladakhi men were fascinated.

As the expedition continued, the two Kirghiz officers assigned to escort them proved to be decent fellows who willingly questioned the local inhabitants about possible ruins, caves, or tombs. The rich finds of Sir Aurel Stein and the ruined cities in the Takla Makan desert around Khotan were well known, but only some ancient Chinese copper coins had been unearthed in these mountains north of the Sanju Pass.

This area was famous for its oases, and the air grew decidedly hotter as they approached the first one. The sturdy Ladakhis stripped off their heavy sheepskins. Sensing water ahead, the men and animals hurried along the dusty loess-covered trail and soon reached the first village of the Sanju Oasis. Further on, the river gorge widened and the high rugged mountains on either side of it became low undulating hills that stretched away to the north. Marching eastward, they could no longer see Ladakh, the kingdom of the mountain passes and sparkling snows. Roerich wrote:

We said farewell to the mountains. Of course we shall find others, few worse than these—but it is sad to descend from them. The desert cannot bestow on us what the heights have whispered.

As a farewell, the mountain yielded up something unusual for us! With the very last rock that we could still touch, we spied the very messengers of the transmigration of peoples. And they have a special meaning, for these are the same designs we encountered previously. Here in Turkestan, we found the same Neolithic designs of the ibexes with huge twisted horns, the same archers, and the same circles of dancing people that we found etched in the rocks bordering Ladakh and other places in Western Tibet.

The Roerichs speculated that these dated back to the shamanistic form of worship celebrated throughout the higher regions of Asia. Rev. Francke had written about their ritual use in ancient Tibet, and George was able to document that the ancient Mongols venerated ibex and used them prominently in their fire cult.

10

THE SILK ROAD AND CHINESE HOSPITALITY

"It is time for breakfast and we want to stop, but some riders are galloping toward us, beckoning us to come farther," wrote Nicholas in his diary. They were the headmen of Sanju, accompanied by a messenger from the magistrate of Guma, the nearest city. "The men dismounted, and stroking their beards in the approved Turkestani fashion, congratulated us on our successful arrival, and begged us to ride up to the next poplar grove where there was a feast awaiting! Then the headman, a Turkestani soldier, presented us with the large, red visiting card of the Guma Amban and announced they were there to escort us to Khotan, making sure we would be properly received by local authorities along the route. We went with them and found everything the country produces was spread before us on finely designed felts."

Mounds of melons and apricots, juicy pears, red and blue tinted eggs, roast chicken, and mutton were provided, as well as Turkestani bread and steaming tea. The feast on colorful felts, and the entire scene, reminded Roerich of a French Impressionist painting or of the Russian countryside and his excavating days.

This was not a painting, however, nor was it Russia; nonetheless, "Here are the same caftans and beards and colored girdles and small caps

145

bordered with wolf fur or beaver. Surprisingly, many of these bearded men know at least one Russian word and are very pleased if they own some small Russian object. Yet, they know almost nothing about America. It would be good if we had books on America, written in Turkestani, to give them. We must give it some thought."

The Roerichs cheerfully accepted the honors and thoroughly enjoyed the feast while the delegation stood around them in a semicircle, gravely watching. Then, accompanied by the first of several detachments of guards that would attend them during their seven months in Chinese Turkestan, the caravan continued down the gradually sloping valley. The open plains were covered with fields of barley and corn; poplars and apricot groves were everywhere. The entire area appeared to be a thriving agricultural oasis, with numerous irrigation ditches to water the fields.

The first village was situated in a heavy grove of poplars, willows, and fruit trees. In the large shady garden reserved for them, a neatly dressed crowd of villagers waited, anxious to observe every detail as the caravan made camp. Then, while the Roerichs stood under the shade trees, enjoying the soft grass beneath their feet, the villagers milled around the tents. When Nicholas presented the friendly headman with a wristwatch, the old man beamed with satisfaction and immediately reciprocated by sending over peaches, pears, and delicious watermelons.

During the month they were resting in Ladakh and waiting for pack animals, they had received their first mail with news of the Master Institute and the museum. Catching up on the activities of the little circle of coworkers in America gave them much to talk about. After parting from the Roerichs in Europe, the Horches had returned to New York and moved the institute into its new location on Riverside Drive. A passageway had been opened connecting the two buildings. While the Roerichs had been exploring in Sikkim, leading representatives of New York's art, music, and literary world had gathered to celebrate the institute's grand opening. The school was already gaining a unique reputation for teaching "unity of the arts" and for being the art center devoted to the work of a living artist whose theories were influencing America. A collections catalog had been prepared.

Because Roerich's paintings had toured America, many visitors were flocking to the art center. Enthusiastic admirers who wanted to be more involved with the work had initiated The Society of Friends of the Roerich Museum. Charles Wharton Stork, an eminent poet and playwright from Philadelphia, was selected president. They soon published *Archer*, a magazine containing articles devoted to Roerich's aims and purposes, lists of events at the museum, and announcements of contests. Branches of the society were opened throughout Europe.

Meanwhile, Frances Grant had formed the News Information Agency to supply leading newspapers and magazines with material dealing with the creative arts. The agency quickly evolved into the Roerich Press, publishing data of the expedition, and later Roerich's books, as well as works by outstanding writers such as James Cousins and Ivan Narodny.

Corona Mundi, the international art center, was sending paintings to tour museums, colleges, and libraries. The institute had added classes, including classes for the handicapped, and increased the faculty. The concert and lecture series had been expanded, and the summer study program had developed into a summer school at Moriah, New York, offering "rare cultural privileges—both for studies under an eminent faculty in all arts, and the educational opportunities of lectures, exhibitions and concerts." Located near Lake Champlain, Moriah had probably been chosen because its name so closely resembled Morya.

The little circle continued their study sessions, but without the Roerichs, it was not the same. Grant remembered, "Everything was possible with them here, but without them, things were difficult." Sina and Frances were both strong-minded women, opinionated and successful, and without the calming presence of the Roerichs, their egos sometimes intervened. While Sina, Maurice, and his sister Esther spoke Russian, the others did not, and although some of the letters from the Roerichs arrived in both languages, Frances often felt excluded when Sina had to translate the Roerichs' words.

The teachings encouraged them to exert their will to rise above petty differences, and they had the opportunity to do so, daily. As the Master explained to Helena:

> In the formation of new communities, it is necessary to have in mind a troublesome specific human trait—I am speaking of envy. From rivalry, there gradually arises the viper of envy, and in the same nest are falsehood and hypocrisy.
>
> The viper is small in size and its birth is sometimes impossible to notice. Therefore, at the formation of a community, it is necessary to foresee the differences between its members and to show that like the limbs of the body, none can be duplicated nor compared.

Thinking of his friends in New York, Roerich recorded advice in his diary on how to handle a journey like this one. Perhaps the third paragraph reveals another of the unmentioned reasons for the expedition:

> You, my young friends, I remind you to provide yourselves with clothes for heat and especially for cold. The cold approaches quickly and sharply. Suddenly you cease to feel your extremities. Always have a little medicine chest at hand. The chief considerations are the teeth and stomach; also prevention against colds. Have bandages for cuts and bruises. All of this has already been of use in our caravan. Any kind of wine on the heights is very harmful. Against headaches—pyrimidine. One should not eat much. Tibetan tea is very useful for it is really hot soup that warms one very well. It is light and nourishing. The soda, which is used in the tea, keeps lips from painful chapping.

Do not overfeed the dogs and horses, otherwise bleeding will begin and you will have to do away with the animal. The whole path is strewn with the traces of blood. One must make sure, in advance, that the horses have already been on the heights. Many untried ones perish at once. On such difficult passes, all social differences are erased—all remain just people, equally working, equally near danger. Young friends, you must know all conditions of caravan life in the desert. Only in such ways will you learn to fight with the elements, where each uncertain step is already an actual death. Here you forget the number of days and the hours. Here the stars shine as heavenly runes.

The foundation of all teachings is fearlessness. Keenness of thought and resourcefulness of action are not learned in bittersweet, suburban summer camps. Not during lectures, in well-heated auditoriums do you realize the power of the work of matter, but upon the cold glaciers where you can understand that each end is but the beginning of something still more significant and beautiful.

When Roerich was unable to paint or even take photographs, he frequently made quick pencil studies in small sketchbooks, labeling each color in tiny Russian script. His passion for mountains was inexhaustible, and he observed that the atmosphere worked magic on everyone: "Without exception, people stop their disputes and all differences disappear as they sense the beauty of these no man's heights. They help each other with their smallest needs and then share the warmth of campfires."

The caravan traditions impressed him: "Often we saw bales of unguarded goods left behind by unknown owners. Perhaps an animal fell or became too fatigued to carry the goods, so it was left for later. And the property was safe, for no one would violate this ethic of the caravan. We smiled, imagining what would happen if we left property unguarded on a city street. Yes, one enjoys greater safety in the desert.... There is a special delight in knowing that one is safer and less molested in a distant, unpeopled place, than on the streets of a Western city." He remembered that when he had entered the East End of London one night, a policeman had inquired if he was armed and prepared for danger. He seemed in far more danger on nights in the suburbs of Montparnasse or Hoboken than on the paths in the Himalayas or the Karakorum.

Roerich was exhilarated by the challenges of pitting himself against nature: "When the dangers of nature are essentially so joyous and arouse the vigor to purify the consciousness so greatly, it is a pity to descend from the unpeopled spaces into the whirl of the human crowd. Some people shy away from danger, but in me, it awakens an unknown resourcefulness."

The Roerich Central Asian Expedition was now so far into Chinese Turkestan that the mountains were lost somewhere behind in gray mists. Missing them tremendously, he asked his diary:

> How now to live and whither to direct my eye? We have emerged into a completely different country. Here Ladakhi heroism is no more, nor their clear singing with strong, agreeable voices. No more the *sub-urgans* and *kurgans* of fearlessness.
>
> It is hot in this forgotten oasis. Around us we find only peaceful, agricultural, ignorant Sarts and the slow Turkis who have completely forgotten that their people took part in the marches of Genghis Khan and Tamerlane.

Day by day they inched toward the formidable Takla Makan, an oval-shaped desert rimmed on three sides by lofty mountain ranges, among the most notable in Central Asia. The long, bleak, serrated Kunluns were to the south, the T'ien Shans to the north, and to the west, were the sky-piercing Pamirs, clustered masses of snow-covered mountains whose passes reach 20,000 feet. Takla Makan was 250 miles from north to south and 1,500 miles from east to west.

Seeing this vastness of mountain ranges and fierce deserts on a map, one might think nature had intended this region to serve as a barrier dividing the great Eastern and Western civilizations. But in the thirteenth century, the Mongol Empire had extended from the China Sea to the Danube, and European ambassadors, Christian and Buddhist missionaries, pilgrims with their scriptures and sacred statues, and commercial travelers like Marco Polo had all traversed the patrolled Silk Road. Rather than dividing East and West, this region had linked them. By approximately AD 160, Buddhist teachings were widespread throughout Central Asia. Trained artisans had established Buddhist centers and exerted their influence by bringing Hellenistic art into Asia from thousands of miles away. Concealed in tumuli, graves, and caves, priceless relics of those times now awaited the excavator's spade.

October 9, 1925, was Nicholas's fifty-first birthday. What a happy day it must have been for him, for they had reached the region that had spawned the very tribesmen—the Scythians and the Sarmatians—into whose graves he may have dug so many years ago. He told his diary:

Soon we start on the old Silk Road. Now we can begin to search for antiquities. These places—and Khotan as well—are mentioned in the literature written three or four hundred years before the birth of Christ. We left Sanju oasis accompanied by the chirping birds, the joyous gurgling of the irrigation canals and the bleating of the goat herds. Then we turned and climbed the sandy incline of a riverbed and found ourselves in the real desert. The hot air vibrated on the horizon, heavy enough to interweave new formations in the sands spread out around us. But not a step of the great hordes that passed this way was revealed. Just as the waves of the seas do not show the traces of a passing boat, so the desert forgets the movement upon it. All eradicable signs are ebbed away.

The whole mercilessness of the desert starts here. A Kirghiz points to the hazy pink northeast and says, "There is the great Takla Makan!" He points out the hills that conceal buried cities, and still farther, those foothills of the heavenly mountains [the T'ien Shan]. And farther still lies the great Altai, which the Blessed Buddha reached. We inquire about antiquities only to be told that much has been carried away—but still more waits hidden beneath the sands. One can find it only gropingly. And now the wind blows up, and from the depths new *stupas* emerge and new temples and walls of unknown houses. The locals themselves are indifferent to it all.

For days they proceeded along the Silk Road toward China, named perhaps not only for the silk transported, but also for the lacy, iridescent designs in the wind-whirled, pearly dust and sand of the road. By midmornings it was so hot that the stirrups burned their feet through their boots. "What must it be like in summer?" Roerich wondered. There was great sadness one evening when one of their mountain dogs, Amdong, perished from the heat.

The legendary beauty of China seduced them. It was a land walked by both Buddha and Confucius. Almost half of the entire Buddhist literature of teachings had been written in China, and Tibetan art was said to have its roots both there and in India. In fact, Roerich found it difficult to recall any architectural, sculptural, or painted monuments that did not originate from the delicate treasures of either China or India.

Ten miles from Khotan, they stopped to rest. Then they decided to rent a house, ignoring warnings they had been given to avoid Khotan because of the Tao-tai (governor). Other explorers, Przhevalsky for instance, had written of unpleasant experiences in Khotan, and even Marco Polo had condemned its customs. However, Nicholas felt confident they need not be concerned about the tyranny of any dangerous despot, civil unrest, or political intrigue. Certainly, he had not come so far just to be turned away by rumors of an evil governor.

His sense of security was increased because they were traveling with a passport from the Peking government, and had English and French passports as well. Furthermore, he had a special recommendation from the Chinese ambassador in Paris, a letter from the United States consul in Calcutta, and letters from the Victoria and Albert Museum in London, the Archaeological Society in Washington, and six other American institutions. The greatest comfort, however, came from knowing they were a peaceful painting expedition, traveling under the flag of the United States. The former Chinese diplomat and officer accompanying the caravan would vouch for them, and they even had copies of all of the books published about Roerich's paintings. But none of these would be enough.

Compared with what the expedition was about to endure in Chinese Turkestan, the harsh ordeals of the Karakorum route would seem safe and simple. Only fourteen years after the overthrow of the Manchu Dynasty, the China they were entering was a loosely allied group of principalities, where law was maintained by force. Although a republic had been established, the government did not function and had been replaced by the military and warlords with semiprivate armies and shifting alliances.

In Khotan, and later in Urumchi, the capital of Sinkiang, the hypocrisy, ignorance, stupidity, and duplicity of devious Chinese bureaucrats severely challenged the Roerichs. Since these experiences demanded that they control their tempers, develop greater patience, and search deeper within for peace, the Master advised them: "Master the problem of remaining cool throughout the entire Battle. The Battle of Light is just the beginning—millions are in it without knowing the final outcome. But you know, and this knowledge should make you wise and prompt a worthy decision.... Truly, creative patience and CHEERFULNESS are the two wings of the workers."

The first hints of trouble came when they attempted to rent a house, but they pushed their uneasiness aside and quickly established headquarters. Khotan was an ancient site and there was much that they wanted to explore, especially where shifting sands had uncovered new remains near the Rawak stupa and a recent landslide had exposed some old structures. Besides the scientific work, Nicholas was eager to capture the beauty of the Karanghu Tagh Mountains in and around Khotan.

Chinese Turkestan, however, was on the brink of war. As the Roerichs became embroiled in political rivalries and power struggles, they were asked, "Is it possible that in America and Europe they do not know about Sinkiang?" To which, with hindsight, Roerich later replied, "If we had known one-half of the reality, we would never have continued through China."

Their Ladakhi caravanners were the first to complain: "Too much trouble in the bazaars." They wanted to return to Ladakh. Even though those wonderful hillmen would be needed as the expedition continued into China, Roerich regretfully paid them for their splendid service and sent them off. Now they had to muster a new caravan of men and animals, and, amid this, friends and acquaintances began warning them that the Tao-tai, known to hate all "foreign devils," seemed to be conspiring against them.

When the Roerichs presented their official papers, they were accused of having false passports. Their possessions were searched, their arms seized, all scientific work prohibited, and they were put under surveillance. Roerich was given permission to paint in the house but not outside it; photography and sketching were forbidden. The Tao-tai suspected them of spying. They narrowly escaped the fate of an American explorer, Owen Lattimore, who arrived a few months later and was locked straight into jail.

Roerich pondered in his diary:

One can imagine how much the Chinese intellectuals and students have to stand. . . . I sorrow for them and can well imagine how they must blush for these others. I recall the tales of how Chinese officials searched Sven Hedin's trunks, looking for Russian soldiers; how Dr. Filchner, the German, had to sign a waiver that he had no claims against the Chinese for robbery; how badly Przhevalsky fared; how Kozlov was forced to enter the court of the Amban protected by twenty Cossacks to quell the lawlessness. It is sad to realize the new political regime has not brought this country out of gloomy medieval-ism. If the Amban chooses not to wipe his nose with a handkerchief, that endangers no one as much as his ignorance.

It is necessary to find ways to depart, in spite of the frost. We hired a camel caravan to carry our baggage to Kashgar, and once more the courtyard of the house and garden were filled with men and kneeling camels—a welcome sight to every explorer, but most especially to us at this time. Our old Chinese interpreter whispers, "The Chinese shoot from the rear—we'll be safer if you tell the escorting soldiers with guns to go ahead." Our Expedition banner is ready. It will be carried out in front. Tzung sewed it in red and yellow with a black inscription: "Lo, an American Art Officer."

"Lo" was one of the ways "Roerich" was said in Chinese, and by some strange circumstance it was also the word for danger.

The Roerichs were denied permission to leave, and their next four months were filled with anxiety and deceit. When they sought domestic help, they were shocked at the suggestion that they purchase the people they needed. They were told it would only be possible for them to leave Khotan if they retraced their steps over the Sanju Pass, which was now impassable until June. Roerich asked his diary, "Why, in point of fact, is Khotan considered a commercial center of Chinese Turkestan? We do not see any commerce. We live on a big road branching off to other provinces and into the depths of China, but seldom do we hear the camel bells or the cries of the donkeys. The rug industry has deteriorated considerably and the jade has disappeared. The antiques in Khotan seem exhausted and what is brought for our approval is mostly imitation."

Roerich had read the fourth-century writings of Fa-hsien, who was alive when Khotan was thriving. Rich, generous, and hospitable Buddhists lived there then, who took great joy in their music. It seemed to Roerich that fierce screaming had replaced the melodious songs. He remembered his enjoyment of the singing of the Ladakhis, so full of rhythm and freshness. "Only when people are greatly depressed does their singing cease."

Although much of the time passed in complete frustration and disappointment,[1] spurred by his ardent hope that the time of Maitreya was near, he managed to complete his *Maitreya* series.

On December 1, 1925, Nicholas recorded in his diary, "I cannot imagine a more remarkable contrast than when the shades of the desert are compared with those of the Himalayas and Ladakh. Sometimes it seems that my eyesight is gone or that my eyes are filled with dust. And where are the crystals of purple, blue, and green? And where is the abundance of fiery yellow and vivid red? It is like a gray and dusty storeroom! The sands cut the skin like glass and eat the tissues. My eyes have become so accustomed to tonelessness and not glimpsing any colors, that they slid into a void."

When the haze cleared from the night sky, the stars were beautiful. Occasionally, when the sand stopped blowing, the faint blue range of the Kunluns was visible, reminding him of the charm of those mountains. Mornings, there was frost and the creeks were covered with ice. When the first snow fell, Helena fed the birds, and as masses of them flew around her, Nicholas's thoughts went to the Hindus, who also fed the birds during the long winter months.

Just north of the Kunluns was said to lie a "Valley of the Immortals," home of holy men whose wisdom was focused on saving humanity. The Roerichs heard that many who tried to locate them lost their way and failed. Interesting tales were told of huge vaults inside the mountains, where treasures had been stored since the beginning of history, and of tall men who disappeared into the rocks. These stories, and others like them, tantalized the family and took their minds off their captivity. All memory returned, however, the instant they glanced into the courtyard where their drivers were continually bemoaning their lot while milling about restlessly with their donkeys and camels.

A lama companion told them a learned Buddhist had wanted to arrange a discussion with George on the subject of Buddhism. At the time, the lama had been uncertain that George knew enough to speak on the foundations of the teachings, since many foreigners who called themselves Buddhists were unable to judge the truthfulness of the books and commentaries they read. Now that he perceived the depth of George's knowledge, he was impressed enough to regret his uncertainty, saying, "George knows more than many learned lamas. I have gradually and unnoticeably questioned you, and you, too, have explained everything. It is a pity I did not know this in Ladakh."

On January 1, 1926, their things were packed, the camels were ready, and the Roerichs were preparing to depart quietly from Khotan, when a messenger arrived with the announcement that the Tao-tai specified that they could not go to Kashgar. They would be allowed to leave only if they went by way of the Tun-huang desert, famous for the Caves of the Thousand Buddhas and notorious for the bandits. Had the circumstances been different, the Roerichs would have been thrilled by this opportunity to visit the oldest, greatest, and most extensive rock temple complex in all of Central Asia.[2] But Roerich was furious. "With our arms taken away, it is impossible for us to go through the desert. Every expedition and every merchant who crosses that desert needs guns with him."

This change of route would make a great difference. It would prevent them from seeing Yarkand, Kashgar, Aksu, or Kusha and deprive them of the opportunity to get much needed dental care, to receive money they were expecting, and to exchange their American checks at the Kashgar banks. Roerich fumed:

> Our conference with the Tao-tai exceeded all limits of our patience. We explained that many of our plans would have to be altered. We had been expecting to meet our American friends [the Lichtmanns] in Urumchi and instead they must be notified that this is not possible. We told the Tao-tai that his conduct was offending the dignity of America. But he was adamant and informed us we could either go back to India over the Sanju Pass or cross through the robber-infested desert (of which he, himself, had warned). He would detain us in Khotan until we made our choice. This forced detention amounts to arrest—and without provocation.
>
> Then the Tao-tai repeated everything he had said previously. He insisted that our passport issued by order of the Peking government, was not valid. "Is it possible that Mr. Chang Lo, the Chinese representative to the League of Nations, does not know how to give a passport?" The Tao-tai had never even heard of the League of Nations!

The disputes continued and Roerich felt as if he had fallen into a chasm of ignorance and madness.

> And so we returned to our house arrested. We sat upon our packed trunks and ended New Year's Day by composing a letter to the Consuls of Kashgar: "On the eve of leaving for Kashgar, without cause, the Roerich Expedition has been arrested by the Chinese officials of Khotan. In view of the absence of a United States Consul, we are addressing ourselves herewith to the representatives of foreign governments in the city of Kashgar with an urgent demand that they give the most serious consideration to obtaining permission for the Expedition to proceed to Kashgar at once. In the event that permis-

sion of the Kashgar Tao-tai be insufficient, we beg you to telegraph the governor-general of the Province of Urumchi at our expense."

Helena was depressed over the dangerous situation. After setting out with an open heart, she wondered if there really was hope for humanity. Although the mission provided the only medical care for hundreds of miles around, the missionaries were so unpopular with the Chinese that they were periodically subjected to intense persecution. Not long before the Roerichs' arrival, the attacks had become so severe that the missionaries had decided to abandon their work. Throughout the entire expedition, Helena's healing abilities had benefited their caravanners and others along the route. People frequently approached their campsite in need, and the Roerichs were often taken somewhere to see sick ones. While still in Khotan, she had healed the Tao-tai's son—though that had not helped them escape their captivity.

George was also downcast: "The China we expected from museums and lectures has nothing in common with this!" Their Chinese translator begged them to keep quiet, fearing they would all be shot. Even the lama whispered, "The Chinese always behave the same."

To his diary, Roerich explains: "And so we live. Once we receive a piece of information from the heights and once from the abyss. Today a soldier stopped our Chinese at the bazaar, caught hold of his horse by the bridle and demanded money from him. Yesterday one of our 'guards' stopped a woman on the road and tried to demand money from her. And in such a country they have left us without arms! So we sit on our trunks amidst untold infamy. They brought us information from the bazaar that the Tao-tai is introducing the opium trade in Khotan."

Yet even in these days of seeming inactivity, there still were enough signs to remind them of their missions:

Here is a remarkable little casket (like the one to carry Chintamani)! And there is Maitreya! . . . After everyday life problems are discussed, most conversations seem to ascend to the order of things. There are periods, which could be called the "snowballs of events," when each circumstance rolls one toward the common end. For seventeen years now, we have been observing the manifestations of the hastening of evolution.

Between the cradle of the future and the tomb of that which passes away, electrons of untold energy are gathering into new formations. And I, as the painter-hermit of the mountain abodes, am tracing the battle and victory of Maitreya with surety. Confidentially, it is the lines and signs of those approaching ones that I trace, as I keep track of what is passing away!

Even with such problems, the Roerichs believed that all forces were working together to lift evolution. In his diary, Nicholas quoted Sri Aurobindo: "We say to humanity: The time has come when you must take the great step and rise out of a material existence into the higher, deeper, and wider life towards which humanity moves. The problems that have troubled mankind, can only be solved by each person conquering the kingdom within. The solution does not lie in harnessing the forces of Nature to provide more comfort and luxury, but rather by mastering the forces of the intellect and the spirit. Man must liberate the freedom within—as well as without—and conquer external Nature from inside himself."

Even with knowledge of the bigger picture, Roerich grumbled, "How is our consciousness enriched by sitting in Khotan? It becomes clear that a life such as that in Khotan should not exist. Imagine the lives of 100,000 people plunged into complete darkness, divested of all light. In this darkness, vice, lies, treachery, and ignorance are being born. Mutual strangulation is going on just below the surface in the bazaars. The people have managed to retain their small livelihoods only by cheating and deceit. The understanding of quality is gone, all promptness is forgotten, and the joy of creative originality has perished. How can this continue?"

A few days later, their mail from America caught up with them. It had taken almost as long to travel from Ladakh to Khotan as it had from New York to Ladakh, but the letters were a breath of fresh air. Roerich replied, "Beloved friends, with joy we read about all works, exhibitions, lectures, the school, the promoting of art among the people; all of this is so imperatively needed. You are bringing true joy into the lives of the youth and are kindling heart-fires."

The next day a telegram arrived, saying, "Washington undertakes necessary measures," but Roerich was not

*Helena and George Roerich,
Khotan-Yarkand, Chinese Turkestan,
February 1926*

comforted: "Our arms are not returned and I cannot attempt to sketch in unknown territories without them; I have a great many reasons for this, including my experience with wild dogs and people. It is insulting to ignore all our documents and deprive us of our means of defense. Many expeditions have faced this kind of oppression, but somehow it seldom gets noticed. I am placing full responsibility upon the government of China."

A second telegram arrived from America, but it was distorted beyond understanding. They were advised an order had been issued that all of their mail be opened before delivery. When money arrived from the

Shanghai bank, they were thoroughly distressed to realize they were unprotected and unarmed while possibly all Khotan knew of their money. Their Chinese translator told them that, in the past, opening a stranger's letter was punished by the removal of an eye, or the cutting off of a hand.

Finally a letter came from Major Gillan, a spy in the Great Game and the British consul in Kashgar, reassuring them that everything possible was being done. The next day another arrived, notifying them that the governor-general of Kashgar was allowing them to proceed immediately.

The lama, who regarded the insolence and cruelty as typical Chinese behavior, accurately advised them that they would be told that nothing at all had happened. Blaming everything on the governor-general of Sinkiang, the officials repeatedly assured them of friendship. Roerich said: "Since they are saying all that occurred was just fantasy, the officials now have the challenge of deciding on what pretext to return our seized arms. For three months we have passed through a wonderful schooling, but much of what we learned remains unclear. The local people warned us at the beginning not to believe the officials, and when we inquired why, they answered us, 'Because they are fools.' But there is some sort of warped reason even in the actions of hopeless fools. Now it occurs to me that not only stupidity is hidden here, but criminality as well."

At the end of the month, Major Gillan finally arranged their freedom on condition that their guns and rifles remain locked away. Before anyone could interfere, they completed the final preparations—not knowing if they would be allowed to enter Urumchi. Since they had never unpacked after their last attempt to leave, all that was necessary was to hire a trustworthy caravan headman. They found one who provided them with seventy-four packhorses and agreed to get them to Kashgar in fourteen days. A military officer was ordered to furnish them with a guard of mounted soldiers to accompany them to Yarkand. He seemed uneasy as they inquired about the day of their departure, as if conscious that a grave injustice had somehow been committed.

Two Chinese carriages were secured: one to carry Tumbal, their fierce Tibetan mastiff, traveling in the charge of a servant; the other for the case of firearms and their elderly Chinese interpreter, who was so depressed by the insulting attitude of the officials that he had taken to smoking opium. (By the time they reached Urumchi, it was necessary to dismiss him.)

On departure day, their courtyard was filled with trusted friends they had made despite the difficult and strained situation. Their route now read Yarkand, Kashgar, Kuchar, Karashahr, and hopefully Urumchi.

11

THE ROAD TO URUMCHI

The family was relieved to be traveling again. Roerich grieved as they left the Kunluns behind. Although he freely acknowledged the Himalayas as his favorites, to him each mountain range had its own endearing personality. "If we were able to create our own planet, it would be very mountainous!" he told his diary.

With the armed escort and their "Lo" flag in the lead, the caravan took on a fresh appearance as they headed for the land of the Sarts. Their escort had reported for duty mounted and armed with old Mausers and dressed in voluminous gray coats and fur caps with large earflaps. The commanding officer also carried an antiquated Chinese sword. Roerich thought they all looked old enough for retirement and wondered who would be guarding whom. The banner proved a wise addition, winning them greater respect than had all of their various papers and passports combined. It was quickly planted wherever they stopped for the night.

As they marched along, people frequently inquired, "What is this America?" Roerich enjoyed responding, "It is a far, far-away land, a land taken from a fairy tale, where anything is possible. Where wool is needed from all over the world and the guts from all the sheep of the Sarts would not make enough sausages to feed them; where people move and speak and write with the aid of machines, and do not count money on counting boards, but have instruments that do it for them."

"Have you pictures of America?" people would ask, then struggle to snatch the photos from his hands and beg to keep them. Photographs of skyscrapers were especially cherished, as were colored labels and scraps of paper. He was frequently asked for a book about America written in Turkish or Arabic so their mullah could read it to them.

Marching over the sands, Roerich was surprised to hear long-bearded Muslims ask if a Ford could pass on that narrow Chinese road, if a Ford could outrun a Kalmyk horse, or how much dirt a Ford could lift. The way that "Ford" was used made Nicholas wonder if they thought it was a man, a machine, or perhaps an abstract concept. He speculated that the name carried a momentum sweeping Asia with possibilities for a new life. Ford could do everything.

"Again the evening sands turn purple and the bonfires are lit," Roerich wrote in his diary. "The caravan animals are much delayed with our belongings, but we will wait quite at ease as though these things which complicate life so much do not exist." He discovered that their escort and some of the Chinese caravanners were confirmed opium smokers, and protested this great calamity. "And the light of the moon and the silence of the night are again permeated with human poison." Even though it was decided to dismiss the smokers at the first opportunity, the opium problem plagued them continually throughout China.

Nicholas further described their journey: "Again the desert, but now traces of snow are everywhere. The silvery tones more severe. Though the snowy mountains on our left seem more ethereal and have greater variety, the sands are as wearisome as ever. I have seldom been so tired. In the twilight, a message is relayed that the oasis ahead is dry. Well, we shall go on somehow. About eight o'clock, in the darkness, under a dull moon, we enter Pialma. The Swedish missionary awaits us and tells us of other cases like ours with the Chinese officials—the same hypocritical instability and the same insolent changing of decisions."

On one day, a moist bluish-white fog enveloped them. The sands seemed to merge into the horizon, broken only by an occasional bush, a partially covered skeleton, or the ruins of a tower.

They speak of buried cities and point toward the desolate Takla Makan desert. A sort of reverence and superstitious fear seems to resound when they pronounce the names of that great desert, or the Lob Nor salt marsh nearby.

We pass two narrow files of caravans on their way to Pialma for fuel, and then there is nothing else—no sounds, no colors—just the pearly dust blowing like a pale curtain. Our ancient carriages proceed rhythmically on the slowly turning purple wheels. The Chinese officer has donned the most amazing yellow cape, lined with red—it appears to be flame-colored as it protects him from the wind.

I spot the silhouette of a small man walking boldly in the distance. From his gait I can tell he is not a Sart . . . nor a Chinese—for they do not take solitary walks through the desert. We make out a gray cloak and a cap with ear-laps, then, as he gets closer, we recognize he is Ladakhi.

Roerich's heart lifts: "Yes, a Ladakhi! They will go anywhere alone like that." They talked, and soon discovered mutual acquaintances. As the man continued on his way, Roerich mused on the courage it takes to cross the desert alone on foot—and about his own sense of ease and closeness with people from Ladakh. "I wanted to keep this passing friend with us."

The next morning began with a radiant glow. Though it was the end of January, it felt like spring. "The Turkis are working better today and for this they shall receive a sheep. Poor things, they have so little, they appreciate any gift. It seems the proprietor of the caravan is pressing them so hard that they all seem irritable." Roerich felt good and was happily devoting a part of each day to painting. There were many such days of contentment as they traveled the ancient Chinese road where jade, silk, silver, and gold had been transported for centuries.

One day a local Amban and his retinue joined them; hearing the cheerful camel bells and piercing chanting from their picturesque caravan reminded Nicholas of the hordes of Genghis Khan. Eventually, they arrived at a village, where a second Amban stepped out from behind the mud walls and ceremoniously welcomed the Chinese potentate. Then, holding hands, the two disappeared through large red gates. Watching through the sandy-pearly mist, Roerich saw their black silhouettes elongate on the clay wall, creating a scene from an old Chinese painting. To end that beautiful day, all religions were represented around the nightly campfire: chants of Allah! Allah! resounded from the Muslims preparing for their month of fasting, and two Ladakhis from the caravan started singing prayers to Maitreya.

As they continued toward Yarkand, dense clouds of mist moved in and gusts of wind blew from the north. "We journeyed through sandy corridors and deep creeks for a long time, not seeing much because of the all-pervading sand. Then gray salt marshes slowly started to appear among low hillocks of a bluish-brown tone. We approached some high shores topped by a lofty frozen bridge, and the scenery became beautiful: some dams lay before us and a lovely cluster of houses and walls."

A house had been prepared for them in Yarkand when they arrived in February 1926, but it was not adequate, so they stopped at the Swedish Mission with the Andersons and enjoyed exchanging tales with the missionaries. Over supper, they discussed the curative herbs growing wild in the surrounding fertile country and the large variety of vegetables being cultivated. Roerich observed that while people discussed the absence of trees, with just a little digging, he had found enough great stumps to indicate former forests.

A wonderful store of coal was also nearby. Analysis of some samples proved it was of the best quality. Roerich speculated that oil might be found in the neighborhood, and radium in the mountains. Since there was plenty of water during the summer, only a little diligence and resourcefulness would be required to start mining. If the Chinese would not fear everything new and if their officials were selected on merit and not just their capacity to steal, or were less immersed in gambling, opium, and hemp hashish, the plain would truly flourish with the help of only a few Ford tractors.

Leaving the friendly missionaries behind was difficult for the Roerichs, especially when their baby held Helena's finger, staring happily at her with his blue eyes. They departed, nevertheless, and were soon marching again, watching the last patches of snow disappear as the billowing sand and dust again arose to choke them.

Then they reached Kashgar, on the edge of the Takla Makan. It was a pleasant oasis, though high winds off the Takla Makan enveloped it in

The house where the Roerichs stayed in Yarkand, February 1926

huge clouds of sand that, legend had it, camouflaged the men from the sky who lived there.

The Roerichs were surprised to discover a little hospital, even better equipped than the Swedish Mission. The Russian doctor allowed them to replenish their medical supplies, and the local authorities were also helpful. No problems arose over the passports, and everyone seemed to concur with Roerich's indignation about their treatment in Khotan. As the family listened, many volunteered stories about plundering Chinese officials and showed them photographs of "victims of justice," rows of people with fingers chopped off or the tendons in their feet cut. Nicholas wrote his circle of coworkers in New York: "When you are seated in a peaceful Chinese restaurant in America, remember the robbers—the Tao-tais and the Ambans—who are keeping their people in complete subjugation. Let the sight-seeing motors to Chinatown remind you of the millions of people here who are perishing in the darkness of ignorance."

Letters from the States were waiting in Kashgar. Reading them, the Roerichs were transported back to America, sitting with their friends for a few brief minutes and catching up with the activities. The schools, lectures, and books were all progressing so well that the two buildings were no longer adequate. After much designing and planning, construction had begun on a grandiose, ultramodern twenty-four-story skyscraper that would house all the institutions, the expedition paintings, a theater, a library, a restaurant, and several extremely large meeting spaces. There was to be a private sanctuary at the very top, apartments for them all, and inexpensive rental accommodations for artists, writers, and musicians.

Roerich replied enthusiastically to this exciting news: "To all friends greetings! A good year! My dear friends, at New Year, did you turn back or were you striving forward? In this call must be a command for those who desire to work, to devote themselves to the educational work. Build constantly. Build the towers high!"

His book *Adamant* had been published in Japanese, and he asked how it looked and praised the idea of an international literary contest:

Although we go beyond mail communication, we wish to see all of your work directed into the future, towards those masses whom art penetrates with such difficulty. Toward universities, schools, the people's and workers' clubs, libraries, village communities, railroad stations, prisons, hospitals, orphan asylums. There is a new consciousness growing; work to expand your creativity and see each obstacle as a birth of possibilities.

Speak to the people about this. Say nothing should impede them, that each barrier should be turned into a happy opportunity. . . . Let pupils create freely in all branches—in art, in ballet, and in singing. Let them polish their creative gifts until they are singing their own song and creating their own dance.

Once the mail from America was digested, the Roerichs returned to their present surroundings in Kashgar, where the golden rays of the sun were reflecting off the ancient walls around them—walls that seemed to have withstood all the injustices of time. Perhaps Confucius, the Teacher of Ten Thousand Generations, had passed by these very walls as he traveled in his little cart. They drank tea with the British consul, Major Gillan, and his wife, then went to view some fantastic sand formations created over eons by water and earthquakes.

In the oldest part of Kashgar, they found the remains of an exceptionally large stupa—now a formless mass with the tower missing. Only the bricks lying at the base testified that it once stood as grand as the stupa in Sarnath. Buddhist caves were nearby, bearing silent witness to the importance of Kashgar as a once-revered center of Buddhism.

Six miles outside the city was the Miriam Mazar. They had often seen *mazars* before—low tombs, found in old Kirghiz cemeteries, with semispherical vaulted roofs, each surrounded by poles with horsetails hanging from the ends. Ancient mazars are frequently Buddhist; this one, however, was exceptional because it was believed to be the tomb of Mary, the Blessed Virgin, Mother of Christ. A surprising legend told that she had fled to Kashgar after the persecution of Jesus in Jerusalem. As the Roerichs viewed her reputed grave, they could see that it was much worshipped.

They were plagued with money problems, for the amount needed in exchange for their traveler's checks was often more than post offices and banks could supply. The currency everyone honored was heavy silver Mexican dollars, but if they exchanged rupees for taels or sars, the Roerichs always lost. "Among the sars which were given to us with such difficulty in Kashgar, many are valueless. There should be ten letters written on each bill but often the tenth is torn off—which means no one will accept it. Whether in change from the bazaar or the bank, money needs to be carefully examined." Wooden chips inscribed with signs were even offered to them, with assurances that it was real money

Permission to enter Urumchi was finally received, but with frustrating conditions. They would be allowed to enter, but their guns would have to remain sealed and Roerich would not be allowed to paint outdoors. He was advised to try to paint anyway and see if the police actually prohibited it. It was also alarmingly close to the time of the spring thaw and flooding rivers. Urumchi lay eleven hundred miles to the northeast, and only donkey carts were available, meaning it would take fifty-five days to cross the desert instead of forty with horses. Roerich grumbled:

> This is especially absurd when you realize that a whole day of exhausting travel is equal to two hours' ride by automobile or to an hour by aeroplane.
>
> With this flatness of land, the roads here could be easily utilized for automobiles and planes would not need aerodromes. Perhaps a

steel bird with a message of good cheer and necessary supplies would awaken the people's consciousness. A crevice of reason would open above these paths traversed by dusty and overloaded donkeys. I remember reading that Sir Aurel Stein was afraid the building of railroads and other signs of civilization would disturb the primitiveness of this country. And I have always been against the ugly evidences of civilization. But this country is so paralyzed that it needs a supermeasure of enlightenment. Buddhists know the reason for this apathy, for in the books of *Kanjur* it is said that if a country should reject the teaching of Buddha, the trees would wither, the grass droop, and the welfare disappear.

A new escort of soldiers arrived and Roerich complained, "They look more like insects than people." However, his mood improved greatly as soon as the opal silhouettes of mountains appeared against the yellow sky. With immense relief, he wrote, "Welcome beloved mountains!"

Another unpleasant experience awaited them. As an additional consequence of their arrest and long detention in Khotan, the river had already risen. "Some people gallop to meet us and warn of the water that has begun to overflow the road. This makes it necessary to detour twenty miles. Now we will be delayed by floods everywhere. We lost the best time for travel."

From Kashgar to Aksu to Kuchar the road was most tedious; dust penetrated everything, and they floundered through areas of deep quicksand and passed lifeless forests of gnarled, half-burnt desert poplars, left by travelers who set trees afire for campfires rather than chopping them down. The daytime heat was intense enough to kill anything: "It is very simple to give an idea of our passage today! On a round dish, place a good bit of gray dust; throw in a few pieces of gray wool and stick in fragments of matches. Let ants crawl over the bumpy plain, and in order to create realism, blow pillars of dust on it."

The sight of the snowcapped T'ien Shans, the Heavenly Mountains, lifted their spirits. There the Buddha was believed to have received his initiation, whereupon they burst into flames. After his prayers, the flames were extinguished by a snowfall.

The mountains marked the limits of the desert. Beautiful Buddhist cave temples and monuments—pilfered and ravaged over the years—had once filled the areas surrounding Kuchar. From what little remained, Roerich could detect that the ancient artists had been highly evolved and masterful with design and decoration. Well aware that this art was highly respected in Asia, he was saddened that careless European explorers had gouged out entire portions for museums, leaving only rubbish behind. And so many of the Buddhist monuments in Muslim lands had been purposely destroyed with knives or fires. The intolerance and useless destruction was beyond his understanding.

Ancient Buddhist caves in Toghrak-Dong, Chinese Turkestan, March 1926

I can sanction the removal of separate objects which have already lost their identity, but to arbitrarily hack a still standing composition apart? . . . Italian frescoes are not treated in that manner. Would it not be better to study all these monuments while carefully retaining them and fostering the right conditions for preservation? When fragments of frescoes are removed, they quickly disintegrate because of climate changes.

I remember seeing whole cases of frescoes destroyed by rats in Berlin, and in other countries, monumental pieces were piled up with no indication of their original purpose and meaning. Individual works of art need to move freely on our planet, but deeply conceived compositions must be preserved. Soon the speedy steel birds will fly all over the world putting all distances within reach. Let our winged guests be greeted by evidences of high creation rather than these ragged skeletons. . . . When the regeneration of Asia shall come, she will ask, "Where are our best treasures, constructed by the creative spirit of our ancestors?" Even the Sphinx has not escaped this abuse.

Over the next few days, the Roerichs' thoughts dwelt on Buddhism and their yearning to locate old monuments. One evening, as they approached a lonely inn at sunset, something about the shadows on the sandy rocks high above gave them the impression of cave openings. And so they were. The little structures and stupas beside the caves were covered by the same avalanche of rocks that had blocked some higher caves, but three passageways stood clear. Although the ceilings and walls were almost destroyed, inscriptions in Turki could still be recognized on the scattered relics. Nicholas thought they were fifth to eighth century. But the hollow echo from the floor below was the most tantalizing, for it indicated more caves. The caves faced east, and they imagined hermits sitting in the doorways, viewing the expansive mountains. A little mountain stream ran through a wooden trough under the caves; they watched as a Sart woman filled her pail with water, just as the hermits must have done.

A few days later Roerich noted in his diary: "One of the most beautiful days. Up to 7:00 it is freezing, and then the hot sun appears. First we find a valiant desert, in pearly tones. Then, a crossing brings us to the most unusual sand formations, like congealed ocean waves, hundred-towered castles, cathedrals, and rows and rows of yurts—all in endless variety. After we fed the horses, we noticed two caves with traces of colored decorations, so we dismounted and hurried over the sandy mounds."

He suspected these were the celebrated caves explored and documented by LeCoq, but they were much more impressive than the photos. Perhaps the silence intensified everything. "One has to imagine all these cavern-shrines vividly and brilliantly frescoed, as they were before the walls darkened, with the statues of the Blessed One and the Bodhisattvas restored to their niches." They found traces of hundreds of Buddhas in one cave, and in another a Buddha still reclined across part of the remaining ceiling. They could feel hollow spaces under the floors and suspected that unopened compartments lay below.

It was the beginning of the month-long fast of Ramadan. The Muslims in their party fasted during the day but were free to eat during the night, and on the eve of the fast they traditionally played and danced to keep from sleeping when they could eat. At one o'clock in the morning, the drums, trumpets, and singing began, making the dogs bark and run wild for the rest of the night. A few nights later, a fierce *buran* (high wind) struck with the power of a flying dragon and roared until daybreak. Their tent flapped so violently that they expected it to blow away. As suddenly as it started, the wind stopped, and the peace of the sapphire blue sky and mother-of-pearl and opal desert once again surrounded them.

March 24, 1926, dawned hot and the Roerichs awoke with America on their minds. It was the anniversary of the founding of their institutions. Happily, they wrote to the little circle:

Our dear friends, we are sending our thoughts to America, to the
Museum and the school and for the festivities of the day. The distance
does not really exist, and we feel as if we are present at your annual
meeting. Traversing these spaces, we are frequently reminded of
the plains of Mississippi and Missouri and the immeasurable steppes
of Russia.

Just now, we are rejoicing, for we are in the company of people
who trade with America. This demonstrates that cooperation with
Asia already exists. Both continents remember their former unity as
though divided by a cosmic catastrophe. How much of the Mongolian
we found in the Mayans and the red-skinned Indians! How much
equal expanse there is in America and Asia. And now, in this
moment of regeneration, Asia remembers its distant ties. Greetings to
America, we wonder when we shall see you dear friends again.

They were now heading toward the villages of the Kalmyk. Despite a
veil of faint, foggy mist, the ridge of the magnificent T'ien Shan Mountains
loomed to the north, emanating such a beautiful quality of ethereal blue
that Roerich was struck by the perfection of their name—Heavenly. The
expedition was about to enter the region of Central Asia that came closest
to matching in size and shape the Tibetan descriptions of Shambhala.

Enclosed by mountain ranges, this huge oval-shaped area could be
viewed as an enormous lotus blossom surrounded by a ring of snowy mountains. The small kingdoms around the basin fringes may well have been the
ninety-six principalities of Shambhala's outer region. Approaching the
area, the expedition heard many exciting legends, such as the story of a
dark-complexioned, serious woman who came out of subterranean passages
and went about helping people, or the unusual looking horsemen seen near
a cave and then vanishing—probably through a subterranean passage into
their own land. Stories of underground irrigation canals, dwellings and
passages and ancient Buddhist cave-temples gave an unusual aura to the

land, reminding the Roerichs of India and Tibet, home of those anxious to serve humanity.

The family stopped to meet the chief prince of the Karashahr Kalmyk, the Toin Lama. Considered an incarnation of one of the most learned priests in Shigatse, Tibet, he was born in the higher valleys of the T'ien Shan and had an outstanding personality. When the Roerichs and the lamas accompanying them informed the prince of the predictions of Maitreya's timely coming, he listened with astonishment and replied, "If you come from the West and know this greatest knowledge, then verily the great time has come! We are all ready to sacrifice our possessions and everything that may be of use to Shambhala. All of our riders will be mounted when the Blessed Rigden Jyepo needs them."

The family had long anticipated stopping in the T'ien Shans, which had been worshipped as the gods' haunt for fifteen centuries before the birth of Confucius. Dozens of Taoist, Confucian, and Buddhist temples stood there, as well as two steles over a thousand years old, with inscriptions that were still legible. According to tradition, pilgrims climbed the famous brick-paved road to the summit at dawn to view the world emerging, pristine gold in the first light.

The Roerichs planned to view the lovely frescoes and inner shrine of the Tai Miao Temple and browse through the bazaar where yellow mud tigers, brass work, and Kwan Yin figures were sold. Finally they would continue up the winding six-mile road called the Broad Way to Heaven, where prayers and pleas were incised into the rocks. They also looked forward to visiting a large monastery situated to the north, and to spending time in Kalmyk encampments.

There was another route to Urumchi, which went through the Turfan Depression, the hottest spot in China (504 feet below sea level) and was four days longer. "Why go through unbearable heat," they asked themselves, "when we could go through the mountains?" However, the expedition would need special permission from Karashahr to go through the mountains, and the Roerichs knew the local authorities felt uneasy about scientific explorations. At first, the Karashahr authorities seemed favorably disposed, and the Roerichs left the meeting believing that no obstacles would be put in their way. But, unfortunately, that impression was false. Late one evening, they received a visit from the postmaster and the secretary of the magistrate, who informed them that the Urumchi authorities had sent orders to deny the expedition permission to cross the mountains.

The Roerichs again found themselves pawns in the middle of a grave political situation. Surrounded by a dense crowd of threatening Torguts, they were prepared to break open the sealed arms box to defend themselves. Roerich ordered their Chinese guard to tell the crowd to disperse or expect to be fired on. George described what happened: "The officer was greatly surprised at our firm stand and ordered his soldiers to guard our camp. It was an exciting scene; when the Chinese soldiers pushed with their whips and rifles, the crowd slowly dispersed. Then the Torguts suddenly became friendly, and hinted that the whole affair was staged by the officers as an harassment, to force us to abandon our plans." Roerich recorded in his diary:

Hardly has evening fallen before a new villainy occurs. We are told we will not be permitted to go over the pass and ordered to continue on the long, tiresome highway, through the sands and heat. An added insult; an added imposition; an added derision of the artist and the man. Is it possible that we will not see the monasteries? Is it possible that we must go by way of the dry sands, and be deprived of all that beauty? ... We hurry to speak to all of the officials. ... They are either not at home, or indisposed. A secretary tells us the governor fears for us on account of the great snows in the mountain pass. We explain that the snow is no longer there, but to be safe, we could take a lower pass.

The authorities' decision, of course, was negative. In his diary, an angry, disappointed Roerich complained: "These Chinese are capable of ruining every day; they are capable of transforming each day into a prison and a torture. In spite of the heat, the humidity and dust, we must go the long way. Helena says she will die from the heat, but the Chinese smile and notify us that their governor has a very small heart."

Frustrated, the Roerichs sent a telegram to the governor-general of Urumchi: "Please wire instructions to the Magistrate at Karashahr to allow Roerich Expedition to proceed to Urumchi by mountain way. Health of Mrs. Roerich does not allow her to continue journey through the hot, sandy desert of the long road. The mountain road permits us to reach Urumchi sooner."

Again to his diary: "The sense of surveillance and compulsion is abominable. How can I work when the warlords, with their 'very small hearts,' stand behind my back? Our whole mood is spoiled and we are again waiting as though in some medieval Chinese dungeon."

Not knowing if their telegram was really sent, they decided to await the outcome at a monastery. Their escorting soldiers chided them, and the Toin Lama said he was afraid to get involved. To their little group in America, Roerich wrote:

> Friends, you will think I am exaggerating somewhat. If anything, I should be glad to understate, but the occurrences are monstrous.
>
> Again, a crowd of Kalmyks come with Chinese soldiers who have orders to demand our immediate departure. They are noisy and threatening. This means that I cannot work, nor can we visit the monastery. The whole purpose of the Expedition vanishes. The only thing to do is to leave Chinese soil as soon as possible. Within two hours, we demand our passports and a letter stating the reasons for our expulsion. The passports arrive with an official letter stating that the expulsion is by command of the governor of Karashahr, who accuses

us of making maps. They offer to give us carts so we can leave more quickly.

I tell them that I am fifty-two years old; that I was honorably received by twenty-two countries, and that for the first time in my life, I am subjected to expulsion. Who would expect this treatment from an area of semi-independent Turguts? What kind of independence can this be—it is nothing but humiliating slavery: to cast out a guest violates all the customs of the East!

And where shall we go? Back to the heat of the desert? And can Helena endure it? Her heart is absolutely unable to bear the heat. And where is the nearest border in order to hide from the Chinese torturers?

Karashahr quickly became a black city for them. Roerich told the diary: "Verily I should much rather paint than write of these harmful, malevolent evils. But apparently it has to be so. Probably this will be useful somehow. America awaits my paintings of the Buddhist heights, but let the Chinese government explain why we were not permitted to go to the monasteries. In Sikkim, they met us with trumpets and banners; but here on Chinese soil, we are met with ropes. . . . Let us get away from this Chinese threat quickly. Before us lie the islands of Japan; and perhaps this is the time to visit the long-dreamed-of Easter Islands, and see their mysterious stone giants."

Prohibited from visiting the temples, painting, or even approaching the Heavenly Mountains, they were doomed to creep along hot sands for twelve days to reach Urumchi.

Instead of mountains, instead of monasteries, instead of Maitreya— again we have yellow steppes around us. What right do the Chinese have to deprive us of seeing beauty?

And to think in only four days, we could have gone amidst the far-off snows, through the solitary mountains. Even from this distance, those mountains are so beautiful! With pearly vistas, they stand dark bronze, with greenish, carmine spots, and blue, sapphire, purple, yellow, and reddish brown glinting against the gray sky. The dark shingled slopes of the desert behind seem strewn with light yellow bushes. A whole carpet of Asia! Today the first small pine appeared. For seventy-four miles, we saw only one inn and it had a bad well, one hundred feet in depth. And during the whole day, we passed only two small caravans of emaciated mules.

Rather than a big Chinese road, it seems we are in undiscovered country. We drag ourselves along this burning, stony desert, while hot air quivers on the horizon. The nonexistent lakes and the mirages melt into a gray pitiless plain as they merge in the heat with the far-off mountains. It is worse when we think, we might already be in Urumchi, reading our mail with good news from America, if not for the despotism of a stupid monster.

After tramping in the foothills for another three days, the family began to feel the refreshing cool mountain air from the eastern side of the T'ien Shans. Finally they were on the outskirts of Urumchi, the capital of Sinkiang, the most inland city in the world. The road was suddenly so clogged with traffic that George wondered if the numerous riders, leading their strings of camels and horses, had sprung from underground: "We passed a long convoy of heavily loaded carts and soldiers in dark gray uniforms. The squeaking noise of the huge wheels, the trampling of the horses and the high pitched shouts of the drivers blended into one discordant cacophony. These were baggage trains for troops dispatched to the Kansu border."

War had been declared, and the atmosphere was heavily charged with anxiety. The governor-general was hastily mobilizing troops, and the arsenal was feverishly preparing ammunition and repairing firearms. Disquieting reports came from the Mongolian border, where clashes were occurring between Mongolian frontier troops and Kirghiz tribesmen. Some ten thousand men had already gone, and more were being trained in Urumchi. It was definitely not the time to study Buddhist ruins or paint.

Three greatly relieved Roerichs were met by friends and escorted to a house reserved for them in the former Russian Concession. A long argument ensued at the courtyard entrance when a Chinese officer tried to requisition their carts and wagons for military purposes. He finally agreed to delay the matter. Their quarters were quite unsuitable to accommodate all their men, baggage, and horses, so they decided to hunt for better accommodations—a difficult task in the confusion of the walled city.

12

⸙

Wayfarer, Let Us Travel Together

Urumchi's Russian community provided a rare treat for the Roerichs. During most of the two years of the expedition, they had barely been in contact with the Western world and knew little about current events. For friends and the exchange of ideas, they essentially had each other and the knowledgeable lamas accompanying them. Along the route they met missionaries, and travelers shared their evening fires. Now Nicholas encountered a woman who remembered him from his school days in St. Petersburg. "We used to watch you through a crack in the door when you came to see Kuindjy," she confessed.

Ah, how long ago that was! For Roerich, it was lovely to find one who shared his remembrances of Arkhip Kuindjy, his revered and beloved art teacher, the fearless liberal who had inspired students with his lectures, aided needy students, and fed lunch to most of the birds of St. Petersburg. "The memory of Kuindjy does not tarnish with time or rust," Roerich told his diary.

The courtyard of the Russian settlement was always crowded. The family enjoyed watching the children of varied nationalities, some playing pegs while others swung on gym bars. Roerich, who loved seeing the world's peoples living harmoniously, heard of a club being organized and rejoiced in his journal, "It is so simple, and human, and joyous to behold."

A low white house with two rooms and a foyer had been prepared for the family, but when they learned that two foreigners were being evicted so they could move in, they decided to live in a yurt outside of the city. Their caravanners were afraid robbers would attack there, so Nicholas and George went to speak to the town dignitaries (the Fan and the Tu-t'u), who assured them that the trouble they had experienced in the past would not be repeated here. But at that very moment, the chief of police and a translator were searching their living quarters and questioning Helena about the artwork.

They moved out near the snowcapped Altas Bogdo-Ulas, sacred mountains to the south of Urumchi. A late April snowfall made it necessary to light the stoves, and a delighted Roerich wrote: "During the night everything became white. By six in the morning, all was covered with snow, and we awoke to find billows of milky clouds creeping along the Bogdo-Ulas. It is a long time since we have seen mountains with all their fine crystal-sharp lines covered in snow."

After speaking with an old friend (probably a White Russian who had also left Russia under difficult circumstances), Nicholas, the romantic idealist, mused, "An inexpressible charm lies in the fact that people leave their native places and on invisible wings make the earth small and accessible. This accessibility is the first step toward reaching other worlds, farther away."

While all around them people were speaking of war, pillage, and the approaching heat, the Roerichs shared in conversations of a more satisfying nature, for many people here had broad interests similar to their own own.

> In the silence of the suburb of Urumchi, in a comprehensive way, we
> speak about the tasks of the evolution of humanity, about the move-
> ment of nations, about knowledge, about the significance of color and

sound. . . . It is gratifying to hear this open-minded reasoning. . . . We learn that some islands have merged into the depths and out of the depths have arisen new ones, powerful ones.

During the time we were marching through mountains and deserts, some smaller stars have become of first magnitude and a whole island, with a population of ten thousand, sank into the sea. Lakes have dried up and new unexpected currents gushed forth. The cosmic energy confirms the steps of the evolution of humanity. Yesterday's "inadmissible" fairy tale is already being investigated by science. The refuse is being burned and the ashes are fertilizing the seedlings of new conquests. The conversations we hear are very significant. . . . The Olets and the Torguts know about Issa, and this makes all denials of the legend even harder to understand. Every enlightened lama speaks about it as confidently as any other historical fact.

We were interested to be reminded of Mohammed's prophetic mission that began on Mount Hira. That after Archangel Gabriel had informed Mohammed he was to be God's messenger, he was told that people would consider him a blasphemer, and he would face hostility, harassment, exile, and war. But this warning only served to strengthen his resolve and bring him peace.

It was now Easter, and saying, "Christ is risen," many lamas streamed into the house to share the joyous occasion. Roerich inquired in his diary, "Well, western clergymen, would you rejoice with the Buddhists on their holidays?" The Roerichs unpacked the thankas and Buddhist paintings they had been collecting and hung them so everyone could enjoy their beauty. All admired the resonant colors and deep meanings of the figures, and earnest discussions of Shambhala and Maitreya filled the house.

The following morning, a Mongolian lama friend arrived. Overjoyed, Roerich wrote: "The spiritual teachings we have gathered from the south are the same as he brings from the north. His eyes brimmed with tears when he told us exactly what fills the consciousness of those people and what they await. Another friend was near Lan-chow for six months, and each day he heard the significance of the future Maitreya mentioned. 'We have known these things for a long time,' said the lama, 'but we did not know how it would come about. And now the time has come. But we cannot tell everyone, only those Mongols and Kalmyks who comprehend.' The lama is such a humble man that until he spoke about various proofs, I would not have expected him to have such vast knowledge; he even spoke of the spiritual significance of the Altai to Russia."

Meanwhile, conditions on the border continued to worsen. The wireless and telegraph were strictly censored, and private individuals were seldom permitted to use them. Newspapers and other printed materials were forbidden throughout the province, and foreign magazines, papers, and correspondence were censored before delivery. The English diplomatic representative advised the Roerichs that the frontiers were practically closed. All foreigners, even the Chinese from China proper, were being viewed with great suspicion, and were often arrested and deported. It was especially difficult for those Chinese who had been educated at foreign universities and were trying to implement their modern ideas in China.

Due to the numerous bands of brigands and deserters who had abandoned their posts, the routes to Peking were in turmoil. The expedition was advised that the only safe artery open to foreigners was by way of Chuguchak and through Siberia. The Roerichs heard that their friend Allen Priest had gone to Siberia through the Altai Mountains. If the way was secure through Siberia, they would abandon their plans for Peking, go to Lake Zaisan, on to Omsk, and then to Moscow.

So the couple applied to their friend Alexander Bystrov, the Soviet consul in Urumchi, for transit visas. They explained they were on a mission for the Mahatmas, who wanted to create a Buddhist federation. Therefore, it was necessary for them to enter the USSR. From there, they planned to go to Mongolia, get in touch with the Panchen Lama, and embark upon a spiritual journey for the liberation of Tibetans. Advised it would take him about two weeks to receive an answer, longer than they had expected to be in Urumchi, they accepted the hospitality of the director of the Russo-Asiatic Bank and stayed in his house and courtyard.

They passed their days meeting with local officials and exploring the city. Detachments of troops marched through the streets daily, usually preceded by a band of musicians and several standard-bearers carrying huge red, yellow, and multicolored flags. George thought the soldiers looked like a motley collection of uniformed ruffians. Often the Roerichs noticed little boys carrying rifles and marching with the troops. They learned these boys had been entrusted with the rifles while the real owners enjoyed a smoke in a nearby restaurant.

Wherever the Roerichs went, they heard about the Mongolian Altai Mountain. They also heard tales of the Katun River, where it was said that the last war of the world would occur—to be followed by a time of peaceful labor. There were also stories of a village of Russian "Kerjaks" (Old Believers), who preserved the ways of the old Christian faith and lived in complete isolation from "worldly men."

Eight days passed before the weary family was honored with a luncheon and informed their passports would be ready the next day. When they returned to the banker's house, their guns were already there. The next day a scroll was delivered, which, when unrolled, was as long as Nicholas was tall. To their surprise, it was their passport, with their equipment and personal effects itemized and the artistic and scientific aims of the expedition spelled out. "Such stupidity—to write on a passport the number and description of all objects," Roerich fumed in his diary. "How many changes might take place on the journey!" But all that really mattered was that they were finally able to depart from Chinese Turkestan.

Before leaving Urumchi, Roerich drew up a will, which he left with the Soviet consul. It stipulated that in the event of his death, if Helena were no longer alive, all of the expedition's property and the paintings would go to the Soviet government. Considering that the paintings already belonged to the institutions in New York, one might speculate that this action was actually to ensure Soviet good will—or maybe it was a foreshadowing of the time to come when the Roerichs might well have wished that none of the paintings were in America.

All they could find for the journey were three carts, into which they crammed the drivers, a Tibetan lama, and Ramsana, their Ladakhi right-hand man. Their dog, Tumbal, had been left behind at the mission. If they were really going to leave China, they would have to whittle their possessions down until everything fit in the carts. Grateful they still had their horses, an exasperated Roerich complained to his diary, "Oh, how many difficulties with the packing! Possessions—enemies of man! Will we really leave tomorrow?"

Of course, the answer was no. Now there was trouble with the wagon drivers, a surly lot, who wanted to set their own pace. Roerich complained, "The old driver informed me that he will not go according to our conditions, but as God desires. I ask them to translate this to him, 'that he can also return as God wills.'"

Finally they left Urumchi and the Kalmyk villages behind them, while the majestic beauty of the three snowy peaks of the Bogdo-Ulas shone joyously and full of light. On their left, the snowy ridges of the T'ien Shans sparkled purple and blue, and the air was filled with the scent of wild mint and wormwood. When the moon rose, it was so luminous that the glow of the Chinese dusk paled at once and the Bogdo-Ulas drowned in the mist. The T'ien Shans would keep them company for another three days until the expedition started into the bleak steppes, salt marshes, and saline lakes of Dzungaria.

Helena regretfully summed up their China experience: "If only the Chinese had received us well, so much would have been changed." As Roerich reviewed the whole episode, he asked, "And is it possible that none of you Chinese of Sinkiang, who consider yourselves civilized, are indignant at the license of the Khotan official? Is it possible that I will have to leave the boundaries of Chinese Turkestan with the firm conviction that this country is not fit for cultural intercourse? We sincerely wish to say a word of sympathy for China or to justify her! But we will proceed instead, feeling like prisoners who have escaped from the nest of robbers." They would experience similar feelings of disappointment and frustration again ten years later.

Their first night out, they arose at 2:30 a.m. and spurred the ill-tempered drivers enough that they were ready to leave in two hours. Dawn broke cloudy, then the clouds changed into opalescent fissures, and a rain began that cooled everything off. Nicholas wrote in his diary: "The fresh grass was richly green and fragrant after the rain, but our mood was somewhat disturbed by the continual custom houses and inspections of our passports." By day's end, their arms had been inspected three times and the passports deciphered by an illiterate opium smoker representing the governor: "He read our five-foot-long passport syllable by syllable, and asked us to take our guns out of their cases. Then he timidly touched a revolver, paced for a long time, mumbled something to the innkeeper, and left. Can such an official be included in the evolution of humanity? Simply the dregs. But these stupidly annoying dregs are capable of obscuring the shining mountains and transforming every peaceful mood into the feeling of a prison. Away with such ignorance! And what for? Why do we go on these highways when we could turn and go into the mountains and cross without any inspections whatsoever?"

One of the expedition's original objectives had been to survey and record the graves and other vestiges of nomad culture along the northern rims of the T'ien Shans, the Jair Mountains, and the Altai, none of which had been recorded by other archaeological expeditions. Now, however, Roerich realized that the ancient trade routes had been so thoroughly excavated and plundered that the probability of finding anything was small.

The comparatively untouched province stretching from Urumchi to the steppes of Russia was another story. The entire border of Dzungaria and Mongolia was a vast cache of the past. Burial mounds were known to contain ancient nomad chiefs, with their most precious possessions. Dzungaria's sands, however, also teemed with gangs of well-armed bandits back from the civil wars. Although Chinese soldiers and local militiamen guarded the mountain trails, frequent raiding and murder were quite common.

After all the Roerichs had endured, they were more intent on reaching the Siberian border as quickly as possible than on excavating in the terrible heat, so they began traveling at night. Over the next several days they passed through numerous Kalmyk and Kirghiz encampments where immense herds of horses and cattle grazed. Grave sites were everywhere, some surrounded by mysterious concentric rounds of standing stone slabs or other relics of the nomads' past. Stopping to dig or explore, or gather support for the pan-Mongolian New Russia, however, was out of the question.

Up at four. How beautiful! The mountains become pink. A purplish mist is rising and the grass is luxuriant. We leave on a wonderful road, enjoying the fresh, sweet scent of the silver jilda. The birds are singing unlike anything we have heard for a very long time. We cross a plain strewn with mounds of graves while the silvery blue mountains stand there like a forbidding wall. At half-past nine, we reach Yan-zi-hai; and just in time, for the sun is already scorching hot and everything is searing.

Jubilant, we enter a small clay hut where we shall rest until twelve tonight, and then in the coolness we shall proceed to Shiho by moonlight. We can already feel the nearness of Russia; it is something almost tangible. Either the village streets are broader, or there are more plowed fields. And the inns are cleaner! Once more we sit in a little clay hut; the swallows are busy with their nests under the beams. It seems that we are back twenty-five years along the plain of Russia.

Helena speaks of other huts where we sat in Russian villages or under the walls of the monastery of Suzdal. Or later, when we were in the cells of Siena and San Gimignano, Italy. When we stop and think of all that we have seen, it is truly amazing!

The Roerichs had requested that the Lichtmanns meet them in Moscow but had never received a reply:

We have been waiting for news from our friends in America for months now. Where and whence are we going to receive it? Up to May 16th, we still did not receive an answer to a telegram that we sent April 12th. The condition of the telegraph station, of the wires, of the insulators, all spelled "Resign all hope." The words that did arrive were distorted beyond recognition, as if written in code.

The crest of the T'ien Shans is disappearing, while far ahead toward the north, the light line of the Tarbagatai Mountains starts to appear. In the steppe, Chinese tombs like little *kurgans* are crumbling and we learned of Tsagan-Khutukhta, a new face of Maitreya. How instructive it is to compare the images from behind the Himalayas with those from the North! While not deviating from the truth, each country adds its own details and observations; and though he is called Tsagan-Khutukhta here, he is still coming.

The pulse of evening makes us uncomfortable, and after a drama with the drivers (who would rather rest than continue on), we decide to extinguish the lights, muffle the harness bells, load up our arms and depart despite the rain. For twelve hours (with two hours to feed the horses), we march through deep sands—difficult for the horses and carriages. We see few inns and there is no food. The sands change into the dark-pebbled hills of the Jair Mountains. Everything becomes clear. Blinding threatening clouds whirl and thunder begins ahead of us. We stop on a little hill near a wretched Chinese temple.

The ridge of the Heavenly Mountains stretches in front of us, merging into the mist for the last time. They are so heavenly in tone, so rich with their white crests. Dear mountain snows, we shall see you again only in my paintings!

Finally, after carts breaking down, rude drivers and officials, and several nights without sleep, they arrived at the no-man's land separating the Chinese and Soviet frontiers. It was here that raiding bands of Kirghiz most frequently molested travelers. Roerich told his diary:

More border hassles; one carriage wheel broken. And here we sit again in our tents. Perhaps it will be the last time for a long time. The full golden moon looks unflinchingly through the flap of the tent; it brings back to us such pleasant memories of tents and beloved moun-

Members of the expedition repair a broken wheel.
Center, wearing a pith helmet: *Roerich. Dzungaria, May 1926*

tains. Today we passed a few nomad monasteries, and saw that Maitreya is revered there. But to avoid complications with the Chinese, we did not stop. What a pity, what a pity!

How solemn is this night of the end and the beginning! Farewell, Dzungaria! Here we descended and ascended green hills, and righted our fallen carriages. As a farewell, she reveals herself with abundant grass and flowers such as we have not seen for a long time: wild peonies, crimson red, yellow lilies, golden heads of a fiery orange color, irises, briar-roses. And her blue snow mountains, and the chrysoprase of the hills. The air is pervaded with the breath of spring.

The Kirghiz escort rode near us; they chased the wolves that crossed the road and picked a bunch of red peonies for Helena. The Kirghiz look just like the Scythians, who adorned the ancient vase we had; they wear identical caps, leather trousers, and half caftans. Only one more crossing and we will pass beyond the peak where a small heap of stones signifies the end of China!

And so they were back in their motherland, along with the many new paintings and albums of sketches Roerich had accumulated. Ironically, the first village they came to was named Rurikowsky. What more appropriate welcome than a village named after Prince Rurik. Exhilarated, Roerich wrote: "The white walls of the border post of Kuzeun, U.S.S.R. greets us! Welcome spring soil, in thy new attire! Continuous grass and little goldenheads. Soldiers approach us with questions. They are generally anxious to do what is best for us. We would expect crudeness and ignorance in an isolated little post like this, unmarked on the map; but they apologize for taking our time and for bothering us. The head of the post comes out with his assistant, and his family, and we are invited to remain overnight."

The boat that would carry them across the broad, smooth-flowing Irtysh River was to depart in three days. The soldiers at the post rejoiced to have this time in their company. Now, with the ordeals of China behind them, Helena started to receive transmissions from Master Morya for Book Three of the Agni Yoga series, titled *Community*. It opened:

> Wayfarer, friend, let us travel together. Night is near, wild beasts are about, and our campfire may go out. But we can conserve our forces if we agree to share the night watch.
>
> Tomorrow our path will be long and we may become exhausted. Let us walk together. We shall have joy and festivity. I shall sing for you the song your mother, wife and sister sang. You will relate for me your father's story about a hero and his achievements. Let our path be one.
>
> Be careful not to step upon a scorpion, and warn me of any vipers. Remember we must arrive at a certain mountain village. Traveler, be my friend.
>
> We are dissipating superstition, ignorance and fear. We are forging courage, will and knowledge. Every striving toward enlightenment is welcome. Every prejudice caused by ignorance is exposed. Thou who dost toil, are the roots of cooperation and community alive in thy consciousness? If this flame has already illumined thy brain, then adopt the mountains as signs of our Teaching. Greetings to workers and seekers!

Master Morya went on to explain that a planetary body can be just as sick as any other organism and that the spirit of the planet is affected by the condition of its body. Earth was suffering as from a fever because it had been cut off from the other worlds that could send assistance; therefore, poisonous, suffocating gases were accumulating in the lower strata of the subtle world.

On the first of June, 1926, they boarded the *Lobkov*, a boat in better condition than they had expected. They felt so refreshed by the sea breezes, the cool days and nights, and the delight of speaking their mother tongue with people who had open, curious minds that they were glad they had not decided to go to Omsk by train. Though the wind soon became a cold downpour and there was no heat, Helena was tremendously pleased, for she had worried that it might be too hot on the boat.

Here on the frontier, they again found people who spoke of Buddha, who understood Buddhism as a teaching rather than a religion. These people appreciated Buddha as a man, an actual historical personality, and were interested in the manuscripts of Issa. Roerich asked, "What accounts for this vital, clear thinking?" He wondered if he would have appreciated everyone so much had he not just come from China.

They stopped for three days in Omsk and were surprised to read newspapers stating that the Roerich expedition had "found" the legend of Christ. "How could we find something that has been known for so long?" Nicholas wondered: "What we found was greater than a legend, for we found that the story of the life of Issa, the Teacher, is accepted and alive throughout the entire east. On the borders of Bhutan, in Tibet, Sikkim, Ladakh, and Mongolia. Even in the Kalmyk encampments it is accepted as a firm, calm realization. That which is a sensation for the West is frequently old knowledge for the East."

The family toured their first Russian museum in many years and found Roerich's own paintings on exhibit—it was like seeing old friends: "To our surprise, we found two of my paintings: *Boats* (1903) from the suite called *Building the City*, and a sketch titled *Benevolent Tree*, both from the unfinished group which stood near the walls of my studio. A local schoolteacher walked up in astonishment and asked me, 'Are you Roerich?' 'Yes!' I replied. 'But you were killed in Siberia in 1918!' And here once again, we encountered the same fairy tale that had reached us in London and America; many heard of my obituaries and funeral services."

Roerich thought that perhaps all the prayers had helped, for even though their family had been chanted for and mourned, nevertheless they had succeeded joyously in traversing the mighty oceans and ascending the great heights.

Finally, at midnight June 13, 1926, they were in Moscow. With them were a message from the Mahatmas and a small box filled with soil from the Himalayas—earth on which Buddha might have stood. While wondering if they would meet Maurice and Sina Lichtmann there, a weary sounding Nicholas wrote in his journal: "Friends, upon the completion of this journey, I shall rejoice to transfer my complete drawings to you, along with these brief notes. But for this, it is necessary to settle down somewhere for a time and arrange the notes and albums. But where and when?"

13

THE ALTAI:
SACRED MAGNET FOR THE FUTURE

Before the family arrived in Moscow, Vladimir Shibayev, Roerich's secretary, had been corresponding with a close relative of Helena's, hoping to locate and reclaim the Roerichs' confiscated collection of Old Master paintings and artifacts. But the Russia from which the Roerich family had fled in 1916 bore little resemblance to the Union of Soviet Socialist Republics they now entered, ten years later. The Tsar and his family had been brutally murdered, and all possessions of the rich ruling class had been given to the poor. Education had become compulsory, and brothels were closed. Little of the past remained.

Although bitter struggles, severe hardships, and continual turmoil had filled the intervening years, by 1925 the "policy of recovery" had relieved the worst of the economic shortages and restored a semblance of health to the country. A kind of freeness had occurred on the heels of Lenin's New Economic Policy. Major transformation was occurring politically, economically, culturally, and spiritually. Small-scale and light industries were largely in the hands of private entrepreneurs or cooperatives. Some people in the top echelons of government were Buddhists or involved with spiritual organizations such as the

Masons and the Rosicrucians. With the support and encouragement of the Roerichs' old friend Lama Dorzhiev, the Soviets were entertaining the idea of influencing Tibet and turning it toward a "Red" Buddhism.

Although many writers and artists had greeted the early years of the new regime with high fervor, Roerich had not been among them. In 1919, his article "Violators of Art" had been published by the Russian Liberation Committee in London and widely circulated. In it, he challenged the Bolsheviks' claim that they were the "Medicis of Petrograd," guardians of art and science encouraging "the cultural achievements of the Soviet Government." Roerich had warned readers not to be deceived, labeling the Bolsheviks

> Judas Iscariots with their thirty pieces of silver.... Vulgarity and hypocrisy. Betrayal and bribery, the distortion of all the sacred conceptions of mankind. That is Bolshevism.
>
> The shameless monster which is deceiving mankind; a monster who has gained possession of the sparkle of precious stones. But do not be afraid to come nearer and look! The stones are imitations. Only a weak eye will fail to see that the glitter is false and the world and real spiritual culture are perishing in this glitter. Wake up and recognize what you know!

Roerich's views had been stated so emphatically that they were unlikely to have been forgotten by those he had implicated—who had been involved with the formation of the new government and now held many of the key political positions. Nevertheless, the Roerichs still had friends in Russia. The Mahatmas saw this special time as a window of opportunity and hoped that a message from them to the heads of state might help Russia turn toward a new path. In sending the Roerichs back to deliver it, Master Morya advised them:

It is wise to draw the line between past and future. It is impossible to calculate all that has been done. . . . It is better to say, "Yesterday is past; let us learn how to meet a new dawn." We all grow, and our works are expanding with us. It is unworthy to rummage in yesterday's dust. . . .

He, who affirms the Community, contributes to the hastening of the evolution of the planet. Fear and immobility signify a return to primitive forms. If you pay attention to history, you will perceive clear jolts of progress, and see that these jolts graphically coincide with manifestations of the idea of community—cooperation. When the banner of cooperation was unfurled, dictatorships were destroyed, new scientific forms were developed, new techniques of labor arose, and benevolent boldness shone forth. . . . In our picture of Community, everyone is working in full readiness, and our resources are intensified for the Common Good.

Encouraged by the wisdom of these teachings, the family decided that if they could safely return to Russia, they would. Now, in Moscow, they were welcomed by G. V. Chicherin, People's Commissar for Foreign Affairs and Nicholas's old school friend; A. V. Lunacharsky, Commissar of Education, who was interested in Buddhism; and several others, including Lenin's wife, Nadezhda Krupskaya. They listened to the Roerichs' tales of India and the research they had done in Asia, and accepted the small chest of sacred Himalayan soil ceremoniously presented to Chicherin, to be placed on the grave of "Mahatma Lenin." The Mahatmas' message read:

In the Himalayas, we know what you are accomplishing. You abolished the church, which was a breeding ground of lies and superstitions. You destroyed the bourgeoisie who had become agents of prejudice. You demolished the educational prisons. You destroyed the hypocritical family. You did away with the army, which had ruled as over slaves. You crushed the spiders of greed. You closed the night dens of cutthroats. You freed the land of wealthy traitors. You recognized that religion is the teaching of universal matter. You recognized the insignificance of private ownership. You foresaw the evolution of community. You pointed out the importance of knowledge. You bowed down before beauty. You brought the entire power of the Cosmos to the children. You opened the windows of the palaces. You saw the urgency of building homes for the Common Good.

We stopped the revolt in India because it was premature; but We recognized the timeliness of your movement, and We send you all our help, affirming the Unity of Asia.

Once Roerich had executed the Mahatmas' mission, he presented his *Maitreya* series and the painting *The Time Has Come* to Lunacharsky. Then he set about seeing friends and relatives and conducting some business of his own. He also hoped to display the work he had created during the expedition. Two years earlier, in November 1924, Roerich had formed the Beluha Corporation to take advantage of the easing economic conditions and attempt to begin business transactions with the Soviets. During the expedition, Roerich had seen many rich natural resources waiting to be developed: timber, coal, oil, ores, metals, minerals. In 1927, the Ur Corporation was incorporated; the purpose of both companies was to try to get these resources to market and manufacture, which would benefit the New Country. Both corporations, however, were so ineffective that they were later abandoned.

Now Roerich felt he had a perfect opportunity to discuss the prospects of mining in Siberia with the Soviet authorities. With Herbert Hoover's Quaker Relief Fund feeding the perishing millions in the Ukraine, the well-remembered Roerichs, now with American connections, were very newsworthy. But the press pounced upon them. Accusations were hurled at the couple for desertion, for fleeing from the Bolsheviks, and for serving the capitalists of the world. Their "mysterious devotion" to Buddhism received the most severe criticism. Though the family tried to make light of these charges, they were understandably wary and troubled. *Pravda* printed an article, reprinted in the English language papers, saying the Soviets were considering equipping Roerich with Soviet passports and Browning revolvers so that he could lead a two-year scientific expedition to Tibet.

The publicity did broadcast the news of their arrival in Moscow to their friends and acquaintances. Roerich was able to speak with some young Russian painters, engaging them with stories of their American brother artists in Cor Ardens and Los Cinco Pintores. And, again, a brotherhood of artists was formed, called Amaravella. One artist who was there, Boris Smirnov-Rusetsky, remembered the meeting until his death in 1993. He often recalled how deeply Roerich's talk and the Agni Yoga teachings had affected the young artists. For many years thereafter, when free expression and symbolism in art were considered criminal acts deserving punishment, the Roerichs' support and the Agni Yoga teachings were all the artists had for encouragement.

Some weeks later, Roerich and George were sitting in the CHEKA reception room waiting to see Felix Dzherzhinsky, the head of that organization, when Dzherzhinsky suddenly dropped dead in his office.[1] After watching the funeral procession with all the important dignitaries pass beneath their hotel window, the family expediently packed and prepared to leave. With their supplies and equipment replenished, the Roerichs and the Litchmanns climbed into two hired cars and departed for the Altai Mountains. They had been in Moscow for two months.

Upon her return to New York, Sina told the American press that the Moscow visit was a great success. All doors flew open at the sound of the Roerich name, and they were met with absolute hospitality and friendship everywhere. But the many conflicting stories lead one to wonder what exactly did happen.[2]

For anyone hoping to escape notice, the Altai Mountains were the perfect place to go. Partially on Soviet territory and partially in Mongolia, the range stretches from the West Siberian Plain southeast to the Gobi Plain, forming the northern boundary of the Gobi. With a tradition as holy as Shambhala, the mountains are regarded as sacred. The highly revered Mount Belukha rises in the center of the Katun Range. This was to be the location of the New Russia (called Zvenigorod by the Masters), the Buddhist spiritual country. Although the range has been described as cruel and unapproachable, to Roerich it was, "austere yet beautiful," and their arrival was greeted by an auspicious double rainbow stretching across the entire sky, above the mighty river Ob. Their Master explained: "The sun's smile amidst the clouds brings forth the radiant rainbow. Thou shall remember the Aura of the Teacher smiling through the dewdrops on that future day of glory."

Passing beside the Shambatyon and Katun Rivers, the group saw rocks hurling through the rapids with tremendous force. Even though followers of Master Morya were said to be living already on the opposite shore, none of the group was reckless enough to wade across to investigate. They were watching for signs of the new city, but saw nothing obvious. They did notice an abundance of caves containing bones with carved inscriptions. Without a light to gauge the depth, the Roerichs felt sure these caves were the same secret passages that the Spiritual Ones of Asia used to reach Tibet, the Kunluns, Altyn-Taga, Turfan, and other places.

In *Heart of Asia*, Roerich explained:

> The Altai played a most important part in the migration of nations and is an untouched treasure with Belukha, the ruler, nourishing all rivers and fields, ready to yield its riches. The so-called graves of the Tchud and those burial places marked with inscriptions on rocks, all direct our attention to that time when, whether impelled by glaciers or escaping the sands, nations from the far southeast col-

lected themselves into an avalanche and overran and regenerated Europe. I believe the entire area is a sacred and powerful magnet for the future.

On the 17th of August we beheld Belukha; so clear and reverberant; "the Queen of the White Snows" of whom even the deserts whisper. Verily, she is Zvenigorod, the City of the Bells that I painted while still in Russia. And beyond Belukha, the crests of the Kunluns, so beloved in my heart, appear far in the distance. "The Queen of the White Snows" stands alongside "the Five Treasures of the Snows" and all the other sacred names written and unwritten, spoken and unspoken.

During their weeks in the Altai, the Roerichs stayed in the home of an Old Believer, Vakhramey Semyonovich Atamanov. Writing of Atamanov, Nicholas noted: "Like many of the wise ones who know the secret traditions, Vakhramey is not astonished at anything; he knows the ores, the ways of the deer and the little bees. He loves herbs and flowers and understands them indisputably.... His face lights up as he gathers a great bunch of varied-colored grasses that reach up and touch his gray beard. He delights in them, pets them, and caresses them as he speaks of their usefulness. Here is verily the same Panteleimon, the Healer, whom I first painted in 1916."

Completely versed in the sacred shamanistic lore of the region, Vakhramey was a treasured resource. Whatever secrets he revealed to the group remained secret however, for neither Roerich nor Sina Lichtmann disclosed a word in their diaries. Even George, so meticulous with his lists and descriptions, completely omitted mention of the trip to Altai. Sina wrote only, "We went out exploring today, and discovered many wonderful things." Nor did the Lichtmanns ever divulge anything when they returned to New York. The press was informed that the Roerich expedition was on its way to Abyssinia!

Nicholas and Helena, Altai, August 1926

Instead, Roerich wrote of the cave of the legendary Tchud tribe, who escaped bondage by going underground. He said stones encircled its entrance and it resembled other huge tombs he had seen from the period of the great migrations in such places as the foothills of the northern Caucasus. He further wrote that when the Central Asia expedition was crossing the Karakorum Pass, their Ladakhi groom had told them they were riding above caves where many treasures had been stored by a wonderful tribe who went underground because they abhorred the sins of the earth. The reverberation of the horses' hooves had sounded the same as it had when they approached Khotan. The caravanners had told them that people could reach distant countries through those passages.

To his diary, Roerich commented: "Great is the belief in subterranean people. Through all Asia, through the vast spaces of the deserts, from the Pacific to the Urals, I have heard the same wondrous tales of vanished holy people. 'Long ago people lived here; now they have gone inside; they found a passage and entered the subterranean kingdom. And only rarely do they appear on earth again. Such people come to our bazaar with strange, very ancient money. No one can even remember when such money was used.'"

When Nicholas inquired if he could see some of these subterranean people, he was told, "Yes, if your thoughts are similarly high and in contact with these holy people—because sinners stay upon earth, while the pure and courageous ones pass on to something more beautiful."

The Roerichs were introduced to several village schoolteachers, who lowered their voices and inquired if the group had come from India. Upon hearing their affirmative reply, all eyes lit up with eagerness as they asked for information of the Mahatmas, whispering, "There are many of us and we exist solely for these teachings." They spoke of an old monk who had died recently after traveling throughout India and the Himalayas. Among his possessions was a manuscript containing much about the Mahatmas, and indicating the monk had been intimately acquainted with this usually secret subject.

Much needed to be accomplished if the Roerichs were to return to the Altai someday and establish their pan-Mongolian country. Although they were now starting for Mongolia in the hope of finding the Panchen Lama, he wrote: "Mongolia (Land of Brave Men) attracts our attention. Tales creep to us of Kobdo, near the Northwest frontier, where a goodly number of temples and mud houses are built near the lake. Everyone seems interested in conveying at least something to us of the spirit of Mongolia, the land of magnetic storms, mirages of the sun, and cruciform moons."

Geographically, the area loosely called Central Asia is outlined by the Caspian Sea on the west, Siberia on the north, and northern Iran and

Afghanistan on the south. China lies to the east, Mongolia to the northeast. The Pamirs and the Himalayas rise in the south, and the T'ien Shans and the Altai are on the eastern flank. This vast expanse of arid plain and desert is the greatest landmass on earth. Inner and Outer Mongolia are the heartland of the Asian continent. In 1921, following the Russian Revolution, Mongolia peacefully converted from a centuries-old, completely pastoral society populated by nomads to a socialist state. Though after the revolution, the capital city was renamed Ulan Bator Khoto (City of the Red Warrior), most people continued to call it Urga.

From the Altai, the Roerich party went by train to the Buriat Republic and then arranged for autos to carry them into Mongolia. With the Altai behind, George resumed his journal: "Around 4:00 in the afternoon, we started our journey toward the immense and boundless steppes of Mongolia, motoring through the country of the greatest conquerors of Asia. The road rose imperceptibly until we had crossed several ridges of low, grass-covered hills, and then we saw the true signs of Buddhist Mongolia: the suburgans or stupas, which stood sparkling, like a white necklace."

The next day, when they tried to cross a swift current where there was no ferry, it became obvious that the cars were going to create more problems than they would solve:

> One at a time, the cars were carried on barges; the driver made a careless movement and one almost slid into the river, but it was rescued just in time. . . . Our progress was very slow, for after the recent heavy rains the route was sandy, extremely muddy, and slippery. It was often necessary to get out and push the cars along the slopes, greatly handicapped by the lack of headlights on one of them.
>
> In the full darkness of a moonless evening, we reached the river Iro and persuaded the ferryman to take us across. We camped in the open, near to some wretched Mongol tents, from which two old

women emerged, covered with rags. The night was cold and we had to light camp fires. A white mist arose from the river surface to envelop the far bank. Dark silhouettes of the forest-clad mountains stood to the south and we heard the conchshell of a nearby lamasery call the lamas for evening prayer. We were up before dawn and drove south toward a low pass. Though newly constructed, the road was so muddy and sandy that our cars sank deep into the mud and had to be rescued by horsemen.

We continued on, and found several cars traveling from Urga, stranded on the banks. They had endeavored to cross the river, but it flooded their engines. They all warned us that it was foolhardy to try and cross, but we decided to try it; so we crammed all the luggage inside the cars and covered the radiators with several sheets of waterproof canvas. Luckily, several horsemen came to our aid again. They tied ropes from the front of the cars to the pommels of their saddles and when we were all set, the drivers started the cars and the horsemen rushed towards the opposite river bank, shouting wildly. Water splashed high into the air but the two cars were pulled safely across the river.

They were heading toward the Tola Valley and the magnificent Bogdo-Ula, which rises 3,000 feet above Urga and forms the southern boundary of the forests in that part of Mongolia. Believed to be the birthplace of Genghis Khan, some scholars also believe he died there. The mountain dominates the entire valley and has a unique history. In AD 1778 when Mongolia was under Chinese domination, the Bogdo-Ula was declared sacred and the Emperor legalized the cult of the sacred mountains. He ordered that incense and silk be sent there biannually and that ceremonial offerings be made by the spiritual leader, the Bogdo-gegen, the Living Buddha of Mongolia. Hunting and tree chopping were outlawed, and fishing forbidden. The area became a true natural reserve and haven for fauna large and small. One could observe herds of reindeer, mountain deer, wild bears, wolves, foxes, and hundreds of different birds, all quite tame and unafraid of humans. Over time, the Bogdo-gegen brought apes, bears, rare birds, and even an elephant to live in this sanctuary.

Though students of history considered Genghis Khan "the Scourge of God" for his acts of brutality, Roerich had never agreed. He recognized that Genghis had given the world a wise code of laws so usable that it was still Mongolia's base of justice. Now Nicholas was pleased to discover that many in Mongolia shared his viewpoint.

Closely in touch with Tibet, Mongolia had been a stronghold of Lamaism for centuries. Even after the revolution, the Lamaist church continued to exist and membership was maintained in the World Buddhist Association. The old ways, however, were quickly dying out; there were only about one hundred priests in the entire country. Most of the lavish temples and sanctuaries had become museums. Roerich was anxious to offer the New Country as a safe asylum for the priests.

Eager to visit the Ganden Lamasery, the only sanctuary in Mongolia where Lamaism still functioned, the Roerich party also wanted to see the state library, with its monumental collection of theological works including the hundreds of volumes of the Kanjur and the Tanjur printed in rare woodblock form. The ancient brilliant textiles discovered by the Russian explorer General P. K. Kozlov were of special scientific interest; traced back to Greece, Iran, Scytho-Siberia, and China, the designs were evidence of the far-reaching trade of Central Asian nomads. Because of their strong resemblance to the well-documented silks excavated from the Tarim Basin by Sir Aurel Stein, the materials could be fairly well dated to the first century BC. The textiles' composition affirmed for Roerich that different provinces of Central Asia had borrowed their inspiration from a common source. The Mongol Scientific Committee's current research and excavations of tumuli throughout the Noin-Ul Mountains were substantiating that and throwing fresh light on nomadic culture.

The sprawling city of Urga resembled a permanent settlement surrounded by a large colony of yurts. Most of the population lived in yurts during the cold winters. The glittering, gilded roofs of monasteries, the cathedral, and other religious buildings enhanced Urga's appearance. With wonderful luck, the Roerichs found a four-room house with two spacious courtyards and stables for rent. There was room to establish headquarters and space for brother Boris and the Lichtmanns.[3] Dr. Konstantin Ryabinin, their dear friend from Russia, and Roerich's other brother, Vladimir, soon joined the expedition, renting a place nearby.

With many opportunities to attend dances, festivals, and services at the colorful temples, they were entranced by everything they saw and heard. The family spent their days productively: Helena had time to write, Nicholas to paint, George to share rare time with the lamas, and all three were able to study Kalachakra. "These rituals and music are remnants of the past," George wrote, "and harken back to shamanistic antiquity. Its peculiar charms touch me deeply." The family also needed time to organize and carefully study the route for the last phase of the expedition: the great crossing of Central Asia, through Mongolia and Tibet, back to India.

Touring near a temple in Urga one day, they spotted an open place surrounded by a stockade, unusual for Mongolian dwellings. They inquired, and were startled to hear that it was a site for the future temple of Shambhala. An unknown lama had purchased it. Roerich told his diary: "Not only do many learned lamas in Mongolia know of Shambhala, but even many laymen and members of the Government can relate the most striking details. When we showed some of the Shambhala prophecies to a member of the Government, he exclaimed in astonishment, 'But this agrees with the prophecy foretold by a young boy on the Iro River. Verily, the Great Time is coming!'"

The Roerichs were surprised to hear the same stories of the Mahatmas they had previously heard in India. Roerich wrote, "Such are the ties of Asia. Who carries the news? By what secret passageways do these un-

Roerich with lamas of the Ganden Monastery, Urga, Mongolia,

known messengers travel? While one may be living an ordinary routine daily life in Asia, confronted with difficulties, crudeness and many trying cares, still at any moment a knock may come at the door, bringing important news."

The first theological school for study of Kalachakra, the higher metaphysics of Buddhism, had been established in Urga in 1741. Since the Panchen Lama had escaped, he had been spreading these hidden teachings of Shambhala everywhere, therefore it was experiencing a powerful revival. Numerous Kalachakra colleges had been established in Inner Mongolia, Buddhist China, and even Buriatia. As George explained in his journal: "Learned abbots and meditating lamas are said to be in constant communication with the mystic fraternity of Shambhala, for it guides the destinies of the Buddhist world. A western observer is apt to

belittle the importance of this name, or to relegate the voluminous literature about Shambhala (and the still more vast oral tradition) into the
class of folklore or mythology; but those who have studied both literary
and popular Buddhism know the terrific force that this name possesses
among the masses of Buddhists of higher Asia. For over the course of
history, it has not only inspired religious movements, but even moved
armies, whose war cry was 'Shambhala.'"

The troops of the great war hero Sukhe Bator, who had liberated
Mongolia from centuries of Chinese domination, marched to such a song.
The Roerichs were startled to hear the cavalry singing of the war of
Northern Shambhala as they marched by, summoning the warriors of
Mongolia to rise for the holy war and liberate their country from the
oppressors. "Let us die in this war and be reborn as warriors of Shambhala"
resounded through the streets as the soldiers passed.

Urga's largest temple had been dedicated to Maitreya, and a colossal
statue of him towered some fifty feet above the surrounding altars, candles,
incense burners, and a Wheel of Life. George wrote:

> One of the most important religious events is the Maidari procession,
> an imposing parade of Maitreya, the Coming Buddha, which encircles
> the entire city sometime during the third or fourth moon of the
> Mongol year. Its approach is heralded by the concentrated look of the
> tremendous crowd, and by the dim, yet ever rising powerful sound of
> the trumpets, the cymbals, and the many deep voices chanting
> prayers. The air becomes so dusty that the monks, and the richly
> bedecked horses that transport the holy images, the huge palanquins,
> and the silk umbrellas of bright hued silk, all seem to move in a yel-
> lowish cloud.
>
> Hundreds of thousands of feet trample on the dusty road to the
> accompaniment of long trumpets sounding out their deep, sonorous
> notes, clear ringing tones of the clarinets, the clashing of cymbals,

and the bass voices of the drums. Majestic abbots, resplendent in gold cloth, their high lama hats, and purple mantles can be seen marching ahead of the novices in shabby garments. In one massive crowd, garbed in rainbow colors, are officials and commoners, with ropes of pearls and precious stones set in gold, all following the images of the One who incarnates all the hopes of Buddhist Mongolia. Some onlookers prostrate themselves in the dust as the images pass, others murmur prayers and jostle to get in closer.

Aware that he was watching the last remnants of old Mongolia, George was struck by the contrast of the somber khaki uniforms of the Mongolian cavalrymen, the colorfully costumed crowd, and the clergy in their deep purple robes.

Worshiper near the Temple of Maitreya, Urga, Mongolia

Professor Roerich presented the government with a painting of Rigden Jyepo, the ruler of Shambhala, and was moved by the emotion with which it was accepted. He was told a special memorial temple might be built where it would occupy the central altar. He was asked how he knew of this vision, for it was the same as one seen several months earlier by one of their most revered lamas. "Our lama saw a great crowd of people from many nations; all of them were facing the West. A majestic rider appeared on a fiery steed, encircled by flames, with the banner of Shambhala in his hand—it was the Blessed Rigden Jyepo Himself—who bade the crowd to turn from the West and face the East."

"Two roads of life are evident in Asia," Roerich explained. "Do not be confused. They are making a great effort to preserve their monuments to study and learn from them. Mongolia reveals its outer self to the casual passerby with an astonishing wealth of color, costumes, and age-old traditions that are blended with brilliantly staged ceremonials. But on closer observation, I found serious research being conducted and was pleasantly impressed by their attitude towards their past. Proof of the Great Truth may lie over the next hill."

1. *Mother of the World*, 1930s.
Tempera on canvas, 98 x 65.5 cm. Nicholas Roerich Museum, New York.

2. Krishna. From "Kulu" series, 1929.
Tempera on canvas, 74 x 118 cm. Nicholas Roerich Museum, New York.

3. Tibet. Himalayas, 1933.
Tempera on canvas, 74 x 117 cm. Nicholas Roerich Museum, New York.

4. *Shirin and Khosrov*, 1938.
Tempera on canvas, 45.7 x 78.7 cm. Museum of Oriental Art, Moscow.

5. *Tidings of the Eagle*, 1927.
Tempera and oil on panel, 31.5 x 41 cm. Nicholas Roerich Museum, New York.

6. *Sophia—the Wisdom of the Almighty*, 1932.
Tempera on canvas, 107.5 x 153 cm. Nicholas Roerich Museum, New York.

7. *Most Sacred (Treasure of the Mountain)*, 1933.
Tempera on canvas, 73.5 x 117 cm. Nicholas Roerich Museum, New York.

8. *Great Wall*, 1935.
Tempera on canvas, 91.4 x 60 cm. International Centre of the Roerichs, Moscow.

9. *St. Panteleimon the Healer*, 1931.
Tempera on canvas, 44.5 x 78.5 cm. Nicholas Roerich Museum, New York.

10. *Treasure of the World*. From "His Country" series, 1924.
Tempera on canvas, 88.5 x 116.5 cm. Nicholas Roerich Museum, New York.

11. *Star of the Morning*, 1932.
Tempera on canvas, 61.5 x 97 cm. Nicholas Roerich Museum, New York.

12. *Padma Sambhava*. From "Banners of the East" series, 1924.
Tempera on canvas, 74 x 117 cm. Nicholas Roerich Museum, New York.

13. *Madonna Oriflamma*, 1932.
Tempera on canvas, 173.5 x 99.5 cm. Nicholas Roerich Museum, New York.

14

᭙

ACROSS THE GOBI

Locked in the heart of Central Asia, Tibet challenged Roerich's imagination as no other country did. In 1904, Tibet and Great Britain had signed a treaty granting the British government control of entry, but it had maintained Tibet's policy toward strangers. It was almost possible to count on both hands the foreigners who had entered the kingdom: Sir Charles Bell, a friend of the Dalai Lama; Lieutenant Colonel F. M. Bailey, the political officer in Sikkim; some English officials; the adventurers who were climbing Mount Everest; and a few others. The two famous women—Helena Blavatsky, Russian spiritualist and Theosophist, and Alexandra David-Neel, the intrepid French explorer and scholar of Buddhism—who had managed to penetrate the country had only done so disguised and under the greatest secrecy.

Tibet was forbidden to most outsiders, and Lhasa, its capital, was even more closely protected. Not one of the great explorers who had set out to reach Lhasa had been admitted. The Russian explorer Colonel Przhevalsky and his men had gotten within 150 miles before they were halted by Tibetan officials and ordered to leave the country. Neither Sven Hedin nor Sir Aurel Stein had gotten even that close.

217

If the Roerichs were able to visit Lhasa, it would be a brilliant achievement. While in Urga in the fall and winter of 1926, they met with a representative of the Dalai Lama who was willing to try to secure permission for them to enter Tibet and visit Lhasa. After waiting three months, they received an encouraging reply. Official passports would be issued, as well a letter of introduction to the Dalai Lama. The family was thrilled, for mysterious Tibet was where Mme Blavatsky had met her Masters and obtained the *Stanzas of Dzyan.*

Meanwhile, the Lichtmanns had gone back to America and then managed to return to Urga, bringing the mountain of supplies needed to continue the expedition. Everything from tents to toilets, guns to paints, canvas to canned goods, had been brought from America. The Roerichs were completely outfitted to resume "encircling inner Asia" to search for future fields of artistic and scientific work—and Shambhala.

As the route to Tibet was unmapped, all they knew was that if they steered toward central Tibet, their path must cross the formidable, but uniquely interesting, Gobi. Roerich was aware that the regions of Mongolia and the central Gobi were an explorer's and archaeologist's paradise—with whole cities hidden beneath the sands—but nothing could be planned beforehand. Even the stretch of the journey after Tibet would not be known in advance. As George explained, "The chaotic state of affairs in inner Asia and China made all sorts of unexpected events possible and the only thing left to us was to trust Providence and proceed on our journey, leaving details to be decided on the spot."

So with the good wishes of the Mongolian authorities, the expedition set off on April 23, 1927, heading southwest toward a Mongolian frontier post and the Yum-Beise monastery. The gear and supplies were packed in three trucks, and light baggage was strapped to the running boards of the two Dodge touring cars that would carry the group.

The Lichtmanns said their good-byes; they were returning to New York with plans for the new Roerich Museum building. It was to be the

One of the touring cars with the light luggage tied on the running boards

first skyscraper museum, a unique cultural center that would house all the Roerich institutions; apartments in the upper floors would enable it to pay for itself and allow educators, musicians, writers, and artists to live in the building and enjoy the cultural events held there. Construction was to be paid for by a bank loan, which they estimated could be paid off in ten years; after that, the income would be used for cultural programs. With Louis Horch's good reputation, obtaining the loan should not be any problem.

The banner of Maitreya, fastened to a Mongolian spear, had joined the flags leading the procession. The party had grown considerably, now consisting of the Roerichs, their caravanners, several lamas, Dr. Ryabinin, the chief of transport, several army men, and two Cossack girls, Ludmila and Iraida Bogdanova, who were to help Helena. (The sisters became part of the Roerich household and continued with them for the next thirty years.) George wrote:

> A part of the way, we covered by motor. The heavily freighted auto-mobiles looked like battle-tanks with our fellow travelers, the Buriat and Mongol lamas, sitting on top, colorfully dressed in their coned caps and yellow, blue and red robes. We intended to continue this way till beyond the border, for people had told us we could easily cross the Gobi by car, but it was impossible. With difficulty, we covered the nearly 600 miles to Yum-Beise in twelve days. There was no actual road, and with troublesome river crossings, stony ridges, and car prob-lems some days we did no more than ten or fifteen miles. Here and there we traveled on a camel path, but most of the trip we had to scout our way through virgin land. When our guide took us to an ancient, destroyed city fifty miles to the west, by mistake, we learned two important things: that all existing maps were inaccurate, and that we could not trust the local guides.

After endless negotiations, they managed to reach the Chinese border and continued by camel from there. Roerich wrote: "Draw a line from the South Russian steppes and the northern Caucasus across the steppes of Semipalatinsk, Altai, and Mongolia, then turn south, and you will have the main artery of our migration.... The Central Gobi seems limitless. White—pink—blue—and slate black. The fierce gales bury the flat slopes under a layer of stones, and we soon learned not to be caught by it. The danger of continuing on this route was that the wells might be dry or filled with dead animals; the only other way would be toward the east, but that area was infested with Chinese bandits."

George described the region:

The Gobi between Yum-Beise and An-hsi represents a succession of mountain ridges of crystalline rocks, intersected by desert. Most of the mountain ridges belong to the Altai system, which stretches northwest by southeast across the arid region situated between the southern branches of the Khangai Mountains and the eastern slopes of the T'ien Shans and the Barkol Mountains. I am confident that if explored properly, the numerous canyons that flank the desert ridges would offer ample opportunities to discover fossils.

Although Dr. Roy Chapman Andrews has thoroughly investigated the country to the northeast, scant attention has been given the southwest area we are taking. Only a few of the European travelers have touched this desolate region, and much remains to be done to reconstruct its geological past. Our headman Portniagin, and some of the other Mongols, say they have crossed the eastern part of the Mongolian Gobi, but have never seen a country so barren and desolate as where we are now.

After leaving Russia, Nicholas seemed to lose interest in keeping his diary. His notations dwindled to only a few lines, but George continued to document everything fully. On June 1, 1927, the expedition arrived at the edge of the central Gobi and set up camp on the silvery banks of the Shih-pao-ch'ang. "It is good," Roerich noted. "The Nan-Shan Mountains glow at sunrise, the mountain streams murmur, and the herds of goats and rams gleam white in the sun. Riders speed by us—is there any news? Rumors fill the air; they try to frighten us by giving us many reasons why we should wait here until September: the grass must thicken, the camels must fatten, their wool must grow, the treacherous swamps of Tsaidam must dry out, and the Blue River must subside."

Waiting would also give them time to study future routes and complete preparations for their great march in August. As always, there was much to keep each of them busy. George was learning the language and customs of the local Mongols while inquiring about routes across the salt swamps of Tsaidam and the uplands of Tibet. Nicholas painted, while Helena and her two assistants sorted the baggage, making lists of supplies needed for the arduous trip ahead. Portniagin, the headman, handled the transport problems, saddlery, and other odds and ends.

Just as Portniagin was leaving to buy provisions and handle the cables to and from America, their Tibetan guide rode into camp on a fine black horse, driving a big herd of horses and mules to add to the caravan. They were advised that Lhasa had requested that all European travelers be prevented from coming any closer, but since the expedition carried Tibetan passports and letters of introduction, and was escorted by a deputy of the Tibetan representative in Urga, the Roerichs were confident this would not apply to them.

Ten difficult days followed. They had problems obtaining more animals. A local Chinese businessman, who called Roerich "the American King," tried to cheat them at every opportunity. And Helena and several of the caravanners suffered health problems. Therefore, they decided to move their camp into the upper Sharagolji Valley, where there was less drought and better conditions. They climbed 9,000 feet, crossed the "Three Mountain Pass," and entered the valley beside the snow-clad Humboldt Mountains (locally called the Doyugu), then continued until they set up camp in the foothills of Ulan Davan (16,000 feet).

In *Heart of Asia*, Roerich remembered it this way: "A long march for the camels. The song of Shambhala rings again through the air. Even here on the stony mountain passes and frozen uplands, we are not left without signs of Shambhala. Bending over a stony slope, our lamas were collecting pieces of white quartz and carefully designing them into something on the neighboring rocks. It was the monogram of Kalachakra they had embedded into the sands. 'Henceforth, this white inscription that invokes the Great Teaching will be visible from afar to all travelers.'"

The six weeks in camp waiting for the camel caravan season to begin were a special time. The Mongols, whose solitary tents were scattered wherever water and grass was best for their herds, loved occasions to socialize. The Roerichs had a great tent erected and invited everyone to join in the Festival of Maitreya, observed annually on July 5. The long service was conducted by the expedition lamas, and as they chanted together all hearts gladdened. In return, the group was invited to join the

Camped on the road to Tibet waiting for the camel caravan season to begin

several days of festivities when the scattered people came together to enjoy themselves.

It was a peaceful time. Roerich painted the Bogdo-Ulas several times, then sketched and painted *Guardian of the Entrance, The Great Horseman*, and others. The Humboldt peaks glowed white with snow, and the air was invigorating. The stillness reminded them of the Himalayan heights. At night, the group held wonderful discussions on the new prayer to Shambhala, the prophecies of the Panchen Lama, or the need for a pan-Asiatic language to reconcile, at least elementally, the three hundred dialects of Asia. Roerich yearned to convey to the West through his paintings and books—and through the establishment of the New Country—the importance that Maitreya, Shambhala, and Gessar Khan have in Asia.

They were camped in the area where the Mahatma had rested on his way to Mongolia forty years before, so they decided to commemorate the spot with a suburgan of Shambhala. Everyone gaily joined in the construction, building the understructure of stones, reinforced with clay and grass. The top was made of wood, covered with tin from a gasoline tank, and the entire surface was given a sturdy coat of Humboldt lime and reverently painted with red, yellow, and green designs by a Buriat lama using Roerich's paints. The suburgan was completed July 24. "The Elder Lama of Tsaidam comes to consecrate it," wrote Roerich.

> In front of the tent of Shambhala, the lamas prayed for the coming of the Blessed Rigden Jyepo and placed a polished mirror before the image. Water was poured onto the mirror and the glass seemed to come alive with strange figures appearing on the surface. When it blurred, it resembled one of the magic mirrors in ancient stories.
>
> A procession walked around the shrine with burning incense while the lama held onto a thread suspended from the roof. The altar was filled with gifts of turquoise, coral, and beads, an image of the Buddha, a silver ring with a most significant inscription, prophecies

for the future, and other precious objects that had been placed there by an old lama who had helped with the construction. We also lay the Ak-dorje and the Maitreya Sangha within.

After a long service, the white thread that connected the lama and the suburgan was severed, and the monument stood there alone in the purple of the desert, forever to shine brightly, defended only by invisible powers.

That night news arrived that Colonel N. V. Kordashevski, a Lithuanian and long-time friend of the Roerichs who was to head the

Suburgan to Shambhala, Sharagolji, Nan-Shan Mountains

convoy, was crossing the Gobi after leaving Peking. Of vital importance, they also heard that the Panchen Lama and his Chinese escort were on the way to nearby Kumbun monastery and that his luggage was already there. "Toward evening on the 28th, N. V. came galloping along with his sword and the ring. We hardly had time to hear him, when a devastating torrent swept down the canyon. A flash flood in place of the peaceful stream, the result of the strange night-tumult in the mountains. The torrent swept away the kitchen, the dining tent, and George's tent. Much was destroyed and many Mongol yurts were swept away. We walked in water up to our waist; many irreplaceable things were destroyed. N. V. told us that on the eve of his departure, for some inexplicable reason, the thankas sent to us by Y. were destroyed by fire. It is significant!"

August 5 was another exceptional day:

Something remarkable! We are in our camp in the Kukunor district, not far from the Humboldt Chain. It was morning, about 9:30 when some of our caravaneers noticed a remarkably big black eagle flying above us.[1]

Seven of us began to watch this unusual bird and at the same moment, another of our caravaneers noticed something flying far above it. And he shouted in his astonishment. We all saw it. Something shining and beautiful glistening in the rays of the sun—a huge oval moving at great speed flying from north to south. And then it disappeared in the intense blue sky, behind the Ulan Davan, the red pass in the Humboldt chain.

It was in view long enough for them to get field glasses from the tents, so they saw it quite distinctly: "An oval form with a shiny surface, one side of which was brilliant from the sun. And the lama whispered: 'A good sign. A very good sign. We are protected. Rigden Jyepo himself is looking after us!'"

Other things happened during this extraordinary time. Some Roerich wrote about, others were whispered by a few of the party or repeated by the coworkers in New York. For instance, one warm day, when traveling in the desert, their caravan guide covered his nose and mouth with a scarf, explaining that precautions were needed. "We are approaching the forbidden lands of Shambhala," he said. "We will soon encounter Sur—the poisonous gas that guards the frontier." Lowering his voice, he continued, "We are close to the place where all the people and animals of the Dalai Lama's caravan started to tremble while traveling with him from Tibet to Mongolia. The Dalai Lama reassured everyone and explained that they had approached the forbidden zone of Shambhala, and unfamiliar aerial vibrations were touching them."

Another time, the group was roaming through the desolate rocks of the desert when many of them became simultaneously aware of an exquisite breath of perfume in the air—like the best Indian incense. "From where does it come?" they asked, "for we are surrounded by barren rocks." The high lama with them whispered, "Can you smell the fragrance of Shambhala?" They also came to an area the caravanners refused to enter, yet the Roerichs rode into it and remained there for a few days. Upon their return, the Asians prostrated themselves, exclaiming they must be gods, for no mere people could have penetrated that territory without divine credentials.

Since Roerich's travel diary was kept for himself and the coworkers in New York, it is doubtful that he thought it might ever be published or read around the world for decades to come. We must, therefore, assume he did not intend to cause the frustration many feel while studying *Altai-Himalaya, A Travel Diary*, wishing he had confided the entire story behind the mysterious accounts of these few days. What they uncovered in the desert remains a mystery, for unlike other explorers who trumpeted their finds and filled the newspapers with stories of their adventures, the Roerich expedition sought much that was only spoken of in secrecy.

Perhaps they found Shambhala, ancient cities or artifacts, or even a figurine of the Great Mother. Due to the diligent work of several Russians now translating the Roerichs' diaries and the writings of others involved with the expedition, more may come to light.

On August 19, 1927, they broke camp and started for the salt desert of Tsaidam, accompanied by several Mongols traveling in the same direction. They crossed a 17,000-foot pass without difficulty, pausing to view the panorama of mountains and rocky crags ahead. This was the trail taken by the Dalai Lama in 1904, and it was comforting to come upon the many sacred sites marking his journey.

Then, the dreaded salt desert of Tsaidam stretched before them. They decided to cross it at night: "We could not stop but had to continue for a hundred and twenty miles without a halt. In the darkness of the night, the road was invisible and fortunately, we crossed the most dangerous spots without realizing it. There were bottomless pits on either side of the narrow path, and if a horse had tripped, it would have been impossible to save him—one false step and we would have been finished. It was forbidding, but we made it and crossed Tsaidam in a new direction—the shortest way."

In his diary, Roerich wrote: "None of it was as the maps had indicated. After we were across, I chanced to look toward the west and saw endless pink sands glowing there. Although entirely unexplored, the maps show it as completely desert area; but this does not seem true to me. There may be much of the remarkable in the folds of those hills; maybe the ancient Buddhist monasteries expanded in that direction, with interesting hermitages and monumental caves. The Mongols seldom mention these regions, but they do tell stories of caravans lost in the sands and of buried cities."

By the time they neared the Tibetan border, both Helena and the recently arrived Tibetan commercial agent were experiencing heart problems, no doubt exacerbated when robbers attacked the caravan. Colonel Kordashevski led a counterattack that drove them off, and when the expedition expected another attack the next day, "in blew a terrific snow-storm mingled with thunder, and the superstitious robbers dispersed."

Roerich described their approach to the border: "We looked for Tibetan outposts, but instead, we saw something shining against the gray background of the hilly desert." Attempting to identify it, they wondered, "Is it a huge tent?" But the white spot was too big for a tent. "Perhaps it is snow?" But why would there be so much snow in only one place? As they approached, it seemed to increase in size, and whatever it was, "was truly superb." Getting closer, they realized they were looking at a huge pyramid, formed by the drippings of a gigantic geyser of Glauber salt. "A real fortune for the druggist," Roerich remarked. "A snowy mass—glistening in the sun—verily, a sacred boundary."

They had reached Tibet at last.

15

Into Tibet

For the next twenty-one days, the expedition marched across the dreary, inhospitable northern plain of Tibet. Sitting 15,000 feet above sea level, it stretches from the Kunlun Mountains in the north to the Trans-Himalayas in the south. The contrast in temperature between sun and shade can be so great that it is possible to severely blister and develop chilblains at the same time.

One day they spotted a black tent by some foothills toward the west. A reconnoitering party was sent out and reported it was Camp Yatung, an outpost of Tibetan militia. As they watched, a horseman rushed out of the tent and galloped southwest. "Soon a group of militiamen approached us; their chief inquired about our passports and invited us to stop for the day. He checked our passports, and appearing to find everything in order, promised to send the papers to his superior and dispatch mounted messengers to Nag-chu to announce our arrival."

The chief neglected to mention that the British colonial administration had ordered that Nagchu, the first big settlement on the road to Lhasa, be notified immediately of the expedition's arrival, or that the Roerichs had been under surveillance since they had first secured permission to visit Ladakh, northern India, and Tibet. The secret service had received occasional reports throughout most of the journey, and after the expedition crossed into the U.S.S.R. their "friend" Lieutenant Colonel Bailey, the political officer in Sikkim, and others, had begun to take notice. On October 6, 1927, Bailey wrote the following confidential memo to the Indian foreign secretary in Simla:

> With reference to the enclosure to your Memorandum #38(2)-X, dated July 1927, I have the honour to suggest that I should write and warn the Tibetan Government that Professor Roerich intends visiting Tibet and that he is a Bolshevik. I met Professor Roerich in Darjeeling in May 1924 and his son George stayed a few days with me in April 1924 in Gantok. At that time they were anti-Bolshevik. In your telegram No.1007-S, dated the 18th May 1927, mention was made of "Roe-Alex." Am I right in presuming that this is a mutilation of the name "Roerich?"

He received this confidential reply dated Simla, 11th October:

> Reference your letter No. 907-P, dated 6th October 1927. The Government of India approve your suggestion that you should now warn the Tibetan Government of Roerich's intention to visit Tibet and inform them of his Bolshevik tendencies. Your assumption that "Roe Alex" is a mutilation of "Roerich" is correct.
>
> Sd/- J.G. Acheson,
> Deputy Secretary to the Government of India

The actual story of what next occurred can best be summarized by this communiqué sent from Tibet to Lieutenant Colonel Bailey, one year later.

> Translation of a letter from the Ministers of Tibet to Lieutenant Colonel F. M. Bailey, C.I.E., Political Officer in Sikkim, dated the 6th

day of the 9th month of the Earth-Dragon Year (corresponding to the 19th October 1928).

The reason of sending this letter by the Ministers of Tibet. In your letter of last year, dated the 16th day of the 9th Month of the Fire-Hare Year (10th November 1927), you informed us that one Russian Professor named Nicholas Roerich, an artist, intended to visit Tibet: that he was a Bolshevik: that he was said to have been in Urga at the time: that we were well aware of the condition of the country where Bolshevism was spread: and that you hoped the news would reach us in plenty of time.

Meanwhile we informed you that a party headed by Ral-drag had arrived on the frontier of Shangri. To this we received a reply from you dated the 15th day of the 12th month of the Fire-Dragon Year (5th February 1928), saying that he (Professor Roerich) stayed in America for some years and that he was a red Russian. You know that foreigners are not allowed to come to Tibet casually and in the case of Roerich, particularly after the fact of his being a red Russian was brought to our notice, we could not allow him to come to Tibet. Accordingly we had him stopped at Nagchukka and persuaded him to go back from there. Meanwhile there had been an unusually heavy snow fall in the northern region and many ponies and camels belonging to the party died in the intense cold. They also ran short of foodstuff. They fell sick owing to the rigors of the climate. In other words, they were put to great hardship and it was simply impossible for them to go back. They therefore of their own accord, went to India through Sikkim following the Changtang route. We sent you a detailed report about this on the 1st day of the 4th month (20th May 1928).

So the Roerich Expedition had been held in confinement on the roof of the world, pawns in a political situation that left them defenseless. In *Heart of Asia*, an unaware Roerich described it this way:

This place will remain in our memory forever. The dull upland, arctic in character, was full of small mounds and was bordered by the drear outlines of sliding hills. The general's first welcome was the acme of kindness and friendliness. He told us that in consideration of our passports and letter, he would permit us to proceed to Lhasa via Nagchu, the northern fort of Tibet. He requested we move our camp closer to his headquarters and prepare to stay for three days. . . . In all our meetings, the general was very friendly and probably was not guilty of what followed. When a week passed without reply, he informed us it was necessary for him to depart on duty, but that he would leave a major and five soldiers with us, to give all necessary instructions to the local elders.

The general left, and instead of three days, we remained in this dull place at 15,000 foot altitude, for five months. The situation became catastrophic. A severe winter set in, with whirlwinds and snow. What happened, and where, we could not discover, for all letters sent to us by the Dalai Lama and Governor of Nagchu were returned to us and often torn up. We repeatedly wrote to the American Consul in Calcutta, to the British Resident, Colonel Bailey in Gangtok, and to our institutions in New York, requesting the Governor of Nagchu to send all this by wire from Lhasa to India. And we were told that the telegram lines between Lhasa and India no longer existed—a downright lie!

When we asked the major's permission either to return back or to proceed to the general's headquarters, we were refused permission, as if they actually wished our destruction. Our money was exhausted. Of course the American dollars that we had with us were absolutely useless. Moreover, we had no more medicine and our provisions were at an end. Under our very eyes, the whole caravan perished.

Each night the freezing, starving animals approached our tents, as though knocking for the last time before their death. And in the morning we found them near our tents, dead. Our Mongols dragged them beyond the camp, where packs of wild dogs and condors and vultures were already awaiting their prey. Of a hundred and four animals, we lost ninety-two. On the Tibetan uplands, we also left the bodies of five of our fellow-travelers: three lamas, one a Buriat and two from Mongolia; and Chimpa, from Tibet, and finally the Tibetan major's wife, who died from inflammation of the lungs. Even the natives could not stand the severe conditions. Our caravan had only summer tents, as we never imagined we would pass the winter in the most severe climate in Asia.

Mrs. Roerich's pulse reached 145, and our doctor called it "the pulse of a bird." My pulse was 130, instead of the usual 64. The pulses of George and the two Bogdanovas remained about normal. The doctor prophesied the most dark prospects and wrote medical certificates, stating that to detain an expedition under such conditions was equal to attempt at murder.

Of this stay in Nag-chu, I could write a whole book of the saddest reminiscences, but in any case, on March 6th, we finally started for India, compelled to go by the most difficult, circuitous way. With us also went the unsolved problems as to how the Government of Lhasa could refuse to recognize the passport issued by its own official. And whether one could detain a peaceful American Expedition, with three women members, at the most dangerous heights, in summer tents, for an entire winter. And why it was necessary for the Tibetans to imperil our health, starve the entire caravan to death, and destroy all our cinema films through acute changes in temperature.

Not only was the expedition camped in the coldest spot in all of Asia, but the area was also in the grip of an unusual cold spell. When the grass was snowed under and the animals began to starve, the local population thought the weather must be punishment for the behavior of their government. In his journal, George wrote: "Packs of hungry dogs are beginning to be troublesome, attacking our men outside the camp. The militiamen keep them away by throwing stones but after withdrawing, the dogs only collect in another place. At night we can hardly sleep for the continuous barking and howling."

On January 19, 1928, permission was granted for them to march on to Nagchu, where all caravans awaited orders from Lhasa. The group finally made it to Nagchu and was able to buy "bad flour, some *tsampa*, Chinese conserves in tins, very bad sugar, Chinese vermicelli, frozen turnips, and frozen tangerines." After their long diet of *tsampa* (a barley grain mixture) and mutton, these things seemed to be extraordinary delicacies. They were also glad to secure fifteen bags of food for their poor riding horses.

At last, on March 4, the expedition was finally allowed to leave. Nicholas wrote in his diary, "Everyone rose very early. The day promised to be fine. Having distributed the baggage among the different headmen who supplied yaks for the caravan, we started. Thus ended a five-month stay. Our Colonel was so weak after his illness that he asked us to leave him behind to await his end, but we persuaded him to mount his horse and try and follow the caravan."

The most arduous, roundabout route had been mapped, a wide loop west of Lhasa taking them through the Chang-Thang Mountains, over passes of 20,600 feet, across the Brahmaputra, and into Sikkim. Nevertheless, they were leaving. George wrote:

> It was still night when everyone rose and packed his bedding, but the dawn was soon softly coloring the sky, veiling the snow peaks of the Chang-Thang Range behind a deep blue. Nag-chu's streets were still completely deserted, but columns of smoke were rising above the houses, and our yak drivers were squatting on the pavement near the big fires outside the gates of our headquarters, taking their tea and

*Perishing camp of the expedition during the winter detention at Chu-na-khe, Tibet,
October–December 1927*

tsampa. Then the loading began; it took us almost three hours, but
finally the yak caravan started.

At 8:30, when everything was finished and the last section of
the heavy caravan had disappeared across the river, we set out accompanied by two men from the village. Our Mongol servants, who were
returning to Tsaidam, had presented us with ceremonial scarves and
bade us farewell. They were sorry to see us go and feared trouble from
the officials. While in Nag-chu, I had spoken to the local authorities
on our men's behalf and was promised that they would be given every

assistance on their return journey. We issued them certificates in Tibetan, requesting the civil and military authorities of Tibet to give them help and protection on Tibetan territory, and a high Tibetan lama, who was traveling to Tsaidam, agreed to take them with his caravan. Some four months later, I was gratified to hear that all of them had reached their native pastures safely.

Having crossed the river, still frozen hard, we ascended a spur and then Nag-chu was forever obscured from our view.... We had finally escaped and were returning to India! We knew the way ahead would be difficult. Food was in short supply everywhere and it would be necessary to assemble a new team of men and animals for every stage of the journey—which might mean a delay of anything from a few days to a week or two. But we were on our way back and by following a westerly course, we would arrive in some fifty days. Next day we had to fight our way through the snows that blocked the Ta-sang La. The ascent was not steep but long, and it took us four hours to get to the top of the pass. Heavy clouds covered the sky. The yaks had a bad time on the pass, many got stuck in the snow, and had to be dragged out by their drivers—a tiresome job at these altitudes. The horses stumbled knee-deep in snow. We passed a Golok lama on the top of the pass. The poor fellow was struggling in the snows, his horse having fallen while climbing the pass. Several tea caravans were stranded, unable to proceed farther, all their caravan animals having perished.

Roerich tried again to obtain permission to go to Lhasa, but to no avail. Local officials along the way were at a loss about what to do with this group of foreigners who had no proper papers. After much hesitation, the viceroy of India authorized their return to Darjeeling.

With Tibet plunged into famine by the intense cold, their arrival at many of the villages was met with hostility and exasperation. At one point, their guide informed the natives that George was "a big Lhasan official, accompanying the American Mission," and with his knowledge of Tibetan, and enormous fur cap, George was able to maintain the disguise.

Nonetheless, their traverse of Tibet's unmapped territory proved to be rich and fruitful. George wrote: "After a sixteen mile march, we camped in a narrow valley sheltered by undulating, grass hills. The place was called Do-ring or 'The Lone Stone' because of the curious megalithic monuments found in the vicinity. While sanctuaries and the crude stone altars of the primitive Bon-po religion were known to exist here, monuments of this kind had never been found before."

His father was more enthusiastic: "We especially rejoiced in discovering typical *menhirs* and *cromlechs* in the Trans-Himalayan region of Tibet. It was remarkable to see long rows of stones, and stone circles standing, which vividly transported me to Carnac and the coast of Brittany. Erected perhaps by prehistoric Druids, who were connected in some way to the ancient Bon-po. In any case, this discovery rounded out our search for traces of the great migrations."

They also found graves thought to date to the Neolithic era. Arranged in a stone square, each grave was laid out from east to west with a large boulder standing at the eastern extremity. The Tibetan authorities objected too strenuously to any excavation for them to attempt anything more than photography.

In the same district, we also saw women wearing head-gear that was exactly like the Slavonic kokoshnik: red, adorned with turquoise and silver coins, or ornamented with beads—it was quite unusual for Tibet. Apparently some remnants had survived here that had been transplanted by an alien tribe, for the local dialects spoken were also different than anything in the area. And there were other interesting analogies. Since the unicorn is found in Chinese art and on Tibetan thankas, I showed a picture of one to a Tibetan, and he insisted there was an antelope with one horn like that, in a region nearby. And indeed the British explorer Bryan Hodson had exported a specimen of a special antelope with one horn. Perhaps we have proved the heraldic myth, here near the Himalayas.

And there were many other interesting facts: without drawing any conclusions, I will tell you that the tribes of Northern Tibet strongly suggested some European types to me. I saw nothing of the Chinese, Mongolian, or Hindu about them; before me passed faces similar to the ones painted by the old French, Dutch, and Spanish artists. It seemed that people from Lyons, the Basques, and the Italians were looking at me with their large, straight eyes, aquiline noses and characteristic wrinkles, thin lips, and long, black hair.

A special surprise came when the expedition passed through Tingri, where the hermit Milarepa had lived in the eleventh century. Milarepa, the St. Francis of the Snow Country, was one of Roerich's greatest inspirations. Stopping to explore, they were rewarded by discovering the "Brothers and Friends of the Hidden," a secret brotherhood of followers who lived on the same ice-clad slopes Milarepa had graced. In the city itself, they located some wall paintings depicting Milarepa sitting in front of his cave in a huge snow mountain, with his right hand cupped to his ear, listening to his devas. While painted images of Milarepa seemed common, the Roerichs were pleased to find an exceedingly rare crude bronze statue to purchase.

Finally, the group was climbing over the 16,970 feet of Sepo La and passing the stone cairn marking the summit between Tibet and the Indian empire. Once again, India spread before them. The long expedition was over. Relief, thanksgiving, joy, disappointment, and a mixture of other powerful emotions assailed them as they gradually descended in the bitter cold, passing huge snow masses, glaciers, and tremendous peaks. George wrote, "Farewell Tibet, land of gales and winds and inhospitable rulers!

We are heading toward the wonderland of Sikkim with its rhododendron forests and deodars."

Farewell also to the dreams of the New Country and Roerich's destiny to unite the world's Buddhists under the Panchen Lama and himself.

With spring in full glory, India must have been a feast. They rode through fresh woods, crossed over mountain slopes thickly covered with evergreen shrubs, and smelled fragrant pines. Lush groves of colorful rhododendron bloomed around them. The family had been away from civilization for more than a year, and in all that time they had seldom removed their dust-covered fur coats, boots, and hats. Everything seemed so unfamiliar that they could easily understand when the Mongol horses shied at trees and objected to the stable. Nicholas recounted in his diary, "Two camels are survivors of the entire ordeal, they traveled more than 5,000 miles with us, and crossed the Himalayas. But because camels are unknown from Nag-chu to Gangtok, they attracted large crowds of onlookers everywhere." The camels were presented to His Highness the Maharaja of Sikkim, who put them on his estate at Dobtra.

"The remaining part of the way to Gangtok was easy and the hospitable house of the British Resident, Colonel Bailey, was waiting to greet us," wrote an unsuspecting George. "We spent two delightful days there." So, aside from the feelings that doubtless started churning inside the colonel when he heard the heartrending tales of horror, hunger, and frustration, the Baileys were gracious hosts who had lively discussions with their company. Perhaps Bailey was able to assuage some of his guilt by being "kind enough" to provide the party with much needed baths, clean clothing, and food before they continued.

By May 16, 1928, they were back in civilization. Letters and telegrams to America were their greatest priority. A justifiably proud Roerich announced the expedition to Central Asia as victorious. Their journey had yielded many discoveries about Buddhism, and much scientific and artistic data. Some of the newly created paintings were already in New

Crossing the Brahmaputra, Tibet, April 1928

York; the last batch had been sent from Mongolia. Roerich announced: "In spite of the tremendous difficulties, including political upheavals and unfavorable seasons for traveling, during which we were often obliged to continue on, we achieved a signal success and brought back a unique record of the regions of Inner Asia."

The Master explained, "Truly, the experience of journeying gives the best key to the realization of cosmic lives. The true traveler reflects lucidly on the path which lies behind and clearly expresses the desired direction. He will appraise former circumstances and will foresee the better possibilities."

The expedition officially disbanded in Darjeeling, its members taking their recollections of the stupendous snow passes, roaring moun-

Warm, clean, and well fed at the home of British Resident, Lt. Col. F. M. Bailey and his wife. Seated, left to right: *Mrs. F. M. Bailey, Nicholas Roerich, Helena Roerich,* Standing: *Col. N. V. Kordashevski, George Roerich, Dr. Ryabinin, name not recorded, Lt. Col. F. M. Bailey. May 26, 1928*

tain streams, and never-ending deserts home as tales to tell forever. Helena had written two books, *Foundations of Buddhism* and *On Eastern Crossroads,* translated a portion of *The Mahatma Letters to A. P. Sinnett* into Russian,[1] and added the third book, *Community,* to the Agni Yoga series.

Now the family was back in Talai-Pho-Brang, being amused and confounded by the rumors that had filtered to Sikkim. Roerich had been described as "a French and American King," "Commander of a Russian Corps," and "King of all Buddhists." The Mongols had decided the word

American was really "Ameri-Khan" (Ameri, the King) and therefore visualized Roerich as a kind of warrior. "When we heard the fairy tales told about us from Lhasa, we could identify ourselves only with difficulty. It was said I carried on a war with the Amban of Sinkiang, and the Tao-tai of Khotan had passed the word that our expedition brought a small cannon that would destroy the entire population (about 100,000 people) in ten minutes."

The New Yorkers had received Roerich's telegram with enormous relief. Five months had passed with no word from the expedition; their cables and registered letters had been returned and all investigation had failed to uncover anything. At their wits' end, Svetoslav, the trustees, and the American friends had waited and prayed, trying not to imagine the worst. Once the telegram arrived, Svetoslav quickly set sail for Bombay; Frances Grant notified the media and then prepared to accompany Sina Lichtmann, who was following close behind Svetoslav.

A photo taken earlier of George and Professor Roerich, both sporting spats, hats, and overcoats, with their hands snugly in their pockets, appeared in the Art section of *Time* magazine:

ROERICH'S RETURN

Nicholas Konstantinovich Roerich nursed his chilblains. Jailbirds were glad, as were school children, teachers, art students, functionaries at his Roerich Museum in Manhattan. They were glad because at last he was safe and recuperating from his five-year expedition in and around Tibet, in snow and desert. Where other expeditions dig and collect for science, he saw and painted for art. Snug with him at Darjeeling in northeast India last week were bales of his paintings. He has depicted the whole panorama of Tibet, scenery, people, customs. Some of his scenes are realistic; most are interpretative. A philosopher-painter, he prefers to translate a situation as he realizes it. Soon he will take his pictures to the United States for display in his museum, then in jails and school houses for the benefit of the crass as well as of the well-bred. To know what he is trying to say with paintings, many will need the aid of the scientific notes that he made incidentally on his trip.

Harvard men were glad: George Roerich, Nicholas's son, was well. Brilliant young Orientalist, he studied there. Perfect in more than a score of Asiatic dialects, on this expedition he was his father's facile interpreter and pacifier of obstreperous brigands. He is a painter, too. His brother Svetoslav is a portraitist. Svetoslav has just reached Darjeeling from the United States.

Women were glad: Mrs. Nicholas Roerich, mother and wife of the men, had the stamina to accompany them through five years of privation. Last week at Darjeeling she was still weak from starvation, long marches, high climbing, winters in thin tents. Two other women had endured with her.

Archaeologists were glad: In the Altai Mountains, along northern Tibet, Dr. Roerich found tombs like those of Ancient Goths in eastern Europe. Buckles ornamented with Goth-like double eagles strengthened his theory. Tibetans told him that the country around Lhasa was anciently called Gotha.

Scientists were glad: Roerich notebooks were crammed with important observations—magnetic, meteorological, geological, topical, botanical, zoological.

Devil worshipers were glad: The Roerichs found a Buddhism twisted topsy-turvy, the black faith of Bon Po. They worship demons, hate Buddhists, have peculiar saints with a central, legendary protector similar to Buddha. The swastika is one of their symbols.

Swedes were glad: The Roerichs descend from Swedes who a thousand years ago founded the Russian empire.

Russians were glad: The Roerichs were born there. . . . Fantastic flat decorations are his forte and peculiarity. In this manner he has tried to picture Russia's and Asia's past. His pieces number about 3,000. Seven hundred and fifty are in the Roerich Museum in Manhattan. They are weird, mystical, fascinating.

Artists were glad: Nicholas Roerich has shown them a way of becoming successful. Returned to St. Petersburg from Paris he wanted to found a school. He hobnobbed with intellectuals; joined societies, shouted out his art theories, got an audience.... New United States friends organized the Roerich Museum for him to hold his swift paintings.... Other productions are in the Louvre, Luxembourg, Victoria and Albert museums. Finally moneyed friends started to build him a twenty-four story skyscraper on Riverside Drive. It will be completed next July.

In June, barely recovered from the dreadful Tibetan experience, Roerich wrote His Holiness the Dalai Lama, identifying himself as a scientific man from the great kingdom of America and calling for certain explanations to enable him to present a report to his government. He wanted to know, "inter alia," why his expedition was detained for five months in the Chang-Thang region in terrible conditions and why the local people had been forbidden to sell food to his group, resulting in the casualty of many men and animals.

Uneasy over the idea that Roerich might be a representative of America and not a Communist as they had been told, Tibetan officials acknowledged his letter but were at a loss about what to tell him. They quickly contacted Colonel Bailey: "Please let us know whether these Americans were really sent to make inquiries into the matter (by the American Government). As the hope of Tibet centers on the British Government, please let us have your advice as to how a reply should be sent to their letter. An early reply is requested."[2]

"Point eight" of one communiqué that then passed between Bailey and the Home Office reads:

The Tibetan Government desires our advice with regard to the reply which they should give to Professor Roerich's letter. It is not easy to suggest a suitable reply, especially as they were acting under our instructions in refusing him entering into Tibet. I would suggest that the Tibetan Government might reply that since the outbreak of the revolution in Russia they have issued stringent orders against the entry of any foreigners into Tibet by the Northern Route, and for this reason refused to have any dealings with the Roerich expedition which followed that route to Tibet. I do not think it would be advisable to inform the Tibetan Government by letter that they should send such a reply. They can be informed by telephone when I go to Gyantse next year or I can inform the Tibetan Trade Agent there verbally. For the present I may be empowered to send a reply to them acknowledging their letter and telling them that I have referred the matter to the Government of India.

By August, Sina and Frances had passed through the Suez Canal, seen Akbar's Fatehpur Sikri, and toured the Ellora and Ajanta caves. In India's heat, the trip was long and tiresome for the young women, despite their excitement. They were ready to be reunited with their dear Roerichs. Along with the many papers they were bringing from New York was a note from Horch, asking that Roerich confirm in writing that he, Horch, had purchased all of the paintings and drawings Roerich had completed in Finland plus those from 1924 to 1928. A letter explained this request was "a pure formality that did not in any way affect or change the original arrangements regarding the expedition and its results." Louis Horch had clearly explained to both Lichtmann and Grant that the request was merely for technical reasons, since the paintings actually belonged to the museum. Should difficulties arise during construction of the skyscraper, however, the note would confirm Horch's great assets.

Frances later claimed she thought the request strange, but was assured that the document would be destroyed as soon as the building was completed, if no difficulties had arisen from the bank, the contractors, et cetera. No sooner had the two women arrived in Darjeeling than Horch announced his intention to make the skyscraper twenty-nine stories rather than the originally planned twenty-four, necessitating an extra three hundred thousand dollars, but he would lend this money personally and repay himself from the apartment rents. This decision greatly distressed the Roerichs, but little could be done from India, so they soon dropped the matter.

Frances and Sina immediately took over the job of consulting Indian lawyers to see how just compensation could be demanded from the Tibetan government for the losses sustained by the expedition. Frances wrote to the trade agent at Gyantse, but she got no further than Roerich had, for again, the Tibetan government forwarded copies of all correspondence to Colonel Bailey, who forwarded it to the government of India, which didn't know what to do.

Frances's and Sina's attention, however, was quickly concentrated on sorting, arranging, and cataloging the precious materials that had been so carefully loaded and unloaded daily onto the yaks, camels, donkeys, or horses. The young women felt privileged to be touching and viewing the tremendous collection of paintings, plus all the data and the assortment of Mongolian, Tibetan, and Hindu objects. They could easily visualize everything on display in the International Art Center and the Tibetan Library, where the sacred collection of the Kanjur and Tanjur would be exhibited.

They decided to publish Roerich's travel diary, so his notes needed to be put in some order and transcribed. Years later, Frances could still remember how happy she was to be seated at her typewriter by six each morning, transcribing Roerich's notes. Her drive and enthusiasm were such that he had to reassure her it would all get done soon enough.

Nicholas with Sina and Frances, who came to help, autumn 1928

Plans were formulated to establish the Urusvati Himalayan Research Institute, a "permanent Institute which might dedicate itself to the scientific study of this region of Asia, untouched in its opportunities." Their idea was to establish bases throughout the area so that specialists could conduct research in archaeology, arts, biology, botany, astrochemistry, and other sciences. The plans reached fruition later that year when the institute was founded by the Roerich Museum.

But now that the expedition was over, what about the Masters? In his travel diary and in *Heart of Asia*, Roerich wrote:

Approaching the picturesque banks of the Brahmaputra, one can find more indications and legends about Shambhala. . . . Until quite recently several ashrams of the Mahatmas of the Himalayas existed near Shigatse and further in the direction of the sacred lake Mano-saravar. Knowing this, and the facts that surround those remarkable sites, filled me with a special emotion. It was wondrous and strange to pass through the same places where They passed. There are still old people who remember meeting Them personally—calling Them by the names of Asaras and Khuthumpas. Some remember that a reli-gious school was founded there by the Mahatmas of India. . . .

We stood in the same courtyard where an episode occurred with a letter which was destroyed and then miraculously restored by a Master. We passed the caves where They had stayed and crossed the same rivers and in these same jungles of Sikkim stood outside Their outwardly modest Ashram.

To outsiders, who have not felt the energy of these places, the question of the Mahatmas is inconceivable. But traversing the Trans-Himalayas, I discovered it is not just a mountain range, but rather a whole mountainous country, filled with secret areas created by the ranges, the valleys, and the streams. As I wandered through those labyrinths, I realized that hidden places were accessible only through some happy "chance." Old volcanos, geysers, hot springs, and the pres-ence of radio-activity offered many unsuspected delightful discoveries. Often I stood beside a stark glacier and saw that the neighboring valley was rich with growth that must have been nourished by a hot spring.

While in the barren uplands of Dungbure, we spotted boiling springs with magnificent vegetation nearby. Strawberries, hyacinths, and many other flowers were in bloom. There were several such val-leys in the Trans-Himalayas. Near Lhasa it is said that hot springs may be found in some courtyards, supplying hot water to the entire house-hold. Having traveled through these unusual uplands, and seen the peculiar magnetic currents and electric phenomena, and heard and witnessed much, I feel that I know a great deal about the Mahatmas.

With every step, I was convinced that if the hermit can remain safely hidden within his cave, then it is possible for people to dwell undisturbed in a remote valley. There was so much unexplored in these regions, that maps were only useful for helping to gauge distance. While Europeans argue about the existence of the Mahatmas, the Hindus are significantly silent, for many not only know about Them, but have seen Them and have actual proof of Their deeds and appearances. Because the people of Asia had always yearned for Them, the Mahatmas created a special existence there, manifesting Themselves when it was necessary and passing unnoticed otherwise; leaving Their imprint only upon the hearts and minds of those who know. They are not a fairy tale, imagination, or invention, the Mahatmas are living forms.

I do not wish to persuade or try to convince anyone of Their existence. A great many people have seen Them, have talked to Them, and received letters and material objects from Them. If someone ignorantly asks, "But isn't it all just a myth?" advise them to study the book *The Reality of the Origin of the Grecian Myths*, written by Professor Zelinsky of the Warsaw University. Real knowledge will only enter through open doors—if prejudice exists, it will be outgrown through inner development. For us personally, it was more important to verify that this belief was accepted throughout immense distances and that many people were ready and waiting for the future evolution. Throughout central Asia, we found that the same sacred respect and impregnability surrounded both the concept of Teacher and Guru. Only in the East, where Teachers are said to be conductors of electricity and unifiers of knowledge, is the importance of this relationship understood.

Many Hindu, Chinese, and Japanese scholars are familiar with the Mahatmas, but their reverence is so great that it prevents them from revealing anything to the uninitiated. The sacred meaning of the word "Guru," Teacher and Spiritual Guide, makes the subject of the Mahatmas almost unapproachable, and for this reason, many who traveled in Asia have not mentioned Them. They were prevented from meeting this most precious concept by ignorance of the languages, or diverse interests, or bad luck in not meeting the right people. If one visits a museum or temple without special permission, he may never know that the most sacred things are in the hidden storeroom.

If you are in a hurry, or just curious, it might be difficult to understand even a simple chemical experiment, let alone anything as complicated as the Mahatmas. And what good would it do to just have your curiosity satisfied? How many people are there who would love to receive a letter from the Mahatmas! But after it provided a moment of astonishment and confusion, would it really change their lives? Probably not.

The average scientist talks about the Mahatmas as pure illusion; but Sir William Crooks or Sir Oliver Lodge would not speak so. Vivekananda and many Hindus who know Them safeguard Their names to such an extent that they are willing to deny Their existence rather than betray or reveal. But now people are knocking on the doors for this great knowledge; many of the younger generation simply want to start a correspondence with a Guru or find a real teacher. Everyone knocks in his own way. Many find disillusionment because they knocked on the wrong door, or lacked sufficient energy and the necessary determination to continue knocking.

What laboratory could analyze the intent of those who approach this method of knowledge? Yes, verily, it needs to be a laboratory, where labor and perseverance and fearlessness are the keys to the gates. The teachings of the Mahatmas speak about the scientific foundations of existence. They direct one toward the conquest of energy. They speak of those victories of labor which shall transform life into a constant festival. The things suggested by Them are not ephemeral or illusionary, but real, for without superstition or prejudice they pertain to the most all-embracing study of possibilities of life. The true followers of the Mahatmas are not sectarians or hypocrites—on the contrary, they are vital people, who are attempting to conquer life.

16

NEW YORK: THE ROERICH MUSEUM

The governments of India, England, and Tibet were not nearly as concerned about the Mahatmas as they were about the Roerichs. Although they had lived in the United States less than three years and did not hold American passports, they had traveled under the American flag and spent American money. They were Russian nationals who had recently been in Moscow, but did not have Soviet passports and had not acquired Soviet citizenship. When permission to tour India and conduct an expedition across Central Asia had been requested, no one had inquired into immigration. If they had come to India as tourists, they were expected to leave.

Nevertheless, it was very clear to the Roerichs that they were home. Nicholas told people that "India was his land of heart's desire," often explaining his "spiritual kinship" had begun in childhood; Rabindranath Tagore had even identified "Isvara," Roerich's ancestral estate, as the Sanskrit word for ashram. Of all the mountain ranges they had seen, none equaled the Himalayas, and where else but in the land of the Mahatmas could they await the Coming One and the time of Shambhala?

Kulu Valley

So, while the status of citizenship was a dilemma for everyone, the couple adopted India. In September 1928, Roerich was reluctantly granted permission to stay because Helena still suffered from the hardships of the expedition. Not knowing how long they would be allowed to remain, they decided to use wisely the time they did have. Once rested, they began traveling toward the western part of the Himalayas, to Naggar and Manali and into the Kulu Valley. Ancient Kuluta was known as the cradle of culture; some said it was the most beautiful spot on earth. Roerich wrote:

> The sacred Kulu Valley lies hidden on the border of Lahul and Tibet, forming the northern part of the Punjab. The most significant names and events have gathered there, in the Silver Valley (and it well merits that name, whether under the cover of sparkling snow in winter, or in spring when the fruit trees are laden with snow-white blossoms).
>
> The law-giver Manu himself gave his name to Manali, and the great Arjuna opened a miraculous passage when he went to the hot springs. The Pandavas came to Naggar after the great war described in the *Mahabharata*, and Rishi Vyasa compiled the book itself

there. Much of historical importance happened by the Beas River. Thousands of pilgrims come because Padma Sambhava had been there, and a hill nearby still carries the name of Alexander the Great, who passed by.

In this ancient place, three hundred and sixty gods and protectors, including Akbar the Great, Buddha, Maitreya, and all the great teachers and kings, are memorialized with temples and statues. . . . In this Silver Valley, Krishna joyfully called all things to life. . . . And the fruit trees responded by blossoming. Under an apple tree, covered with rose colored blossoms, he played his divine songs of regeneration on his silver flute.

And his painting *Krishna—Spring in Kulu* captured it all.

At Christmastime, the family was visiting in Kulu when they saw a house high up on the hill that they knew was for them. But they were told that it was on the Rajah of Mandi's estate and not available. But they knew if a thing was destined, it would be. And so it must have been. They leased the house first, and then succeeded in purchasing it— along with rights and obligations, including a con-

Nicholas Roerich in Kulu Valley

tractual agreement about the water rights, shared with the god Jamlu and the British government. Called the Hall Estate, the house sat near the top of a mountain, reached by a narrow winding road closed by snowdrifts in winter. A carved statue of Guga Chohan, the protector of the valley, stood beneath a deodar tree guarding the terraces, stone walls, and majestic blue pines and other healing trees.

The Roerichs happily immersed themselves in the local traditions, taking part in all local celebrations. Their respect for the vegetable kingdom and love of trees touched their gardeners, who were ordered to avoid shortening the life of any plants or trees. "In ancient Kuluta, we found an abundance of all we needed!" Roerich joyously recorded. There was land nearby to start the Urusvati Himalayan Research Institute, and the Rotang Pass, the path to Tibet and Central Asia, lay just to the north. By spring, they were so well settled that Roerich was ready to return to New York.

Nicholas and George sailed for Europe in spring 1929 and then on to New York. In their absence, Maurice's sister Esther came to stay with Helena and the Bogdanova sisters. (She remained for two years.) When Frances and Sina had returned to the States in November 1928, they had carried the precious cargo of carefully crated additional expedition paintings and treasures for Corona Mundi. Sacred items and writings had also been sent, to be sealed in the cornerstone of the skyscraper museum in a rare four-hundred-year-old Rajput casket of handwrought iron, inlaid with elaborate gold and silver.

Construction of the new building was almost completed; preparations for its dedication and opening were coordinated through frequent cables and letters. Roerich suggested representatives of foreign countries and leaders of art and culture who would be interested in attending the dedication ceremonies, set for October 17, 1929.

Chicago's Louis Sullivan had designed the first skyscraper in the 1800s, believing it portrayed the new spirit of the twentieth century and exemplified American progress and greatness. His skyscraper created great

Carefully packed crates of paintings going to America

controversy, but many architects working on tiny Manhattan Island immediately grasped its potential and began to build high instead of wide. Skyscrapers were touted as the solution to New York's congestion, and the city began "going tall," with one building following another into the air. When the Master Institute needed to expand, the trustees wanted their new building to be the "outward visage of the spirit of America and its creative idioms."

After Sina and Maurice had returned with the plans formulated in Urga, Harvey Wiley Corbett had been selected as architect. Then everything was moved into temporary offices so the institute buildings (and three adjacent structures) could be demolished. Now, a new Roerich Museum building was rising on the corner of Riverside Drive and 103rd Street. Construction of the first fifteen stories had gone fairly smoothly. Then difficulties arose.

When Roerich's opinion was needed, he was on the border of Tibet, completely out of touch—maybe forever. So without Roerich's knowledge, Louis Horch sanctioned changes and made revisions that greatly altered and improved the building from the original plans. Corner windows were added to let in more light. The stupa Roerich had planned for the capstone was replaced by a black zigzag design on the water tank. Faced entirely with brick, the building began with a dark purple tone, shading into mauve at its upper terraces and tower. The exterior walls were planned to give the effect of a growing thing, and the tower commanded a thirty-mile view of the Hudson.

As soon as Sina and Frances were back from India, they were caught up in the excitement of inviting hundreds of the world's distinguished and important people to join the ceremony of the laying of the cornerstone. One invitation went to John G. Sargent, attorney general of the United States. Sargent forwarded the invitation to J. Edgar Hoover, director of the Federal Bureau of Investigation, who scribbled on a memo, "The Atty. Gen. asks 'What is it?'" This memo and the invitation became the first items in the FBI files on Roerich. Over the years, despite the fact that several folders eventually bulged with interviews, news clippings, and documents of activities of Roerich and the Master Institute (under close scrutiny and surveillance), no one ever reached a conclusion about what "it" was.

Few attended the ceremony, held in the unfinished Hall of Nations under banners of all nations flying from the steel network canopy, but telegrams and letters poured in. The highlight came when the gold- and silver-inlaid Rajput casket was cemented into the gray granite cornerstone.

Directly afterward, charged with the mission of establishing friendly relations with South American artists, Frances Grant (who spoke Spanish) sailed for Latin America with some Roerich paintings. She followed the route President Hoover had taken when he opened the doors with his "good neighbor" policy: down the western coast to Peru and Chile, across the Andes to Argentina, Uruguay, and then Brazil. She received enthusiastic responses everywhere.

Her return coincided with the Roerich men's arrival, and she joined those greeting them enthusiastically at the pier. A police escort rushed their party past the skyscraper to the temporary headquarters, and then to a tea in Roerich's honor at the Hotel Biltmore. The following evening, the city saluted him at the official reception in the museum. The reception committee roster listed 158 names. The press covered the event lavishly. Under the headline "Women Rule Far East," the *New York American* reported:

> Women are fast assuming the reins in the Far East, Professor Nicholas Roerich, head of the Roerich American Expedition to Central Asia, declared yesterday.
>
> The blue-eyed, rosy-cheeked little man of fifty-four, who has just returned from a three-year Expedition into the wilds of Tibet and Mongolia with his wife and son, George, mildly tells of climbing 17,000 foot mountain peaks, of being held in captivity by Tibetan bandits for more than a year.
>
> Speaking of the Mongolians and the Tibetans, he said: "The women have more energy than the males. They are better business dealers, too. While the male seldom has more than one wife, the wife often has five husbands. They know little of America but have heard of Henry Ford and President Hoover. They hope some day to achieve a state such as they vision America to be."

During the next several days, the man who referred to himself as the "hermit artist" whirled through enough social gatherings to make him ache. He spoke to more people at one time than he probably had during the entire past five years altogether. He was feted, lauded, honored, and celebrated with accolades. On behalf of New York's seven million people, Mayor Jimmy Walker praised Roerich as a "messenger of unity" among men, and thanked him for the great things he had done for humanity, saying that the understanding of peace and the message of brotherhood had been brought to remote peoples of the world by Roerich's "Mission of Good Will": "It is men like Professor Roerich who make us come to the realization that there are no foreigners, no alien races in the world, but that humanity represents one great brotherhood. Professor Roerich is teaching the world to achieve peace and happiness through art and the appreciation of beauty. We in America feel signally honored that he has chosen New York as the permanent abode of his remarkable collection of paintings."

A few days later, Roerich was received in a private audience at the White House, where he presented President Hoover with a Himalayan painting and summarized his expedition and his impressions, concluding, "The people of Central Asia praised America in the highest way, considering it the land of 'Shambhala' . . . the land of the enlightened future, the land of the new era."

Reporters from newspapers around America came to interview Roerich, who enjoyed telling a Mongolian myth passed down over generations: Two brothers dwelt together in a rich and fertile land, each with his own family and servants. One day, the land was torn apart by a streak of lightning; the ocean poured in and the brothers were separated. Over time, they each founded races. The myth ended with the prophecy that the time will come when the brothers are reunited. Then Roerich would tell the reporters that when he showed photos of the Pueblo Indians to the Mongolians, they immediately called them cousins.

How New Yorkers and Roerich's followers felt about his return is best told by Herbert Corey's article in his column "Manhattan Days and Nights":

The story of Prof. Nicholas Roerich is more than a week over-due because I have not known precisely what to write. I'm not sure that I know even yet. Other men travel to remote parts of the earth and risk their lives and come back and write books. But no other man, so far as I am aware, is like Nicholas Roerich. . . . When he went to the Himalayas he was the head of a cult. Roerich might resent that statement. It is the fact that his disciples are ardent. Some of them almost to the verge of incoherence. When he returned to New York after five years, they were just as devoted. Yet he does not preach, so far as I know. He imposes no doctrine on his followers. He is a searcher for truth and beauty. That's all. It is difficult to understand the grip he has on his people. There can be no doubt of the reality of it.

Gladys Baker, a special correspondent for the *Birmingham News*, filled the huge first page of the Sunday supplement with this article of unusual sensitivity and perception. "Knowing the reticence and likewise the greatness of the man, whose name has become a by-word throughout America," she had asked to see his paintings before she began the interview.

Graciously acceding to my request, he took me at once up narrow stairs to the fourth story. We paused in front of a locked chamber which, for the present, guards the famous Asiatic series. . . . It was only after the last canvas had been turned to the wall that I spoke with the artist. Something of the restfulness of the August afternoon, something of the mood of the paintings, of scenes and profound thoughts, which his brush had so recently described, was with him. Because this was Roerich, as he knows himself, and is known by his intimates, I would not have had it otherwise. . . . Seated opposite Prof. Roerich I was able to regard him with that close and almost unconscious scrutiny which interviewers, by years of practice, bring to bear on the subject whose personality forms the background of their observations. Though his career stamps him definitely as a man of action, a man who makes his visions tangible, none of these qualities present themselves in his physical appearance. To begin with, Prof. Roerich is of small stature and slightly built.

His snowy-white hair, which has already left bare the temples and his gray Van Dyke, add another decade of years to the five decades chalked up against him in the matter of birthday anniversaries. He is uniformly quiet and relaxed in voice, gesture, and mannerisms. I could observe no single trace of that nervousness which usually marks the man whose imagination and quick impulses compel him to set his face on untrod paths.

In conversation he proceeds slowly, though without hesitancy. When he crosses a room he walks with unhurried pace as though eternity stretched before him. More than any other feature do his eyes transmit this spirit of ease and tranquility, indicating a nature unharrassed by the harsh outlines of a keyed-up civilization in the midst of which he lives and exemplifies his creed, which calls for practical activity and constructive service.

The eyes of Roerich bespeak the seer, the priest, the poet. They are as baffling in analysis as that inscrutable quality in his paintings which defies concrete description. Though I made a definite effort to do so, it was impossible to even know their color. . . . But I would not give the impression that only in the matter of the pigment are the eyes of Roerich his most arresting feature. It is something, which lies behind them—an age-old knowing which emanates so surely from the man that one is tempted to believe with the occultists that each person possesses individual vibrations. Without assuming that each man has his special "aura," how else is one able to explain the rays of peace, goodwill, and higher purpose which seem to enfold one by merely coming within the radius of the man's presence? And this, mind you, before a single word has been spoken.

Sitting with this gentle, quiet man and listening to conversation which showed the trend to which his thought turns most naturally, it was difficult to realize that a good part of his life has been spent in bold and spirited adventuring. . . .

From what one has read and heard of Nicholas Roerich it is not difficult to sum up his philosophy. Leaning strongly to the original teachings of Gautama Buddha he has also forged into his spiritual armor the essence of all great religious principles.

"You will find," he said, "the same golden threads woven into the tapestry of them all." One of these golden threads he holds to be the theory of reincarnation. When I asked him directly if he himself believed that the soul rides on the winds of the centuries and comes back to inhabit a new garment of the flesh, he replied, "I do not believe in reincarnation—I know it. Without such an explanation, life would be meaningless and futile." He reminded me that Jesus had taught reincarnation and that the belief was also current at that time among the people. Well informed on all subjects on which he converses, he underlined his statements with authentic quotations from the Testaments. . . .

Nicholas Roerich, Naggar, India.
In background: *triptych* Fiat Rex *(1931)*

In summing up the personality of Nicholas Roerich, I am inclined to believe his chief characteristic, and one which permeates the whole of his creations, is that spirit of humility, found only in the truly great.

He was taking the measure of his own heart when he wrote in *Morya's Flowers*:

> When I get knowledge, I think there is someone who knows better.
> When I can, I think there may be some
> Whose power strikes firmer and deeper—
> And behold! I know not, and I cannot.
> Thou who comes in the dead of the night,
> Tell me, in the silent way
> What have I willed and what accomplished in my life.
> Put thy hand upon my head
> And then I shall regain my will and my power.
> And what I will in my dream at night
> Will be remembered in the hours of the morning.

A few months ago the name of Nicholas Roerich was presented to the Nobel Commission for the peace prize through the Department of International Law of the University of Paris. The committee at this time pointed out his eligibility to the great award by reason of the fact that for the last twenty years, through his writing, painting, researches, and lectures, his propaganda for peace has reached into twenty-one countries carrying the unified message of international brotherhood.

The official opening of the Master Institute building on October 17, 1929, was described as "one of the most brilliant events in the history of art in America." No expense had been spared, and the tremendous publicity brought thousands of congratulatory messages streaming in from all over the world. Representatives attended from universities, scientific and artistic institutions, and museums; the mayor of New York City, congressmen, cabinet members, and envoys from France and Italy attended as well.

The new building was entered from Riverside Drive through two large brass doors with framed panes of glass. The Tibetan Library, the Hall of the East, and the galleries of the International Art Center flanked the entrance. Murals painted by a Tibetan lama adorned the Hall of the East. Though the museum was located on the second and part of the third floors, paintings hung everywhere. Roerich had personally directed the lighting and hanging of each of the 750 paintings.

The spacious quarters of Corona Mundi International Art Center and a large adjoining office for Nettie Horch shared the main floor with a restaurant, built despite Roerich's objections, that could seat four hundred people and a theater that came to be called Roerich Hall. The third floor was chiefly occupied by the Master Institute of United Arts and the School of the Roerich Museum. There were sixteen studios— large ones for painting and ballet classes and

Roerich at the front entrance of the Master Institute

standard-size ones for the various departments of music, painting, drawing, interior decor, and drama.

At Roerich's request, the St. Sergius Chapel had been constructed to house a collection of religious paintings of the Early Masters and the fine icon collection that Sina and Maurice had brought back from Moscow. These were said to be the first Russian icons to be exhibited publicly in America. This chapel proved to be a favorite with the thousands of visitors to the building. Private apartments for the trustees and additional apartments for artists and writers were above. They were advertised as "fine modern quarters at a very reasonable rental for people who want to live in the Roerich Museum building while enjoying the cultural privileges extended free of charge to its residents."

The building was considered outstanding in its practicality; the apartments were predicted to be one of the greatest successes in the country. The twenty-ninth floor was not mentioned to the public, for it had been built exclusively for the trustees, who generally met there weekly for discussions and to read whatever came from Professor and Mme Roerich. They went there when they wanted privacy. The Trustees' Room was graciously furnished with fine old statues, antique tables, and chairs. It also contained a steel closet built expressly to store Helena's precious writings. In it were the manuscripts she had completed before the expedition, the ones Sina and Maurice had transported from Moscow and Urga, and the books Esther Lichtmann brought back from her two extended visits in India.

The archives, all important documents, the original manuscripts of *Altai-Himalaya*, *Shambhala*, and the Agni Yoga series were also stored there. Eventually, the trustees felt that, since anyone could get a duplicate key and enter that room, a better way should be found to safeguard Mme Roerich's manuscripts. When they wrote to Helena in India, she replied that she, too, had been apprehensive and asked that Nettie Horch be responsible for their safekeeping, perhaps renting a special vault. Mrs.

The Tibetan Library, with sacred collection of Kanjur and Tanjur

Horch informed the other trustees that she had done so and transferred everything from the closet.

On October 23, 1929, only six days after the opening, prices on the New York Stock Exchange started to plummet. By 3:00 p.m., when the second largest number of shares in history had been traded, the time of lavishness was over. The following day, Wall Street looked as if it were under siege. Hundreds of small investors—waiters, cooks, shopkeepers, housemaids, seamstresses—crowded into the narrow street, demanding to know if their money was safe. When the market closed on October 24, there was a three-billion-dollar loss, and a record 12,894,650 shares had changed hands. Representatives of thirty-five brokerage firms jointly issued a statement, assuring everyone that "the worst had passed," that the market was "fundamentally sound" and "technically in better condition than it had been in months."

When the final quotation clicked across the tickers the night of October 29, the New York Stock Exchange alone had lost over ten billion dollars, twice the amount of currency in circulation in the entire country at the time. Americans were in shock. How uncanny it must have been for Roerich to be in materialistic America in time to see the end of "the get rich overnight" era. In *Hierarchy*, their teacher explained:

> With the loss of spiritual understanding, the planet loses its equilibrium and the consequences are inevitable; for there is no karmic effect without cause and no cause without effect. The manifestation called forth by the loss of spiritual striving will certainly spur those impulses which will bring regeneration to the planet. The appearance of physical changes will give the understanding of Agni Yoga to the planet. The financial crash will cause a revaluation of values. The distortion of religions will result in a search for a new spiritual achievement.
>
> Therefore, verily the crumbling of the old world is a new affirmation, for through the coming of new values We bring the salvation of the spirit to the world.

Asked to address students at New York University, Roerich spoke of the "vital value of art": "Anyone, who took the time to look, could have anticipated this blow-up of paper profits, for almost worthless objects had reached enormous values, and vice-versa. Now everyone is left holding piles of paper, litter. Many times during the time of the Russian revolution, we saw bankers and financial concerns swept away, but artists and collectors survived. Life itself demonstrates that creative work survives, as do scientific discoveries—and thoughts."

Between one and three million Americans were immediately and directly affected by the crash—many almost totally wiped out. The market continued to slump downward until mid-November. Even the beginning of a sluggish return did little to change the aftereffects. The

Depression had begun. In New York there was an immediate increase in requests for aid from charitable organizations; scholarships became a necessity at the Master Institute. Rents in the Master Apartment Hotel were lowered.

Fortunately, the many friends of the Roerich Museum were both wealthy and generous. People like Major Stokes, Mrs. Lionel Sutro, Mrs. Katherine Campbell, Mr. and Mrs. Charles Crane, and others had regularly helped financially in advancing Roerich's visions. Now they stepped forward with donations, scholarships, and contributions and promised greater support in the future. Nevertheless, things looked rocky for the Master Institute. As the Depression set in, the opportunities for generating income from culture diminished greatly.

In *Roerich, Fragments of a Biography*, Maurice Lichtmann's sister Esther (using the pen name Jean Duvernois) gave an emotional insight into the impact the building had on the city when she wrote:

> Recently, approaching New York at night, along the shore of the Hudson . . . I spotted the tallest building on the entire shore of Riverside Drive; its top was glowing in a white light—it was our house. Suddenly, I was unable to proceed further. The hundreds of automobiles that were rushing around me completely blinded me, and a dampness impeded my vision as I made my way out of the avalanche of autos, stopped my car on the side, dried my eyes and with unforgettable emotion, looked at the lighted white "*Stupa*"—the daughter of the desert. And I said to myself, "This is that guiding white stone from our beloved mountains of Altai! For it is ours, created by our genius; for our glory, and for further growth, the treasure of our mind and spirit is raised to this height."

17

THE PACT AND BANNER OF PEACE

The Depression notwithstanding, Roerich had still another dream for his American friends to transform into reality. He had been working on it since 1904, when he and Helena had traveled throughout Russia investigating and painting old churches and monasteries. Because he believed culture to be humankind's highest expression, the lack of concern over its preservation had been one of the most painful aspects of his travels. It hurt him to review all that had been destroyed by war—the libraries of Louvain and Oviedo, for example, or the Cathedral of Rheims, not to mention hundreds of museums, laboratories, schools, and private collections filled with irreplaceable treasures.

As he thought of ways to prevent this senseless waste, he decided to rally all nations together with a pact. Since pacts were signed and generally forgotten, his would also have a banner to fly above any building containing an artistic treasure; announcing, as did the Red Cross flag, that something needed protection from bombing.

With the Depression extending throughout Europe, many were predicting war. Over two million Germans were jobless; their nation faced bankruptcy while Hitler gathered strength and popularity. Roerich felt an urgent need for action and presented his ideas to his loyal coworkers, who, obliging as ever, were willing to start the wheels rolling.

On Sunday, March 16, 1930, the *New York Times* printed a letter from Roerich. Under the headline "Special Flag is Suggested to Protect Art Treasures," he wrote of the loss of "precious milestones of human achievement" due to the "world's misunderstandings":

> Against such errors of ignorance, we should take immediate measures. . . . No one can deny that the flag of the Red Cross proved to be of immeasurable value in reminding the world of humanitarianism and compassion. For this reason, a plan for an international flag has been outlined through America to all the foreign governments, which would protect all treasures of art and science.
>
> The plan is to create a flag to be raised above museums, libraries, universities, and other cultural centers, so they will be respected as international and neutral territory. When it was first propounded, we were not surprised to find that it met with unanimous interest and enthusiasm. Experienced statesmen wondered why it had not been thought of before. When we asked Roerich Museum honorary advisers Dr. George Chklaver, Doctor of International Law at Paris University, and Professor Albert Geouffre de la Pradelle, member of the Hague Peace Court and vice president of the Institute of International Law of Paris, to frame this idea into an international formula, they returned a splendidly formulated project of internation-al agreement, along with many answers full of pan-human sympathy.
>
> This international flag is for the protection of beauty and science and to prevent the repetition of the atrocities of the last war to cathedrals, museums, libraries, and other lasting memorials of the creation of the past. And to elevate the universal understanding of evolutionary discoveries and act as a guardian of culture. . . . We

often repeat that the cornerstone of future civilization rests upon beauty and knowledge. Now we must act upon this thought and act quickly. The League of Nations, which has progressed toward international harmony, will not be opposed to this flag, for it expresses their aims of a world unity. It has been submitted to the State Department and the Committee on Foreign Relations.

That the idea was originally conceived in the United States is not an accident. By its geographical position, the United States is least personally affected by such measures of protection. Hence the proposition comes from a country whose own art treasures are in no particular danger, better illustrating that this flag is a symbol of peace, not of one country, but of civilization as a whole. The flag is designed with three magenta spheres within a magenta circle on a white ground, as a symbol of eternity and unity. . . .

It is imperative to take immediate measures to preserve the noble heritage of our past for a glorious posterity that can only come if all countries pledge themselves to protect the creations of culture. After all, these belong to the whole world and this plan may be the way to create the next vital step towards a universal culture and peace.

For Helena, the Banner of Peace and the unity of women in the name of the new era of culture were the two historical tasks at hand. From India, she repeatedly encouraged the coworkers to set aside their problems and petty differences and take on these causes. "You must understand the majesty of this formidable time. You must realize that everything is in conflagration behind you and that the only salvation lies ahead. . . . The time will come when the Banner of Peace and the Banner of Culture will cover the whole world. Can you sense the beauty and power of this symbol?" Much concerning the higher ramifications of the pact and Banner were included in *Hierarchy*, which the Master and Helena were writing. The Banner of Peace would open the gates to a better future, for salvation lies in culture. "Humanity cannot flourish without the knowledge of the greatness of culture."

Until late spring of 1930, the pact met with much opposition. Then it began gathering support. Senator Borah agreed to take the plan to Washington, and support was growing in Belgium, where the First International Roerich Pact Conference was scheduled. On their return to India, Nicholas and George would be going through Europe, seeking support, catching up with the latest scientific experiments, and planning for the newly established Urusvati Himalayan Research Institute.

At departure time, their Indian visa applications were knotted in red tape and confusion but they were not unduly alarmed, feeling everything could be straightened out in London. However, once there, they started to feel a little desperate when the troubles continued. After several weeks of requests, petitions, and memoranda, their appeals were denied—on accusations of Bolshevism. D. Petrie, head of the Indian Secret Service, wrote to London quite candidly that he had enough troubles without trying to keep suspicious people like the Roerichs under surveillance.

On May 23, 1930, an official of the Home Office answered George's request to return to his work as director of Urusvati by informing him that India was not a suitable place for people to research matters relating to archaeology, art, and science if their sympathies lay with the Soviets. That Roerich's wife was ill and that everything they owned was there did not matter; India's door was firmly closed to them. Roerich wired New York for help and a tremendous outcry of protest was raised, but it did nothing to change Britain's position. The press got nowhere in their attempt to reunite this "great figure" with his wife.

So father and son were faced with the challenge of finding a way home. As Roerich tried every approach, he must have seen the irony in the situation, for other countries were liberally heaping honors upon him and "attesting to his inspiration as a force for cultural advances and the betterment and ennoblement of human life." The president of France received him and placed the Palace of Fine Arts at his disposal should he care to exhibit his paintings. In September, the International Museums Committee of the League of Nations, some four hundred representatives from the governments of France, Belgium, and Italy and from many cultural societies, met in Bruges and organized a permanent association to further the worldwide adoption of the Roerich Peace Pact and the Banner of Peace.

Then, some progress was made. On the day after Nicholas's fifty-sixth birthday, the governor of Pondicherry, French India, allowed the two men to enter his country. They remained a few months and began a little excavating. Then the viceroy of India agreed to allow them into India with a three-month visa. They reached Kulu on December 11, 1930, and were finally reunited with their dear Helena Ivanovna. When the three months elapsed, the British, wanting to escape another uproar of public sentiment, relented and permitted Roerich to remain in Naggar on condition that he go no farther into India than the Punjab's southern border. Finally things in Kulu settled down, and Roerich and George began work at Urusvati.

Early the next year, the Roerich Museum Press published a slim book proudly entitled *Roerich Museum, A Decade of Activity, 1921–1931*. Now everyone could read how the Roerichs' vision had been cultivated like a "garden of beauty." The school had indeed flowered; the creative spirit of thousands had been awakened, nurtured, and developed. From India, Roerich wrote:

Dear co-workers,

On this day of greeting . . . I do not attempt simply to praise you, because is it possible to praise a man who is completely devoted to the idea of culture? Is it possible to praise a man for honesty? Can one give praise for spirituality? Or inspiration through beauty? Because all these are the basis for a cultural worker. Praise is always relative. But fact is absolute and today we mark a decade of arduous labor in the name of Culture. I wish to measure that which is undeniable.

Glancing back upon all labors, upon all our battles with ig-norance, it becomes apparent that the creative work proceeds in-cessantly. . . . Can we recall even one year that was spent in rest or self-indulgence? Can we name even one month, out of these one hundred and twenty months, when thought and labor did not mold new possibilities? When endless obstacles were not turned into oppor-tunities . . . and our energy was not devoted towards the Good?

As I have always said, Culture is the reverence of Light. Even the grass and the plants strive towards light. How inspiredly and exaltedly must people then strive to one Light if they consider them-selves higher than the vegetable kingdom.

This very night, above the chain of the Central Himalayas, an extraordinary illumination is glowing. It is not lightning; the sky is clear. It is the luminous glow noted very recently over the Himalayas by scientists. In the name of Light, in the name of Light borne by the human heart, let us work and create and study. Greetings to you all on this memorable day.

The little volume triumphantly enumerated the activities and people who had shared in the work. It listed Roerich's hundreds of paintings, described the Asiatic expedition, and acknowledged the honors bestowed upon him from around the world. It also cited many of the programs that had been carried into settlement homes, schools, and women's asso-ciations. Thousands of lectures had been delivered over the radio, in libraries, at schools, to art clubs, societies, and institutions, and even in Sing Sing penitentiary.

Roerich's desire to create a common cultural bond and encourage finer understanding between all parts of the globe had resulted in thirty-nine paintings being exhibited in leading museums throughout Latin America. Branches of Roerich societies were also started around the world. The Latin American Institute had been founded in Brazil, and a

European Center of the Roerich Museum was inaugurated in Paris, with plans underway to establish others in Buenos Aires, Belgrade, and Riga.

The list of eighty-six honorary advisors reads like a Who's Who of the world's renowned educators, artists, and cultural leaders, including Sir Jagadis Bose, India; Albert Einstein, Germany; Dr. Edgar Hewitt, Santa Fe; Charles Hovey Pepper, Boston; Leopold Stokowsky, Philadelphia; Deems Taylor and Claude Bragdon, New York; Rabindranath Tagore, India; and Ignacio Zuloaga, Spain. Hundreds of concerts, recitals, performances, and contests had been held, and many volumes of books written by Roerich and others had been published.

Under the guidance of Frances Grant, the Museum Press published the *Roerich Museum Bulletin*, a monthly magazine devoted to disseminating information about all movements for international friendship through culture around the world, and the *Archer*, a magazine for members of the Roerich societies. A series of commemorative stamps was sold to raise funds for the publication of the New Era Library Series. The *Message of 1929* and *Message of 1930* had been published to keep everyone informed of the activities and participants for those years. On and on, the museum's accomplishments and committees continued, until the book ended with an inspiring message by Roerich, "On the Threshold of the New Decade."

More than 2,400,000 people had toured the new building in their first year, and over sixty diverse groups had used the meeting halls. The New York Chapter of Rosicrucians had moved their Grand Lodge and AMORC (Ancient Mystical Order Rosae Crucis) reading rooms into the building. Their first meeting was such a success that they overflowed into two of the largest meeting rooms, and their entire membership enthusiastically pledged their support. The Rosicrucians considered Roerich one of their own, giving him the honorary title of "European Legate of the Rosicrucian Order in America." He was also called the representative-at-large of the Great White Brotherhood.

Riverside Drive, New York, 1929. The Master Institute is the tallest building

People from all over the world flocked to see the museum, Sarah Delano Roosevelt, mother of New York governor Franklin D. Roosevelt, included. Like so many society women of her day, she was drawn to the occult practices in vogue. Iowa-born Henry A. Wallace, who became secretary of agriculture after Roosevelt was elected president, shared her interests. Wallace, who called himself a practical agriculturist, was mystically inclined. Searching for something deeper than his religion offered, he had joined the Theosophical Society, explored occultism and astrology, and incorporated some American Indian rituals into his life. He confided to a friend that he was searching for methods of bringing the "Inner Light" into outward manifestation.

Wallace, who saw the Depression as an opportunity for a spiritual reformation, became a great admirer of Roerich's art, ideas, and principles and was soon a frequent visitor to the museum. Everyone felt honored by his interest. Either Frances or Maurice received a note from him almost weekly. He wrote and spoke with Frances so often, that some wondered if their interest in each other might have gone beyond the paintings and teachings.

Admiring the way the museum continued to function despite their severe money problems, Wallace volunteered to champion the Pact of Peace and the Banner. He wrote from Washington: "I believe so profoundly in the things for which the Banner of Peace stands that I am only too happy to offer you any cooperation in my personal capacity to help to make your efforts along this line successful." The support Wallace offered was considerable. He eagerly lobbied Congress, and after the 1932 election kept President Roosevelt thoroughly briefed on the Pact. Roosevelt's interest is shown in this handwritten note (undated) to Cordell Hull, his secretary of state:

> Dear Cordell
> As you know I am *very* keen about the Roerich Peace Pact and I hope we can get it going via "the Americas"—Will you and Henry Wallace talk this over and have something for me when I get back.
>
> FDR

By 1932, the Pact had made enough progress to be considered by many government bodies, international jurists, and cultural groups. Pope Pius, King Albert of Belgium, King Alexander of Yugoslavia, President Masaryk of Czechoslovakia, and others took up the cause alongside universities, scientific bodies, and national academies. When the Second International Conference met in Bruges, thirty-two countries were represented, and the *Fondation Roerich pro Pace, Arte, Scientia et Labore* was established.

Then the stock market took another plunge and more fortunes were jeopardized, Louis Horch's among them. Manufacturer's Trust started proceedings for foreclosure on the museum building mortgages and took action to put the building into receivership. Henry Wallace expressed his concern in many ways. When questioned about the situation by a member of the State Department, he wrote a "Memorandum in Regard to the Receivership of the Roerich Museum," stating that the Master Institute had "continued its activities and even increased the scope and measure from the educational and cultural point of view." He continued:

> In line with this Receivership, however, I may state that I know from the Roerich Museum officials that a complete legal victory has been won by them, and a definite plan has now been drawn up whereby the building returns entirely into the hands of the Museum, which had never once defaulted in interest payments on the building.
>
> The reason why wide attention has been drawn to this case is the fact that the Roerich Museum has been acclaimed for its fight in bringing about a revelation of the existing receivership practices and "rackets" worked in conjunction with the New York Banks, due to the lure of high receivership fees and other malpractices.
>
> I may also state that this case—fought as a precedent by the Roerich Museum—has provided a basis for the new legislation in regard to Real Estate and Receiverships now promoted by Governor Lehman of New York, which are aimed to wipe out forever the insidious practices which have held in the real estate field, and which have long terrorized real estate owners.

The 1934 decision ending the litigation ordered the Roerich Museum to incorporate as an educational corporation but allowed it still to be governed by the Roerich Museum interests.

In September, Wallace became Protector of the Third International Roerich Peace Banner Convention, held in Washington, assuring America's participation with the pact. Fourteen American senators were honorary members and twenty-seven nations attended. Frances Grant gave a rousing speech, saying, "The East has said that when the Banner of Shambhala encircles the world, verily the New Dawn will follow.... Let us determine that when the Banner of Peace encircles the world, it will presage a New Morning of human brotherhood."

Wallace, who followed her to the podium, was deeply troubled by the severe drought the southern Great Plains was experiencing. In late January, a dust storm had swept across the Texas Panhandle, Oklahoma, and Kansas with sixty-mile-an-hour winds and a ten-thousand-foot high dirt cloud, damaging property and destroying crops. The high winds continued into the spring, carrying off much of the soil from land standing barren where the crops had failed. Rainfall was scanty and insufficient. The sky took on a violet-greenish hue, cars were stranded in highway ditches, and cattle huddled against the dust as they would against wind-driven snow. Lights had to be turned on in the afternoon. Farmers were left with commitments to pay for expensive machinery bought on credit and no income.

The civic-minded Wallace family had been helping farmers in Iowa for generations. Henry, who described himself as "first and last a friend of the farmer," was aware that unusual measures were needed. As a usual practice, the Department of Agriculture sent botanists throughout the world to bring back pressed plants and seeds for cultivation. Two years earlier, Knowles A. Ryerson, Division of Plant Exploration and Introduction, had discussed the need for grasses to stabilize the topsoil with Joseph F. Rock, botanist and daring explorer of the Tibetan border. But Rock had said the severe fighting between the Tibetans and the Chinese to the north of Yunnan precluded all travel in those regions.

Now Wallace talked over his concerns with Frances Grant, and she repeated some of Roerich's tales of parts of Central Asia where grass grew in areas that never received rain. If Professor Roerich would be willing to lead the Department of Agriculture team to the right places, perhaps

Mongolian grasses could help. Several cables and letters were exchanged and Roerich was invited to America to discuss the plan in person. This brought up the passport situation again, but Wallace solved it easily. In February 1934, Professor Roerich and George stopped to see the consul of the American Embassy in Paris, the following letter in hand:

> Dear Mr. Marriner:
>
> This will introduce to you Professor Nicholas Roerich and his son, George Roerich, citizens of the Russian Empire who have taken out their first papers for American citizenship, but who have spent much of their time in recent years in scientific exploration in Central Asia.
>
> Professor Roerich, as you doubtless know, has a worldwide reputation as an artist and archaeologist. His son George graduated from Harvard and is a specialist in Oriental languages. I know both of them personally and would appreciate any courtesies which you could afford them in obtaining their necessary visas.
>
> Thanking you, I am
> Sincerely yours,
> Secretary Wallace

Leaving Helena with Esther Lichtmann and Svetoslav for companionship, Nicholas and George returned to the United States. On March 16, 1934, "on behalf of the United States," the artist was officially asked to undertake the assignment. Wallace wrote to him that his "unusual understanding of Central Asia," growing out of his many years of experience, would result in successful studies, to which Roerich replied:

> Dear Mr. Secretary,
>
> I have received your letter of March 16th, in which you invite me, on behalf of the Department of Agriculture, to act as leader and

protector of the botanical expedition organized by the United States Department of Agriculture to search for drought resistant grasses in the central Asian field.

For the past thirty-five years I have been working in the interests of the United States and during the last decade, I have been working in behalf of this country as an officer of an American institution, leading the American Expedition into Asia, and following this, as head of the Himalayan Research Institute, an American Educational corporation. Thus, your proposal coincides with my closest interests and is a natural continuation of my years of activity in this field.

It is therefore with pleasure that I accept your invitation, and I confidently anticipate that the work of this expedition will lead to new scientific benefits for America.

Now, the question is, did Wallace know about the plans for the "New Country"—the "New Russia"? If he did, and many so believe, then by sending the Roerichs back into the very area where they wanted to be, he was endorsing the plan. They would finally be able to assemble an army, find the Panchen Lama, who was now in Peking, ride triumphantly into the Altai, and establish the New Country. When Roerich wrote to Wallace, "Your proposal coincides with my closest interests and is a natural continuation of my years of activity in this field," it was his heartfelt expression of truth.

Nicholas and George stayed in America for five weeks, during which time the necessary papers were drawn up and signed and provision made for financial consideration to cover their costs. According to Frances Grant, Wallace stated that he was ready to give his life to the service of the cultural and spiritual work of the Roerich Museum.

A one-year contract was drawn up between the Department of Agriculture and the Roerich men, with Wallace providing all necessary papers and letters of recommendation to the American consuls in the Far

East and to the leading statesmen and governmental officials there. Frances was designated liaison officer. All communication between the Roerichs, Secretary Wallace, and the Department of Agriculture was to go through her. Wallace agreed to put Grant in touch with Mary Rumsey, one of the pioneers in the establishment of agricultural and dairy cooperatives in America. He also agreed to obtain letters of recommendation from Henry Ford and Averell Harriman, chairman of the board of Union Pacific and an administrative officer of the National Relief Association.

Enthusiastic about the cooperative movement becoming a bond between the United States, China, and Mongolia, Wallace asked Roerich to come up with some definite figures and statistics on starting a small cooperative with China. That the secretary was interested in cooperatives was a stroke of luck for the Roerichs. If agricultural cooperatives could be organized with Mongolian or Chinese banks operating jointly with the United States government or leading American enterprises, they could also operate jointly with the New Russia.

When all the planning was concluded, the Secretary remarked that he was elated to have met Professor Roerich personally and expressed a great liking for George. Before leaving, the Roerichs met with Dr. Howard G. MacMillan, head botanist for the expedition. They discussed budgets, equipment, and maps, and made plans to meet in Asia. Then the two Roerichs departed for China via Yokohama, Japan.

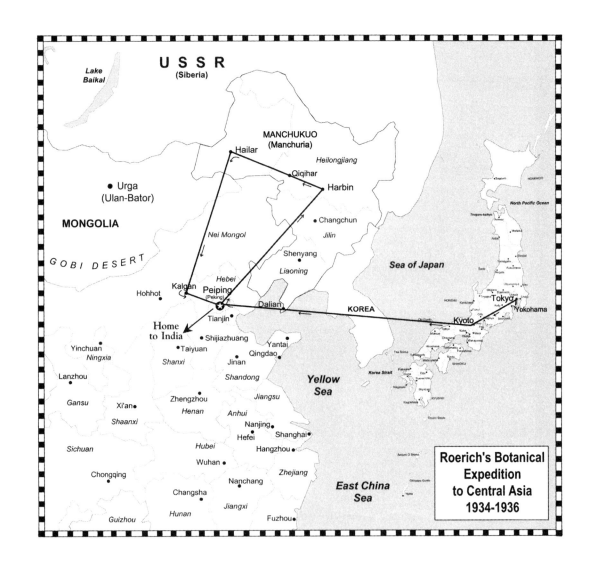

18

THE ASIAN BOTANICAL EXPEDITION

Anyone going into the Far East in 1934 was walking into an area churning with chaos and turmoil. The tangled skein involved a volatile combination of spies, double agents, Bolsheviks bent on converting the world to Communism, displaced soldiers who had become bandits, and over 70,000 White Russians, as well as the Japanese and Chinese with their conflicting interests. It also involved Manchukuo, the new country formed by Japan from the three eastern provinces of China that had previously been Manchuria. Manchukuo had a population of over thirty million in a territory of 460,000 square miles extending from the Amur River to the Great Wall of China.

When Manchukuo declared its autonomy on March 9, 1932, Prince Teh (Henry Pu-yi) was appointed chief executive. At age three, he had been enthroned as Emperor Hsuan-t'ung of China. At age five, the uprising that brought Sun Yat-sen to power had caused him to "voluntarily" abdicate. Politicians and historians have called Manchukuo a puppet state, and Henry Pu-yi a puppet, but to many of his countrymen he symbolized unity and harmony. He was heir to his family's three-hundred-year Manchu Dynasty Dragon Throne, which, according to some, had given

China the best form of government ever. According to Owen Lattimore, the much-traveled scholar of Central Asia and the East, Teh was the only Inner Mongolian prince capable of winning the alliance of all the other princes.

In the 1700s, the Manchu Empire had stretched from Formosa to Nepal, from Manchuria and Mongolia to what became Burma and Thailand. At that time, the rulers had observed a mandate from heaven called *Wangtao*, the Way of the King. Based on Confucius's teachings, it taught that the king was the embodiment of *jen*, "love for fellow men," and was to govern accordingly. The basic concepts were: (1) Everything under heaven worked for the common good. (2) Harmony ruled because the virtuous were elected to office and the able given responsibility. (3) Faithfulness was practiced constantly.

In *History of Chinese Political Thought*, Liang Chi-chao explained: "Unless all men stand together, no man can stand; unless all men strive for the attainment, no man can accomplish it. The real meaning of 'establishing others' and 'elevating others' embraces not merely individuals, but the whole of mankind."

As ruler of Manchukuo, Prince Teh planned to combine *Wangtao* with modern knowledge and technology and restore peace, order, and happiness. A country based on Confucius's principles was worth watching. If it worked, it could offer a new model for humanity. Some hoped Manchukuo would be a place where all nations could live side by side and eventually have a strong, free, democratic economy. Others feared the Soviet Union had plans to invade it, and then all the other Asian countries. The United States was refusing official recognition of the new country.

The situation in China was far worse than when the Roerichs had fled it earlier. The Chinese still hated foreigners, there was still no central government, control remained in the hands of local warlords, and Communist uprisings were fanning the flames. Japan had a long list of grievances against the Chinese and was using them as the excuse to send troops into Manchukuo.

Afterward, many (including Wallace himself) questioned why the elderly Roerich had been chosen to lead an expedition that the Department of Agriculture team was capable of handling. When the State Department questioned why Roerich, a "White Russian with French passport," was representing the United States in a hotbed of Red Russian/White Russian hostility, Wallace ignored them. But what qualifications did the Russian artist have? Certainly he had no diplomatic skills. His greatest qualifications were his perspective on life and his dream of world unity.

Conjecturing in *The Way to Shambhala* that the grasses were merely a subterfuge, Edwin Bernbaum quotes an article from *Newsweek* magazine: "Around the Department of Agriculture the Secretary's assistants freely admitted that in addition to searching for grass, Wallace also wanted Roerich to look for the signs of the Second Coming." Then Bernbaum speculates, "Wallace could only have been thinking of the prophecy of Shambhala and associating the future king of the kingdom with the coming Messiah." How else to understand Roerich's reasons for accepting such a strenuous trip?

Some said that Roerich saw it as an opportunity to establish a separate state in Siberia—with himself as ruler. Frances Grant claimed he did it out of "appreciation" for Wallace's help. Ever the scientist and archaeologist, Roerich might have agreed with Roy Chapman Andrews that the key to understanding our world of today waited in Central Asia—where the true story of our past could be found, "for no other region on earth would yield such important results in every branch of natural science." Without doubt, Roerich would have been pleased to be the one to find the key to the mystery of humans on earth. Possibly he wanted to bring spiritual help and encouragement to Prince Teh and Manchukuo. For the Master said to "manifest solicitous attention to each one who is ready to proceed toward the Light."

It may be that under the cover of seed hunting, Wallace and President Roosevelt were sending Roerich to get first-hand information of Teh's work without revealing American interest. But taking into account the Roerichs' prior difficulties in Chinese Turkestan, Wallace's choice and loyalty make no sense. Whatever the truth, Roerich was being given the chance to penetrate the areas from which he had been previously barred. He was to spread the word of the Banner and Pact and go forward to fulfill his destiny: locating the exiled Panchen Lama and then establishing and ruling the Buddhist spiritual country, New Russia.

Whatever the reasons, Roerich bungled it. Obviously, he could have quietly entered this country not recognized by America. But he strode in, presented the emperor with the insignia of the Roerich Museum, and requested to be housed as an official state guest. His request was denied. Now, with the expedition only two months along, the Department of State received a communiqué stating that Roerich had embarrassed the American government by being received in audience by the emperor. Yet could art-loving Roerich really have been expected to enter an area filled with magnificent art treasures from the former imperial palaces and Forbidden City without trying to see them? So matters got very complicated.

There was no way the American government could allow Roerich to do the things he was doing and still act as if he were America's representative. Over the next year, many telegrams and hundreds of pages of conflicting letters and reports flew back and forth to Washington as George Roerich and the botanists, Dr. Howard MacMillan and James L. Stephens, continually frustrated each other.

In his "Report of Activities for Period May–July, 1934," George wrote that the Roerichs were met in Japan at 11:00 p.m. on May 10, 1934, at the Yokohama pier by the Director of the Bureau for Culture and Arts of the Imperial Minister of Public Instruction. Whisked through customs and driven to Tokyo, they spent their next days making courtesy calls to the United States Embassy and to various governmental offices and institutions, such as the Foreign Office, the Ministry of Public Instruction, museum authorities, and the Imperial University.

On May 15, the Japan-American Society gave a luncheon to honor Roerich. U.S. Ambassador J. C. Grew, Prince Tokugawa, and Mr. K. Horinouchi of the Foreign Office attended. According to George, Ambassador Grew advised Roerich that "because of the very delicate situation with the new state in Manchuria, it is better to use personal connections in negotiations with local authorities." (Translated, this means the ambassador advised Roerich not to mention that his trip was funded by America.) But Roerich felt much would be denied them without the aid of his American connection.

Over the next few days, while the authorities studied the submitted exploration plans, the Roerichs visited the Imperial Botanical Gardens several times and Japanese scientific institutions involved with explorations into Manchuria, Mongolia, and northern China. Wallace's request that they collect data on "native *materia medica*" fit perfectly with their own desire to learn more of the vast lore on Oriental herbs, especially those for treating cancer. Then, Nicholas was given cards of introduction to the Manchukuo legation in Tokyo, visas, and instructions for the authorities along the route. Also, exploration privileges, which had been denied to Roy Chapman Andrews because he was suspected of wanting to prospect for oil and minerals would be granted. When they departed from Tokyo, they left the Banner of Peace happily flapping in the breezes above the museum and a message of greeting for MacMillan and Stephens, who were expected shortly.

Before leaving for Manchuria, the Roerichs stopped in Kyoto for two days to see the Tibetan book collection at the Otani Daigaku Library and visit the great Kanjur Monastery.[1] Roerich later wrote: "George found a Tibetan medical manuscript in the possession of one of the old lamas, and succeeded in copying it—it is most fortunate that he is completely familiar with Mongolian and Tibetan, because it is invaluable for this work. In the monastery, we saw numerous great Images, and heard the lamas speak of the coming 'War of Shambhala,' adding, 'But a man of

Nicholas Roerich in Japan, 1934

great heart is needed for it.'"

Their translator, Mr. S. Kitagawa, joined them in Kyoto and accompanied them through Korea and the Manchukuo frontier, receiving official greetings and easing their baggage and the firearms they carried through customs. Along the route, a cable was delivered from Knowles A. Ryerson (Department of Agriculture) saying that MacMillan and Stephens were planning to arrive in Yokohama two days earlier than expected. With no desire to wait for them, George left a note. The Roerichs entered Manchukuo while MacMillan was catching up with his lost luggage in Japan and arranging things for the expedition.

Thoroughly upset, MacMillan wrote to Washington claiming that Roerich had stepped on the wrong toes in Japan and had compounded everyone's nervousness by telling them he was about to conduct an "expedition into the unknown for certain purposes." But those toes had already been bruised in 1924 when the Roerichs were returning to the United States to straighten out their visa problems. Traveling aboard a Japanese ship, they had received a cable, read by the Japanese, from Roerich's brother Boris, who indiscreetly mentioned the

New Country. Now the repercussions would be felt, for Roerich, though he didn't know it, had been on their list of suspicious people for ten years.

Left in the dark about their plans, MacMillan was understandably frustrated by not being able to connect with the Roerichs. He construed their being met by Japanese officials instead of U.S embassy people as a blatant disregard of protocol and sent many accusations and grievances back to Wallace, concluding his report:

> The further I go on this expedition the more I have contemplated several factors in the character of it. Whatever we may have thought of this when I was in New York, each one started off in good faith and with nothing but conviction to make it succeed. We are not a month on our way, and not yet joined as a party and with still more time to elapse before that can be brought about. So far as the State Department officials are concerned in this section, the Roerichs are in bad favor. I know they will be informed in Dairen, and the Minister in China will be told. Those people should know. What the Japanese will decide as far as the Roerich status is concerned I do not know. But when you think of the decidedly nervous state they are in, the normal suspicion with which they regard even the innocent, not to say the bland, it should surprise no one if the Japanese suddenly decide to be through with all and sundry that have any connection with them, no matter how remote.[2]

From then on, MacMillan continually sent voluminous reports filled with every rumor he heard. His relationship with the Roerichs worsened as time went by. From Harbin, George categorically refuted and denied every accusation MacMillan made, but since the Roerichs were probably doing the very things George denied, one has to question what was truth and what was not when reading these concluding paragraphs:

The frequent statements made by Mr. MacMillan about alleged suspicions of anything connected with the name of Roerich are pure slander. We never visited any White Russian summer resort in the vicinity of Hailar. The information about a Cossack guard on the door is ridiculous. Mr. MacMillan never came near our house in Harbin. MacMillan's statement in his letter of August 11, para 4, is again entirely wrong. We had to postpone our departure due to the fact that there were breaches on the railway line and trains ran nine hours late. The station authorities, however, had instructions to conceal the actual state of affairs along the line, and continued to sell tickets. Mr. MacMillan and his companion made no attempt to meet the Leader of the Expedition [Roerich] during the journey to Hailar, although traveling in the same [railway] car. There was no guard stationed at the door of the compartment occupied by Prof. Roerich and the other members of the Expedition.

There was no Cossack army or uniforms on the Expedition. The statement that we had promised that all including the two botanists were going to the Khingen Mountains is again absolutely false. Such statement was never made. On our return to Hailar, Mr. MacMillan again made no attempt to visit the Leader of the Expedition, although Mr. Sato, the Japanese botanist accompanying MacMillan, visited us in Hailar, and even came to the station to see us off.

The whole correspondence gives a very definite impression that Mr. MacMillan's statements were written with the object to handicap the Expedition and slander the good name of Roerich.

The relationship never improved. They never met nor worked together. In fall of 1934, still protecting the Roerichs, the Department of Agriculture recalled MacMillan and Stephens for serious insubordination and disobedience.

With so much internal dissension and so much fear, confusion, and political intrigue abounding in the area, it is little wonder that reporters, the military, the botanists, and the Roerichs all had different versions of what happened on the expedition. But there is no doubt that between December 1934 and September 1935, Nicholas wrote a book titled *Sacred Watch*, an essay titled "The Desert Will Bloom Again," and seventy-two other essays, which were compiled into *The Invincible*, his eleventh book. In the preface, he wrote that, despite the attacks of numerous adversaries, he remained faithful to his task and to the goal he had set for himself: to stand invincibly on watch over culture, dedicating his entire life to the battle with ignorance, superstition and prejudices, steadfastly molding the steps of consciousness of the new human.

There is also no doubt that between 1934 and 1936 he created sixty studies and 195 glorious paintings and drawings in watercolor, gouache, or tempera. Further, in 1934, he created a greater number of paintings with the name Shambhala in the title than at any previous time: *Shambhala Go* (subtitled *Shambhala Gate*) he painted twice, and *Entrance to Shambhala*, *Shambhala Lam* (*Kurul Davan*), and *Shambhala Lam* (*Pass to Shambhala*). Painting, writing, planning, organizing for the New Russia, and riding around searching for grass seeds, he was thoroughly occupied.

Nicholas's brother Vladimir lived in the White Russian community in Harbin. During the winter, Nicholas and George stayed with him. The Russian expatriates interpreted Roerich's zeal for Buddhism, the Banner, and the Agni Yoga teachings as an attempt to change the dogma of their church and "correct the religion of their forefathers." Whatever he did or said seemed to create dissension and misunderstanding within the Russian community. When the Japanese initiated a campaign in the émigré news-papers against Roerich, he played right into their hands by distributing a handbill saying that art and herbs were his purpose for being there, and that an understanding of Chinese art would help bring peace to the world. It also had a photo of him wearing the regal robes of the Dalai Lama, which no doubt he planned to wear when he was the administrative head of the New Russia. Gossip and aspersions spread like wildfire. When *Sacred Watch* was published, the Japanese censors banned it and arrested its editors.

Helena, thoroughly disturbed, wrote to a friend: "I am writing all this with pain in my heart, for I love my country and I suffer for its shortcomings. . . . It is time to stop this senseless wasting of people who are real forces of the highest energies and in whom the entire significance of evolution is contained. . . . It is time to change our thinking. We are standing on the edge of an abyss! And only a Miraculous Banner can carry us across and put us at the Gates of the Miraculous Castle. Let us accept the Benevolence which is sent to us!"

She advised everyone to read George Grebentchikoff's article "I Protest," in which he wrote, "Russia's Roerich leads his coworkers of all nationalities, creeds, and positions who are ready for any sacrifice that they may fulfill his ever beautiful call to Light. Perhaps it is possible that Roerich does not deserve to have the Russians themselves—no matter how they each believe or where they live—listen to his slanderers and allow them to pollute the atmosphere. Roerich is our national pride, one of the luminaries of today's culture, one of the very few who have constantly maintained a high position both spiritual and cultural."

A year after the expedition began, the *Peking & Tientsin Times* printed this perspective on things:

ROERICH EXPEDITION TO INNER MONGOLIA
PARTY OF WHITE RUSSIANS MAKE EXTENSIVE TOUR

Inner Mongolia, the "hotbed of internal intrigue," is greeting with mingled wonderment and amusement at the activities of a botanical expedition sent into Inner Mongolia by the United States Department of Agriculture but staffed largely with White Russians, according to foreign travelers who have returned to Tientsin from desert territory.

The expedition is headed by Professor Nicholas Roerich, founder of the Roerich Museum in New York and revered by White Russian émigrés as an artist, journalist, and author of peace plans. This seventy-year-old bearded patriarch, who is accompanied by his son, George Roerich, and a collection of four White Russian guards and Mongol Buriat helpers, arrived in Inner Mongolia two months ago in search of plants that could be developed for use in the United States where lack of rain played havoc with crops last year.

He first sought to make his headquarters at the Palace of Prince Teh, just inside the Inner Mongolia frontier and 200 miles north of Kalgan, but Prince Teh is reported to have replied that he already had enough problems striving to accommodate the Japanese "medical mission" which has come to live with him, not to mention the frequent visits of Japanese military authorities. Professor Roerich and his retainers, whose luxuriant beards are a source of constant wonderment to the Mongols, thereupon took quarters at the nearby home of Swede Larsen, who has been adopted into the royal family, and is popularly known as the "Duke of Mongolia."

With the arrival of a batch of new motor trucks, which have been sent from Kalgan to the explorer's headquarters, Professor Roerich is planning to push his expedition farther into the interior through the Gobi desert along the fringe of Sovietized Outer Mongolia and thence southwards into the Ordos Plateau in Suiyuan province, returning about November. It is said that he will not attempt to enter Outer Mongolia owing to the danger of being shot by Reds. Rather, he will strive to avoid areas where suspicions would be likely to be aroused by his penetration and movements. Professor Roerich has already sent to his White Russian representative in Peiping, Mr. A. P. Friedlander, numerous specimen plants and seeds for transshipment to the United States, and has written him to the effect that he has already made several important discoveries of plants which are likely to assist the United States Department of Agriculture to combat the drought menace.

Professor Roerich's headquarters are at present situated about a hundred miles from the Outer Mongolia frontier where a "no-trespassing" sign hangs out for all White Russians, Japanese, and others unsympathetic to the Red cause. His expedition, according to reports, includes no Americans, the Professor himself being a Russian with French citizenship. A colorful personage, it will be recalled that the Professor was, a year ago, granted an interview with Henry Pu-yi, the Emperor Kang Teh of Manchukuo, to whom he presented a medal of his own invention and design. The Professor is also a frequent contributor to the White Russian press in the Far East. His wife is at present staying in Kalgan, awaiting her husband's return from the Mongolian wilderness.

While the simple Mongolian mind cannot understand why the United States is sending an expedition half way round the world to collect a few Mongolian weeds, the Japanese are reported to be watching the movements of the expedition with greatest interest. The area of northern Chahar, nominally under Chinese control, in which the expedition is operating, is today the scene of ever-increasing Japanese penetration, according to foreigners who have been visiting the district. Japanese army trucks from Manchukuo come and go over the Inner Mongolian plateau at will, paying frequent visits to the Mongol princes. Manchukuo, it is said, caught between Japanese pressure and Chinese promises of autonomy, is striving to play off one nation against the other in hopes of improving their own lot. No longer is Inner Mongolia the buffer between Manchukuo and southern Outer Mongolia. Waves of Japanese influence have long since washed over this barrier and are beating against the Outer Mongolian frontier where extraordinary precautions are taken against the entry of Japanese agents or anti-Red propaganda.

The importance of Kalgan as the gateway to this region of international rivalry may be gauged by the presence in the town of both Japanese and Soviet consulates, despite the fact that the population of both nationalities is negligible. The recently established Japanese military mission is also highly active and has imported several motor trucks for Mongolian tours.[3]

When Wallace heard this, he cabled Roerich: "I do not know whether there is any foundation whatsoever for the insinuations of political activity on your part in Mongolia, but I ask that you be engaged, both actually and apparently, in doing exactly what you are supposed to do as an employee of the United States Department of Agriculture in searching for seeds valuable to our country. With times as troubled as they are, with due consideration for safety, I request that you travel to safer areas." "Actually and apparently"—an alarmed Wallace was requesting that Roerich stop what he was presently doing and begin doing only what an employee of the United States Department of Agriculture was "supposed" to do.

Then a Soviet military attaché supplied a United States military attaché with this item:

George Roerich, formerly a Czarist officer, has recruited assistance for his expedition from among the followers of the bandit Semenoff. The expedition was refused arms by the Commanding Officer, Fifteenth Infantry at Tientsin, but succeeded in getting that decision overruled, and Commander of the garrison was directed to turn over rifles, revolvers, and a considerable quantity of ammunition to Roerich and the Semenoff bandits.

The armed party is now making its way toward the Soviet Union, ostensibly as a scientific expedition, but actually to rally former White elements and discontented Mongols.

The American officer wrote to the War Department to refute or confirm the report. Since George had been fifteen when the Roerich family fled Russia and after that had been in Moscow for only two months in 1926, the idea of his being a former Czarist officer seems far-fetched, and he had no connection with the bandit Semenoff.

Roerich wired Wallace on August 24, 1935:

> Hope our radiogram 19th received stop Referring recommendations going Sining impossible reach there before end September due bad condition roads floods and necessity obtaining extra truck for gasoline stop New permission authorities also required stop Also essential bring personally present extensive collections seeds herbarium Peiping for shipment stop Much of seeding season will be lost during journey Koko-nor where seeding season closes about end September due altitudes stop Local seed collecting proceeding unhampered with good results stop Could terminate local collecting towards middle September and proceed as indicated Department's letter July 9th Please advise Roerich

With the State Department, the War Department, the Japanese, the military, and the press all looking to him for answers, the entire affair was becoming too politically explosive, too volatile for Wallace, who had political aspirations of his own. He called the whole matter to a halt and wired Roerich: "Impracticability transferring to Sining described in your cablegram of August 24th noted proceed immediately to Peiping complete work there as rapidly as possible and proceed not later than October 15th by most direct to India finishing there by February 1st."

Eventually, Washington received 435 seed and plant specimens, plus 170 herbarium specimens of various genera and species, and a trunk full of drug plant material. No one knew what to do with any of it.

19

A Dark Spot

Two weary Roerichs returned to Kulu Valley, India, in the fall of 1935, the plans, hopes and dreams of many years postponed yet again. The Masters' direction had been to begin small, but somehow the endeavor had escalated into something far larger than Roerich knew what to do with. Perhaps while traveling home, his thoughts had gone back to April 15, 1935, when he was camped in the Gobi.

On that day, representatives of twenty-two Latin American countries had assembled in Washington and commemorated Pan American Day by meeting with President Roosevelt and signing the Roerich Peace Pact. A joyous Helena had written to Roosevelt, "The people of the Americas will recall this Day as a symbol of the great destiny of One United America . . . and as the Reconstruction of the World proceeds at a gigantic pace, this day will go down in history."

Yet as Nicholas would soon discover, while the pact signing was a step toward world peace and the preservation of culture, it also stirred the forces of negativity into greater action. With America still in the grip of the Depression, the museum was facing tremendous financial difficulties, and the "Day in Washington" had been possible only because of generous

President Franklin D. Roosevelt (center) *and representatives of all American republics watch as Henry Wallace* (right) *signs the Roerich Peace Pact. The White House, Washington, D.C., 1935*

donations. For several years, Master Morya had been forewarning of a betrayal, but with such loyal friends and coworkers, it was hard to imagine from where it would come.

As Roerich was on his way back to India, Louis Horch announced that the Horches and Esther Lichtmann were breaking with the Roerichs: they would no longer follow Roerich's advice and direction, and would govern themselves. If the others at the institutes did not like that, they could go to the Himalayas and join the Roerichs.

About the time Nicholas and George were staying with Vladimir Roerich in Harbin during the winter of 1934–35, Helena, in India, had initiated a correspondence with President Roosevelt. She wrote that the entire world was standing at the threshold of reconstruction and the fate of many countries was being weighed on the cosmic scales. She reminded

Roosevelt of the tall stranger whose flaming speech had roused the Constitutional Assembly in Philadelphia prior to America's revolution in the 1700s. The man had disappeared as soon as the vote for a free America was taken, before anyone could greet him. Helena said that, down through the ages, such help had been extended to others, such as Napoleon and George Washington, and offered to aid Roosevelt in that way:

> You, Mr. President, have realized that it is impossible to build the welfare and the future of the Country from the outlived measures that have reduced the world to its present state of destruction, and so are indefatigably and courageously seeking new ways of constructiveness. You will be a true great Leader because You have understood that the Bird of Spirit of humanity cannot fly on one wing, and have given Woman her due place. Hence from the same One Source Who had offered Assistance in the past, the Mighty Hand is sending Fiery Messages to You in the White House.
>
> The map of the World is already outlined and the worthiest place in forming the New Epoch is offered to You to accept or reject. The destiny of the Country is in your hands.

Roosevelt accepted her offer of assistance, and Helena sent him nine letters over a two-year period, covering a wide range of topics, including the warning that America should not disarm because intentions were being nurtured from two sides to involve her in war. Her eighth letter, written in December 1935, best explains the situation at the institutes:

> I am writing to you in full confidence but with an open heart that is filled with deep sorrow. For several months now I have been seeking to find the way to warn you that after fourteen years of collaboration with us, two of the people who have conveyed my messages to you have proved to be traitors who have betrayed my trust.

Last April, having succumbed to covetousness and ambition, regarding certain financial matters (silver), they transmitted their personal advice to you pretending that it came from the Original Source through me. My Source warned me about the treason committed and I was ordered to question them both and they confessed to me in writing, that they did convey their own message to you, while giving you the impression that it came from the Original Source through me.

I was shocked and indignant at such treason and immediately cabled prohibiting them to convey any other message without my full knowledge and previous sanction. They both knew very well that all questions had to be referred to me, the more so as one of them was expected to return here this summer, bringing along any possible questions. When they saw my indignation at their action and realized the grave consequences, fear and revenge moved them to turn to the path of open treason and not only break all relations with us but start an odious campaign to discredit our name and destroy us as witness to their deceitful action.

In their present hatred they stop at nothing. Mr. H. took advantage of my husband's absence on the expedition to remove his name as Founder of the Institutions. Further, Mr. H., who had our full power of attorney since 1932, and who always attended to our personal accounts and taxes and led us to think that all tax matters were in order, suddenly after nine years, tells the Tax Department that for the years when we were in Tibet, that expedition funds were personal funds. As a result of his actions, without previous notification, a lien was placed on our property in America (our paintings). These are but two instances of what they have done to discredit our name. Such is the revenge of these people whose treason has been disclosed.

I am writing all of this to forewarn you that Messages can no longer be transmitted through these people. But no matter how difficult the times are for us at present, we know that truth and justice will prevail. The path is not easy for those who bring new ideas and lay the steps for the new consciousness of humanity. But ideas move the world and thus evolution takes place.

I am especially grieved that I could not warn you before and was unable to communicate, for my heart was longing to convey the Great Words on the coming significant year. No human reasoning can solve the present problems of the world. Only Those, Who stand on vigil, know whither the Wheel of Necessity rolls.

May the Blessing of the Highest rest with you. I know that your great heart will understand.

She signed it with her initials and then added a P.S.: "If you approve this new channel, Messages could be sent again." Helena's final letter was sent to him January 11, 1936.[1]

Sometime during the previous year Horch had decided to end his eight-year retirement and return to work as a foreign exchange broker. He had opened an office in downtown Manhattan and reestablished his former connections. According to Frances Grant, Horch seemed anxious to get Wallace to supply him with useful information. Frances related a conversation she

Helena Roerich, 1934

claimed had taken place while she, Horch, and a few others were having dinner at Wallace's house, in which Horch had suggested that Wallace give Horch advance information on certain events. The other trustees had been aghast at Horch's action. From then on, Frances took special pains to keep the men apart, for she wanted nothing to "impair the fine and friendly feeling which Mr. Wallace constantly expressed for Professor Roerich."

Grant reported that Horch frequently told her she was foolish not to use her friendship with Secretary Wallace for personal advantage and financial enrichment, quoting him as saying, "If I were his friend, I would already have a good position in the government. You could easily get one and he could pass on tips pertaining to the stock exchange and lots of money could be made in this way. You are very stupid not to use his friendship to help yourself and all of us."

Frances and both of the Lichtmanns believed that a friendship with a member of the president's cabinet should not be abused; it would be most unethical and definitely against their spiritual principles to ask Secretary Wallace for any position, let alone for a tip to speculate and make money on the stock exchange.[2]

Relationships between the trustees had been severely strained by the grave financial responsibilities they faced and the lengthy litigation the museum endured. One indication of the stress was Sina and Maurice's deteriorating marriage. All had put aside their differences, however, for the pact signing ceremony in Washington. Immediately after the ceremony, they had cabled Helena and hailed the Roerichs as "the great leaders of culture and spirit," while thanking them for "the glorious opportunities" they were continuing to bring the institutions. All of the trustees had expressed assurances of love and deep gratitude for the constant wisdom and advice the Roerichs provided.

When Esther Lichtmann had wanted to return from India for two months to be in Washington for the ceremony, the trustees had told her they could not afford to pay for the trip. But Horch took the money from somewhere and arranged it. Once Esther was back in New York, she said she had come especially to help Horch in his business. Since Frances and Sina were aware that Esther knew nothing of banking, they began to question her motives, accusing her of "embarking on some mysterious trip and enterprise with Horch." Next, Esther and Horch began taking trips together to Washington and other places, then announced they were going to Europe to "further the cause of the Roerich Peace Pact and Banner." Now the other trustees were disturbed by more than the expenses; they wanted to know why Esther was accompanying Horch at all.

The pair left, saying they would be gone only three weeks. Three weeks turned into almost two months. Esther then began insisting on returning to India, but never did. When she told her brother, Maurice, that she had no time to see him because she had to help Horch, Frances began to suspect that Esther had allied herself with the Horches. And She did manage, however, to find time to visit all the wealthy museum donors, telling them that Professor Roerich was little known in Europe and insinuating that the Peace Pact was barely recognized.

While the pair was in Europe, Nettie Horch, confiding her opinions of her husband's activities with Esther to no one, announced that she was creating a Master Institute of Arts and Sciences in some of the empty rooms on the third floor of their building. Then, she began presenting a few lectures and classes. After the pair returned, Nettie arranged for all mail to go directly to her. She had a tap put on the telephone lines, and, according to Grant, told the teachers and students lies and distortions about Professor Roerich.

Next, Nettie wrote to Sina and resigned from the Agni Yoga Committee, saying she no longer wished to be involved in any way. She demanded that Sina take over the bookkeeping and files, and remove the Agni Yoga publication office from the fourth floor. Accordingly,

Sina moved the business office of the Master Institute and Urusvati down to the third floor. She discovered that Nettie had done no work for months, and many accounts and reports were missing. Later, a museum guard reported that, under Esther's direction, books had been burned in the basement. It appeared to Frances that each day the Horches created some new disturbance, attacking Sina Lichtmann and the school in some way.

The stockholders had originally allotted the trustees five years to rebuild and strengthen the school before expecting repayment of the debt. At the time, everyone had agreed that, with a united effort, five years would be adequate. Now nothing was bringing in revenue, and there was no cooperation. The normal functions of the school were so badly disrupted that concerts and lectures couldn't continue. Horch adamantly refused to allow the Master Institute to function as before, demanding that all activities be concentrated on the third floor. Frances felt as if she were confined in a fortress and besieged by enemies on all sides.

Roerich had been back in Kulu Valley for a few months, when, on January 30, 1936, readers of the Washington *Daily News* and other papers around the country opened their evening papers to read:

SPY RUMOR ENDS ROERICH EXPEDITION
AGRICULTURE DEPARTMENT RECALLS RENOWNED ARTIST

Announcement that the Agriculture Department had disbanded an Asiatic plant-hunting expedition headed by Nicholas Roerich and terminated the governmental services of Roerich himself today revealed that the internationally famous artist had become entangled in the turbulent politics of China and Manchukuo.

Officials here disclosed that informal protests against the expedition had been received from high authorities of the area in which it had been working.

The case was almost unprecedented in the history of the department, it was declared, though hundreds of similar exploring groups have been sent to virtually every country in the world.

BRUSQUE STATEMENT

Notice of Roerich's dismissal came in reply to rumors that the expeditions would resume. "A rumor has reached the Department of Agriculture," the announcements said, "that it would again employ the Roerichs for plant exploration in Asia. This rumor is entirely unfounded. The Department stopped the seed-collecting expedition in Western China on September 22, 1935. All connections of the Roerichs with the Department have been terminated, and the Department has no intention of re-employing them."

RETICENT

Officials refused to detail the protests against Roerich. It was learned, however, that the complaints declared he was believed to have become involved in the tense and potentially dangerous politics of Manchukuo, the Japanese-contolled state on which many serious international problems focused.

Agriculture officials said they had been informed that Roerich had finally come to be regarded as a "spy" by some officials of Manchukuo. This was given as one of the principal factors in the department's decision that it had best end the expedition.

DEPARTMENT SILENT

State Department officials professed to have no official knowledge of the "espionage" complaints against Roerich. It has been known for some time that a definite coldness existed between the State Department and Roerich, and officials were reluctant to discuss his case. If there had been grounds for spy charges, experts pointed out, it would be most unusual for the country concerned to communicate officially with this Government. Instead, the person suspected of espionage customarily would be arrested in the foreign country and either placed in jail or deported.

NOW IN INDIA

Roerich was given until February 1 to return and complete his reports. But he is now in India, the department declared, so the termination has been imposed effective Saturday. They said the noted artist was chosen to lead the expeditions largely because of his high reputation and his minute knowledge of the Great Plains.

Roerich at one time spent five years in the region, painting 500 pictures. Born in Russia in 1874, he came to this country only in 1920. He was traveling on a French passport with the expedition, the Agriculture Department said.

FOUNDED ROERICH PACT

Roerich has painted more than 3,000 pictures, of which over 1,000 hang in the museum bearing his name in New York. In addition, he has written a number of books, largely along philosophic lines, and had been interested in archaeology. Followers of his religious philosophy have been organized in several cities.

He is given credit for the final approval in 1934 of the Roerich Pact, an international agreement, tentatively approved by twenty-one nations to protect artistic, scientific, historical and cultural monuments in time of war.

The following day, the *New York Herald Tribune* and other papers carried this story:

MUSEUM FIGHT REVEALED AS
UNITED STATES DROPS ROERICH
BATTLE FOR CONTROL OF RIVERSIDE INSTITUTION
IS AT INJUNCTION STAGE
WALLACE APOLOGY ASKED: HORCH FOES
CHARGE ITEM WAS TIMED TO THWART THEM

A bitter fight for control of the Roerich Museum at Riverside Drive and 103rd Street broke into the open yesterday following the release in Washington of an apparently routine announcement from the Dept. of Agriculture that an Asiatic plant-hunting expedition headed by Nicholas Roerich, founder of the museum, had been disbanded.

Immediately Herbert Plaut and Harold Davis, attorneys for Mr. Roerich and for four other trustees of the museum, charged Secretary of Agriculture Henry A. Wallace had "timed" the announcement to come on the eve of injunction proceeding against Louis L. Horch, president of the museum.

Mr. Plaut was incensed particularly because the Washington announcement recalled rumors that Mr. Roerich had become involved in the turbulent politics of China and Manchukuo and that charges of espionage were allegedly leveled against him.

ASKS WALLACE APOLOGY

He sent the following telegram to Secretary Wallace:

Evening papers carried today a statement: "Agriculture officials said it was even alleged that Mr. Roerich had finally come to be regarded as a 'spy' by certain officials in Manchukuo. This was given as one of the principal factors in the department's decision." On behalf of Mr. Roerich, whom we represent, we demand that you publicly retract these statements and insinuations with an apology. We demand you explain why the press release from your department and these quoted statements come on the eve of the injunction proceedings in the New York Supreme Court against your friend, Louis L. Horch."

No reference to allegations against Mr. Roerich were contained in the Department of Agriculture announcement, which merely said that the department had stopped the seed-collecting expedition in western China on September 22, 1935. According to The United Press, the notice of Mr. Roerich's dismissal came in reply to rumors that the expedition would resume operations. Since September, Mr. Roerich has been residing in the northern Punjab province of India, where, according to friends, he has been engaged in cancer research.

ROERICH OUT AS TRUSTEE

Last night Mr. Horch revealed that Mr. Roerich had not been a trustee of the Roerich Museum "for several months." He declined to say why Mr. Roerich's connections with the museum had been severed, but said that the action followed re-organization last February when the twenty-nine story skyscraper of culture was foreclosed.

The row between the museum trustees started December 15, when Mr. and Mrs. Maurice Lichtmann and Miss Frances R. Grant, three of the seven trustees, learned that Mr. Horch had summoned a stockholders' meeting for the next day. Protesting they had not been notified, they obtained an injunction to restrain Mr. Horch from performing any actions that might be voted at the meeting. Orders were served on Mr. Horch, but his attorneys obtained an adjournment until today, when the case will be heard before Special Term, Part III, of the Supreme Court.

Today's struggle marks a new crisis in the brief and unhappy career of the museum, founded in 1926 by disciples of Roerich as a skyscraper center to art and education. There were seven original trustees. Mr. Horch, the principal donor, gave more than one million dollars to the place. Mr. Roerich, who became the honorary president, contributed more than one thousand of his paintings. The other trustees were Mrs. Horch, Madam Roerich, Frances R. Grant and Mr. and Mrs. Lichtmann. Each of the trustees held one share of stock, entitling them to one vote in the museum's management.

Yesterday Mr. and Mrs. Lichtmann and Miss Grant charged that Mr. Horch had ousted Mr. and Mrs. Roerich as trustees, naming in their stead his brother-in-law, Sidney Newberger, and Miss Esther Lichtmann, a sister of Mr. Lichtmann. The Roerichs said they had turned over their shares to Mr. Horch a few years ago under a deposit agreement, but had retained the right to vote. Today they will seek to regain their stock.

Within the next few days many newspapers did in fact carry a retraction, but it was so small, and so far in the back of the papers, that the trustees decided to sue the *New York Sun* (the first paper to carry the story) for libel. Three days after the first story appeared, the *New York Herald Tribune* and others reported:

ROERICH'S NAME TO BE STRICKEN FROM MUSEUM

CORPORATION HEAD EXPLAINS MASTER INSTITUTE

OF UNITED ARTS WILL SUPPLANT IT

DEFIANT TRUSTEES ADMIT HORCH $1,000,000 GIFT

Justice Samuel I. Rosenman reserved decision yesterday in Supreme Court on application by opponents of Louis L. Horch, president of the Master Institute of United Arts, formerly the Roerich Museum, for an order to restrain Mr. Horch from carrying out plans voted at a stockholder's meeting last month.

The application was sought by counsel for five original trustees of the Roerich Museum, including Professor Nicholas Roerich, its founder, and his wife. It was stated that the meeting was held without their knowledge, although they controlled five of the seven shares of stock.

EXPLAINS CHANGE IN NAME

Meanwhile Mr. Horch announced all the "vital" activities of the museum would be continued under the auspices of the Master Institute. He has ordered the name "Roerich Museum" removed from the facade of the twenty-nine story skyscraper and has deleted "Roerich" from the title of several cultural projects. This was necessary, he explained, to keep them tax-free. He said there would be no curtailment of museum activities, but that an expansion of work is under consideration.

In court yesterday Jonas J. Shapiro, counsel for Mr. Horch, charged that the pro-Roerich trustees were never more than nominal stockholders and were pressing their fight for control because they feared they would lose their rent-free apartments in the building. He said that when the corporation was organized Mr. Horch believed that all the trustees had to be stockholders and therefore the stock was divided equally among them. He asserted that they never had contributed financially to the museum and argued that they never really believed they were more than nominal owners of the stock.

$1,000,000 GIFTS CITED

Herbert Plaut, counsel for Professor Roerich and his supporters, said that the museum corporation was organized in 1922 and that Mr. Horch contributed to it. He admitted that his clients had endorsed over to Mr. Horch their stock certificates but said that each trustee retained the right to vote.

Mr. Plaut said he had received no reply to the telegram he sent to Secretary Wallace. . . . On behalf of Professor Roerich and Mrs. Roerich who are in India, he was prepared to bring action for libel against "certain officials" because of the "innuendos" which he said were contained in the announcement.

Roerich was being attacked from all sides. Wallace had accused him of spying and "leaked" the stale news that his conduct in Manchukuo and Central Asia had embarrassed America. Horch was attempting to oust the Roerichs, Grant, and the Lichtmanns so he could take complete control of the museum and his million-dollar investment. Hardly a day passed that Mrs. Horch did not approach the teachers or students, trying to influence them against Sina and the school in general. She continued giving classes on the fourth floor, where Frances accused her of "pretending to conduct school."

Realizing the situation had gone far beyond anything that could be healed and anticipating what might be coming next, Sina asked on behalf of Mme Roerich that Nettie return all of the Roerichs' manuscripts. She was told that neither Nettie nor Esther had any. Then Sina put the request in writing and received the same response. Greatly alarmed, she quickly contacted their lawyer, Mr. Plaut, and cabled India.

Helena immediately replied that it was imperative to protect the tremendous body of work from any evil intentions. The manuscripts must be recovered because they contained valuable material she had written with the Master from 1923 to 1935. It could only be published under her direct supervision. She pointed out that some of it was so far ahead of the consciousness of the time that publication was not to be for many years.

Mr. Plaut wrote a demand letter and was told that whatever notebooks Mme Roerich had given Mrs. Horch had been gifts. Therefore, there was no reason to return them. Since all were handwritten in Russian, which Nettie could not read, Frances thought it "sounded absolutely incredible" to say they were presented as gifts. There was also abundant evidence in letters, cables, and trustee meeting minutes that could prove the notebooks had been sent to New York for safekeeping. Mr. Plaut attempted to secure the books with a search warrant. When that failed, he started proceedings to sue for their return.

At the same time, other developments were proceeding. Mr. Jackson, an attorney, had begun negotiating with the federal government for a settlement of the back taxes. The trustees brought charges against Horch to recover the shares of stock they had entrusted to him for safekeeping, and Horch sued Roerich to recover money owed him for the thousands of dollars of IOU's in Horch's possession.

For several years, none of the suits won anyone anything except tremendous bitterness, frustration, and disappointment. In court and out, matters never seemed to go in Roerich's favor. Frances claimed she saw "the same sinister hand at work in that." Cases dragged on, lawyers were inefficient, things were bungled and postponed. Refusing to explain, the IRS turned down all attempts at settlement. In 1937, the court decided that since Horch was the only one of the trustees who had put in money, he had the right to keep all the shares in the Master Institute. Sina and

Frances were given two days to move out all belongings of the Master Institute, Urusvati, and the Roerich Museum Press.

Everything was finally moved to new quarters on 72nd Street, where, though crowded and uncomfortable, Sina started holding classes for the few remaining students. The barely functioning Roerich Museum Press occupied a part of the same space. Even after the institutions were moved, Frances and Sina somehow still thought they could keep their "life tenure" apartments. When the situation became too unpleasant, they finally gave up.

When they heard that the bulk of the paintings had quietly disappeared from the walls, they rushed to inspect, and found only a few scattered ones remaining. In spite of their loud protests and hysterical demands for explanations, two days later the halls were completely empty. Upon reporting this to the police and the district attorney's office, they were told the district attorney had no jurisdiction over such matters. Horch's attorneys insisted that, since the paintings belonged to Horch, he had the right to remove them. The Roerichs' loyal followers maintained that "the entire Museum was stolen by criminals, people without any scruples, people who deliberately ousted the rightful shareholders and trustees from the Institutions and who succeeded in winning the courts and the judges over to their side."

They then gathered signatures of protest, trying to win in the court of public opinion, but the newspapers seemed to lose interest in the affair. In India, feeling powerless, the Roerichs sent constant guidance and advice to encourage the little group in the struggle. At the very beginning, Helena had written: "I most sincerely wish for you to become a real warrior, and to temper your spirit under the rain of those hostile arrows. There is a peculiar joy in receiving hostile arrows. Thus, at this moment a betrayal has been discovered where I least of all expected it. My heart was wounded, but somewhere in the depth of it joy is already rising. It is the joy of a warrior, the joy of a possibility of fighting for Truth, and above all the joy of one more liberation!"

She reminded them, "The power of faith, the power of love, that is the fire which transmutes all our feelings. . . . Only the transmutation of energies, i.e., feelings or qualities of thought, can take us out of the magic circle of karma. Hence, let us uplift our vibrations through high emotions." And the Master, too, reminded them that "the law of Karma flows immutably."

Many wondered why Roerich never returned to the United States to clear his name. With Wallace opening the doors, Lichtmann and Horch had visited the undersecretary of state, Mr. Hornbeck. In the presence of the chief of the Visa Division, they showed photostats of tax notices to prove Roerich was in default in the amount of $48,000 and claimed that if Roerich came to America, "He would cause a great deal of trouble." In reporting the conversation, Hornbeck noted, "Throughout the conversation they made it understood that what they want is that Roerich be kept out of the country." When Hornbeck heard that three members of the museum board were still for Roerich and three were against him, he asked what had caused that. Horch and Miss Lichtmann replied that it was their "discovery that Roerich was an impostor and a cheat." When he inquired if there was anything for which they would be inclined to prosecute Roerich, they said no. Yet, they maintained that Roerich was a dangerous person who mixed politics with art and would be a troublemaker wherever he went. On December 4, 1939, they were still persisting with their efforts to prevent Roerich's return to the United States. The undersecretary sent the following memo to Wallace:

My dear Mr. Secretary:

I refer to our conversation concerning Professor Nicholas Roerich who it was understood, would endeavor to obtain a visa at one of our consular offices. A telegraphic report from the Consulate General at Calcutta states that Professor Roerich is said to still be residing at Naggar, Punjab and that it has been impossible to learn anything regarding his plans. The Consul General has been requested to inform all consular offices in India that if the Professor should apply, a visa should not be issued to him without previous authorization from the Department.

Upon receiving the above information, one department head wryly asked how dangerous Roerich could be if he was only charged with tax evasion and suggested that matters might get settled if he was allowed entry. But as far as Wallace was concerned, Roerich was persona non grata in America. He had written the Roerichs ordering that neither the professor nor anyone in the family was ever to attempt to contact him or President Roosevelt again, and recommended that Roerich's name be removed from the Pact and Banner of Peace. Helena wrote:

And so we drink the chalice of poison tendered by the hands of our former co-workers. But in spite of this, strength and courage live in our hearts. For what is achievement without betrayal? The symbol of Judas is eternal and is inevitably present at the consummation of a great achievement. But after Golgotha, comes the resurrection, and the great exaltation of the spirit. This was indicated in the Mysteries, and causes joy to flame in our hearts. We know the Great Pledge of the Stronghold of Light, we treasure the signs of Trust, and we know the victorious shield. Our spirit cannot be frightened by any battles; we have even learned to love them, because what else can so temper the spirit and test our abilities and bring us great experiences for the crown of fulfillment? And so, we may once more say, "Blessed be the obstacles, by them we grow."

In 1939, the school moved to the Fisk Building at 250 West 57th Street, occupying two studios and an office. Sina had divorced Maurice and married Dudley Fosdick, a coworker who had been welcomed into the teachings and was devoted to the fight. He, Sina, and two members of the school faculty became directors of the newly formed Roerich Academy of Arts. Their faith, and that of a few other supporters like Mrs. Campbell and Miss Fritschi, was unwavering.

They began accumulating paintings from friends and private collectors, so that one day there would be another museum of Roerich's art in America. They held to the hope that "the time was not far off when the battle for justice would be won and the Roerich Museum would be returned to its former status." They saw the whole affair as "a dark spot on the history of culture in America."

20

KULU VALLEY

Regardless of the situation in New York, an exhausted Roerich, now sixty-three, was back in Kulu Valley in 1937. The hopes, plans, and dreams of uniting all Buddhists and establishing a spiritual country in the Altai were put on hold for another time, perhaps another lifetime. Restricted to the Punjab, his expeditions were very short. When his health was poor, he lectured himself:

> Don't be ill.... During half a century, there were many illnesses, but how much danger was passed. We were lost, we froze—the things have been difficult! But the will did not weaken. We crossed difficult passes, sometimes it seemed that we could ascend no higher, but the height proved surmountable. Sometimes on a narrow ledge, the rock seemed as if it would break away, but all the passes and the ledge are still there. One became dizzy when looking at the rapidly rushing blocks of ice in the river, but they were at a salutary distance. Do not be ill, there are great days yet to be seen.

His thoughts dwelt on Buddha, the Agni Yoga teachings, his paintings, Shambhala, old friends, and current scientific discoveries. Urusvati, the Himalayan Research Institute, exchanged information with many scientific organizations in Asia, Europe, and America and traded botanical and zoological collections with the University of Michigan, Punjab University, the Paris Museum of Natural History, Harvard, and the U.S.S.R. Academy of Sciences.

As Director of Urusvati, George studied and translated the books and cherished articles his family had brought back from their expeditions. Svetoslav continued to paint, producing, among other works, numerous portraits of Nicholas and Helena. He also headed the Urusvati Botany Department and researched the medicinal plants of Tibet. A biochemistry laboratory was opened to study cosmic rays under high altitude conditions, cancer, and other subjects.

Kulu Valley was perfect for their needs. As Helena explained:

We selected the location of the center in the Himalayas quite deliberately and purposefully, for innumerable possibilities are offered by these heights, and the attention of the scientific world is directed here. In the sphere of magnetic currents which bring precious new energies to humanity, science is still in its infancy, and modern instruments are nothing but toys. But the discovery of new cosmic rays is possible here, for the finest and most valuable energies are found in this pure mountain atmosphere.

We pay attention to all meteoric precipitation which falls on these snowy summits and is carried into the valleys by the mountain streams. The astronomical observations are exceptionally good and the rarest medical plants, grasses, and botanic species are also here. . . . Since the source of knowledge is found throughout the entire Cosmos, a scientific center should belong to the whole world and include co-workers of all nationalities. And the scientists of the

Urusvati, the Himalayan Research Institute, 1935

world should be as united in their cooperation as the Cosmos is indivisible in all its functions.

In October 1937, the first Baltic Congress of Roerich Societies met in Riga, Latvia. It celebrated his fifty years of achievements and published a beautiful volume relating his attempts to further beauty and culture by working to conquer ignorance and hatred. In spite of the negative publicity from America, Roerich's fame as an artist, his humanitarian outlook, his support of India's freedom fighters, and Urusvati's activities turned remote, hilly Naggar into a cultural center and a beacon to the world. So many Indian scientists, artists, writers, and political figures were personally and professionally acquainted with him that it became standard procedure for scientific congresses and art conferences to send him invitations and salutations. But the great respect paid him by progressive circles of Indian society and his contact with the United States only made the British more suspicious, and he remained under surveillance.

Visitors to their home remarked that Helena, dressed in her long Edwardian skirt, looked like a tsarina, while Nicholas's most striking feature was his white beard, which he sometimes wore square, but usually wore pointed or even double pointed. He liked to wear a skullcap and a long jubba cloak, with a gold chain around his neck that gave him the look of a priest from an Orthodox church.

Most of the family's activities were viewed with distrust by their British neighbors, perhaps Great Game veterans. The Roerichs were accused of being Bolshevik spies and Russian Buddhists and criticized for welcoming Hindu priests, lamas, and wandering holy men to their door, for calling themselves Americans, for paying their serving staff more than the local wages, and for many other things. Gossipers labeled their actions "queer" and thought it "interesting" that they had traveled into trouble spots and chosen such an inaccessible location for their research headquarters. Who knows what would have been said if any of them had gone into Helena's study and seen the paintings of Master Morya surrounded by a most incredible light or holding a sacred censer to purify the world.

George F. Waugh, Lt. Col., U.S.A. (Ret.), wrote a long letter to the United States secretary of state passing on the innuendoes and rumors he had heard. In summation, he wrote, "The principle question one meets is what are they doing here, why do they want to stay, and where does their money come from."

When Jawaharlal Nehru and his daughter, Indira Gandhi, visited for a week, Svetoslav sketched him and later painted his portrait. (He subsequently painted Indira, and her son Rajiv when he was prime minister.) As rumbles of war in Europe reached India, Nehru, convinced that a victory for Hitler would spell doom for the entire world, frequently quoted

Trotsky: "It is clear that the twentieth century is the most disturbed century within the memory of humanity; any contemporary of ours who wants peace and comfort before everything else has chosen a bad time to be born."[1]

Interior of Helena's study in Kulu Valley, India, 1930s

As the opening shots of World War II were heard, Helena wrote that it was necessary for the first battles with the Prince of Darkness to take place in the subtle spheres before the Lord of Shambhala could act through his earthly warriors. The chaos would eventually usher in the Golden Age: "The threatening time has come. Very threatening—and a great sorting out is taking place. There is a shifting in the consciousness of people, an awakened striving toward the reconstruction of life, on a new basis and on a large scale."

And the Master said, "Therefore, verily, the crumbling of the old world is a new affirmation, for through the coming of new values we bring the world the salvation of spirit."

In June 1940, Roerich wrote in his diary:

First we seemed cut off from Vienna, then from Prague. Now it is Warsaw and gradually the contacts with the Baltic republics have

Left to right: *Jawaharlal Nehru, Svetoslav Roerich, Indira Gandhi, Nicholas Roerich*. With umbrella: *Helena Roerich. Naggar, India, 1942*

become difficult. Sweden, Denmark, and Norway have disappeared from the list. Bruges has gone silent, as have Belgrade, Zagreb, and Italy. Paris is not there and the Far East is silent. Even Switzerland seems a possessed country and it is not even possible to write to Russia any longer in response to the inquiries for herbs. Who knows how many letters have gotten lost or been destroyed by the hands of the censor. It is sad to see our work crippled and no improvement near.

Worried and grieving over the world's chaotic happenings, he immersed himself in the solidness of his mountains, painting and repainting his cherished Himalayas over and over again, in all kinds of weather and at every time of day. He produced huge canvases with masses of color which, as Svetoslav explained, "carried the message of the Teacher calling the disciples to awaken and strive towards a new life—a better life, a life of Beauty and Fulfillment."

Roerich painted military campaigns and the sorrows of war and gave them titles like *Armageddon*, *Heroes Awakened*, *Alexander Nevsky*, and the *Campaign of Igor*. In a letter to another artist, he wrote: "Above all earthly havoc Art and Religion remain, and if human beings reveal exalted feelings, they manifest through these two channels. At the moment there are few joys on the earthly plane, and the human heart is very much in need of rejoicing. We artists should be grateful to fate for giving us one of the best channels to bring people happiness of the heart. To someone else, these words might appear as nebulous abstractions, but for artists, they represent reality."

Still creating his own world, Roerich lost himself in the romance of India: "Here is the Abode of the Rishis. Here resounded the flute of Krishna. Here thundered the Blessed Gautama Buddha. Here originated all the *Vedas*. Here lived the Pandavas. Here Gessar Khan. Here Aryavarta. Here is Shambhala. Himalayas—Jewel of India. Himalayas—Treasure of the World. Himalayas—the sacred Symbol of Ascent."

Indian artist and lecturer B. M. Goswamy observed:

Roerich's whole view was different. India was not as he perceived her. It is difficult for us to think of Gautama the Buddha's "thundering." This is one of the last descriptions that comes to mind when one thinks of his gentle words, and yet this is how Roerich wants us to think of Buddha and, therefore, of the Himalayas. The Himalayas were not home to the Pandavas, nor did Krishna's flute ever resound

329

in them, and yet, it is these images which are invoked by Roerich's enthusiasm for the great ranges that he so tirelessly traversed.

In Roerich's mind the view of the Himalayas merged with his belief in, and longing for, the Second Coming. In his writing and his painting alike, he seemed to be making prophetic pronouncements in his consistently emphatic tone. One turns to Roerich's writing and sees that while the flow of words is quite remarkable, the sequence of thoughts was as hard to follow as the jagged peaks of the mountains. Roerich was not beyond turning everything to his own purpose—even modifying facts in his impassioned desire to get the message across.

One sees fairly clearly that he aimed to bring the grandeur and the majesty of the mountain ranges into relief no matter if the facts had to be modified or nuances changed. It is as if his paintings, writings, and discourses were all calculated to merge and form the background to his conviction that the Second Coming was near and would manifest itself in the Himalayas. The paintings advanced this end as did the countless mysterious tales he collected and retold. And the sense of joy he felt at the fact that some of the mountain peaks were still "pure" because they were unconquered, is better understood with the perspective that it is in these ranges that the splendid legions of Maitreya would one day stand forth.

Now seventy, with his family in their beloved India, Roerich was heartened by the Master's teachings. Concerned for the millions who were dying in Russia, he and Svetoslav arranged exhibitions, sold paintings, and sent the proceeds to the Russian Red Cross and the Red Army. George spoke of joining the ranks when the military action reached the Russian front. The Roerichs encouraged Sina and those still loyal to them in New York to establish the American-Russian Cultural Association, something very close to their hearts. They solicited Ernest Hemingway,

*Svetoslav Roerich painting the mountains his
father loved in Kulu Valley, India*

Rockwell Kent, Charlie Chaplin, Norman Bel Geddes, and many others to work with them toward cultural cooperation.

Then the war was over. As Roerich contemplated the pointless destruction of the world's culture, it aroused his passion to resume work on the Pact and Banner. In August 1946, Helena wrote to Sina about establishing a new Banner of Peace Committee: "It is time to understand that the greatest Banner in history is being unfurled. Never before has the Banner of Peace, the sign of the New World, been manifested. Let the people understand the Sign of Salvation. The firmament trembles. The currents are red-hot! The Banner of Peace, our Banner, is as a Beacon of Light during the storm. And the sowing of Culture is an antidote for poison."

A few months later the All-Indian Conference of Cultural Unity endorsed the banner, while India demanded that the British "Quit India," and massive demonstrations took place in every major town and hundreds of villages. Roerich applied for permission to return to the U.S.S.R. and was refused. Perhaps as the death tolls climbed to thousands, he realized that the only island of peace he would ever find was inside himself and in the world he and Helena created around them.

In her company, with their sons, the Bogdanova sisters, and the guests who came up the mountain to visit, Roerich turned to the simple joys of life. He greeted the early sun, took long walks in the mountains, watched the flowers grow in his gardens, and contributed generously to local fairs and celebrations. Most of his time was spent in his studio. Of his life with Helena, he fondly wrote in his diary: "Forty years—no less than forty. On such a long voyage, meeting many storms and menaces—from without. Together we overcame all obstacles. And obstacles turned into possibilities. I dedicated my books to 'Helena, my wife, friend, fellow traveler, inspirer!' Each of these concepts was tested in the fire of life. And in Petersburg, Scandinavia, England, America, and in all Asia we worked, we studied, we broadened our consciousness. Together we created, and not without reason is it said that the work should bear two names—a feminine and a masculine."

When India became independent at midnight, August 15, 1947, waves of violence erupted, reverberating in every direction. By October, the entire country—particularly the Punjab territory west of Kulu—was a churning mass of migration and horror. All work ceased, the telegraph was silent, no mail was delivered. From the Hall Estate, the Roerichs could hear shooting, and as the neighbors from below requested shelter, Roerich retreated to his bed, heartsick and ill. He had been ailing since June with prostate cancer; surgery had been performed and bed rest prescribed.

An unfinished canvas, *The Master's Command*, stood on his easel. On it, weighed down by the worries of the world, a figure perches among some enormous mountain cliffs that rise far above the winding stream in the valley. A large white bird—resembling an albatross—hovers close. Bird and man are surrounded by rich brown and intensely blue mountains. In the distant golden sky, streaked with coral, hope awaits.

December 13 was Shiva's birthday, the most solemn day of the Hindu calendar. At 3:00 a.m., Roerich had endured enough; his heart, and possibly his kidneys, had failed. Perhaps the beauty he knew was possible would be found in his next incarnation, or perhaps he could achieve more from the other side. Helena wrote to Sina: "The heart could not endure the pressures and the terrible pain of seeing the oppression of all that belongs to culture, all that brings salvation for the coming generation. Our Light, Our Beloved left as he lived—simply, beautifully, and majestically. The world is truly orphaned by the departure of this beautiful Spirit!"

Three days later, in front of his last earthly home—facing the Himalayas—the flames of a mighty fire consumed the frail body of the singer of the Holy, the artist who had loved to dig up graves, kurgans, and tumuli. His funeral pyre burned for two days, emanating the aromatic oils of deodar and sandalwood. Then a slab of mountain rock was installed on the spot and inscribed, "The body of Maharishi Nikolai Roerich, a great friend of India, was cremated here on 30th Magh, 2004th year of the Vikram era, corresponding to the 15th December 1947. Om Ram."

On the reverse side, the stonemason had aptly chiseled, "This fragment of a mountain cliff was brought here from far away."

A few days later, when George cabled the sad news to his friend Robert Horniman in Great Britain, he reported that his mother could have gone too, but the Master had said she still had some important work to do. Valentina Dutko, a beloved friend who did much of Helena's translating, further reported that "Master was with Helena," and as she watched her husband leave his body, he was "surrounded by truly beautiful colors and light."

After her husband's death, Helena wrote, "My spiritual loneliness on Earth is great. The loving understanding and spiritual harmony that bound me with him made all the difficult situations easier and brightened the future. With his departure, my isolation from all that is personal and earthly is even stronger. There is left only a deep desire to bring forth all the collected treasures and give whatever is possible to hungry souls."

In 1949, two years after Roerich's passing, following Helena's advice, Sina Fosdick found a new location for the museum. She remembered, "As if Helena were not in India, but together with us in America, she guided us by pointing out better locations. And after searching for many weeks, even though its owner at first refused to sell it, the ideal house came to us through a series of unusual happenings. So with the help of our generous co-workers, we assembled a good collection of Roerich paintings."

Eight years after Roerich's passing, mere days before what would have been his eighty-first birthday, following several years of serious pain and frail health, Helena had two heart attacks and died in her sleep. She and George had moved to Kalimpong, where she worked heroically to consolidate the spiritual legacy for future safekeeping. According to her wish, her body was cremated on the top of a mountain facing holy Kanchenjunga, the wonderful country of the Great Snows, the Abode of Light. Her ashes were placed under a Buddhist chorten. Her sons and daughter-in-law (Svetoslav had married in 1945) were deeply touched when people from all over Asia came to pay their respects. Hindus, Chinese, Afghans, Tibetans, Mongols, Nepalis, Bhutanese, and even some Japanese joined in the procession. Helena had previously told friends that the Master had said if she had died earlier, certain things would have had to be postponed for two hundred years or more: "I exist due only to the Ray of the Great Master, who said it was necessary for me to remain because no one could replace me as I work under the highest Cosmic Sign, and this century was in need of my attainment."

On December 19, 1958, the Roerich Museum was chartered in a five-story brownstone just a few blocks away from the skyscraper. With Sina as director, renewed cultural activities began, and the work for the future continued.

Though their bodies burned away, much still remained. After all of the living—the drama, the striving, the intensity—when lives end, one may wonder, "What endures?" Of the countless millions who roam the earth, live out their days and then pass over, what stays behind to verify their existence? Many blessed ones are remembered for generations by those who knew and loved them. The more famous or infamous are recalled for what they did or said; a comparatively meager few are remembered because they expanded consciousness and added more beauty to the world.

"With every affirmation of the Beautiful and of the highest, we are creating that quality for the future life," wrote Roerich in *Shambhala*. "The most gratifying and uplifting way to serve the coming evolution is by spreading the seeds of beauty. If we are to have a beautiful life and some happiness . . . it must be created with joy and enthusiasm for service to art and beauty. . . . If the culture of spirit is to win, beauty must invade new regions."

Reflecting on the books, the paintings, and all that the Roerichs gave to the world, one can

Svetoslav and George Roerich
beside their mother's ashes

recognize that their lives were lives of devotion—devotion to overcoming obstacles, to beauty, to service, and to following the will of their Master. They advocated that one never stop exploring his or her depths for the greater levels of strength, resourcefulness, and creativity waiting there. Their actions gave proof to their words. Spiritual pioneers, searching for something greater than themselves, the Roerichs cut a path through the darkness for all of us. Perhaps in our time, we will get to Shambhala and live in peace. In the meantime, as the Roerichs' names are added to those exceptional ones who have contributed to our world, we might ask ourselves what we are willing to do for the coming generations. And then begin doing it!

Madame Roerich's chair

EPILOG

After the elder Roerichs were gone, Svetoslav and his wife, Devika Rani, first lady of the Indian cinema and niece of Rabindranath Tagore, lived in Bangalore, India; they had no children. He is widely known as a painter. George never married. He was allowed to return to the Soviet Union by special permission from Nikita Khrushchev—bringing the banned Agni Yoga teachings with him into the spiritually hungry country. Although in poor health and with a weak heart, he joined the staff of the Institute of Oriental Studies of the Academy of Science. He continued his scientific work and research there and enriched the institute with his firsthand knowledge and expertise. He is recognized as a prominent Buddhist scholar and scientist.

Fulfilling Nicholas's last wish, George presented 418 paintings to Russia. Sixty of them went to the Novosibirsk Picture Gallery and the rest to the Russian Museum in St. Petersburg. Roerich's childhood home, Isvara, is open to the public, and the house in Kulu has been made into a memorial museum.

The Agni Yoga teachings had been outlawed in the Soviet Union until Mikhail Gorbachev opened the door with *perestroika* and many of

Raisa Gorbachev, Svetoslav Roerich, Mikhail Gorbachev, Devika Rani Roerich.
Kremlin, Moscow, May 14, 1987

Russia's cultural treasures were returned. At that time, Svetoslav met with Gorbachev and his wife, Raisa, herself an Agni Yoga student. The meeting resulted in a Roerich Fund being established in Moscow for the creation of a cultural center and museum. Gorbachev, calling Nicholas Roerich "one of the cultural pillars of Russia," contributed a palace and the rubles necessary to establish the Moscows International Roerich Centre.

Into the center went four tons of paintings, correspondence, and unpublished manuscripts, which had been stored with Svetoslav in Bangalore. With the Roerich legacy safely back in Russia, a heavy burden of responsibility must have been lifted from Svetoslav's shoulders. He died within the next few years, and Devika Rani passed on soon afterward.

Sina Fosdick, first director of the Nicholas Roerich Museum,
surrounded by Roerich paintings at the present location of the museum

Over the years, Horch steadily sold paintings out of the museum's storeroom and gave away many for tax write-offs. About one hundred went to the Rose Art Gallery at Brandeis University. Some of the paintings on display in the Roerich Museum were actually bought from Horch and donated back to the museum. The largest such collector was one of Helena Roerich's disciples, Baltzar Bolling. At his request, Helena had given him a list of the paintings she thought were important to rescue, and he kindly donated about a dozen of them.

Mme Roerich's notebooks were never returned. Due to the wisdom of the Horch's daughter, Oriole, however, they were not destroyed. They are deposited in the library of Amherst College along with other material she gave.

The Agni Yoga books have been translated into numerous languages. Agni Yoga societies meet around the world.

Over the years, many of Roerich's thousands of paintings and drawings have been photographed and cataloged. The largest collection on display in America is at the Nicholas Roerich Museum in New York. Prints of his paintings and books written by and about both Roerichs are available through the museum: 319 West 107th Street, New York, NY 10025. The museum web site address is www.roerich.org.

An old Tibetan story tells of a young man who set off on the quest for Shambhala. After crossing many mountains, he came to the cave of an old hermit, who asked him, "Where are you going across these wastes of snow?"

"To find Shambhala," the youth replied.

"Ah, well then, you need not travel far," the hermit said. "The kingdom of Shambhala is in your own heart."

—Jacques Bacot, quoted by Edwin Bernbaum
in *The Way to Shambhala*

NOTES

PROLOG

    1. Karma is the law of retribution: whatever is sown is reaped.

CHAPTER 1: An Inner Urgency for Artistic Creation

    1. The Panchen Lama, or Panchen Rimpoche (the Precious Teacher), and the Dalai Lama, or Gyalpo Rimpoche (the Precious King), are titles indicating the difference between spiritual and worldly power. The Dalai Lama had greater political power and ruled over Tibet. The Panchen Lama, believed to be the ruler of Shambhala, had greater spiritual power and was more knowledgeable regarding sacred scriptures.

CHAPTER 2: Magnetic Mysticism

    1. The term "Great Game" was adopted from Rudyard Kipling's book *Kim*. It was the Victorian Cold War.

    2. Many of the messages were eventually published by the Agni Yoga Society: *Leaves of Morya's Garden, New Era Community, Agni Yoga, Infinity, Hierarchy* and other volumes.

    3. *Agni*, fire; *yoga*, union with God: the yoga that can link humans with the highest divine principles.

4. Talashkino was an experimental village established by Princess Maria Tenisheva to educate the serfs and teach them the long-lost skills needed to create folk arts. The village became an artists' colony, drawing together many people. Much of Talashkino interested Nikolai, especially the research necessary before the arts could be taught. The Talashkino products became so popular that they created a revival of interest in the arts of medieval Russia. Roerich designed furniture and staged elaborate productions for the theater there. In 1912, he completed his fresco *Queen of Heaven* on the chapel wall and ceiling. It was the prototype for the Mother of the World, which he later painted several times.

5. Once in America, Nikolai used the name Nicholas and Elena became Helena.

6. *Nicholas Roerich, 1874–1947*, Nicholas Roerich Museum.

CHAPTER 3: Culture Is of the Spirit

1. Kuindjy had been dismissed from the faculty for having a bad influence on the students. When his students walked out with him, they were offered their diplomas contingent upon the work they would present. Nikolai presented *The Messenger*.

2. About half of the paintings were eventually recovered. While in California, Roerich discovered that thirty-five were in the Oakland Museum, and six others were in private collections. They were finally returned to Russia in 1976 and are on display in the Oriental Art Museum in Moscow.

3. Taken from Jonson's diary, courtesy of the archives of the Jonson Gallery of the University Art Museum, University of New Mexico, Albuquerque.

4. *El Palacio*, Vol. XI, No. 8, October 15, 1921.

CHAPTER 4: Santa Fe

1. Several years later, Hewitt's dream of making the area a national park was fulfilled with the creation of Bandelier National Monument.

2. The "Advanced School of Mysticism" referred to was the little study group, about ten in all, consisting of the Lichtmanns and Sina's mother, Sophie Shafran, Frances Grant, and a few others.

3. Tretyakov so liberally used his wealth as encouragement that after forty years of collecting he had amassed the most fabulous art collection in Russia. A few years before his death, he donated the entire collection of 1,757 paintings to Moscow, in appreciation for his family's success there.

CHAPTER 5: The Master School of United Arts

1. From an interview with the Hudson sisters. The names of the people in the party were lost over time.

2. Andrews, *Under a Lucky Star*.

CHAPTER 7: Where Can One Have Such Joy?

1. A stupa is a dome- or cone-shaped monument erected over relics of a revered person.

2. Bose was knighted in 1916 for his work with wavelengths and his experiments with plants.

CHAPTER 10: The Silk Road and Chinese Hospitality

1. See Roerich's *Altai-Himalaya* and *Heart of Asia* for a more detailed account.

2. The Caves of the Thousand Buddhas had recently been "robbed" over a twenty-year period of hundreds of Buddhist manuscripts, sacred texts, paintings, silks, and priceless art relics. Sir Aurel Stein and other archaeologists had startled the world by spiriting them out of Chinese Turkestan into Western museums. The texts included the Diamond Sutra, the world's earliest printed book—the sixteen-foot-long scroll bears an exact date: May 11, 868, according to the Christian calendar.

CHAPTER 13: The Altai

1. CHEKA was the precursor to the KGB.

2. For another perspective on the Roerichs' trip to Moscow, see *Tournament of Shadows* by Karl E. Meyer and Shareen Blair Brysac.

3. Boris planned eventually to join the group in America, but in 1927 he was arrested by the Soviets for smuggling "contraband" and could not leave the country after that.

CHAPTER 14: Across the Gobi

1. In later books Roerich remembered the bird as a vulture.

ρ ϡ ϡ

CHAPTER 15: Into Tibet

✳ 1. The collected letters of Master Morya and Master Koot Humi.

2. This correspondence was taken from British secret files.

CHAPTER 18: The Asian Botanical Expedition

1. The monastery was named in the eighteenth century when the Chinese emperor gave it a complete collection of the sacred books of Kanjur.

2. From records of the United States Department of State, Division of Far Eastern Affairs.

3. Two obvious false statements—Roerich was sixty, not seventy, and Helena was in India, not Kalgan—call into question the accuracy of the rest of the report.

CHAPTER 19: A Dark Spot

1. Copies of her letters to the president were stored among his other papers at the Franklin D. Roosevelt Memorial Library, in Hyde Park, New York. None of his replies to her are there, but her letters make it clear that he did reply.

2. Horch was hired by the Department of Agriculture within the next two years to administer foreign exchange transactions with imports.

CHAPTER 20: Kulu Valley

1. Ali; *An Indian Dynasty*.

BIBLIOGRAPHY

Since a large portion of my material was taken from personal interviews and letters, crumbling scrapbooks, microfilmed newspapers, old diaries, and magazines, it is highly improbable that anyone will track these sources. Therefore, I have chosen not to document this work with many notes. I am, however, listing all of the books; many are obtainable, though out-of-print, and make fascinating reading.

BOOKS

Aberle, David F. *The Kinship System of the Kalmuk Mongols*. Albuquerque: University of New Mexico Press, 1953.

Ajaya and Rama. *Living with the Himalayan Masters*. Honesdale, PA: Himalayan International Institute, 1978.

Agni Yoga Society. *Agni Yoga*. Agni Yoga Series. New York: Agni Yoga Society Inc., 1929.

———. *Hierarchy*, 1931.

———. *Infinity*, 1930.

———. *Leaves of Morya's Garden: The Call*, 1924.

———. *Leaves of Morya's Garden: Illumination*, 1925.

———. *New Era Community*, 1926.

347

Ali, Tariq. *An Indian Dynasty*. New York: Putnam, 1985.

Andrews, Roy Chapman. *Under A Lucky Star*. New York: The Viking Press, 1944.

———. *On the Trail of Ancient Man*. New York: Garden City Publishing Co., 1926.

Atlantic Monthly. *Brief Lives*. New York: Little, Brown, 1971.

Aurora Art Publishers. *Nikolai Roerich*, Masters of World Painting. Leningrad: 1976.

Axelbank, Albert. *Mongolia*. Tokyo: Kodansha International Ltd., 1971.

Bailey, Alice A. *The Unfinished Autobiography*. New York: Lucis Publishing Co., 1951.

Bailey, F. M. *No Passport to Tibet*. London: Rupert Hart-Davis, 1957.

Barborka, Geoffrey A. *H. P. Blatvatsky, Tibet and Tulku*. Adyar, India: Theosophical Publishing House, 1974.

Barford, P. M. *The Early Slavs*. Ithaca, NY: Cornell University Press, 2001.

Barroll, Clare. *The Iron Crown*. New York: Charles Scribner, Sons, 1975.

Beecham, Thomas. *An Independent Biography*. New York: E. P. Dutton, 1962.

Belikov, P., and V. Knyazeva. *Roerich*. Unpublished translation by Courtney Collier. Moscow, Russia, 1972.

Bennett, J. G. *An Introduction to Gurdjieff*. New York: Stonehill Publishing, 1973.

Benz, Ernst. *Buddhism or Communism*. New York: Anchor Books, 1965.

Bernbaum, Edwin. *The Way to Shambhala*. New York: Anchor Press/Doubleday, 1980.

Berry, Scott. *Monks, Spies and a Soldier of Fortune*. New York: St. Martin's Press, 1995.

Blavatsky, Helena P. *The Secret Doctrine*. Adyar, India: Theosophical Publishing House, 1978.

Bonnefield, Matthew P. *The Dust Bowl*. Albuquerque: University of New Mexico Press, 1978.

Bosse, Malcolm. *The Warlord*. New York: Simon & Schuster, 1983.

Bowers, Fabion. *Scriabin*. Tokyo: Kodansha International Ltd., 1969.

Bowlt, John E. *The Silver Age: Russian Art of the Early 20th Century and The World of Art Group*. Newtonville, MA: Oriental Research Partners, 1979.

Bragdon, Claude. *The Beautiful Necessity*. Wheaton, IL: The Theosophical Publishing House, 1978.

Buckle, Richard. *In Search of Diaghilev*. New York: Theo. Nelson & Sons, 1956.

———. *Nijinsky*. New York: Simon & Schuster, 1971.

Cable, M., and F. French. *The Gobi Desert*. New York: Macmillan, 1944.

Cavendish, Marshall. *The Great Composers*. London: Chartwell Books, 1975.

Chaliapin, Fyodor. *An Autobiography as Told to Maxim Gorky*. New York: Stein & Day Publishing, 1969.

Chaudhuri, N. C. *Thy Hand Great Anarch*. England: The Spartan Press, 1988.

Chauvenet, Beatrice. *Hewitt and Friends*. Albuquerque: Museum of New Mexico Press, 1983.

Childress, D. H. *Lost Cities of China, Central Asia and India*. Steele, IL: Adventures Unlimited Press, 1987.

Cohn, Stephen F. *Burkharin and the Bolshevik Revolution*. New York: Alfred A. Knopf, 1973.

Cooper, Irving S. *Theosophy Simplified*. Adyar, India: Theosophical Publishing House, 1979.

Cronin, Jr., E. W. *The Arun*. Boston: Houghton Mifflin, 1979.

Crowther, Geoff, et al. *India, a Travel Survival Kit*. Victoria, Australia: Lonely Planet Publishing, 1984.

Decter, Jacqueline. *Nicholas Roerich: The Life and Art of a Russian Master*. Rochester, VT: Park Street Press, 1989.

Department of Languages, Art and Culture. *Nicholas K. Roerich 1874–1947*. (Commemoration Volume). Simla, India: Department of Languages, Art and Culture 1975.

Dictionary of American Biography. New York: Charles Scribner's Sons, 1973.

Duvernois, Jean. *Roerich: Fragments of a Biography*. New York: 1933.

Foster, Barbara, and Michael. *Forbidden Journey: the Life of Alexandra David-Neel*. San Francisco: Harper & Row Publishing, 1987.

Garden, Mary. *Mary Garden's Story*. New York: Simon & Schuster, 1951.

Gorbacheva, Raisa M. *I Hope: Reminiscences and Reflections*. New York: HarperCollins Publishers, 1991

Hall, Nelson. *Miracle in the Evening: An Autobiography of Norman Bel Geddes*. New York: Doubleday, 1960.

Harrar, Heinrich. *Seven Years in Tibet*. New York: E. P. Dutton & Co., Inc., 1954.

Hart, Duff. *The Heights of Riming*. New York: Atheneum, 1981.

Hedin, Sven. *Across the Gobi*. New York: Greenwood Press, 1968.

———. *Central Asia and Tibet*. New York: Greenwood Press, 1969.

Hopkirk, Peter. *Setting the East Ablaze*. New York: W. W. Norton & Co., 1985.

———. *Trespassers on the Roof of the World*. Los Angeles: J. P. Tarcher, Inc., 1982.

Hurt, R. D. *The Dust Bowl*. Chicago: Nelson Hall, 1981.

Jenkins, Peter. *Across China*. New York: Fawcett Crest, 1986.

Kawakami, K. K. *Manchuokuo, Child of Conflict*. New York: Macmillan, 1933.

Larson, F. A. *Larson, Duke of Mongolia*. Boston: Little, Brown Co., 1930.

Lincoln, W. Bruce. *In War's Dark Shadow*. New York: Dial Press, 1983.

Maclean, Fitzroy. *Holy Russia*. New York: Atheneum, 1979.

———. *To the Back of Beyond*. Boston: Little, Brown, 1975.

Mahatmas, M. and K. H. *The Mahatma Letters to A.P. Sinnett*. Madras, India: Theosophical Publishing House, 1979.

Martin, John. *A Picture History of Russia*. New York: Bonanza Books, 1948.

Mead, Marion. *Madame Blavatsky: The Woman Behind the Myth*. New York: Putnam's Sons, 1980.

Meyer, Karl E., and Shareen B. Brysac. *Tournament of Shadows*. Washington, D.C.: Counterpoint, 1999.

Migot, Andre. *Tibetan Marches*. New York: E. P. Dutton & Co., 1955.

New Century. *Cyclopedia of Names*. New York: Appleton Crofts Century, 1954.

Norgay, Tenzing, and J. R. Ullman. *Tiger of the Snows*. New York: Bantam Books, 1955.

Novotny, Ann. *Strangers at the Door*. Riverside, CA: The Chatham Press, Inc., 1971.

Paelian, Garabed. *Nicholas Roerich*. Sedona, AZ: Aquarian Educational Group, 1974.

Phillips, E. D. *The Royal Hordes*. New York: McGraw-Hill, 1961.

Prophet, Mark and Elizabeth. *Lords of the Seven Rays*. Livingstone, MT: Summit University Press, 1986.

Praeger, Frederick. *Encyclopedia of Art*. Vol. 5. Secaucus, NJ: Praeger, 1971.

Przhevalskii, N. A. *From Kulga Across the Tian Shan to Lob-Nor*. New York: Greenwood Press, 1969.

Corona Mundi. *Roerich: A Monograph*. New York: Corona Mundi, 1934.

Roerich, George N. *Trails to Inmost Asia*. New Haven, CT: Yale University Press, 1931.

Roerich, Helena. *Letters of Helena Roerich ,1929–1938*. New York: Agni Yoga Society, Inc., 1954.

———. *At the Threshold of the New World*. Prescott, AZ: White Mountain Education Association, 1998.

Roerich, Nicholas. *Adamant*. New York: Corona Mundi, 1922.

———. *Altai-Himalaya*. Brookfield, CT: Arun Press, 1983.

———. *Heart of Asia*. New York: Roerich Museum Press, 1930.

———. *Himalayas, Abode of Light*. Bombay: Nalanda Kitabistan Publications, 1947.

———. *Himavat, Diary Leaves*. Allahabad, India: Kitabistan 1946.

———. *The Invincible*. New York: Nicholas Roerich Museum, 1974.

———. *Shambhala*. New York: Nicholas Roerich Museum, 1978.

———. *Talashkino*. St. Petersburg: Edition Sodrougestvo, 1906.

Roerich Museum Press. *Roerich Museum: A Decade of Activity, 1921–1931*. New York: Roerich Museum Press. 1931.

———. *Message of 1929*. New York: 1930.

———. *Message of 1930*. New York: 1931.

Roerich Committee. *The Roerich Pact and the Banner of Peace*. New York: 1947.

Saint-Hilaire, Josephine. *On Eastern Crossroads*. New York: Frederick A. Stokes Co., 1930.

Saraydarian, T. *Talks on Agni Yoga*. Sedona, AZ: Aquarian Educational Group, 1987.

Selivanova, Nina. *The World of Roerich*. New York: Corona Mundi, 1922.

Sheean, Vincent. *Lead, Kindly Light*. New York: Random House, 1949.

Sturley, D. M. *A Short History of Russia*. New York: Harper & Row Publishing, 1964.

Tagore, Rabindranath. *A Tagore Reader*. New York: Macmillan, 1961.

Tampy, Padmanaban. *Gurudev Nicholas Roerich*. India.

351

Theosophical Publishing House. *A Brief Life of Annie Besant*. Madras, India: Theosophical Publishing House. 1909.

Thomas, Gordon. *The Day the Bubble Burst*. New York: Doubleday, 1979.

Tomas, Andrew. *On the Shores of Endless Worlds*. New York: G. P. Putnam's Sons, 1974.

———. *Shambhala: Oasis of Light*. London: Sphere Books, 1977.

Vana, zDenek. *The World of the Ancient Slavs*. Detroit: Wayne State University Press, 1983.

MAGAZINES AND NEWSPAPERS

Art and Archaeology up to 1927

El Palacio, 1921–1922, Museum of Fine Arts, Santa Fe, New Mexico

National Geographic, early 1920s

New York Times, 1920–1936

Science in the U.S.S.R., 1986

LIBRARIES AND COLLECTIONS

Art Institute of Chicago, Chicago, Illinois

Federal Bureau of Investigation

Harwood Foundation, Taos, New Mexico

Hewitt Files, History Library, Laboratory of Anthropology, Santa Fe: New Mexico

Herbert Hoover Library, West Branch, Iowa

Archives of Jonson Gallery of the University Art Museum, University of New Mexico, Albuquerque

Library of Congress files

National Archives, Washington, D.C., *Records and Reports of Roerich Expedition*

New Mexico State Library, Santa Fe, New Mexico

Roerich Museum scrapbooks

Franklin D. Roosevelt, Hyde Park, New York

Rosicrucian Research Library

United States Departments of Agriculture, Immigration, Justice, and State

Henry A. Wallace Memorial Library

OTHER SOURCES

Grant, Frances, "Clear-cut Description of the History of the Roerich Museum . . . and the Break Which Occurred in 1935," (unpublished notes).

————. Interview by the author, May–August, 1987

INDEX

Quest Books

encourages open-minded inquiry into
world religions, philosophy, science, and the arts
in order to understand the wisdom of the ages,
respect the unity of all life, and help people explore
individual spiritual self-transformation.

Its publications are supported by
the Kern Foundation,
a trust committed to Theosophical education.

Quest Books is the imprint of
the Theosophical Publishing House,
a division of the Theosophical Society in America.
For information about programs, literature,
on-line study, membership benefits, and international centers,
See www.theosophical.org
Or call 800-669-1571 or (outside the U.S.) 630-668-1571.

RELATED QUEST TITLES

Nicholas Roerich: Messenger of Beauty (video)

Shambhala: The Fascinating Truth Behind the Myth of Shangri-la,
Victoria LePage

To order books or a complete Quest catalog, call 800-669-9425.

Praise for Ruth Drayer's
Nicholas and Helena Roerich

"Drayer's brilliant book brings us all closer to an important insight: 'Truth, Beauty, and Peace are essential and basic to life.' [It] guides us through the powerful artistic and spiritual insights seen and sensed in Russia, Europe, America, and India by truly genius artists and mystics. Unique and compelling, it is an extraordinary contribution to the bridge between heart, art, and the new millennium. Simply a must for those who see and feel spirit through art!"

—Don Campbell, author,
Music: Physician for Times to Come and *The Mozart Effect*

"With profound research and exacting detail, Drayer has done a wonderful job of compiling this long-hidden story set during the turbulent years of intrigue between nations.... Battling political powers and the suspicion that threatened their lives and blocked their journey, Nicholas and Helena Roerich struggled to introduce spiritual realities to the world while seeking Shambhala, the long-unidentified, most holy region of the world. This book reveals their courage and endurance and the significance of their dedication as never before."

—Rev. Carol Parrish-Harra, Ph.D., Dean, Sancta Sophia Seminary;
author, *Adventures in Meditation*

"A beautifully written and illustrated book that reveals the spectacular life of a genius, master artist, and world humanitarian and his mystical wife. Both lives were dedicated to living ethics."

—Joleen D. Du Bois, President, White Mountain Education Association;
publisher, E. I. Roerich's *At the Threshold of the New World*

"This beautiful book will help to broaden the Roerichs' appeal from a specialized audience into the mainstream."

—Daniel Entin, Director, Nicholas Roerich Museum, New York

"Nicholas and Helena Roerich were two of the leading second-generation exponents in the modern revival of the ancient Wisdom Tradition, applying that tradition especially in the realms of art and culture.... Drayer has presented her readers with an absorbing direct view of the lives of these two remarkable twentieth-century figures, whose work continues to echo powerfully in our time."

—John Algeo, Vice President, International Theosophical Society

"This fine, absorbing, and well-written book . . . is impossible to leave, mentally or physically. I can recommend it very highly."

—Lloyd Nick, Director,
Oglethorpe University Museum of Art,
Atlanta, Georgia

"The legacy of these two world servers, Nicholas and Helena Roerich, has opened windows and doors, letting light into dark places and inspiring human minds and hearts to unfold in conformity with the next step forward on the path of spiritual evolution. . . ."

—Mary Bailey, Past President, Lucis Trust

"A penetrating chronicle. . . . Drayer's meticulous conveyance of the material, detail, and spiritual vision pursued by this celebrated Russian artist/philosopher/mystic and his inspired wife led into the world where ancient Buddhist perspectives and premodernist artistic idealism merge."

—Tiska Blankenship, Former Director and Curator,
Jonson Gallery, University of New Mexico Art Museum,
Albuquerque, New Mexico

"This intriguing and inspiring book describes the Roerichs' journeys and world service as they penetrated the inner and higher worlds, questing to unite humanity through bridges of beauty, art, and culture. Striving to present their philosophies through art, their work parallels the lives of other world teachers who upheld the vision of a world united. . . ."

—Lesley Vann, Director,
Sid Richardson Child Development Center

"We greatly admire the work of Nicholas and Helena Roerich and are inspired and heartened by this book. Many people in this country have never heard about these people who were so vital to the culture of the twentieth century. We feel it is important to 'spread the word' and thank you for your efforts."

—Evelyn Hancock, The Lifebridge Foundation

"Helena and Nicholas will touch your heart, stir your dreams, and remind you of the power and perseverance of the human spirit."

—David Raynr, independent filmmaker

Blackstone's

Police Operational Handbook

Blackstone's

Police Operational Handbook 2010

Police National Legal Database

Editor: Ian Bridges

Consultant Editor: Fraser Sampson

OXFORD

UNIVERSITY PRESS

OXFORD
UNIVERSITY PRESS

Great Clarendon Street, Oxford ox2 6DP

Oxford University Press is a department of the University of Oxford.
It furthers the University's objective of excellence in research, scholarship,
and education by publishing worldwide in

Oxford New York

Auckland Cape Town Dar es Salaam Hong Kong Karachi
Kuala Lumpur Madrid Melbourne Mexico City Nairobi
New Delhi Shanghai Taipei Toronto

With offices in

Argentina Austria Brazil Chile Czech Republic France Greece
Guatemala Hungary Italy Japan Poland Portugal Singapore
South Korea Switzerland Thailand Turkey Ukraine Vietnam

Oxford is a registered trademark of Oxford University Press
in the UK and in certain other countries

Published in the United States
by Oxford University Press Inc., New York

© West Yorkshire Police Authority 2010

The moral rights of the authors have been asserted
Database right Oxford University Press (maker)

Crown copyright material is reproduced under Class Licence
Number C01P0000148 with the permission of OPSI
and the Queen's Printer for Scotland

First published 2006
Second edition published 2007
Third edition published 2008
Fourth edition published 2010

British Library Cataloguing in Publication Data

Data available

Library of Congress Cataloging-in-Publication Data

Blackstone's police operational handbook 2010 : police national legal database/
editor, Ian Bridges ; consultant editor, Fraser Sampson.
    p. cm.
  ISBN 978–0–19–957605–0
1. Criminal law—England. 2. Criminal law—Wales. 3. Police—England—
Handbooks, manuals, etc. 4. Police—Wales—Handbooks, manuals, etc.
I. Bridges, Ian. II. Title: Police operational handbook 2010.
  KD7869.6.B55 2009
  344.4205'23—dc22

                                                            2009046859

Typeset by MPS Limited, A Macmillan Company
Printed in Great Britain
on acid-free paper by
L.E.G.O. S.p.A.

10 9 8 7 6 5 4 3 2 1

Preface

This is the fourth edition of the *Blackstone's Police Operational Handbook*, which has been specifically designed to meet the needs of the operational police officer, police community support officer, special constable, or other practitioner who has to interpret and apply the criminal law within our community.

Due to the phenomenal success of the previous editions and the positive comments that we have received it is apparent that the format and contents of the handbook are meeting the needs of our readers and proving to be an invaluable addition to the police officer's 'tool kit'.

Formulated and written by staff from the Police National Legal Database (PNLD) <http://www.pnld.co.uk>, the book covers a wide range of offences and clearly explains and interprets the relevant legislation. It follows the style of the database by providing the wording of the offences, points to prove, meanings, explanatory notes, relevant cases, and practical considerations. In order to assist the officer further, the law/guidance notes are all presented in a 'bullet point', easy-to-understand format; thus at a glance, a quick and informed decision can be made in a host of everyday policing situations.

Although every effort has been made to include as many 'commonly dealt with offences' as possible, the size of the handbook dictates how many offences can be included. However, the number and variety of offences given within the areas of crime, assaults, drugs, sexual offences, public disorder, firearms, road traffic, licensing, and PACE powers and procedures; together with the guidance chapters and useful appendices, should be more than sufficient to cover most eventualities.

The handbook is fully up to date as of 1 July 2009 and includes all recent legislative developments and further changes to the law from the Criminal Evidence (Witness Anonymity) Act 2008, Finance Act 2008, Criminal Justice and Immigration Act 2008, Forced Marriage (Civil Protection) Act 2007, Mental Health Act 2007, Serious Crime Act 2007, UK Borders Act 2007, Road Safety Act 2006; updates to the Police and Justice Act 2006, PACE Codes of Practice; plus guidance on the Proceeds of Crime Act 2002 regarding 'criminal lifestyle' offences and the confiscation of property.

Preface

As a result of the Serious Organized Crime and Police Act 2005, officers are now expected to know what offences are indictable or either way—the mode of trial icons (within each offence) provided in the book give this important information.

Whilst every care has been taken to ensure that the contents of this handbook are accurate, neither the publisher nor the authors can accept any responsibility for any action taken, or not taken, on the basis of the information contained within this handbook.

Please email <police.uk@oup.com> with any comments or queries.

Ian Bridges

Editor

July 2009

Acknowledgements

The Police National Legal Database (PNLD) (<http://www.pnld.co.uk>) is an ACPO managed (not-for-profit) organization, which is subscribed to and well known by all police forces in England and Wales, the Crown Prosecution Service, and other recognized organizations from within the criminal justice system.

The handbook, which is a natural development from our premier electronic database, would not have been created without the foresight and determination of Heather Croft (Business Director), the hard work of Ian Bridges (Legal Adviser), and the support and guidance from staff at the Oxford University Press and Fraser Sampson (Consultant Editor).

Thanks are also extended to the PNLD legal advisers who have contributed to the production of the *Blackstone's Police Operational Handbook*.

Contents

Contents

Contents

Contents

Contents

Contents

Contents

Contents

Contents

APPENDICES

Table of Cases

Table of Cases

Table of Cases

Table of Cases

Table of Cases

European Court of Human Rights

Table of Statutes

Table of Statutes

Table of Statutes

Table of Statutes

Table of Statutes

Table of Statutes

Table of Statutes

Table of Conventions

Abbreviations

A-G	Attorney-General
ACPO	Association of Chief Police Officers
AOABH	Assault Occasioning Actual Bodily Harm
ASBO	Anti-Social Behaviour Order
BB gun	Ball Bearing gun
BTP	British Transport Police
CCTV	Closed-circuit television
CJ	Criminal Justice
CJA	Criminal Justice Act
COP	Code of Practice
CPC	Certificate of Professional Competence
CPR	Cardiopulmonary Resuscitation
CPS	Crown Prosecution Service
CRB	Criminal Records Bureau
CS spray	Named after the initials of the inventors—Corson and Staughton
CSO	See PCSO
DEFRA	Department for Environment, Food and Rural Affairs
DNA	Deoxyribonucleic acid
DPP	Director of Public Prosecutions
DSA	Driving Standards Agency
DVLA	Driver and Vehicle Licensing Agency
ECHR	European Court of Human Rights/European Convention on Human Rights
EPO	Emergency Protection Order
EU	European Union
FMU	Forced Marriage Unit
GBH	Grievous Bodily Harm
GHB	Gamma-hydroxybutrate
GV	Goods Vehicle
HGV	Heavy Goods Vehicle
HIV	Human Immunodeficiency Virus

HMCS	Her Majesty's Courts Service
HMRC	Her Majesty's Revenue & Customs
HOC	Home Office Circular
NAFIS	National Automated Fingerprint Identification System
NHS	National Health Service
NIP	Notice of Intended Prosecution
NPIA	National Policing Improvement Agency
OAPA	Offences Against the Person Act 1861
OFCOM	Office of Communications
PACE	Police and Criminal Evidence Act 1984
PCSO	Police Community Support Officer
PCV	Passenger Carrying Vehicle
PNC	Police National Computer
PND	Penalty Notices for Disorder/Police National Database
POA	Public Order Act 1986
PSV	Public Service Vehicle
RNID	Royal National Institute for Deaf People
SCGC	Self-Contained Gas Cartridge system
SIO	Senior Investigating Officer
SOCA	Serious Organized Crime Agency
SORN	Statutory Off Road Notification
TFPN	Traffic Fixed Penalty Notice
TW	Traffic Warden
TWOC	Taking a Conveyance Without Owner's Consent
UK	United Kingdom
VEL	Vehicle Excise Licence
VOSA	Vehicle and Operator Services Agency
YOI	Young Offenders' Institution

Icons List

SSS **Stop, search, and seize powers** under the Police and Criminal Evidence Act 1984, s 1 or stop, search, and seize powers under a statutory authority given within that chapter.

E&S **Entry and search powers** under the Police and Criminal Evidence Act 1984, ss 17, 18, and 32.

PND **Penalty Notices for Disorder offences** under the Criminal Justice and Police Act 2001, s 1.

TFPN **Traffic Fixed Penalty Notices** under the Road Traffic Offenders Act 1988.

RRA **Racially or Religiously Aggravated offences** under the Crime and Disorder Act 1998 ss 28–32.

CHAR **Offences where evidence of bad character can be introduced** under the Criminal Justice Act 2003, s 103.

TRIG **Trigger offences**—when police can test (request to take samples) for presence of Class A drugs, under the Criminal Justice and Court Services Act 2000, Sch 6.

PCSO **Instances/offences when PCSO can use their standard powers** (or discretionary power(s) if Chief Constable of the force concerned has designated the power(s) in question to PCSO), under the Police Reform Act 2002.

Mode of trial
Indictable, either way, or summary.

Penalty
Sentence (maximum) allowed by law.

Prosecution time limit
The time limit allowed for submission of the file (laying of the information).

Chapter 1

Introduction

1.1 **Human Rights**

Since its introduction the Human Rights Act 1998 has greatly affected operational policing, legislations, and court decisions.

The Human Rights Act 1998 guarantees and encompasses the fundamental rights and freedoms contained in the European Convention. The following summarized sections relate to the police and criminal justice system:

Section 2

Requires a court to take account of the opinions and decisions of the European Court of Human Rights; the Commission and Committee of Ministers when determining a question relating to a **Convention right**.

Section 3

Demands that all United Kingdom legislation must be construed and given effect in such a way as to be compatible with Convention rights.

Section 4

Permits the High Court or Court of Appeal to make a declaration of non-compatibility on any question of United Kingdom law.

Section 6

Makes it unlawful for a **public authority** to act in a way incompatible with a Convention right. This includes a failure to act.

Section 7

Provides for an aggrieved party to take proceedings where a public authority has breached (or proposes to breach) s 6, but only if that person is (or would be) a victim of the unlawful act.

Section 8

Empowers a court to grant such remedy or **relief** within its powers as it considers just and appropriate.

Section 11

Preserves any other right or freedom enjoyed under United Kingdom law.

1.1 Human Rights

Meanings

Convention Right

Means the following rights and freedoms given in **Sch 1**:
- Articles 2 to 12 and 14 of the **Convention**;
- Articles 1 to 3 of the First Protocol;
- Article 1 of the Thirteenth Protocol.

Public authority

This includes:
- a court or tribunal;
- any person (eg a police officer) certain of whose functions are functions of a public nature.

Relief

Includes an award of damages or payment of compensation which can be given through the civil courts, such as the county court or the High Court.

Convention

Means the Convention for the Protection of Human Rights and Fundamental Freedoms, agreed by the Council of Europe at Rome on 4 November 1950 as it has effect for the time being in relation to the UK.

Protocol

Means a protocol to the Convention which the UK has ratified or has signed with a view to ratification.

Schedule 1—Articles

Article 2—Right to life

This right shall be protected by law. No one shall be deprived of life intentionally. Deprivation of life shall not be regarded as being in contravention of this Article if force is used, being no more than absolutely necessary, in order to—
- defend from unlawful violence;
- effect a lawful arrest;
- prevent the escape of a person lawfully detained;
- a lawful action to quell a riot or insurrection.

Article 3—Prohibition of torture

No one shall be subjected to torture or to inhuman or degrading treatment or punishment.

Article 4—Prohibition of slavery and forced labour

No one shall be held in slavery or servitude or be required to perform forced or compulsory labour.

Article 5—Right to liberty and security

No one shall be deprived of these rights save in the following cases and in accordance with a procedure prescribed by law—
- lawful detention (after conviction) by a competent court;
- lawful arrest or detention for failing to comply with the lawful

order of a court or in order to secure the fulfilment of any obligation prescribed by law;
- lawful arrest or detention for the purpose of bringing the person before the competent legal authority on reasonable suspicion of having committed an offence or when it is reasonably considered necessary to prevent his committing an offence or fleeing after having done so;
- detention of a minor by lawful order for the purpose of educational supervision or his lawful detention for the purpose of bringing him before the competent legal authority;
- lawful detention for the prevention of the spreading of infectious diseases, of persons of unsound mind, alcoholics or drug addicts, or vagrants;
- lawful arrest or detention to prevent unauthorized entry into the country or with a view to deportation or extradition.

This Article also deals with:
- promptly being informed as to the reason for arrest/charge;
- entitlement to trial within a reasonable time or release pending trial;
- entitlement to take proceedings for unlawful detention and the right to compensation in these instances.

Article 6—Right to a fair trial

Everyone is entitled to a fair and public hearing within a reasonable time by an independent and impartial tribunal established by law. Protection shall be given against publicity (for all or part of the trial) in the interests of: morals, public order, national security, juveniles, the private lives of the parties, or if it would prejudice the interests of justice.

Furthermore, everyone charged with a criminal offence shall—
- be presumed innocent until proved guilty according to law;
- be informed promptly, in a language which they understand, of the detail, nature, and cause of the accusation against them;
- have adequate time and facilities for the preparation of their defence;
- be allowed to defend themselves in person or through legal assistance of their choosing or be provided with free legal assistance (if insufficient funds) when the interests of justice so require;
- be allowed to produce/examine witnesses for/against him;
- have the free assistance of an interpreter if he cannot understand or speak the language used in court.

Article 7—No punishment without law

No one shall be found guilty of a criminal offence arising out of actions which at the time were not criminal, neither shall a heavier penalty be imposed.

Article 8—Right to respect private/family life

Everyone has the right to respect for their private and family life, home, and correspondence, except where a public authority acts in accordance with the law **and** it is necessary in a democratic society in the interests of national security, public safety, or the economic well-being of the country, for the prevention of disorder or crime, for the protection of health or morals, or for the protection of the rights and freedoms of others.

Article 9—Freedom of thought, conscience, and religion

Everyone has this right, including the freedom to change their religion or belief. These rights can be limited in certain circumstances.

Article 10—Freedom of expression

Everyone has the right to hold opinions and express their views either on their own or in a group without interference by a public authority.

These rights can only be restricted in specified circumstances.

Article 11—Freedom of assembly and association

Everyone has the right to assemble with other people in a peaceful way, to associate with other people, including the right to form and join trade unions for the protection of their interests.

These rights may be restricted, but only in specified circumstances.

Article 12—Right to marry

Men and women of marriageable age have the right to marry and to found a family, according to the national laws governing the exercise of this right.

Article 14—Prohibition of discrimination

The enjoyment of the rights and freedoms set forth in this Convention shall be secured without discrimination on any ground such as sex, race, colour, language, religion, political or other opinion, national or social origin, association with a national minority, property, birth, or other status.

1st Protocol—Article 1 Protection of property, entitled to peaceful enjoyment of possessions

1st Protocol—Article 2 Right to education

1st Protocol—Article 3 Right to free elections

13th Protocol—Article 1 Abolition of the death penalty

Explanatory notes

- Examples of public authorities include: central and local government, the police, immigration officers, prisons, courts and tribunals, and the core activities of private utilities companies that were once publicly owned.
- Section 7(8) stipulates that nothing in the Act creates a criminal offence.
- A criminal trial judge does not have the power to award damages for an alleged breach of a Convention right.
- Infringement of an individual's human rights will be open to examination in every criminal trial, civil or care proceedings, and tribunals.

Related cases

R (on the application of Saunders) v IPCC [2008] EWHC (Admin) 2372, QBD Article 2 imposes a duty to investigate adequately a death resulting from the actions of police officers. In this instance the IPCC were investigating a fatal shooting by the police and no steps were taken to prevent the officers conferring prior to giving their first accounts. Held: that collaboration during the production of witness statements did not breach the Article 2 duty. However this practice was criticized, particularly since the defence provided by s 3 Criminal Law Act 1967 (see **1.2.1**) is personal to the individual officer as to what s/he honestly believed at the time.

Osman v UK (1998) 29 EHRR 245, ECHR The court must be satisfied that the authorities knew, or ought to have been aware, of the existence of a real and immediate risk to the life of an identified individual, from the criminal acts of a third party. Failure to take action within the ambit of their powers which reasonably might be expected to avoid the risk meant the positive obligation under Article 2 would be violated.

R (on the application of Bennett) v HM Coroner for Inner South London [2006] EWHC Admin 196, QBD If a police officer reasonably decides to use lethal force within the law of self-defence or s 3 (see **1.2.1**), then the reasonableness of the use of force has to be decided on the basis of the facts which the user of the force honestly believed to exist and an objective test as to whether he had reasonable grounds for that belief.

Practical considerations

- Police officers should take particular note of s 6, which makes it unlawful for them to act in a way which is incompatible with a Convention right. In order to ensure compliance with this requirement, officers should make themselves familiar with these 'rights' which have been incorporated into this legislation.
- The proportionality and necessity test asks 'were the measures taken **necessary** in a democratic society and in **proportion** to the ultimate objective?' This test should always be borne in mind by a police officer when dealing with an incident, members of the public, or an individual (eg is the force being used proportionate and necessary to prevent disorder, protect life/property, or deal with offenders).
- This test is reflected in the statutory power of arrest (see **12.2**)—unless an officer can show that arrest was **necessary** (eg there was no alternative) then the arrest power cannot be used.
- Before using their powers a police officer should consider this test in their decision-making process and ask themselves—
  - What is the objective to be achieved?
  - Is it urgent or (if desirable) could it be delayed?
  - If action is needed now what are the alternative means of dealing with this incident/individual?
  - Is the proposed action proportionate to the intended aim and the means to be used?
  - Can the least intrusive means be deployed?
  - If not, does a lawful power exist?
- The use of force must always be justified and reasonable otherwise an assault will be committed and any action taken could be rendered unlawful (see **1.2.1**).

- Where excessive force is used there is the possibility of a breach of Article 3 (inhuman or degrading treatment).
- If force is used disproportionately, this may amount to a breach of Article 8, as this Article guarantees not just the right to privacy, but also the right to physical integrity—the right not to be hurt in an arbitrary or unjustifiable way.
- There must be some objective justification for the decision or action taken.
- An important point, often overlooked, is the need to strike a proper balance between the interests and rights of the community at large as well as considering the rights of the individual.
- Lawful interference with an individual's human rights, especially depriving them of these rights, must be necessary and proportionate to the aim required to be achieved (eg lawful arrest/detention of a suspect meets the legitimate aim for the prevention and detection of crime).
- Always consider whether the aim can be met with minimal impact on the rights of the suspect and any other person likely to be affected.
- Article 15 allows governments to 'derogate' from the Convention in time of war or other public emergency threatening the life of the nation.

Links to alternative subjects and offences

1.2 Use of Force Resolution

If a police officer uses force, this must be justified and reasonable and be based on a lawful authority—otherwise it will be an assault and would therefore become an unlawful act.

1.2.1 Lawful authorities for using reasonable force

Statute, common law, and human rights set out the circumstances in which the use of force will be lawful, but each case will be decided upon its own peculiar facts.

Statute

The Criminal Law Act 1967 allows the use of reasonable force in the prevention of crime or making an arrest, and applies to any person, whereas the Police and Criminal Evidence Act 1984 (PACE) relates to the use of reasonable force by a police officer whilst exercising their PACE powers.

Criminal Law Act 1967

(1) A person may use such force as is **reasonable** in the circumstances in the prevention of **crime,** or in effecting or assisting in the lawful arrest of offenders or suspected offenders or of persons unlawfully at large.

(2) Subsection (1) above shall replace the rules of the common law on the question when force used for a purpose mentioned in the subsection is justified by that purpose.

Criminal Law Act 1967, s 3

Meanings

Crime

This refers to crimes committed against domestic law or statute, it does not cover crimes recognized as international law and not given effect in domestic law either by statute or judicial decision (*R v Jones and others; Ayliffe & others v DPP, Swain v DPP* [2006] UKHL 16) (see **4.4**).

Reasonable force

Statutory test for self-defence, preventing crime or making an arrest

(1) This section applies where in proceedings for an offence—
(a) an issue arises as to whether a person charged with the offence ('D') is entitled to rely on a defence within subsection (2), and

---

    (b) the question arises whether the degree of force used by D against a
person ('V') was reasonable in the circumstances.

(2) The defences are—

    (a) the common law defence of self-defence; and

    (b) the defences provided by section 3(1) of the Criminal Law Act 1967
[*use of force in prevention of crime or making arrest* (above)].

(3) The question whether the degree of force used by D was reasonable in
the circumstances is to be decided by reference to the circumstances as
D believed them to be, and subsections (4) to (8) also apply in connection with deciding that question.

(4) If D claims to have held a particular belief as regards the existence of any
circumstances—

    (a) the reasonableness or otherwise of that belief is relevant to the ques-
tion whether D genuinely held it; but

    (b) if it is determined that D did genuinely hold it, D is entitled to rely on
it for the purposes of subsection (3), whether or not—

        (i) it was mistaken, or

        (ii) (if it was mistaken) the mistake was a reasonable one to have made.

(5) But subsection (4)(b) does not enable D to rely on any mistaken belief
attributable to intoxication that was voluntarily induced.

(6) The degree of force used by D is not to be regarded as having been
reasonable in the circumstances as D believed them to be if it was
disproportionate in those circumstances.

(7) In deciding the question mentioned in subsection (3) the following
considerations are to be taken into account (so far as relevant in the
circumstances of the case)—

    (a) that a person acting for a legitimate purpose may not be able to
weigh to a nicety the exact measure of any necessary action; and

    (b) that evidence of a person's having only done what the person hon-
estly and instinctively thought was necessary for a legitimate purpose
constitutes strong evidence that only reasonable action was taken by
that person for that purpose.

(8) Subsection (7) is not to be read as preventing other matters from being
taken into account where they are relevant to deciding the question
mentioned in subsection (3).

(9) This section is intended to clarify the operation of the existing defences
mentioned in subsection (2).

(10) In this section—

    (a) '**legitimate purpose**' means—

        (i) the purpose of self-defence under the common law, or

        (ii) the prevention of crime or effecting or assisting in the lawful arrest
of persons mentioned in the provisions referred to in subsection
(2)(b);

    (b) references to **self-defence** include acting in defence of another per-
son; and

    (c) references to the **degree of force used** are to the type and amount
of force used.

Criminal Justice and Immigration Act 2008, s 76

Case law

Whether the force used in self-defence, preventing crime, or in making an arrest is reasonable or excessive will be determined by the court taking into account all the circumstances. It is important to consider the words of Lord Morris in *Palmer v R* [1971] AC 814, HL which emphasize the difficulties faced by a person confronted by an intruder or in taking any defensive action against attack:

If there has been an attack so that defence is reasonably necessary, it will be recognised that a person defending himself cannot weigh to a nicety the exact measure of his defensive action. If the jury thought that in a moment of unexpected anguish a person attacked had only done what he honestly and instinctively thought necessary, that would be the most potent evidence that only reasonable defensive action had been taken.

> **Police and Criminal Evidence Act 1984**
>
> Where any provision of this Act—
> (a) confers a power on a constable; and
> (b) does not provide that the power may only be exercised with the consent of some person, other than a police officer, the officer may use **reasonable force**, if necessary, in the exercise of the power.
>
> Police and Criminal Evidence Act 1984, s 117

Common Law

Although this area of law is addressed by statute (Criminal Law Act 1967, s 3(2)—above), self-defence under common law is still relevant and may be a consideration (see **2.1.2**).

Human rights

- In addition, under the provisions of the European Convention on Human Rights (see **1.1**), a further dimension in respect of the necessity and proportionality must be considered alongside the common law or statutory powers.
- Apart from using no more force than is absolutely necessary, the further consideration of proportionality will bring other factors into the equation, such as whether the force used is—
  - proportionate to the wrong that it seeks to avoid or the harm it seeks to prevent;
  - the least intrusive or damaging option available at the time.
- Striking a fair balance between the rights of the individual and the interests, rights of the community at large must be carefully considered.
- Any limited breaching of an individual's human rights must be both necessary and proportionate to the legitimate aim to be pursued (eg the lawful arrest or detention of that person is to pursue the legitimate aim of the prevention and detection of crime). Note, however, that certain Articles such as Article 3 cannot be lawfully breached.
- Therefore, any use of powers to cause inhuman or degrading treatment may amount to a breach—words alone may contribute

to the demeaning treatment (eg of prisoners), and under extreme circumstances the use of words alone may suffice.
- If force is not used proportionately, then this may amount to a breach of various Articles of the ECHR (see **1.1** for details)—
  - ◆ Article 2: Use of lethal force, unless the level of force used was strictly proportionate to the lawful aim pursued;
  - ◆ Article 3: If excessive force is used—inhuman or degrading treatment;
  - ◆ Article 8: Guarantees not only the right to privacy/family life, but also the right not to be hurt in an arbitrary or unjustifiable way.

1.2.2 **Evidential considerations**

Police officers should choose the most reasonable, proportionate option available to them after taking the person's behaviour, circumstances and other factors into account.

Force used by an officer at an incident must be justified. Here are some points to consider when preparing your evidence—

Upon arrival

- In uniform or plain clothes?
- Officers at scene/en route?
- Type of vehicle used?
- Observations and perceptions?
- Type of incident?

Upon approach

- Observations and perceptions now?
- Any communications made?
- *Threat assessment* (see **1.2.3**).
- Potential to escalate?

Attitude of individual(s)/group

- Reaction to police instructions?
- Any threats made?

Response of police

- Means used (or attempted) to control situation—
  - ◆ presence, stance taken;
  - ◆ communication skills;
  - ◆ physical control skills:
    - ▪ offensive or defensive.
- Resulting injuries (if any)—all parties?

If the evidence is prepared thoroughly, applying this format, then apart from giving evidence at court in a professional manner, complaints and civil litigation against the force or individual officers would also be reduced.

1.2.3 **Resolution tactics**

Gathering information

Obtain as much information and intelligence as possible, this may come from—
- what an officer—
  - sees;
  - hears;
  - is aware of;
  - feels;
  - is told by a third person;
- local or force systems;
- communications staff;
- experience from previous encounters with suspect.

A police officer's feelings are important and relevant, it is quite acceptable to feel frightened and have reservations. If this is admitted it may help the court or other person(s) to understand why the officer(s) reacted as they did.

Threat assessment

After gathering sufficient information/intelligence, the officer(s) will be able to make a more affective assessment of the threat they face.

These threats to the officer(s) are most likely to emanate from the behaviour of the person(s) they are dealing with. Some issues to consider are—

Person(s) reactions
- Compliant.
- Threats—verbal or by body language.
- Resistant being either—
  - passive;
  - reactive;
  - aggressive;
  - assaults;
  - weapons used.

Factors to consider
Person(s)
- Number of person(s) involved.
- Sex, age, size.
- Potential strength and skill threat.
- Injuries (if any)/physical state.
- Whether consumed alcohol or taken drugs.
- Mental state—aggressive or making threats.
- Their perception, reactions to situation.

Environmental
- Objects/weapons—available or possessed.
- Vehicles at scene.

1.2.3 Resolution Tactics

- Locus features—
  - shelters;
  - concealed/hidden areas;
  - alleys/side roads;
  - properties—licensed premises, schools, private;
  - potential to escalate with other persons in the area;
  - other dangers not mentioned.

Police officer(s)
- Number of officers at scene.
- Number of officers available to assist—distance away/warned.
- Sex, age, size.
- Strength and skill level.
- Physical state—exhaustion level or injured.
- Experience and specialist knowledge.
- Morale, confidence to deal with incident.
- Overall perception of threats, danger, situation.

Once all these factors have been established the threat assessment can be categorized. In order to avoid complacency or complications by grading the incident, it is best to rate it as being either a high or unknown risk.

Use of force options

It is impossible to give all the different combinations of options available to deal with conflict. However, each of the techniques described represents a tactical option. You should always consider the consequences of your actions, including the risk of causing long term and/or significant injury. An option that carries a high risk of serious injury to the person(s), is less likely to be justified where the threat posed carries a limited risk to others.

The tactical option chosen must always be proportionate to the threat faced in all the circumstances.

Response options available
- Mere presence and/or containment.
- Use of communication skills.
- Primary control—empty hand tactics, pressure points, use of handcuffs and baton.
- Secondary control—incapacitants (eg CS spray or Taser).
- Defensive and offensive—escalation in use of unarmed skills and restraints.
- Deadly force—likely to cause serious injury or even death.

Having considered all the above aspects, you are more likely to make the right decision in relation to the action you take.

These tactics can also be applied to a non-conflict policing situation in order to avoid danger or conflict.

There is a need to constantly reassess the situation, because if anything changes, any original intended action may no longer be appropriate.

Links to alternative subjects and offences

1.3 **Managing Crime Scenes**

These guidelines have been adopted as a result of accepted 'best practice' although police officers must always be familiar with force policy and procedures and ensure that these are complied with.

Anybody asked to protect/guard a crime scene must ensure that they are fully briefed about the circumstances of the offence being investigated.

A person chosen to perform this duty must never underestimate the responsibility of this role and its importance to the enquiry, and be aware that at a future date they may be called upon to give evidence at court.

The primary role (and responsibility) of managing a crime scene is to—

• protect the scene from contamination by others; and
• preserve the integrity of everything which could be used as evidence.

Protecting the crime scene

The extent of the scene—

• needs to be established;
• the perimeter clearly marked with tape—denoting that it is a crime scene (remembering that is always easier to reduce the size than expand it later);
• the area needs to be secure and effectively cordoned off;
• if the scene is insecure and problems arise in trying to maintain a sterile scene, then assistance should be provided from the enquiry team.

Explanatory notes

Cordon off a crime scene

• When investigating crime, the police do not have a right to restrict movement on private land. However, in the circumstances of one case (wounding in a private shopping mall), the police were held to have been entitled to assume consent to cordon off the crime scene (*DPP v Morrison* [2003] EWHC 683, HC).
• Sections 34–36 of the Terrorism Act 2000 give the police a power to cordon off an area for a terrorist investigation—for example to carry out a meticulous search for evidence in the wake of a bomb blast.

Maintaining a scene log

An accurate log must be contemporaneously recorded providing—

• a chronological report of any matters of note;
• full details of all authorized people attending, including time/date entering or leaving the scene;
• details/description of any person taking an unusual interest in the area of the crime (together with any vehicle used);
• any suspicious activities in or around the scene should be brought to the attention of the enquiry team as soon as possible.

Managing the scene

A person performing this role must be briefed as to—
- preventing any unauthorized access;
- preventing access to people who are not wearing protective suits;
- updating the SIO or scene manager with any significant matters or developments;
- what can and cannot be said to people.

Dealing with the media

Person(s) protecting the scene of a crime must—
- be mindful of their appearance as they may be filmed or photographed by the media;
- avoid joking with colleagues, which although innocent, may cause offence;
- avoid being seen smoking or chewing gum;
- prevent journalists from breaching the cordon;
- avoid restricting journalists from taking pictures of the scene or talking to members of the public who may be present as long as they remain outside the cordon (the editor will be responsible for determining which pictures are used and details included);
- not offer opinions or views to members of the press. Any enquiries should be directed to the press office.

Preserving the integrity of exhibits

Preservation of a crime scene is of paramount importance in order to ensure that evidence is recovered and its integrity maintained.

Consideration should always be given to—
- weather conditions;
- type of surface;
- visible evidence (eg fingerprints, blood, shoe marks, property);
- other matters (eg Have repairs been carried out? Will the forensic evidence be of any value?).

Any evidential prints/marks or objects that are found outside must be covered in order to protect them from the elements.

Make sure a contact telephone number for the victim is included with the details for the 'scenes of crime officer'.

Fingerprints

- Smooth, clean, and dry surfaces provide the best opportunity for finding and recovering fingerprints. Ensure such items/areas are preserved for examination by the 'scenes of crime officer'.
- Recover removable items found outside and place them against an internal wall to dry. Wet items should not be placed against radiators.
- Any pieces of paper, envelopes, or bin liners left by the offender(s) are often a good source of fingerprints.
- Fingerprints from scenes of crime can now be searched nationally on the National Automated Fingerprint Identification System (NAFIS).

- Details of any genuine suspects should be given to either the attending 'scenes of crime officer' or to the Fingerprint Bureau (eg suspect's name, date of birth, and CRB details, if known).

DNA

- DNA can be present in bloodstains and in saliva. Consequently police officers should be mindful that this can be present in discarded chewing gum, drink cans or bottles, and cigarette ends.
- DNA can also be recovered from saliva, hair, and skin (dandruff) left in masks or balaclavas, or from the handles of tools. Also, semen or other body fluids in sexual offences.
- The national DNA Database is maintained by the Forensic Science Service which collates two profile types of DNA that are—
  - ◆ left at the scene of the crime by the offender—'Scene Samples';
  - ◆ of people arrested and charged or cautioned with a recordable offence—'Criminal Justice (CJ) Samples'.
- Ensure that a DNA CJ sample is obtained from all people who are arrested for a 'recordable offence'.

Shoes

- Shoe marks found at the scene should be preserved (they must show some pattern detail to be of any evidential value). In this regard consider shoes worn by all burglary suspects.
- Surfaces where footwear marks might be present, but not immediately obvious (eg windowsills, linoleum, work surfaces), the mark may be revealed by techniques used by 'scenes of crime officers'.
- Some forces maintain a computerized database of shoes marks and offenders' shoe impressions.

Glass

- Glass can rarely be of strong evidential value, but can be corroborative.
- Consider calling a 'scenes of crime officer' to serious crime scenes where a suspect is in custody, before glass is cleared away.
- Consider also combing a suspect's hair and retaining clothing and shoes for traces of glass as soon as they arrive in custody.

Other items

- Fibres, paint, tool, and glove mark evidence can also connect an individual to a scene.

Forensic procedure

- Evidential items should be placed in brown paper bags, sealed, labelled, and continuity maintained.
- Remember special packaging requirements apply to certain categories of exhibits (eg bladed weapons and fire accelerants) for which specific advice may be obtained from your 'scenes of crime officers'.

- Further details regarding preserving the integrity of evidence in relation to accelerants can be found in arson (see **4.5.2**).

Prisoner handling
- In appropriate cases clothing should be taken from detainees at the earliest opportunity.
- Beware of contamination. Prisoners should be treated as a crime scene and dealt with by officers who have not been to the scene of the offence.
- If more than one prisoner is arrested, ensure they are transported in different vehicles.

Vehicle crime
- Stolen vehicles and vehicles used in crime invariably yield forensic evidence which may be linked to other crimes and provide a valuable source of intelligence.
- Depending on force procedure, where practicable, all stolen vehicles, or those used in crime, should be recovered to a suitable location where there is good lighting and the vehicle can be dried before examination.

Mobile phones
- If the mobile phone is switched on, record what is on the display.
- Do not push buttons other than to turn it off.
- Turn the mobile off.
- Seal in tamper-proof box, making sure buttons cannot be pressed.
- Submit to appropriate forensic supplier, with full details.
- Be aware that fingerprint powder can damage electronic equipment (seek advice).

Continuity
- Unfortunately, many cases are lost because police officers have failed to maintain evidential continuity of exhibits.
- You should be able to account for the exhibit's movements at every stage (point in time), between seizure and production in evidence.
- Ensure that this is maintained and reflected in the Criminal Justice Act witness statements, exhibit logs, and labels.
- Major investigations will have a trained exhibits officer appointed.

Links to alternative subjects and offences

1.4 **Identification Issues**

The area of law dealing with physical identification is quite involved and cannot be dealt with in sufficient detail in this book. However, a brief overview of the subject can be given and the details provided are only meant to be a rough guide.

PACE Code of Practice D

Part 3 of this code deals with identification by witnesses: making a record of first description and then detailing the various identification procedures where the suspect is known/not known.

Record of first description

- A record shall be made of the suspect's description as first given by a potential witness.
- This record of first description must—
  - ◆ be made and kept in a form which enables details of that description to be accurately produced from it, in a visible and legible form, that can be given to the suspect or the suspect's solicitor in accordance with this Code; and
  - ◆ unless otherwise specified, be made before the witness takes part in any identification procedures.
- A copy of the record shall be made where practicable, be given to the suspect or their solicitor before any identification procedures are carried out.
- A detailed description can be very important and should be obtained as soon as possible. If no formal identification of a suspect is made, a factual description may be given in evidence by a witness. This may, for example, be a distinctive tattoo which may help a jury decide if a defendant was responsible for the offence. Although a description is not classed by the courts as a form of identification (*R v Byron The Times,* 10 March 1999).

Identity of suspect not known

- In these cases, a witness may be taken to a particular area to see whether they can identify the person they saw.
- Although the number, age, sex, race, general description, and style of clothing of other people present at the location (and the way in which any identification is made) cannot be controlled, the formal procedure principles shall be followed as far as practicable. Care must be taken not to direct the witness's attention to any individual unless, taking into account all the circumstances, this cannot be avoided.
- Another means of identification can be the showing of photographs, where the witness will be shown no fewer than 12 photographs at a time, which will, as far as possible, be of a similar likeness. An officer of sergeant rank or above shall be responsible for supervising and

directing the showing of photographs. Ensure that the procedure
for the showing of photographs as given in COP D, Annex E is
complied with.
- Although a witness must not be shown photographs, computerized
  or artist's composite likenesses or similar likenesses or pictures
  (including 'E-fit' images) if the identity of the suspect is known
  to the police and the suspect is available to take part in a video
  identification, an identification parade, or a group identification.

Identity of suspect known and available

If the suspect's identity is **known** to the police and they are **available**, the
following identification procedures may be used—
- video identification (COP D, Annex A);
- identification parade (COP D, Annex B);
- group identification (COP D, Annex C).

Video identification

This is when the witness is shown moving images of a known suspect, together with similar images of others who resemble the suspect.
In certain circumstances still images may be used.

Identification parade

This is when the witness sees the suspect in a line of others who resemble
the suspect.

Group identification

This is when the witness sees the suspect in an informal group of people.

Arranging identification procedures

- The arrangements for, and conduct of, the above identification
  procedures and circumstances in which an identification procedure
  must be held shall be the responsibility of an officer not below
  inspector rank who is not involved with the investigation,
  'the identification officer'.
- Generally, another officer or police support staff, can make arrangements
  for, and conduct, any of these identification procedures. Although
  the identification officer must be available to supervise effectively,
  intervene, or give advice.
- Officials involved with the investigation cannot take any part in these
  procedures or act as the identification officer (except where required
  by these procedures).
- This does not preclude the identification officer from consulting with
  the officer in charge of the investigation to determine what procedure
  to use.
- When an identification procedure is required, in the interest of
  fairness to suspects and witnesses, it must be held as soon as
  practicable.

When an identification procedure must be held

- This is whenever—
  - ◆ a witness has identified a suspect or purported to have identified them prior to any of the above identification procedures having been held; or
  - ◆ there is a witness available, who expresses an ability to identify the suspect, or where there is a reasonable chance of the witness being able to do so, and they have not been given an opportunity to identify the suspect in any of the above procedures, and the suspect disputes being the person the witness claims to have seen.
- An identification procedure shall then be held unless it is not practicable or it would serve no useful purpose in proving or disproving whether the suspect was involved in committing the offence (eg when it is not disputed that the suspect is already well-known to the witness claiming to have seen them commit the crime).
- Similarly an identification procedure may be held if the officer in charge of the investigation considers it would be useful.

Selecting the type of identification procedure

- If an identification procedure is to be held, the suspect shall initially be offered a video identification unless—
  - ◆ a video identification is not practicable; or
  - ◆ an identification parade is both practicable and more suitable than a video identification; or
  - ◆ a group identification is the more appropriate method.
- A group identification may initially be offered if the officer in charge of the investigation considers it is more suitable than a video identification or an identification parade and the identification officer considers it practicable to arrange.
- The identification officer and the officer in charge of the investigation shall consult with each other to determine which option is to be offered.
- An identification parade may not be practicable because of factors relating to the witnesses: their number, state of health, availability, and travelling requirements.
- A video identification would normally be more suitable if it could be arranged and completed sooner than an identification parade.
- A suspect who refuses the identification procedure first offered shall be asked to state their reason for refusing and may get advice from their solicitor and/or if present, their appropriate adult.
- The suspect, solicitor, and/or appropriate adult can make representations about why another procedure should be used.
- A record should be made of the reasons for refusal and representations made.
- After considering any reasons given, and representations made, the identification officer shall, if appropriate, arrange for the suspect to be offered an alternative which the officer considers suitable and practicable.

1.4 Identification Issues

- If the officer decides it is not suitable and practicable to offer an alternative identification procedure, the reasons for that decision shall be recorded.

Notice to suspect

Prior to identification procedures being arranged, the following shall be explained to the suspect—

- the purposes of the identification procedures;
- their entitlement to free legal advice;
- the procedures for holding it, including their right to have a solicitor or friend present;
- that they do not have to consent to or co-operate in these identification procedures;
- if they do not consent to or co-operate in these identification procedures, their refusal may be given in evidence and police may proceed covertly without their consent or make other arrangements to test whether a witness can identify them;
- if appropriate, special arrangements for juveniles; mentally disordered or mentally vulnerable people;
- if they significantly alter their appearance between being offered and any attempt to hold an identification procedure, this may be given in evidence and other forms of identification may be considered;
- a moving image or photograph may be taken of them when they attend any identification procedure;
- if, before their identity became known, the witness was shown photographs, a computerized or artist's composite likeness or similar likeness or image by the police;
- if they change their appearance before an identification parade, it may not be practicable to arrange another one and alternative methods of identification maybe considered;
- that they or their solicitor will be provided with details of the first description of the suspect given by any witnesses who are to attend identification procedures.

This information must be in a written notice handed to the suspect, who should then be asked to sign a second copy and indicate if they are willing to take part or co-operate with the identification procedure.

Identity of suspect known but not available

- When the **known** suspect is not **available** or has ceased to be available, the identification officer may make arrangements for a video identification.
- If necessary, the identification officer may follow the video identification procedures but using still images.
- Any suitable moving or still images may be used and these may be obtained covertly if necessary. Alternatively, the identification officer may make arrangements for a group identification.
- The identification officer may arrange for the suspect to be **confronted** by the witness if none of the options referred to above are practicable. If this method of identification is used ensure compliance with COP D, Annex D.

- A confrontation does not require the suspect's consent.
- Requirements for information to be given to, or sought from, a suspect or for the suspect to be given an opportunity to view images before they are shown to a witness, do not apply if the suspect's lack of co-operation prevents this action.

Meanings

Known

Where there is sufficient information known to the police to justify the arrest of a particular person for suspected involvement in the offence.

Available

A suspect being immediately available or will be within a reasonably short time and willing to take an effective part in at least one of the identification procedures which it is practicable to arrange.

Confrontation

This is when the suspect is directly confronted by the witness.

Related cases

R v Turnbull (1976) 63 Cr App R 132, HL This case set out guidelines for dealing with a case involving disputed identification. The jury must examine the circumstances in which the identification was made, in particular—

A—Amount of time under observation.
D—Distance between witness and suspect.
V—Visibility at all times (in what light).
O—Observation impeded/obstructed in any way (traffic, objects or people).
K—Known or seen before, how often, and in what circumstances.
A—Any reason to remember the suspect, if only seen occasionally and not well-known.
T—Time lapse between observation and subsequent identification to police.
E—Error or material discrepancy between description given to police and actual appearance.

In every case where a witness describes a suspect, it is essential to consider these points, all of which should be included in any written statement.

R v Forbes (2001) 1 Cr App R 31, HL When identification is disputed by the suspect, an identification parade shall be held (if the suspect consents) unless unusual appearance, refusal, or other practical alternatives apply. A parade may also be held if the officer in charge of the investigation considers that it would be useful, and the suspect consents. Otherwise there will be a breach of COP D.

R v Smith and others [2008] EWCA Crim 1342, CA Code D provides safeguards that are equally important where a police officer has been asked to attempt to identify someone from a CCTV recording or image.

1.4 Identification Issues

When viewed by the officer a written record must be made as to: initial reactions, recognition or doubt, words used, and factors relating to the image that caused that recognition to occur.

Practical considerations

- Where practicable, the 'first description' from the witness should be recorded in the police officer's pocket notebook, before asking the witness to make any identification.
- Do not assume that the description has been recorded elsewhere.
- Avoid using 'closed' questions (those which only need a 'yes' or 'no' answer) when obtaining description details.
- Care must be taken not to direct the witness's attention to any individual.
- However, this does not prevent a witness being asked to look in a particular direction, if this is necessary to—
  - make sure that the witness does not overlook a possible suspect simply because the witness is looking in the opposite direction; and
  - to enable the witness to make comparisons between any suspect and others who are in the area.
- Where there is more than one witness, every effort should be made to keep them separate.
- A written record should be made of any identification including—
  - date, time, and place when the witness saw the suspect;
  - whether any identification was made;
  - if so, how it was made and the conditions at the time;
  - if the witness's attention was drawn to the suspect (reason for this); and
  - anything said by the witness or the suspect about the identification or the conduct of the procedure.
- It is best practice, for any officer who recognizes a suspect from either a 'still' photograph or CCTV image, to avoid being involved in the arrest of that individual, thereby ensuring they are available to take part in any forthcoming identification procedure, should the identification be disputed.

Links to alternative subjects and offences

Chapter 2
Assaults and Violence

2.1 Assault (Common/Actual Bodily Harm)

What is often thought of (and referred to) as a common assault under s 39 of the Criminal Justice Act 1988 is in fact two separate matters: an assault and/or a battery. This area of law and the meaning of assault are dealt with first, before covering the more serious assault occasioning actual bodily harm under the Offences Against the Person Act 1861. Any defences which may be available (to all assaults) are then discussed.

2.1.1 Common assault—battery

Offence

Common **assault** and **battery** shall be summary offences

Criminal Justice Act 1988, s 39

Points to prove

Assault
- ✓ date and location
- ✓ unlawfully
- ✓ assaulted
- ✓ another person

Battery
- ✓ all points above
- ✓ the application of unlawful force (eg by beating)

Meanings

Assault

Any act, which **intentionally** or **recklessly**, causes another person to apprehend immediate and **unlawful** personal violence (*Fagan v Metropolitan Police Commissioner* [1968] 3 All ER 442, QBD).

Battery

An act by which a person intentionally or recklessly applies force to the complainant.

Intent (see **4.1.2**)

Reckless (see **2.3.1**)

Unlawful (see **2.3.1**)

Explanatory notes

- There are two offences covered by this legislation: 'assault' and 'assault by beating' (battery).
- There is also a civil wrong of assault/battery.
- An 'assault' does not have to involve an actual application of force: it may involve a threat alone, although if violence is threatened, there must be the ability to carry out the threat at the time. Words alone will never amount to an assault. A mere omission to act cannot be an assault.
- In both offences there has to be either an intentional causing of apprehension of immediate unlawful violence or subjective recklessness as to that apprehension.

Defences (see **2.1.2**).

Related cases

McMillan v CPS [2008] EWHC (Admin) 1457, QBD A police officer firmly took hold of the arm of a drunken female to ensure her safety. Force had not been used and it was not against her will. Held not to be an assault as the officer had acted in line with generally acceptable standards of conduct.

Wood v DPP [2008] EWHC (Admin) 1056, QBD A police officer grabbed a person's arm to stop them walking away, with no intention to arrest that person. This action amounted to an unlawful assault.

Haystead v Chief Constable of Derbyshire [2000] 3 All ER 890, QBD A mother was punched by her boyfriend and as a result dropped and injured the baby she was carrying. The defendant was convicted of assault by battery directly on the mother, and indirectly on the baby.

Mepstead v DPP [1996] Crim LR 111, QBD Touching someone to draw their attention may be lawful.

2.1.1 Common Assault—Battery

Fagan v Metropolitan Police Commissioner [1968] 3 All ER 442, QBD It is irrelevant whether the battery is inflicted directly by the body of the offender or with a weapon or instrument such as a car.

Practical considerations

- If racially or religiously aggravated, consider the more serious racially/religiously aggravated offence (see **7.10**).
- An individual should be charged with either 'assault' or 'battery'—the inclusion of both in the same charge is bad for duplicity and could result in the charge being dismissed (*DPP v Taylor* [1992] QB 645, QBD and *DPP v Little* (1994) 95 Cr App R 28, CA).
- Ensure that visible injuries are photographed.
- Include in your CJA witness statement evidence as to intent or recklessness.
- Ascertain whether any of the defences could apply.

Assault

- Unless extenuating circumstances apply, the police/CPS will invariably invite the aggrieved party to take their own action either by criminal prosecution or by civil action.
- Where a court decides that the assault or battery has not been proved or that it was justified, or so trifling as not to merit any punishment, they must dismiss the complaint and forthwith make out a certificate of dismissal. This certificate releases the defendant from any further proceedings (civil or criminal) (Offences Against the Person Act 1861, s 44).
- It the conduct involves threatening acts, words, gestures, or a combination of these, then consider alternative offences under the Public Order Act 1986, breach of the peace or harassment (see **7.8**).

Battery

- Ascertain the degree/severity of injury before charging.
- CPS guidelines specify the following injuries should normally be charged as battery: grazes; scratches; abrasions; minor bruising; swellings; reddening of the skin; superficial cuts; and a 'black eye'.
- Consider ss 47, 20, or 18 of the Offences Against the Person Act 1861 for more serious injuries.

 Summary   6 months

 6 months' imprisonment and/or a fine not exceeding level 5 on the standard scale.

2.1.2 Assault occasioning actual bodily harm (AOABH)/defences to assaults

Offence

Whosoever shall be convicted upon an indictment of any assault **occasioning actual bodily harm** shall be guilty of an offence.

Offences Against the Person Act 1861, s 47

Points to prove

✓ date and location
✓ unlawfully
✓ assaulted
✓ another person
✓ occasioning him/her
✓ actual bodily harm

Meaning of actual bodily harm

Actual bodily harm has been defined as 'any hurt which interferes with health or comfort but not to a considerable degree'.

Explanatory notes

- CPS guidance states that this offence is committed when a person assaults another, thereby causing actual bodily harm to that other person.
- Bodily harm has its ordinary meaning and is that which is calculated to interfere with the health or comfort of the victim, but must be more than transient or trifling.
- Examples of 'actual bodily harm' physical/mental injuries are given in **Practical considerations**.
- A conviction can be obtained if actual bodily harm is caused to the victim by some action which is the natural and reasonably foreseeable result of what the defendant said or did.

Defences to assault

Accident

(as long as malice is not present)

Consent

- This can be expressly given to an application of force (such as tattooing or an operation), providing the activity is not illegal itself (injection of illegal drugs); it can also be implied (by getting into a crowded train where contact is unavoidable).

- A belief by the defendant that consent had been given (or would have been given—emergency surgery to save life) can be a defence, even based on unreasonable grounds, provided that the belief is honestly held.
- Submitting to an assault is not the same as consent. Similarly, consent is negated if given due to duress or fraud (a trick), but the burden of proof is on the prosecution to prove that this was how consent was obtained.
- Consent cannot be given by a child or young person if they fail to understand the true nature of the act (what is involved).
- Consent cannot be given to an assault that inflicts bodily harm of a substantial nature, such as in **sado-masochism** (*R v Brown & others* [1994] 1 AC 212, HL).
- However, some body mutilation in limited and **non-aggressive** circumstances may be acceptable (*R v Wilson* [1996] 2 Cr App R 241, CA).

Lawful sport

- Properly conducted lawful sports are considered to be for the public good and injuries received during the course of an event kept within the rules are generally accepted.
- Players are taken to have consented to any injuries which they might reasonably expect to suffer during the course of the match or contest.
- Criminal charges and proceedings should only be instigated in situations where the player acted outside the rules of the sport and the conduct was sufficiently serious as to be properly regarded as criminal.

Lawful correction

The Children Act 2004, s 58 ensures that parents no longer have the right to use force in the course of reasonable chastisement of their child that would go beyond a s 39 'common assault'.

Section 58 states that in relation to the following offences under—

- sections 18 or 20 (wounding and causing grievous bodily harm);
- section 47 (assault occasioning actual bodily harm);
- section 1 of the Children and Young Persons Act 1933 (cruelty to persons under 16)

the battery of a child cannot be justified on the ground that it constituted reasonable punishment.

Self-defence (case law)

In cases of self-defence—'A jury must decide whether a defendant honestly believed that the circumstances were such as required him to use force to defend himself from an attack or threatened attack; the jury has then to decide whether the force used was reasonable in the circumstances' (R v Owino [1996] 2 Cr App R 128, CA and *DPP v Armstrong-Braun* (1999) 163 JP 271, CA).

Self-defence (statutory test)

Section 76 of the Criminal Justice and Immigration Act 2008 provides a statutory test as to whether force used in self-defence, preventing crime or making an arrest may be considered reasonable in the circumstances (see **'Reasonable force' 1.2.1** for details).

Related cases

H v DPP [2007] EWHC 960, QBD It is not necessary to identify which particular injury had been caused by which defendant provided that some injury resulting in actual bodily harm had been caused by the defendant.

DPP v Smith [2006] 1 WLR 1571, QBD Cutting hair, or applying some unpleasant substance that marked or damaged the hair was capable of being assault causing actual bodily harm. Harm is not limited to injury and includes hurt or damage.

R v Barnes [2004] EWCA Crim 3246, CA Provided guidance on the defence of consent in contact sports (see '**Defences to assaults—Lawful sports**').

T v DPP [2003] EWHC (Admin) 266, QBD Actual bodily harm can also include loss of consciousness (even if there is no other physical injury) because it involves an impairment of the victim's sensory functions.

R v Chan-Fook [1994] All ER 552, CA Lodger was assaulted and then locked in an upstairs room. His fear of further assault was such that he attempted to escape by climbing out of a window and in doing so was injured. Fear alone was not a psychiatric injury and could not therefore amount to AOABH.

R v Brown & others [1994] 1 AC 212, HL Sado-masochists engaged in torture with each other cannot give consent, even though the 'victims' were all willing participants.

Actual Bodily Harm can include causing—
• a psychiatric illness (*R v Ireland* [1998] AC 147, HL);
• mental 'injury' (*R v Chan-Fook* [1994] 2 All ER 552, CA—above);
• shock (*R v Miller* (1953) 118 JP 340, Assize Court).

R v Savage [1992] 1 AC 699, HL and DPP v Parmenter [1991] 3 WLR 914, HL No need to prove any intent to cause injury for assault occasioning actual bodily harm.

R v Donovan (1934) 25 Cr App R 1, CA A person cannot generally consent to someone else using excessive violence against them.

Practical considerations

• If racially or religiously aggravated, consider the more serious racially/religiously aggravated offence (see **7.10**).
• Ensure that visible injuries are photographed.
• Include in your CJA witness statement details of injuries, circumstances of the incident, and any evidence as to intent or recklessness.
• Obtain medical evidence (hospital or doctor).
• Could any of the defences apply or be relied upon by the defendant later?
• CPS charging standards and guidance give examples of injuries which could amount to 'actual bodily harm'—
  ♦ loss or breaking of a tooth or teeth;
  ♦ temporary loss of sensory functions (includes loss of consciousness);

- extensive or multiple bruising;
- displaced broken nose;
- minor fractures;
- minor cuts (not superficial), may require stitches (medical treatment);
- psychiatric injury (proved by appropriate expert evidence) which is more than fear, distress, or panic.

- Consider ss 20 or 18 of the Offences Against the Person Act 1861 for more serious injuries (see **2.3**).

 Either way

 None

 6 months' imprisonment and/or a fine not exceeding the statutory maximum.

Indictment: 5 years' imprisonment.

Links to alternative subjects and offences

2.2 Assault/Resist/Impersonate and Obstruct—Police or Designated/Accredited Person or Emergency Workers

This area of law addresses offences involving assault with intent to resist or prevent lawful arrest; assault or resist or wilfully obstruct either a police constable, designated or accredited person while in the execution of their duty; and obstruct or hinder emergency workers.

2.2.1 Assault with intent to resist or prevent lawful arrest

Section 38 of the Offences Against the Person Act 1861 creates the offence of 'assault with intent to resist or prevent lawful arrest'.

Offences

Whosoever shall **assault** any person with **intent** to resist or prevent the lawful apprehension or detainer of himself or of any other person for any offence shall be guilty of an offence.

Offences Against the Person Act 1861, s 38

Points to prove

✓ date and location
✓ assaulted
✓ with intent to resist/prevent
✓ the lawful apprehension/detention of
✓ self/some other person (including defendant)
✓ for the offence or other relevant reason

Meanings

Assault (see **2.1.1**)

Intent (see **4.1.2**)

Resist or prevent

The Oxford English Dictionary offers the following meanings—

- *resist*—'to strive against, oppose, try to impede or refuse to comply with';
- *prevent*—'stop from happening or doing something; hinder; make impossible'.

2.2.1 Assault with Intent to Resist or Prevent Lawful Arrest

Explanatory notes

- The assault itself need not be any more serious than a common assault (which could be considered as an alternative charge).
- The intention to resist the lawful arrest (either of themselves or another person) must be proved.
- Prevent means to 'stop or render impossible'.

Defences to assault (see 2.1.2)

Related cases

R v Self (1992) 95 Cr App R 42, CA The resisted arrest/detention must have been a lawful one. This can be problematic where s 24A 'citizen's arrests' are made and the arresting person did not have any lawful power to arrest/detain.

R v Lee (2000) 150 NLJ 1491, CA It is not a defence to this offence to hold an honest belief that a mistake is being made by the arresting/detaining officers.

Practical considerations

- It must be proved that—
  - ◆ the arrest/detention was lawful, and
  - ◆ the person concerned knew that an arrest was being made on himself or another.
- Intention (at the time of commission of the offence) can be proved by—
  - ◆ interviewing defendant—admissions made and explanations as to their state of mind, actions, and intentions, and/or
  - ◆ inferences drawn from the circumstances of the offence, evidence from witnesses, property found on defendant or in their control and any other incriminating evidence.
- If this offence is committed by the person initially being arrested, the power of arrest comes from the original offence. Otherwise consider assaulting a police officer in the execution of their duty, or breach of the peace.
- Could any of the general assault defences apply?
- Consideration must be given to CPS guidelines on charging standards and the specific guidance for CPS with intent to resist arrest.

 Either way None

 Summary: 6 months' imprisonment and/or a fine not exceeding the statutory maximum.

Indictment: 2 years' imprisonment

2.2.2 **Assault constable in execution of duty**

The Police Act 1996 consolidates certain legislation relating to the police. Section 89(1) provides the offences of assaulting a constable or person assisting a constable acting in the execution of their duty.

Offences

Any person who **assaults** a constable in the execution of his duty, or a person assisting a constable in the **execution of** his **duty**, commits an offence.

Police Act 1996, s 89(1)

Points to prove

✓ date and location
✓ assaulted a constable or person assisting a constable
✓ in the execution of their duty

Meanings

Assault (see **2.1.1**)

Execution of duty

The officer must be acting lawfully and in the execution of their duty (see related cases).

Explanatory notes

- The duties of a constable have not been defined by any statute (see related cases).
- This offence also applies to police officers from Scotland or Northern Ireland (while in England or Wales) who are acting within statutory powers or executing a warrant.
- Section 30 of the Police Act 1996 defines the jurisdiction of a constable as being throughout England and Wales and the adjacent UK waters. Special constables have the same jurisdiction, powers, and privileges of a constable.

Defences to assault (see 2.1.2).

Related cases (see 2.1.1 for more cases)

DPP v Hawkins [1988] 1 WLR 1166, QBD An arrest was rendered unlawful by a failure to provide reason for arrest as soon as practicable after arrest. The reason could not be given retrospectively.

2.2.2 Assault Constable in Execution of Duty

Collins v Wilcock [1984] 3 All ER 374, QBD A police officer was assaulted after holding the arm of a prostitute in order to detain her just to answer some questions. This act went beyond acceptable lawful physical contact and so constituted a battery; as a result the officer had not been acting in the execution of their duty when assaulted by the prostitute.

Robson v Hallett [1967] 2 All ER 407, QBD An officer may be a trespasser (and therefore not acting in the execution of their duty) if permission to enter or remain on property is withdrawn, but reasonable time must be given to leave property.

Mepstead v DPP [1996] Crim LR 111, QBD Touching someone to draw their attention may be lawful.

DPP v L [1999] Crim LR 752, QBD An unlawful arrest does not mean that the custody staff subsequently act unlawfully in detaining the person.

Practical considerations

- It is vital to prove that the officer was acting lawfully in the execution of their duty at the time of the assault.
- Officers should ensure they are acting within their powers and following relevant requirements or procedures, otherwise they may no longer be acting within the execution of their duty.
- In general, it will be for the defence to show, on the balance of probabilities that the constable was not acting in the execution of their duty.
- The offence does not require proof that the defendant knew or ought to have known that the victim was a constable or that they were acting in the execution of their duty.
- A plain clothes officer should produce identification, as a failure to do so could mean that the officer was acting outside the execution of their duty.
- Section 68 of the Railways and Transport Safety Act 2003 stipulates that the s 89(1) and s 89(2) (see **2.2.3**) offences apply to BTP constables as they apply to other constables in England and Wales.
- Officers should comply with s 28 of PACE as to information to be given on arrest (see **12.2.2**).
- Does any of the general assault defences apply?
- Consideration must be given to CPS guidelines and the specific guidance for this offence relating to injuries received amounting to a battery (see **2.1.1**).
- If the injuries justify a s 47 charge (see **2.1.2**) for a member of the public, then this will also be the appropriate charge for a constable.

 Summary

 6 months

 6 months' imprisonment and/or a fine not exceeding level 5 on the standard scale.

SSS Stop, search, and seize powers

RRA Racially or religiously aggravated offence

2.2.3 **Resist/obstruct constable in execution of duty**

The Police Act 1996 consolidates legislation relating to the police and deals with the offences of resisting or wilfully obstructing a constable in the execution of their duty.

Offences

Any person who **resists** or **wilfully obstructs** a constable in the **execution** of his duty, or a person assisting a constable in the execution of his duty, commits an offence.

Police Act 1996, s 89(2)

Points to prove

✓ date and location
✓ resisted/wilfully obstructed a constable or person assisting
✓ in the execution of constable's duty

Meanings

Resists (see 2.2.1)

Wilful obstruction
In this context it has to be deliberate obstruction.

Execution of duty (see 2.2.2)

Explanatory notes

- Resists does not imply that any assault has taken place and where a person in the process of being lawfully arrested tears himself away from the constable or person assisting, this will constitute resistance.
- The obstruction must be some form of positive act which prevents or impedes the officer in carrying out their duty.
- For the constable's duty and jurisdiction, see **2.2.2**.
- It must be proved that the officer was acting in the execution of their duty.

Related cases

Moss & others v McLachlan (1985) 149 JP 167, QBD A constable is under a general duty to prevent a breach of the peace occurring.

Lewis v Cox [1984] Crim LR 756, QBD A wilful act has to be deliberate and prevent or make it more difficult for the constable to carry out their duty. It is sufficient for defendant to be aware that their actions cause this.

2.2.4 Impersonate Constable or Wear/Possess Uniform

Rice v Connolly [1966] 2 All ER 649, QBD A citizen is entitled to refuse to answer questions or assist/accompany a police officer where no lawful reason exists and therefore this conduct does not automatically amount to resistance/obstruction.

Sekfali and others v DPP [2006] EWHC 894, QBD Citizens have no legal duty to assist the police, but most would accept that it is a moral and social one; however running away and fleeing can amount to an obstruction.

Smith v DPP (2001) 165 JP 432, QBD An officer can take someone aside to aid entry to premises even if there is no obstruction being caused.

Practical considerations (see 2.2.2)

 Summary 6 months

 1 month imprisonment and/or a fine not exceeding level 3 on the standard scale.

2.2.4 Impersonate constable or wear/ possess article of police uniform

Section 90 of the Police Act 1996 deals with the offences of impersonating a member of a police force or special constable or wearing/being in possession of any article of police uniform.

> **Offences**
>
> (1) Any person who **with intent** to **deceive** impersonates a **member of a police force** or **special constable**, or makes any statement or does any act calculated falsely to suggest that he is such a member or constable, shall be guilty of an offence.
> (2) Any person who, not being a constable, wears any **article of police uniform** in circumstances where it gives him an appearance so nearly resembling that of a member of a police force as to be calculated to deceive shall be guilty of an offence.
> (3) Any person who, not being a member of a police force or special constable, has in his possession any article of police uniform shall, unless he proves that he obtained possession of that article lawfully and has possession of it for a lawful purpose, be guilty of an offence.
>
> **Police Act 1996, s 90**

Points to prove

s 90(1) offence

- ✓ date and location
- ✓ impersonated
- ✓ special constable/member of police force
- ✓ with intent to deceive

or

- ✓ with intent to deceive
- ✓ made a statement/did an act
- ✓ which calculated falsely to suggest
- ✓ that you were a special constable/member of a police force

s 90(2) offence

- ✓ date and location
- ✓ not being a constable
- ✓ wore article(s) of police uniform
- ✓ in circumstances which made you appear to resemble
- ✓ being a member of police force
- ✓ so as to be calculated to deceive

s 90(3) offence

- ✓ date and location
- ✓ not being a special constable/member of police force
- ✓ possessed article(s) of police uniform

Meanings

With intent (see **4.1.2**)

Deceive

Means to induce a person to believe a thing to be true which is in fact false, in this case that the person is a police officer.

Member of a police force

This includes a member of the staff of the NPIA who is a constable.

Special constable

Means a special constable appointed for a police area.

Article of police uniform

Means any article of uniform or any distinctive badge or mark or document of identification usually issued to members of police forces or special constables, or anything having the appearance of such an article, badge, mark or document.

Explanatory notes

- Section 68 of the Railways and Transport Safety Act 2003 states that s 90 (impersonation of constable) applies to a constable/special constable of the BTP as it applies in relation to other constables in England and Wales.

- In s 90(2) 'calculated to deceive' has been held to mean 'likely to deceive' (*Turner v Shearer* (1973) 1 All ER 397), although this does not require the defendant to have a specific intent to deceive as with the more serious offence under s 90(1).

> **Defence**—applicable to s 90(3) only
>
> Proof that they obtained possession of the article of police uniform lawfully and possession of it was for a lawful purpose.

Practical considerations

- The burden of proof in relation to the defence of lawful possession under s 90(3) is on the defendant, to prove on the balance of probabilities.
- For the s 90(1) and s 90(2) offences it is not necessary to prove intent to deceive a specific individual, or to prove that the person obtained any form of benefit or advantage as a result of the deception.

 Summary 6 months

 s 90(1)—6 months' imprisonment and/or fine not exceeding level 5 on the standard scale.

s 90(2)—A fine not exceeding level 3 on the standard scale.

s 90(3)—A fine not exceeding level 1 on the standard scale.

2.2.5 **Assault/resist/obstruct designated or accredited person in execution of duty**

Section 46 of the Police Reform Act 2002 refers to offences in respect of suitably designated and accredited people as follows—

> **Offences**
>
> (1) Any person who assaults—
>   (a) a **designated person** in the execution of his duty,
>   (b) an **accredited person** in the execution of his duty,
>   (ba) an **accredited inspector** in the execution of his duty, or
>   (c) a person assisting a designated or accredited person or an accredited inspector in the execution of his duty,
>   is guilty of an offence.

(2) Any person who resists or wilfully obstructs—
   (a) a designated person in the execution of his duty,
   (b) an accredited person in the execution of his duty,
   (ba) an accredited inspector in the execution of his duty, or
   (c) a person assisting a designated or accredited person or an accredited inspector in the execution of his duty,
is guilty of an offence.

Police Reform Act 2002, s 46

Points to prove

✓ date and location
✓ assaulted or resisted/wilfully obstructed
✓ a designated/accredited person/accredited inspector or person assisting
✓ while in the execution of their duty

Meanings

Designated person

Means a person designated under ss 38 or 39 of this Act.

Accredited person

Means a person accredited under s 41 of this Act.

Accredited inspector

Means a weights and measures inspector accredited under s 41A of this Act.

Explanatory notes

- References to the execution of their duties relate to exercising any power or performing any duty by virtue of their designation or accreditation.
- A designated person can be either: a PCSO, investigating officer, detention officer or escort officer employed by the police authority and under the direction/control of the designating chief officer of that force (s 38); or employees of companies contracted to provide detention and escort services so designated by a chief officer (s 39).
- An accredited person is a person whose employer has entered into arrangements for carrying out a community safety function under a community safety accreditation scheme set up by the chief officer for that police area under s 40 and has been granted accreditation by the chief officer under s 41. It can also be a person contracted out under Pt 4 with powers under Sch 5 of the Police Reform Act 2002.
- Under s 41A a chief officer of police may grant accreditation to a weights and measures inspector who is an inspector of weights and measures appointed under s 72(1) of the Weights and Measures Act 1985.

Defences to assault (see 2.1.2)

41

Related cases (see also **2.2.2** and **2.2.3**)

R v Forbes and Webb (1865) 10 Cox CC 362 It is not necessary that the offender knows the person is a designated or accredited person.

Practical considerations (see also **2.2.2** and **2.2.3**)

Given the extensive and detailed restrictions on the powers of these individuals, the precise activities that were involved at the time will be closely scrutinized by a court. It will be critical to establish that the person was acting within the lawful limits of their powers at the time.

 Summary 6 months

 Assaulted/assaulted a person assisting

6 months' imprisonment and/or a fine not exceeding level 5 on the standard scale.

Resisted/wilfully obstructed or resisted/obstructed a person assisting

1 month imprisonment and/or a fine not exceeding level 3 on the standard scale.

2.2.6 Obstruct/hinder emergency workers and persons assisting

The Emergency Workers (Obstruction) Act 2006 creates offences of obstructing/hindering certain emergency workers responding to an emergency, and obstructing/hindering persons assisting such emergency workers.

Offences against emergency workers

A person who without reasonable excuse obstructs or hinders another while that other person is, in a **capacity** mentioned in subsection (2) below, responding to **emergency circumstances**, commits an offence.

Emergency Workers (Obstruction) Act 2006, s 1(1)

Points to prove

- ✓ without reasonable excuse
- ✓ obstructed or hindered
- ✓ emergency worker as described in s 1(2) who is
- ✓ attending/dealing/preparing to deal
- ✓ with emergency circumstances as given in s 1(3) and 1(4)

Meanings

Capacity (of emergency worker)

(2)   The capacity referred to in subsection (1) above is—

    (a) that of a person employed by a fire and rescue authority in England and Wales;

    (b) in relation to England and Wales, that of a person (other than a person falling within paragraph (a)) whose duties as an employee or as a servant of the Crown involve—

        (i)   extinguishing fires; or

        (ii)   protecting life and property in the event of a fire;

    (c) that of a person employed by a relevant NHS body in the provision of ambulance services (including air ambulance services), or of a person providing such services pursuant to arrangements made by, or at the request of, a relevant NHS body;

    (d) that of a person providing services for the transport of organs, blood, equipment or personnel pursuant to arrangements made by, or at the request of, a relevant NHS body;

    (e) that of a member of Her Majesty's Coastguard;

    (f) that of a member of the crew of a vessel operated by—

        (i)   the Royal National Lifeboat Institution, or

        (ii)   any other person or organisation operating a vessel for the purpose of providing a rescue service,

or a person who musters the crew of such a vessel or attends to its launch or recovery.

Emergency circumstances

(3)   For the purposes of this section and section 2 of this Act, a person is responding to emergency circumstances if the person—

    (a) is going anywhere for the purpose of dealing with emergency circumstances occurring there; or

    (b) is dealing with emergency circumstances or preparing to do so.

(4)   For the purposes of this Act, circumstances are 'emergency' circumstances if they are present or imminent and—

    (a) are causing or are likely to cause—

        (i)   serious injury to or the serious illness (including mental illness) of a person;

        (ii)   serious harm to the environment (including the life and health of plants and animals);

        (iii)   serious harm to any building or other property; or

        (iv)   a worsening of any such injury, illness or harm; or

    (b) are likely to cause the death of a person.

Emergency Workers (Obstruction) Act 2006, s 1

Offences against person assisting

(1) A person who without reasonable excuse obstructs or hinders another in the circumstances described in subsection (2) below commits an offence.

2.2.6 Obstruct/Hinder Emergency Workers and Persons Assisting

> (2) Those circumstances are where the person being obstructed or hindered is assisting another while that other person is, in a capacity mentioned in section 1(2) of this Act, responding to emergency circumstances.
>
> Emergency Workers (Obstruction) Act 2006, s 2

Points to prove

✓ without reasonable excuse
✓ obstructed or hindered
✓ a person who was assisting
✓ an emergency worker as described in s 1(2) who was
✓ attending/dealing/preparing to deal
✓ with emergency circumstances as given in s 1(3) and 1(4)

Explanatory notes

- In s 1(2) a 'relevant NHS body' is an NHS foundation trust, National Health Service trust, Special Health Authority, Primary Care Trust, or Local Health Board.
- A person may be convicted of the offence under ss 1 or 2 of this Act notwithstanding that it is effected by: means other than physical means; or action directed only at any vehicle, vessel, apparatus, equipment or other thing or any animal used or to be used by a person referred to in that section.
- For the purposes of ss 1 and 2, circumstances to which a person is responding are to be taken to be emergency circumstances if the person believes and has reasonable grounds for believing they are or may be emergency circumstances.
- Further details on this 2006 Act are dealt with in HOC 3/2007.
- The 2006 Act does not include police or prison officers because obstruction of a police constable is an offence under the Police Act 1996 (see **2.2.3**). This 1996 Act also covers prison officers by virtue of s 8 of the Prisons Act 1952 which stipulates that prison officers, whilst acting as such, shall have all the powers, authority, protection and privileges as a constable.
- See **2.2.5** for assault or resist/wilfully obstruct a suitably designated or accredited person.

 Summary   6 months

 Fine not exceeding level 5 on the standard scale.

Links to alternative subjects and offences

2.3 **Wounding/Grievous Bodily Harm**

Sections 20 and 18 of the Offences Against the Person Act 1861 deal with the offences of 'wounding or inflicting grievous bodily harm' and the more serious 'wounding or causing grievous bodily harm with intent'.

2.3.1 **Wounding or inflicting grievous bodily harm**

Section 20 of the Offences Against the Person Act 1861 provides the offence of 'wounding or inflicting grievous bodily harm'.

Offences

Whosoever shall **unlawfully** and **maliciously wound** or **inflict** any **grievous bodily harm** upon any other person, either with or without any weapon or instrument shall be guilty of an offence.

Offences Against the Person Act 1861, s 20

Points to prove
- ✓ date and location
- ✓ unlawfully
- ✓ maliciously
- ✓ wounded **or** inflicted grievous bodily harm
- ✓ upon another person

Meanings

Unlawfully

Means without excuse or justification at law.

Maliciously

- Means malice (ill-will or an evil motive) must be present.
- 'Maliciously requires either an actual intention to do the particular kind of harm that was done or **recklessness** whether any such harm should occur or not; it is neither limited to, nor does it require, any ill-will towards the person injured' (*R v Cunningham* [1957] 2 All ER 412, CA).

Recklessness

Is one element of the term 'maliciously'; in *R v Cunningham* [1957] 2 All ER 412, CA it was held that the prosecution have to prove that the defendant was aware of the existence of the risk but nonetheless had gone on and taken it.

Wound

Means any break in the continuity of the whole skin.

Inflict

- Inflict does not have as wide a meaning as 'cause'—grievous bodily harm can be inflicted without there being an assault.
- 'Grievous bodily harm may be inflicted either by: directly and violently assaulting the victim; *or* something intentionally done which although in itself is not a direct application of force to the body of the victim, does directly result in force being applied to the body of the victim so that he suffers grievous bodily harm' (*R v Wilson and Jenkins* [1983] 3 All ER 448, HL).

Grievous bodily harm

- Means 'serious or really serious harm' (*R v Saunders* [1985] Crim LR 230, CA).
- Bodily harm can include inflicting/causing a psychiatric harm/illness (silent/heavy breathing/menacing telephone calls—*R v Ireland* [1998] AC 147, HL).
- It could include psychiatric injury, in serious cases, as well as physical injury (stalking victim—*R v Burstow* [1997] 4 All ER 225, HL).

Explanatory notes

- If it appears that the target of the attack was not the actual victim, then the 'doctrine of transferred malice' provides that if a person mistakenly causes injury to a person other than the person whom he intended to attack, they will commit the same offence as if they had injured the intended victim. The doctrine only applies if the crime remains the same and the harm done must be of the same kind as the harm intended (*R v Latimer* (1886) 17 QBD 359, QBD).
- As wounding and grievous bodily harm are both different, the distinction as to which offence is appropriate should be made.

Defences

May be available to a s 20 offence (see **2.1.2**).

Related cases

R v Barnes [2004] EWCA Crim 3246, CA Conduct outside of what a player might regard as having accepted when taking part in contact sports may fall outside defences to assaults. Apart from proving unlawful and malicious, consider the foresight of the risk of harm. Case examined the defences in contact sports (see **2.1.2**).

R v Wilson & Jenkins [1983] 3 All ER 448, HL Frightened by the defendant the victim jumps through a window and breaks a leg. Grievous bodily harm has been 'inflicted' by the offender by inducing substantial fear, even though there is no direct application of force.

2.3.1 Wounding or Inflicting Grievous Bodily Harm

R v Martin [1881–85] All ER 699, CA Defendant came out of a theatre, extinguished the lights, and placed a bar across the doorway. Panic was intended to be the natural consequences of his actions but, if in the ensuing panic, people suffered serious injuries the defendant will have 'inflicted GBH' on those people.

Attorney-General's Reference (No 3 of 1994) [1997] Crim LR 829, HL The doctrine of transferred malice was accepted where the defendant stabbed his girlfriend knowing she was pregnant and the knife penetrated the foetus.

R v Cunningham [1957] 2 All ER 412, CA Meaning of 'maliciously' and recklessness test (above).

R v Savage [1992] 1 AC 699, HL and DPP v Parmenter [1991] 3 WLR 914, HL In s 20 wounding/GBH cases—
- A s 47 assault (AOABH) can be an alternative verdict if it includes implications of assault occasioning actual bodily harm.
- 'Cunningham malice' will suffice. It is enough that the defendant should have foreseen that some physical harm might result—of whatever character.

R v Brown & others [1994] 1 AC 212, HL Consent cannot be given to an assault that inflicts bodily harm of a substantial nature such as in sado-masochism.

R v Wilson [1996] 2 Cr App R 241, CA Some body mutilation in limited and non-aggressive circumstances may be acceptable.

R v Dica [2005] EWCA Crim 2304, CA Inflicting grievous bodily harm by infecting the victim with HIV through unprotected consensual sexual intercourse.

R v Konzani [2005] EWCA Crim 706, CA For a valid defence, there has to be a willing and informed consent to the specific risk of contracting HIV—this cannot be inferred from consent to unprotected sexual intercourse.

Practical considerations

- Consider the more serious racially/religiously aggravated offence (see 7.10).
- In cases of 'transferred malice' the charge must specify at whom the intent was aimed (eg 'A wounded C with intent to cause GBH to B').
- It is not strictly necessary to describe any weapon or instrument used in the actual charge, but it is good practice to do so, particularly if the article has been recovered and is to be produced at court.
- The distinction between 'wound' and 'GBH' must be identified and considered, as they do not have the same meaning.
- Where both a wound and grievous bodily harm have been inflicted, choose which part of s 20 reflects the true nature of the offence (*R v McCready* [1978] 1 WLR 1376, CA).
- The prosecution must prove under s 20 that either the defendant intended, or actually foresaw, that the act would cause harm.

- The prosecution has to prove that the defendant was aware of the existence of the risk but nonetheless went on to take it. It is not necessary to prove these elements in relation to the extent of the specific injuries received.
- The s 18 offence requires intent while s 20 is 'unlawfully and maliciously'.
- A s 47 assault can be an alternative verdict to s 20 if it includes implications of AOABH.
- Consideration must be given to CPS advice and the specific guidance for unlawful wounding/inflicting GBH—
  - The distinction between charges under s 18 and s 20 is one of **intent**. The gravity of the injury resulting is not the determining factor, although it may provide some evidence of intent.
  - Wounding means the breaking of the continuity of the whole of the outer skin, or the inner skin within the cheek or lip. It does not include the rupturing of internal blood vessels.
  - Wounds within this definition are sometimes minor, such as a small cut or laceration. Such minor injuries should more appropriately be charged under s 47. Section 20 should be reserved for those wounds considered to be serious (thus equating the offences with the infliction of grievous, or serious, bodily harm under the other part of the section).
  - Grievous bodily harm means serious bodily harm. Examples of this are—
    - injury resulting in permanent disability or permanent loss of sensory function; injury which results in more than minor permanent, visible disfigurement;
    - broken or displaced limbs or bones, including fractured skull, compound fractures, broken cheekbone, jaw, ribs, etc;
    - injuries which cause substantial loss of blood, usually necessitating a transfusion; injuries resulting in lengthy treatment or incapacity;
    - psychiatric injury. As with assault occasioning actual bodily harm expert evidence is essential to prove the injury.
- Obtain medical evidence to prove extent of injury.
- Obtain photographs of victim's injuries.

 Either way   None

 Summary: 6 months' imprisonment and/or a fine not exceeding the statutory maximum.

Indictment: 5 years' imprisonment.

2.3.2 **Wounding or grievous bodily harm—with intent**

Section 18 of the Offences Against the Person Act 1861 creates the offences of 'wounding or causing grievous bodily harm with intent'.

Offences

Whosoever shall **unlawfully** and **maliciously** by **any means whatsoever wound** or **cause** any **grievous bodily harm** to any person with **intent** to do some grievous bodily harm to any person, or with intent to **resist or prevent** the lawful apprehension or detainer of any person, shall be guilty of an offence.

Offences Against the Person Act 1861, s 18

Points to prove

✓ date and location
✓ unlawfully and maliciously
✓ caused grievous bodily harm or wounded a person
✓ with intent to
✓ do grievous bodily harm or resist/prevent lawful apprehension/detention of self/another

Meanings

Unlawfully (see 2.3.1)

Maliciously (see 2.3.1)

Any means whatsoever

This is given its literal meaning. The only thing that must be proved is a connection between the means used and the harm caused.

Wound (see 2.3.1)

Cause

This has been defined as 'anything that produces a result or effect'.

Grievous bodily harm (see 2.3.1)

Intent (see 4.1.2)

Resist or prevent (see 2.2.1)

Explanatory notes

• Cause has a wider meaning than 'inflict'. All that needs to be proved is some connection between the action (the means used) and the injury (sometimes called the chain of causation). There does not need to be a direct application of force.
• The issue of causation is separate from the test for intent.

- An example would be where the defendant intends to assault a person and kicks down a door, making the victim jump out of the window to escape thereby suffering harm/injuries. There is clearly a causal link between the actions of the defendant and the victim's injuries and the chain of causation is unbroken.
- Intent must be proved either from verbal admissions on interview and/or other and incriminating evidence (eg subsequent actions).
- The statutory test under s 8 of the Criminal Justice Act 1967 must be considered (see **4.1**).
- In relation to the offence of wounding or causing GBH with intent to resist or prevent the lawful arrest/detention of any person the following points must be proved—
  - the arrest/detention must be lawful;
  - the person concerned must know that an arrest is being made on them or another person.

Defences (see 2.1.2).

Related cases

R v Belfon [1976] 3 All ER 46, CA For the offence of wounding with intent the prosecution must prove that the defendant—
- wounded the victim;
- the wounding was deliberate and unjustified;
- with intent to cause really serious bodily harm;
- and the test of intent is subjective.

R v Roberts (1972) 56 Cr App R 95, CA A victim of an ongoing sexual assault jumped out of a car to escape and was seriously injured in doing so. The court considered the actions of a victim which could affect the 'chain of causation' and applied a 'causation test' to determine whether the harm/injury was the natural result of what the assailant had said or done—
- If victim's actions are reasonable ones which could be foreseen and were acceptable under the circumstances, then the defendant will be liable for injuries resulting from them.
- If the harm/injury to the victim is really brought by a voluntary act on the part of the victim which could not reasonably be foreseen, then the chain of causation between the defendant's actions and the harm/injury received will be broken and the defendant will not be liable for them.

Practical considerations (see also 2.3.1)

- Section 18 does not come under racially or religiously aggravated assaults (see **7.10.2**). However, the courts must consider such matters when determining sentence.
- The essential ingredient here is **intent**: either a specific intent to cause grievous bodily harm or intent to resist arrest.
- Proof is required that the defendant specifically intended to cause grievous bodily harm. Knowledge that grievous bodily harm was a virtually certain consequence of their action will not amount to an

2.3.2 Wounding or Grievous Bodily Harm—with Intent

intention, but it *will* be good evidence from which a court can infer such an intention.
- Other factors which may indicate the specific intent include—
  ◆ a repeated or planned attack;
  ◆ deliberate selection of a weapon or adaptation of an article to cause injury, such as breaking a glass before an attack;
  ◆ making prior threats;
  ◆ using an offensive weapon against, or kicking, the victim's head.
- Proof is required that the wound/GBH was inflicted maliciously. This means that the defendant must have foreseen some harm—although not necessarily the specific type or gravity of injury suffered or inflicted.
- Generally an assault under this section may take one of four different forms—
  ◆ wounding with intent to do grievous bodily harm;
  ◆ causing grievous bodily harm, with intent to do grievous bodily harm;
  ◆ wounding with intent to resist or prevent the lawful arrest/ detention of self/any person;
  ◆ maliciously causing grievous bodily harm with intent to resist or prevent the lawful arrest of self/any person.
- Where evidence of intent is absent, but a wound or grievous bodily harm is still caused, then both s 18 and s 20 should be included on the indictment.
- Consideration must be given to CPS advice and the specific guidance for wounding/causing GBH with intent—
  ◆ The distinction between charges under s 18 and s 20 is one of **intent**. The gravity of the injury resulting is not the determining factor, although it may provide some evidence of intent.
- In cases involving grievous bodily harm, remember that s 20 requires the infliction of harm, whereas s 18 requires the causing of harm, although this distinction has been greatly reduced by the decisions in *R v Ireland* [1998] AC 147, HL and *R v Burstow* [1997] 4 All ER 225, HL (see **2.3.1**).
- A s 18 offence includes wounding or causing grievous bodily harm with intent to resist or prevent the lawful detention of any person. This part of s 18 is of assistance in more serious assaults upon police officers, where the evidence of an intention to prevent arrest is clear, but the evidence of intent to cause grievous bodily harm is in doubt.
- Section 6(3) of the Criminal Law Act 1967 permits a conviction of s 20: inflicting grievous bodily harm in respect of a count for s 18 causing grievous bodily harm with intent as 'cause' includes 'inflict' (*R v Wilson and Jenkins* [1983] 3 All ER 448, HL).
- Obtain medical evidence to prove extent of injury.
- Obtain photographs of victim's injuries.

SSS	E&S

♿	Indictable only	🕐	None
🎚	Life imprisonment		

Links to alternative subjects and offences

2.4 **Child Cruelty and Taking a Child into Police Protection**

The Children and Young Persons Act 1933 deals with and tries to prevent any child or young person being exposed to moral or physical danger. Section 1 of the Act creates offences relating to the treatment of children below the age of 16 years by persons with responsibility for them.

This topic area deals with child cruelty and taking a child into police protection.

2.4.1 **Child cruelty**

Offences

If any person who has attained the age of 16 years and has **responsibility** for any **child** or **young person** under that age, wilfully assaults, ill-treats, neglects, abandons, or exposes him, or causes or procures him to be assaulted, ill-treated, **neglected**, abandoned, or exposed, **in a manner likely to cause** him unnecessary suffering or **injury to health** (including injury to or loss of sight, or hearing, or limb, or organ of the body, and any mental derangement), that person shall be guilty of an offence.

Children and Young Persons Act 1933, s 1(1)

Points to prove

✓ date and location
✓ being a person
✓ 16 years or over
✓ having responsibility
✓ for a child/young person
✓ wilfully
✓ assaulted/ill-treated/neglected/abandoned/exposed the child/ young person or caused/procured/the child/young person to be assaulted/ill-treated
✓ in manner likely
✓ to cause unnecessary suffering/injury to health

Meanings

Responsibility (s 17)

• The following shall be presumed to have responsibility for a child or young person—
  (a) any person who—

- (i) has **parental responsibility** for the child/young person; or
- (ii) is otherwise legally liable to maintain the child/young person; and
(b) any person who has care of the child/young person
- A person who is presumed to be responsible for a child or young person by virtue of (a) shall not be taken to have ceased to be responsible by reason only that they do not have care of the child/young person.

Parental responsibility

Means all the rights, duties, powers, responsibilities, and authority which by law a parent of a child has in relation to that child and their property.

Child

Means a person under 14 years of age.

Young person

Means a person who has attained the age of 14 but is under the age of 17 years.

Neglect in a manner likely to cause injury to health

- A parent or other person legally liable to maintain a child or young person, or the **legal guardian** of such a person, is deemed to have neglected in a manner likely to cause injury to health if they have failed to provide adequate food, clothing, medical aid, or lodging, or if, having been unable to do so, they have failed to take steps to procure it to be provided under relevant enactments.
- A person may be convicted of this offence—
  - ♦ even though actual suffering or injury to health, or the likelihood of it, was prevented by the action of another person;
  - ♦ notwithstanding the death of the child or young person in question.

Legal guardian

In relation to a child or young person, means a **guardian** of a child as defined in the Children Act 1989.

Guardian

In relation to a child or young person, includes any person who, in the opinion of the court having cognizance of any case in relation to the child or young person or in which the child or young person is concerned, has for the time being the care of the child or young person.

Explanatory notes

- The term 'ill-treated' is not specifically defined, but will include bullying, frightening, or any conduct causing unnecessary suffering or injury to physical or mental health.
- Under s 58 of the Children Act 2004, battery of a child cannot be justified on the ground that it constituted reasonable punishment (see **2.1.2** 'Defences to assaults')

Practical considerations

- The circumstances that satisfy this offence may justify a more serious charge, such as manslaughter (see **2.7.2**), or causing/allowing the death of a child or vulnerable adult (see **2.7.4**).
- Section 548 of the Education Act 1996 prevents teachers in any school from giving corporal punishment.
- The prosecution must prove a deliberate or reckless act or failure to act. The test is **subjective**, not based on the notion of a reasonable parent or person in charge.
- If a child has been ill-treated by one or both parents, but there is no evidence to suggest which one, it may be possible to consider them jointly responsible.
- Consideration should be given to taking the child/young person into police protection (see **2.4.2**)

E&S

 Either way   None

Summary: 6 months' imprisonment and/or a fine not exceeding the statutory maximum.

Indictment: 10 years' imprisonment and/or a fine.

2.4.2 Taking a child at risk into police protection

The Children Act 1989 comprehensively reformed the law in relation to child welfare. Section 46 of the Act provides for the removal and accommodation of children by police in cases of emergency. The following relates to police powers to take children under 18 years old who are at risk of significant harm into police protection.

Powers

(1) Where a constable has reasonable cause to believe that a **child** would otherwise be likely to suffer significant harm, he may—

    (a) remove the child to suitable accommodation and keep him there; or

    (b) take such steps as are reasonable to ensure that the child's removal from any **hospital**, or other place, in which he is being accommodated is prevented.

(2) For the purposes of this Act, a child with respect to whom a constable has exercised his powers under this section is referred to as having been taken into police protection.

(3) As soon as is reasonably practicable after taking a child into police protection, the constable concerned shall—
  (a) inform the local authority within whose area the child was found of the steps that have been, and are proposed to be, taken with respect to the child under this section and the reasons for taking them;
  (b) give details to the authority within whose area the child is ordinarily resident ('the appropriate authority') of the place at which the child is being accommodated;
  (c) inform the child (if he appears capable of understanding)—
    (i) of the steps that have been taken with respect to him under this section and of the reasons for taking them; and
    (ii) of the further steps that may be taken with respect to him under this section;
  (d) take such steps as are reasonably practicable to discover the wishes and feelings of the child;
  (e) secure that the case is inquired into by an officer designated for the purposes of this section by the chief officer of the police area concerned; and
  (f) where the child was taken into police protection by being removed to accommodation which is not provided—
    (i) by or on behalf of a local authority; or
    (ii) as a refuge, in compliance with the requirements of section 51, secure that he is moved to accommodation which is so provided.
(4) As soon as is reasonably practicable after taking a child into police protection the constable concerned shall take such steps as are reasonably practicable to inform—
  (a) the child's parents;
  (b) every person who is not a parent of his but who has parental responsibility for him; and
  (c) any other person with whom the child was living immediately before being taken into police protection,
  of the steps that he has taken under this section with respect to the child, the reasons for taking them and the further steps that may be taken with respect to him under this section.
(5) On completing any inquiry under subsection (3)(e), the officer conducting it shall release the child from police protection unless he considers that there is still reasonable cause for believing that the child would be likely to suffer significant harm if released.
(6) No child may be kept in police protection for more than 72 hours.
(7) While a child is being kept in police protection, the designated officer may apply on behalf of the appropriate authority for an emergency protection order to be made under s 44 with respect to the child.
(8) An application may be made under subsection (7) whether or not the authority know of it or agree to its being made.
(9) While a child is being kept in police protection—
  (a) neither the constable concerned nor the designated officer shall have parental responsibility for him; but

(b) the designated officer shall do what is reasonable in all the circumstances of the case for the purpose of safeguarding or promoting the child's welfare (having regard in particular to the length of the period during which the child will be so protected).

(10) Where a child has been taken into police protection, the designated officer shall allow—

(a) the child's parents;

(b) any person who is not a parent of the child but who has parental responsibility for him;

(c) any person with whom the child was living immediately before he was taken into police protection;

(d) any person in whose favour a contact order is in force with respect to the child;

(e) any person who is allowed to have contact with the child by virtue of an order under s 34; and

(f) any person acting on behalf of any of those persons,

to have such contact (if any) with the child as, in the opinion of the designated officer, is both reasonable and in the child's interests.

Children Act 1989, s 46

Meanings

Child

Means a person under the age of 18.

Hospital

Any health service hospital within the meaning of the National Health Service Act 2006; **and** any accommodation provided by a local authority and used as a hospital by or on behalf of the Secretary of State under that Act, but not where high security psychiatric services are provided.

Explanatory notes

- The spirit of the legislation is that all the parties including the parents, the child, and the local authority are kept informed and given reasons for any actions. The child's wishes must be listened to but do not have to be acted upon.
- The police have a duty to protect the child until more formal arrangements can be made. It is possible for a child to be in police protection without physically moving them from their present location. For example, if a child is in hospital having been battered, they may be taken into police protection while leaving the child in the hospital.
- This power is appropriate for detaining and returning children missing from home so long as they are at risk from significant harm.

Related cases

Langley and others v Liverpool City Council [2006] 1 WLR 375, CA Section 46 gives the police power to remove and accommodate children in cases of emergency. If practicable removal should be authorized by an emergency protection court order under s 44 and carried out by the local authority. If such an order is in force the police should not exercise their s 46 powers, unless there are compelling reasons for doing so.

Practical considerations

- HOC 44/2003 provides guidance as follows—
  - The designated officer under s 46(3)(e) will usually be an officer of the rank of Inspector.
  - These powers should only be used when the child would be likely to suffer significant harm.
  - Except in exceptional circumstances (eg imminent threat to a child's welfare), no child is to be taken into police protection until the investigating officer has seen the child and assessed their circumstances.
  - An Emergency Protection Order cannot be obtained prior to the birth of a child, even if it is believed that it will be at risk of significant harm after it is born.
  - Consider entry powers under s 17 PACE (see **12.3.2**) as no power of entry is provided under these police protection powers.
  - A police station is not suitable accommodation for these purposes, but may be used as a temporary or emergency measure until suitable accommodation is identified.
  - If it is necessary for a child to be brought to a police station every effort should be made to ensure their physical safety, comfort, access to food and drink, and access to toilet and washroom facilities.
- The Children Act 1989 includes other powers to protect children—
  - s 43—Child assessment orders;
  - s 44—Emergency protection orders;
  - s 47—Duty of local authority to investigate welfare;
  - s 48—Warrant/powers to ascertain if child requires protection;
  - s 50—Recovery of abducted children.
- Similarly the Children Act 2004 has measures to safeguard and promote the welfare of children and obliges a range of parties providing children's services, including the police, to co-operate to improve the well-being of children. This involves the establishment of a Local Safeguarding Children Board for each area, to which the police are a Board partner, and an information database whereby information can be shared between all partners.
- For further advice on instances involving child abuse see **13.2**.

Links to alternative subjects and offences

2.5 **Threats to Kill**

Section 16 of the Offences against the Person Act 1861 provides the offence of threats to kill.

Offences

A person who, without lawful excuse makes to another a threat **intending** that the other would fear it would be carried out, to kill that other or a third person shall be guilty of an offence.

Offences Against the Person Act 1861, s 16

Points to prove

✓ date and location
✓ without lawful excuse
✓ made threat to kill
✓ intending to cause fear threat would be carried out

Meaning of intending (see **4.1.2**)

Explanatory notes

- The offence of 'threats to kill' is a serious offence, particularly given its potential effect on the victim.
- There is no need to show that the defendant intended to kill anyone. The relevant intent has to be that the person receiving the threat would fear the threat (to kill them or a third person) would be carried out.
- An unborn child (foetus in utero) is not a 'third person' for this purpose. Therefore, a threat to a pregnant woman to kill her unborn baby is not an offence under this section.

Defences

- The specific statutory defence to this offence is having a lawful excuse. Such excuse could arise from a number of sources, including the prevention of crime or self-defence.
- The defence will only apply if it was reasonable in all the circumstances to make the threat.

Related cases

R v Rizwan Mawji [2003] EWCA Crim 3067, CA Where a threat to kill was made to a victim by email and they printed that email, it could be adduced in evidence after they had given oral evidence without offending the rules of hearsay.

R v Williams (1987) 84 Cr App R 299, CA On a charge of threats to kill, evidence of a previous assault is admissible by the judge as it went to the seriousness of the threat and tended to prove that the accused intended his victim to take the threat seriously.

R v Cousins [1982] 2 All ER 115, CA A lawful excuse can exist if a threat to kill is made for the prevention of crime or for self defence, provided that it is reasonable in the circumstances to make such a threat.

R v Tait [1990] 1 QB 290, CA An unborn child is not a third person as it is not distinct from its mother. Therefore, a threat to kill the child in the womb or cause a miscarriage will not commit this offence. However, a threat to kill the baby at birth will be an offence under this section.

Practical considerations

- Generally the threats to kill are often made during a heated argument or a moment of aggression and as a result the case usually fails to pass the evidential test required before bringing a prosecution owing to lack of proof of the required intent.
- The onus is on the prosecution to prove that there was no lawful excuse for making a threat. The jury should be directed to any facts that could give rise to a defence of lawful excuse which was reasonable. It is for the jury to decide what is reasonable and what amounts to a threat.
- Consider hearsay and bad character admissibility under the Criminal Justice Act 2003.
- Proof of the mens rea ('guilty mind'), as to the intention that the other person would fear the threat would be carried out to kill that person or a third person is required.
- Evidence of previous history between the parties is admissible as tending to prove that the defendant intended his words to be taken seriously.
- Detail in your file and CJA witness statements the following points—
  - ♦ nature of the threats made—exact words used and in what context, include any previous threats made.
  - ♦ the fact that the threat was **understood** by the person to whom it was made and that the person feared the threat would be carried out.
  - ♦ describe the full circumstances of the incident, antecedent history details of the relationship between the defendant and complainant.
- Does the defendant have a lawful excuse (defence) for making the threat?
- Consider whether or not there are any 'aggravating' circumstances such as racial or religious motivation or terrorism.

 SSS   **E&S**

 Either way   None

 Summary: 6 months' imprisonment and/or a fine not exceeding the statutory maximum.

Indictment: 10 years' imprisonment.

Links to alternative subjects and offences

2.6 **False Imprisonment, Kidnapping, and Child Abduction**

Contained within this topic area are the common law offences of kidnapping and false imprisonment and child abduction under the Child Abduction Act 1984. Officers should be familiar with this area of law for when they deal with any violent domestic incidents, sexual offences, or other cases where people are taken against their will.

2.6.1 **False imprisonment**

False imprisonment is an offence at common law.

Offences

The unlawful and total restraint of the personal liberty of another, whether by constraining them or compelling them to go to a particular place or by confining them in a prison or police station or private place or by detaining them against their will in a public place.

Common Law

Points to prove

✓ date and location
✓ imprisoned, detained, or arrested
✓ another person
✓ against his/her will
✓ unlawfully

Explanatory notes

- The wrongful act ('actus reus') of false imprisonment is the act of placing an unlawful restriction on the victim's freedom in the absence of any legal right to do so.
- There must also have been an element of intent ('mens rea') to restrain, either deliberately or recklessly.
- There is no offence if the victim is not physically restrained, unless the offender detains/intends to detain them by use of fear/threats. Unlawfully locking someone in a vehicle may be sufficient for this offence.

Defences

That the taking or detaining was in the course of a lawful arrest or detention under PACE (see **12.2**) or acting under another statutory or common law power.

Related cases

Bird v Jones (1845) 7 QB 742, QBD Preventing a person from proceeding along a particular way is not false imprisonment.

R v James The Times, 2 October 1997, CA The victim's fear that she was being restrained had to arise from the defendant's intentional or reckless act to frighten her into staying where she was. If the victim's lack of will to escape was simply a by-product of an assault then the offence of false imprisonment is not committed.

R v Rahman (1985) 81 Cr App R 349, CA False imprisonment consists of the unlawful or reckless restraint of a person's freedom of movement from a particular place. 'Unlawful' is not restricted to the contravention of a court order.

Austin v Commissioner of Police of the Metropolis [2009] UKHL 5, HL Detaining thousands of people during a protest demonstration for several hours had not been a deprivation of their liberty in breach of Article 5 (see **1.1**). Under the particular circumstances it was a restraint on their movement (which is not protected under the Human Rights Act) and was compared to holding back a football crowd after the match had ended or the holding of motorists in a queue after an accident. Any steps taken to restrict the liberty of any individual had to be used in good faith, be necessary, and proportionate to the situation, thus preserving the general principle that the restriction should not be arbitrary. Provided those criteria are met it is open to a court to find that crowd control measures in the interests of the community did not infringe Article 5.

Practical considerations

- A parent has no right to imprison their own child, although a parent is allowed to detain a child for purposes of reasonable parental discipline. Whether it is reasonable in all the circumstances is for a jury to decide.
- A victim could bring a civil action for damages (invariably after unlawful arrest by the police). Consider kidnapping (**2.6.2**) or child abduction (**2.6.3**) as alternatives.

 Indictable   None

Life imprisonment and/or unlimited fine

2.6.2 **Kidnapping**

Kidnapping is another offence at common law.

Offences

The taking or carrying away of one person by another, by force or **fraud**, without the consent of the person so taken or carried away, and without lawful excuse.

Common Law

Points to prove

- ✓ date and location
- ✓ without lawful excuse
- ✓ by force/fraud
- ✓ took/carried away
- ✓ another person
- ✓ without their consent

Meaning of fraud

Means deceit/guile/trick. It should not be confused with the narrower meaning given to it for the purposes of consent in sexual offences.

Explanatory notes

- The important points to prove are the deprivation of liberty and carrying away even where a short distance is involved—and the absence of consent.
- In the case of a child it is the child's consent that should be considered (rather than the parent/guardian) and in the case of a very young child, absence of consent may be inferred.

Defences

Consent or lawful excuse.

Related cases

R v Hendy-Freegard [2007] EWCA Crim 1236, CA The victim must have been deprived of their liberty by the kidnapper for the offence to be made out. Inducing a person by deception to move from one place to another unaccompanied by the 'kidnapper' could not constitute a taking and carrying away or deprivation of liberty.

R v Wellard [1978] 3 All ER 161, CA The defendant purported to be a police officer and escorted/placed a female victim into his car a short distance away. Ingredients for the offence of kidnapping are that the victim was deprived of their liberty; and carried away from the place where they wanted to be without lawful excuse.

R v Cort [2003] 3 WLR 1300, CA The defendant went to bus stops telling lone women that the bus they were waiting for had broken down and offering/providing lifts in his vehicle. The fact that the defendant had lied about the absence of the buses meant that, although they had got into the car voluntarily, the women had not given true consent to the journey and the offences of kidnap (and attempts) were complete.

Practical considerations

- A man or woman may be guilty of this offence in relation to their spouse or partner.
- Under s 5 of the Child Abduction Act 1984 (see **2.6.3**), except by or with the consent of the DPP no prosecution shall be instituted for an offence of kidnapping if it was committed—
  - ◆ against a child under the age of sixteen;
  - ◆ by a person connected with the child under s 1 (see **2.6.3**).
- In all other cases the consent of the DPP is not required.

 Indictable None

Life imprisonment and/or unlimited fine

2.6.3 **Child abduction**

The Child Abduction Act 1984 provides the law in relation to the abduction of children. There are two distinct offences: s 1—a person connected with that child (parent/guardian) and s 2—committed by other persons.

Person connected with child

> **Offences**
>
> Subject to subsections (5) and (8) below, a **person connected** with a child under the age of 16 commits an offence if he **takes** or **sends** the child out of the United Kingdom without the **appropriate consent**.
>
> Child Abduction Act 1984, s 1(1)

Points to prove

- ✓ date and location
- ✓ being a parent/person connected with
- ✓ a child under 16 years of age
- ✓ took/sent that child
- ✓ out of the United Kingdom
- ✓ without the appropriate consent

2.6.3 Child Abduction

Meanings

Person connected (s 1(2))

A **person connected** with a child for the purposes of this section is—

(a) a parent of the child; or
(b) in the case of a child whose parents were not married to each other at the time of birth, there are reasonable grounds for believing that he is the father of the child; or
(c) the guardian of the child; or
(ca) a special guardian of the child; or
(d) a person in whose favour a residence order is in force with respect to the child; or
(e) has custody of the child.

Takes

A person is regarded as **taking** a child if they cause or induce the child to accompany them or any other person or causes the child to be taken.

Sends

A person is regarded as **sending** a child if they cause the child to be sent.

Appropriate consent (s 1(3))

(a) This means the consent of each of the following—
  (i) the child's mother;
  (ii) the child's father, if he has parental responsibility for him;
  (iii) any guardian of the child;
  (iiia) any special guardian of the child;
  (iv) any person in whose favour a residence order is in force with respect to the child;
  (v) any person who has custody of the child; or
(b) the leave of the court granted under or by virtue of any provision of Pt 2 of the Children Act 1989; or
(c) if any person has custody of the child, the leave of the court which awarded custody to him.

Explanatory notes

The offence is committed subject to—

- the statutory defences given below;
- a child being in the care of a local authority or voluntary organization or place of safety whilst subject to adoption proceedings.

Defences

(4) A person does not commit an offence under this section by taking or sending a child out of the United Kingdom without obtaining the appropriate consent if—
  (a) he is a person in whose favour there is a residence order in force with respect to the child, and he takes or sends the child out of the United Kingdom for a period of less than one month; or

(b) he is a special guardian of the child and he takes or sends the child out of the United Kingdom for a period of less than three months.

(4A) Subsection (4) above does not apply if the person taking or sending the child out of the United Kingdom does so in breach of an order under Pt 2 of the Children Act 1989.

(5) A person does not commit an offence under this section by doing anything without the consent of another person whose consent is required under the forgoing provisions if—

    (a) he does it in the belief that the other person—

        (i) has consented; or

        (ii) would consent if he was aware of all the relevant circumstances; or

    (b) he has taken all reasonable steps to communicate with the other person but has been unable to communicate with him; or

    (c) the other person has unreasonably refused to consent.

(5A) Subsection (5)(c) above does not apply if—

    (a) the person who refused to consent is a person—

        (i) in whose favour there is a residence order with respect to the child; or

        (ia) who is a special guardian of the child; or

        (ii) who has custody of the child; or

    (b) the person taking or sending the child out of the United Kingdom is, by so acting, in breach of an order made by a court in the United Kingdom.

Child Abduction Act 1984, s 1

Abduction of Child by Other Person

An offence in relation to the taking or detaining of a child where the offender is not connected with that child states:

Offences

Subject to subsection (3), a person other than one mentioned in subsection (2) below, commits an offence if, without lawful authority or reasonable excuse, he **takes** or **detains** a child under the age of 16—

(a) so as to remove him from the lawful control of any person having lawful control of the child; or

(b) so as to keep him out of the lawful control of any person entitled to lawful control of the child.

Child Abduction Act 1984, s 2(1)

Points to prove

✓ date and location
✓ without lawful authority/reasonable excuse
✓ detained or took

2.6.3 Child Abduction

> ✓ a child under 16 years of age
> ✓ so as to remove him/her
> ✓ from/out of the lawful control
> ✓ of a person having/entitled to lawful control
> ✓ of that child

Meanings

Takes

A person is regarded as taking a child if they cause or induce the child to accompany them or any other person or causes the child to be taken.

Detains

A person is regarded as detaining a child if they cause the child to be detained or induces the child to remain with them or any other person.

Explanatory notes

- The offence is committed subject to a statutory defence of consent (s 2(3)—below).
- This offence does not apply to persons listed in s 2(2) namely—
  - the child's father and mother—where the father and mother of the child in question were married to each other at the time of the birth;
  - the child's mother—where the father and mother of the child in question were not married to each other at the time of the birth;
  - any other person mentioned in s 1(2)(c) to (e) above.
- **Remove from lawful control** can be satisfied if the child is induced to take some action that they would not normally have done.

Defences

It shall be a defence for that person to prove—
(a) where the father and mother of the child in question were not married to each other at the time of his birth—
  (i) that he is the child's father
  (ii) that, at the time of the alleged offence, he believed, on reasonable grounds, that he was the child's father, or
(b) that, at the time of the alleged offence, he believed that the child had attained the age of 16 years.

Child Abduction Act 1984, s 2(3)

Related cases

R v Mohammed [2006] EWCA Crim 1107, CA (see 6.7.2 'Related cases')

R v Leather [1993] Crim LR 516, CA Children playing in the park were induced by the defendant to go to another part of the park to look for a stolen bike (which did not exist). No force was used and no attempt was made to restrain them. However, as the children had been deflected from what they would otherwise have been doing into some activity induced by the accused it was held that they had been taken and removed from lawful control.

R v A (Child Abduction) [2000] 2 All ER 177, CA The jury has to be satisfied that the defendant caused the child to accompany them. However, they do not have to be the sole or even the main cause for the child going with them (though the actions must be more than a peripheral or inconsequential cause).

Foster and another v DPP [2005] 1 WLR 1400, QBD Section 2 has two separate offences and alternative charges cannot be made. The mens rea of s 2 is an intentional or reckless taking or detention. It is immaterial that the child consents to removal from lawful control, but the s 2(3)(b) defence is available if it is believed that the child was 16 or over.

Practical considerations

- Consider the more serious offence of kidnapping (see **2.6.2**), but s 5 states that the DPP must consent before a prosecution is brought for a s 1 offence.
- The s 1 offence (person connected with child) can only be committed by those people listed in s 1(2) **and** they must take or send that child out of the UK; the prosecution must rebut the defence of consent and the consent of the DPP is required before proceedings may be commenced.
- A Convention agreement exists between the UK and other countries regarding liaison between the different civil jurisdictions in those countries in order to recover the abducted child.
- Section 2 (other people not connected with the child) will cover the situation where an agent snatches a child for an estranged parent. The parent in such a case may commit the offence of aiding and abetting or the principal offence.

 Either way None

 Summary: 6 months' imprisonment and/or a fine not exceeding the statutory maximum.

Indictment: 7 years' imprisonment.

Links to alternative subjects and offences

2.7 **Suspicious Deaths**

Police officers investigating sudden/suspicious deaths should have a basic knowledge of the relevant law and their powers. Apart from informing supervision, following Force policies/procedures and requesting the assistance of scenes of crime officers, be mindful of scene preservation and the obtaining of forensic evidence (see **1.3**).

Murder; manslaughter; corporate manslaughter, causing or allowing the death of a child/vulnerable adult; 'over-laying' of an infant; infanticide; child destruction; and concealment of birth are all dealt with in this part of the chapter.

2.7.1 **Murder**

The offence of murder comes under the common law and is defined as—

> **Offence**
>
> Where a person of sound mind and discretion unlawfully kills any reasonable creature in being and under the Queen's peace, with intent to kill or cause grievous bodily harm.
>
> Common Law

Points to prove
- ✓ date and location
- ✓ unlawfully killed a human being
- ✓ with intent to kill or cause grievous bodily harm

Meanings

Sound mind and discretion

Every person of the age of discretion is presumed to be sane and accountable for his actions, unless the contrary is proved. This means anyone who is not insane or under 10 years old.

Unlawfully

Means without lawful authority, legal justification, or excuse.

Kills

This is 'the act' ('actus reus') which is the substantial cause of death (stabbed, shot, strangled, suffocated, poisoned, etc).

Reasonable creature in being

Any human being, including a baby born alive having an independent existence from its mother.

2.7.1 Murder

Under the Queen's peace

This is meant to exclude killing in the course of war. A British subject takes the Queen's peace with them everywhere in the world.

Intent

An intention to kill or to cause grievous bodily harm is the 'mens rea' of murder (see **4.1.2**).

Cause/causation

If there is an 'intervening factor' between the defendant's actions and the death of the victim, the jury will consider whether the defendant's act **contributed significantly** to the death.

Grievous bodily harm (see 2.3)

Explanatory notes

- It shall be conclusively presumed that no child under the age of 10 years can be guilty of any offence (Children and Young Persons Act 1933, s 50).
- If a defendant wishes to plead insanity, they will be judged on M'Naghten's Rules from *M'Naghten's Case* (1843) 10 Cl & F 200. This examines the extent to which, at the time of the commission of the offence, the person was 'labouring under such defect of reason from disease of the mind that either: (a) the defendant did not know what they were doing, **or** (b) they did know what they were doing but did not know it was wrong'.
- The onus is on the prosecution to prove that the killing was unlawful.
- If a person intentionally causes grievous bodily harm and the victim subsequently dies as a result, the defendant is guilty of murder.
- Traditionally it required 'malice aforethought', but practically it is the relevant intent that will determine whether an unlawful killing is murder or manslaughter.
- The jury will consider whether the defendant's act **contributed significantly** to the death by applying the 'substantial test' as set out in the case *R v Smith* [1959] 2 All ER 193, Court Martial CA.
- Whether the defendant intended or foresaw the results of their actions will be determined by a number of factors including the statutory test under the Criminal Justice Act 1967, s 8 (see **4.1.2**).

Defences to murder

Insanity

See the meaning of 'sound mind and discretion' and explanatory notes as to 'insanity'.

Lawful killing

Means with lawful authority; legal justification or excuse (see **1.2.1**). Self-defence.

At war

This is self explanatory, not being under the 'Queen's peace' (see 'Meanings').

Specific defences

Provocation

Where on a charge of murder there is evidence on which the jury can find that the person charged was provoked (whether by things done or by things said or by both together) to lose his self-control, the question whether the provocation was enough to make a reasonable man do as he did shall be left to be determined by the jury; and in determining that question the jury shall take into account everything both done and said according to the effect which, in their opinion, it would have on a reasonable man.

Homicide Act 1957, s 3

Diminished responsibility

Where a person kills or is party to the killing of another, he shall not be convicted of murder if he was suffering from such abnormality of mind (whether arising from a condition of arrested or retarded development of mind or any inherent causes or induced by disease or injury) as substantially impaired his mental responsibility for his acts and omissions in doing or being party to the killing.

Homicide Act 1957, s 2(1)

Suicide pact

Means a common agreement between two or more persons having for its object the death of all of them, whether or not each is to take his own life, but nothing done by a person who enters into a suicide pact shall be treated as done by him in pursuance of the pact unless it is done while he has the settled intention of dying in pursuance of the pact.

Homicide Act 1957, s 4(3)

Related cases

R v Rahman and others [2007] EWCA Crim 342, CA The victim had died from a stab wound to the back during an attack by a number of people each of whom had been armed with various types of instrument, but the identity of the person who had actually inflicted the fatal wound was unknown. The case dealt with joint enterprise to inflict unlawful violence, where a principal killed with an intention to kill which was unexpected and unforeseen by the others.

R v Hatton [2005] EWCA Crim 2951, CA Self-defence—not possible if mistake induced by intoxication.

R v Byrne [1960] 3 All ER 1, CA An abnormality of mind (diminished responsibility defence) is a 'state of mind so different from that of ordinary, reasonable human beings that they would call it abnormal'.

2.7.1 Murder

R v Cheshire [1991] 1 WLR 844, CA Even though medical negligence was the primary cause of death, the shooting had been a major contributory factor and the wounds inflicted were a significant cause of death.

R v Smith [1959] 2 All ER 193, Court Martial CA Only if the second cause is so overwhelming as to make the original wound merely part of the history can it be said that the death does not flow from the wound.

R v Malcherek and R v Steel (1981) 73 Cr App R 173, CA A defendant (who causes injury) necessitating medical treatment could not argue that the sole cause of death was the doctor's action in switching the life support system off.

R v Moloney [1985] 1 All ER 1025, HL The jury has to decide whether the defendant **intended** to kill or cause grievous bodily harm.

R v Smith [2001] 1 AC 146, HL Provocation requires some act by the victim, which causes the defendant a sudden temporary loss of self-control. The considerations for the jury in such cases are technically complex and require a consideration of both subjective and objective elements.

Practical considerations

- The defendant's act must be the substantial cause of death.
- The killing must be causally related to the acts of the defendant and not through an intervening factor which breaks the chain of causation.
- If there is doubt whether death was caused by some supervening event (such as medical negligence when treated), the prosecution do not have to prove that the supervening event was not a significant cause of death.
- Intention—mens rea ('guilty mind')—has to be proved (see **4.1.2**).
- The date of the offence is the actual date of death.
- Consent of the Attorney-General is required where—
  - the injury was sustained more than three years before death; **or**
  - the accused has been previously convicted of the offence alleged to be connected with the death.
- If a person is suffering from a terminal disease and receives a wound that hastens their death, this killing would (with the required intent) be murder or manslaughter.
- A murder or manslaughter committed by a British citizen outside the UK may be tried in this country as if it had been committed here (Offences Against the Person Act 1861, s 9, and the British Nationality Act 1948, s 3).
- Motivation will form a key part of any prosecution and will also be relevant in considering the availability of special or general defences.
- Motivation, such as revenge, would mean that a person has had time to think/reflect so negating the defence of provocation (no sudden and temporary loss of self-control) and increasing the likelihood that the defendant foresaw the consequences of their actions and therefore that they intended them to happen.
- Note that the only mens rea that will suffice for attempted murder is an intent to kill and the defence of diminished responsibility cannot be used in answer to such a charge.

• Section 2(1) of the Suicide Act 1961 creates the **offence** of aiding and abetting a suicide: 'A person who aids, abets, counsels or procures the suicide of another, or an attempt by another, shall be liable on conviction on indictment to imprisonment for a term not exceeding 14 years.'

 Indictable None

 Life imprisonment

2.7.2 **Manslaughter**

> **Offence**
>
> Manslaughter is the **unlawful killing** of another human being which can either be a **voluntary** or **involuntary** manslaughter offence.
>
> Common Law

Points to prove

✓ date and location
✓ unlawful act or gross negligence
✓ killed a human being

Meanings

Unlawful killing (see **2.7.1**)

Voluntary manslaughter

This occurs when a murder charge is reduced to voluntary manslaughter by reason of one of the specific defences to murder (see **2.7.1**).

Involuntary manslaughter

Is an unlawful killing without an intention to kill or cause grievous bodily harm. Apart from the required intent, the elements of the offence are the same as for murder (see **2.7.1**). Manslaughter can be caused by:

• **unlawful act** (not omission): The unlawful act must be unlawful in itself (eg another criminal offence such as an assault or a threat to kill) and must involve a risk that someone would be harmed by it;
• **gross negligence** (involving breach of duty): Gross negligence manslaughter requires a breach of a duty of care owed by the defendant to the victim under circumstances where the defendant's conduct was serious enough to amount to a crime.

2.7.2 Manslaughter

Related cases

R v Evans [2009] EWCA Crim 650, CA Considered the duty required in gross negligence manslaughter. Where a person has contributed to a state of affairs which they knew or ought reasonably to have known had created a threat to life then a duty arose for them to act by taking all reasonable steps to save the life at risk.

R v Kennedy [2007] UKHL 38, HL This case considered deaths where the victim was a consenting adult who self-administered drugs of their own free will and also considered their actions in preparing or passing the drugs. In the case of a fully informed and responsible adult it was not possible to find someone guilty of manslaughter where they had been involved in the supply of a Class A drug, which was then freely and voluntarily self-administered by the victim causing their death.

Attorney-General's Reference (No 3 of 1994) [1997] Crim LR 829, HL A baby was born prematurely after an intentional stabbing which penetrated and damaged the foetus. The baby only lived for 120 days. The doctrine of 'transferred malice' was not wide enough to encompass murder, but was sufficient for manslaughter.

R v Roberts, Day (I) and Day (M) [2001] Crim LR 984, CA Intention to cause GBH is murder but an intention only to do some lesser harm is manslaughter.

R v Adomako Sulman & others [1993] 4 All ER 935, HL Manslaughter by gross negligence requires—
* that the defendant owed a duty of care to the victim;
* a breach of that duty;
* which caused the victim's death; and
* in circumstances where the defendant's conduct was so bad as to amount to a criminal act.

R v Misra and Srivastava [2004] All ER (D) 150, CA Grossly negligent medical treatment, which exposes the patient to the risk of death and causes the death of the victim would be manslaughter.

Practical considerations

* Consider corporate manslaughter (see **2.7.3**) in work-related deaths involving negligence by the company/organization.
* The previous convictions or past behaviour of the defendant in homicide cases may well be relevant, both to the issue of mens rea/intent and also to sentence.
* The burden of proof in relation to claiming diminished responsibility or acting in pursuance of a suicide pact lies with the defendant.
* Acts having fatal consequences for another person can arise in a number of forms— from workplace accidents to calculated acts of violence.
* Motivation will form a key part of any prosecution and will also be relevant in considering the availability of special or general defences.
* Motivation such as revenge would mean that a person has had time to think/reflect so negating the defence of provocation (no sudden and temporary loss of self-control) and increasing the likelihood that

the defendant foresaw the consequences of their actions and therefore that they intended them to happen.

- Note that the only mens rea that will suffice for attempted murder is the intention to kill and the defence of diminished responsibility cannot be used in answer to such a charge.
- Section 2(1) of the Suicide Act 1961 creates the **offence** of aiding and abetting a suicide (see **2.7.1**).

 SSS E&S

 Indictable None

 Life imprisonment

2.7.3 **Corporate manslaughter**

The Corporate Manslaughter and Corporate Homicide Act 2007 sets out the offence of corporate manslaughter for an organization, where a gross failure in the way its activities were managed or organized resulted in a person's death.

> **Offence**
>
> (1) An **organisation to which this section applies** is guilty of an offence if the way in which its activities are managed or organised—
>   (a) causes a person's death, and
>   (b) amounts to a gross breach of a relevant duty of care owed by the organisation to the deceased.
>   Corporate Manslaughter and Corporate Homicide Act 2007, s 1

Points to prove

- ✓ date and location
- ✓ being an organization to which s 1 applies
- ✓ managed or organized its activities
- ✓ in a way that caused the death of a person
- ✓ by an act or omission
- ✓ which amounted to a gross breach of a relevant duty of care owed to that person

---

Meanings

Organizations to which s 1 applies

The organizations to which this section applies are—
- a corporation;
- a department or other body listed in **Sch 1**;

2.7.3 Corporate Manslaughter

- a police force;
- a partnership, or a trade union or employers' association, that is an employer.

Schedule 1

This Schedule lists over 40 Government departments and other similar bodies, examples of these are: CPS; DEFRA; Department for Transport; Department of Health; Foreign and Commonwealth Office; HMRC; Home Office; Ministry of Defence; and the Serious Fraud Office.

Explanatory notes

- An organization will be guilty of this offence if the way in which its activities are managed or organized causes a death and amounts to a gross breach of a duty of care owed to the deceased.
- The conduct must fall far below what would reasonably have been expected for it to be a gross breach. Any breaches of health and safety legislation will have to be taken into account—and how serious and dangerous those failures were.
- A duty of care exists for example in respect of the systems of work and equipment used by employees, the condition of worksites or premises occupied by the organization or to products or services supplied to customers. This Act does not create new duties, they are already owed in the civil law of negligence and the offence is based on these.

Practical considerations

- Officers dealing with fatal/potentially fatal work incidents that appear to involve negligence by the company or organization should inform the Health and Safety Executive (see **Appendix 1**), as well as protecting the scene for a potential corporate manslaughter criminal prosecution.
- Currently this offence does not apply to the death of a person detained in police custody. However, when s 2(1)(d) is in force it will apply to a police force.
- Section 2 deals with the '**relevant duty of care**' owed to a person; and s 2(1)(d) states that a duty owed to a person within s 2(2), is someone whose safety the organization is responsible for, namely someone who is—
  - ◆ detained at a custodial institution or in a custody area at a court or police station;
  - ◆ detained at a removal centre or short-term holding facility;
  - ◆ being transported in a vehicle, or being held in any premises, in pursuance of prison escort arrangements or immigration escort arrangements;
  - ◆ living in secure accommodation in which they are placed;
  - ◆ a detained patient.
- Juries will consider how the fatal activity was managed or organized throughout the organization, including any systems and processes for managing safety and how these were operated in practice.

A substantial part of the failure must have been at senior level. Senior level means the people who make significant decisions about the organization or substantial parts of it. This includes both centralized, headquarters functions as well as those in operational management roles.

- Directors, senior managers or other individuals cannot be held liable for this offence, it will be the organization that will be prosecuted. However, individuals can still be prosecuted for gross negligence manslaughter (see **2.7.2**) and for health and safety offences. Individuals will continue to be prosecuted where there is sufficient evidence and it is in the public interest to do so.
- Consent of the DPP is needed before a case of corporate manslaughter can be taken to court. Cases will be prosecuted by the CPS and Health and Safety charges will probably be dealt with at the same time.

 Indictment   None

 An unlimited fine.

2.7.4 **Death of a child or vulnerable adult**

Section 5 of the Domestic Violence, Crime and Victims Act 2004 creates the offences of causing or allowing the death of a child or a vulnerable adult by means of an unlawful act.

Offences

A person ('D') is guilty of an offence if—

(a) a **child** or **vulnerable adult** ('V') dies as result of the **unlawful act** of a person who—
   (i) was a member of the same household as V, and
   (ii) had frequent contact with him,
(b) D was such a person at the time of that act,
(c) at that time there was a significant risk of **serious physical harm** being caused to V by the unlawful act of such a person, and
(d) either D was the person whose act caused V's death or—
   (i) D was, or ought to have been, aware of the risk mentioned in paragraph (c),
   (ii) D failed to take such steps as he could reasonably have been expected to take to protect V from the risk, and
   (iii) the act occurred in circumstances of the kind that D foresaw or ought to have foreseen.

Domestic Violence, Crime and Victims Act 2004, s 5(1)

2.7.4 Death of a Child or Vulnerable Adult

Points to prove

- ✓ date and location
- ✓ being a member of the same household and having had frequent contact with a person who was at that time a child/vulnerable adult
- ✓ caused that person's death or
- ✓ was, or ought to have been, aware that there was a significant risk of serious physical harm being caused to that person
- ✓ by the unlawful act of a member of their household
- ✓ which occurred in circumstances of the kind that the defendant foresaw or ought to have foreseen and
- ✓ the defendant failed to take such steps as they could reasonably have been expected to take to protect them from that risk

Meanings

Child

Means a person under the age of 16 years.

Vulnerable adult

Means a person aged 16 or over whose ability to protect themselves from violence, abuse or neglect is significantly impaired through physical or mental disability or illness, through old age or otherwise.

Unlawful act (see 2.7.2)

Act

This includes a course of conduct and also includes omission.

Member of the same household

This includes people who do not live in that household, providing they visit often and for such periods of time that they are regarded as a member of it.

Serious physical harm

Means grievous bodily harm (see **2.3**).

Explanatory notes

The meaning of a vulnerable adult also includes a temporary vulnerability as well as one which is permanent.

Related Cases

R v Khan and others [2009] EWCA Crim 2, CA This offence imposes a duty on members of the same household to protect children/vulnerable adults where their ability to protect themselves was impaired and vulnerability may be short- or long-term. Furthermore, the defendant was aware of the risk of serious harm and foresaw or ought reasonably to have foreseen that an unlawful act or course of conduct would result in death, and failed to take reasonable steps to prevent the risk.

R v Stephens and Mujuru [2007] EWCA Crim 1249, CA S seriously assaulted M's daughter causing her serious injury, but neither S nor M sought medical intervention for her. Later S inflicted a severe blow to M's daughter's head resulting in her death. The question of M knowing that a significant risk of serious physical harm to her daughter existed was a matter of fact for the jury to decide and the term 'significant risk' is to be given its ordinary meaning.

Practical considerations

- If the defendant was not the mother or father of the deceased then they may not be charged with this offence if they were under the age of 16 at the time of the act that caused the death. Similarly, they could not have been expected to take any such preventative steps to protect the victim before attaining that age.
- Charges can be brought against all members of a household who had responsibility for the death of a child or vulnerable adult.
- Despite this 'catch all' offence the death should still be thoroughly investigated to establish whether the person is responsible for murder or manslaughter.
- The offence is limited to an unlawful act, so it will not apply to accidental or cot deaths. Similarly the offence only applies to household members who had frequent contact with the victim, but is not restricted to family members or carers. It also imposes a duty to protect the victim from harm. However, the question of who is a household member will lie with the courts.

 SSS   **E&S**

 Indictable   None

 14 years' imprisonment and/or a fine

2.7.5 **Over-laying/suffocation of infant under 3 in a bed**

The Children and Young Persons Act 1933 makes specific provision for circumstances where a child has been suffocated while sharing a bed with an adult.

Offence

For the purposes of this section, where it is proved that the death of an infant under three years of age was caused by suffocation (not being suffocation caused by disease or the presence of any foreign body in the throat or air passages of the infant) while the infant was in bed with some other person who has attained the age of sixteen years, that other person shall, if he was, when he went to bed, under the influence of drink, be deemed to have neglected the infant in a manner likely to cause injury to its health.

Children and Young Persons Act 1933, s 1(2)(b)

Points to prove

- ✓ date and location
- ✓ being a person 16 years or over
- ✓ caused the death of an infant under 3 years of age
- ✓ by suffocation
- ✓ while the infant was in bed with that person
- ✓ person under the influence of drink
- ✓ when they went to bed

Explanatory notes

- The circumstances that satisfy this offence might justify a more serious charge, such as manslaughter (see **2.7.2**) and causing/allowing the death of a child (see **2.7.4**).
- Further details relating to s 1 are given at **2.4.1**.

 Either way   None

 Summary: 6 months' imprisonment and/or a fine not exceeding the statutory maximum.

Indictment: 10 years' imprisonment and/or a fine.

2.7.6 **Infanticide**

This offence is committed by the mother of a child (under 12 months old), who by any wilful act or omission, causes the death of her child whilst mentally unbalanced (such as post-natal depression) due to childbirth or lactation.

Offence

Where a woman by any wilful act or omission causes the death of her child being a child under the age of twelve months, but at the time of the act or omission the balance of her mind was disturbed by reason of her not having fully recovered from the effect of giving birth to the child or by reason of the effect of lactation consequent upon the birth of the child, then, notwithstanding that the circumstances were such that but for this Act the offence would have amounted to murder, shall be guilty of a felony, that of infanticide, and may for such offence be dealt with and punished as if she had been guilty of the offence of manslaughter of the child.

Infanticide Act 1938, s 1(1)

Points to prove

✓ date and location
✓ a woman
✓ caused the death of her own child (being under 12 months of age)
✓ by wilful act/omission
✓ whilst balance of her mind disturbed

Practical considerations

- On a count of infanticide, the accused may be convicted of an offence of child destruction under the Infant Life (Preservation) Act 1929 (see 2.7.7).
- The date of offence will be the date death occurs.
- This offence reduces the act to a lesser offence of manslaughter as the responsibility for her actions may have been reduced by the disturbance of her mind caused by childbirth.

SSS E&S

 Indictable   None

 Life imprisonment

2.7.7 **Child destruction**

This is committed by any person, by any wilful act, intentionally destroying a child capable of being born alive, either at or before birth.

.ffence

Any person who, with intent to destroy the life of a child capable of being born alive, by any wilful act causes a child to die before it has an existence independent of its mother, shall be guilty of an offence

Infant Life (Preservation) Act 1929, s 1(1)

Points to prove

- ✓ date and location
- ✓ with intent to destroy the life of a child capable of being born alive
- ✓ by a wilful act (specify)
- ✓ caused the child to die
- ✓ before it had existence independent of mother

Explanatory notes

Capable of being born alive

Evidence that a woman had at any material time been pregnant for a period of 28 weeks or more shall be prima facie proof that she was at that time pregnant with a child capable of being born alive.

Related cases

Rance v Mid-Downs Health Authority [1991] 1 QB 587, QBD An abortion carried out when the baby was capable of being born alive at that stage of the pregnancy would have been unlawful.

Practical considerations

- It has been held that a foetus of between 18 and 21 weeks is not 'capable of being born alive' since it would be incapable of breathing even with the aid of a ventilator, and a termination of a pregnancy of that length is not an offence under this Act.
- No person shall be found guilty of this offence if it is proved that the act was done in good faith for saving the life of the mother.
- A registered medical practitioner does not commit this offence if the pregnancy is terminated in accordance with the provisions of s 5(1) of the Abortion Act 1967.
- Section 58 of the Offences Against the Person Act 1861 relates to administering drugs or using instruments to procure a miscarriage (abortion) at any time between conception and the birth of the child alive, whereas this Act prohibits the killing of any child capable of being born alive.

Indictable None

 Life imprisonment

2.7.8 **Concealment of birth**

Although this is not an offence of unlawful killing it is related to topics already discussed and concerns the offence of concealing the birth of a child, by secretly disposing of or hiding the body.

Offence

If any woman shall be delivered of a child, every person who shall, by any secret disposition of the dead body of the said child, whether such child died before, at, or after its birth, endeavour to conceal the birth thereof, shall be guilty of a misdemeanour, and being convicted thereof shall be liable, at the discretion of the court, to be imprisoned.

Offences Against the Person Act 1861, s 60

Points to prove

✓ date and location
✓ endeavoured to conceal the birth of a child
✓ by secret disposition of the dead body of the child

Related cases

R v Brown (1870) LR 1 CCR 244 'If the body were placed in the middle of a moor in winter, or on the top of a mountain, or in any other secluded place, where the body would not likely to be found', it would amount to a secret disposition.

R v Berriman (1854) 6 Cox 388 Concealment of a foetus only a few months old would not be an offence—'the child must have arrived at that stage of maturity at the time of birth that it might have been a living child'.

Practical considerations

- The offence is specific in that it must be a 'secret disposition'; the test being whether there is a likelihood that the body would be found.
- Where the body is put in a secluded place, even though it is not actually concealed from view, it may nevertheless be a secret disposition.

2.7.8 Concealment of Birth

- However, where a body was left in an area which is used regularly this would not be a secret disposition. Similarly, the same would apply to leaving a body in a dustbin awaiting collection.
- The defendant must be shown to have done some act of disposition **after** the child has died. If the living body of a child is concealed and then it dies where it is concealed, clearly a more serious offence of homicide should be considered.

 Either way

 None

 Summary: 6 months' imprisonment and/or a fine not exceeding the statutory maximum.

Indictment: 2 years' imprisonment.

Links to alternative subjects and offences

Chapter 3

Crime: Dishonesty

3.1 **Theft**

The Theft Act 1968 provides for the offence of theft and several other key offences of which theft is a constituent part. Section 1 of the Act provides for the offence of theft, while s 11 covers the offence of removing articles from places open to the public and s 23 concerns advertising rewards for the return of stolen or lost goods.

3.1.1 **Theft**

Theft is defined by s 1 of the Act, while ss 2–6 explain the elements contained within that definition.

> **Offence**
>
> A person is guilty of theft if he **dishonestly appropriates property belonging to another** with the **intention of permanently depriving** the other of it; and 'thief' and 'steal' shall be construed accordingly.
>
> Theft Act 1968, s 1(1)

Points to prove

✓ dishonestly
✓ appropriates
✓ property
✓ belonging to another
✓ intention to permanently deprive the other of it.

Meanings
Dishonestly
Section 2 defines what will not be considered as 'dishonest'.

3.1.1 **Theft**

- It is not considered dishonest if a person takes possession of property belonging to another, whether for themselves or a third person, believing that they have a legal right to deprive the other of it.
- It is not considered dishonest to take property belonging to another believing that, if the other had known about it and the circumstances, they would have consented.
- It will not be dishonest if, not being a trustee or personal representative, a person takes possession of property believing that, by taking reasonable steps, the owner could not be discovered.
- It is for the court to decide if a person acted dishonestly (see '**Related cases**' *R v Ghosh*).
- Taking property belonging to another may be dishonest even if the perpetrator is willing to pay for it.

Appropriates

'Appropriates' is defined in s 3.
- If a person assumes the rights of an owner over property they are deemed to have appropriated it. This includes where they obtain the property without stealing and later assumes such rights by keeping or dealing with it as the owner.
- Where property (or a right or interest in it) is transferred to a person for its true value, any later assumption by the acquirer as to the rights of ownership will not amount to theft simply because the transferor had no right to transfer it.

Property

'Property' is defined by s 4.
- It includes money and all other property (real or personal) including 'things in action' and other intangible property.
- Land, or things forming part of it, and taken from it by a person or on their instructions, can only be stolen if—
  - ♦ the person is a trustee or personal representative, or is authorized by power of attorney, as a company liquidator, or in some other way, to sell or dispose of land belonging to somebody else, and they appropriate it or anything forming part of it, by dealing with it in breach of the confidence entrusted in them, or
  - ♦ when the person is not in possession of the land, they appropriate anything forming part of it by severing it, causing it to be severed or after it has been severed, or
  - ♦ when, being in possession of the land under a tenancy, they appropriate all or part of a fixture or structure let for use with that land.
- Mushrooms (and other fungi), flowers, plants (including shrubs and trees), and fruit or foliage from a plant are all capable of being 'property' for the purposes of theft. Picking mushrooms, flowers, fruit, or foliage **growing wild** on land is not theft unless it is done for reward, sale, or other commercial purpose.
- Wild creatures, tamed or untamed, are regarded as property. However, a wild creature which is not tamed or normally kept in captivity (or the

carcass of such animal) cannot be stolen unless it has been taken into possession by or on behalf of another, and such possession has not been lost or given up, or it is in the process of being taken into possession.

Belonging to another

'Belonging to another' is defined by s 5.

- Property belongs to any person having possession or control of it, or having a proprietary right or interest in it (such interest not being valid only because of an agreement to transfer or grant it).
- Where property is subject to a trust, ownership includes the right to enforce that trust, and any intention to break it is regarded as intending to deprive a person having such right.
- Where a person receives property from or on account of another, and is under an obligation to the other to retain and deal with that property or its proceeds in a particular way, the property or proceeds shall be regarded (as against them) as belonging to the other.
- When a person obtains property because of another's mistake, and they are obliged to repay all or part of it, its proceeds or value then, to the extent of that obligation, the property or proceeds are regarded as belonging to the person entitled to restoration, and any intent not to repay it is an intention to deprive them of it.

Intention to permanently deprive

'Intention to permanently deprive' is defined by s 6.

- Appropriation of property belonging to another without meaning them permanently to lose it still has the intention of 'permanently depriving' them of it, if the appropriator intends to treat it as their own to dispose of regardless of the other's rights.
- Borrowing or lending the property may amount to treating it as their own if it is for a period and in circumstances equating to an outright taking or disposal.
- Where a person has possession or control of another's property, for their own purposes and without the other's permission, loans it to a third person with unachievable conditions for its return, they treat it as their own to dispose of regardless of the other's rights (eg pawning property belonging to another when not able to redeem it).

Explanatory notes

- It is immaterial whether the appropriation is made with a view to gain, or is made for the thief's own benefit.
- 'Things in action' include a cheque drawn to a payee, giving them an action (demand for payment), which they may enforce against the payer. It is, therefore, the property of the payee.
- 'Intangible property' includes patents, applications for patents, copyrights.
- 'Tenancy' means a tenancy for any period and includes a tenancy agreement, but a person who, when a tenancy ends, remains in

possession as statutory tenant or otherwise will be treated as having possession under the tenancy.

- Possession, in general terms, means having the right to use property as your own without having any legal title to it (eg hiring a car—you have possession while legal ownership remains with the hire company).
- Possession may be 'actual' (an item in your hand or pocket) or 'constructive' (an item at your home while you are elsewhere).
- Control means having the power to use or manage items without having legal title to them (eg a delivery service having control of letters and packages for delivery—it does not actually own any of them and may not even have 'possession' at all times).
- Proprietary right or interest means ownership or having legal title of property or similar rights.
- An obligation to make restoration of property belonging to another must be a legal obligation, not a moral or social one.
- Simple and genuine borrowing of property is insufficient to constitute theft because the necessary 'mens rea' is missing, unless the person intends to return the property in such a state that it loses its value or goodness (eg exam papers borrowed for copying would not be 'stolen' as they had not lessened in their intrinsic value).
- The theft or attempted theft of mail bags or postal packages, or their contents, whilst in transit between British postal areas is, even if it happens outside England and Wales, triable in England and Wales.

Related cases

R v Ghosh [1982] 2 All ER 689, QBD To determine dishonesty, the court must decide what is dishonest according to the ordinary standards of reasonable and honest people, and whether that person realized that what they were doing was dishonest by those standards.

R v Hinks [2000] 4 All ER 833, HL H influenced, coerced or encouraged the complainant who was naive, gullible and of limited intelligence to hand over large sums of money. Receiving a valid gift is appropriation; if the circumstances surrounding the acceptance of the property would be considered dishonest (by a reasonable person), then that conduct becomes theft.

R v Skivington [1967] 1 All ER 483, CA It is not considered dishonest if a person believes they have the legal (as opposed to moral) right to deprive the other of the property.

Lawrence v Metropolitan Police [1972] 2 All ER 1253, HL It is not necessary for the prosecution to prove that the property was taken without the consent of the owner. If consent is shown it does not mean that there is no dishonesty if the consent was obtained without full knowledge of the circumstances.

R v McPherson [1973] Crim LR 191, CA It is an appropriation if, at the time the property is taken, there is an intent to steal.

DPP v Gomez (1993) 96 Cr App R 359, HL Goods taken with the consent of someone empowered to give it can nevertheless be an 'appropriation'. Consent to the removal of items that are obtained by fraud, deception, or false representation amounts to the dishonest appropriation of goods.

R v Ngan [1998] 1 Cr App R 331, CA The appropriation must take place in England and Wales.

R v Arnold [1997] 4 All ER 1, CA Where property is received from, or on account of, another and the recipient is under an obligation to retain and deal with it (or its proceeds) in a particular manner, the property (or proceeds) are regarded as belonging to the other.

R v Fernandes [1996] 1 Cr App R 175, CA A person in possession or control of another's property, who dishonestly and for their own purpose, deals with it in a manner which they know is risking its loss may be regarded as having the intention to permanently deprive.

National Employers MGIA Ltd v Jones [1987] 3 All ER 385, CA For a buyer to gain 'good title' to property that they buy, the seller must have a lawful right to it in the first place. Therefore someone who innocently buys goods that turn out to have been stolen does not become the lawful owner.

Practical considerations

- All five of the elements contained within the theft definition must be proved to obtain a conviction.
- In the absence of a reliable admission of dishonesty, this evidence will have to be proved by other evidence. Such things might include: Where was the property found? Had it been hidden? What were the subsequent actions of the defendant?
- Other matters that should be addressed include—
  ♦ Evidence of who owns the property and/or that the defendant does not.
  ♦ Does the offender have any claim on the property?
  ♦ Does the offender own any similar property/have the means to have paid for it?
  ♦ Any attempts to alter the property or change its appearance.
  ♦ Proof that only some of the property was stolen is sufficient for a conviction.
  ♦ The current location of the property.
  ♦ The value of the property stolen/recovered.
- The fact that a man and woman are married or are civil partners, does not preclude one from stealing property belonging to the other.
  ♦ A person is not exempt from answering questions in recovery proceedings on the grounds that to do so would incriminate them or their spouse or civil partner.
  ♦ However, a statement or confession made in recovery proceedings is not admissible in proceedings for an offence under this Act as evidence against them or their spouse or civil partner.

- Consider issuing a PND for retail/commercial thefts under £200 (see **7.1**).
- Consider additional evidence (eg security video, CCTV footage).

SSS   E&S   PND   CHAR   TRIG

Either way   None

Summary: 6 months' imprisonment and/or a fine not exceeding the statutory maximum.

Indictment: 7 years' imprisonment and/or a fine.

3.1.2 **Removal of articles from places open to the public**

Section 11 of the Theft Act 1968 covers the offence of removing articles from places open to the public.

Offence

Subject to subsections (2) and (3) below, where the public have access to a building in order to view the building or part of it, or a **collection** or part of a **collection** housed in it, any person who without lawful authority removes from the building or its grounds the whole or part of any article displayed or kept for display to the public in the building or that part of it or in its grounds shall be guilty of an offence.

Theft Act 1968, s 11

Points to prove

- ✓ date and location
- ✓ without lawful authority
- ✓ removed from building/grounds of building
- ✓ to which public have access
- ✓ to view building/collection/part thereof
- ✓ the whole/part of article displayed/kept for display to public

Meaning of collection

This includes a collection got together for a temporary purpose, but references in this section to a collection do not apply to a collection made or exhibited for the purpose of effecting sales or other commercial dealings.

Explanatory notes

- Access to grounds alone is insufficient. The public must have access to a building to view it, part of it or a collection or part of it housed therein.

 SSS   Stop, search, and seize powers

 PND   Penalty notice for disorder offences

 E&S   Entry and search powers

TRIG   Trigger offences

 CHAR   Offences where bad character can be introduced

- Payment for the privilege of viewing the collection is irrelevant, as is whether such payment merely covers expenses or makes a profit.
- Articles displayed are not confined to works of art, the test being that the article, which may be priceless or valueless, is displayed or kept for public display.
- Note that this offence does not require any intent to permanently deprive the owner of the article taken.

Defences

A person does not commit an offence under this section if he believes that he has lawful authority for the removal of the thing in question or that he would have it if the person entitled to give it knew of the removal and the circumstances of it.

Theft Act 1968, s 11(3)

Defence notes

The burden is on the prosecution to prove the absence of genuine belief on the part of the defendant.

Related cases

R v Durkin [1973] 2 All ER 872, CA It has to be proved that the collection was intended to be permanently available for exhibition to the public. That intention was sufficiently manifested in this case by the local authority's practice of periodically displaying to the public at the gallery the pictures in their permanent collection.

Practical considerations

- Ascertain the dates on which the building/articles is/are on display.
- Public access to a building for other purposes (eg a shopping mall) when a collection is displayed as an incidental to the main purpose of access (shopping) is unlikely to fall into this section.
  - However, if the collection was displayed in a separate part of the building with access given purely to view it, it would fall into this section.
- Removal need not be during the times the public have access, it can occur even when the buildings/grounds are closed. However, per s 11(2), if the display is temporary, removal must take place on a day when the public have access to the buildings/grounds in order to view.
- Does the defendant have any claim on the property?
- Current location of the article(s).
- Value of property taken/recovered.
- Obtain CJA witness statements.
- Consider additional evidence (eg security video, CCTV footage).

Either way   None

 Summary: 6 months' imprisonment and/or a fine not exceeding the statutory maximum.
Indictment: 5 years' imprisonment and/or a fine.

3.1.3 **Advertising rewards for the return of stolen/lost goods**

Section 23 of the Theft Act 1968 deals with the offence of advertising rewards for the return of stolen or lost goods.

Offences

Where any public advertisement of a reward for the return of any goods which have been stolen or lost uses any words to the effect that no questions will be asked, or that the person producing the goods will be safe from apprehension or inquiry, or that any money paid for the purchase of the goods or advanced by way of loan on them will be repaid, the person advertising the reward and any person who prints or publishes the advertisement shall be guilty of an offence.

Theft Act 1968, s 23

Points to prove

✓ advertiser/printer/publisher
✓ publicly advertised
✓ offer of reward for return of lost/stolen goods
✓ used words implying
✓ no questions asked/producer safe from apprehension/inquiry or any money paid will be repaid/loan repaid

Explanatory notes

- This is an offence of strict liability and does not require any specific mens rea.
- The offence applies not just to the person advertising the reward, but the person who prints or publishes the advertisements is also liable.
- A charge under this section may consist of any one or more of the elements contained in the section.

Related cases

Denham v Scott [1983] Crim LR 558, QBD A weekly paper published an advertisement offering reward for return of stolen goods and implying that no questions would be asked. This offence is one of strict liability and an employee of a company which publishes such an advertisement can also be guilty of the s 23 offence.

Practical considerations

- What inducement was included in the advertisement?
- Obtain a copy of the advertisement.
- Obtain evidence of origin of advertisement (eg invoice from printer).
- Any evidence of who placed the advert?
- Obtain CJA witness statement.

 Summary   6 months

 A fine not exceeding level 3 on the standard scale.

Links to alternative subjects and offences

3.2 **Robbery**

The Theft Act 1968 provides for the offence of theft and several other offences of which theft is a constituent part. Section 8 provides for the offences of robbery and assault with intent to rob, whilst s 21 concerns the offence of blackmail.

3.2.1 **Robbery**

Offence

A person is guilty of robbery if he **steals,** and immediately before or at the time of doing so, and in order to do so, he uses **force** on any person or puts or seeks to put any person in fear of being then and there subjected to force.

Theft Act 1968, s 8(1)

Points to prove
- ✓ stole property
- ✓ immediately before/at the time of doing so
- ✓ and in order to do so
- ✓ used force on a person or put/sought to put person in fear of immediate force

Meanings

Steals (see **3.1.1**)

Force

Means the ordinary meaning and whether force has been used is a matter for the court to decide (*R v Dawson & James* (1976) 64 Cr App R 170, CA).

Explanatory notes
- The offence of theft must be proved before robbery can be substantiated.
- Section 8(2) deems that a person guilty of robbery is guilty of an offence.
- Force or the threat of force must be used immediately before or at the time of the theft.
- A threat to use force has to be made with the intention that something should happen immediately.
- The purpose of the use of force is to facilitate the theft; using force to escape is not robbery.

- If the offence is carried out by a number of assailants, but only one uses violence towards the victim, the others cannot be held responsible for the violence unless a prior agreement between them to use that degree of violence in order to achieve their objective is shown.
- In order to seek to put somebody in fear, the state of mind of the offender is what is important (rather than that of the victim).
- If a person, while stealing or attempting to steal mailbags or postal packages, or their contents, whilst in transit between British postal areas, commits robbery or attempted robbery, the offence is triable in England and Wales, even if it is committed outside England and Wales.

Defence

An honest belief that a legal claim of right to the property exists is a defence to robbery (*R v Skivington* [1967] 1 All ER 483, CA).

Related cases

R v DPP [2007] EWHC 739 (Admin) QBD A large group surrounded the victim then, after asking for a mobile phone/cash, removed a drink and wallet from his pockets and snatched a packet of crisps from his hands. The victim was shocked, but did not feel scared, threatened or put in fear. It is the intention of the perpetrator rather than the fortitude of the victim which dictates whether it is an offence of robbery. A threat of force can be from words, or implied by actions/conduct or both.

R v Hale (1979) 68 Cr App R 415, CA Appropriation is a continuing act and a defendant who takes items from a shop or a housekeeper and uses violence on the proprietor/owner during the course of the appropriation (eg when approached by the owner) may be guilty of robbery.

R v Clouden [1987] Crim LR 56, CA Very little force is required and a push or nudge to put the victim off balance to enable a theft to take place can be sufficient.

Smith v Desmond & Hall [1965] 1 All ER 976, HL The threat or use of force can be on any person, in order to make a set of circumstances arise, so that the theft can take place (eg threatening a signalman making him stop a train further down the track so that its contents can be stolen).

Corcoran v Anderton (1980) 71 Cr App R 104, CA Use of force applied indirectly (eg pulling at a handbag held by the victim) can under some circumstances amount to robbery as force is transferred to the person.

Practical considerations

- Is there evidence of a theft?
- Ownership of any property stolen.
- Value of property stolen/recovered.

3.2.2 Assault with Intent to Rob

- The fear of being subjected to force must be genuine and can be proved in the victim's statement (although it is the defendant's **intention** to cause fear that is the key element).
- Specific words used by the defendant will be critical.
- It is not necessary to prove that somebody was actually put in fear, only that the accused sought to put somebody in fear of force.
- The force used must be to enable the theft to take place.
- The use of force after the theft is complete is not robbery.
- A threat of force can also be implied, as long as the victim believes that force will be used against them and therefore allows the theft to take place.
- An assault committed as an afterthought following a theft is not robbery, but it is assault and theft.
- Obtain CJA witness statements.
- Consider blackmail (see **3.2.3**) when the threats are for force to be used on a future occasion.
- Any additional evidence (eg security video, CCTV footage).

 Indictment   None

 Life imprisonment

3.2.2 **Assault with intent to rob**

Offence

A person guilty of **robbery**, or of an assault with **intent** to rob, is guilty of an offence.

Theft Act 1968, s 8(2)

Points to prove

✓ assault
✓ intended to rob

Meanings

Robbery (see 3.2.1)

Intent1 (see 4.1.2)

Explanatory notes

- This offence is committed if a victim is assaulted in order to rob them, but the robbery is not completed because of interference or

---

 SSS Stop, search, and seize powers

TRIG Trigger offences

E&S Entry and search powers

 CHAR Offences where bad character can be introduced

resistance, or it could not be completed because the assailant demanded property which the victim did not have.

- If a person, whilst stealing or attempting to steal mailbags or postal packages, or their contents, whilst in transit between British postal areas, commits assault with intent to rob, the offence is triable in England and Wales, even if it is committed outside England and Wales.

Defence (see 3.2.1)

Practical considerations

- What was the purpose of the assault?
- Was there an unsuccessful attempt to steal property from the victim?
- There is no need for actual violence, as an assault does not require it. However, where no force is actually used immediately before or at the time of the unsuccessful attempt to rob, consider a charge of attempted robbery under s 1 of the Criminal Attempts Act 1981 (see **4.1.1**).
- If the assault occurs when the assailant has a firearm in their possession consider charging with an offence under the Firearms Act 1968 (see **8.3**).
- What was the degree of violence used towards the victim?
- Obtain CJA witness statements.
- Consider any additional evidence (eg security video, CCTV footage).
- If the defence to robbery is available to the defendant, consider the assault in isolation.

 Indictment   None

Life imprisonment

3.2.3 **Blackmail**

Section 21 of the Theft Act 1968 deals with the offence of blackmail.

Offences

A person is guilty of blackmail if, with a view to gain for himself or another or with intent to cause loss to another, he makes any unwarranted demand with menaces; and for this purpose a demand with menaces is unwarranted unless the person making it does so in the belief—

(a) that he has reasonable grounds for making the demands; **and**

(b) that the use of the menaces is a proper means of reinforcing the demands.

Theft Act 1968, s 21(1)

SSS Stop, search, and seize powers   **E&S** Entry and search powers   **CHAR** Offences where bad character can be introduced   101

TRIG Trigger offences

Points to prove

✓ with view to gain for self/another or intent to cause loss to another
✓ made unwarranted demand with menaces

Meanings

Intent (see **4.1.2**)

Menaces

The ordinary meaning of menaces applies (eg threats).

Explanatory notes

- The nature of the act or omission demanded is immaterial.
- It is also immaterial whether the menaces relate to action to be taken by the person making the demand or a third party.
- The words 'with a view to gain' and 'with intent to cause loss' do not have the same meaning. They are alternative, separate, and distinct phrases.
- The posting, making, or receipt of the threat must occur in this country.

Defences

In the belief—

- that they had reasonable grounds for making the demands; **and**
- that the use of the menaces is a proper means of reinforcing the demands.

Defence notes

- Belief in both s 21(a) and (b) must be present for this defence. If only one is present the offence of blackmail will still be made out.
- The onus is on the defendant to prove the belief, but the prosecution must cover this defence in interview or by other means to negate it.

Related cases

R v Clear (1968) 52 Cr App R 58, CA Person threatened need not be frightened, but the menaces must be enough to unsettle the mind of an ordinary person when the threat and demand are made.

Treacy v DPP [1971] 1 All ER 110, HL A letter containing a demand with menaces posted in England and delivered abroad is sufficient for this offence.

R v Bevans [1988] Crim LR 237, CA Gain is not restricted to money; merely obtaining something they did not previously have will suffice.

R v Harvey [1981] Crim LR 104, CA Conduct including threats cannot be proper means of reinforcing a demand.

Practical considerations

- The menaces do not need to relate to action to be taken by the person making the demand.
- Cover the defence in interview or other means in order to negate it.
- Obtain CJA witness statement.
- If the evidence for 'gain' or 'loss' is vague, consider s 1 of the Malicious Communications Act 1988 (see **7.12**).
- Identify any evidence of contact/threats made to the complainant by the defendant (eg notes, letters, telephone calls).
- Consider confiscation of cash and property as this blackmail offence is listed as a 'criminal lifestyle' offence under Sch 2 of the Proceeds of Crime Act 2002 (see **5.6** for details).

Indictment   None

14 years' imprisonment

Links to alternative subjects and offences

3.3 **Burglary**

The Theft Act 1968 provides for the offence of theft and several other offences of which theft is a constituent part. Section 9 of that Act creates the offence of burglary.

Offences

(1) A person is guilty of burglary if—
  (a) he enters any **building** or part of a building as a **trespasser** and with **intent** to commit any such offence as is mentioned in subsection (2) below; or
  (b) having entered any building or part of a building as a trespasser he steals or attempts to **steal** anything in the building or that part of it or inflicts or attempts to inflict on any person therein any **grievous bodily harm.**
(2) The offences referred to in subsection (1)(a) above are offences of stealing anything in the building or part of a building in question, of inflicting on any person therein any grievous bodily harm or of doing unlawful **damage** to the building or anything therein.

Theft Act 1968, s 9

Points to prove

✓ entered a building/part of a building
✓ as a trespasser
✓ with intent
✓ to steal property therein/inflict grievous bodily harm on person therein/do unlawful damage to the building or anything therein

or

✓ having entered a building/part of a building
✓ as a trespasser
✓ stole or attempted to steal anything therein/inflicted or attempted to inflict grievous bodily harm on any person therein

---

Meanings

Building

'Building' includes an outhouse, a shed, an inhabited vehicle, or a vessel irrespective of whether the resident is there or not.

Trespasser

Trespass means to pass over a limit or boundary or to unlawfully enter another's building or land. An offender must either know or be reckless as to whether they are a trespasser. Entry gained by fraud is still trespass.

Intent (see **4.1.2**)

Steal (see **3.1**)

Grievous bodily harm (see **2.3.1**)

Damage (see **4.4**)

Explanatory notes

- There does not have to be a forced entry into the building, merely proof that the person has entered as a trespasser.
- Entry into a building may be an actual physical entry, by use of an instrument (eg a hook on a stick through an open window) or by an innocent agent (eg a child under 10 years old).
- The offence does not differentiate between different types of building—but the punishment does (see below).
- A person who has entered one part of a building legally and then enters into another part of the same building as a trespasser falls within this section.
- In s 9(1)(a) the original intention need not be completed—it is sufficient that the intention existed at the time of entry.
- In s 9(1)(b) no specific intention is required at the time of entry as the intruder commits one of the acts having entered as a trespasser.

Related cases

R v Saw and others [2009] EWCA Crim 1, CA Burglary of a home is a serious criminal offence. Police officers should consider not just an offence against property, but also and often more alarmingly or distressingly an offence against the person. The court listed commonly encountered aggravating features in a burglary that should be included in the file so they can be expressly addressed by the court, rather than as an addition to those identified in the sentencing guidelines.

S v DPP [2003] EWHC 2717 (Admin), QBD S stood outside a building knowing that a burglary was ongoing. Watching and knowing a crime is being committed is not sufficient to establish joint enterprise/guilt. It should be considered whether S had encouraged the crime or had participated through joint enterprise (eg acted as lookout) but had not done so. Merely being present was not sufficient for burglary.

R v Brown [1985] Crim LR 212, CA The least degree of entry is sufficient to constitute this element of the offence, eg putting a hand or instrument through an open window or letterbox.

B & S v Leathley [1979] Crim LR 314, CC A freezer container may be a building under this section.

R v Walkington [1979] 2 All ER 716, CA A person who enters a building as a trespasser with the intention of committing a relevant offence therein, but gets caught before they manage to commit that offence, will still commit burglary.

3.3 Burglary

R v Wilson & Jenkins [1983] 3 All ER 448, HL If force is applied either directly or indirectly then harm is inflicted, eg a victim who is so intimidated by an intruder that they jump from a window thereby causing injury then harm has been caused although no actual force is used.

Practical considerations

- Ensure a degree of entry into the building can be proved, otherwise consider other offences relevant to the circumstances.
- If satisfied the offender entered the building gather evidence as to right to be there—CJA witness statements.
- A building may include structures made of wood, steel or plastic, but it would not include a tent (inhabited or not), articulated trailer (on wheels), open-sided bus shelter or carport.
- An inhabited caravan would be a building under this legislation.
- A static caravan permanently connected to mains water, sewers, and gas/electricity would probably be a building even when it was not occupied.
- A touring caravan parked in the driveway of a house is a vehicle. However, if it was no longer used for touring, and instead used for storage as a garden shed, it may well then be a building.
- A person who enters a shop legally and then goes into a store room may be a trespasser.
- A person who has legally entered premises and later becomes a trespasser because of hostilities by them does not become a trespasser under this legislation. They must have been a trespasser at the time of entry into that part of the building.
- A person acting as a lookout should be treated as a joint principal.
- Is there any other evidence available (eg security video, CCTV)?
- Is there any evidence of the intent for an offence under s 9(1)(a)? For theft this may be easy to prove (eg the possession of burgling tools), but it may be more difficult for grievous bodily harm, or damage.
- The type of building may affect the sentence.
- Burglary dwelling—if any person in the dwelling was subjected to violence or the threat of violence then the case is triable on indictment only.
- If the defendant had a firearm/imitation firearm with them, then consider also s 17(2) of the Firearms Act 1968 (see **8.3.5**).

 Either way   None

 Summary: 6 months' imprisonment and/or a fine not exceeding the statutory maximum.

Indictment: 10 years' imprisonment (dwelling—14 years' imprisonment).

SSS Stop, search, and seize powers **E&S** Entry and search powers **CHAR** Offences where bad character can be introduced **TRIG** Trigger offences

Links to alternative subjects and offences

3.4 **Aggravated Burglary**

The Theft Act 1968 provides for the offence of theft and several other offences of which theft is a constituent part. Section 10 creates the offence of aggravated burglary, where the trespasser has with them, at the time of committing the burglary, one or more of the specified weapons.

> ### Offences
> A person is guilty of aggravated burglary if he commits any **burglary** and at the time **has with him** any **firearm** or **imitation firearm,** any **weapon of offence,** or any **explosive.**
>
> Theft Act 1968, s 10

Points to prove
✓ committed burglary
✓ had with them
✓ firearm/imitation firearm/weapon of offence/explosive

Meanings

Burglary (see **3.3**)

Has with him

This phrase has a narrower meaning than 'possession' (see **8.3.6**).

Firearm (see **8.1.1**)

Includes an airgun or air pistol (see **8.7.2**).

Imitation firearm

Anything which has the appearance of being a firearm, whether capable of being discharged or not.

Weapon of offence

Any article made or adapted for use for causing injury to or incapacitating a person, or intended by the person having it with him for such use.

Explosive

Means any article manufactured for the purpose of producing a practical effect by explosion, or intended by the person having it with him for that purpose.

Related cases

R v Daubney (2000) 164 JP 519, CA Defendant must know that they had the article with them.

R v Kelly (1993) 97 Cr App R 245, CA A burglar who used a screwdriver to break into premises then, when challenged by the occupants, used that same screwdriver to threaten them, was held to have a weapon of offence with him at the time.

R v O'Leary (1986) 82 Cr App R 341, CA In a s 9(1)(a) burglary (enters with intent), if the burglar has with them an article (listed above), the offence is committed at the time of entry. However, under s 9(1)(b) (having entered), the point at which aggravated burglary is committed is when they commit the theft or grievous bodily harm with the article—not at the time of entry.

R v Klass [1998] 1 Cr App R 453, CA Entry into a building with a weapon is an essential element of this offence. Therefore, if there is only one weapon and it is with an accomplice who remains outside the building, neither of the offenders would commit aggravated burglary.

R v Stones [1989] 1 WLR 156, CA A burglar in possession of a knife for self-protection while carrying out a burglary may be tempted to use it if challenged and would therefore commit this offence.

Practical considerations

- Was the burglary committed under s 9(1)(a) or (b)? This affects the point in time at which the offence occurred.
- If there is more than one offender, is there evidence that somebody actually entered the building with the weapon? If not, charge with burglary or the relevant offence.
- What reason did the offender have for possessing the article?
- Where it is unclear whether the offender had the article with them at the relevant time, charge them with burglary and charge possession of the article separately.
- The offence may be committed where the offender takes possession of an article in one part of a building and then enters another part of the building with it.
- Obtain evidence of ownership and right of entry into building.
- Obtain CJA witness statements.
- Is there any other evidence (eg security video, CCTV footage)?

SSS	E&S	CHAR	TRIG

Indictable   None

Life imprisonment

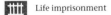

| **SSS** Stop, search, and seize powers | **E&S** Entry and search powers | **CHAR** Offences where bad character can be introduced | 109 |
| **TRIG** Trigger offences | | | |

Links to alternative subjects and offences

3.5 Dishonestly—Abstract Electricity/Retain a Wrongful Credit

A further offence provided for by the Theft Act 1968 of which theft is a constituent part is abstracting electricity. Section 13 deals with the offence of dishonestly abstracting electricity and section 24A the offence of dishonestly retaining a wrongful credit.

3.5.1 Dishonestly abstracting electricity

Offence

A person who dishonestly uses without due authority, or dishonestly causes to be wasted or diverted, any electricity commits an offence.

Theft Act 1968, s 13

Points to prove
- ✓ dishonestly
- ✓ used without due authority or caused to be wasted/diverted
- ✓ electricity

Meanings

Dishonestly

This means a state of mind as opposed to the conduct (although the conduct will often be a feature from which dishonesty can and will be inferred) (*Boggeln v Williams* [1978] 2 All ER 1061, QBD).

Uses

Consumption of electricity that would not have occurred without an action by the accused.

Without due authority

Means without the proper authorization.

Explanatory notes

- This section is made necessary by the fact that electricity does not fit into the definition of property under s 4 for theft (see **3.1.1**) and, therefore, it cannot be stolen. This also means that entering a building and abstracting electricity (or intending to) will not be burglary.

3.5.1 Dishonestly Abstracting Electricity

- A tramp who obtains warmth by an electric fire, which is already switched on, would not commit this offence, but if they switched the fire on they would commit this offence.
- Employees using their employer's electrically powered machinery for their own use would commit an offence under this section.
- It is not necessary for anybody to benefit from the wasted or diverted electricity. A person who, out of spite, switches on an electrical appliance before leaving a building would commit this offence.

Related cases

R v McCreadie & Tume [1992] Crim LR 872, CA It is sufficient for the prosecution to show that electricity was used without the authority of the electricity authority and that there was no intention to pay for it (eg squatters).

Boggeln v Williams [1978] 2 All ER 1061, QBD A householder who bypasses the electric meter after their supply has been disconnected dishonestly causes the electricity to be diverted.

Practical considerations

- Obtain evidence of dishonest use, waste, or diversion of electricity (eg note the state of the meter, cash box missing).
- The person using the electricity does not have to be the person who reconnects the supply (eg a person using electricity with no intention to pay for it after a disconnected supply has been unlawfully reconnected by a third person would commit this offence).
- Check for sign of break-in to the premises, which may negate or support the story of the householder.
- Utilities bill may assist to prove diversion to bypass the meter.
- There is no requirement for the electricity to be supplied through the mains (eg it may be supplied from a car battery). Thus a person who takes a pedestrian controlled electric vehicle which is not classed as a conveyance (see **4.3.1**) may commit this offence.
- Obtain CJA witness statement from electricity supplier.

 Either way   None

 Summary: 6 months' imprisonment and/or a fine not exceeding the statutory maximum

Indictment: 5 years' imprisonment.

3.5.2 **Dishonestly retain a wrongful credit**

Offence

A person is guilty of an offence if—

(a) a **wrongful credit** has been made to an account kept by him or in respect of which he has any right or interest;

(b) he knows or believes that the credit is wrongful; and

(c) he dishonestly fails to take such steps as are reasonable in the circumstances to secure that the credit is cancelled.

Theft Act 1968, s 24A(1)

Points to prove

✓ knowing/believing
✓ wrongful credit made to account
✓ kept by them in which they had right or interest
✓ dishonestly
✓ failed to take reasonable steps to cancel the credit

Meanings

Wrongful credit

A credit to an account is wrongful to the extent that it derives from—

• theft (see **3.1.1**);
• blackmail (see **3.2.3**);
• fraud (see **3.9.1**); or
• stolen goods (see **3.6**).

Credit

Means a credit of an amount of money.

Explanatory notes

• In determining whether a credit to an account is wrongful, it is immaterial (in particular) whether the account is overdrawn before or after the credit is made.
• Any money dishonestly withdrawn from an account to which a wrongful credit has been made may be regarded as stolen goods.

Practical considerations

• Where did the credit originate?
• Obtain supplementary evidence (eg bank statements, cheque book).
• What steps could/have been taken to cancel the credit.
• Obtain CJA witness statement.

3.5.2 Dishonestly Retain a Wrongful Credit

 Either way

 None

 Summary: 6 months' imprisonment and/or a fine not exceeding the statutory maximum.

Indictment: 10 years' imprisonment.

Links to alternative subjects and offences

3.6 **Handling Stolen Goods**

Section 22 of the Theft Act 1968 creates various combinations of offences of handling stolen goods knowing or believing them to be stolen.

> **Offences**
>
> A person handles stolen **goods** if (otherwise than in the course of the stealing) **knowing** or **believing** them to be stolen goods he **dishonestly receives** the goods, or dishonestly **undertakes** or assists in their **retention**, removal, disposal or **realisation** by or for the benefit of another person, or he **arranges to do so**.
>
> Theft Act 1968, s 22(1)

Points to prove
- ✓ otherwise than in the course of stealing
- ✓ knowing/believing goods to be stolen
- ✓ dishonestly received them or
- ✓ dishonestly undertook/assisted
- ✓ in the retention/removal/disposal/realization of them
- ✓ or arranged to do so
- ✓ by/for the benefit of another

Meanings

Goods

Includes money and every other description of property except land, and includes things severed from the land by stealing (see **3.1.1**).

Knowing

Means actually having been told by somebody having first-hand knowledge (eg the thief or burglar) that the goods had been stolen (*R v Hall* (1985) 81 Cr App R 260, CA).

Believing

Means the state of mind of a person who cannot be certain that goods are stolen, but where the circumstances indicate no other reasonable conclusion (*R v Elizabeth Forsyth* [1997] 2 Cr App R 299, CA).

Dishonestly

A court must decide what is dishonest according to the ordinary standards of reasonable and honest people, **and** whether that person knew that what they were doing was dishonest by those standards (*R v Ghosh* [1982] 2 All ER 689, QBD).

3.6 Handling Stolen Goods

Receives

Means gaining **possession** or control of the goods.

Possession

Means either actual physical possession or constructive possession (storing the goods in premises belonging to them).

Undertakes

Includes where the person agrees to perform the act(s) that constitute the offence.

Retention

Means keeping possession of, not losing, continuing to have (*R v Pitchley* [1972] Crim LR 705, CA).

Realisation

Means the conversion of the goods, invariably into money (*R v Deakin* [1972] Crim LR 781, CA).

Arranges to do so

Means arranging to receive, retain, remove, dispose or convert the stolen goods. This can be done without actually seeing or having had anything to do with the goods.

Explanatory notes

- Where a person is being proceeded against for handling stolen goods only, s 27(3)(a) provides for '**special evidence**' (eg their previous dealings with stolen goods within the 12 months prior to the current incident) to be introduced into the proceedings. No charge or conviction regarding the previous incident is necessary.
- Similarly, s 27(3)(b) allows the introduction of evidence of a previous conviction for theft or handling within 5 years of the present incident. In this case a notice must be served on the defence 7 days prior to use of the evidence in court.
- Where the only evidence on a charge of handling stolen goods is circumstantial in that an accused person is in possession of property recently stolen (doctrine of recent possession), a court may infer guilty knowledge if: (a) the accused offers no explanation to account for their possession, or (b) the court is satisfied that the explanation they offer is untrue.
- Any benefit to the receiver is irrelevant.
- Someone who handles stolen goods, whilst having no knowledge or reason to believe them to be stolen, will not commit this offence.
- Actions taken for the benefit of another are only relevant in the offence of handling stolen goods—they have no significance in relation to the receiving of such goods.

Related cases

R v Kousar [2009] EWCA Crim 139, CA A wife who knew her husband was storing stolen business merchandise in the matrimonial home, acquiesced in its being there, and did not demand its removal, was not in control or possession of the goods.

R v Duffus (1994) 158 JP 224, CA The 'special evidence' under s 27(3)(a) or (b) can only be introduced to assist in proving that the accused knew or believed that the goods were stolen.

R v Ghosh [1982] 2 All ER 689, QBD Case sets out a two-stage test (see 'Meanings—*Dishonestly*' above).

National Employers Mutual Ltd v Jones [1987] 3 All ER 385, CA Paying value for goods that subsequently turn out to be stolen does not transfer good title to the buyer.

R v Nicklin [1977] 2 All ER 444, CA Where a particular form of handling is specified in the charge the defendant cannot then be found guilty of another form with which they have not been charged.

R v Brown [1969] 3 All ER 198, CA 'Assists' includes permitting the storage of stolen goods in premises and denying knowledge of their whereabouts.

R v Figures [1976] Crim LR 744, CC Handling of goods stolen abroad is only an offence in this country if the handling takes place here. If the handling is complete before coming here there is no offence under this section.

R v Bloxham (1982) 74 Cr App R 279, HL A person who innocently buys goods for value and later discovers they were, in fact, stolen goods cannot commit the offence of assisting in their disposal by selling them as they benefited from their *purchase* not their sale.

Practical considerations

- Ownership of the goods and evidence of theft must be established.
- Check for any evidence of previous dealings with stolen goods within previous 12 months.
- Check previous convictions for theft or handling within previous 5 years.
- Consider need for 7 days' notice of intent to use previous convictions.
- Check for communications between the handler, the thief or any potential buyers/distributors.
- Check for evidence of removal or alteration of identifying features.
- Obtain evidence of the true value of the goods.
- If the facts fit both theft and handling stolen goods, use the relevant alternate charges and let the court decide which offence, if any, is committed.
- Goods are not regarded as still being stolen goods after they have been returned to a person having lawful possession or custody, or after the person having a claim to them ceases to have a right to restitution regarding the theft.

3.6 Handling Stolen Goods

- Several people may be charged on one indictment, concerning the same theft, with handling all or some of the goods at the same or various times, and all such persons may be tried together. This does not apply to a summary trial.

 Either way

 None

 Summary: 6 months' imprisonment and/or a fine not exceeding the statutory maximum.

Indictment: 14 years' imprisonment.

Links to alternative subjects and offences

SSS   Stop, search, and seize powers   E&S   Entry and search powers   CHAR   Offences where bad character can be introduced

TRIG   Trigger offences

3.7 **Going Equipped**

The Theft Act 1968 provides for several other key offences of which theft is a constituent part. Section 25 creates the offences of going equipped for any burglary or theft.

Offences

A person shall be guilty of an offence if, when not at his **place of abode**, he **has with him** any **article** for use in the course of or in connection with any **burglary or theft**.

Theft Act 1968, s 25(1)

Points to prove

✓ not at place of abode
✓ had with them
✓ article(s) for use in course of/in connection with
✓ a burglary/theft

Meanings

Place of abode

This normally means the place or site where someone lives. Using its natural meaning it normally includes the garage and garden of a house, but it is ultimately a matter for the court or jury to decide.

Has with him

This phrase has a narrower meaning than 'possession' (see **8.3.6**).

Article

This has a wide meaning. It may include a whole range of items and substances, from treacle and paper to assist in breaking a window quietly, a car jack for spreading bars, or pieces of spark plug ceramic for breaking car windows.

Burglary (see **3.3**)

Theft (see **3.1.1**)

Includes taking a conveyance without owner's consent (see **4.3.1**).

Explanatory notes

- A direct connection between the article and a specific act of burglary or theft does not need to be proved.
- You do not need to prove that the person found with the article intended to use it themselves—intended use by another will suffice.

3.7 Going Equipped

Related cases

R v Bundy [1977] 2 All ER 382, CA A 'place of abode' includes a person living rough in a car when on a site with the intention of abiding there. However, that same person in the same car would not be at their place of abode when travelling from one site to another.

R v Tosti & White [1997] Crim LR 746, CA A person charged with going equipped, when the offence of burglary or theft has not been completed, may also be charged with that offence or with attempting to commit it.

National Employers Mutual Ltd v Jones [1987] 3 All ER 385, CA For a buyer to gain a good title to property the person selling the property must have a lawful right to the property in the first instance. No such right could ever exist if the goods were originally stolen. In this case the insurance company was the true owner and entitled to the car.

Practical considerations

- What articles were with or available to the defendant?
- Where were the articles?
- What were their possible/intended uses?
- Did the defendant have a lawful purpose for having the article(s) in their possession at that particular time/place?
- Has the defendant used such articles in committing offence previously?
- Obtain CJA witness statements.
- This offence caters for some preparatory acts prior to the commission of one or more of the specified acts.
- This offence can only be committed before the intended burglary or theft, not afterwards.
- Possession of the article(s) after arrest is not sufficient for this offence.
- When two or more people are acting in concert the possession of housebreaking implements by one of them would be deemed to be possession by all of them.
- A person who has a relevant article with them, but has not yet decided whether to use the article, does not have the necessary intent to commit the offence.
- Taking a conveyance without the owner's consent is, for the purposes of this section, to be treated as theft.
- Once it has been proved that the defendant had a relevant article with them, the defendant will need to prove possession for a purpose other than burglary or theft.

 Either way   None

 Summary: 6 months' imprisonment and/or a fine not exceeding the statutory maximum.

Indictment: 3 years' imprisonment.

SSS Stop, search, and seize powers **E&S** Entry and search powers **CHAR** Offences where bad character can be introduced **TRIG** Trigger offences

Links to alternative subjects and offences

3.8 **Making off without Payment**

The Theft Act 1978 creates specific offences relating to fraudulent conduct. Section 3 creates the offence of making off without payment (also known as 'bilking') when on-the-spot payment is required or expected for goods or a service and the perpetrator intends to avoid payment.

Offence

Subject to subsection (3) below, a person who, knowing that **payment on the spot** for any **goods** supplied or service done is required or expected from him, **dishonestly** makes off without having paid as required or expected and with **intent** to avoid payment of the amount due shall be guilty of an offence..

Theft Act 1978, s 3

Points to prove

✓ knowing immediate payment is required/expected
✓ for goods supplied/services done
✓ dishonestly
✓ made off
✓ without having paid as required/expected
✓ with intent to avoid payment of amount due

Meanings

Payment on the spot

This includes payment at the time of collecting goods on which work has been done or in respect of which service has been provided.

Goods (see **3.6**)

Dishonestly (see **3.6**)

Intent (see **4.1.2**)

Explanatory notes

• The term 'goods supplied or services done' will include making off without payment for fuel at a self-service petrol station, meals at restaurants or hotel accommodation/services where the charge is levied after supplying the goods/service.
• If a motorist forgets to pay for petrol and drives off, but later remembers that they had not paid, and then returns to the filling station to pay, they may not commit the offence due to lacking the necessary intent.

- Where there is an agreement to defer payment, any such agreement would normally eliminate the expectation of payment on the spot.

Defence

Subsection (1) above shall not apply where the supply of the goods or the doing of the service is contrary to law, or where the service done is such that payment is not legally enforceable.

Theft Act 1978, s 3(3)

Defence notes

A payment not being legally enforceable may be where the service provider breaks a contract (eg a taxi driver who fails to complete a journey) or where the contract cannot be enforced through the courts.

Related cases

R v Brooks & Brooks (1983) 76 Cr App R 66, CA 'Making off' involves leaving the place or passing the point where payment is expected or required.

R v Vincent [2001] Crim LR 488, CA If an agreement to defer payment is obtained dishonestly it would not reinstate the expectation for payment on the spot.

Practical considerations

- What goods or services have been provided?
- The goods or services provided must be specified in the charge.
- It is important to prove that the person knew that 'payment on the spot' was required.
- Did the accused have money or means with which to pay the bill?
- Is the payment legally enforceable?
- There must be an intention to avoid payment completely and not merely intent to defer or delay it.
- Obtain CJA witness statement.
- Is there any further evidence (eg CCTV footage)?

 Either way

 None

 Summary: 6 months' imprisonment and/or a fine not exceeding the statutory maximum.

Indictment: 2 years' imprisonment.

Links to alternative subjects and offences

3.9 **Fraud Offences**

The Fraud Act 2006 provides for the offence of fraud and other fraudulent offences of which dishonesty is a constituent part. Sections 1 to 4 detail the three different ways of committing fraud, s 12 the liability of company officers and s 13 evidential matters in relation to fraud.

3.9.1 **Fraud offence**

Section 1 creates the general offence of fraud, and ss 2 to 4 detail three different ways of committing fraud by false representation; failing to disclose information; or by abuse of position.

Offences

(1) A person is guilty of fraud if he is in breach of any of the sections listed in subsection (2) (which provide for different ways of committing the offence).

(2) The sections are—
   (a) section 2 (fraud by false representation),
   (b) section 3 (fraud by failing to disclose information), and
   (c) section 4 (fraud by abuse of position).

Fraud Act 2006, s 1

Points to prove

False representation

✓ date and location
✓ dishonestly made a false representation
✓ intending to make a gain for yourself/another OR
✓ intending to cause loss to another/expose another to a risk of loss

Failing to disclose information

✓ date and location
✓ dishonestly failed to disclose to another
✓ information which you were under a legal duty to disclose
✓ intending, by that failure
✓ to make a gain for yourself/another OR
✓ to cause loss to another/expose another to a risk of loss

Fraud by abuse of position

✓ date and location
✓ occupying a position in which you were expected

> ✓ to safeguard, or not to act against, the financial interests of another
> ✓ dishonestly abused that position
> ✓ intending to make a gain for yourself/another OR
> ✓ intending to cause loss to another/expose another to a risk of loss

Meanings

Fraud by false representation (see 3.9.2)

Fraud by failing to disclose information (see 3.9.3)

Fraud by abuse of position (see 3.9.4)

Gain and loss

(1) The references to gain and loss in sections 2 to 4 are to be read in accordance with this section.
(2) 'Gain' and 'loss'—
    (a) extend only to gain or loss in money or other property;
    (b) include any such gain or loss whether temporary or permanent;
    and 'property' means any property whether real or personal (including things in action and other intangible property).
(3) 'Gain' includes a gain by keeping what one has, as well as a gain by getting what one does not have.
(4) 'Loss' includes a loss by not getting what one might get, as well as a loss by parting with what one has.

Fraud Act 2006, s 5

Dishonestly (see 3.6)

Intention (see 4.1.2)

Explanatory notes

- Section 1 creates the general offence of fraud, and ss 2 to 4 detail three different ways of committing the fraud offence.
- All three fraud offences require an intention to make a gain for oneself or another OR cause loss to another/expose another to a risk of loss.
- Similarly in all of these fraud offences intention must be proved (see **4.1.2**).
- Property covers all forms of property, including intellectual property, although in practice this is rarely 'gained' or 'lost'.
- If any offences are committed by a company, the company officers may also be liable under s 12 (see **3.9.5**).
- Section 13 deals with evidential matters under this Act, conspiracy to defraud or any other offences involving any form of fraudulent conduct or purpose (see **3.9.6**).

3.9.2 **Meaning of fraud by false representation**

Meanings

Fraud by false representation

(1) A person is in breach of this section if he—
   (a) dishonestly makes a false representation, and
   (b) **intends**, by making the representation—
      (i)   to make a **gain** for himself or another, or
      (ii) to cause loss to another or to expose another to a risk of
            loss.
(2) A representation is false if—
   (a) it is untrue or misleading, and
   (b) the person making it knows that it is, or might be, untrue or
       misleading.
(3) '**Representation**' means any representation as to fact or law,
     including a representation as to the state of mind of—
   (a) the person making the representation, or
   (b) any other person.
(4) A representation may be express or implied.
(5) For the purposes of this section a representation may be regarded
     as made if it (or anything implying it) is submitted in any form
     to any system or device designed to receive, convey or respond to
     communications (with or without human intervention).

Fraud Act 2006, s 2

Gain and loss (see **3.9.1**)

Dishonestly (see **3.6**)

Intention (see **4.1.2**)

Explanatory notes

- The offence of fraud by false representation comes under fraud
  s 1 (see **3.9.1**) and **not** s 2.
- The gain or loss does not actually have to take place.
- There is no restriction on the way in which the representation may be
  expressed. It can be spoken, written (hardcopy or
  electronically) or communicated by conduct.
- An example of a representation by conduct is where a person
  dishonestly uses a credit card to pay for goods. By tendering the card,
  they are falsely representing that they have the authority to use it for
  that transaction. It is immaterial whether the retailer accepting the
  card is deceived by this representation.
- The practice of 'phishing' (eg sending an email purporting to come
  from a legitimate financial institution in order to obtain credit card
  and bank account details, so that the 'phisher' can access and fraudulently use those accounts) is another example of false representation.

- Subsection (5) is given in broad terms because it may be difficult to distinguish situations involving modern technology and/or human involvement. It could well be that the only recipient of the false statement is a machine or a piece of software, where a false statement is submitted to a system for dealing with electronic communications and not to a human being (eg postal or messenger systems). Another example of fraud by electronic means can be entering a number into a 'chip and pin' machine.

3.9.3 **Meaning of fraud by failing to disclose information**

Meanings

Fraud by failing to disclose information

A person is in breach of this section if he—

(a) **dishonestly** fails to disclose to another person information which he is under a legal duty to disclose, and
(b) **intends**, by failing to disclose the information—
   (i) to make a **gain** for himself or another, or
   (ii) to cause **loss** to another or to expose another to a risk of loss.

Fraud Act 2006, s 3

Gain and loss (see **3.9.1**)

Dishonestly (see **3.6**)

Intention (see **4.1.2**)

Explanatory notes

- The offence of fraud by failing to disclose information comes under fraud s 1 (see **3.9.1**) and **not** s 3.
- A legal duty to disclose information may include duties under both oral and/or written contracts.
- The concept of 'legal duty' may derive from statute, a transaction that requires good faith (eg contract of insurance), express or implied terms of a contract, custom of a particular trade/market, or a fiduciary relationship between the parties (eg between agent and principal).
- This legal duty to disclose information may be where the defendant's failure to disclose gives the victim a cause of action for damages, or the law gives the victim a right to set aside any change in their legal position to which they may consent as a result of the non-disclosure. An example of an offence under this section could be where a person intentionally failed to disclose information relating to their physical condition when making an application for life insurance.

3.9.4 **Meaning of fraud by abuse of position**

Meanings

Fraud by abuse of position

(1) A person is in breach of this section if he—
  (a) occupies a position in which he is expected to safeguard, or not to act against, the financial interests of another person,
  (b) **dishonestly** abuses that position, and
  (c) **intends**, by means of the abuse of that position—
      (i)   to make a gain for himself or another, or
      (ii) to cause **loss** to another or to expose another to a risk of loss.
(2) A person may be regarded as having abused his position even though his conduct consisted of an omission rather than an act.

Fraud Act 2006, s 4

Gain and loss (see **3.9.1**)

Dishonestly (see **3.6**)

Intention (see **4.1.2**)

Explanatory notes

- The offence of fraud by abuse of position comes under fraud s 1 (see **3.9.1**) and **not** s 4.
- The offence of committing fraud by dishonestly abusing their position applies in situations where they are in a privileged position, and by virtue of this position are expected to safeguard another's financial interests or not act against those interests.
- The necessary relationship could be between trustee and beneficiary, director and company, professional person and client, agent and principal, employee and employer, or even between partners. Generally this relationship will be recognized by the civil law as importing fiduciary duties. This relationship and existence of their duty can be ruled upon by the judge or be subject of directions to the jury.
- The term 'abuse' is not defined because it is intended to cover a wide range of conduct. Furthermore, the offence can be committed by omission as well as by positive action.
- Examples of offences under this section are—
  - Purposely failing to take up the chance of a crucial contract in order that an associate or rival company can take it up instead to the loss of their employer.
  - A software company employee uses their position to clone software products with the intention of selling the products to others.
  - Where a carer for an elderly or disabled person has access to that person's bank account and abuses their position by transferring funds for their own gain.

3.9.5 **Liability of company officers for offence by company**

Liability

(1) Subsection (2) applies if an offence under this Act is committed by a body corporate.

(2) If the offence is proved to have been committed with the consent or connivance of—

    (a) a director, manager, secretary or other similar officer of the body corporate, or

    (b) a person who was purporting to act in any such capacity,

he (as well as the body corporate) is guilty of the offence and liable to be proceeded against and punished accordingly.

(3) If the affairs of a body corporate are managed by its members, subsection (2) applies in relation to the acts and defaults of a member in connection with his functions of management as if he were a director of the body corporate.

Fraud Act 2006, s 12

Explanatory notes

- This section provides that if people who have a specified corporate role are party to the commission of an offence under the Act by their body corporate, they will be liable to be charged for the offence as well as the corporation.
- Liability for this offence applies to directors, managers, company secretaries and other similar officers of companies and other bodies corporate.
- Furthermore, if the body corporate is charged with an offence and the company is managed by its members, the members involved in management can be prosecuted too.

3.9.6 **Admissible evidence**

Evidence

(1) A person is not to be excused from—

    (a) answering any question put to him in **proceedings relating to property**, or

    (b) complying with any order made in proceedings relating to property,

on the ground that doing so may incriminate him or his spouse or civil partner of an offence under this Act or a related offence.

(2) But, in proceedings for an offence under this Act or a **related offence**, a statement or admission made by the person in—

    (a) answering such a question, or

    (b) complying with such an order,

is not admissible in evidence against him or (unless they married or became civil partners after the making of the statement or admission) his spouse or civil partner.

(3) '**Proceedings relating to property**' means any proceedings for—

    (a) the recovery or administration of any property,

    (b) the execution of a trust, or

    (c) an account of any property or dealings with property,

    and 'property' means money or other property whether real or personal (including things in action and other intangible property).

(4) '**Related offence**' means—

    (a) conspiracy to defraud;

    (b) any other offence involving any form of fraudulent conduct or purpose.

Fraud Act 2006, s 13

Explanatory notes

- This means that during any proceedings for—

    ♦ the recovery or administration of any property,

    ♦ the execution of a trust, or

    ♦ an account of any property or dealings with property,

    a person cannot be excused from answering any question or refuse to comply with any order made in those proceedings on the grounds of incrimination under this Act; conspiracy to defraud; or an offence involving any form of fraudulent conduct or purpose.

- However, any statement or admission made in answering such a question, or complying with such an order, is not admissible in evidence against them or their spouse or civil partner (unless they married or became civil partners after the making of such a statement or admission).

- Although this section is similar to s 31(1) of the Theft Act 1968 where a person/spouse/civil partner is protected from incrimination, while nonetheless being obliged to co-operate with certain civil proceedings relating to property, it goes beyond that section by removing privilege in relation to this Act, conspiracy to defraud and any other offence involving any form of fraudulent conduct or purpose.

- A civil partnership is a relationship between two people of the same sex ('civil partners') registered as civil partners under the Civil Partnerships Act 2004 and ends only on death, dissolution or annulment.

Related cases

R v Minet [2009] All ER (D) 215, CA M was in financial difficulties with his plumbing business and made fraudulent transactions using his customers' card details. This was a clear breach of trust. M had been allowed into the victims' homes and been entrusted with their credit cards and details. He had clearly been under an obligation to deal honestly with them.

Kensington International Ltd v Congo and others [2007] EWCA (Civ) 1128, CA Case provides guidance relating to disclosure, evidence, and other aspects of s 13.

R v Ghosh [1982] 2 All ER 689, QBD A court/jury must decide whether, according to the standards of reasonable and honest people, what was done was dishonest. If it was dishonest by those standards the court/jury must then decide whether the defendant realized that what they were doing was, by those standards, dishonest.

DPP v Gomez (1993) 96 Cr App R 359, HL If consent to take property is obtained by fraud then the property is obtained dishonestly and may fall into this offence or theft.

Practical considerations

- The words used may be spoken or written. Alternatively, there may be nothing done or said in circumstances where a reasonable and honest person would have expected something to be said/done (eg to correct a mistake).
- The fraud may be proved by admissions, the defendant's actions or a combination of both.
- Acts may be dishonest even if the perpetrator genuinely believed them to be morally justified.
- Schedule 2 of the Act concerns transitional provisions and any deception offences committed before the Act commenced (15th January 2007) should be dealt with under the repealed ss 15, 15A, 16, and 20(2) of the Theft Act 1968 and ss 1 and 2 of the Theft Act 1978.
- If committed by a body corporate with the consent or connivance of one of its officers they, as well as the body corporate, are liable to be proceeded against (see **3.9.5**).

 Either way

 None

 Summary: 12 months' imprisonment and/or a fine not exceeding the statutory maximum.

Indictment: 10 years' imprisonment and/or a fine.

Links to alternative subjects and offences

3.10 **Articles for use in Fraud**

The Fraud Act 2006 provides for the offence of fraud and other fraudulent offences of which dishonesty is a constituent part.

3.10.1 **Possess or control article for use in fraud**

Sections 6 deals with the offence of having in their possession or under their control an article for use in fraud.

Offences

A person is guilty of an offence if he has in his **possession** or under his control any **article** for use in the course of or in connection with any **fraud**.

Fraud Act 2006, s 6(1)

Points to prove

✓ date and location
✓ had in your possession/under your control
✓ an article
✓ for use in the course of/in connection with a fraud

Meanings

Possession (see **8.1.1**)

Article

Means an article—
• made or adapted for use in the course of or in connection with an offence of fraud; or
• **intended** by the person having it with them for such use by them or by some other person.
It also includes any program or data held in electronic form.

Fraud (see **3.9.1**)

Intention (see **4.1.2**)

Explanatory notes

• Having the article after the commission of the fraud is not sufficient for this offence.

- The prosecution must prove that the defendant was in possession of the article, and intended the article to be used in the course of or in connection with some future fraud. It is not necessary to prove that they intended it to be used in the course of or in connection with any specific fraud; it is enough to prove a general intention to use it for fraud.
- Similarly it will be sufficient to prove that they had it with them with the intention that it should be used by someone else.
- Examples of electronic programs or data which could be used in fraud are: a computer program that can generate credit card numbers; computer templates that can be used for producing blank utility bills; computer files containing lists of other people's credit card details or draft letters in connection with 'advance fee' frauds.

 Either way None

 Summary: 12 months' imprisonment and/or a fine not exceeding the statutory maximum.

Indictment: 5 years' imprisonment and/or a fine.

3.10.2 Making or supplying article for use in fraud

Section 7 deals with the offences of making or supplying an article for use in fraud.

Offences

A person is guilty of an offence if he makes, adapts, supplies or offers to supply any **article**—

(a) knowing that it is designed or adapted for use in the course of or in connection with **fraud**, or

(b) **intending** it to be used to commit, or assist in the commission of, fraud.

Fraud Act 2006, s 7(1)

Points to prove

✓ date and location
✓ made/adapted/supplied/offered to supply
✓ an article
✓ knowing that it was designed/adapted for use in the course of/in connection with fraud

OR

✓ intending it to be used to commit/assist in the commission of fraud

3.10.2 Making or Supplying Article for use in Fraud

Meanings

Article (see **3.10.1**)

Fraud (see **3.9.1**)

Intention (see **4.1.2**)

Explanatory notes

- The offence is to make, adapt, supply or offer to supply any article, knowing that it is designed or adapted for use in the course of or in connection with fraud, or intending it to be used to commit or facilitate fraud.
- Such an example would be where a person makes devices which when attached to electricity meters cause the meter to malfunction. The actual amount of electricity used is concealed from the provider, who thus suffers a loss.

Practical considerations

- A general intention to commit fraud will suffice rather than a specific offence in specific circumstances (eg credit card skimming equipment may provide evidence of such an intention).
- Proof is required that the defendant had the article for the purpose of or with the intention that it be used in the course of or in connection with fraud, and that a general intention to commit fraud will suffice.
- Consider s 12 (see **3.9.5**) as to liability of company officers for offences under this Act if they are committed by a body corporate. Similarly s 13 deals with evidential matters for offences under this Act.

 Either way

 None

 Summary: 12 months' imprisonment and/or a fine not exceeding the statutory maximum.

Indictment: 10 years' imprisonment and/or a fine.

Links to alternative subjects and offences

3.11 **Obtaining Services Dishonestly**

The Fraud Act 2006 provides for the offence of fraud and other fraudulent offences of which dishonesty is a constituent part. Section 11 makes it an offence for any person, by any dishonest act, to obtain services for which payment is required, with intent to avoid payment.

Offences

(1) A person is guilty of an offence under this section if he obtains services for himself or another—
   (a) by a **dishonest act,** and
   (b) in breach of subsection (2).
(2) A person obtains services in breach of this subsection if—
   (a) they are made available on the basis that payment has been, is being or will be made for or in respect of them,
   (b) he obtains them without any payment having been made for or in respect of them or without payment having been made in full, and
   (c) when he obtains them, he knows—
      (i) that they are being made available on the basis described in paragraph (a), or
      (ii) that they might be,
   but **intends** that payment will not be made, or will not be made in full.

Fraud Act 2006, s 11

Points to prove

✓ date and location
✓ obtained services for yourself/another by a dishonest act
✓ services were available on the basis that payment made for/in respect of them
✓ you obtained them without any payment/in full
✓ when you obtained them you knew that they were being/might be made available on the basis described above
✓ but you intended that payment would not be made/made in full

---

Meanings

Dishonest act (see 3.6)

Intention (see 4.1.2)

Explanatory notes

• This section makes it an offence for any person, by any dishonest act, to obtain services for which payment is required, with intent to avoid payment.

- This offence replaces the offence of obtaining services by deception in s 1 of the Theft Act 1978, although the new offence contains no deception element.
- It is not possible to commit the offence by omission alone and it can be committed only where the dishonest act was done with the intent not to pay for the services as expected.

Practical considerations

- The person must know that the services are made available on the basis that they are chargeable, or that they might be.
- There is nothing to suggest that the services obtained need to be lawful for this offence to be committed (eg services of a prostitute).
- There must be some action or communication by the defendant rather than an error wholly initiated by the supplier of the service which is unaffected by behaviour on the part of the defendant.
- The offence is not inchoate, it requires the actual obtaining of the service, for example data or software that is only available on the Internet once you have paid for access rights to that service.
- Examples of this offence would be where a person—
  - dishonestly uses false credit card details or other false personal information to obtain the service;
  - climbs over a wall and watches a football match without paying the entrance fee—such a person is not deceiving the provider of the service directly, but is obtaining a service which is provided on the basis that people will pay for it;
  - attaches a decoder to a television set in order to view/have access to cable/satellite channels for which they have no intention of paying.
- Consider s 12 (see **3.9.5**) as to liability of company officers for offences under this Act if they are committed by a body corporate.

 Either way   None

Summary: 12 months' imprisonment and/or a fine not exceeding the statutory maximum.

Indictment: 5 years' imprisonment and/or a fine.

Links to alternative subjects and offences

E&S   Entry and search powers

Chapter 4
Crime: General

4.1 Criminal Attempts/Meaning of Intent/Encourage or Assist Crime

4.1.1 Criminal attempts

In certain circumstances where an offence is not actually committed, the **attempt** to do so is an offence in itself. The Criminal Attempts Act 1981 creates an offence of 'attempting' to commit certain crimes. It is imperative to prove intent (mens rea) for attempt offences, as well as other offences requiring intent. Intent is thus discussed in detail.

Offence

(1) If, with **intent** to commit an **offence to which this section applies,** a person does an act which is more than merely preparatory to the commission of the offence, he is guilty of attempting to commit the offence.

(2) A person may be guilty of attempting to commit an offence to which this section applies even though the facts are such that the commission of the offence is impossible.

(3) In any case where—
   (a) apart from this subsection a person's intention would not be regarded as having amounted to an intent to commit an offence; but
   (b) if the facts of the case had been as he believed them to be, his intention would be so regarded

then, for the purposes of subsection (1) above, he shall be regarded as having had an intent to commit that offence.

Criminal Attempts Act 1981, s 1

4.1.1 Criminal Attempts

Points to prove

✓ date and location
✓ with intent
✓ attempted
✓ **(wording of the offence attempted)**

Meanings

Intent (see **4.1.2**)

Offence to which this section applies

This section applies to any offence which if it were completed, would be triable as an indictable offence, **other than**:

- conspiracy (at common law or under s 1 of the Criminal Law Act 1977 or any other enactment);
- aiding, abetting, counselling, procuring, or suborning the commission of an offence;
- offences under s 4(1) (assisting offenders) or s 5(1) (accepting or agreeing to accept consideration for not disclosing information about a relevant offence) of the Criminal Law Act 1967.

More than merely preparatory (see 'Explanatory notes'—below)

Explanatory notes

- Therefore, a person may attempt an offence that is either indictable or triable either way. However, offences that are 'summary only' cannot be attempted, together with the above specific exclusions.
- Whether an act is more than merely preparatory to the commission of an offence is ultimately for the jury/court to decide. However, two tests have been set out over the years and have been accepted by the higher courts. These are—
    - The test set out in *R v Eagleton* (1855) Dears CC 515: whether there was any further act on the defendant's part remaining to be done before the completion of the intended crime.
    - The decision in *Davey v Lee* (1967) 51 Cr App R 303: the offence of attempt is complete if the defendant does an act which is a step towards the commission of the specific crime, which is immediately (and not just remotely) connected with the commission of it, the doing of which cannot reasonably be regarded as having any other purpose than the commission of the specific crime.
- Remember—a criminal attempt is not the same as having the intent to commit the offence. If an act is only preparatory (eg obtaining an insurance claim form to make a false claim), then it is not an attempt. There would have to be some other act such as actually filling the form out and posting it. Mere intent is not enough.
- A typical example is *R v Geddes* [1996] Crim LR 894. Here G had hidden materials on school premises, which could be used for

---

kidnapping a child. There was no evidence he had started to carry out his intended action. The Court of Appeal determined that his actions were merely preparatory to the offence and did not go far enough to amount to an attempt. Compare this case with *R v Tosti and White* [1997] EWCA Crim 222 in which examining a padlock was considered to be more than a preparatory act.

• Attempting the impossible can be sufficient for a criminal attempt, as illustrated in the case of *R v Shivpuri* [1986] UKHL 2 (below).

Related cases

R v Ilyas (1984) 78 Cr App R 17, CA When a criminal attempt begins, an act has to be more than merely preparatory.

Davey & others v Lee (1967) 51 Cr App R 303, CA What constitutes an attempt— see above.

R v Shivpuri [1986] UKHL 2, HL S was arrested by customs officers in possession of a suitcase in which S believed he had hidden heroin. The 'drugs' turned out to be harmless powder, but by receiving and hiding the powder in the suitcase, S had done an act that was more than merely preparatory to the commission of the import of heroin offence (even though it was harmless powder). S was guilty of attempting to import heroin—by attempting the impossible under s 1(2).

Attorney-General's Reference (No 1 of 1992) [1993] 2 All ER 190, CA Attempted penetration not necessary for attempted rape.

R v Williams (1991) 92 Cr App R 158, CA No attempt needed for perverting the course of justice charge.

Practical considerations

• Criminal attempt offences can only occur where the principal offence is either an indictable offence or one that is triable either way.
• Even though damage under £5,000 can be dealt with at magistrates' court, a suspect can still be charged with attempting to damage property under £5,000, because the attempt damage offence is still an 'either way' offence. It is not a purely summary offence in the normal sense (*R v Bristol Justices ex parte Edgar* [1998] 3 All ER 798).
• In circumstances where a person commits the full offence of aiding and abetting, the offender should be charged as principal to the main offence where the offence is indictable or either way.
• When investigating attempted murder consideration must be given to the CPS advice offered in the assault charging standards (see 'Assault' 2.1 and 'Murder' 2.7).
• Powers of arrest, search, mode of trial, penalty, and time limits are the same as those relating to the principal offence.
• Consider confiscation of cash and property for an offence of attempting, conspiring, or inciting the commission of a 'criminal lifestyle' offence under Sch 2 of the Proceeds of Crime Act 2002 (see 5.6 for details).

4.1.2 **Meaning of Intent**

CHAR Where substantive theft/sexual offences apply

TRIG **Only** in relation to attempt of the following offences—

- **Theft—s 1** (see **3.1**)
- Robbery—s 8 (see **3.2**)
- Burglary—s 9 (see **3.3**)
- Handling stolen goods—s 22 (see **3.6**)
- Fraud—s 1 (see **3.9.1**)

  Either way   None

Summary: 6 months' imprisonment and/or a fine not exceeding the statutory maximum.

Indictment: 5 years' imprisonment.

4.1.2 **Meaning of intent**

The mens rea, which is Latin for 'guilty mind', has to be proved—more so in 'attempts' than in any other offence.

Intent

This can be proved by drawing on various sources of information—

- admissions made by the defendant in interview which reveal their state of mind at the time of commission of the offence;
- answers given by the defendant to questions regarding their actions and intentions at the time of the offence;
- by inference from the circumstances of the offence;
- evidence from witnesses;
- actions of the defendant before, during and after the event, and property found on them or in their control (such as a vehicle for transporting property).

To prove intent, you need to take all of the above into account. However, the important thing is that you have to **prove** the defendant's **state of mind** at the time.

Statutory test

A jury/magistrates' court must consider the circumstances and decide whether the defendant would have intended or foreseen the results which occurred by way of a **subjective test**.

A court or jury in determining whether a person has committed an offence—

(a) shall not be bound by law to infer that he intended or foresaw a result of his actions by reason only of its being a natural and probable consequence of those actions; **but**

(b) shall decide whether he did intend or foresee that result by reference to all the evidence, drawing such inferences from the evidence as appear proper in the circumstances.

Criminal Justice Act 1967, s 8

Subjective test

The difference between 'objective' and 'subjective' tests are important here. *Blacks Law Dictionary* defines the terms as—

• *Objective*: 'Of, relating to, or based on externally verifiable phenomena, as opposed to an individual's perceptions, feelings, or intentions.' This is sometimes used in the context of the 'reasonable person' test—What would a reasonable man or woman perceive to be the rights or wrongs of the matter in question or the likely outcome?

• *Subjective*: 'Based on an individual's perceptions, feelings, or intentions, as opposed to externally verifiable phenomena.' In a legal context this is more or less the opposite of objective. Instead of the hypothetical reasonable person, subjectivity requires a court to establish whether the offender was in fact conscious of a risk or other factor.

Strict liability

For some rare criminal offences, 'strict liability' will be enough to secure a conviction. The liability for committing this type of offence does not depend on an intention (such as causing harm) or particular state of mind (eg recklessness), but is based on the breach of a duty. Beyond road traffic offences, the occasions where strict liability offences will be encountered by police officers are very limited.

4.1.3 **Encourage or assist crime**

Part 2 (ss 44–67) of the Serious Crime Act 2007 abolishes the common law offence of incitement and creates three encouraging or assisting crime offences. This area of law is far too wordy and involved to give full details, but sufficient law is provided to give an idea as to what is involved.

Offences

A person commits an offence if—

(a) he **does an act capable of encouraging or assisting** the commission of an offence; and

(b) he **intends** to encourage or assist its commission.

Serious Crime Act 2007, s 44(1)

4.1.3 Encourage or Assist Crime

Points to prove

✓ date and location
✓ did an act which was capable of encouraging or assisting
✓ in the commission of an offence namely (*detail offence*)
✓ intending to
✓ encourage or assist in its commission

Meanings

Does an act

This includes a reference to a course of conduct.

Capable of encouraging or assisting

(1) A reference in this Part to a person's doing an act that is capable of encouraging the commission of an offence includes a reference to his doing so by threatening another person or otherwise putting pressure on another person to commit the offence.
(2) A reference in this Part to a person's doing an act that is capable of encouraging or assisting the commission of an offence includes a reference to his doing so by—
 (a) taking steps to reduce the possibility of criminal proceedings being brought in respect of that offence;
 (b) failing to take reasonable steps to discharge a duty.
(3) But a person is not to be regarded as doing an act that is capable of encouraging or assisting the commission of an offence merely because he fails to respond to a constable's request for assistance in preventing a breach of the peace.

Serious Crime Act 2007, s 65

Encouraging or assisting commission of an offence

Reference in Pt 2 to encouraging or assisting the commission of an offence is to be read in accordance with s 47.

Intends (see **4.1.2**)

Explanatory notes

- A person is not taken to have intended to encourage or assist the commission of an offence merely because such encouragement or assistance was a foreseeable consequence of that person's act.
- If a person (D1) arranges for a person (D2) to do an act that is capable of encouraging or assisting the commission of an offence, and D2 does the act, D1 is also to be treated for the purposes of this Part as having done it.
- Section 47 provides further meanings, assumptions, and in particular sets out what is required to prove intent or belief and whether an act would amount to the commission of an offence.

Defences of acting reasonably

(1) A person is not guilty of an offence under this Part if he proves—
    (a) that he knew certain circumstances existed; and
    (b) that it was reasonable for him to act as he did in those circumstances.

(2) A person is not guilty of an offence under this Part if he proves—
    (a) that he believed certain circumstances to exist;
    (b) that his belief was reasonable; and
    (c) that it was reasonable for him to act as he did in the circumstances as he believed them to be.

(3) Factors to be considered in determining whether it was reasonable for a person to act as he did include—
    (a) the seriousness of the anticipated offence (or, in the case of an offence under section 46, the offences specified in the indictment);
    (b) any purpose for which he claims to have been acting;
    (c) any authority by which he claims to have been acting.

Serious Crime Act 2007, s 50

Practical considerations

- Other sections worthy of note in Pt 2 of the Act are as follows—
    - s 45 Encouraging or assisting an offence believing it will be committed
    - s 46 Encouraging or assisting offences believing one or more will be committed
    - s 47 Proving an offence under Pt 2
    - s 48 Further provision as to proving a s 46 offence
    - s 49 Supplemental provisions
    - s 51 Protective offences: victims not liable
    - s 56 Persons who may be perpetrators or encouragers.
- A person may commit an offence under Pt 2 whether or not any offence capable of being encouraged or assisted by his act is committed.
- Consider confiscation of cash and property for an offence under s 44, which is listed as a 'criminal lifestyle' offence under Sch 2 of the Proceeds of Crime Act 2002 (see **5.6** for details). Similarly aiding, abetting, counselling, or procuring the commission of the s 46 offence is also listed under Sch 2.

 s 46 Indictment   None

 ss 44 or 45 Triable in same way as anticipated offence   Variable as to trial venue

 ss 44–46 Penalty As given in the anticipated offence, subject to s 58.

Links to alternative subjects and offences

4.2 **Vehicle Interference and Tampering with a Motor Vehicle**

The Criminal Attempts Act 1981 and the Road Traffic Act 1988 created offences designed to protect motor vehicles from the actions of others name-ly vehicle interference and tampering with motor vehicles. Although the defendant may be trying to take the vehicle without the owner's consent, the law does not allow 'criminal attempts' for purely summary offences

4.2.1 **Vehicle interference**

Offences

(1) A person is guilty of the offence of vehicle interference if he **interferes** with a **motor vehicle** or **trailer** or with anything carried in or on a motor vehicle or trailer with the **intention** that an offence specified in subsection (2) below shall be committed by himself or some other person.

(2) The offences mentioned in subsection (1) above are—
   (a) theft of the motor vehicle or part of it;
   (b) theft of anything carried in or on the motor vehicle or trailer; and
   (c) an offence under section 12(1) of the Theft Act 1968 (taking a conveyance)

   and if it is shown that a person accused of an offence under this sec-tion intended that one of those offences should be committed, it is immaterial that it cannot be shown which it was.

Criminal Attempts Act 1981, s 9

Points to prove

✓ date and location
✓ interfere with a
✓ motor vehicle/trailer/part of/anything carried in/on it
✓ with intent that an offence of
✓ theft/taking and drive away without consent
✓ should be committed

Meanings

Interferes (see **'Related cases'**—below*)*

Motor vehicle

Means a mechanically propelled vehicle intended or adapted for use on a road (see **10.1.3**).

4.2.2 Tampering with Motor Vehicles

Trailer

Means a vehicle drawn by a motor vehicle (see **10.1.3**).

Intention (see **4.1.2**)

Explanatory notes

This offence 'fits' between the offence of going equipped (an offence which may be committed prior to any contact with a 'conveyance') and the offence of taking a conveyance without the owner's consent or theft (which is dependent on whether or not an intention to permanently deprive can be established).

Related Cases

Reynolds and Warren v Metropolitan Police [1982] Crim LR 831, CC Interference has to be more than merely looking into vehicles and/or touching them.

Practical considerations

- Has the suspect possession of any implements for use in the offence that would not necessarily complete the offence of going equipped?
- Is there any CCTV evidence available?
- Check on the availability of witness evidence for CJA statements.

SSS

 Summary

 6 months, but if endanger road user: none.

 3 months' imprisonment and/or a fine not exceeding level 4 on the standard scale.

4.2.2 **Tampering with motor vehicles**

Offences

If while a **motor vehicle** is on a **road** or on a parking place provided by a local authority, a person—
(a) gets on to the **vehicle**, or
(b) tampers with the brake or **other part of its mechanism**
without lawful authority or reasonable cause he is guilty of an offence.

Road Traffic Act 1988, s 25(1)

Points to prove
✓ date and location
✓ without lawful authority or reasonable cause
✓ got on to/tampered with
✓ the brakes/other mechanism of a motor vehicle
✓ on a road/parking place provided by local authority

Meanings

Motor vehicle/vehicle (see **10.1.3**)

Road (see **10.1.1**)

Tamper

Means improperly interfering with something.

Other part of its mechanism

Means any mechanical part and not just those of a similar type to the brake.

Explanatory notes

- The motor vehicle must be on a road (see **10.1.1**) and/or on a parking place provided by the local authority.
- It is for the prosecution to prove the above and that the accused got onto or tampered with the motor vehicle without lawful authority or reasonable cause.

Defences

People with lawful authority and reasonable cause will have a defence. Lawful authority might take the form of a police officer or firefighter releasing the brake of a vehicle to move it in an emergency.

Practical considerations

- Has the suspect possession of any implements for use in the offence that would not necessarily complete the offence of going equipped?
- Is there any CCTV evidence available?
- Check on the availability of witness evidence for CJA statements.

 Summary   6 months

 Fine not exceeding level 3 on the standard scale.

Links to alternative subjects and offences

4.3 **Taking a Conveyance Without Owner's Consent**

The following topic covers three aspects: taking a conveyance without the owner's consent (TWOC), aggravated vehicle-taking, and the taking of pedal cycles. TWOC can also be known as unlawful taking of a motor vehicle (UTMV) or taking and driving away (TDA).

4.3.1 **Taking a conveyance without owner's consent**

Offences

Subject to subsections (5) and (6) below, a person shall be guilty of an offence if, without having the consent of the **owner** or other lawful authority, he **takes** any **conveyance** for his own or another's use or, knowing that any conveyance has been taken without such authority, drives it or allows himself to be carried in or on it.

Theft Act 1968, s 12(1)

Points to prove

There are several sets of circumstances depending on the role taken in the offence. Following relates to initial taker only:
✓ date and location
✓ without the consent
✓ of the owner/other lawful authority
✓ took a conveyance
✓ for your own/another's use

Meanings

Owner

If the conveyance is subject to a hiring or hire purchase agreement means the person in possession of the conveyance under that agreement.

Takes

Some movement of the conveyance is essential (*R v Bogacki* [1973] 2 All ER 864).

Conveyance

Means any conveyance constructed or adapted for the carriage of a person or persons whether by land, water, or air, **except** that it **does not include** a conveyance constructed or adapted for use only under the control of a person not carried in or on it.

4.3.1 Taking a Conveyance without Owner's Consent

Explanatory notes

- An important point is that the conveyance must be capable of carrying a person. A machine such as a small domestic lawn mower is not a conveyance, but one upon which the operator sits would be.
- A horse is an animal and therefore not 'constructed or adapted', so it is not a 'conveyance'.
- Pedal cycles are catered for in s 12(5) (see **4.3.3**).
- You must prove the use or intended use as a means of transport. If the conveyance is not used in this way (eg pushing a car away from a drive entrance to remove an obstruction), then there is no 'taking'.
- If it is used to ride on while being pushed then there may be a taking (*R v Bow* [1977] Crim LR 176).
- A dinghy on a trailer that is to be used as a dinghy at some future time is still 'taken' for the taker's/another's own use. Use has been held to mean 'use as a conveyance' and future intended use is sufficient (*R v Marchant and McAllister* (1985) 80 Cr App R 361).
- The term 'carried in or on' requires some movement of the conveyance. In *R v Miller* [1976] Crim LR 147, a man found sitting in a boat that had been moored was found not guilty of the offence. The normal movement of the waves was deemed insufficient for the ingredients of the offence. However, the vertical movement of a hovercraft would be sufficient, because that is not a 'natural' movement taking place independently of the use of the conveyance.
- The term 'consent of the owner' does not arise simply on occasions where specific permission has been given. Problems tend to arise where the owner has given some form of conditional consent; case law suggests that if the borrower of a car, for instance, makes a reasonable detour to their journey, then that detour will still be made 'with the consent of the owner'. However, using the conveyance for a wholly or substantially different purpose may well be an offence. This element is also relevant to one of the statutory defences (below).
- To prove the term 'allows himself', it is necessary to show that the defendant knew that the conveyance had been taken without the consent of the owner or other lawful authority. The person may not know that when they get into the conveyance, but if they find out subsequently, they are expected to make some attempt to leave.
- The essential difference between this offence and the offence of theft is that in this offence there is an absence of any intention to permanently deprive the owner of their property.

Defences

A person does not commit an offence under this section by anything done in the belief that he has lawful authority to do it or that he would have the owner's consent if the owner knew of his doing it and the circumstances of it.

Theft Act 1968, s 12(6)

Defence notes

- The prosecution must prove that the defendant did not believe that they had lawful authority (such as a police or local authority power of removal, or repossession by a finance company).
- Apart from the belief that the owner would have consented if they had known of the using of the conveyance, it must also be shown that they believed that the owner would have consented had they known of the circumstances of the taking and the using of it.

Related cases

R v Bogacki [1973] 2 All ER 864, CA 'Taking' must involve movement.

R v Pearce [1973] Crim LR 321, CA 'Taking' should be given its ordinary meaning.

R v Wibberley [1965] 3 All ER 718, CA Use of company vehicle outside working hours.

McKnight v Davies [1974] Crim LR 62, CA The taking is complete when consent is exceeded.

Whittaker v Campbell [1983] 3 All ER 582, QBD Consent of owner is valid even if obtained by fraud.

R v Peart [1970] 2 All ER 823, CA Misrepresentation must be fundamental to void consent.

R v Marchant and McAllister (1985) 80 Cr App R 361, CA Intended use sufficient.

Practical considerations

- If on the trial of an indictment for theft of a conveyance, the jury are not satisfied that the accused committed theft, they may find the accused guilty of the s 12(1) offence.
- As the offence is only summary, there is no such thing as an 'attempted taking of a conveyance' (see **4.1.1**).
- Consider the more serious offence of aggravated vehicle-taking (see **4.3.2**).
- In the interview, the situation where the person becomes aware that the conveyance has been taken after they had entered it should be covered along with any subsequent efforts to leave the conveyance.
- The Act allows for the extension of **prosecution time limits**, where proceedings shall not be commenced after the end of the period of 3 years beginning with the day on which the offence was committed. Subject to the 3 year maximum period, proceedings may be commenced at any time within the period of 6 months beginning with the **relevant day**.
- The '**relevant day**' means the day on which sufficient evidence is available to justify proceedings.

4.3.2 Aggravated Vehicle-Taking

SSS **E&S** **CHAR** **TRIG**

  Summary   Complex—see **'Prosecution time limits'** above

6 months' imprisonment and/or a fine not exceeding level 5 on the standard scale. Discretionary disqualification.

4.3.2 **Aggravated vehicle-taking**

The Aggravated Vehicle-Taking Act 1992 inserted s 12A into the Theft Act 1968 thereby creating the various offences of 'aggravated vehicle-taking'.

Offences

(1) Subject to subsection 12A(3) *[defence]* a person is guilty of aggravated taking of a vehicle if—
  (a) he commits an offence under section 12(1) (taking a conveyance without consent) (in this section referred to as the 'basic offence') in relation to a mechanically propelled vehicle, and
  (b) it is proved that, at any time after the vehicle was unlawfully taken (whether by him or another) and before it was recovered, the vehicle was driven or injury or damage was caused, in one or more of the circumstances set out in paragraphs (a) to (d) of subsection 12A(2).
(2) The circumstances referred to in subsection (1)(b) are—
  (a) that the vehicle was driven dangerously on a road or other public place;
  (b) that, owing to the driving of the vehicle, an accident occurred by which injury was caused to any person;
  (c) that, owing to the driving of the vehicle, an accident occurred by which damage was caused to any property, other than the vehicle;
  (d) that damage was caused to the vehicle.

Theft Act 1968, s 12A

Points to prove

✓ date and location
✓ without the consent
✓ of the owner/other lawful authority
✓ took (being the initial taker)
✓ a mechanically propelled vehicle for
✓ your own/another's use
(The 'basic offence')

And after it was taken and before it was recovered—
✓ the vehicle was driven dangerously on a road/public place **or**
✓ accident which caused injury to person(s), damage to any property or the vehicle

---

Meanings

Dangerously (see **10.7.1**)

A vehicle is driven dangerously if—
- it is driven in a way which falls far below what would be expected of a competent and careful driver; **and**
- it would be obvious to a competent and careful driver that driving the vehicle in that way would be dangerous.

Accident

Means 'any unintended occurrence which has an adverse physical result' and the legislation does not specify that it has to occur on a road or even in a public place.

Damage

Means any damage not just criminal damage.

Explanatory notes

- 'Owner' has the same meaning as s 12(1) (see **4.3.1**).
- Consider the offence of dangerous driving (see **10.7.1**).
- A vehicle is recovered when it is restored to its owner or to other lawful possession or custody.
- It would appear that a vehicle has been recovered once the police, owner, or some other person with the authority of the owner, takes responsibility for the vehicle. However, if the police have been informed of the location of a taken vehicle, it has yet to be decided whether 'recovered' is from the time of the call or the time the police arrive at the scene and take physical control.
- This offence only applies to mechanically propelled vehicles and not to all conveyances.
- Passengers in a vehicle involved in such an offence can also be liable to prosecution. Their culpability would be increased depending upon the extent or degree of encouragement they may have given to the driver.

Defences

A person is not guilty of an offence under this section if he proves that, as regards any such proven driving, injury or damage as is referred to in subsection (1)(b) (aggravating factors) above, either—
(a) the driving, accident or damage referred to above occurred before he committed the basic offence; or
(b) he was neither in, nor on, nor in the immediate vicinity of, the vehicle when that driving, accident or damage occurred.

Theft Act 1968, s 12A(3)

Related cases

Dawes v DPP [1995] 1 Cr App R 65, QBD Injury to a person or damage to property owing to driving or damage caused to the taken vehicle (whether by driving or not) needs to be proved.

4.3.3 Take Pedal Cycle without Consent

R v Wheatley and Another [2007] EWCA Crim 835, CA Passengers can also be liable and the degree of their culpability will depend upon the amount of encouragement they give the actual driver of the vehicle.

Practical considerations

- The fact that the person who originally took the vehicle is not the person who caused the accident resulting in personal injury is irrelevant—the initial taker can still be prosecuted for the aggravated offence. Nor is there any requirement that the driver of the 'taken vehicle' has to be at fault when a personal injury accident occurs (*R v Marsh* [1996] 8 CL 54).
- Always bear in mind the above defences when interviewing.
- The aggravated offence never becomes statute barred as it is an either way offence. Even if the damage caused is under £5,000 and the offence is triable only summarily, it is still an either way offence.
- By virtue of s 12A(5), a person who is found not guilty of this offence can still be found guilty of taking a vehicle without consent as an alternative.

 Either way   ⏱ None

Summary: 6 months' imprisonment and/or a fine not exceeding the statutory maximum.

Indictment: 2 years' imprisonment, **but** where a person dies as a result of an accident involving the offence, 14 years' imprisonment.

4.3.3 **Take pedal cycle without consent**

Taking or riding a pedal cycle without the consent of the owner or other lawful authority is an offence.

Offences

Taking a conveyance shall not apply in relation to pedal cycles; but, subject to subsection (6) below *[defences]*, a person who, without having the consent of the owner or other lawful authority takes a pedal cycle for his own or another's use, or rides a pedal cycle knowing it to have been taken without such authority, shall be guilty of an offence.

Theft Act 1968, s 12(5)

Points to prove
- ✓ date and location
- ✓ consent of the owner

✓ takes/rides
✓ pedal cycle
✓ for own or other's use

Explanatory notes

- A pedal cycle is neither propelled by mechanical power nor is it electrically assisted.
- There are many types of 'hybrid' vehicles, such as motorized scooters that may qualify as mechanically propelled vehicles or conveyances. Ultimately this is a question of fact for the court to decide.

Defences (see **4.3.1**)

Related Cases

Sturrock v DPP [1996] RTR 216, QBD Where it is admitted that no consent had been given there is no need for an owner to be identified or any statement taken. The court can infer that the bicycle has an owner.

Practical considerations

- The prosecution must prove that the accused did not have lawful authority, such as a police or local authority power of removal, or repossession by a finance company.
- As this is a summary offence, there is no offence of 'attempting to take a pedal cycle' (see **4.1.1**).

  Summary   6 months

  Fine not exceeding level 3 on the standard scale.

Links to alternative subjects and offences

4.4 **Criminal Damage**

The offence of criminal damage is designed to protect people's property from the unlawful actions of others. Section 1 of the Criminal Damage Act 1971 creates the offence of simple 'criminal damage'.

Offences

A person who without lawful excuse **destroys** or **damages** any **property belonging to another intending** to destroy or damage any such property or being **reckless** as to whether any such property would be destroyed or damaged shall be guilty of an offence.

Criminal Damage Act 1971, s 1(1)

Points to prove

- ✓ date and location
- ✓ without lawful excuse
- ✓ destroyed/damaged
- ✓ property to value of
- ✓ intending to
- ✓ destroy/damage such property **or**
- ✓ being reckless whether it was destroyed/damaged

Meanings

Destroyed

Means property which is incapable of being repaired and can only be replaced.

Damaged

Means property that has suffered some physical harm, impairment, or deterioration.

Property (s 10(1))

Means property of a tangible nature, whether real or personal, including money and—

(a) including wild creatures which have been tamed or are ordinarily kept in captivity, and any other wild creatures or their carcasses if, but only if, they have been reduced into possession which has not been lost or abandoned or are in the course of being reduced into possession; but

(b) not including mushrooms growing wild on any land or flowers, fruit or foliage of a plant growing wild on any land.

Belonging to another

This is property that belongs to another person who has custody or control of it, or who has a right or an interest in it, or has a charge over it.

Intending (see **4.1.2**).

Reckless

The test set out in *R v G and R* [2003] UKHL 50 applies, which states that a person acts 'recklessly' for the purposes of s 1 with respect to—
• circumstances where that person is aware of a risk that exists or will exist;
• a result when they are aware of a risk that it will occur;
and it is, in the circumstances known to them, unreasonable to take the risk.

The **first part** provides for those existing or future circumstances known to the defendant which, in the circumstances as known to them, made it unreasonable to take the risk they took. An example would be a tramp taking shelter in a barn full of dry hay: aware of the risk they light a fire to boil water for a cup of tea, and set the barn alight.

The **second part** of the test applies if the person is aware that the result of their actions are a risk and, in the circumstances as known to them, it would be unreasonable to take that risk. An example would be an adult who lets off a large rocket and ignores instructions which state that the firework should be launched from a tube embedded in the ground and instead launches it from a bottle standing upright on the pavement. As a result the rocket goes through the window of a house opposite and causes a fire

The case of *G and R* involved two children aged 11 and 12 who set fire to a shop when lighting newspapers in a yard at the back. It was argued in their defence that, although the act might have been an obvious risk to the average person, it might not be obvious to such young children. The House of Lords agreed and overturned the previous 'objective' test in the case of *R v Caldwell* [1981] 1 All ER 961.

Explanatory notes

The important thing to prove or disprove (in addition to the damage itself) is the state of mind (intent) or that they were reckless in their actions, in destroying/damaging the property.

Defences

Lawful excuse

(1) This section applies to any offence under section 1(1) and any offence under section 2 or 3 other than one involving a threat by the person charged to destroy or damage property in a way which he knows is likely to endanger the life of another or involving an intent by the person charged to use or cause or permit the use of something in his custody or under his control so to destroy or damage property.

(2) A person charged with an offence to which this section applies shall, whether or not he would be treated for the purposes of this Act as having a lawful excuse apart from this subsection, be treated for those purposes as having a lawful excuse—

(a) if at the time of the act or acts alleged to constitute the offence he believed that the person or persons whom he believed to be entitled to consent to the destruction of or damage to the property in question had so consented, or would have so consented to it if he or they had known of the destruction or damage and its circumstances; or

(b) if he destroyed or damaged or threatened to destroy or damage the property in question or, in the case of a charge of an offence under section 3, intended to use or cause or permit the use of something to destroy or damage it, in order to protect property belonging to himself or another or a right or interest in property which was or which he believed to be vested in himself or another, and at the time of the act or acts alleged to constitute the offence he believed—

   (i) that the property, right or interest was in immediate need of protection; and

   (ii) that the means of protection adopted or proposed to be adopted were or would be reasonable having regard to all the circumstances.

(3) For the purposes of this section it is immaterial whether a belief is justified or not if it is honestly held.

Protect life or property

(4) For the purposes of subsection (2) above a right or interest in property includes any right or privilege in or over land, whether created by grant, licence or otherwise.

(5) This section shall not be construed as casting doubt on any defence recognised by law as a defence to criminal charges.

Criminal Damage Act 1971, s 5

Defence notes

Damage caused to protect life, prevent injury, or stop unlawful imprisonment of a person is also a valid defence (*R v Baker & another The Times*, 26 November 1996).

Related cases

R v Jones and others; Ayliffe and others v DPP, Swain v DPP [2006] UKHL 16, HL Defendants took part in protests at military bases against the war in Iraq and damaged the perimeter fence and vehicles. Claimed damage done to prevent the international crime of aggression and so was a 'lawful excuse' under s 5. Held: The right of citizens to use force or cause damage on their own initiative is limited when not defending their own person or property and furthermore it does not cover customary international law.

Johnson v DPP [1994] Crim LR 673, QBD When lawful excuse is the defence, two questions need to be asked. The first is an objective question (eg whether the act of damage was done in order to protect property); and second, a subjective question (whether the defendant believed that the property was in immediate need of protection and the means of protection used were reasonable).

Chamberlain v Lindon [1998] 2 All ER 538, QBD Requirement of immediacy (under s 5(2)(b)(i) above) will still be satisfied if the threat to property (or rights in property) is already taking place. Here, the defendant was charged with criminal damage after destroying a wall erected by his neighbour which obstructed a right of access to his property. The defendant had a lawful excuse for his action because the obstruction to his rights had already happened and he believed rights would be further prejudiced if the wall remained in place.

Drake v DPP [1994] Crim LR 855, QBD Damage must affect the integrity of the object damaged.

'A' (a Juvenile) v R [1978] Crim LR 689, CC Spitting on a police uniform did not constitute damage.

Hardman & others v Chief Constable of Avon & Somerset [1986] Crim LR 330, CC Cost of cleaning (here a pavement artist's water-soluble drawing on a street) may still amount to 'damage'.

Practical considerations

- If property has been destroyed, the value specified in the charge should reflect the full replacement cost.
- Charging that property was both 'destroyed' and 'damaged' is an unnecessary duplication, so wherever possible a choice should be made.
- Consider applying for a warrant (under s 6) to search for and seize anything in custody or control of suspect on their premises. Having reasonable cause to believe, has been used **or is intended for use** without lawful excuse to either: destroy or damage property— belonging to another or in a way likely to endanger the life of another.
- If the destruction or damage has been caused by fire, an offence of arson under s 1(3) should be charged (see **4.5.1**).
- Consider the more serious offence of racially or religiously aggravated criminal damage (see **7.10**).
- Where the value of the damage is below £5,000, the offence would normally be tried at a magistrates' court.
- If the full offence is not committed consider attempt criminal damage (see **4.1**).
- The same incident may involve separate activities, some causing ordinary damage and some damage by fire (for example, protestors break into a laboratory building, smash laboratory equipment and set fire to some files). In such circumstances they are separate offences and best charged as such.
- There is a special offence of criminal damage to an ancient monument under the Ancient Monuments and Archaeological Areas Act 1979, s 28. The advantage of using this offence is that the owner can also be liable for damaging the protected monument which they own.
- Consider the offences of having an article with intent to commit damage (see **4.7**) or made threats to cause damage (see **4.6**).

4.4 Criminal Damage

- Section 48 of the Anti-social Behaviour Act 2003 enables certain local authorities to serve a 'graffiti removal notice' on the owners of street furniture, buildings, structures, apparatus, plant, or other objects in or on any street, statutory undertakers, and educational institutions whose property is defaced with graffiti that is either detrimental to the local amenity of the area or deemed to be offensive. The notice will require the owners to remove the graffiti within a specified period of time (minimum 28 days).

SSS **E&S**

PND Police only

RRA **PCSO**

♿ Either way   🕐 None

🏛 **Summary:** *Value below £5000:* 3 months' imprisonment and/or a fine not exceeding level 4 on the standard scale. *Value of or exceeding £5000:* 6 months' imprisonment and/or a fine not exceeding the statutory maximum.

Indictment: 10 years' imprisonment.

Links to alternative subjects and offences

SSS Stop, search, and seize powers   **E&S** Entry and search powers   **PND** Penalty notice for disorder offences

RRA Racially or religiously aggravated offence   **PCSO** Police community support officers

4.5 Damage with Intent to Endanger Life and Arson

The offence of damage with intent to endanger life is also known as aggravated damage. This and arson are serious offences because of their potential to have disastrous effects on other people's lives and the wider community.

This section is presented in two parts: damage with intent to endanger life and then arson.

4.5.1 Damage with intent to endanger life

Section 1(2) of the Criminal Damage Act 1971 creates the serious offence of destroying or damaging property intending that, or being reckless as to whether life would be endangered.

Offences

A person who without lawful excuse, **destroys** or **damages** any **property**, whether **belonging to** himself or **another**—

(a) **intending** to destroy or damage any property or being **reckless** as to whether any property would be destroyed or damaged; and

(b) intending by the destruction or damage to endanger the life of another or being reckless as to whether the life of another would be thereby endangered;

shall be guilty of an offence.

Criminal Damage Act 1971, s 1(2)

Points to prove

✓ date and location
✓ without lawful excuse
✓ destroy/damage
✓ property
✓ whether belonging to self or another
✓ with intent destroy/damage or reckless destroy/damage AND
✓ intending by destruction/damage to endanger life of another or
✓ being reckless as to whether such life would thereby be endangered

Meanings

Lawful excuse (see 'Defence' below)

Intent (see **4.1.2**)

4.5.1 Damage with Intent to Endanger Life

Destroy (see **4.4**)

Damage (see **4.4**)

Property (see **4.4**)

Belonging to another (see **4.4**)

Endanger life

Does not require an attempt to kill or injury to occur. It is sufficient that life was endangered.

Reckless (see **4.4**)

Explanatory notes

- Consider attempt murder or manslaughter (see **4.1** and **2.7**).
- No actual injury need occur; all that is required is evidence that life was endangered. For example, if a jealous person cuts the brake pipe of his rival's car, no harm may actually come to the intended victim, but the potential for harm exists. Either intention to endanger the life of another or recklessness in that regard must be proved and the potential for harm to someone other than the defendant must be proved.
- The actual damage caused must also be the cause of the danger. For example, shooting at a person in a room (through a window) both endangers life and damages the window, but it is not the damage that endangers the life.

Defences

- Lawful excuse could be attempting to effect a rescue in order to save life, but in doing so it could endanger life.
- Statutory lawful excuse defence for damage given in s 5 (see **4.4**) specifically precludes damage with intent to endanger life and arson.

Related cases

R v Webster & others [1995] 2 All ER 168, CA Two similar cases relating to the offence of 'damage with intent to endanger life'. In the first case, the defendants pushed a coping stone from a bridge onto a moving railway carriage. No one was injured. Court decided that the principal intention of the defendants was for the stone to directly injure the passengers, therefore the offence of 'damage intending to endanger life' had not been committed. However, the court substituted a conviction for the offence of 'recklessness causing damage which could endanger life', (eg the debris that flew around the carriage following the incident). In the second case, the defendants threw bricks at a police car from a stolen car, aiming for its windscreen. The windscreen broke and injured one of the officers. In that case, the victim's resultant loss of vision would be sufficient for a conviction for the offence of causing damage with intent to endanger life. Establishing intention is important, so ascertain in interview what the offender's intentions were or what the perceived outcome of their actions would be.

R v Merrick [1995] Crim LR 802, CA M cut an electric mains and left live cabling exposed for 6 minutes; was convicted of damaging property, being reckless as to whether life was endangered. On appeal, M argued that he had weighed up the work and decided there was no significant risk, therefore he was not 'reckless'. Conviction was upheld on the reasoning that if M had wanted to make sure that he was outside the definition of 'reckless', remedies to eliminate risk would have to be taken **before** starting the work. It was too late to take action once the risk had been created.

R v Hardie [1984] 3 All ER 848, CA Recklessness after defendant has taken drugs is insufficient as defendant could not form the necessary mens rea.

R v Steer [1988] AC 111, HL Actual damage caused must give rise to the danger to life, not just the act of causing the damage.

Practical considerations

- The same incident may involve separate activities, some causing ordinary damage and some damage by fire (for example, protestors break into a laboratory building, smash laboratory equipment, and set fire to some files). In such circumstances they are separate offences and best charged as such.
- Damage by fire is arson (see **4.5.2**).

 Indictable   None

Life imprisonment

4.5.2 **Arson**

Section 1(3) of the Criminal Damage Act 1971 creates the offence of 'arson'.

Offence

An offence committed under this section by destroying or damaging property by fire shall be charged as arson.

Criminal Damage Act 1971, s 1(3)

Points to prove

Arson

✓ date and location
✓ without lawful excuse

> ✓ destroy/damage
> ✓ by fire
> ✓ property with intent to destroy/damage it or
> ✓ being reckless whether such property was destroyed/damaged
>
> *Arson—endanger life*
> ✓ all points to prove for arson (above) **and**
> ✓ intending by destruction/damage to endanger life of another **or**
> ✓ being reckless as to whether such life would be endangered

Meanings

Destroy (see **4.4**)

Damage (see **4.4**)

Property (see **4.4**)

Explanatory notes

For the offence to be complete, some of the damage must be by fire; this does not include smoke damage. It is enough, however, that wood is charred (*R v Parker* [1839] 173 E R 733).

Defence

There is no specific defence for arson.

Related cases

R v Drayton [2005] EWCA Crim 2013, CA A charge of causing criminal damage by fire under s 1(3) still constitutes a charge of arson even if 'arson' is not specifically stated in the charge.

Practical considerations

- Intention or recklessness must be proved. A burglar who accidentally dropped a lighted match used for illumination could be reckless.
- The same incident may involve separate activities, some causing ordinary damage and some damage by fire. These are separate offences and should be so charged.
- Most arsons involve the use of '**accelerants**' such as petrol or lighter fuel to start the fire. If it is suspected that accelerants might have been used, special procedures need to be implemented in order to obtain forensic samples.
- An accelerant is used to increase the speed of a chemical reaction. For police purposes, this usually means something to speed up the spread of a fire during an arson attack. Accelerants (such as petrol) are volatile and will evaporate if left in the open air. Do not confuse accelerants with oils and greases, which demand different treatment.

- Procedures for the careful preservation and packaging which must be carried out to enable the detection of accelerants can be divided into three basic areas—
  - clothing,
  - at the scene,
  - fragile items.
- Submit the control sample of the suspected accelerant in a clean metal container with a well fitting cap, sealed inside a **nylon bag**. If no metal can is available, use a clean glass container but protect any rubber insert in the cap with a nylon film. For this purpose cut up part of one of the nylon bags, and use the rest as a control—see below. Isolate from all other samples.
- Control sample of nylon bag used to seal any sample: in a case where a nylon bag has been employed to seal a sample, a control nylon bag from the same batch as the one used to contain the samples should be submitted. This should be sealed but should only contain air.
- Important—never dry out items suspected of containing fire accelerants before packaging. Never store or transport items for examination for the presence of fire accelerant materials in close proximity to a control sample of fire accelerant or anything taken from the defendant. Even a suspicion of contamination will destroy the evidential value of the samples.

 Either way   None

 Summary: 6 months' imprisonment and/or a fine not exceeding level 5 on the standard scale.

Indictment: Life imprisonment.

Links to alternative subjects and offences

4.6 **Threats to Destroy or Damage Property**

Section 2 of the Criminal Damage Act 1971 creates specific offences relating to threats to destroy or damage property.

Offences

A person who without **lawful excuse** makes to another a threat, **intending** that the other would fear it would be carried out—
(a) to **destroy** or **damage** any **property** belonging to that other or a third person; or
(b) to destroy or damage his own property in way which he knows is likely to **endanger** the **life** of that other or a third person
shall be guilty of an offence.

Criminal Damage Act 1971, s 2

Points to prove

✓ date and location
✓ without lawful excuse
✓ threatened to destroy/damage property of a person
✓ intending
✓ a person would fear that the threat would be carried out

Threaten damage own property to endanger life

✓ date and location
✓ without lawful excuse
✓ threatened to destroy/damage
✓ your own property
✓ in a way you knew
✓ was likely to endanger life of another
✓ intending a person would fear threat would be carried out

Meanings

Lawful excuse (see 'Defences' 4.4)

Intending (see 4.1.2)

Destroy (see 4.4)

Damage (see 4.4)

Property (see 4.4)

Endanger life (see 4.5.1)

Explanatory notes

- It is not necessary to show the other person is actually in fear that the threat will be carried out; what has to be proved is that the defendant intended the other to fear it will be carried out.
- It does not matter that the defendant may not actually intend to carry out the threats and/or the victim may not even believe them. The offender's **intention** to create such a fear is sufficient— and necessary—to complete the offence.
- The test for whether the action amounts to a threat is objective ie 'would the reasonable person conclude that a threat had been made?' (*R v Cakmak and others* [2002] EWCA Crim 500). Only intention will do; unlike s 1 there is no mention of reckless in this section.
- The threat must be to another person, and can relate to a third party—such as 'I will smash up your son's car if you don't do what I say'—the threat is to one person about their or a third person's property.
- In s 2(b) above, the offender can threaten to damage their own property in a way that is likely to endanger the life of another, such as a landlord threatening to burn down a house he owns if a tenant will not leave.
- In relation to the meaning of 'threats in criminal damage', two points must be considered—
  - ◆ the type of conduct threatened; and
  - ◆ the threat itself.
- There is no specific requirement for the threatened act to be immediate and a threat to do damage to a property at some time in the future may well suffice; each case will depend on the circumstances surrounding it.

Defence

Having a lawful excuse will be a defence under s 5 (see **4.4**).

 SSS E&S

 Either way

 None

 Summary: 6 months' imprisonment and/or a fine not exceeding the statutory maximum.

Indictment: 10 years' imprisonment.

Links to alternative subjects and offences

4.7 **Custody/Control of Articles with Intent to Damage and Sale of Paint Aerosols to Persons Under 16**

Even when criminal damage has not been committed or threatened, there may still have been an offence arising out of the possession of articles where there is an intention to cause damage. An offence of selling paint aerosols to children, is designed to address the increasing problem of criminal damage to property by way of graffiti.

4.7.1 **Custody/control of articles with intent to damage**

Section 3 of the Criminal Damage Act 1971 creates the offence of 'going equipped' intending to destroy or damage property.

Offences

A person who has **anything** in his **custody** or under his **control intending** without **lawful excuse** to use it or **cause** or **permit** another to use it—
(a) to destroy or damage any property belonging to some other person or
(b) to destroy or damage his own or the user's property in a way which he knows is likely to **endanger** the **life** of some other person;
shall be guilty of an offence.

Criminal Damage Act 1971, s 3

Points to prove

✓ date and location
✓ had in custody/control
✓ an article/object/substance/anything at all
✓ intending
✓ without lawful excuse
✓ to destroy/damage or to cause/permit another to use the article etc
✓ property belonging to another/own or user's property knowing life of another is likely to be endangered

---

Meanings

Anything

Means its natural/everyday meaning and can range from explosives to a box of matches or a hammer.

4.7.1 Custody/Control of Articles with Intent to Damage

Custody or control

It must be proved that the defendant had custody or control of the article in question. This is a wider term than possession and could cover occasions where the defendant does not have the article with them.

Intent (see **4.1.2**)

Lawful excuse (see **4.4**)

Cause

Means some degree of dominance or control, or some express or positive authorization, from the person who 'causes'.

Permit

Requires general or particular permission, as distinguished from authorization, and the permission may be express (eg verbal/written) or implied (eg the person's actions). A person cannot permit unless they are in a position to forbid and no one can permit what they cannot control.

Destroy (see **4.4**)

Damage (see **4.4**)

Property (see **4.4**)

Belonging to another (see **4.4**)

Endanger life (see **4.5.1**)

Explanatory notes

- The offence is split into two parts, but certain elements are common to both. Intent to use/cause/permit must be proved in all cases, as must the element of having anything in the defendant's custody/control and the absence of lawful excuse.
- The act intended does not have to be immediate; it can be at some time in the future (eg someone storing bomb-making materials for future use).
- The only difference between s 3(a) and s 3(b) offences is that in (b) there is an element of knowledge of the likelihood of endangering the life of someone else and the offender's own property can be the object of the intended damage (eg a person carrying a can of petrol to set fire to their own house with their partner inside).

Defence

Having a lawful excuse (see **4.4**).

Related cases

R v Fancy [1980] Crim LR 171, CC The intention must be to commit some specific damage.

R v Buckingham (1976) 63 Cr App R 159, CC Intention for an 'immediate use' is not necessary; an intention to use some time in the future will suffice.

Either way None

 Summary: 6 months' imprisonment and/or a fine not exceeding the statutory maximum.

Indictment: 10 years' imprisonment.

4.7.2 **Sale of aerosol paints to children**

Section 54 of the Anti-social Behaviour Act 2003 makes it an offence to sell aerosol spray paints to persons under 16. The objective is to reduce the incidence of graffiti criminal damage caused by young persons using cans of aerosol spray paint.

Offence

A person commits an offence if he sells an **aerosol paint container** to a person under the age of sixteen.

Anti-social Behaviour Act 2003, s 54(1)

Points to prove
✓ date and location
✓ sale
✓ an aerosol paint container
✓ to a person under the age of 16

Meaning of aerosol paint container

Means a device which contains paint stored under pressure, and is designed to permit the release of the paint as a spray.

Defences

(4) It is a defence for a person charged with an offence under this section in respect of a sale to prove that—
  (a) he took all reasonable steps to determine the purchaser's age, and
  (b) he reasonably believed that the purchaser was not under the age of sixteen.
(5) It is a defence for a person charged with an offence under this section in respect of a sale effected by another person to prove that he (the defendant) took all reasonable steps to avoid the commission of an offence under this section.

Anti-social Behaviour Act 2003, s 54

4.7.2 Sale of Aerosol Paints to Children

Practical considerations

- You will need to show that the sale was concluded, rather than simply the advertising or negotiating.
- There is no need to prove any intention by the purchaser or any specific knowledge/suspicion of intended knowledge on the part of the seller.
- Age to be proved by a birth certificate and testimony that it belongs to the person producing it.

 Summary   6 months

 A fine not exceeding level 4 on the standard scale.

Links to alternative subjects and offences

4.8 Intimidation of a Witness/Juror and Perverting the Course of Justice

Witnesses and/or jurors involved in the investigation or trial of criminal offences are protected from intimidation and/or threat by s 51 of the Criminal Justice and Public Order Act 1994. This area of law is presented in two parts: intimidation of a witness/juror, and perverting the course of justice.

4.8.1 Intimidation of a witness/juror

Offences

Intimidation

(1) A person commits an offence if—
   (a) he does an **act** which intimidates, and is intended to intimidate, another person ('the victim'),
   (b) he does the act knowing or believing that the victim is assisting in the **investigation of an offence** or is a witness or **potential** witness or a juror or **potential** juror in proceedings for an offence; and
   (c) he does it **intending** thereby to cause the investigation or the course of justice to be obstructed, perverted or interfered with.

Threats

(2) A person commits an offence if—
   (a) he does an act which harms, and is intended to harm, another person or, intending to cause another person to fear harm, he threatens to do an act which would harm that other person,
   (b) he does or threatens to do the act knowing or believing that the person harmed or threatened to be harmed ('the victim'), or some other person, has assisted in an investigation into an offence or has given evidence or particular evidence in proceedings for an offence, or has acted as a juror or concurred in a particular verdict in proceedings for an offence; and
   (c) he does or threatens to do it because of that knowledge or belief.

Criminal Justice and Public Order Act 1994, s 51

Points to prove

Intimidate a witness/juror

✓ date and location
✓ knew/believed person was
✓ assisting investigation of offence or a witness/potential witness or juror/potential juror

4.8.1 Intimidation of a Witness/Juror

- ✓ in proceedings for offence
- ✓ did an act which
- ✓ intimidated that person and was intended to do so
- ✓ intending to cause investigation/course of justice to be obstructed or perverted or interfered with

Harm/threaten a witness/juror

- ✓ date and location
- ✓ knew/believed person or another had assisted in investigation/ given evidence in proceedings/acted as juror/concurred in particular verdict
- ✓ because of that knowledge/belief
- ✓ threatened/did an act which
- ✓ harmed/was intended to harm/would have harmed person

Meanings

Investigation into an offence

Means such an investigation by the police or other person charged with the duty of investigating offences or charging offenders.

Offence

Includes an alleged or suspected offence.

Potential

In relation to a juror, means a person who has been summonsed for jury service at the court at which proceedings for the offence are pending.

Intending

Intimidation offence

If, in proceedings against a person for an offence under subsection (1), it is proved that he did an act falling within paragraph (a) with the knowledge or belief required by paragraph (b), he shall be presumed, unless the contrary is proved, to have done the act with the intention required by paragraph (c) of that subsection.

Criminal Justice and Public Order Act 1994, s 51(7)

Threatened/harmed offence (see 4.1.2)

Act

In proceedings against a person for an offence under subsection (2) (**threats**) if it can be proved by the prosecution that within the **relevant period** he did or threatened to do an act described by (a) above with the knowledge or belief of (b) above, then he shall be presumed, unless the contrary is proved, to have done the act (or threatened to do the act) with the motive required by (c) above.

Criminal Justice and Public Order Act 1994, s 51(8)

The relevant period

In this section 'the relevant period'—

(a) in relation to a witness or juror in any proceedings for an offence, means the period beginning with the **institution of the proceedings** and ending with the first anniversary of the conclusion of the trial or, if there is an appeal or reference under ss 9 or 11 of the Criminal Appeal Act 1995, of the conclusion of the appeal;

(b) in relation to a person who has, or is believed by the accused to have, assisted in an investigation into an offence, but was not also a witness in proceedings for an offence, means the period of one year beginning with any act of his, or any act believed by the accused to be an act of his, assisting in the investigation; and

(c) in relation to a person who both has, or is believed by the accused to have, assisted in the investigation into an offence and was a witness in proceedings for the offence, means the period beginning with any act of his, or any act believed by the accused to be an act of his, assisting in the investigation and ending with the anniversary mentioned in paragraph (a) above.

Criminal Justice and Public Order Act 1994, s 51(9)

Institution of proceedings

For the purposes of the definition of the relevant period in subsection (9) above—

(a) proceedings for an offence are instituted at the earliest of the following times:

(i) when a justice of the peace issues a summons or warrant under s 1 of the Magistrates' Courts Act 1980 in respect of the offence;

(ii) when a person is charged with the offence after being taken into custody without a warrant;

(iii) when a bill of indictment is preferred by virtue of s 2(2)(b) of the Administration of Justice (Miscellaneous Provisions) Act 1933;

(b) proceedings at a trial of an offence are concluded with the occurrence of any of the following, the discontinuance of the prosecution, the discharge of the jury without a finding, the acquittal of the accused or the sentencing of or other dealing with the accused for the offence of which he was convicted; and

(c) proceedings on an appeal are concluded on the determination or abandonment of the appeal.

Criminal Justice and Public Order Act 1994, s 51(10)

Explanatory notes

- For equivalent offences in some civil proceedings see s 39 and s 40 of the Criminal Justice and Police Act 2001.
- In respect of the relevant period, this subsection means that the statutory presumption can only be used during the relevant period. It is still possible to bring a prosecution for this offence many years after that period, but the prosecution will not have the advantage of being able to use this presumption.

4.8.1 Intimidation of a Witness/Juror

- Section 51(3) states that, in relation to both offences, it will be immaterial whether or not the act is (or would be) done, or that the threat is made—
  - (a) otherwise than in the presence of the victim, or
  - (b) to a person other than the victim.
- Two cases regarding the above provision have determined the following—
  - ◆ Relating to both offences, the person making the threats still commits an offence if they use a third party to convey them to the witness/juror. The 'messenger' could be an innocent agent (eg a victim's relative), who simply passes on a message without understanding its meaning or effect (*Attorney-General's Reference (No 1 of 1999)* [2000] QB 365).
  - ◆ The threats can be made by telephone, letter, or by other means. It is not necessary for the offender and victim to be in the same place at the same time (*DPP v Mills* [1996] 3 WLR 1093).
- Section 51(4) provides that the harm done or threatened may be financial as well as physical (whether to the person or a person's property) and the same applies with regard to any intimidatory act that consists of threats.
- Section 51(11) states that this offence is in addition to, and does not necessarily replace any offence which currently exists at common law (eg perversion of the course of justice, which is usually charged as an attempt, conspiracy, or incitement).

Related cases

Van Colle and another v Chief Constable of Hertfordshire [2008] UKHL 50, HL Following a series of threats and incidents, a prosecution witness for a trial was murdered days before giving evidence. Established, in the absence of special circumstances, the police owed no common law duty of care to protect individuals from harm caused by criminals. Police are not required to take action unless an assessment of the threat finds the need to warrant further action (*Osman v UK* (1998) 29 EHRR 245, for test in relation to Article 2 claim—see **1.1**).

R v Normanton [1998] Crim LR 220, CA Spitting, although a common assault, is not harm for the purposes of this legislation unless it causes some physical or mental injury, such as an infection.

R v Waters [1997] Crim LR 823, CA As the witness had threats made against him and his family, he was no longer willing to support the prosecution. Although giving oral evidence at trial, he claimed to be unable to identify his attackers. Accepted that he was prevented from giving oral evidence through fear so the original statement was admitted under s 23(3)(b) of the CJA 1988.

R v Singh (B), Singh (C) and Singh (J) [2000] Cr App R 31, CA There must be evidence that the investigation had started at the time of the intimidation.

Practical considerations

The case *R v Davis* [2008] UKHL 26 concerned the use of anonymous witness evidence at trial. As a result, the House of Lords judgment placed restriction on the court's ability to allow evidence to be given anonymously during criminal trials.

Following on from this case, the Criminal Evidence (Witness Anonymity) Act 2008 was quickly introduced which abolished the common law rules relating to witness anonymity, save for withholding information for public interest immunity reasons. It provides for the making of witness anonymity orders in relation to witnesses in criminal proceedings.

Although this Act is a temporary measure and is due to expire on 31 December 2009, albeit subject to extension by order, this area of law is in the Coroners and Justice Bill and is expected to become law prior to the expiry of the current Act.

 Either way None

 Summary: 6 months' imprisonment and/or a fine not exceeding the statutory maximum.

Indictment: 5 years' imprisonment and/or a fine.

4.8.2 **Perverting the course of justice**

Offence

Committed where a person or persons—
- acts or embarks upon a course of conduct
- which has a tendency to, and
- is intended to pervert,
- the course of public justice.

Common Law

Points to prove

✓ date and location
✓ with intent to pervert
✓ the course of public justice
✓ do an act/series of acts
✓ tending to pervert course of public justice

Explanatory notes

- Examples where conduct is capable of amounting to this offence are—
    - making false allegations;
    - perjury;
    - concealing offences;
    - obstructing the police;
    - assisting others to evade arrest;
    - failing to prosecute;
    - procuring and indemnifying sureties;
    - interference with witnesses, evidence, and jurors;
    - publication of matters calculated to prejudice a fair trial.
- A positive act is required (eg failing to respond to a summons was insufficient to warrant a charge of perverting the course of justice).
- Any act or course of conduct that tends or is intended to interfere with the course of public justice can amount to an offence. In order to get a conviction, it is not sufficient to prove that the conduct actually did, or had a tendency to pervert the course of justice. The evidence must prove that the offender intended that it would do so.
- It is not necessary for the offender's motives to be the procurement of a false verdict or the defeat of the ends of justice. Trying to introduce genuine evidence by unlawful means is perverting the course of justice (eg a witness takes incriminating photos but refuses to give evidence). Steps are then taken by the investigator to get another witness to introduce them as evidence (*Attorney-General's Reference (No 1 of 2002)* [2002] EWCA Crim 2392).

Related cases

R v Headley (1996) 160 JP 25, CA Deliberate inaction is not perverting the course of justice. H was the brother of a man who was stopped by police and asked to produce driving documents. The man gave H's details. H was subsequently summonsed, convicted, and fined in his absence. When the truth was discovered, H was convicted of perverting the course of justice. His appeal was upheld as he had done nothing to pervert the course of justice.

R v Kiffin [1994] Crim LR 449, CA It is possible to pervert course of justice even if no offence could be shown to have been committed. In this case, removing account books/records subject of PACE warrant application out of jurisdiction.

R v Toney [1993] 1 WLR 364, CA Perverting the course of justice need not be by improper means. T attempted to persuade a witness to alter his evidence at T's trial. There was no evidence of improper means, but T was still convicted of perverting the course of justice.

Practical considerations

- This offence is sometimes referred to as 'attempting to pervert the course of justice', but the word 'attempting' in a common law indictment was misleading because it is a substantive rather than an inchoate (incomplete) offence. It should be charged as 'doing acts tending and intended to pervert the course of justice' (*R v Williams* (1991) 92 Cr App R 158).

- Perverting the course of justice is usually charged as an attempt, conspiracy, or incitement.
- There has been comment by the courts where this offence has been used for relatively minor attempts to pervert the course of justice and it is charged alongside an offence that is serious enough to permit the offender's conduct to be taken into account when sentencing for the main offence. In *R v Sookoo* [2002] EWCA Crim 800, a shoplifter had attempted to hide his identity and inevitably failed, the prosecutors should not include a specific count of perverting the course of justice. Such conduct may serve to aggravate the original offence and the judge may increase the sentence as a result. However, in *R v Pendlebury* [2003] EWCA Crim 3426, P gave a positive breath test but a false name to police and had four previous convictions for doing the same thing. He argued that he should not be charged with perverting the course of justice but it should simply be an aggravating factor. Held that P's conduct was not too trifling to amount to the offence because it was the third occasion on which he had given false particulars against a background of persistent and serious offending.
- A more appropriate use for this offence will be where a great deal of police time and resources are involved in putting the matter right, or there may be cases where innocent members of the public have their names given and they have been the subject of questioning and even detention.

 E&S

 Indictment   None

 Life Imprisonment

Links to alternative subjects and offences

Chapter 5

Drugs

5.1 Produce/Supply a Controlled Drug and Supply of Articles

The Misuse of Drugs Act 1971 was designed and intended to regulate the flow and use of controlled drugs. The Act designates which drugs are controlled and assigns them to certain categories (A, B or C). If the drug is a controlled drug it will then be unlawful, with exceptions, to import, export, produce, supply, or possess the drug in question. Section 4 deals with producing or supplying a controlled drug and s 9A supplying or offering articles for the purpose of administering or preparing controlled drugs.

5.1.1 Produce/supply a controlled drug

Section 4 of the Misuse of Drugs Act 1971 relates to the production and supply of controlled drugs. Section 4(1) provides a prohibition on the production, supply and offering to supply controlled drugs. Offences that result from a contravention of this prohibition are set out in s 4(2) and (3).

Offences

(1) Subject to any **regulations under section 7** of this Act for the time being in force, it shall not be lawful for a person—
  (a) to **produce** a **controlled drug**; or
  (b) to **supply** or offer to **supply** a controlled drug to another.
(2) Subject to **section 28** [*defence of lack of knowledge*] of this Act, it is an offence for a person—
  (a) to produce a controlled drug in contravention of subsection (1) above; or
  (b) to be concerned in the production of such a drug in contravention of that subsection by another.

---

(3) Subject to section 28 of this Act, it is an offence for a person—
   (a) to supply or offer to supply a controlled drug to another in contravention of subsection (1) above; or
   (b) to be concerned in the **supplying** of such a drug to another in contravention of that subsection; or
   (c) to be concerned in the making to another in contravention of that subsection of an offer to supply such a drug.

Misuse of Drugs Act 1971, s 4

Points to prove

s 4(2)(a) offence

✓ date and location
✓ produced a controlled drug
✓ of Class A/B/C

s 4(2)(b) offence

✓ date and location
✓ concerned in the production
✓ by another of
✓ a controlled drug
✓ of Class A/B/C

s 4(3)(a) offence

✓ date and location
✓ supply or offered to supply (type of drug)
✓ a controlled drug
✓ of Class A/B/C

s 4(3)(b) offence

✓ date and location
✓ was concerned in
✓ supplying (type of drug)
✓ a controlled drug
✓ of Class A/B/C

s 4(3)(c) offence

✓ date and location
✓ was concerned in making an offer
✓ to supply (type of drug)
✓ a controlled drug
✓ of Class A/B/C

Meanings

Regulations under s 7

Misuse of Drugs Regulations 2001, regs 5 and 6—see '**Defences**'.

5.1.1 Produce/Supply a Controlled Drug

Produce

Means producing it by manufacture, cultivation, or any other method, and 'production' has a corresponding meaning. Stripping a cannabis plant of its leaves comes within the term 'any other method' for the purposes of production (*R v Harris & Cox* [1996] Crim LR 36).

Controlled drug

Drugs are classified as Class A, Class B, or Class C in Sch 2 to the Act. Essentially the classification affects the punishment. The PNLD website at <http://www.pnld.co.uk> lists the classes of drugs according to the chemical names and/or the 'trade name', and also the 'street' or 'slang' names by which most officers and defendants will know the drugs.

Supply

Furnishing or providing a person with something that that person wants or requires for that person's purposes. Including where an offender is looking after drugs whether voluntarily or involuntarily if they intend returning them to the person for whom they were being 'minded' or even anyone else (*R v Maginnis* [1987] 1 All ER 907 (voluntary minding) and *R v Panton* [2001] EWCA Crim 611 (involuntary minding, for example after threats have been made against them)).

Section 28 (see 'Defences').

Explanatory notes

- The offence of offering to supply a controlled drug is complete when the offer is made. It does not matter whether the defendant intended ever to follow the offer through (see *R v Goddard* [1992] Crim LR 588).
- Section 37 (interpretation) states that supplying includes distributing.
- The purpose of the Misuse of Drugs Regulations 2001 is to control the lawful use, possession and type of drugs used for medicinal, research and other legitimate reasons (see 'Defences' below).
- In *R v Hunt* [1987] 1 All ER 1, HL it was made clear that the onus is on the prosecution to prove all elements, including the fact that the drug could not be lawfully possessed by the defendant in the circumstances, or that it was not in a lawful form (some classified drugs are chemically mixed into a form which can be bought over the counter as a remedy for simple ailments).
- *R v Maginnis* [1987] 1 All ER 907, HL involved possession of a packet of cannabis which was being kept for a friend (a drug trafficker). The return of the drugs to the trafficker was deemed to be **supply**.
- Undercover or 'test purchase' officers may find themselves in circumstances where they are offered or are asked to mind controlled drugs. Such officers are trained to a National Standard and comply with ACPO guidelines. Where appropriate, authority is obtained under Pt 2 of the Regulation of Investigatory Powers Act 2000, before surveillance takes place.

Defences

Section 28 of the Misuse of Drugs Act 1971

This applies to offences s 4(2) and (3), s 5(2) and (3), s 6(2) and s 9 of this Act and provides that it shall be a defence if the defendant—

- proves that they neither believed nor suspected nor had reason to suspect that the substance or product in question was a controlled drug; or
- proves that they believed the substance or product in question to be a controlled drug or a controlled drug of a description such that, if it had been that controlled drug or a controlled drug of that description, they would not at the material time have been committing any offence to which this section applies.

Regulation 5—Licences to produce, supply, possess

Where any person is authorised by a licence of the Secretary of State issued under this regulation and for the time being in force to produce, supply, offer to supply or have in his possession any controlled drug, it shall not by virtue of section 4(1) or 5(1) of the Act be unlawful for that person to produce, supply, offer to supply or have in his possession that drug in accordance with the terms of the licence and in compliance with any conditions attached to the licence.

Regulation 6—General authority to supply and possess

(1) Notwithstanding the provisions of section 4(1)(b) of the Act, any person who is lawfully in possession of a controlled drug may supply that drug to the person from whom he obtained it.

(2) Notwithstanding the provisions of section 4(1)(b) of the Act, any person who has in his possession a drug specified in Schedule 2, 3, 4 or 5 which has been supplied by or on the prescription of a practitioner, a registered nurse, a supplementary prescriber or a person specified in Schedule 8 for the treatment of that person, or of a person whom he represents, may supply that drug to any doctor, dentist or pharmacist for the purpose of destruction.

(3) Notwithstanding the provisions of section 4(1)(b) of the Act, any person who is lawfully in possession of a drug specified in Schedule 2, 3, 4 or 5 which has been supplied by or on the prescription of a veterinary practitioner or veterinary surgeon for the treatment of animals may supply that drug to any veterinary practitioner, veterinary surgeon or pharmacist for the purpose of destruction.

(4) It shall not by virtue of section 4(1)(b) or 5(1) of the Act be unlawful for any person in respect of whom a licence has been granted and is in force under section 16(1) of the Wildlife and Countryside Act 1981 to supply, offer to supply or have in his possession any drug specified in Schedule 2 or 3 for the purposes for which that licence was granted.

(5) Notwithstanding the provisions of section 4(1)(b) of the Act, any of the persons specified in paragraph (7) may supply any controlled drug to any person who may lawfully have that drug in his possession.

(6) Notwithstanding the provisions of section 5(1) of the Act, any of the persons so specified may have any controlled drug in his possession.

(7) The persons referred to in paragraphs (5) and (6) are—
   (a) a **constable** when acting **in the course of** his **duty** as such;
   (b) a person engaged in the business of a carrier when acting in the course of that business;
   (c) a person engaged in the business of a postal operator (within the meaning of the Postal Services Act 2000) when acting in the course of that business;
   (d) an officer of customs and excise when acting in the course of his duty as such;
   (e) a person engaged in the work of any laboratory to which the drug has been sent for forensic examination when acting in the course of his duty as a person so engaged;
   (f) a person engaged in conveying the drug to a person who may lawfully have that drug in his possession.

Misuse of Drugs Regulations 2001, regs 5 and 6

Related cases

R v Prior [2004] EWCA Crim 1147, CA An offer to supply can be related to an immediate or future supply no matter how unspecified the offer itself may be. It is immaterial who took the initiative (whether it is the offeror or offeree).

R v Hodgson [2001] EWCA Crim 2697, CA Evidence of the number of visitors, for short periods, to a property may be evidence from which drug dealing may be inferred.

R v Leeson [2000] 1 Cr App R 233, CA It does not matter whether a person thinks they are dealing in a specific type of controlled drug if they are in fact dealing in another. The fact is that they are still dealing in a controlled drug. The wording of the dealing offence is such that the type of controlled drug does not matter.

R v Shivpuri [1986] 2 All ER 334, HL Attempting to supply something that in fact was not a controlled drug can nevertheless be a criminal attempt.

R v Russell [1992] Crim LR 362, CA Making crack from cocaine is 'producing'.

R v Gill (Simon Imran) (1993) 97 Cr App Rep 2, CA An 'offer to supply' fake drugs is an offence.

Practical considerations

• Consider offences under ss 23 or 24 of the Offences Against the Person Act 1861—
  ◆ s 23—Whosoever unlawfully and maliciously administers to, or causes to be administered to, or taken by, any other person any

poison or other destructive or noxious thing, so as to endanger the life of that person, or so as to inflict grievous bodily harm upon that person is guilty of an offence (Indictment—10 years' imprisonment);

♦ s 24—Whosoever shall unlawfully and maliciously administer to or cause to be administered to or taken by any other person any poison or other destructive or noxious thing, with intent to injure, aggrieve, or annoy such person, shall be guilty of an offence (Indictment—5 years' imprisonment).

- Section 4A of the Misuse of Drugs Act 1971 aggravates the offence of supplying a controlled drug where the offender (drug dealer) uses a courier (under 18) in the vicinity of school premises (including school land).
- HOC 82/1980 recommends that cultivation of cannabis (see **5.4.1**) be charged under this section instead of s 6 of the Misuse of Drugs Act 1971 in view of s 37(1) of this Act which provides a definition of 'produce'. The term has a much wider meaning than just chemically making a drug.
- The specific power to search, detain a person or vehicle/vessel and seize any drugs is given in s 23(2) (see **5.5**). Ensure that s 2 of PACE (see **12.1.2**) is complied with, because any breaches of s 2 will mean that the search is unlawful and may affect the admissibility of any evidence obtained.
- Section 110 of the Powers of Criminal Courts (Sentencing) Act 2000 provides for a minimum sentence of 7 years' imprisonment for a third successive conviction for an offence of trafficking in a Class 'A' drug. Trafficking includes an offence under s 4(2) or (3) (production and supply of controlled drugs).
- Producing/cultivating magic mushrooms, being a Class A drug (see **5.4.2** for further details).
- Consider confiscation of cash and property for the s 4(2) and (3) offences of unlawful production/supply of controlled drugs; these are listed as 'criminal lifestyle' offences under Sch 2 of the Proceeds of Crime Act 2002 (see **5.6** for details).

 Either way   None

 Class A drug
Summary: 6 months' imprisonment and/or the statutory maximum fine.

Indictment: Life imprisonment and/or a fine.

Class B drug

Summary: 6 months' imprisonment and/or the statutory maximum fine.

Indictment: Imprisonment for a term not exceeding 14 years and/or a fine.

Class C drug

Summary: 3 months' imprisonment and/or fine not exceeding £2,500.

Indictment: Imprisonment for a term not exceeding 14 years and/or a fine.

5.1.2 Supply articles to administer or prepare drugs

Section 9A of the Misuse of Drugs Act 1971 creates a prohibition on the supply or offering to supply articles for administering or preparing a controlled drug.

Offences

(1) A person who **supplies** or **offers** to supply any article which may be used or adapted to be used (whether by itself or in combination with another article or other articles) in the **administration** by any person of a **controlled drug** to himself or another, believing that the article (or the article as adapted) is to be so used in circumstances where the administration is unlawful, is guilty of an offence.

(3) A person who supplies or offers to supply any article which may be used to prepare a controlled drug for administration by any person to himself or another believing that the article is to be used in circumstances where the administration is unlawful is guilty of an offence.

Misuse of Drugs Act 1971, s 9A

Points to prove

✓ date and location
✓ supplied/offered to supply article(s)
✓ which might be used/adapted
✓ for administration of a controlled drug
✓ to self/another
✓ believing article(s)
✓ was/were to be used
✓ in circumstances where administration unlawful

Meanings

Supplies (see **5.1.1**)

Offers (see '**Related cases**' **5.1.1**)

Controlled drug (see **5.1.1**)

Administration
Includes administering it with the assistance of another.

Explanatory notes

The Misuse of Drugs Act 1971 generally penalizes the possession or supply of a drug, rather than the administration. However, the administration of a drug will be unlawful for the purpose of this section when its possession is unlawful.

Defences

(2) It is not an offence under subsection (1) above to supply or offer to supply a hypodermic syringe, or any part of one.
(4) For the purposes of this section, any administration of a controlled drug is unlawful except—
  (a) the administration by any person of a controlled drug to another in circumstances where the administration of the drug is not unlawful under section 4(1) of this Act, or
  (b) the administration by any person of a controlled drug to himself in circumstances where having the controlled drug in his possession is not unlawful under section 5(1).

Misuse of Drugs Act 1971, s 9A

Practical considerations

- The scope of the 'article(s)' is wide and includes, for example plastic bottles which are intended to be used or adapted for smoking controlled drugs.
- Certain healthcare professionals are specifically exempted from s 9A by reg 6A of the Misuse of Drugs Regulations 2001.
- It is not an offence to supply or offer to supply a hypodermic syringe, or any part of one.
- Consider s 23 or s 24 of the Offences Against the Person Act 1861 for the offences of unlawfully and maliciously administering any poison or other noxious thing (see **5.1.1**).
- Section 9 of the Misuse of Drugs Act 1971 deals with opium, and subject to s 28 (lack of knowledge defence) provides the following offences: smoke or use prepared opium; frequent a place used for

5.1.2 Supply Articles to Administer or Prepare Drugs

opium smoking; have in their possession any pipes or other utensils made or adapted for use in connection with the smoking or preparation for smoking of opium, which have been used by them or with their knowledge and permission in that connection or which they intend to use or permit others to use in that connection.

 Summary   6 months

 6 months' imprisonment and/or a fine not exceeding £5000.

Links to alternative subjects and offences

5.2 Possession of/with Intent to Supply a Controlled Drug

The Misuse of Drugs Act 1971 makes a distinction between people who are lawfully allowed to possess controlled drugs and people who are **unlawfully** in possession of such drugs. Possession (unless exempt) of a controlled drug is unlawful, as is possession of controlled drugs with intent to supply.

5.2.1 Possessing a controlled drug

Offence

(1) Subject to any **regulations under s 7** of this Act for the time being in force, it shall not be lawful for a person to have a **controlled drug** in his **possession**.

(2) Subject to section 28 of this Act and to subsection (4) below, it is an offence for a person to have a controlled drug in his possession in contravention of subsection (1) above.

Misuse of Drugs Act 1971, s 5

Points to prove

✓ date and location
✓ possess [name of drug]
✓ a controlled drug of Class A/B/C

Meanings

Regulations under s 7 (see **5.1.1**)

Controlled drug (see **5.1.1**)

Possession

Proof of unlawful possession requires the following three elements—

• the drug must be in the custody or control (actual or constructive) of the defendant;
• the defendant must know or suspect the existence of the drug in question;
• the drug must be a controlled drug within the meaning of the Act.

5.2.1 Possessing a Controlled Drug

Explanatory notes

Constructive possession is when the defendant does not have immediate physical possession of the drugs but has almost as much control over them. An example would be a person who leaves drugs in a railway 'left luggage' locker and retains the keys. Although no longer having 'actual' custody of the drugs, they have a high degree of control over them which amounts to possession. If the defendant handed the keys to an innocent agent who holds them as a favour, the defendant still has constructive possession. Similarly, if that other person knows that drugs are in the locker then, by keeping the keys, they are also in constructive possession of the drugs.

Defences

- Section 28 (lack of knowledge defence) and Regulations under s 7 (see **5.1.1**).
- In any proceedings for an offence under subsection (2) above in which it is proved that the accused had a controlled drug in his possession, it shall be a defence for him to prove—
  (a) that, knowing or suspecting it to be a controlled drug, he took possession of it for the purpose of preventing another from committing or continuing to commit an offence in connection with that drug and that as soon as possible after taking possession of it he took all such steps as were reasonably open to him to destroy the drug or to deliver it into the custody of a person lawfully entitled to take custody of it; or
  (b) that, knowing or suspecting it to be a controlled drug, he took possession of it for the purpose of delivering it into the custody of a person lawfully entitled to take custody of it and that as soon as possible after taking possession of it he took all such steps as were reasonably open to him to deliver it into the custody of such a person.

Misuse of Drugs Act 1971, s 5(4)

Defence notes

- The Misuse of Drugs Act 1971 makes a distinction between people who are lawfully allowed to possess controlled drugs (even though their use may be restricted) such as doctors, dentists, or police officers and people who are **unlawfully** in possession of drugs.
- The defence under s 5(4) is to cater for situations such as—
  - a parent discovers their child has a controlled drug in their bedroom, takes possession of it, and flushes it down the lavatory;
  - a passer-by discovers heroin lying on the pavement, takes possession of it and then gives it to the police.

Related cases

R v Hunt [1987] 1 All ER 1, HL Prosecution must prove all elements of unlawful possession under Misuse of Drugs Regulations.

R v Altham [2006] EWCA Crim 7, CA Using cannabis to alleviate chronic pain was still unlawful possession.

Practical considerations

- For produce/supply a controlled drug (see **5.1.1**).
- The Misuse of Drugs Regulations 2001 allow some drugs to be in the possession of an individual for certain legitimate reasons (eg medicinal, research) (see **5.1.1**).
- The drug should be tested in the first instance to prove that it is in fact a controlled drug and what class of drug it is.
- HOC 40 of 1998 makes it clear that most drugs should be sent off to Forensic for testing, with certain exceptions.
- The specific power to search, detain a person or vehicle/vessel and seize any drugs is given in s 23(2) (see **5.5**). Ensure that s 2 of PACE (see **12.1.2**) is complied with, because any breaches of s 2 will mean that the search is unlawful and may affect the admissibility of any evidence obtained.
- Cannabis and its derivatives have been reclassified back to a Class B controlled drug. HOC 1/2009 draws attention to this, together with the changes to penalties and recording codes for cannabis offences.
- Possession of cannabis under s 5(2) can now be dealt with by PND (see **7.1.1**).
- For possession of magic mushrooms, which is a Class A drug, see **5.4.2** for further details.

 (Cannabis)

 Either way   None

  Class A

Summary: 6 months' imprisonment and/or a fine not exceeding the statutory maximum.

Indictment: 7 years' imprisonment and/or a fine.

Class B

Summary: 3 months' imprisonment and/or a fine not exceeding level 4 on the standard scale.

Indictment: Imprisonment for a term not exceeding 5 years and/or a fine.

Class C

Summary: 3 months' imprisonment and/or a fine not exceeding level 3 on the standard scale.

Indictment: 2 years' imprisonment and/or a fine.

5.2.2 **Possession with intent to supply**

The Misuse of Drugs Act 1971 creates a specific offence of possessing a controlled drug with intent to supply it.

Offence

Subject to section 28 of this Act, it is an offence for a person to have a **controlled drug** in his **possession**, whether lawfully or not, with **intent** to **supply** it to another in contravention of **section 4(1)** of this Act.

Misuse of Drugs Act 1971, s 5(3)

Points to prove

✓ date and location
✓ possess
✓ [name of drug]/an unspecified controlled drug of class A/B/C
✓ with intent to supply

Meanings

Controlled drug (see **5.1.1**)

Possession (see **5.2.1**)

Intent (see **4.1.2**)

Supply (see **5.1.1**)

Section 4 (see **5.1.1**)

Explanatory notes (see **5.1.1** and **5.2.1**)

Defences

Section 28 (lack of knowledge defence)—see **5.1.1**.

Related cases (see also **5.1.1** and **5.2.1** cases)

R v Batt [1994] Crim LR 592, CA Cash found with drugs not evidence of intent to supply.

R v Kearley [1992] 2 All ER 345, HL Hearsay evidence alone will not prove intent.

R v Gordon [1995] Crim LR 142, CA Evidence must be relevant to the specific offence charged.

R v Maginnis [1987] 1 All ER 907, HL Giving drugs back to the owner can be 'supplying'.

R v Scott [1996] Crim LR 653, CA Lifestyle may prove possession, but not intent to supply.

R v Lambert [2001] UKHL 37 A judge must treat this defence as an evidential burden on the defendant rather than a legal requirement to be proved on the balance of probabilities.

Practical considerations (see also 5.1.1 and 5.2.1)

- What is and what is not admissible evidence of 'possession' and 'intent to supply' is the subject of numerous cases. For example, in *R v Griffiths* [1998] Crim LR 567, the defendant was charged with 'possession with intent to supply' a huge amount of drugs which were found in his home. The defence conceded that whoever 'possessed' the drugs must be a dealer and therefore intending to supply. Possession was really the only disputed issue. The court accepted that evidence of large sums of cash in the defendant's house along with the drugs may be used as part of the prosecution case to show that the defendant was, indeed, the person in possession of those drugs.
- It would appear that lifestyle/paraphernalia can sometimes be used to help prove the 'possession' element but not the 'intent to supply' element where dealers are being prosecuted.
- Provided a controlled drug is involved, it does not matter that a dealer thought they were supplying another controlled drug.
- The specific power to search, detain a person or vehicle/vessel and seize any drugs is given in s 23(2) (see **5.5**). Ensure that s 2 of PACE (see **12.1.2**) is complied with, as any breaches will mean that the search is unlawful and may affect the admissibility of any evidence obtained.
- Consider confiscation of cash and property for the s 5(3) offence of possession of controlled drug with intent to supply; this is listed as a 'criminal lifestyle' offence under Sch 2 of the Proceeds of Crime Act 2002 (see **5.6** for details).

 Either way None

 Class A

Summary: 6 months' imprisonment and/or a fine not exceeding the statutory maximum.

Indictment: Life imprisonment and/or a fine.

5.2.2 Possession with Intent to Supply

Class B

Summary: 6 months' imprisonment and/or a fine not exceeding the statutory maximum.

Indictment: Imprisonment for a term not exceeding 14 years and/or a fine.

Class C

Summary: 3 months' imprisonment and/or a fine not exceeding level 4 on the standard scale.

Indictment: Imprisonment for a term not exceeding 14 years and/or a fine.

Links to alternative subjects and offences

5.3 Occupier or Manager Permitting Premises to be Used for Drugs and Closure Notices/Orders

It is illegal for occupiers and managers of premises to permit certain activities relating to drugs to take place on those premises.

5.3.1 Occupier/manager permit drug use on premises

Offences

A person commits an offence if, being the **occupier** or concerned in the **management** of any premises, he **knowingly permits** or suffers any of the following activities to take place on those premises, that is to say—

(a) **producing** or attempting to produce a **controlled drug** in contravention of **section 4(1)** of this Act;

(b) **supplying** or attempting to supply a controlled drug to another in contravention of section 4(1) of this Act, or offering to supply a controlled drug to another in contravention of section 4(1);

(c) preparing opium for smoking;

(d) smoking cannabis, cannabis resin or prepared opium.

Misuse of Drugs Act 1971, s 8

Points to prove

✓ date and location
✓ being the occupier/concerned in managing of premises
✓ knowingly
✓ permitted/suffered to take place
✓ on premises
✓ the production/attempted production **or**
✓ supplying/attempted to supply/offering to supply
✓ to another
✓ Class A/B/C drug namely [name of drug if known] **or**
✓ the preparing of opium for smoking **or**
✓ the smoking of cannabis, cannabis resin, or prepared opium

5.3.1 Occupier/Manager Permit Drug Use on Premises

Meanings

Occupier

Whether a person is in **lawful** occupation of premises has created some difficulty. In *R v Tao* [1976] 3 All ER 65, a college student who paid rent for a room on the campus was deemed to be the occupier of that room; Lord Justice Roskill commented that it would be 'somewhat astonishing' if a squatter could not be an 'occupier' under the Act. Similarly there may be different occupiers at different times or an occupier who only had that status for certain periods. The question was always one of fact (*R v Coid* [1998] Crim LR 199, CA).

Management

Implies a degree of control over the running of the affairs of the venture or business. If a person controls premises by running, planning, or organizing them they will be managing. Sharing or assisting in the running of premises is sufficient for the purposes of 'being concerned in the management'.

Knowingly (see **9.1.3**)

Permits (see **10.14.1**)

Suffers

Means an unwillingness or failure to prevent.

Producing (see **5.1.1**)

Controlled drug (see **5.1.1**)

Section 4(1) (see **5.1.1**)

Supplying (see **5.1.1**)

Explanatory notes

- As long as the defendant is aware that the premises are being used to supply controlled drugs, it does not matter for the purposes of establishing guilt, which type of drug is involved (*R v Bett* [1998] 1 All ER 600). However, there is a difference so far as the penalty is concerned. Therefore, it is desirable, if possible, to identify the class of drugs and name them in the charge (of course, in the majority of cases the drugs will have been seized and this issue will not cause any difficulty).
- This offence is limited to the activities specified at (a) to (d). It is not committed, for example, by a landlord who knows that one of their tenants is in their room injecting themselves with amphetamines. They may commit the offence if, for example—
  - a drug is being supplied to others on the premises;
  - a controlled drug is being produced on the premises;
  - the occupants are smoking cannabis.

- The Misuse of Drugs Regulations 2001 allows some drugs to be in the possession of an individual for certain legitimate reasons (eg medicinal, research) (see '**Defences**' **5.1.1**).

Related cases

R v Lunn [2008] EWCA Crim 2082, CA It is more serious where the manager of a public house allows premises to be used for drugs compared to the owner of a private house; this is because it is drug taking in public, thus making it appear to be an acceptable activity and may encourage others to partake.

R v Auguste [2003] EWCA Crim 3929, CA During a police raid a block of cannabis resin and two reefers were found. Although several men were in the house, there was no smell of cannabis having been smoked. Held: Activity of actually smoking cannabis must be carried out before this offence is committed.

R v Brock and Wyner (2001) 2 Cr App R 3, CA The offence under s 8(b) has two elements: (i) knowingly permits—knowledge of the dealing, which could be actual knowledge or the defendant closing their eyes to the obvious; or (ii) suffers—unwillingness to prevent the dealing, which could be inferred from the failure to take reasonable steps to prevent it. A defendant's **belief** that they had taken reasonable steps does not provide them with a defence.

R v Bett [1999] 1 All ER 600 The type of drug is immaterial to prove guilt but the defendant must be aware that the premises are being used to supply controlled drugs.

Practical considerations

- Whenever the decision to search premises can be planned in advance, a warrant should be obtained under the Misuse of Drugs Act 1971, s 23(3) (see **12.4**).
- A key power for the police when dealing with Class A drug offences on premises is the closure procedure. There are two practical aspects to consider: closure notices and closure orders (see **5.3.2**).
- Consider confiscation of cash and property for the s 8 offence of premises relating to controlled drugs; this is listed as a 'criminal lifestyle' offence under Sch 2 of the Proceeds of Crime Act 2002 (see **5.6** for details).

 Either way   None

 Class A/B
  Summary: 6 months' imprisonment and/or the statutory maximum fine.

  Indictment: 14 years' imprisonment and/or a fine.

Class C

Summary: 3 months' imprisonment and/or a fine of £2,500 maximum.

Indictment: 14 years' imprisonment and/or a fine.

5.3.2 Premises closure notices/orders (Class A drugs)

Section 1 of the Anti-social Behaviour Act 2003 gives police power to issue a closure notice where premises are being unlawfully used in the production or supply of a Class A controlled drug, and this use is associated with the occurrence of disorder or serious nuisance to members of the public. Section 4 of this Act creates offences of remaining in or entering property subject to a closure notice or order.

Offences

(1) A person commits an offence if he remains on or enters **premises** in contravention of a **closure notice**.

(2) A person commits an offence if—

    (a) he obstructs a constable or an **authorised person** acting under section 1(6) or 3(2),

    (b) he remains on premises in respect of which a **closure order** has been made, or

    (c) he enters the premises.

Anti-social Behaviour Act 2003, s 4

Points to prove

Obstruction

✓ date and location
✓ obstructed
✓ a constable/an authorized person
✓ acting under
✓ s 1(6) (service)/s 3(2) (enforcement)

Closure notice

✓ date and location
✓ remained on/entered premises
✓ in contravention of a closure notice
✓ under s 1
✓ issued by a constable/authorized person

> *Closure order*
> ✓ date and location
> ✓ entered/remained on premises
> ✓ in respect of which a closure order
> ✓ under s 2
> ✓ made by magistrates on a date

Meanings

Premises

Includes any land or other place (whether enclosed or not); any outbuildings which are or are used as part of the premises.

Closure notice (see below procedure)

Closure order (see below procedure)

Authorised person

Means a person authorized by the chief officer of police for the area in which the premises are situated.

Defences

A person does not commit an offence under subsection 4(1) or subsection 4(2)(b) or (c) if he has a reasonable excuse for entering or being on the premises (as the case may be).

Anti-social Behaviour Act 2003, s 4(4)

Closure notice procedure

Grounds

(1) This section applies to premises if a police officer not below the rank of superintendent (the authorising officer) has reasonable grounds for believing—

    (a) that at any time during the relevant period the premises have been used in connection with the unlawful use, production or supply of a Class A controlled drug, and

    (b) that the use of the premises is associated with the occurrence of disorder or serious nuisance to members of the public.

Authorisation

(2) The authorising officer may authorise the issue of a closure notice in respect of premises to which this section applies if he is satisfied—

    (a) that the local authority for the area in which the premises are situated has been consulted;

    (b) that reasonable steps have been taken to establish the identity of any person who lives on the premises or who has control of or responsibility for or an interest in the premises.

5.3.2 Premises Closure Notices/Orders (Class A Drugs)

(3) An authorisation under subsection (2) may be given orally or in writing, but if it is given orally the authorising officer must confirm it in writing as soon as it is practicable.

Requirements

(4) A closure notice must—
  (a) give notice that an application will be made under section 2 for the closure of the premises;
  (b) state that access to the premises by any person other than a person who habitually resides in the premises or the owner of the premises is prohibited;
  (c) specify the date and time when and the place at which the application will be heard;
  (d) explain the effects of an order made in pursuance of section 2;
  (e) state that failure to comply with the notice amounts to an offence;
  (f) give information about relevant advice providers.

Service

(5) The closure notice must be served by a constable.
(6) Service is effected by—
  (a) fixing a copy of the notice to at least one prominent place on the premises,
  (b) fixing a copy of the notice to each normal means of access to the premises,
  (c) fixing a copy of the notice to any outbuildings which appear to the constable to be used with or as part of the premises,
  (d) giving a copy of the notice to at least one person who appears to the constable to have control of or responsibility for the premises, and
  (e) giving a copy of the notice to the persons identified in pursuance of subsection (2)(b) and to any other person appearing to the constable to be a person of a description mentioned in that subsection.
(7) The closure notice must also be served on any person who occupies any other part of the building or other structure in which the premises are situated if the constable reasonably believes at the time of serving the notice under subsection (6) that the person's access to the other part of the building or structure will be impeded if a closure order is made under section 2.

Anti-social Behaviour Act 2003, s 1

Meanings

Relevant period

The relevant period is the period of three months ending with the day on which the authorizing officer considers whether to authorize the issue of a closure notice in respect of the premises.

Production (see **5.1.1**)

Supply (see **5.1.1**)

Class A controlled drug (see **5.1.1**)

Relevant advice providers

Relates to information about the names of and means of contacting persons and organizations in the area that provide advice about housing and legal matters.

Explanatory notes

- Section 1(1) sets out the relevant grounds before an officer of at least the rank of superintendent can authorize the issue of a closure notice.
- For the purpose of fixing a copy of the notice to at least one prominent place on the premises, a constable may enter any premises to which this section applies, using reasonable force if necessary.
- It is immaterial whether any person has been convicted of an offence relating to the use, production, or supply of a controlled drug.
- The police have a power under s 1 to close down premises, sometimes called 'crack houses', being used for the supply, use or production of Class A drugs where there is associated serious nuisance or disorder.
- Various steps and consultations must be made before the police can apply to the magistrates' court for a closure order under s 2 (which must be heard by the magistrates within 48 hours of the closure notice being served).
- No drug-specific criminal offence has to be proved (at least, not beyond the level of reasonable suspicion) before a closure notice can be served or a closure order made. But if evidence is found that an occupier or manager knowingly permitted the premises to be used for drugs offences, then charges might be considered under s 8 of the Misuse of Drugs Act 1971 (see **5.3.1**).
- The local authority for the area in which the premises are situated must be consulted before a closure notice is served.

Closure orders procedure

Sections 2 to 4 of the Anti-social Behaviour Act 2003 relate to closure orders.

Court procedure

(1) If a closure notice has been issued under section 1 a constable must apply under this section to a magistrates' court for the making of a closure order.

(2) The application must be heard by the magistrates' court not later than 48 hours after the notice was served in pursuance of section 1(6)(a).

(3) The magistrates' court may make a closure order if and only if it is satisfied that each of the following paragraphs applies—

    (a) the premises in respect of which the closure notice was issued have been used in connection with the unlawful use, production or supply of a Class A controlled drug;

(b) the use of the premises is associated with the occurrence of disorder or serious nuisance to members of the public;

(c) the making of the order is necessary to prevent the occurrence of such disorder or serious nuisance for the period specified in the order.

Anti-social Behaviour Act 2003, s 2

Enforcement

(1) This section applies if a magistrates' court makes an order under s 2.

(2) A constable or an authorised person may—

(a) enter the premises in respect of which the order is made;

(b) do anything reasonably necessary to secure the premises against entry by any person.

(3) A person acting under subsection (2) may use reasonable force.

(4) But a constable or authorised person seeking to enter the premises for the purposes of subsection (2) must, if required to do so by or on behalf of the owner, occupier or other person in charge of the premises, produce evidence of his identity and authority before entering the premises.

(5) A constable or authorised person may also enter the premises at any time while the order has effect for the purpose of carrying out essential maintenance of or repairs to the premises.

Anti-social Behaviour Act 2003, s 3

Explanatory notes

- The police can apply for a closure order once a s 1 closure notice has been served.
- The court must hear the application within 48 hours of the closure notice being posted on the property.
- The court must be satisfied that not only have the premises been used for the unlawful supply, use, or production of Class A drugs but also that closure will prevent future disorder or serious nuisance.
- The court order can ensure closure of the premises for up to 3 months and may allow and/or specify access to a part of the building or structure. This order applies to all people, including owners and residents.

Practical considerations

- Reasonable steps must be taken to establish the identity of any person who lives on the premises or who has control of or responsibility for or an interest in the premises.
- If the drugs are not Class A, consider issuing closure notices/orders in respect of premises associated with persistent disorder or nuisance under ss 11A to 11L (see **7.13.4**).

Summary 6 months

6 months' imprisonment and/or a fine not exceeding level 5 on the standard scale.

Links to alternative subjects and offences

5.4 Cultivating Cannabis and 'Magic Mushrooms'

This part of the chapter deals with the offence of cultivating cannabis (Class B drug) and possessing or producing 'magic mushrooms' (Class A drug).

5.4.1 Cultivating cannabis

Although s 6 of the Misuse of Drugs Act 1971 makes it an offence to cultivate cannabis plants, HOC 82/1980 recommends that the cultivation of cannabis be charged under s 4(2) (produce/supply a controlled drug—see **5.1.1**) for the offences of 'producing cannabis' or being 'concerned in the production of cannabis'; further details and reasons are given in '**Practical considerations**'.

Offence

(1) Subject to any **regulations under s 7** of this Act for the time being in force, it shall not be lawful for a person to cultivate any plant of the genus **cannabis**.

(2) Subject to **section 28** of this Act, it is an offence to cultivate any such plant in contravention of subsection (1) above.

Misuse of Drugs Act 1971, s 6

Points to prove

✓ date and location
✓ cultivation of cannabis plant(s) a Class B drug

Meanings

Regulations under section 7

This allows cultivation of the cannabis plant under licence (see '**Defences**').

Cannabis

This includes the whole plant.

Section 28 (see '**Defences**')

Explanatory notes

• The mere growing of the cannabis plant is regarded as an act of 'production'.

- It is necessary to prove that the defendant gave some attention to the plant in order to show 'cultivation'—watering, heating, and lighting would be common examples.

Defences

- Section 28 (lack of knowledge)—see **5.1.1**.
- Where any person is authorized by a licence of the Secretary of State issued under this regulation and for the time being in force to cultivate plants of the genus Cannabis, it shall not by virtue of section 6 of the Act be unlawful for that person to cultivate any such plant in accordance with the terms of the licence and in compliance with any conditions attached to the licence.

Misuse of Drugs Regulations 2001, reg 12

Defence notes

- Acting without a valid licence or failing to comply with the conditions of the licence is an offence under s 18 of the Misuse of Drugs Act 1971 (although other more serious offences may also have been committed).
- Certain people can lawfully possess/supply a controlled drug and/or can be licensed to do so (see **5.1.1**).
- There is no general defence of medical necessity to the offence of production/possession/supply of cannabis (*R v Quayle and others: Attorney-General's Reference (No 2 of 2004)* [2005] EWCA Crim 1415, CA).

Practical considerations

- HOC 82/1980 recommends that the cultivation of cannabis be charged under s 4(2) 'producing cannabis' or being 'concerned in the production of cannabis' (see **5.1.1**) (produce/supply a controlled drug), because under s 37(1) the definition of 'produce' has a much wider meaning than just chemically making a drug and means: by manufacture, cultivation or any other method. Stripping a cannabis plant of its leaves comes within the term 'any other method' for the purposes of production (*R v Harris and Cox* [1996] Crim LR 36).
- Any equipment used at 'cannabis farms', which usually consists of hydroponic equipment to provide the lighting and heating, electrical fans, air ventilation systems, transformers and other equipment, can be seized under s 19 of PACE (see **12.3.4**).
- Instead of storing this bulky equipment, which has been seized as evidence, consider s 22 of PACE which states that photographs of the equipment will be sufficient evidence.
- In order to ascertain whether a building is being used as a 'cannabis farm' consider the use of a thermal camera or heat-seeking equipment

which can detect high infrared values; this is because the buildings emit a lot of heat due to the intensive use of heating and lighting equipment used for the growing environment.

- The use and cultivation of 'skunk', being a far stronger strain of cannabis, has greatly increased. Studies by the Home Office have found that 80% of cannabis seized is of the skunk variety, which has been linked to causing mental health problems.
- Cannabis and its derivatives have been reclassified back to a Class B controlled drug. Possession under s 5(2) (see **5.2.1**) can now be dealt with by PND (see **7.1.1**).

 Either way None

 Summary: 6 months' imprisonment and/or a fine not exceeding the statutory maximum.

Indictment: 14 years' imprisonment and/or a fine.

5.4.2 **'Magic mushrooms'**

Section 21 of the Drugs Act 2005 added fungus (of any kind) that contains psilocin or an ester of psilocin, commonly known as 'magic mushrooms' to the Class A drugs schedule under the Misuse of Drugs Act 1971.

Offences

Possess
Possess a Class A controlled drug (see **5.2.1** for full wording)

Misuse of Drugs Act 1971, s 5(2)

Produce
Produce a Class A controlled drug (see **5.1.1** for full wording)

Misuse of Drugs Act 1971, s 4(2)(a)

Points to prove

Possess
- ✓ date and location
- ✓ possess a fungus containing psilocin or an ester of psilocin (magic mushrooms)
- ✓ being a Class A controlled drug

> *Produce*
> ✓ date and location
> ✓ produce a fungus containing psilocin or an ester of psilocin (magic mushrooms)
> ✓ being a Class A controlled drug

Meanings

Possess (see 5.2.1)

Controlled drug (see 5.1.1)

Produce (see 5.1.1)

Explanatory notes

- Section 21 of the Drugs Act 2005 has made 'magic mushrooms' a Class A drug.
- Regulation 4A of the Misuse of Drugs Regulations 2001 (see '**Defences**') provides four circumstances where a person could possess 'magic mushrooms' and would not be liable for committing a s 5(1) possession of a Class A controlled drug offence.

Defences

- The Misuse of Drugs Act, s 5(1) defences (see 5.2.1).
- Section 5(1) of the Act (which prohibits the possession of controlled drugs) shall not have effect in relation to a fungus (of any kind) which contains psilocin or an ester of psilocin where the fungus—
  (a) is growing uncultivated;
  (b) is picked by a person already in lawful possession of it for the purpose of delivering it as soon as is reasonably practicable into the custody of a person lawfully entitled to take custody of it and it remains in that person's possession for and in accordance with that purpose;
  (c) is picked for either of the purposes specified in paragraph (2) and is held for and in accordance with the purpose specified in paragraph (2)(b), either by the person who picked it or by another person; or
  (d) is picked for the purpose specified in paragraph (2)(b) and is held for and in accordance with the purpose in paragraph (2)(a), either by the person who picked it or by another person.
  (2) The purposes specified for the purposes of this paragraph are—
  (a) the purpose of delivering the fungus as soon as is reasonably practicable into the custody of a person lawfully entitled to take custody of it; and
  (b) the purpose of destroying the fungus as soon as is reasonably practicable.
  Misuse of Drugs Regulations 2001, reg 4A

5.4.2 'Magic Mushrooms'

Practical considerations

- Section 110 of the Powers of Criminal Courts (Sentencing) Act 2000 provides for a minimum sentence of 7 years' imprisonment for a third successive conviction for an offence of trafficking in a Class A drug committed after 30 September 1997. Trafficking includes an offence under s 4(2) or (3) (production and supply of controlled drugs).
- The specific power to search, detain a person or vehicle/vessel and seize any drugs is given in s 23(2) (see **5.5**). Ensure that s 2 of PACE (see **12.1.3**) is complied with, as a breach of s 2 will mean the search is unlawful and may affect the admissibility of any evidence obtained.
- Simple possession of magic mushroom spores is not illegal, owing to the fact that they do not contain psilocin (the 'controlled drug') until they are actually cultivated.

 Either way   None

 Possess—s 5(2) offence
Summary: 6 months' imprisonment and/or a fine not exceeding the statutory maximum.

Indictment: 7 years' imprisonment and/or fine.

 Produce—s 4(2)(a) offence
Summary: 6 months' imprisonment and/or a fine not exceeding the statutory maximum.

Indictment: Life imprisonment and/or a fine.

Links to alternative subjects and offences

SSS Stop, search, and seize powers   **E&S** Entry and search powers   **TRIG** Trigger offences
PCSO Police community support officers

5.5 **Drug-Related Search Powers**

The police can exercise specific search powers under s 23 of the Misuse of Drugs Act 1971 which confers powers on a constable to stop, detain, and search a person, vehicle, or vessel for controlled drugs and various offences for failing to comply.

Offences

A person commits an offence if he—
(a) **intentionally obstructs** a person in the exercise of his powers under this section; or
(b) **conceals** from a person acting in the exercise of his powers under subsection (1) any such books, documents, stocks or drugs as are mentioned in that subsection; or
(c) without **reasonable excuse** (proof of which shall lie on him) fails to produce any such books or documents as are so mentioned where their production is demanded by a person in the exercise of his powers under that subsection.

Misuse of Drugs Act 1971, s 23(4)

Points to prove

✓ date and location
✓ concealed from constable/authorized person **or**
✓ without reasonable excuse
✓ failed to produce books/documents
✓ relating to dealings in production/supply
✓ of controlled drugs
✓ when so demanded by a
✓ constable/authorized person **or**
✓ intentionally obstructed a person in exercise of s 23 powers

Meanings

Intentionally obstructs

Where a person deliberately does an act which, though not necessarily aimed at or hostile to the police, makes it more difficult for the police to carry out their duty and they intentionally do the act knowing that their conduct will have an obstructive effect *(Lewis v Cox* [1984] Crim LR 756, QBD).

Conceals

The *Oxford English Dictionary* defines this as to hide, keep secret from, or refrain from disclosing or divulging.

5.5 Drug-Related Search Powers

Reasonable excuse

The *Oxford English Dictionary* defines this as likely or appropriate justification for an action.

Explanatory notes

The s 23(4)(b)–(c) offences refer to statutory powers under s 23(1) to inspect chemists and other suppliers of controlled drugs.

> #### Power to search, detain, and seize drugs
>
> If a constable has **reasonable grounds** to suspect that any person is in possession of a **controlled drug** in contravention of this Act or of any regulations made thereunder, the constable may—
> (a) search that person, and detain him for the purpose of searching him;
> (b) search any **vehicle** or **vessel** in which the constable suspects that the drug may be found, and for the purpose require the person in control of the vehicle or vessel to stop it;
> (c) seize and detain, for the purposes of proceedings under this Act, anything found in the course of the search, which appears to the constable to be evidence of an offence under this Act.
>
> Misuse of Drugs Act 1971, s 23(2)

Meanings

Reasonable grounds (see **12.1**)

Controlled drug (see **5.1.1**)

Vehicle (see **10.1.3**)

Vessel

Includes a hovercraft within the meaning of the Hovercraft Act 1968.

Explanatory notes

This power is exercisable *anywhere* and must be conducted in accordance with the related COP and PACE (see **12.1**).

Related cases

R v Bristol [2007] EWCA Crim 3214, CA If the power to search a person for drugs under s 23 is used, then s 2 of PACE will also apply (see **12.1.2**). As the officer had failed to state his name and police station, s 2 was breached, so the search was unlawful and the conviction was set aside (following *Osman v DPP* (1999) 163 JP 725, QBD).

Practical considerations

Personal safety

- Contact with the blood or saliva of drug abusers (particularly those users who inject) carries a risk of infection with serious diseases such as AIDS, HIV, and Hepatitis.
- Every effort should be made to avoid such fluids entering your own body through cuts, eyes, or the mouth. Should such contact occur, the possibility of infection is minimized by the contact area being thoroughly washed immediately and medical advice sought as soon as practicable.

Searching of suspects

- Care should always be taken to avoid unguarded needles piercing the skin, if such an event does occur seek medical advice as soon as practicable.
- When conducting a search initially request the suspect/prisoner to turn out their own pockets, before patting the outside of pockets to detect the presence of a syringe.
- Drug abusers will go to extreme lengths to conceal drugs on or in their bodies. Drugs are commonly found in body orifices. Certain circumstances must prevail before an intimate search may be conducted.
- Search a person minutely, small amounts of drugs can be concealed, for example, in the lining of clothing, under plasters supposedly covering an abrasion, or stuck to the skull under the hairline.
- Searching inside a person's mouth does not constitute an intimate search.

Handling of drugs

- Certain drugs may be absorbed through the skin, it is therefore always advisable to wear gloves when handling drugs.
- **Never under any circumstances taste the drugs.**
- There will be occasions when the name of the drug seized is unknown and doubt as to whether it is controlled. Always seek advice and assistance from a supervisory officer or the drug squad.

Drug abusers' equipment

- Abusers use a wide range of paraphernalia to prepare and administer their drugs. the following list (which is not exhaustive) may provide evidence of that activity where premises are searched—
  - syringes and needles; scorched tinfoil and spoons; small mirrors, razors and straws; tubes of tinfoil; ligatures; lemon juice or citric acid; cigarette papers and home-made cigarettes; bloodstained swabs; square folds of paper which may contain powder; cling film; small self-sealing bags; weighing scales; hookah pipes.

5.5 Drug-Related Search Powers

General

- Section 23(3) of the Misuse of Drugs Act 1971 allows a justice of the peace (subject to conditions) to issue a warrant authorizing any constable for the police area in which the premises are situated to search the premises for evidence of offences relating to controlled drugs (see **12.4**).
- Grounds for carrying out a search must always be capable of justification. Mere appearance is insufficient—there must be something about their manner, deportment, conversations, and the surrounding circumstances that reasonably gives rise to that suspicion. Ensure compliance with PACE powers generally (see **12.1**).
- Section 23(2) expressly authorizes detention of a suspect for the purpose of searching. It does not give the officer a general right to question the suspect, however, they may ask questions incidental to the exercise of that power.
- Section 23(2)(b) does not give an officer the right to stop a vehicle or to search it simply because they suspect the vehicle (not the occupants) has been used in connection with a drug offence on a previous occasion (*R v Littleford* [1978] CLR 48).
- Nothing in s 23(2) prejudices any other powers to search, seize or detain property which may be exercisable by a constable apart from this subsection.
- Consider road traffic legislation as a means of causing a stop (see **10.2**).
- Compliance with PACE and the COP are required with regard to the grounds for searching of people, the conduct of the search and completion of a search record (see **12.1**).
- When the s 23 search powers are used, ensure that the s 2 PACE requirements are met (see **12.1.2**) (eg police officer fails to state name and police station), otherwise the search will be deemed unlawful and may affect the admissibility of any evidence obtained.
- Reasonable force may be used to detain and carry out a search (PACE s 117) (see **1.2**).

E&S

 Either way   None

 Summary: 6 months' imprisonment and/or a fine not exceeding the statutory maximum.

Indictment: 2 years' imprisonment and/or a fine.

Links to alternative subjects and offences

5.6 **Proceeds of Crime**

The Proceeds of Crime Act 2002 allows application for confiscation and restraint orders; it also deals with recovery of property and money laundering.

Section 75 sets out the criteria of whether a person has a criminal lifestyle and so could be subject to a confiscation order; this is to be read in conjunction with Sch 2 (lifestyle offences) and s 6 (confiscation order procedure).

Criminal lifestyle criteria

(1) A defendant has a criminal lifestyle if (and only if) the following condition is satisfied.

(2) The condition is that the offence (or any of the offences) concerned satisfies any of these tests:—
   (a) it is specified in Schedule 2;
   (b) it constitutes conduct forming part of a course of criminal activity;
   (c) it is an offence committed over a period of at least six months and the defendant has benefited from the conduct which constitutes the offence.

(3) Conduct forms part of a course of criminal activity if the defendant has benefited from the conduct and:—
   (a) in the proceedings in which he was convicted he was convicted of three or more other offences, each of three or more of them constituting conduct from which he has benefited, or
   (b) in the period of six years ending with the day when those proceedings were started (or, if there is more than one such day, the earliest day) he was convicted on at least two separate occasions of an offence constituting conduct from which he has benefited.

(4) But an offence does not satisfy the test in subsection (2)(b) or (c) unless the defendant obtains relevant benefit of not less than £5000.

(5) Relevant benefit for the purposes of subsection (2)(b) is—
   (a) benefit from conduct which constitutes the offence;
   (b) benefit from any other conduct which forms part of the course of criminal activity and which constitutes an offence of which the defendant has been convicted;
   (c) benefit from conduct which constitutes an offence which has been or will be taken into consideration by the court in sentencing the defendant for an offence mentioned in paragraph (a) or (b).

(6) Relevant benefit for the purposes of subsection (2)(c) is—
   (a) benefit from conduct which constitutes the offence;

(b) benefit from conduct which constitutes an offence which has been or will be taken into consideration by the court in sentencing the defendant for the offence mentioned in paragraph (a).

Proceeds of Crime Act 2002, s 75

Criminal lifestyle offences

Schedule 2 lists the criminal lifestyle offences—

Drug trafficking

Misuse of Drugs Act 1971

- s 4(2) or (3) (unlawful production/supply of controlled drugs) (see **5.1.1**);
- s 5(3) (possession of controlled drug with intent to supply) (see **5.2.2**);
- s 8 (premises relating to controlled drugs) (see **5.3.1**);
- s 20 (assisting/inducing offence outside UK).

Customs and Excise Management Act 1979: committed in breach of import or export drug restriction—

- s 50(2) or (3) (improper importation of goods);
- s 68(2) (exportation of prohibited or restricted goods);
- s 170 (fraudulent duty evasion).

Criminal Justice (International Co-operation) Act 1990

- s 12 (manufacture/supply substance used for drugs);
- s 19 (using a ship for illicit traffic in controlled drugs)

Money laundering

- s 327 (concealing etc criminal property);
- s 328 (assisting another to retain criminal property).

Directing terrorism

- Terrorism Act 2000, s 56—directing the activities of a terrorist organisation.

People trafficking

- Offence under s 25, 25A, or 25B of the Immigration Act 1971 (assisting unlawful immigration etc) (see **11.3**);
- Offence under s 57, 58, or 59 of the Sexual Offences Act 2003 (trafficking for sexual exploitation);
- Offence under s 4 of the Asylum and Immigration (Treatment of Claimants, etc.) Act 2004 (exploitation).

Arms trafficking

Customs and Excise Management Act 1979: in connection with a firearm or ammunition—

- s 68(2) (exportation of prohibited goods);
- s 170 (fraudulent duty evasion).

Firearms Act 1968, s 3(1)

- dealing in firearms or ammunition by way of trade or business (see **8.1.2**).

Counterfeiting

Forgery and Counterfeiting Act 1981

- s 14 (making counterfeit notes or coins);
- s 15 (passing etc counterfeit notes or coins);
- s 16 (having counterfeit notes or coins);
- s 17 (make/possess materials or equipment for counterfeiting).

Intellectual property

Copyright, Designs and Patents Act 1988

- s 107(1) (make/deal in article which infringes copyright);
- s 107(2) (make/possess article designed or adapted to make copy of a copyright work);
- s 198(1) (making or dealing in an illicit recording);
- s 297A (making or dealing in unauthorised decoders)

Trade Marks Act 1994, s 92(1), (2), or (3)—

- unauthorised trade mark use.

Prostitution and child sex

Sexual Offences Act 1956, s 33 or 34—keeping or letting premises for use as a brothel.

Sexual Offences Act 2003

- s 14 (arranging or facilitating commission of a child sex offence) (see **6.7.1**);
- s 48 (causing or inciting child prostitution or pornography);
- s 49 (controlling a child prostitute or a child involved in pornography);
- s 50 (arranging or facilitating child prostitution or pornography);
- s 52 (causing or inciting prostitution for gain);
- s 53 (controlling prostitution for gain).

Blackmail

Theft Act 1968, s 21—blackmail (see **3.2.3**).

Gangmasters (Licensing) Act 2004, s 12(1) or (2)—acting as a gangmaster without a licence, possession of false documents.

Inchoate offences

- Offence of attempting, conspiring, or inciting the commission of an offence specified in this Schedule (see **4.1.1**);
- Offence under s 44 of the Serious Crime Act 2007 of doing an act capable of encouraging or assisting the commission of an offence specified in this Schedule (see **4.1.3**).
- Offence of aiding, abetting, counselling, or procuring the commission of such an offence.

Explanatory notes

- The criminal lifestyle regime is based on the principle that an offender who gives reasonable grounds to believe that they are living off crime should be required to account for their assets, and should have them confiscated to the extent that they are unable to account for their lawful origin. The criminal lifestyle tests, therefore, are designed to identify offenders who may be regarded as normally living off crime.
- The first test is that s/he is convicted of an offence specified in Sch 2.
- The second test is that the defendant is convicted of an offence of any description, provided it was committed over a period of at least six months, and obtained not less than £5,000 from that offence and/or any others taken into consideration by the court on the same occasion.
- The third test is that the defendant is convicted of a combination of offences amounting to 'a course of criminal activity'.
- This third test is more complicated than the other two. The defendant satisfies it if s/he has been convicted in the current proceedings—
  - of four or more offences of any description from which s/he has benefited, **or**
  - of any one such offence and has other convictions for any such offences on at least two separate occasions in the last six years.

  In addition, the total benefit from the offence(s) and/or any others taken into consideration by the court must be not less than £5,000.
- The purpose of confiscation proceedings under s 6 is to recover the financial benefit that the offender has obtained from his criminal conduct. Proceedings are conducted according to the civil standard of proof, being on the balance of probabilities.
- In certain circumstances the court is empowered to assume that the defendant's assets, and his income and expenditure during the period of six years before proceedings were brought, have been derived from criminal conduct and to calculate the confiscation order accordingly.
- Confiscation orders may be made in the Crown Court following conviction. Where the conviction takes place in the magistrates' court, a confiscation order can only be made if the defendant is either committed to the Crown Court for sentence or for sentence and confiscation under s 70.

Links to alternative subjects and offences

Chapter 6

Sexual Offences and Assaults

6.1 **Rape**

Rape and other sexual offences have been consolidated by the Sexual Offences Act 2003.

6.1.1 **Rape**

The offence of rape is covered by ss 1 (rape) and 5 (rape of a child under 13) of the Sexual Offences Act 2003.

Offences

A person (A) commits an offence if—

(a) he **intentionally penetrates** the **vagina, anus** or **mouth** of another person (B) with his penis,

(b) B does not **consent** to penetration, and

(c) A does not **reasonably believe** that B consents.

Sexual Offences Act 2003, s 1

Points to prove
- ✓ date and location
- ✓ intentionally
- ✓ without consent
- ✓ penetrated anus/vagina/mouth
- ✓ of another person
- ✓ with the defendant's penis
- ✓ not reasonably believing that s/he had consented

6.1.1 Rape

Meanings

Intentionally (see also **4.1.2**)

This is the defendant's aim or purpose in pursuing a particular course of action. If the defendant intended to penetrate but was physically unable to do so or he admitted that it was his intent then the law states that he still had the necessary intent.

Penetration

Means a continuing act from entry to withdrawal.

Vagina

Includes vulva.

Consent

Both s 75 (evidential presumptions about consent) and s 76 (conclusive presumptions about consent) apply to this offence (see 'Defences' below).

Reasonable belief

Whether a belief is reasonable is to be determined having regard to all the circumstances, including any steps A has taken to ascertain whether B consents.

Explanatory notes

- As the definition of vagina includes vulva, then full penetration is not essential to commit rape.
- The offence of rape now includes not only penile penetration of the vagina and anus but also of the mouth as this act could be just as traumatizing and damaging for the victim.
- As penetration can be proved by reference to scientific evidence (sperm, semen, bruising, etc), consent often becomes the major, if not only, issue.
- The offence of rape is gender specific in that only a male (over the age of 10) can commit the offence; the gender of the complainant is irrelevant. This section and s 5 (see **6.1.2**) are the only offences throughout the whole Act that are gender specific because they refer to penile penetration.

Defences

A critical issue in rape cases is consent and s 74 to s 76 deals specifically with these issues.

Consent

A person consents if he **agrees** by choice, and has the **freedom** and **capacity** to make that choice.

Sexual Offences Act 2003, s 74

Evidential presumptions about consent

(1) If in proceedings for an offence to which this section applies it is proved—
   (a) that the defendant did the **relevant act**,
   (b) that any of the circumstances specified in subsection (2) existed, and
   (c) that the defendant knew that those circumstances existed,
   the complainant is to be taken not to have consented to the relevant act unless sufficient evidence is adduced to raise an issue as to whether he consented, and the defendant is to be taken not to have reasonably believed that the complainant consented unless sufficient evidence is adduced to raise an issue as to whether he reasonably believed it.

(2) The circumstances are that—
   (a) any person was, at the time of the relevant act or immediately before it began, using violence against the complainant or causing the complainant to fear that immediate violence would be used against him;
   (b) any person was, at the time of the relevant act or immediately before it began, causing the complainant to fear that violence was being used, or that immediate violence would be used, against another person;
   (c) the complainant was, and the defendant was not, unlawfully detained at the time of the relevant act;
   (d) the complainant was asleep or otherwise unconscious at the time of the relevant act;
   (e) because of the complainant's physical disability, the complainant would not have been able at the time of the relevant act to communicate to the defendant whether the complainant consented;
   (f) any person had administered to or caused to be taken by the complainant, without the complainant's consent, a substance which, having regard to when it was administered or taken, was capable of causing or enabling the complainant to be stupefied or overpowered at the time of the relevant act.

(3) In subsection (2)(a) and (b), the reference to the time immediately before the **relevant act** began is, in the case of an act that is one of a continuous series of sexual activities, a reference to the time immediately before the first sexual activity began.

Sexual Offences Act 2003, s 75

Conclusive presumptions about consent

(1) If in proceedings for an offence to which this section applies it is proved that the defendant did the relevant act and that any of the circumstances specified in subsection (2) existed, it is to be conclusively presumed—
   (a) that the complainant did not consent to the relevant act, and
   (b) that the defendant did not believe that the complainant consented to the relevant act.

(2) The circumstances are that—
   (a) the defendant intentionally deceived the complainant as to the nature or purpose of the relevant act;

    (b) the defendant intentionally induced the complainant to consent to
the relevant act by impersonating a person known personally to the
complainant.

Sexual Offences Act 2003, s 76

Defence notes

Meaning of 'relevant act' (s 77)

References to the term 'relevant act' in ss 75 and 76 vary according to the
offence committed and are where the defendant—

- Penetrates, with his penis, the vagina, anus or mouth of another
person *[Rape (s 1)]*.
- Penetrates, with a part of his body or anything else, the vagina or
anus of another person, where the penetration is sexual *[Assault by
penetration (s 2)]*.
- Touches another person, where the touching is sexual *[Sexual assault
(s 3)]*.
- Causes another person to engage in a sexual activity *[Causing a person
to engage in sexual activity without consent (s 4)]*.

Consent (s 74)

The **freedom** to **agree** is intended to stress that a lack of protest, injury or
consent by the victim does not necessarily signify consent.

- Freedom is not defined in the Act so it must be a matter of fact as to
whether the victim was free to agree or whether pressure or threats
ruled out that agreement.
- A person might not have sufficient **capacity** if they suffer from a mental
disorder or their age prevents them from being able to do so.
- Capacity is not defined so it will be for the court to decide from all the
available evidence.

Evidential presumptions about consent (s 75)

- The term 'substance' in s 75(2)(f) is not defined, so anything capable
of stupefying or overpowering would be covered; this would include
substances such as alcohol, GHB, or Rohypnol.
- Section 75(3) covers the situation where there have been a number
of sexual acts, of which penetration is the culmination, and the
defendant is being prosecuted for them and the threats occurred
immediately before the first sexual act. In that case the presumption
still applies.
- Where the prosecution proves that the defendant did a **relevant
act** (in this case rape) and the situations described in s 75(2) existed
and the defendant knew they existed, then the complainant will be
presumed to have not consented and the defendant will be presumed
not to have reasonably believed the complainant consented.

Conclusive presumptions about consent (s 76)

- Where the prosecution prove that the defendant did a relevant
act and any of the circumstances described above existed then it is
conclusively presumed that the complainant did not consent and

the defendant did not believe that the complainant consented to the relevant act. Therefore, evidence as to the existence of the intentional deception will be critical.

- Deceiving the complainant as to the nature or purpose of the act could be where the complainant is told that digital penetration of her vagina is necessary for medical reasons when in fact it is only for sexual gratification of the defendant.
- Impersonation would cover circumstances where the defendant deceives the complainant into believing that he is her partner causing the complainant to consent to the sexual act.

General

- If none of the situations described in ss 75 and 76 apply, then the prosecution must show that the circumstances of the offence were such that the defendant could not reasonably believe that the complainant consented.
- If the defendant states that he did reasonably believe that the complainant consented then it would be a matter for the jury to decide as to whether a reasonable person would come to the same belief having regard to all the circumstances.
- The circumstances will include the personal characteristics of the defendant. The defendant's age; general sexual experience; sexual experience with this complainant; learning disability; and any other factors that could have affected his ability to understand the nature and consequences of his actions which may be relevant depending on the circumstances of the particular case.
- The Act makes it clear there is an onus on parties involved in a relevant sexual activity to ensure that they have the true consent of the other person(s) and that they took reasonable steps to make sure true consent has been freely given prior to any sexual act taking place.

Related cases

R v Bree [2007] EWCA Crim 804, CA Temporary loss of capacity to choose whether to have sexual intercourse, through consumption of alcohol, means consent is not present. The issues of consent in s 74 with the 'capacity to make that choice' need to be addressed.

R v McAllister [1997] Crim LR 233 The circumstances of a possibly reluctant consent may be infinitely varied, and on each occasion the jury has to decide whether an alleged agreement to a sexual act may properly be seen as a real consent or whether it was obtained by improper pressure which the complainant could not reasonably withstand from the defendant.

Practical considerations

- The Sexual Offences Act 2003 now takes into account surgically reconstructed genitalia.
- For example a male-to-female transsexual could be raped under s 1 and a female-to-male transsexual could commit rape.

- Medical examination could reveal that the person has undergone reconstructive surgery, as transsexuals can legally have their birth certificate changed to reflect their new gender under the Gender Recognition Act 2004.
- Although there is no express reference to reconstructed genitalia in s 1, it can be found in s 79(3).
- Ejaculation does not have to occur for the rape to be committed.
- All reports of rape must be treated as genuine and the victims treated with sensitivity.
- The crime scene should be identified and preserved, ensuring that cross-contamination does not occur (see **1.3**).
- Evidence of the offence should be seized, including clothing and any articles used, such as condoms.
- Consider medical and forensic examination of the victim and offender.
- Obtain evidence of first complaint if appropriate and available.
- Advise the victim not to shower, bathe, drink, or smoke and to retain the clothing they were wearing at the time of the attack.
- Consider CCTV and other potential evidence from independent witnesses.

 Indictable   None

 Life imprisonment.

6.1.2 **Rape of a child under 13**

This is covered by s 5 of the Sexual Offences Act 2003.

Offences

A person commits an offence if—
(a) he **intentionally penetrates** the **vagina**, anus or mouth of another person with his penis, and
(b) the other person is under 13.

Sexual Offences Act 2003, s 5(1)

Points to prove

- ✓ date and location
- ✓ intentionally
- ✓ penetrated the anus/vagina/mouth
- ✓ of a person under 13
- ✓ with the defendant's penis

SSS Stop, search, and seize powers **E&S** Entry and search powers **CHAR** Offences where bad character can be introduced

Meanings

Intentionally (see **6.1.1**)

Penetrates (see **6.1.1**)

Vagina (see **6.1.1**)

Explanatory notes

- There is no issue of consent under this section. Whether the child consented or not is irrelevant making this almost an offence of 'strict liability'.
- This section also includes not only penetration of the vagina and anus but also penile penetration of the mouth as in s 1.
- This section replaces the offence of unlawful sexual intercourse with a girl under 13 in the Sexual Offences Act 1956, s 5.

Related cases

R v G [2008] UKHL 37, HL G, aged 15, had sex with a girl of 12 years old in his room with her full consent and at the time he believed her to be aged 15. Reasonable belief as to consent or age was irrelevant as the offence was absolute and imposed strict liability.

Practical considerations

- Full penetration does not have to occur and it is not necessary to prove any additional consequences (eg that the hymen was broken).
- Once it can be proved that penetration occurred, it will be very hard to show that it was anything other than intentional but it is still a necessary ingredient of the offence.
- Age of child will have to be established by the prosecution, using the child's birth certificate (although other documentation could be used) and testimony of a person who can state that the complainant is the person whom the birth certificate relates to.
- Given the nature of this offence, only a suitably trained or qualified person should interview and obtain evidence from the victim.
- Specific provisions for the police and other agencies to protect the welfare and safety of children are given in the Children Act 2004 (see **2.4**).
- Whilst offences between adults and children will always be viewed as serious, account should be taken of Article 8 (respect for private life) in relation to the criminalization of consenting children.
- The CPS will make charging decisions based on the principles set out in the Code for Crown Prosecutors.
- Consider all the evidential responsibilities highlighted as with the s 1 offence of rape.

6.1.2 Rape of a Child Under 13

 Indictable

 None

 Life imprisonment.

Links to alternative subjects and offences

SSS Stop, search, and seize powers   **E&S** Entry and search powers   **CHAR** Offences where bad character can be introduced

6.2 **Trespass with Intent to Commit a Sexual Offence**

This offence is covered by s 63 of the Sexual Offences Act 2003 and replaces the part of s 9(1)(a) of the Theft Act 1968 that related to burglary with intent to rape.

Offences

A person commits an offence if—
(a) he is a **trespasser** on any **premises**,
(b) he **intends** to commit a **relevant sexual offence** on the premises, and
(c) he knows that, or is **reckless** as to whether, he is a trespasser.

Sexual Offences Act 2003, s 63

Points to prove

✓ date and location
✓ knowingly/recklessly
✓ trespassed on premises
✓ with intent to
✓ commit a relevant sexual offence
✓ on those premises

Meanings

Trespasser (see 3.3)

Premises

Include a structure or part of a structure. This would include premises, yard, garden, vehicle, tent, vessel, or other temporary or moveable structure (eg caravans).

Intent (see 4.1.2)

Relevant sexual offence

Means all the sexual offences included within Pt 1 of the Act (ss 1 to 79 inclusive), including an offence of aiding, abetting, counselling, or procuring such an offence.

Reckless

In these circumstances means that they were aware of the risk that they might be trespassing, but ignored that risk and continued with the course of action they were pursuing.

6.2 Trespass with Intent to Commit a Sexual Offence

Explanatory notes

- A person could enter premises without being a trespasser but become one later. For example, a person enters a shop but then goes into the stockroom; that person then becomes a trespasser because as a potential customer you have the owner's implied permission to enter the shop and browse but you do not have the right to go into the stockroom.
- The old concept of burglary with intent to rape was a limited one and only covered buildings and rape. This offence now caters for a wider interpretation of premises and sexual offences.

Related cases

R v Cunningham [1957] 2 All ER 412 The test for 'subjective recklessness'. It is not sufficient to show that if the defendant had stopped to think, it would have been obvious to them that there was a risk. The prosecution had to prove that they were aware of the existence of the risk but nonetheless had gone on and taken it.

Practical considerations

- The offence is not gender specific, so can be committed by a male on a female or vice versa; equally the victim and defendant could be of the same sex.
- The defendant does not have to commit the relevant sexual offence for this offence to be committed, it is sufficient to have the intent to commit a relevant sexual offence at any time whilst a trespasser.
- Ensure evidence of trespass is obtained.
- Obtain CCTV evidence if available.
- Consider other offences (eg false imprisonment) if insufficient evidence available to prove this offence.

 Either way None

 Summary: 6 months' imprisonment and/or a fine not exceeding the statutory maximum

Indictment: 10 years' imprisonment.

Links to alternative subjects and offences

SSS Stop, search, and seize powers   **E&S** Entry and search powers   **CHAR** Offences where bad character can be introduced

6.3 **Sexual Assault by Penetration**

These offences are covered by s 2 and s 6 (child under 13) of the Sexual Offences Act 2003.

6.3.1 **Assault by penetration of a person aged 13 or over**

Offences

A person (A) commits an offence if—

(a) he **intentionally penetrates** the **vagina** or **anus** of another person (B) with a part of his body or **anything else**,
(b) the penetration is **sexual**,
(c) B does not **consent** to the penetration, and
(d) A does not **reasonably believe** that B consents.

Sexual Offences Act 2003, s 2

Points to prove

✓ date and location
✓ intentionally
✓ sexually penetrated
✓ the anus/vagina of another person aged 13 or over
✓ with a part of the body and/or a thing
✓ without consent
✓ not reasonably believing that s/he had consented

Meanings

Intentionally (see **6.1.1**)

Penetration (see **6.1.1**)

Vagina (see **6.1.1**)

Anything else

This term has not been defined but it is an extremely wide category and will cover anything that can be used to penetrate the body of another.

Sexual

For the purposes of this Part (except section 71), penetration, touching or any other activity is sexual if a reasonable person would consider that—

(a) whatever its circumstances or any person's purpose in relation to it, it is because of its nature sexual, or

(b) because of its nature it may be sexual and because of its circumstances or the purpose of any person in relation to it (or both) it is sexual.

Sexual Offences Act 2003, s 78

Consent (see 6.1.1)

Reasonable belief (see 6.1.1)

Explanatory notes

- Once penetration has been proved, it will be difficult for the defendant to show that it was not their intention to do so. However, as partial penetration will suffice, there may be occasions (such as during a sporting or gymnastic contact) where the defendant claims inadvertent partial penetration by, say, a finger. It would then be for the prosecution to prove otherwise.

- If the defendant states that they reasonably believed that the complainant consented then it will be a matter for the jury to decide as to whether a reasonable person would come to the same belief having regard to all the circumstances.

- The circumstances include the personal characteristics of the defendant; the defendant's age; general sexual experience; sexual experience with this complainant; learning disability; and any other factor that could have affected their ability to understand the nature and consequences of their actions may be relevant depending on the circumstances of the particular case.

- The reasonableness test does not oblige the defendant to have taken any specific steps to ascertain consent, but any taken will be highly pertinent to the case.

- Parties to relevant sexual activity must ensure that they have the true consent of the other person(s) and that they took reasonable steps to make sure true consent had been freely given prior to any sexual act taking place.

- This offence was created in order to reflect the seriousness of assault by penetration, previously being indecent assault, which was perceived not to carry the appropriate penalties for such a serious offence. It carries the same penalty as rape (life imprisonment), thus reflecting its gravity.

- **Section 78 which defines 'sexual'** is a mixed test consisting of an objective test based on what a reasonable person would consider to be sexual and the purpose of the person involved—

  ◆ subsection (a) where there is no doubt that the activity is sexual, such as oral sex or penetration by vibrator, and

  ◆ subsection (b) where the activity could also have some other purpose, apart from a sexual one and also where the defendant's act was not sexually motivated. This would cover situations where the defendant penetrates his victim with an object with the sole intent of committing a violent act not a sexual one (for example, penetration by gun barrel or screwdriver for the purpose of humiliating the victim and the defendant asserting his power over the victim).

- The defendant may not have intended the act to be sexual but from a reasonable person's point of view and because of its nature, a reasonable person would consider that it might be sexual.
- Medical examinations or intimate searches by the relevant authorities (such as police and customs) or such other treatment where penetration is involved but is not sexual (eg in colonic irrigation) will not normally be deemed sexual.
- Unlike rape, this offence can be committed by digital penetration and also penetration by any other part of the body, such as a fist, tongue, and toes.
- Full penetration is not essential to commit the offence.
- Items included in the term 'anything else' can be such objects as bottles, vibrators, and screwdrivers along with other objects and substances.

Defences

Sections 75 and 76 apply to this offence, see **6.1.1 'Defences'** for further details.

Practical considerations

- Any reports of serious sexual assault must be treated as genuine and the victims with sensitivity.
- Evidence of the offence should be seized and includes clothing, condoms, and articles used.
- Ensure cross-contamination does not occur.
- Obtain evidence of first complaint if appropriate and available.
- Advise the victim not to shower, bathe, drink, or smoke and to retain the clothing they were wearing at the time of the attack.
- Consider CCTV and other potential evidence from independent witnesses.

 Indictable   None

 Life imprisonment.

6.3.2 **Assault by penetration of a child under 13**

This offence is the same as s 2 above, except the complainant is under 13 and there is no issue of consent.

SSS Stop, search, and seize powers   **E&S** Entry and search powers   **CHAR** Offences where bad character can be introduced

Offences

A person commits an offence if—
(a) he **intentionally penetrates** the **vagina** or **anus** of another person with a part of his body or **anything else,**
(b) the penetration is **sexual,** and
(c) the other person is under 13.

Sexual Offences Act 2003, s 6

Points to prove

✓ date and location
✓ intentionally
✓ sexually penetrated
✓ anus/vagina of a girl aged under 13
✓ anus of a boy aged under 13
✓ with a part of the body and/or a thing

Meanings

Intentionally (see **6.1.1**)

Penetrates (see **6.1.1**)

Vagina (see **6.1.1**)

Anything else (see **6.3.1**)

Sexual (see **6.3.1**)

Explanatory notes (see **6.3.1** notes)

Practical considerations (also see **6.3.1** considerations)

- This is an offence of strict liability (see **6.1.2**).
- It is not necessary for the victim to know or explain what they were penetrated with.
- The offence can be used in cases where the child does not possess the knowledge to identify the nature of what they had been penetrated with.
- Age of the child to be ascertained by means of birth certificate or similar documentation and the testimony of a person who can confirm the birth certificate relates to the victim.
- Only a suitably trained and qualified person should be used to obtain evidence from a victim of this offence.
- The Children Act 2004 (see **2.4**) makes specific provisions for the police and other agencies to protect the welfare and safety of children.

6.3.2 Assault by Penetration of a Child Under 13

 Indictable

 None

 Life imprisonment.

Links to alternative subjects and offences

SSS Stop, search, and seize powers   **E&S** Entry and search powers   **CHAR** Offences where bad character can be introduced

6.4 Sexual Assault by Touching

6.4.1 Sexual assault by touching a person aged 13 or over

This offence is covered by s 3 of the Sexual Offences Act 2003.

Offence

A person (A) commits an offence if—
(a) he **intentionally touches** another person (B),
(b) the touching is **sexual,**
(c) B does not **consent** to the touching, and
(d) A does not **reasonably believe** that B consents.

Sexual Offences Act 2003, s 3

Points to prove

✓ date and location
✓ intentionally touched
✓ another person aged 13 or over
✓ by touching her/his body
✓ that touching was sexual
✓ not reasonably believing that s/he was consenting

Meanings

Intentionally (see **6.1.1**)

Touches

This includes touching—
• with any part of the body,
• with anything else,
• through anything,
and in particular includes touching amounting to penetration.

Sexual (see **6.3.1**)

Consent (see **6.1.1**)

Reasonable belief (see **6.1.1**)

Explanatory notes

• This section covers non-penetration sexual assaults of another person aged 13 or over. It will cover a wide spectrum of behaviour that would include the defendant rubbing up against the complainant's private parts through the person's clothes for their sexual gratification.

6.4.1 Sexual Assault by Touching a Person Aged 13 or Over

- Touching includes touching through clothes, touching with anything and touching that amounts to penetration. It does not have to involve using the hands and can involve any part of the body being used or touched or even an object such as a sex toy.
- The offence does not require that the defendant intended that the touching be sexual, only that the touching itself was intentional. The sexual aspect of the touching is a separate element.
- Whilst there could not be many examples of 'accidental' or inadvertent penetration, accidental touching occurs all the time. Jostling in a crowded street, travelling on a busy train or bus, and attending sports events can all lead to some form of contact with others.
- It will normally be apparent that the defendant intentionally touched the victim (because of the part of the body touched or used, or because of accompanying circumstances) but there will still be far more room for a defence of lack of intent than in penetration offences.
- In most cases of sexual assault the sexual element will be non-contentious. For example, where a man gropes a female's genitals, it would be hard to imagine a set of circumstances where this would not be sexual and in those cases s 78(a) (see **6.3.1**) will be relied on.
- If with regard to all the circumstances, the purpose and nature of the touching, a reasonable person would consider it sexual then it will be covered by s 78(b). However, it is not certain if the more obscure sexual fantasies would be covered at all by s 78. Would a reasonable person consider the removal of a shoe as sexual, looking at the purpose and nature of it? If not then this would not constitute 'sexual' touching even if the offender received sexual gratification from doing it. This reflects the former common law position with regard to such offences (see **'Explanatory notes'** under **6.3.1** for further details on 'sexual' and s 78).

Defences

Sections 75 and 76 apply—see **6.1.1 'Defences'** for further details.

Related cases

R v H [2005] 1 WLR 2005, CA A female was approached by a man who said to her 'Do you fancy a shag?' and then grabbed at her tracksuit bottoms, attempting to pull her towards him. It was held that in the circumstances surrounding this offence, by applying s 78(b) the touching of the clothing was sexual and amounted to 'sexual assault by touching' for the purposes of s 3.

R v Heard [2007] EWCA Crim 125, CA Police officers took H to hospital who was drunk, emotional, and had cut himself. At the hospital H was abusive, singing noisily, and danced suggestively towards one of the police officers (P). H punched P in the stomach and then took out his penis, rubbing it up and down P's thigh. This touching was intentional, despite his intoxication. H may have lost his inhibitions or behaved out of character, but this did not detract from the fact that his intent to touch P with his penis was deliberate.

Practical considerations

- Reports of serious sexual assault must be treated as genuine and the victims treated with sensitivity.
- As with all serious sexual offences identify any scene, preserve it and seize any articles or associated items relevant to the offence for which the offender has been arrested.
- Prevent any potential for cross contamination.
- Keep the offender and victim separate.
- Consider medical and forensic examination for victim and offender.

 Either way   None

| | **Summary:** 6 months' imprisonment and/or a fine not exceeding the statutory maximum. |

Summary: 6 months' imprisonment and/or a fine not exceeding the statutory maximum.

Indictment: 10 years' imprisonment.

6.4.2 Sexual assault by touching a child under 13

This offence is covered by s 7 of the Sexual Offences Act 2003 and is the same as s 3 but there is no need to prove lack of consent by the child; any such consent is irrelevant.

> ### Offence
>
> A person commits an offence if—
> (a) he **intentionally touches** another person,
> (b) the touching is **sexual**, and
> (c) the other person is under 13.
>
> Sexual Offences Act 2003, s 7

Points to prove

- ✓ date and location
- ✓ intentionally touched
- ✓ a girl/boy under 13
- ✓ and the touching was sexual

6.4.2 Sexual Assault by Touching a Child Under 13

Meanings

Intentionally (see **6.1.1**)

Touches (see **6.4.1**)

Sexual (see **6.3.1**)

Explanatory notes

- Consent is not an issue as this is an offence of strict liability (see **6.1.2**).
- Points raised in **6.4.1** relating to the touching and its sexual nature are still relevant to this offence.

Related cases

R v Weir [2005] EWCA Crim 2866, CA W was on trial for sexual assault by touching a 10-year-old girl. Despite not being the same offence category, a previous caution for taking an indecent photograph of a child was disclosed at court under s 103(2)(b) of CJA 2003. This was allowed as it showed a propensity to commit the s 7 offence.

Practical considerations

- Age of child will be proved by use of the birth certificate or other similar documentation and testimony of a person who can state that the victim is the person whom the birth certificate relates to.
- Only a suitably trained or qualified person should be used to take a statement or obtain evidence from the victim.
- The Children Act 2004 (see **2.4**) makes specific provisions for the police and other agencies to protect the welfare and safety of children.
- If possible identify and preserve a scene and seize any articles suspected of being used in the offence. Always consider the potential for cross-contamination (see **1.3**).

 Either way   None

 Summary: 6 months' imprisonment and/or a fine not exceeding the statutory maximum.

Indictment: 14 years' imprisonment.

Links to alternative subjects and offences

SSS Stop, search, and seize powers   **E&S** Entry and search powers   **CHAR** Offences where bad character can be introduced

6.5 **Sexual Activity with a Child**

This offence is covered by s 9 of the Sexual Offences Act 2003.

Offences

(1) A person aged 18 or over (A) commits an offence if—
   (a) he intentionally touches another person (B),
   (b) the **touching** is **sexual**, and
   (c) either—
      (i) B is under 16 and A does not **reasonably believe** that B is 16 or over, or
      (ii) B is under 13.
(2) A person is guilty of an offence under this section, if the touching involved—
   (a) penetration of B's **anus or vagina**,
   (b) penetration of B's mouth with A's penis,
   (c) penetration of A's **anus or vagina** with a part of B's body, or
   (d) penetration of A's **mouth** with B's penis.

Sexual Offences Act 2003, s 9

Points to prove

Non-penetrative under 13

- ✓ date and location
- ✓ defendant aged 18 or over
- ✓ intentionally touched
- ✓ a girl/boy under 13
- ✓ the touching was sexual

Penetrative under 13

- ✓ date and location
- ✓ defendant aged 18 or over
- ✓ intentionally touched complainant sexually
- ✓ sexual touching involved penetration of—
  - ◆ complainant's anus/vagina with part of D's body or thing **or**
  - ◆ complainant's mouth with D's penis **or**
  - ◆ D's anus/vagina with part of complainant's body **or**
  - ◆ D's mouth with complainant's penis
- ✓ complainant being under 13

Penetrative between 13 and 15

- ✓ per points to prove of '**Penetrative under 13**' except
- ✓ complainant is aged 13/14/15
- ✓ not reasonably believing complainant was 16 or over

> **_Non-penetrative aged between 13 and 15_**
> ✓ date and location
> ✓ defendant aged 18 or over
> ✓ intentionally touched a girl/boy aged 13/14/15
> ✓ not reasonably believing s/he was 16 or over
> ✓ the touching was sexual

Meanings

Touching (see **6.4.1**)

Sexual (see **6.3.1**)

Reasonable belief (see 'Defence')

Explanatory notes

This offence is very similar to s 3 and s 7 (see **6.4**), but the defendant is aged 18 or over and touching involved in s 9(2) is specified in terms of what was used on/in what part of the body. Consent is not mentioned in s 9, but per s 7—if the complainant is under 13 then consent is irrelevant.

Defence

Proving a reasonable belief that the child was 16 or over at the time. However, this is only relevant when the victim is aged between 13 and 15. If under 13 the offence is one of strict liability so far as the element of age is concerned.

Defence notes

- If the victim is aged between 13 and 15 the prosecution must provide evidence that the defendant's belief was not reasonable. For example, that the defendant knew that a girl attended school and had not yet taken her GCSE examinations.
- However, if the defendant and the complainant met for the first time over the Internet, the complainant provided photographs of her in which she looked much older that she in fact was and if she told the defendant that she was 18 and looked 18, then the belief may be reasonable.
- If the prosecution can provide such evidence it is open to the defendant to rebut it, if he can show on the balance of probabilities his belief was reasonably held.

Practical considerations

- This offence is gender neutral.
- Consent is not an issue, but if the complainant is under 13 consent is irrelevant anyway as the offence will then be of strict liability.

6.5 Sexual Activity with a Child

- Identify and preserve any scene.
- Prevent cross-contamination.
- Seize any articles/clothing or associated equipment which is relevant.
- Decisions about charging will be made in accordance with principles set out in the Code for Crown Prosecutors.
- In deciding whether it is in the public interest to prosecute this offence, where there is enough evidence to provide a realistic prospect of conviction, prosecutors may take into consideration factors which include the age and emotional maturity of the parties, whether they entered into the sexual relationship willingly, any coercion or corruption by a person, the relationship between the parties and whether there was any existence of a duty of care or breach of trust.
- The discretion of the CPS not to charge where it is not in the public interest would be partially relevant where the two parties were close in age, for instance an 18-year-old and a 15-year-old, and had engaged in mutually agreed sexual activity.

s 9(1) offence

 Either way   None

 Summary: 6 months' imprisonment and/or a fine not exceeding the statutory maximum.

Indictment: 14 years' imprisonment.

s 9(2) offence

 Indictment   None

 14 years' imprisonment.

Links to alternative subjects and offences

SSS Stop, search, and seize powers   E&S Entry and search powers   CHAR Offences where bad character can be introduced

6.6 Cause/Incite Child to Engage in Sexual Activity

These offences are covered by s 10 (child under 16) where the offender is aged 18 or over, and s 8 (child under 13) of the Sexual Offences Act 2003 to cause/incite the child to engage in sexual activity.

6.6.1 Cause/incite child under 16 to engage in sexual activity

Offences

(1) A person aged 18 or over (A) commits an offence if—
   (a) he **intentionally causes** or **incites** another person (B) to engage in an activity,
   (b) the activity is **sexual**, and
   (c) either—
      (i) B is under 16 and A does not **reasonably believe** that B is 16 or over, or
      (ii) B is under 13.
(2) A person is guilty of an offence under this section, if the activity caused or incited involved—
   (a) penetration of B's anus or vagina,
   (b) penetration of B's mouth with a person's penis,
   (c) penetration of a person's anus or vagina with a part of B's body or by B with anything else, or
   (d) penetration of a person's mouth with B's penis.

Sexual Offences Act 2003, s 10

Points to prove

Non-penetration

- ✓ date and location
- ✓ offender aged 18 or over
- ✓ intentionally
- ✓ caused/incited
- ✓ a girl or boy 13/14/15, not reasonably believing s/he was 16 or over **or**
- ✓ under 13
- ✓ to engage in sexual activity
- ✓ of a non-penetrative nature

Penetration

✓ per first seven points of **'Non-penetration'**
✓ involving the penetration of
✓ her/his anus/vagina **or**
✓ her/his mouth with another person's penis **or**
✓ a person's anus/vagina with part of complainant's body or by complainant with anything else **or**
✓ a person's mouth with complainant's penis

Meanings

Intentionally (see **6.1.1**)

The defendant's aim or purpose in pursuing a particular course of action.

Causes

Defined by the *Concise Oxford Dictionary* as 'be the cause of, make happen'. This infers that the defendant must take some positive action rather than an omission to act. Examples could be the use of force, threats, deception, or intimidation.

Incites

Defined by the *Concise Oxford Dictionary* as 'encourage, stir up, urge or persuade'. Examples could be bribery, threats, or pressure.

Sexual (see **6.3.1**)

Reasonably believe (see **6.5**)

Explanatory notes

• The sexual activity that is caused or incited involves the victim being engaged in that sexual activity. This can be, for example, where the defendant causes or incites the child to sexually touch themselves or for the child to masturbate or strip for the defendant's sexual gratification.
• It may be with a third person (for example, where the defendant causes or incites the child to have oral sex with the penis of another person).
• The incitement itself is an offence so the sexual activity does not have to take place for the offence to be committed.
• Section 10(2) replicates some of the other offences covered in the Act, such as rape, assault by penetration. This duplication is intended to cover every possible scenario that could be envisaged ensuring that offenders do not escape prosecution as a result of a loophole in the law.

6.6.1 Cause/Incite Child Under 16 to Engage in Sexual Activity

- Examples of an adult causing or inciting a child to engage in sexual activity could be promising a reward, persuading the child that it is perfectly acceptable behaviour that other children engage in all the time and they would be abnormal not to agree, or saying that the activity was necessary to check the child's body for bruises, lice etc, or to try on clothes.
- Where the child is under 13, the offender should be charged with the s 8 offence (see **6.6.2**), especially if it involves penetration as it then carries life imprisonment. However, s 10 might be used where the offender is under 18 or the child is under 13 and it only became known during trial that the child was actually under 13. The extension of s 10 to under-13s now means that the trial could continue with the original charge where necessary, thus closing a potential loophole in the law.

Practical considerations

- The age of the child will normally be proved by the production of a birth certificate or other suitable documentation and the testimony of a person who can state that the complainant is the person whom the birth certificate relates to.
- It is not intended to cover health professionals, or anyone providing sex education, advice, or contraception to children.
- This offence could be considered where the offender and victim are very close in age (for example, an offender of 18 and a victim of 15) and are in a relationship and both have entered into a sexual relationship willingly.
- Where the child is aged 13 or over, but under 16, the prosecution must prove that the defendant did not reasonably believe that s/he was 16 or over. If the child is under 13 the offence is one of strict liability.
- If possible identify and preserve crime scene, seize any articles and documentation that is relevant to the offence.
- The obtaining of evidence from a child should be by suitably trained persons.

s 10(1) offence

 Either way   None

 Summary: 6 months' imprisonment and or a fine not exceeding the statutory maximum.

Indictment: 14 years' imprisonment.

SSS Stop, search, and seize powers   **E&S** Entry and search powers   **CHAR** Offences where bad character can be introduced

s 10(2) offence

 Indictment

 None

14 years' imprisonment.

6.6.2 **Cause/incite child under 13 to engage in sexual activity**

This offence is covered by s 8 of the Sexual Offences Act 2003.

Offences

(1) A person commits an offence if—
  (a) he **intentionally causes** or **incites** another person (B) to engage in an activity,
  (b) the activity is **sexual**, and
  (c) B is under 13.
(2) A person is guilty of an offence under this section, if the activity caused or incited involved—
  (a) penetration of B's anus or vagina,
  (b) penetration of B's mouth with a person's penis,
  (c) penetration of a person's anus or vagina with a part of B's body or by B with anything else, or
  (d) penetration of a person's mouth with B's penis.

Sexual Offences Act 2003, s 8

Points to prove

Non-penetration

- ✓ date and location
- ✓ intentionally caused/incited
- ✓ a boy/girl under 13
- ✓ to engage in sexual activity
- ✓ of a non-penetrative nature

Penetration

- ✓ per first four points of 'Non-penetration'
- ✓ involving the penetration of
- ✓ boy/girl's anus/vagina **or**
- ✓ boy/girl's mouth with another person's penis **or**
- ✓ a person's anus/vagina with a part of boy/girl's body or by boy/girl with anything else **or**
- ✓ a person's mouth with the boy's penis

6.6.2 Cause/Incite Child Under 13 to Engage in Sexual Activity

Meanings

Intentionally (see **6.1.1**)

Cause (see **6.6.1**)

Incite (see **6.6.1**)

Sexual (see **6.3.1**)

Explanatory notes

- This offence is the same as the s 10 offence save that the defendant can be of any age and that the victim is under 13. Again this offence is intended to cover every possible scenario.
- In relation to sexual activity caused or incited, the offence covers the same situations as does the offence under s 4 except that, for this offence, consent is irrelevant.
- Provided incitement takes place there is no need to show the sexual activity itself took place.

Practical considerations

- Age of the child will normally be proved by production of a birth certificate or other suitable documentation and the testimony of a person who can state that the complainant is the person whom the birth certificate relates to.
- If possible, identify and preserve crime scene, seize any articles and documentation that is relevant to the offence.
- The obtaining of evidence from a child should be by suitably trained persons.

s 8(1) offence

 Either way   None

 Summary: 6 months' imprisonment and/or a fine not exceeding the statutory maximum.

Indictment: 14 years' imprisonment.

s 8(2) offence

 Indictment   None

 Life imprisonment.

252   **SSS** Stop, search, and   **E&S** Entry and search   **CHAR** Offences where bad
           seize powers   powers   character can be
                                                                           introduced

Links to alternative subjects and offences

6.7 Arranging/Facilitating Commission of a Child Sex Offence and Meeting a Child Following Sexual Grooming

6.7.1 Arrange/facilitate commission of a child sex offence

This offence is covered by s 14 of the Sexual Offences Act 2003.

Offences

A person commits an offence if—

(a) he **intentionally arranges** or **facilitates** something that he intends to do, intends another person to do, or believes that another person will do, in any part of the world, and

(b) doing it will involve the commission of an offence under any of sections 9 to 13.

Sexual Offences Act 2003, s 14(1)

Points to prove

- ✓ date and location
- ✓ intentionally
- ✓ arranged/facilitated
- ✓ an act which the defendant
- ✓ intended to do or
- ✓ intended/believed another person would do
- ✓ in any part of the world
- ✓ and doing it will involve the commission of an offence
- ✓ under ss 9/10/11/12/13

Meanings

Intentionally (see **6.1.1**)

Arranges

Organize or plan, reach agreement about an action or event in advance.

Facilitates

Make it happen, make it easier to achieve or promote.

Explanatory notes

- The defendant does not have to be the one who will commit the sexual offence; it will be enough if they intended/believed that they or another person will commit the relevant offence in any part of the world.
- The offence covers a situation where the defendant takes a person to a place where there is a child in the belief that the person is likely to engage in sexual activity with that child.
- It also caters for situations whereby the defendant arranges for them or another the procurement of a child with whom they propose to engage in sexual activity. For example, the defendant is going on holiday and plans to engage in sexual activity with children whilst there and so arranges through an agency to meet children.
- The sexual activity does not have to occur for the offence to be committed.
- The relevant offences are—
  - ♦ s 9—Sexual activity with a child
  - ♦ s 10—Causing or inciting a child to engage in sexual activity
  - ♦ s 11—Engaging in sexual activity in the presence of a child
  - ♦ s 12—Causing a child to watch a sexual act
  - ♦ s 13—Child sex offences committed by children or young persons.

Defences

(2) A person does not commit an offence under this section if—
  (a) he arranges or facilitates something that he believes another person will do, but that he does not intend to do or intend another person to do, and
  (b) any offence within subs (1)(b) would be an offence against a child for whose **protection** he acts.
(3) For the purposes of subsection (2), a person acts for the protection of a child if he acts for the purposes of—
  (a) protecting the child from sexually transmitted infection,
  (b) protecting the physical safety of the child,
  (c) preventing the child from becoming pregnant, or
  (d) promoting the child's emotional well-being by the giving of advice,
  and **not** for the purpose of obtaining sexual gratification **or** for the purpose of causing or encouraging the activity constituting the offence within subsection (1)(b) **or** the child's participation in it.

Sexual Offences Act 2003, s 14

Defence notes

This is intended to protect those people such as health care workers who are aware that a person is having sex with a child under 16 and give them condoms as they believe that if they do not the child will have unprotected sex. It appears as if the health care worker must warn the person that what they are doing is illegal, but is allowed to give the condoms without committing an offence under this section.

Practical considerations

- The specified offence (under ss 9–13) does not have to take place. If it does occur or would have occurred if it were not for there being facts which made the commission of the offence impossible, then it may be easier to prove the above offence.
- Obtain any evidence which proves the links (eg advertisement, emails, bookings for hotels).
- Seize mobile phone, computer hard drive and any other physical evidence relevant to the offence.
- Consider confiscation of cash and property for the s 14 offence of arranging or facilitating the commission of a child sex offence; this is listed as a 'criminal lifestyle' offence under Sch 2 of the Proceeds of Crime Act 2002 (see **5.6** for details).

 Either way   None

 Summary: 6 months' imprisonment and/or a fine not exceeding the statutory maximum.

Indictment: 14 years' imprisonment.

6.7.2 **Meeting a child following sexual grooming**

This offence is covered by s 15 of the Sexual Offences Act 2003.

> **Offences**
>
> A person aged 18 or over (A) commits an offence if—
>
> (a) A **has met or communicated** with another person (B) on at least two occasions and subsequently—
>   (i) A **intentionally** meets B,
>   (ii) A travels with the intention of meeting B in any part of the world or arranges to meet B in any part of the world, or
>   (iii) B travels with the intention of meeting A in any part of the world,
> (b) A intends to do anything to or in respect of B, during or after the meeting mentioned in paragraph (a)(i) to (iii) and in any part of the world, which if done will involve the commission by A of a **relevant offence**,
> (c) B is under 16, and
> (d) A does not **reasonably believe** that B is 16 or over.
>
> Sexual Offences Act 2003, s 15(1)

Points to prove
- ✓ date and location
- ✓ being a person 18 or over
- ✓ has on at least two earlier occasions met/communicated
- ✓ with a person under 16
- ✓ not reasonably believing that person to be 16 or over
- ✓ intentionally met or travelled intending to meet **or** arranged to meet that person **or** that person has travelled with the intention of meeting you
- ✓ in any part of the world
- ✓ intending to do anything to/in respect of that person
- ✓ during/after the meeting and in any part of the world
- ✓ which if done would involve commission by you
- ✓ of a relevant offence

Meanings

Has met or communicated

The reference to A having met or communicated with B is a reference to A having met B in any part of the world or having communicated with B by any means from, to or in any part of the world.

Intentionally (see **6.1.1**)

Relevant offence

Means an offence under Pt 1 (ss 1–79 inclusive) and anything done outside England and Wales would be an offence within Pt 1.

Reasonably believe (see 'Defences' below)

Explanatory notes

- A defendant must have communicated on at least two earlier occasions or had two prior meetings with the person. The communication could be by telephone, text messaging, or email. These communications do not have to contain sexually explicit language or pornography but could, for example, be something as seemingly innocuous as the offender giving the victim swimming lessons or meeting them incidentally through a friend.
- They must intentionally meet or travel with the intention of meeting or arrange to meet each other. This meeting can take place anywhere in the world as long as some part of the journey took place in England, Wales, or Northern Ireland.
- The meeting itself does not have to take place, arranging will suffice, although the intent to commit the relevant offence (in any part of the world) will have to be proved.

6.7.2 Meeting a Child Following Sexual Grooming

- This offence is intended to deal with predators who groom young children by gaining their trust, lying about their age, then arranging to meet them in order to sexually abuse them. This offence is preventative, in that the relevant sexual offence does not have to occur in order for the offence to be committed.

Defences

Reasonable belief that the victim is 16 or over (see **6.5** 'Defence notes').

Related cases

R v Mohammed [2006] EWCA Crim 1107, CA M befriended a vulnerable 13-year-old girl, who lived in a foster home, and had severe learning difficulties and behavioural problems. They were found together 8 miles from her home and he was arrested. Their mobile phones were analyzed which showed that M had sent intimate messages. M confirmed that she had visited his home; but the abduction was short lived, the girl was willing and initiated contact, and no sexual act had taken place. Motivation was sexual and M had blatantly taken her from the control of carers. Convicted of child abduction and s 15(1).

R v Mansfield [2005] EWCA Crim 927, CA 'The law is there to protect young girls against their own immature sexual experimentation and to punish older men who take advantage of them.'

Practical considerations

- The victim must be under 16 and the prosecution would normally use the child's birth certificate (although other documentation could be used) and testimony of a person who can state that the complainant is the person whom the birth certificate relates to.
- Any articles in the defendant's possession such as condoms, pornography, rope, and lubricant could help to prove intent.
- Only a suitably trained or qualified person should be used to take statements or obtain evidence from the victims with this type of offence.
- The Children Act 2004 (see **2.4**) makes specific provision for the police and other agencies to protect the welfare and safety of children.
- Offence applies to all offences in Pt 1 of the Act (s 1 to s 79).
- All evidence in relation to the grooming should be seized (eg any communications, bookings, or other documents which link the defendant and victim).
- Consider CCTV evidence.
- Seize any computer and mobile phone that could have been used.
- Section 72 allows sexual offences committed outside the UK to be dealt with in England and Wales, as if the person had committed the act in the UK provided certain conditions are met. The conditions are

that the defendant is a UK national or resident who commits an act in a country outside the UK, and the act, if committed in England and Wales, would constitute a sexual offence given in Sch 2.

 Either way   None

 Summary: 6 months' imprisonment and/or a fine not exceeding the statutory maximum.

Indictment: 10 years' imprisonment.

Links to alternative subjects and offences

6.8 Indecent Photographs of Persons Under 18

6.8.1 Take, distribute, publish indecent photographs of person under 18

This offence is covered by s 1 of the Protection of Children Act 1978.

Offences

Subject to sections 1A and 1B *[defences]*, it is an offence for a person—
(a) to take, or permit to be taken, or to **make**, any **indecent photograph** or **pseudo-photograph** of a **child**; or
(b) to **distribute** or show such indecent photographs or pseudo-photographs; or
(c) to have in his possession such indecent photographs or pseudo-photographs, with a view to their being distributed or **shown by himself** and others; or
(d) to publish or cause to be published any advertisement likely to be understood as conveying that the advertiser distributes or shows such indecent photographs or pseudo-photographs or intends to do so.

Protection of Children Act 1978, s 1(1)

Points to prove

s 1(1)(a), (b)
✓ date and location
✓ made/permitted to be taken/took/showed/distributed
✓ indecent photograph(s)/pseudo-photograph(s)
✓ of a child/children

s 1(1)(c)
✓ date and location
✓ possessed
✓ indecent photograph(s)/pseudo-photograph(s)
✓ of child/children
✓ with a view to it (them) being distributed/shown to another

s 1(1)(d)
✓ date and location
✓ published/caused to be published
✓ an advertisement which is likely to convey or be understood
✓ that the advertiser

> ✓ distributes/shows or intends to distribute/show
> ✓ indecent photograph(s)/pseudo-photograph(s)
> ✓ of child/children

Meanings

Make

Includes downloading images from the Internet and storing or printing them (*R v Bowden* [2000] 1 WLR 1427).

Indecent photographs

- Includes indecent film, a copy of an indecent **photograph** or **film**, and an indecent photograph comprised in a film.
- Photographs (including those comprised in a film) shall, if they show children and are indecent, be treated for all purposes of this Act as indecent photographs of children and so as respects pseudo-photographs.

Photograph

References to a photograph include—
- the negative as well as the positive version; and
- data stored on a computer disc or by other electronic means which is capable of conversion into a photograph.
- a tracing or other image, whether made by electronic or other means (of whatever nature)—
  - ◆ which is not itself a photograph or pseudo-photograph, but
  - ◆ which is derived from the whole or part of a photograph or pseudo-photograph (or a combination of either or both); **and**

data stored on a computer disc or by other electronic means which is capable of conversion into the above tracing or image;
Notes: If the impression conveyed by a pseudo-photograph is that of a child, the pseudo-photograph shall be treated as showing a child and so shall a pseudo-photograph where the predominant impression conveyed is that the person shown is a child notwithstanding that some of the physical characteristics shown are those of an adult.

Film

This includes any form of video recording.

Pseudo-photograph

Means an image, whether made by computer graphics or otherwise howsoever, which appears to be a photograph.

Indecent pseudo-photograph

This includes a copy of an indecent pseudo-photograph; and data stored on a computer disc or by other electronic means which is capable of conversion into an indecent pseudo-photograph.

6.8.1 Indecent Photographs of Person Under 18

Child

A person under the age of 18.

Distribute

Means to part with possession to another person, or exposes or offers for acquisition by another person.

Shown by himself

Means shown by the defendant to other people.

Explanatory notes

- The image does not have to be stored in a way that allows it to be retrieved. However, the image must be made deliberately. Innocently opening a file from the Internet may not be an offence, see s 1(4)(b) in 'Defences'.
- The attendant circumstances of the way in which the images have been downloaded, stored, labelled, and filed will be important in demonstrating the extent to which the defendant was or should have been aware of their indecent nature. Other correspondence (by email or otherwise) with the defendant will also be useful here, as will any evidence of a general interest in paedophilia (*R v Mould* [2001] 2 Crim App R (S) 8).

Defences

1(4) Where a person is charged with an offence under subsection 1(b) or (c), it shall be a defence for him to prove—

(a) that he had a legitimate reason for distributing or showing the photographs or pseudo-photographs or (as the case may be) having them in his possession; or

(b) that he had not himself seen the photographs or pseudo-photographs and did not know, nor had any cause to suspect, them to be indecent.

Marriage and partnership

1A(1) This section applies where, in proceedings for an offence under s 1(1)(a) of taking or making an indecent photograph of a child, or for an offence under s 1(1)(b) or (c) relating to an indecent photograph of a child, the defendant proves that the photograph was of the child aged 16 or over, and that at the time of the offence charged the child and he—

(a) were married or civil partners of each other, or

(b) lived together as partners in an enduring family relationship.

1A(2) Subsections (5) and (6) also apply where, in proceedings for an offence under s 1(1)(b) or (c) relating to an indecent photograph of a child, the defendant proves that the photograph was of the child aged 16 or over, and that at the time when he obtained it the child and he—

(a) were married or civil partners of each other, or

(b) lived together as partners in an enduring family relationship.

1A(3) This section applies whether the photograph showed the child alone or with the defendant, but not if it showed any other person.

1A(4) In the case of an offence under s 1(1)(a), if sufficient evidence is adduced to raise an issue as to whether the child consented to the photograph being taken or made, or as to whether the defendant reasonably believed that the child so consented, the defendant is not guilty of the offence unless it is proved that the child did not so consent and that the defendant did not reasonably believe that the child so consented.

1A(5) In the case of an offence under s 1(1)(b), the defendant is not guilty of the offence unless it is proved that the showing or distributing was to a person other than the child.

1A(6) In the case of an offence under s 1(1)(c), if sufficient evidence is adduced to raise an issue both—

(a) as to whether the child consented to the photograph being in the defendant's possession, or as to whether the defendant reasonably believed that the child so consented, and

(b) as to whether the defendant had the photograph in his possession with a view to its being distributed or shown to anyone other than the child,

the defendant is not guilty of the offence unless it is proved either that the child did not so consent and that the defendant did not reasonably believe that the child so consented, or that the defendant had the photograph in his possession with a view to its being distributed or shown to a person other than the child.

Instances when defendant is not guilty of the offence

1B(1) In proceedings for an offence under s 1(1)(a) of making an indecent photograph or pseudo-photograph of a child, the defendant is not guilty of the offence if he proves that—

(a) it was necessary for him to make the photograph or pseudo-photograph for the purposes of the prevention, detection or investigation of crime, or for the purposes of criminal proceedings, in any part of the world,

(b) at the time of the offence charged he was a member of the Security Service or the Secret Intelligence Service, and it was necessary for him to make the photograph or pseudo-photograph for the exercise of any of the functions of that Service, or

(c) at the time of the offence charged he was a member of GCHQ, and it was necessary for him to make the photograph or pseudo-photograph for the exercise of any of the functions of GCHQ.

1B(2) In this section 'GCHQ' has the same meaning as in the Intelligence Services Act 1994.

Protection of Children Act 1978, ss 1(4), 1A, 1B

Defence notes

- The defence given in s 1(4)(b) as to 'not seeing and did not know, nor had any cause to suspect, them to be indecent' would cover situations where an email attachment was opened innocently and not subsequently deleted owing to a genuine lack of IT skills (deleting an email in 'Outlook' may only move it to a 'deleted' directory, much like the 'recycle bin'; this directory needs to be emptied and there may be other 'temporary' directories where it could be held) or innocently downloading an image from the web, then immediately deleting the image without realizing that it was also stored as a back-up copy in a temporary Internet directory.
- In a Crown Court case the 'Trojan Horse' virus defence was successful. In short, expert evidence confirmed the likelihood of this virus being responsible for 14 depraved images saved on the defendant's personal computer. It was accepted that these could have been sent remotely, without the defendant's knowledge. Although this case is not binding on other courts, and each case will be determined according to its own particular facts, officers should be aware of the possibility of this defence being raised.

Related cases

R v Dooley [2005] EWCA Crim 3093, CA If downloaded material was accessible to all club members then it is downloaded with a view to its distribution or showing to others.

R v T (1999) 163 JP 349, CA Courts will not accept an intention by the offender to show photographs to himself as sufficient to prove the offence under s 1(1)(c).

R v Smith and Jayson [2002] 1 Cr App R 13, CA Deliberately opening an indecent computer email attachment or downloading an indecent image from the Internet, so it can be viewed on a screen, is making a photograph.

R v Bowden [2001] 1 WLR 1427, CA Downloading would come within s 1 'to make' as a file is created when the photograph is downloaded.

Practical considerations

- It is not an offence under this Act to possess photographs to show to yourself although this is an offence under s 160 of the Criminal Justice Act 1988 (see **6.8.2**).
- Proceedings for an offence under this Act shall not be instituted except by or with the consent of the DPP.
- Ascertain how the photographs or pseudo-photographs were made, discovered, and whether stored.
- Seize all computer equipment as evidence under s 20 of PACE (see **12.3.4**).

- Section 39 of the Police and Justice Act 2006 inserted Sch 11 into the 1978 Act which now permits forfeiture of indecent images of children and the devices that hold them without the involvement of a court, unless the owner or some other person with an interest in the material objects.
- There are some authoritative factors in deciding whether or not a defence may apply, depending on whether the person(s)—
  - acted reasonably in all the circumstances;
  - reported the photographs or pseudo-photographs as soon as was practicable and to the appropriate authority;
  - stored the photographs or pseudo-photographs in a secure and safe manner;
  - copied or distributed the photographs or pseudo-photographs unnecessarily.

 Either way   None

 Summary: 6 months' imprisonment and/or a fine not exceeding the statutory maximum.

Indictment: 10 years' imprisonment.

6.8.2 **Possession of indecent photograph(s) of person under 18**

Section 160 of the Criminal Justice Act 1988 concerns the offence of simple possession of indecent photographs or pseudo-photographs of a person under 18.

Offence

Subject to **section 160A** it is an offence for a person to have any **indecent photograph** or **pseudo-photograph** of a **child** in his possession.

Criminal Justice Act 1988, s 160(1)

Points to prove
- ✓ date and location
- ✓ possessed
- ✓ indecent photo(s)/pseudo-photograph(s)
- ✓ of a child/children

6.8.2 Possession of Indecent Photograph(s) of Person Under 18

Meanings

Section 160A (see 'Defences' below).

Photographs (see **6.8.1**)

Indecent photograph (see **6.8.1**)

Pseudo-photograph (see **6.8.1**)

Child (see **6.8.1**)

Explanatory notes

Where there is evidence of intent to distribute or show then the offence under s1 of the Protection of Children Act 1978 (see **6.8.1**) should be used.

Defences

160(2) Where a person is charged with an offence under subsection (1) above it shall be a defence for him to prove—
  (a) that he had a legitimate reason for having the photograph or pseudo-photograph in his possession; or
  (b) that he had not himself seen the photograph or pseudo-photograph and did not know, nor had any cause to suspect, it to be indecent; or
  (c) that the photograph or pseudo-photograph was sent to him without any prior request made by him or on his behalf and that he did not keep it for an unreasonable time.

160A(1) This section applies where, in proceedings for an offence under section 160 relating to an indecent photograph of a child, the defendant proves that the photograph was of the child aged 16 or over, and that at the time of the offence charged the child and he—
  (a) were married or civil partners of each other, or
  (b) lived together as partners in an enduring family relationship.

160A(2) This section also applies where, in proceedings for an offence under section 160 relating to an indecent photograph of a child, the defendant proves that the photograph was of the child aged 16 or over, and that at the time when he obtained it the child and he—
  (a) were married or civil partners of each other, or
  (b) lived together as partners in an enduring family relationship.

160A(3) This section applies whether the photograph showed the child alone or with the defendant, but not if it showed any other person.

160A(4) If sufficient evidence is adduced to raise an issue as to whether the child consented to the photograph being in the defendant's possession, or as to whether the defendant reasonably believed that the child so consented, the defendant is not guilty of the offence unless it is proved that the child did not so consent and that the defendant did not reasonably believe that the child so consented.

Criminal Justice Act 1988, ss 160 and 160A

Defence notes

The conditions for the defence are listed under s 160A(1)–(4). If any of these conditions are not satisfied, the prosecution need only prove the offence as set out in s 160. But if the three conditions are satisfied, the defendant is not guilty of the offence unless the prosecution proves that the child did not consent and that the defendant did not reasonably believe that the child consented.

Related cases

R v Porter [2006] EWCA Crim 560, CA The computer hard drives of P were found to contain deleted images which could only be retrieved using specialist software, which P did not have. If a person cannot access deleted images on a computer then he was no longer in custody, control or possession of those images. The jury must decide on this issue having regard to all the relevant circumstances and the defendant's knowledge at the time.

R v Matrix [1997] Crim LR 901 A shop assistant may possess indecent photographs as well as the shop owner.

Atkins v DPP and Goodland v DPP [2000] 2 All ER 425, QBD *Atkins:* Images stored in a temporary directory unbeknown to the defendant did not amount to possession, knowledge was required.

Practical considerations

- Ensure that the photographs or pseudo-photographs are seized.
- Seize the computer or storage mechanism as evidence under s 20 of PACE (see **12.3.4**).
- Section 39 of the Police and Justice Act 2006 inserted Sch 11 into the Protection of Children Act 1978 (see **6.8.1**) which now permits forfeiture of indecent images of children and the devices that hold them without the involvement of a court, unless the owner or some other person with an interest in the material objects.
- Check on the audit chain for the photograph and documents relating to them to ensure possession is the only suitable charge.
- Consent of the DPP required.
- Although this has no direct connection to the above offence, police officers should be aware of s 63 of the Criminal Justice and Immigration Act 2008, which creates the offence of possession of **extreme pornographic images**.
- **Extreme pornographic image** is an image that portrays, in an explicit and realistic way, any of the following, being an act which involves—
  - ◆ threatening a person's life,
  - ◆ serious injury to a person's anus, breasts, or genitals,
  - ◆ sexual interference with a human corpse, or
  - ◆ a person performing intercourse or oral sex with an animal (whether dead or alive), and a reasonable person looking at the image would think that any such person or animal was real.

6.8.2 Possession of Indecent Photograph(s) of Person Under 18

 Either way None

 Summary: 6 months' imprisonment and/or a fine not exceeding level 5 on the standard scale.

Indictment: 5 years' imprisonment and/or a fine.

Links to alternative subjects and offences

E&S Entry and search powers   **CHAR** Offences where bad character can be introduced

6.9 **Exposure and Outraging Public Decency**

6.9.1 **Indecent Exposure**

This offence is covered by s 66 of the Sexual Offences Act 2003.

Offence

A person commits an offence if—
(a) he **intentionally** exposes his **genitals**, and
(b) he intends that someone will see them and be caused alarm or distress.

Sexual Offences Act 2003, s 66(1)

Points to prove

✓ date and location
✓ intentionally
✓ exposed genitals
✓ intending
✓ someone would see them
✓ and be caused alarm/distress

Meanings

Intentionally (see **6.1.1**)

Genitals

Means male or female sexual organs.

Explanatory notes

- Offence would generally exclude naturists and streakers whose intention is not to cause alarm or distress.
- Exposure of the genitals must be intentional and not accidental.
- The offence applies to either sex and is not restricted (as with previous legislation) to the male penis. However, genitals do not include a female's breasts or the buttocks of either sex, so a female flashing her breasts or someone mooning (exposing their buttocks) will not be caught within this offence.
- Offence can be committed anywhere and is not restricted to public places.

Practical considerations

- It is not necessary for a person to have actually seen the genitals or for anyone to be distressed or alarmed. For example, a male exposes his genitals to a female passing by. If his intent was for her to see them and be alarmed or distressed then even if she does not see them or was not distressed then he still commits the offence.
- Proof of the relevant intent (both as to the genitals being seen and alarm or distress being caused thereby) will be critical to a successful prosecution.
- The precise location and the time of day will be important in showing a likely intention by the defendant.
- The accompanying words/conduct of the defendant will be relevant here, along with any preparatory or subsequent actions.
- Is this offence isolated or one of a series?

 Either way   None

 Summary: 6 months' imprisonment and/or a fine not exceeding the statutory maximum.

Indictment: 2 years' imprisonment.

6.9.2 **Outraging public decency**

This is an offence at common law.

> **Offence**
>
> It is an offence to commit an act of a **lewd, obscene,** and **disgusting** nature, which is capable of outraging public decency, in a **public place** where at least two members of the public could have witnessed it.
>
> Common Law

Points to prove

✓ date and location
✓ in a public place
✓ committed an act
✓ outraging public decency
✓ by behaving in indecent manner

  E&S Entry and search powers   **CHAR** Offences where bad character can be introduced

Meanings

Lewd

Means lustful or indecent.

Obscene

Means morally repugnant or depraved.

Disgusting

Means repugnant or loathsome.

Public place

Means a place to which the public have access or a place which is visible to the public.

Explanatory notes

- Consider if statutory offences would be more suitable, such as the Sexual Offences Act 2003, the Public Order Act 1986, or the Obscene Publications Act 1959.
- Such conduct can also be an offence of public nuisance at common law (see **7.13.3**).

Related cases

R v Hamilton [2007] EWCA Crim 2062,CA Video footage showed that H had been filming up women's skirts and he admitted to 'upskirting' by positioning a camera at a certain angle to film up the skirts of women. It was held that a jury could decide if the conduct was lewd, obscene, or disgusting even though no one actually saw the filming.

Rose v DPP [2006] EWHC 852 (Admin), QBD A couple had oral sex in ATM area of bank captured on CCTV, foyer was well lit and passers by could see the act. More than one person must see the act for the offence of outraging public decency.

R v Walker [1996] 1 Cr App R 111, CA Defendant exposed himself and masturbated in front of two young girls in his living room. As public could not see into his living room then it was not a public place for this offence.

Smith v Hughes [1960] 1 WLR 830 Held that the balcony of a private house visible to the public was a sufficiently public place for this offence.

R v Gibson [1990] 2 QB 619 The 'act' does not have to be a 'live' activity, nor does it have to be of a sexual nature. It may be the act of putting a disgusting object on public display, such as displaying a sculpted head with a real human foetus dangling from it in a public art gallery.

6.9.2 Outraging Public Decency

Practical considerations

- More than one person must be able to witness the lewd act.
- Conduct must grossly cross the boundaries of decency and be likely to seriously offend the reasonable person (rather than simply upsetting or even shocking).
- In sexual offences, this offence is reserved for offences where masturbation or sexual intercourse occurs (as with the current fad of 'dogging'). There is no requirement to prove that those persons who witnessed the act were actually disgusted or outraged by it. The test is an objective one based on whether a reasonable person would be disgusted.
- Where the circumstances are appropriate, positive evidence of disgust can be given by a police officer.

 Either way

 None

 Summary: 6 months' imprisonment and/or a fine not exceeding the statutory maximum.

Indictment: Imprisonment and/or a fine.

Links to alternative subjects and offences

6.10 **Voyeurism**

This offence is created by s 67 of the Sexual Offences Act 2003.

Offences

(1) A person commits an offence if—
  (a) for the purpose of obtaining sexual gratification, he observes another person doing a **private act**, and
  (b) he knows that the other person does not **consent** to being observed for his **sexual gratification**.
(2) A person commits an offence if—
  (a) he operates equipment with the intention of enabling another person to observe, for the purpose of obtaining **sexual gratification**, a third person (B) doing a private act, and
  (b) he knows that B does not **consent** to his operating equipment with that intention.
(3) A person commits an offence if—
  (a) he records another person (B) doing a **private act**,
  (b) he does so with the intention that he or a third person will, for the purpose of obtaining **sexual gratification**, look at an image of B doing the act, and
  (c) he knows that B does not consent to his recording the act with that intention.
(4) A person commits an offence if he installs equipment, or constructs or adapts a **structure** or part of a structure, with the intention of enabling himself or another person to commit an offence under subsection (1).

Sexual Offences Act 2003, s 67

Points to prove

Observing s 67(1)

✓ date and location
✓ for purpose of obtaining sexual gratification
✓ observed another person
✓ doing a private act
✓ knowing that the person
✓ does not consent to being observed
✓ for defendant's sexual gratification

Operating equipment to observe s 67(2)

✓ date and location
✓ operated equipment
✓ with the intention of enabling another person

✓ for the purpose of obtaining sexual gratification
✓ to observe a third person doing a private act
✓ knowing that person does not consent
✓ to defendant operating equipment for that intention

Recording a private act s 67(3)

✓ date and location
✓ recorded another person doing a private act
✓ with intention that
✓ defendant or a third person
✓ would for the purpose of obtaining sexual gratification
✓ look at an image of that other person doing the act
✓ knowing that the other person does not consent
✓ to defendant recording the act with that intention

Install equipment/construct/adapt a structure s 67(4)

✓ date and location
✓ installed equipment **or**
✓ constructed/adapted a structure/part of a structure
✓ with intent
✓ to enable defendant or third person
✓ to commit an offence under s 67(1)

Meanings

Private act

A person is doing a private act if they are in a place where they could reasonably expect privacy and their genitals, breasts, or buttocks are exposed or covered with underwear, they are using the toilet, or doing a sexual act that is not normally done in public.

Consent

Defendant must **know** that the person does not consent to being observed for *sexual gratification*. They may have consented to being observed for some other reason.

Sexual gratification

In s 67(1) the sexual gratification must be for the defendant, in the other subsections it could be for a third party's sexual gratification.

Structure

Includes a tent, vehicle or vessel, or other temporary or movable structure.

Explanatory notes

- Previously it was not an offence to watch someone for sexual gratification. This will cater for such situations involving 'Peeping Toms'.
- For s 67(2)–(4), it is irrelevant whether or not any third parties knew that the person did not consent.

- Section 67(2) is aimed at those who install webcams or other recording equipment for their own gratification or for that of others. An image is defined as 'a moving or still image and includes an image produced by any means and, where the context permits, a three-dimensional image'.
- Section 67(4) would cover a person who installed a two-way mirror or a spy-hole in a hotel room. The offender would commit the offence even if the peephole or mirror was discovered before it was ever used.

Related cases

R v Bassett [2008] EWCA Crim 1174, CA Whether a person had a reasonable expectation of privacy would depend on the facts in each case and would be closely related to the nature of the observation taking place. Some parts of the body are those which people would expect privacy for. 'Breasts' to mean female breasts as opposed to the bare male chest.

Practical considerations

- Any equipment used requires seizing.
- CCTV footage may be of use.
- Search for films made and evidence of equipment hire.
- Video tape(s), DVD(s) or other medium/equipment used for storing image can be seized for examination and evidence.

 Either way   None

Summary: 6 months' imprisonment and/or a fine not exceeding the statutory maximum.

Indictment: 2 years' imprisonment.

Links to alternative subjects and offences

E&S Entry and search powers   CHAR Offences where bad character can be introduced

6.11 **Sexual Activity in a Public Lavatory**

This offence is covered by s 71 of the Sexual Offences Act 2003.

Offence

A person commits an offence if—
(a) he is in a lavatory to which the public or a section of the public has or is permitted to have access, whether on payment or otherwise,
(b) he **intentionally** engages in an activity, and,
(c) the **activity is sexual**.

Sexual Offences Act 2003, s 71(1)

Points to prove

✓ date and location
✓ being in a lavatory
✓ to which the public/a section of the public
✓ have/are permitted to have access
✓ whether on payment/otherwise
✓ intentionally
✓ engaged in a sexual activity

Meanings

Intentionally (see **6.1.1**)

Sexual activity

An activity is sexual if a reasonable person would, in all the circumstances but regardless of any person's purpose, consider it to be sexual.

Explanatory notes

- Offence covers lavatories to which the public, or a section of the public, have access, whether or not payment is involved. This would include staff toilets in large/small premises where the public could have access.
- The sexual activity does not have to be specified, it would be enough to record details of what was seen or heard.
- There is no requirement to prove that anyone was alarmed or distressed by the activity.
- This offence replaced the former offence known as 'cottaging'.

Practical considerations

- Sexual in s 71 is different than used throughout the Act, in that it is what a reasonable person would consider sexual, regardless of the person's purpose.
- The offence is gender neutral, so the sexual activity could be committed by a male or female against a male or female.
- If possible obtain independent evidence.

 Summary 6 months

 6 months' imprisonment and/or a fine not exceeding level 5 on the standard scale.

Links to alternative subjects and offences

6.12 Administer Substance and Commit an Offence—with Intent to Commit Sexual Offence

6.12.1 Administer substance intending to commit sexual offence

This offence is covered by s 61 of the Sexual Offences Act 2003.

Offences

A person commits an offence if he **intentionally administers** a substance to, or **causes** a substance **to be taken** by, another person (B)—
(a) knowing that B does not consent, and
(b) with the intention of stupefying or overpowering B, so as to enable any person to engage in a **sexual activity** that involves B.

Sexual Offences Act 2003, s 61(1)

Points to prove

✓ date and location
✓ intentionally
✓ administered a substance to **or**
✓ caused a substance to be taken by
✓ another person
✓ knowing that s/he did not consent
✓ with intention of stupefying/overpowering
✓ so as to enable any person
✓ to engage in a sexual activity involving victim

Meanings

Intentionally (see **6.1.1**)

Administer

In *R v Gillard* (1988) 87 Cr App Rep 189 held to include conduct that brings a substance into contact with the victim's body, directly or indirectly. For example, by injection or by holding a cloth soaked in the substance to the victim's face.

Causes to be taken

This would cover such conduct as slipping a date rape drug directly into a drink or deceiving the victim as to the nature of the substance (eg telling the victim it is a pain killer when in fact it is a sedative).

Sexual (see **6.3.1**)

Explanatory notes

- Offence replaces s 4 of the Sexual Offences Act 1956 (male administer drugs to obtain intercourse with female), but has a much wider remit as it is gender neutral and includes sexual activity not just sexual intercourse.
- This offence is intended to cover situations where so-called 'date rape' drugs (such as Rohypnol or GHB (gamma-hydroxybutrate)) are given to a person in order to allow the defendant or someone else to have sexual activity with them. It also covers the spiking of a person's drink with alcohol when they believed they were drinking a soft drink.
- It does not matter how the substance is administered (eg by drink, injection). The offence has a very wide ambit in that it allows for one person to administer the substance or cause the substance to be taken and another to engage in the sexual activity (although no sexual activity need actually take place).
- The required consent refers to the taking/administering of the substance as opposed to the intended sexual activity. In s 76(2)(f) there is an evidential presumption that the victim does not consent to the sexual activity under s 1 (see **6.1.1**) where a substance which would stupefy or overpower has been administered.

Practical considerations

- The offence is committed whether or not there is any sexual activity as long as the substance was administered and there was the relevant intention.
- If there was no sexual activity, it may be hard to prove this offence. However, consider offences under ss 23 or 24 of the Offences Against the Person Act 1861 as to administering a poison or other noxious thing (see **5.1.1**).
- If there was sexual activity then offender could be charged with other offences, not just this one.
- Consider taking samples and medical examinations where appropriate.
- Gather evidence by seizing any appropriate documentation.
- Seize mobile phones where there is evidence of link between defendants and victims at the relevant time.
- Consider CCTV footage.

Either way

 None

 Summary: 6 months' imprisonment and/or a fine not exceeding the statutory maximum.

Indictment: 10 years' imprisonment.

6.12.2 Commit an offence with intent to commit sexual offence

This offence is covered by s 62 of the Sexual Offences Act 2003.

Offence

A person commits an offence under this section if he commits any offence with the **intention** of committing a **relevant sexual offence**.

Sexual Offences Act 2003, s 62(1)

Points to prove

- ✓ date and location
- ✓ committed any offence
- ✓ with the intention of committing
- ✓ a relevant sexual offence

Meanings

Intention (see 6.1.1)

Relevant sexual offence (see 6.2)

Explanatory notes

- This offence involves the commission of **any** criminal offence, with the intention of the defendant carrying out a relevant sexual offence.
- *Any* offence will be covered (eg burglary, assault, kidnap, blackmail).
- This offence is intended to cater for such situations where the victim is kidnapped, assaulted, poisoned or blackmailed in order that the defendant can thereby rape them or carry out some other sexual act that the victim would not otherwise consent to.
- The offence is committed whether or not the relevant sexual offence actually takes place, for example, if the police find the kidnap victim prior to their being raped.

E&S Entry and search powers

CHAR Offences where bad character can be introduced

Practical considerations

- The first offence does not necessarily have to involve the intended victim of the ulterior sexual offence, for example, where the defendant steals a car from one person in order to drive to the house of another person and rape them.
- If the sexual offence did take place then the defendant would be charged with that relevant sexual offence as well as this one.
- Obtain forensic evidence by identifying and preserving crime scene.
- Ensure there is no cross-contamination.
- Seize any evidence of defendant's knowledge of victim through previous text messages and emails, and if necessary seize phones and computers.

 Either way   None

 Summary: 6 months' imprisonment and/or a fine not exceeding the statutory maximum.

Indictment: 10 years' imprisonment.

Note: If kidnapping or false imprisonment—life imprisonment.

Links to alternative subjects and offences

6.13 Prostitution: Soliciting, Kerb Crawling, and Placing of Adverts

6.13.1 Prostitute soliciting in the street or public place

This offence is contrary to s 1 of the Street Offences Act 1959.

Offence

It shall be an offence for a **common prostitute** (whether male or female) to **loiter** or **solicit** in a **street** or **public place** for the purpose of prostitution.

Street Offences Act 1959, s 1(1)

Points to prove

✓ date and location
✓ common prostitute
✓ loitered **or** solicited
✓ in street/public place
✓ for purpose of prostitution

Meanings

Common

Means that the prostitute has either been previously convicted of this offence or cautioned for such conduct.

Prostitute

Means any person who offers sexual services for reward and includes a person acting as a 'clipper' (a person who offers a sexual service, but does not provide it themselves).

Loiter

Means to dawdle or linger idly about a place, proceeding with frequent pauses (see '**Related cases**').

Solicit

Means to accost and offer oneself.

Street

Includes any bridge, road, lane, footway, subway, square, or passage, whether a thoroughfare or not, which is for the time being open to the public; and the doorways and entrances of premises abutting on a street, and any ground adjoining and open to a street.

Public place

Any highway and any place to which at the material time the public has access, on payment or otherwise, as of right or by virtue of express or implied permission.

Explanatory notes

• Cautioned in this context means someone who has not previously been convicted of loitering or soliciting for the purpose of prostitution is seen loitering or soliciting in a street or public place for that purpose, and receives a warning. The officer seeing them should obtain the assistance of a second officer as a witness.
• Men or women can be prostitutes.

Related cases

Williamson v Wright [1924] SC(J) 570 Implying the idea of lingering, slowing down on one particular occasion does not amount to loitering.

Horton v Mead [1913] All ER 954 An action unaccompanied by words and need not reach the mind of the person intended to be solicited.

Smith v Hughes [1960] 2 All ER 859 A prostitute soliciting from a balcony or window of a house adjoining a street is treated as being in the street for the purposes of this offence.

Behrendt v Burridge [1976] 3 All ER 285 A prostitute sitting on a stool in a window under a light is soliciting.

Weisz v Monahan [1962] 1 All ER 664 The placing of notices in windows offering the services of a prostitute has been held not to be soliciting.

Practical considerations

• When both officers, after having kept them under observation, are satisfied by their demeanour and conduct that the person(s) are in fact loitering or soliciting for the purpose of prostitution the officers will tell them what they have seen and caution the person(s). Details of the caution should subsequently be recorded at the police station.
• There are official guidelines for dealing with prostitution and the key element is for all the agencies to work in partnership. An important role for these agencies is to ensure that individuals do not become involved in prostitution in the first place or to create opportunities to leave prostitution.

- Prosecution should only be used where there is evidence that the person has been offered exit opportunities and they have been ignored and that person has persistently and voluntarily returned to prostitution. This would include when two cautions as described above have been issued and where exit opportunities and support have been offered and ignored.
- Consider seizing CCTV for evidential purposes.

 Summary   6 months

 A fine not exceeding level 2 on the standard scale (after a previous conviction: level 3).

6.13.2 **Soliciting involving motor vehicle (kerb crawling)**

This offence is covered by s 1 of the Sexual Offences Act 1985.

Offences

A person commits an offence if he **solicits** another person (or different persons) for the purpose of **prostitution**—
(a) from a motor vehicle while it is in a street or public place; or
(b) in a street or public place while in the immediate vicinity of a motor vehicle that he has just got out of or off,
persistently or, in such a manner or in such circumstances as to be likely to cause annoyance to the person (or any of the persons) solicited, or nuisance to other persons in the neighbourhood.

Sexual Offences Act 1985, s 1(1)

Points to prove
✓ date and location
✓ solicited
✓ another person (or different persons)
✓ for purpose of prostitution
✓ from or in vicinity of
✓ a motor vehicle
✓ in a street/public place
✓ persistently in such manner/circumstances
✓ as to be likely to cause annoyance
✓ to the other person(s) solicited or nuisance to other persons in the neighbourhood

Meanings

Solicit (see **6.13.1**)

Prostitution (see **6.13.1**)

Motor vehicle (see **10.1.3**)
Meaning as in the Road Traffic Act 1988.

Street (see **6.13.1**)

Public place (see **6.13.1**)

Explanatory notes

It is not necessary that the offender is in the motor vehicle but they must
be in the immediate vicinity and must have just got out of the vehicle.

Practical considerations

Make a record of registration marks of vehicles suspected to be involved
in kerb crawling and a description of the driver.

 Summary   6 months

 A fine not exceeding level 3 on the standard scale.

6.13.3 **Persistently solicit for purpose of prostitution**

Section 2 of the Sexual Offences Act 1985 can be used as an alternative
offence where a motor vehicle is not used.

Offence

A person commits an offence if in a **street** or **public place** he persistently **solicits** another person (or different persons) for the purposes of
prostitution.

Sexual Offences Act 1985, s 2(1)

Points to prove
- ✓ date and location
- ✓ being in a street/public place
- ✓ persistently solicited another person/different people for purpose
  of prostitution

Meanings

Street (see **6.13.1**)

Public place (see **6.13.1**)

Solicits (see **6.13.1**)

Prostitution (see **6.13.1**)

Practical considerations

- Obtain a description of any persons suspected of kerb crawling.
- Ascertain whether CCTV evidence is available.
- As persistent conduct is required, consider the offence of harassment (see **7.11.1**).

 Summary   6 months

 A fine not exceeding level 3 on the standard scale.

6.13.4 **Prostitution—placing of adverts in telephone boxes**

This offence is covered by s 46 of the Criminal Justice and Police Act 2001.

Offence

A person commits an offence if—

(a) he places on, or in the immediate vicinity of, **a public telephone** an **advertisement** relating to **prostitution**, and

(b) he does so with the **intention** that the advertisement should come to the attention of any other person or persons.

Criminal Justice and Police Act 2001, s 46(1)

Points to prove

- ✓ date and location
- ✓ placed
- ✓ on or in immediate vicinity
- ✓ of public telephone
- ✓ an advertisement
- ✓ relating to prostitution
- ✓ with intent
- ✓ that advert should come to attention
- ✓ of another person or persons

Meanings

Advertisement

If it advertises the services of a prostitute, whether male or female, or indicates that premises are premises at which such services are offered.

Public telephone

Means any telephone which is located in a **public place** and made available for use by the public, or a section of the public, and where such a telephone is located in or on, or attached to, a kiosk, booth, acoustic hood, shelter, or other structure, that structure.

Public place

Means any place to which the public have or are permitted to have access, whether on payment or otherwise, other than—

- any place to which children under the age of 16 years are not permitted to have access, whether by law or otherwise, and
- any premises which are wholly or mainly used for residential purposes.

Prostitution (see **6.13.1**)

Intention (see **4.1.2**)

Explanatory notes

- An advertisement will be considered for prostitution if a reasonable person would consider it one. However, this is a rebuttable presumption and the defendant may show that it was not such an advertisement.
- If there is evidence to satisfy the other points to prove (eg it is an advertisement for prostitution and it is in public telephone in public place), then the purpose of the advertisement will require little if any further proof; as the very nature of an advertisement is to bring goods or services to the attention of others and it has been placed where it undoubtedly will be seen by others.

Practical considerations

- Seize any advertisement used to commit the offence.
- Many public telephones are situated on privately owned land, such as railway station concourses or shopping centres, but these will be covered by the Act as the public have access. However, a telephone in a nightclub (children under 16 are not allowed access) or university halls of residence (wholly or mainly used for residential purposes) would not fall within the definition.

6.13.4 Prostitution—Placing of Adverts in Telephone Boxes

 Summary   6 months

 6 months' imprisonment and/or a fine not exceeding level 5 on the standard scale.

Links to alternative subjects and offences

Chapter 7
Public Disorder/Nuisance

7.1 Penalty Notices for Disorder

Penalty Notices for Disorder (PNDs) were established by s 1 of the Criminal Justice and Police Act 2001. The number of offences for which a PND can be issued has more than doubled since s 1 came into force and as a result disposals by PND have increased considerably since their introduction.

7.1.1 Penalty notices for disorder offences

Offences for which a PND can be issued and the current tier (upper or lower) are as follows—

Upper tier

Penalty—£80 for 16 and over (£40 [in pilot forces] for 10–15 years)

Throwing fireworks in a thoroughfare
Explosives Act 1875, s 80 (see **8.8.6**)

Wasting police time or giving false report
Criminal Law Act 1967, s 5(2) (see **11.4.1**)

Disorderly behaviour while drunk in a public place
Criminal Justice Act 1967, s 91 (see **7.2.1**)

Theft (under £200 retail/commercial only) (see 7.1.2 'Theft and criminal damage' for further restrictions)
Theft Act 1968, s 1–7 (see **3.1.1**)

Destroying or damaging property (under £500) (see 7.1.2 'Theft and criminal damage' *for further restrictions*)
Criminal Damage Act 1971, s 1(1) (see **4.4**)

7.1.1 Penalty Notices for Disorder Offences

Possess cannabis and its derivatives, being a Class B
controlled drug
Misuse of Drugs Act 1971, s 5(2) (see **5.2.1**)

Behaviour likely to cause harassment, alarm, or distress
Public Order Act 1986, s 5 (see **7.8**)

Send offensive/false messages on public communications network
Communications Act 2003, s 127(2) (see **7.12.2**)

Breach Fireworks Regulations 2004 prohibitions: curfew; possess under
18/category 4
Fireworks Act 2003, s 11 (see **8.8**)

Sale of alcohol anywhere to a person under 18
Licensing Act 2003, s 146(1) (see **9.1.2**)

Supply of alcohol by or on behalf of a club to a person aged under 18
Licensing Act 2003, s 146(3) (see **9.1.2**)

Buy or attempt to buy alcohol on behalf of a person under 18
Licensing Act 2003, s 149(3) (see **9.1.4**)

Buy/attempt to buy alcohol for consumption by under 18
on relevant premises
Licensing Act 2003, s 149(4) (see **9.1.4**)

Sell or attempt to sell alcohol to a person who is drunk
Licensing Act 2003, s 141 (see **9.2.1**)

Deliver/allow delivery of alcohol to person under 18
Licensing Act 2003, s 151 (see **9.1.6**)

Knowingly give a false alarm of fire
Fire and Rescue Services Act 2004, s 49 (see **7.12.3**)

Lower tier

Penalty—£50 for 16 and over (£30 [in pilot forces] for 10–15 years)

Being drunk in a highway, public place, or licensed premises
Licensing Act 1872, s 12 (see **7.2.2**)

Trespassing on a railway
British Transport Commission Act 1949, s 55

Throw stone, matter, or thing at a train/apparatus on railway
British Transport Commission Act 1949, s 56

Leave/deposit litter
Environmental Protection Act 1990, s 87(1) (see **7.16.1**)—issuing restrictions apply (see **7.16** and **11.1.1**)

Consume alcohol in a designated public place
Criminal Justice and Police Act 2001, s 12 (see **9.4**)

Consume alcohol by a person under 18 or allow on relevant licensed premises
Licensing Act 2003, s 150 (see **9.1.5**)

Person under 18 buys or attempts to buy alcohol
Licensing Act 2003, s 149(1) (see **9.1.4**)

7.1.2 Police operational guidance for issuing PNDs

Police operational guidance on PNDs was issued by the Home Office in March 2005. It is proposed to revise this guidance in the near future. Edited extracts from the current guidance, including subsequent additions, are as shown below.

- The power to issue a penalty notice is additional to existing methods of disposal. The power to arrest should be exercised in the normal way with reporting for process remaining an option for offences where an arrest is considered unnecessary. No one has a right to demand a penalty notice; similarly, no one should be forced to accept one. The notice must be issued to, and received by, the offender. The use of police bail should never be ruled out where further enquiries are needed to inform proper case disposal decisions.
- Officers **may** issue a penalty notice for wasting police time without DPP consent. Where the offender requests a hearing, a summons will be raised in the normal way and the CPS will give delegated DPP consent.

PND aims—instant penalties

- A constable, including a special constable, who has reason to believe that a person aged 16 years of age or over has committed a penalty offence may give that person a penalty notice for that offence.
- The notice may be issued either on the spot (but it does not have to be issued exactly at the time of the offence) by an officer in uniform, or at a police station by an authorized officer. (An authorized officer is any officer authorized to issue penalty notices by the Chief Officer for the area in which they operate.)
- Payment of the penalty involves no admission of guilt and removes both liability to conviction and record of criminal conviction.
- On issue the recipient may elect to pay the penalty or request a court hearing. They must do one or the other within 21 days of the date of issue.
- Failure to do either may result in the registration of a fine of one and a half times the penalty amount which will then be enforced by the courts.

Pre-conditions for issuing a penalty notice

Officers may issue a penalty notice **only** where—

- they have reason to believe a person has committed a penalty offence and they have sufficient evidence to support a successful prosecution (interviews and questioning must be consistent with the practice and procedures established by PACE 1984, Code C);
- the offence is not too serious and is of a nature suitable for being dealt with by a penalty notice;
- the suspect is suitable, compliant, and able to understand what is going on;
- a second or subsequent offence, which is known, does not overlap with the penalty notice offence (but see '**Explanatory notes**' below);
- the offence(s) involve(s) no one below the age of 16 (except in pilot areas for 10–15 year olds);
- sufficient evidence as to the suspect's age, identity, and place of residence exists.

Explanatory notes

- Officers might consider it appropriate to issue a penalty notice in association with any other offence, including where a warning, formal caution, or summons is issued, police bail set, or a charge brought or refused for the second or subsequent offence. This is provided that the subsequent or non-penalty offence can clearly be said not to 'overlap with' or be 'associated with' the first penalty offence. This may occur where a person is suspected of being drunk and disorderly or committing an offence under s 5 of the POA and they are found, upon arrest, to be in possession of a small quantity of cannabis or stolen credit cards for which, respectively, a caution and charge are deemed appropriate.
- Officers might consider it appropriate to issue a penalty notice in addition to dealing with a suspect for a second or subsequent offence in another way. However, discretion should be exercised to ensure that a penalty notice is not issued in addition to dealing with a very serious offence.
- Where a penalty notice is issued for a penalty offence and it subsequently comes to light after the incident that a more serious or non-penalty offence was committed on the same occasion, officers may bring a charge for the subsequent offence. Payment of a penalty discharges the recipient's liability to conviction only for the offence for which the penalty notice was issued. Ultimately, it will be for the CPS to determine, based on the facts of the case, whether a prosecution may be brought in respect of the subsequent offence, and for the courts to decide whether or not to allow such a prosecution.

Offences for which a PND will not be appropriate

Issuing a penalty notice **will not** be appropriate where—

- there has been any injury to any person or any realistic threat or risk of injury to any person (officers may seek the views of any potential victim before making a decision on the most appropriate course of action);
- there has been a substantial financial/material loss to the private property of an individual;
- a penalty offence is committed in association with another penalty notice offence;
- there are grounds for believing that the terms of the Protection from Harassment Act 1997 might apply;
- the behaviour constitutes part of a pattern of intimidation;
- the offence relates to domestic violence;
- it is a football-related offence and it may be appropriate for a court to consider imposing a Football Banning Order;
- the victim is not compliant;
- the licensee has committed an offence (but may be appropriate for bar staff when taking action against premises found or known to be serving alcohol to underage drinkers).

Offenders for which a PND will not be appropriate

- A penalty notice *may not* be issued to a person below 16 years of age (except in the force pilot schemes for 10–15 year olds).
- A penalty notice **will not** be appropriate where the suspect is unable to understand what is being offered to them, for example, those with a mental handicap or mental disorder, or where the suspect is drunk or under the influence of drugs. If a suspect is impaired by the influence of drugs or alcohol, and the officer is satisfied as to their identity and place of residence, it may be appropriate to consider issuing a PND at a later time (eg the next day). The officer should be satisfied that the suspect's offending behaviour has ceased, or take steps to ensure that this is the case. Officers should consider whether a suspect might have a substance addiction problem. In such circumstances a penalty notice may not be an appropriate response and another form of disposal should be considered and where possible, a referral made to an appropriate local scheme, for example, a drug treatment scheme.
- Similarly a penalty notice **will not** be appropriate where the suspect is—
  - ◆ uncooperative;
  - ◆ unable to provide a satisfactory address for enforcement purposes;
  - ◆ known to be already subject to—
    - ■ a custodial sentence, including Home Detention Curfew;
    - ■ a community penalty other than a fine, including Anti-social Behaviour Orders (which may constitute a breach).

7.1.2 Police Operational Guidance for Issuing PNDs

Theft and criminal damage

- PND disposal may only be used for thefts (retail/commercial only) under £200 and criminal damage under £500. (Thefts involving property over the value of £100 would not normally be suitable for PND disposal and explanation as well as the agreement of the victim/retailer would be required.)
- It is expected that in most cases of theft suitable for PND disposal the property will have been recovered, although the value of the property will be relevant in assessing seriousness.
- PND disposal for criminal damage over £300 would be exceptional (except for public property) and require explanation as well as the agreement of the victim/retailer.
- The PND for theft can only be issued by a police officer whereas a PND for damage can only be issued by police and designated community support officers.

Jointly committed offences

An officer may issue a penalty notice **only** where—
- the offence(s) involve(s) no one below the age of 16 years (except pilot areas for 10–15 year olds);
- where a juvenile, aged under 16, and an individual aged 16 years or over are jointly responsible for a penalty offence, a penalty notice will not be appropriate for the offender aged over 16 and existing forms of disposal should be considered. This should avoid any allegations of unfairness resulting from the older offender being able to discharge their liability to conviction.

Identification

An officer may issue a penalty notice **only** where—
- sufficient evidence as to age, identity, and place of residence exists. Age, identity, and address checks must be rigorous. Where doubt as to identity exists officers should exercise the powers under s 24 PACE 1984. Where possible, documentary evidence as to age, identity, and place of residence should be sought in preference to non-physical sources, eg electoral register or PNC checks;
- if fingerprints are taken this will support identification for any PND issued for a penalty offence;
- DNA and fingerprints may be taken with consent for a recordable offence where the suspect is not arrested. If DNA or fingerprints are taken with consent, officers should ensure that the appropriate consent forms are completed.

PNC entry

- Suspects issued with penalty notices will not receive a criminal record, but this does not preclude the retention of information as police intelligence.

- A facility is available on PNC, which allows an entry to be recorded that does not constitute a criminal record but is accessible for police information. This entry will not constitute a criminal record, but will enable DNA, fingerprints, and a photograph to be logged against the entry when appropriate.
- Issue of a PND may be used as evidence of bad character under s 101 of the Criminal Justice Act 2003.

PNDs and a criminal record check

In an Enhanced Disclosure issued by the CRB, a PND could be referred to, if the details of the behaviour leading to the PND were relevant to the matter at hand (eg the applicant's suitability to work with children). However, the mere fact that a PND had been issued would not make it relevant.

PNDs and ASBOs

- Although acceptance of a PND, and subsequent payment of the penalty, discharges liability for that offence, this does not preclude the information being used in the civil context of seeking an ASBO.
- The fact that a PND has been issued can be disclosed in an ASBO hearing as this goes towards establishing a pattern of behaviour.

Links to alternative subjects and offences

7.2 Drunk and Disorderly in Public Places

Section 91 of the Criminal Justice Act 1967 and s 12 of the Licensing Act 1872 deal with offences to do with drunkenness in public places, namely that of being drunk and disorderly and of being drunk in a highway.

7.2.1 Drunk and disorderly

Offence

Any person who in any public place is guilty, while drunk, of disorderly behaviour shall be liable to a summary conviction.

Criminal Justice Act 1967, s 91(1)

Points to prove
- ✓ date and location
- ✓ while in a public place
- ✓ whilst drunk
- ✓ guilty of disorderly behaviour

Meanings

Disorderly manner

Is defined by The *Oxford English Dictionary* as 'unruly or offensive behaviour'.

Public place

Includes any highway and other premises or place to which at the material time the public have or are permitted to have access, whether on payment or otherwise.

Drunk

Means the everyday meaning of 'drunk'. Defined by the *Collins* and *Oxford English Dictionaries* as: 'intoxicated with alcohol to the extent of losing control over normal physical and mental functions' and 'having drunk intoxicating liquor to an extent which affects steady self-control' (*R v Tagg* [2001] EWCA Crim 1230, CA).

Explanatory notes

- It does not apply to a person who is disorderly as a result of **sniffing glue** or **using drugs**. The common meaning of 'drunk' does not cater for such conduct, as confirmed by *Neale v RMJE (a minor)* (1985) 80 Cr App R 20.
- If the offender has taken liquor and drugs, the court must be satisfied that the loss of self-control was due to the liquor and not the drugs.
- Whether or not someone was in a state of drunkenness was a matter of fact for the court/jury to decide.
- A landing in a block of flats, to which access was gained by way of key, security code, tenant's intercom, or caretaker, has been held **not** to be a public place because only those admitted by or with the implied consent of the occupiers had access.

Related cases

Williams v DPP [1993] 3 All ER 365, QBD The landing in a block of flats, with access gained by a key code lock, was held not to have been a 'public place' because entry was restricted to residents, people admitted by residents, and trades people with knowledge of the code.

H v DPP [2005] EWHC (Admin) 2459, QBD Conduct must be disorderly whilst drunk to satisfy the offence. The offence is not committed if the defendant only becomes disorderly after the arrest.

Practical considerations

- This offence can be dealt with by PND (see **7.1.1**).
- Guidance issued by the Home Office provides examples of when it would be inappropriate to issue a PND for this offence (see **7.1.2**).
- Consideration must be given to the CPS advice given in the public order charging standards and the specific guidance for drunk and disorderly.

 Summary   6 months

 A fine not exceeding level 3 on the standard scale.

7.2.2 **Drunk on a highway**

Section 12 of the Licensing Act 1872 creates the offence of being 'drunk and incapable'. It includes offences relating to being drunk on a highway, public place, or licensed premises, whilst in possession of a loaded firearm or being in charge of various conveyances or animals.

7.2.2 Drunk on a Highway

Offences

Every person found **drunk** in any **highway** or other **public place,** whether a building or not, or on any licensed premises, shall be liable to a penalty. Every person who is drunk while in charge on any highway or other public place of any carriage, horse, cattle, or steam engine, or who is drunk when in possession of any loaded firearms, shall be liable to a penalty.

Licensing Act 1872, s 12

Points to prove

Drunk and incapable
- ✓ date and location
- ✓ drunk and incapable
- ✓ highway/public place/licensed premises

Other drunk offences
- ✓ drunk
- ✓ whilst in charge of
- ✓ pedal cycle/carriage/horse/cattle/steam engine **or** when in possession of a loaded firearm
- ✓ on/in a highway/public place

Meanings

Drunk (see 7.2.1)

Highway/Public place (see 7.2.1)

Incapable

Means 'incapable of looking after oneself and getting home safely'.

Carriage

Includes vehicles such as trailers and bicycles (whether being ridden or pushed).

Cattle

Includes sheep and pigs.

Firearm (see **8.1.1**)

Explanatory notes

- A motor vehicle is a 'carriage'. However, it may be more appropriate to consider the offence of driving or being in charge while over the prescribed limit under s 4 of the Road Traffic Act 1988 (see **10.10**).

- Case law suggests that residents in licensed premises cannot be convicted of this offence outside the permitted hours when the premises are closed to the public. However, the duty of the licensee to prevent drunkenness on the premises is unaffected.
- See also the related offences of drunk and disorderly in a public place (see **7.2.1**).
- Section 2 of the Licensing Act 1902 makes it an offence to be drunk in charge of a child who appears to be under the age of 7 years.

Practical considerations

- This offence can be dealt with by means of a PND (see **7.1.1**).
- If this offence involves a firearm consider s 19 of the Firearms Act 1968 which has a far greater penalty (see **8.5**).
- Officers should frequently assess the condition of drunks which can sometimes be life threatening (eg inhalation of vomit).
- Be aware that other medical conditions could give the impression that somebody is drunk (eg diabetic coma). It is best to convey the person to hospital if there are any doubts.
- Section 34 of the Criminal Justice Act 1972 provides a police constable with a power to take a drunken offender to a 'detoxification' or alcohol treatment centre. While a person is being so taken they shall be deemed to be in lawful custody.

 Summary   6 months

Drunk and incapable

A fine not exceeding level 1 on the standard scale.

Drunk in charge of firearm/carriage/horse/steam engine

1 month imprisonment or a fine not exceeding level 1 on the standard scale.

Links to alternative subjects and offences

7.2.2 Drunk on a Highway

7.3 **Breach of the Peace**

'Breach of the peace' provides a number of powers, one of which is to arrest and another is to intervene and/or detain by force, in order to prevent a breach of the peace in both public and private places.

It is not a criminal offence, but a 'complaint' is laid before the court with an application made for the individual to be bound over to keep the peace.

Complaint

Breach of the peace

The power of a magistrates' court on the complaint of any person to adjudge any other person to enter into a recognizance, with or without sureties, to keep the peace or to be of good behaviour towards the complainant shall be exercised by order on complaint.

Magistrates' Courts Act 1980, s 115(1)

Points to prove

✓ behave in a manner
✓ whereby breach of the peace
✓ was occasioned/likely to be occasioned

Meaning of breach of the peace

A breach of the peace may occur where harm is done or is likely to be done to a person, or to their property in their presence, or they are in fear of being harmed through assault, affray, riot, or other disturbance (*R v Howell* [1982] QB 416, QBD).

Court powers

- Section 115 of the Magistrates' Courts Act 1980 provides magistrates' courts with the power to order a person to be 'bound over' to keep the peace and/or be of good behaviour towards a particular person (often a neighbour or partner who has complained about their behaviour).
- The power of a magistrates' court on the complaint of any person to adjudge any other person to enter into a recognizance, with or without sureties, to keep the peace or to be of good behaviour towards the complainant shall be exercised by order on complaint.
- If any person fails to comply with the order, the court may commit that person to custody for a period not exceeding 6 months or until they comply with the order.

Explanatory notes

- The European Court of Human Rights in *Hashman and Harrup v United Kingdom* [2000] Crim LR 185, ECHR found the notion of 'to be of good behaviour' was too vague and uncertain (see '**Related cases**'). A later court 'practice direction' stated that any such order must specify the type of activity from which the offender must refrain.
- In the case of *Steel v United Kingdom* (1998) 28 EHRR 603 it was held that the concept of breach of the peace had been clarified by the courts to the extent that it was sufficiently established that a breach of the peace was committed only when a person caused harm, or appeared likely to cause harm, to persons or property or acted in a manner the natural consequence of which was to provoke others to violence. It was a procedure that came within the ambit of the Human Rights Convention and is lawful so long as the action taken is proportionate to the nature of the disturbance and also having regard to the values of freedom of expression and assembly.
- Notwithstanding that for some purposes proceedings under s115 are treated as criminal proceedings, since the procedure is by way of complaint it is primarily a civil process. The jurisdiction of the justices does not depend on a summons being issued, nor does the absence of a complaint in the form prescribed invalidate the procedure.

Related cases

Austin v Commissioner of Police of the Metropolis [2009] UKHL 5, HL (see 2.6.1).

Hashman and Harrup v United Kingdom [2000] Crim LR 185, ECHR Although they had disturbed a hunt by blowing a horn and shouting at the hounds, the defendants had not acted violently or threatened violence. The court stated that they had behaved *contra bonos mores* (behaviour seen as 'wrong rather than right in the judgement of the majority of contemporary fellow citizens') and should be bound over to be of good behaviour for a year. The ECHR stated that the expression 'to be of good behaviour' was imprecise and did not give sufficiently clear guidance for their future behaviour. Held that Article 10 (freedom of expression) had been violated, binding over for *contra bonos mores* behaviour was incompatible with the Convention and rights such as freedom of expression or assembly.

R (on the application of Hawkes) v DPP [2005] EWHC 3046 (Admin), QBD Verbal abuse not enough to commit breach of the peace.

R (on the application of Laporte) v Chief Constable of Gloucestershire [2006] UKHL 55, HL Three coaches stopped and searched under a s 60 authority (see 8.11.3) on intelligence that occupants would cause disorder at RAF base were returned back to London. Although the police actions were based on a reasonable and honestly held belief in preventing an apprehended breach of the peace, they had acted unlawfully and disproportionately because a breach of the peace was not 'imminent' at the time the coaches were stopped; thus interfering with the protesters' rights under Articles 10 and 11 (see **1.1**).

McGrogan v Chief Constable of Cleveland Police [2002] EWCA Civ 86, CA If a person is detained for an actual or threatened breach of the peace, then continued detention is limited to circumstances where there is a real, rather than a fanciful, fear, based on all the circumstances, that if released the detained person would commit/renew a breach of the peace within a relatively short time. It cannot be justified on the ground that sooner or later the prisoner, if released, is likely to breach the peace. The officer must have an honest belief, based on objectively reasonable grounds, that further detention was necessary to prevent such a breach of the peace. Ensure compliance with the PACE COP (see **12.2.1**).

Practical considerations

- A breach of the peace is not an offence, so a person cannot be granted bail in connection with it.
- A breach of the peace can occur on private premises. If the police have genuine grounds to apprehend such a breach, they have a right to enter private premises to make an arrest or ensure that one does not occur. The right of entry is not absolute, but must be weighed against the degree of disturbance that is threatened.
- Consider the power of entry for protecting life or property under s 17 PACE (see **12.3.2**). Alternatively, one of the parties involved may lawfully invite an officer into the premises in order to deal with the matter (albeit a breach has not occurred).
- A police officer must not remain on private premises once a breach has finished (assuming it is not likely to **re-occur**), but so long as the officer is lawfully on the premises in the first instance, they are entitled to be given the opportunity to withdraw.
- Officers attending private premises with officials such as bailiffs may have to enter them to prevent a breach of the peace while a Court Order is being enforced.
- An individual arrested to prevent a breach of the peace does not have to be taken before a court. There is no power to continue the person's detention beyond the time where a recurrence or renewal of the breach of the peace is likely. If there is such a danger then they should be detained for court (see *McGrogan v Chief Constable of Cleveland Police* [2002] EWCA Civ 86, CA case above).
- Release may occur at any stage: at the scene, after they have been taken from the scene, or at the police station.

 PCSO

 Summary   6 months

 Breach of the order may result in up to 6 months' imprisonment.

Links to alternative subjects and offences

7.4 **Riot and Violent Disorder**

The Public Order Act 1986 provides the statutory offences of riot and violent disorder.

7.4.1 **Riot**

Offences

Where twelve or more persons who are **present together** use or threaten unlawful **violence** for a **common purpose** and the conduct of them (taken together) is such as would cause a **person of reasonable firmness** present at the scene to fear for his personal safety, each of the persons using unlawful violence for the common purpose is guilty of riot.

Public Order Act 1986, s 1(1)

Points to prove
- ✓ date and location
- ✓ 12 or more persons present together used/threatened unlawful violence for common purpose
- ✓ and conduct would cause fear for personal safety
- ✓ to a person of reasonable firmness

Meanings

Present together

Means that all the people concerned were actually present at the scene of the incident aiming for a common purpose.

Common purpose—s 1(3)

The common purpose may be inferred from conduct.

Violence

Includes violent conduct towards property as well as violent conduct towards persons. It is not restricted to conduct causing, or intended to cause, injury or damage, but includes any other violent conduct (eg throwing at or towards a person a missile of a kind capable of causing injury, which does not hit or falls short).

7.4.1 Riot

Person of reasonable firmness

This test is an objective one by which the court can judge the seriousness of the disturbance using a fixed standard—namely whether or not a person of reasonable firmness would be put in fear by the conduct.

Explanatory notes

- It is immaterial whether or not the 12 or more use or threaten unlawful violence simultaneously.
- No **person of reasonable firmness** need actually be, or likely to be, present at the scene.
- A court will not consider this hypothetical person (of reasonable firmness) to be someone who is the target for the people who are involved in the disturbance, but someone who is a bystander to the incident (*R v Sanchez The Times*, 6 March 1996).
- Riot may be committed in private as well as in public places.
- The common purpose can be either lawful or unlawful, and must be proved either by admission or as above by inference from conduct.

Defences

Intention

(1) A person is guilty of riot only if he intends to use violence or is aware that his conduct may be violent.

(2) A person is guilty of violent disorder or affray only if he intends to use or threatens violence or is aware that his conduct may be violent or threaten violence.

(7) Subsection (2) does not affect the determination for the purposes of riot or violent disorder of the number of persons who use or threaten violence.

Effect of drunkenness or intoxication

(5) For the purposes of this section a person whose awareness is impaired by intoxication shall be taken to be aware of that of which he would be aware if not intoxicated, unless he shows either that his intoxication was not self induced or that it was caused solely by the taking or administration of a substance in the course of medical treatment.

Public Order Act 1986, s 6

Defence notes

- Intent or awareness must be proved. Even if intent can only be proved against two people but they were part of a group of, say, 13 who can be shown to have used unlawful violence, the two can still be convicted of riot.
- Intoxication means any intoxication, whether caused by drink, drugs or other means, or by a combination of means.

- The intoxication provision applies to the mental elements of the following public order offences—
    - s 1 riot—unlawful violence,
    - s 2 violent disorder—unlawful violence,
    - s 3 affray—unlawful violence,
    - s 4 threatening words or behaviour, and
    - s 5 harassment, alarm, or distress.

Practical considerations

- Refer to **8.11** for details of powers to stop and search when it is anticipated that serious violence may take place, and to remove masks.
- Consent of the DPP is required.
- When investigating this offence consideration must be given to CPS advice given in the public order charging standards.
- A person who was feeling threatened does not actually have to be a 'person of reasonable firmness', but their evidence may support other evidence that will satisfy the court that a 'person of reasonable firmness' would have been in fear of their personal safety had they been present. Such evidence could be provided by—
    - witnesses including police officers and bystanders (who may or may not be of reasonable firmness);
    - the types of injuries sustained;
    - damage to property;
    - security cameras;
    - news photographs or film footage.

  Indictable only   None

10 years' imprisonment.

7.4.2 **Violent disorder**

Offences

Where three or more persons who are **present together** use or threaten unlawful **violence** and the conduct of them (taken together) is such as would cause a **person of reasonable firmness** present at the scene to fear for his personal safety, each of the persons using or threatening unlawful violence is guilty of violent disorder.

Public Order Act 1986, s 2(1)

7.4.2 Violent Disorder

Points to prove

✓ date and location
✓ used/threatened unlawful violence
✓ 3 persons present together
✓ who use/threaten unlawful violence and their conduct (taken together)
✓ would cause a person of reasonable firmness present at the scene
✓ to fear for their personal safety

Meanings

Present together (see 7.4.1)

Person of reasonable firmness (see 7.4.1)

Violence (see 7.4.1)

Explanatory notes

- It is immaterial whether or not the three or more use or threaten unlawful violence simultaneously.
- No person of reasonable firmness need actually be, or likely to be, present at the scene.
- Violent disorder may be committed in private as well as in public places.
- Three or more persons means that as long as three or more people can be proved to have been present together and using violence, even if intent can only be proved against one person, then that person can be convicted—it is not necessary that 'three or more persons' be charged with the offence. Following *R v Mahroof* [1988] Crim LR 72, CA (see below) it is good practice to specify 'others' in the charge, even if their identity is not known and they were not arrested.

Defences

Intention (see s 6(2) and s 6(7) **7.4.1**)

Effect of drunkenness or intoxication (see **7.4.1**)

Defence notes

Intent

To use or threaten violence must, therefore, be proved for each individual. This means that even if only one person has the intent they can still be charged if it can be proved that at least two others were using or

---

threatening violence and they were present together. Words alone may suffice for the threats.

Intoxication (see 'Defence notes' in 7.4.1)

Related cases

R v Mahroof [1988] Crim LR 72, CA There must be three people involved in the violence or threatened violence. In this case two of the three charged were acquitted and there had been others who had not been mentioned in the charge. If they had, M could have been convicted, but in the absence of three people M's appeal was allowed.

R v Fleming and Robinson [1989] Crim LR 658, CA Following Mahroof—because there was no evidence of three or more people being involved the appeal against conviction was allowed.

Practical considerations

- Refer to **8.11** for details of powers to stop and search when it is anticipated that serious violence may take place, and powers to remove masks.
- Consideration must be given to CPS advice given in the public order charging standards and the specific guidance for violent disorder.

 Either way   None

Summary: 6 months' imprisonment and/or a fine not exceeding the statutory maximum.

Indictment: 5 years' imprisonment and/or a fine.

Links to alternative subjects and offences

7.4.2 Violent Disorder

7.5 **Affray**

The purpose of the offence of affray is to prevent incidents of public disorder and the fear of it. For the offence of affray to be committed, the threat of violence needs to be capable of affecting others.

Offences

A person is guilty of affray if he uses or **threatens** unlawful **violence** towards another and his **conduct** is such as would cause a person of **reasonable firmness** present at the scene to fear for his personal safety.

Public Order Act 1986, s 3(1)

Points to prove

✓ date and location
✓ used/threatened unlawful violence
✓ towards another
✓ and your conduct was such as would cause
✓ a person of reasonable firmness to fear for personal safety

Meanings

Threatens

For the purposes of this section a threat cannot be made by the use of words alone.

Violence

See **7.4**, except affray **does not include** violent conduct towards property.

Conduct

Where two or more persons use or threaten the unlawful violence, it is the conduct of them taken together that must be considered for the purpose of the offence.

Reasonable firmness

• No person of reasonable firmness need actually be, or be likely to be, present at the scene.
• A person of reasonable firmness concept meets the same criteria as riot (see **7.4.1**).

Explanatory notes

• Affray may be committed in private as well as in public places.
• Notionally there are at least three parties involved in an affray—

- ◆ the individual making threats;
- ◆ the person subject of the threats;
- ◆ the bystander of reasonable firmness who does not need to be physically present as long as evidence is available to prove that such a person would be affected.

Defences

Intent (see s 6(2) **7.4.1**)

Effects of drunkenness or intoxication (see 'Defences' **7.4.1**)

Defence notes (see 'Defence notes' **7.4.2**)

Related cases

R v Plavecz [2002] Crim LR 837, CA A doorman pushed a customer out of a nightclub doorway who then fell over. Defendant was charged with assault and affray, but the court stated that where the incident was basically '**one-on-one**' it was inappropriate to use the public order offence of affray.

I v DPP, M v DPP, H v DPP [2001] UKHL 10, HL About 40 young people were 'hanging around' with some carrying petrol bombs. None of them lit or waved a petrol bomb about in a threatening way and there was no actual disturbance. On police arrival the gang scattered and the three defendants threw away their petrol bombs as they ran off. Held: The mere possession of a weapon, without the threatening situation, would not be enough to constitute a threat of unlawful violence. Affray requires that the offender must be 'using/threatening unlawful violence towards another', what amounted to such a threat was a question of fact in each case, but in this instance, there were no threats made and no violence was used.

Practical considerations

- Unlike riot and violent disorder, affray can be committed by one person acting alone. However, where two or more people are involved in the violence or threatened violence, it is the conduct of them taken together that will be used to determine whether or not the offence is made out.
- Refer to **8.11.3** for details of powers to stop and search when it is anticipated that serious violence may take place and to remove masks.
- Consideration must be given to the CPS public order charging standards for affray.
- See **12.1.1** for powers to stop and search for knives and offensive weapons.
- A person who was feeling threatened does not actually have to be a 'person of reasonable firmness', but evidence may support other

evidence that will satisfy the court that a 'person of reasonable firmness' would have been in fear of their personal safety had they been present, such as—

♦ witnesses including police officers and bystanders (who may or may not be of reasonable firmness);
♦ the types of injuries sustained;
♦ damage to property (for affray, the violence must be directed at a person, although accompanying damage may have occurred);
♦ security cameras;
♦ news photographs or film footage.

 Either way None

 Summary: 6 months' imprisonment and/or a fine not exceeding the statutory maximum.

Indictment: 3 years' imprisonment.

Links to alternative subjects and offences

SSS Stop, search, and seize powers

E&S Entry and search powers

7.6 **Fear or Provocation of Violence**

The Public Order Act 1986 deals with offences and powers relating to public order. Section 4 creates the offence of causing fear or provocation of violence, often known as 'threatening behaviour'.

Offences

A person is guilty of an offence if he—
(a) uses towards another person **threatening, abusive** or **insulting** words or behaviour, or
(b) **distributes or displays** to another person any writing, sign or other visible representation which is threatening, abusive or insulting,
with **intent** to cause that person to believe that immediate unlawful violence will be used against him or another by any person, or to provoke the immediate use of unlawful violence by that person or another, or whereby that person is likely to believe that such violence will be used or it is likely that such violence will be provoked.

Public Order Act 1986, s 4(1)

Points to prove

s 4(1)(a) offence

✓ date and location
✓ use towards another person
✓ threatening/abusive/insulting words or behaviour
✓ with intent to *either*
✓ cause that person to believe
✓ that immediate unlawful violence
✓ would be used against them or another
✓ by any person **or**
✓ provoke the immediate use of unlawful violence
✓ by that person/another **or**
✓ that person was likely to believe
✓ that such violence would be used or
✓ likely that such violence would be provoked

s 4(1)(b) offence

✓ date and location
✓ distribute/display
✓ to another
✓ a writing/sign/visible representation
✓ which was threatening/abusive/insulting
✓ with intent to **either**
✓ (continue from this point in above offence—to end)

Meanings

Threatening
Includes verbal and physical threats, and also violent conduct.

Abusive
Means using degrading or reviling language.

Insulting
Has been held to mean scorning, especially if insolent or contemptuous.

Intent see '**Defences**' s 6(3))

Distribute
Means spread or disperse.

Display
Means a visual presentation.

Explanatory notes

• Limited circumstances apply for this offence in private—
  ◆ An offence under this section may be committed in a public or a private place, except that no offence is committed where the words or behaviour are used, or the writing, sign or other visible representation is distributed or displayed, by a person inside a **dwelling** and the other person is also inside that or another dwelling (s 4(2)).
• *Dwelling*—Means any structure or part of a structure occupied as a person's home or as other living accommodation (whether the occupation is separate or shared with others) but does not include any part not so occupied, and for this purpose 'structure' includes a tent, caravan, vehicle, vessel, or other temporary or movable structure (s 8).
• No offence will be committed if the display is inside a dwelling, if it is displayed only to people also inside, although if it is displayed from inside to people outside the dwelling, then an offence under s 4 may be committed.
• Insulting does not mean behaviour that might give rise to irritation or resentment (eg running onto a tennis court at Wimbledon blowing a whistle and stopping the game—*Brutus v Cozens* [1972] 2 All ER 1297, HL). However, each of these will be a question of fact to be decided by the relevant court in the light of all the circumstances.

Defences

Intent
A person is guilty of an offence under s 4 only if he intends [*see 4.1.2*] his words or behaviour, or the writing, sign or other visible representation, to be threatening, abusive or insulting.

Public Order Act 1986, s 6(3)

Intoxication (see 'Defences—intoxication' in 7.4.1)

Related cases

DPP v Ramos [2000] Crim LR 768, QBD If the victim believes that the threatened violence will occur at any moment, this will be sufficient for the 'immediacy' requirement.

Swanston v DPP (1996) 161 JP 203, QBD A witness/officer present when the offence took place can give evidence to prove the threatening behaviour and intent, even if the victim does not give evidence.

Rukwira and Johnson v DPP [1993] Crim LR 882, QBD Dwelling does not include communal landings outside **self–contained** flats.

Atkin v DPP [1989] Crim LR 581, QBD The person threatened should be present. The threatening words must be addressed directly to another person who is present and either within earshot or aimed at someone thought to be in earshot.

Simcock v Rhodes [1977] Crim LR 751, QBD Conduct can be threatening **or** abusive **or** insulting.

Brutus v Cozens [1972] 2 All ER 1297, HL Whether behaviour is insulting or not is a question of fact for justices to decide.

Practical considerations

- Section 17(1)(c)(iii) of PACE gives a constable a specific power to enter and search premises for the purpose of arresting a person for an offence under s 4 (see **12.3.2**).
- If this offence is **racially or religiously aggravated** the more serious offence under s 31(1)(a) of the Crime and Disorder Act 1998 should be considered (see **7.10.4**).
- Consider religious or racial hatred offences (see **7.9**).
- It is not duplicitous if the three alternatives 'threatening, abusive or insulting', are charged, though all three need not be present.
- Consideration must be given to CPS advice given in the public order charging standards.

RRA

 Summary

 6 months

 6 months' imprisonment and/or a fine not exceeding level 5 on the standard scale.

Links to alternative subjects and offences

7.7 Intentional Harassment, Alarm, or Distress

Section 4A of the Public Order Act 1986 creates the offences of intentionally causing a person harassment, alarm or distress by using threatening, abusive, insulting words or behaviour, or disorderly behaviour; or displaying any writing, sign, or other representation that is threatening, abusive, or insulting.

Offences

A person is guilty of an offence if, with **intent** to cause a person **harassment, alarm** or **distress,** he—

(a) uses **threatening, abusive** or **insulting** words or behaviour, or **disorderly behaviour,** or

(b) displays any writing, sign or other visible representation which is threatening, abusive or insulting,

thereby causing that or another person harassment, alarm or distress.

Public Order Act 1986, s 4A(1)

Points to prove

s 4A(1)(a) offence

✓ used threatening/abusive/insulting words/behaviour **or** used disorderly behaviour

✓ towards another person

✓ with intent to cause harassment/alarm/distress

✓ and caused that/another person

✓ harassment/alarm/distress

s 4A(1)(b) offence

✓ displayed threatening/abusive/insulting writing/sign/other visible representation

✓ with intent to cause a person harassment/alarm/distress

✓ and caused that/another person

✓ harassment/alarm/distress

Meanings

Harassment

Means to subject someone to constant and repeated physical and/or verbal persecution.

Alarm

Means a frightened anticipation of danger.

Distress

Means to cause trouble, pain, anguish, or hardship.

Intent (see 4.1.2)

Threatening (see 7.6)

Abusive (see 7.6)

Insulting (see 7.6)

Disorderly behaviour

Not defined; the *Oxford English Dictionary* states 'unruly, unrestrained, turbulent or riotous behaviour'.

Explanatory notes

- This offence is very similar to the offence under s 5 (see **7.8**), but this offence requires proof of **intent** to cause alarm, harassment, or distress.
- An offence under this section may be committed in a public or private place, but no offence is committed if it takes place inside a dwelling and the affected person is also inside that or another dwelling.
- Although this offence can be committed on private premises there is no specific power of entry.

Defences

It is a defence for the accused to prove—

(a) that he was inside a dwelling and had no reason to believe that the words or behaviour used, or the writing, sign or other visible representation displayed, would be heard or seen by a person outside that or any other dwelling, OR

(b) that his conduct was reasonable.

Public Order Act 1986, s 4A(3)

Related cases

R (on the application of R) v DPP [2006] EWHC 1375 (Admin), QBD A 12-year-old boy gestured and shouted obscenities at the police and was arrested for a s 4A offence. Though he may have intended to be insulting and annoying there was no intention to cause the officer alarm or distress. For a police officer to be distressed evidence of real emotional disturbance or upset is required, showing more than is normally experienced during their course of duty.

Dehal v CPS [2005] EWHC 2154 (Admin), QBD D placed a poster on a notice board in a Sikh Temple which contained abusive and insulting comments regarding the teachings being an incorrect translation of the Holy Book. A defence under s 4A(3)(b) was submitted that this amounted to 'reasonable conduct'. Held: This prosecution breached Article 10 (freedom of expression) unless it was necessary to prevent public disorder. It is imperative that there is no restriction placed on a legitimate protest.

Lodge v DPP The Times, 26 October 1988, QBD It is not necessary that the person alarmed was concerned about physical danger to himself, it could be alarm about an unconnected third party.

Practical considerations

- There must be evidence of intent to cause harassment, alarm, or distress and one of those forms of abuse must actually be caused to someone (not necessarily the person who was its original target).
- Where there is no evidence of intent consider s 5 (see **7.8**).
- Where the extent of the behaviour results in the fear or realization of violence consider s 4(1) (see **7.6**) or assault charges (see **2.1**, **2.2** or **2.3**).
- If there is repeated harassment consider s 1 of the Protection from Harassment Act 1997 (see **7.11.1**).
- If a power of entry is required consider s 17 PACE (see **12.3.2**), ongoing breach of the peace (see **7.3**), or s 4 (see **7.6**).
- Consider the behaviour in the context of the circumstances—behaviour that causes distress to an elderly woman may not be distressing to a young man.
- If other people, besides the police officer and the defendant, are present include that fact in your evidence.
- If this offence is racially and/or religiously aggravated consider the more serious offence under s 31 of the Crime and Disorder Act 1998 (see **7.10.4**) or ss 17 to 23 of the Public Order Act 1986 which relate to racial hatred offences (see **7.9**).

 Summary   6 months

 Summary: 6 months' imprisonment and/or a fine not exceeding level 5 on the standard scale.

Links to alternative subjects and offences

7.8 Threatening/Abusive Words/Behaviour

Section 5 of the Public Order Act 1986 creates offences of being threatening, abusive or insulting in a way which is likely to cause harassment, alarm, or distress.

Offences

A person is guilty of an offence if he—

(a) uses threatening, abusive or insulting words or behaviour, or disorderly behaviour, or

(b) displays any writing sign or other visible representation which is threatening, abusive or insulting,

within the hearing or sight of a person likely to be caused **harassment, alarm** or **distress** thereby.

Public Order Act 1986, s 5(1)

Points to prove

✓ date and location
✓ used threatening/abusive/insulting words/behaviour or disorderly behaviour **or**
✓ displayed writing/sign/visible representation being
✓ threatening/abusive/insulting
✓ within hearing/sight of a person likely to be caused
✓ harassment/alarm/distress
✓ with intention/awareness that conduct/actions
✓ would have that effect

Meanings

Threatening, abusive, and insulting (see 7.6)

Harassment, alarm, and distress (see 7.7)

Disorderly behaviour (see 7.7)

Explanatory notes

- What may distress an old woman of 75 years may not distress a young man of 20 years. The conduct has to be **likely to cause** distress. However, you can feel for the safety of someone else, (particularly if you are a police officer), and it does not necessarily have to be for yourself (see *Lodge v DPP 1988* at **7.7**).

- Section 6(4) states that a person is guilty of a s 5 offence only if he **intends** his words or behaviour, or the writing, sign or other visible representation, to be threatening, abusive or insulting, or is aware that it may be threatening, abusive or insulting or (as the case may be) he intends his behaviour to be or is aware that it may be disorderly.
- An offence under this section may be committed in a public or a private place except that no offence is committed when the words or behaviour are used, or the writing, sign or other visible representation is displayed, by a person inside a dwelling and the other person is also inside that or another dwelling.

Defences

It is a defence for the accused to prove—
(a) that he had no reason to believe that there was any person within hearing or sight who was likely to be caused harassment, alarm or distress; or
(b) that he was inside a dwelling and had no reason to believe that the words or behaviour used, or the writing, sign or other visible representation displayed, would be heard or seen by a person outside that or any other dwelling; or
(c) that his conduct was reasonable.

Public Order Act 1986, s 5(3)

Defence notes

Article 6 (right to a fair trial—see **1.1**) does not prohibit rules which transfer the burden of proof to the accused, provided it is only an 'evidential burden' where the defendant only needs to give believable evidence which justifies the defence and does not need to reach any specific standard of proof. Proving the guilt of the defendant still remains with the prosecution (eg s 28 of the Misuse of Drugs Act 1971—see **5.1.1**).

Intoxication (see 'Defence notes' in **7.4.1**)

Related cases

Taylor v DPP [2006] EWHC 1202 (Admin) QBD The wording 'within the sight or hearing of a person' requires evidence that there was someone able to hear or see the conduct but the prosecution does not have to call evidence that the words were actually heard or behaviour seen.

R (on the application of DPP) v Humphrey [2005] EWHC 822 (Admin), QBD Threatening, abusive, or insulting words or behaviour must be within the hearing or sight of a person **likely** to be caused harassment, alarm or distress. Actual harassment, alarm or distress does not have to occur. It is judged on the impact it would have had on the reasonable man or woman.

Norwood v DPP [2003] EWHC 1564 (Admin), QBD Defendant displayed a poster in his flat window, visible from the street, which said 'Islam out of Britain' and 'Protect the British People'. It bore a reproduction of one of the 'twin towers' in flames along with a Crescent and Star surrounded by a prohibition sign. Poster was deemed racially insulting to Muslims, and the circumstances of its location and display were capable of causing harassment, alarm, or distress. The defence of reasonable conduct and the rights of freedom of expression under Article 10 carry with them a duty to avoid unreasonable or disproportionate interference with the rights of others; if they do interfere disproportionately the state has a duty to intervene—as in this case.

Percy v DPP [2001] EWHC (Admin) 1125, QBD Defacing an American flag and stamping on it outside an American airbase was basically a peaceful protest, albeit insulting to some American servicemen. Held that a criminal prosecution was not a proportionate response and breached an individual's right to freedom of expression under Article 10 (see **1.1**).

DPP v Hammond [2004] Crim LR 851, QBD Displaying a sign with anti-homosexual remarks by a preacher was insulting behaviour.

Practical considerations

- Ensure any possible defence raised under s 5(3) is covered in interview or rebutted by other evidence.
- If this offence is racially or religiously aggravated see **7.10**.
  Consider racial and religious hatred offences (see **7.9**).
- The s 5 offence should be distinguished from the similar s 4A offence, which requires specific intent (see **7.7**).
- Words or behaviour are alternatives and one or other should be specified in the charge, and must be proved.
- Consider issuing a PND for this offence (see **7.1**).
- It is not duplicitous if all three alternatives are charged, 'threatening, abusive or insulting', though all three need not be used.
- Also be aware of the Scottish case of *Kinnaird v Higson* 2001 SCCR 427 concerning the way in which the phrase 'fuck off' is used to police officers. What may constitute abusive language in one context or location may not amount to such in another.
- Consider the CPS public order charging standards.

 Summary 6 months

 A fine not exceeding level 3 on the standard scale.

Links to alternative subjects and offences

7.9 **Racial and Religious Hatred Offences**

Sections 17 to 29 of the Public Order Act 1986 relate to racial hatred offences, whereas ss 29A to 29N refer to religious hatred offences.

7.9.1 **Use of words/behaviour or display of written material (racial)**

Section 18 creates the offence of using words or behaviour, or displaying written material, intending or likely to stir up racial hatred.

Offences

A person who uses **threatening**, **abusive** or **insulting** words or behaviour, or **displays** any **written material** which is threatening, abusive or insulting, is guilty of an offence if—
(a) he **intends** thereby to stir up **racial hatred,** or
(b) having regard to all the circumstances racial hatred is likely to be stirred up thereby.

Public Order Act 1986, s 18(1)

Points to prove

✓ used/displayed threatening/abusive/insulting
✓ words/behaviour/written material
✓ intended/likely to stir up racial hatred

Meanings

Threatening, abusive, and insulting (see 7.6)

Display (see 7.6)

Written material
Includes any sign or other visible representation.

Intention (see 4.1.2)

Racial hatred
Means hatred against a group of persons defined by reference to colour, race, nationality (including citizenship), or ethnic or national origins.

Explanatory notes

- Racial hatred includes hatred manifested in Great Britain, but can be directed against a racial or religious group outside Great Britain.
- Insulting does not mean behaviour which might give rise to irritation or resentment (eg running onto a tennis court at Wimbledon, blowing a whistle and stopping the game).
- Offence may be committed in a public or private place, but if committed inside a dwelling see defence given below.
- An intention to stir up racial hatred must be proved, or if having regard to all the circumstances, racial hatred is likely to be stirred up.

Defences

For the accused to prove that he was inside a dwelling and had no reason to believe that the words or behaviour used, or the written material displayed, would be heard or seen by a person outside that or another dwelling.

Public Order Act 1986, s 18(4)

Defence notes

'Dwelling' means any structure or part of a structure occupied as a person's home or other living accommodation (whether the occupation is separate or shared with others) but does not include any part not so occupied, and for this purpose 'structure' includes a tent, caravan, vehicle, vessel or other temporary or movable structure.

Practical considerations

- This section does not apply to words or behaviour used, or written material displayed, solely for the purpose of being included in a programme service.
- If the offence relates to the display of written material, the court may order forfeiture of the material. This forfeiture applies to publishing or distributing written material (see **7.9.2**), distributing/showing/playing a recording (see **7.9.3**), and possession of racially inflammatory material (see **7.9.4**).
- The following applies to all racially aggravated offences—
  - every section from s 18 to s 23 creates a separate offence and one or more such offences may be charged together;
  - if the offence is committed by a body corporate, with the consent or connivance of a director, manager, company secretary, or other similar officer or person acting as such, then under s 28, they as well as the company are guilty of the offence;
  - consider the CPS public order charging standards and guidance for the specific racial hatred offence;
  - consent of Attorney-General/Solicitor-General required for these offences.

Either way ⏱ None

🏛 **Summary:** 6 months' imprisonment and/or a fine not exceeding the statutory maximum.

Indictment: 7 years' imprisonment and/or a fine.

7.9.2 Publishing/distributing written material (racial)

Section 19 of the Public Order Act 1986 creates the offence of publishing or distributing written material intending or likely to stir up racial hatred.

Offences

A person who **publishes** or **distributes written material** which is **threatening, abusive or insulting** is guilty of an offence if—
(a) he **intends** thereby to stir up **racial hatred,** or
(b) having regard to all the circumstances racial hatred is likely to be stirred up thereby.

Public Order Act 1986, s 19(1)

Points to prove

✓ published/distributed
✓ threatening/abusive/insulting written material
✓ intended/likely to stir up racial hatred

Meanings

Publishes or distributes

Means its publication or distribution to the public or a section of the public.

Written material (see 7.9.1)

Threatening, abusive, or insulting (see 7.6)

Intends (see 4.1.2)

Racial hatred (see 7.9.1)

E&S Entry and search powers **RRA** Racially or religiously aggravated offence **PCSO** Police community support officers

Defence

For accused who is not shown to have intended to stir up racial hatred to prove that he was not aware of the content of the material and did not suspect, that it was threatening, abusive or insulting.

Public Order Act 1986, s 19(2)

Practical considerations (see **7.9.1**)

 Either way   None

 Summary: 6 months' imprisonment and/or a fine not exceeding the statutory maximum.

Indictment: 7 years' imprisonment and/or a fine.

7.9.3 **Distributing, showing, or playing a recording (racial)**

Section 21 of the Public Order Act 1986 creates the offence of distributing, showing, or playing a recording of visual images or sounds which are threatening, abusive, or insulting, intending or likely to stir up racial hatred.

Offences

A person who **distributes,** or shows or plays, a **recording** of visual images or sounds which are threatening, abusive or insulting is guilty of an offence if—

(a) he intends thereby to stir up racial hatred, or

(b) having regard to all the circumstances racial hatred is likely to be stirred up thereby.

Public Order Act 1986, s 21(1)

Points to prove

✓ distributed/showed/played

✓ recording of visual images/sounds

✓ which were threatening/abusive/insulting

✓ intended/likely to stir up racial hatred

7.9.4 Religious Hatred Offences

Meanings

Distributes

Showing or playing to the public or a section of the public.

Recording

Means any record from which visual images and sounds may, by any means, be reproduced.

Explanatory notes

This section does not apply to the showing or playing of a recording solely to enable the recording to be included in a programme service (eg electronic communication services such as radio and television).

Defence

For an accused who is not shown to have intended to stir up racial hatred to prove that he was not aware of the content of the recording and did not suspect, and had no reason to suspect, that it was threatening, abusive or insulting.

Public Order Act 1986, s 21(3)

Practical considerations (see also 7.9.1)

- Section 23 creates the offence of possessing racially inflammatory material with intent or likely to stir up racial hatred, with a view to it being included in a programme service.
- Under s 24 a justice of the peace may issue a warrant on suspicion that an offence under s 23 is being committed. The warrant can authorize any constable to enter and search premises—being any place, and including any vehicle, vessel, aircraft, hovercraft, offshore installations, and any tent or movable structure.

 Either way   None

 Summary: 6 months' imprisonment and/or a fine not exceeding the statutory maximum.

Indictment: 7 years' imprisonment and/or a fine.

7.9.4 **Religious hatred offences**

The Racial and Religious Hatred Act 2006 inserted ss 29A to 29N into the Public Order Act 1986 which deals with religious hatred offences.

E&S Entry and search powers   **RRA** Racially or religiously aggravated offence

Section 29B creates the offence of using words or behaviour, or displaying written material, intending or likely to stir up religious hatred.

Offences

A person who uses **threatening** words or behaviour, or **displays** any **written material** which is threatening, is guilty of an offence if he intends thereby to stir up religious hatred.

Public Order Act 1986, s 29B(1)

Points to prove

✓ used threatening words or behaviour or displayed threatening written material
✓ intended to stir up religious hatred

Meanings

Threatening (see 7.6)

Displays (see 7.6)

Written material (see 7.9.1)

Intention (see 4.1.2)

Religious hatred

Means hatred against a group of persons defined by reference to religious belief or lack of religious belief.

Explanatory notes

Racial hatred may be committed in a public or a private place, but if committed inside a dwelling the s 29B(4) defence may apply.

Defence

For the accused to prove that he was inside a dwelling and had no reason to believe that the words or behaviour used, or the written material displayed, would be heard or seen by a person outside that or any other dwelling.

Public Order Act 1986, s 29B(4)

Defence notes (see 7.9.1)

Practical considerations

• This section does not apply to words or behaviour used, or written material displayed, solely for the purpose of being included in a programme service.

7.9.4 **Religious Hatred Offences**

- If the offence under s 29B relates to the display of written material, the court may, under s 29I, order forfeiture of the material. Forfeiture applies to publishing or distributing written material (s 29C), distributing/showing/playing a recording (s 29E), and possession of inflammatory material (s 29G).
- The following apples to religious hatred offences—
  - every section from s 29B to s 29G creates a separate offence and one or more such offences may be charged together;
  - if the offence is committed by a body corporate with the consent or connivance of a director, manager, company secretary, or other similar officer or person acting as such, then under s 29M, they as well as the company are guilty of the offence;
  - consider CPS public order charging standards and guidance for the specific hatred offence;
  - consent of the Attorney-General is required for these offences.
- HOC 29/2007 introduced Pt 3A on religious hatred, stating that for each offence the words, behaviour, written material, recordings or programmes must be threatening and intended to stir up religious hatred. Part 3A was created with the offences of stirring up hatred against persons on religious grounds because Jews and Sikhs have been deemed by courts to be racial groups, but Muslims and Christians are religious rather than racial groups.
- Protection for freedom of expression

Religious hatred

Section 29J states that nothing in Pt 3A shall be read or given effect in a way which prohibits or restricts discussion, criticism or expressions of antipathy, dislike, ridicule, insult or abuse of particular religions or the beliefs or practices of their adherents, or of any other belief system or the beliefs or practices of its adherents, or proselytizing or urging adherents of a different religion or belief system to cease practising their religion or belief system.

Sexual orientation

Section 29JA states that in Pt 3A, for the avoidance of doubt, the discussion or criticism of sexual conduct or practices or the urging of persons to refrain from or modify such conduct or practices shall not be taken of itself to be threatening or intended to stir up hatred.

- Other religious hatred offences under Pt 3A are—
  - publishing or distributing written material—s29C;
  - public performance of play—s 29D;
  - distributing, showing or playing a recording—s29E;
  - broadcasting or including programme in programme service—s29F; and
  - possession of inflammatory material—s 29G.

They are also either way offences and carry the same penalty as s 29B.

Either way None

 Summary: 6 months' imprisonment and/or a fine not exceeding the statutory maximum.

Indictment: 7 years' imprisonment and/or a fine.

Links to alternative subjects and offences

E&S Entry and search powers   RRA Racially or religiously aggravated offence   PCSO Police community support officers   **333**

7.10 Racially/Religiously Aggravated Offences

Sections 28 to 32 of the Crime and Disorder Act 1998 relate to racially or religiously aggravated offences.

7.10.1 Meaning of 'racially or religiously aggravated'

Section 28 states when a specific offence is deemed 'racially or religiously aggravated'.

Definition

An offence is racially or religiously aggravated for the purposes of ss 29 to 32 below if—

(a) at the time of committing the offence, or immediately before or after doing so, the offender demonstrates towards the victim of the offence hostility based on the victim's **membership** (or **presumed** membership) of a **racial or religious group**; or

(b) the offence is motivated (wholly or partly) by hostility towards members of a racial or religious group based on the membership of that group.

Crime and Disorder Act 1998, s 28(1)

Meanings

Membership

In relation to a racial or religious group, includes association with members of that group.

Presumed

Means presumed by the defendant (even if it is a mistaken presumption).

Racial group

Means a group of people defined by reference to race, colour, nationality (including citizenship), or ethnic or national origins.

Religious group

Means a group of people defined by religious belief or lack of religious belief.

Explanatory notes

It is immaterial whether or not the offender's hostility is also based, to any extent, on any other factor not mentioned in s 28(1).

Related cases

Taylor v DPP [2006] EWHC 1202 (Admin) QBD Guidance issued on racially aggravated offences.

R v Rogers [2007] UKHL 8, HL Defendant called three Spanish women 'bloody foreigners' and told them to 'go back to their own country' before pursuing them in an aggressive manner. Held: It is immaterial whether the hostility was based on factors other than simple racism or xenophobia. The denial of equal respect and dignity to people seen as different can be more deeply hurtful, damaging, and disrespectful than if it were based on a more specific racial characteristic.

DPP v M [2004] EWHC 1453 (Admin) QBD The defendant kept using the words' bloody foreigners' before going outside and damaging the window of the kebab shop. The word 'foreigners' satisfied the meaning within s 28(3) and the word 'bloody' meant that the defendant had demonstrated some hostility towards a racial group.

Practical considerations

A police officer is just as entitled to protection under these provisions as anybody else (eg a person committing the offence of threatening behaviour by using racial taunts against the police could be prosecuted for the racially aggravated version of the offence).

7.10.2 **Racially or religiously aggravated assaults**

Section 29 relates to racially or religiously aggravated assault offences.

Offences

A person is guilty of an offence under this section if he commits—
(a) an offence under s 20 of the Offences Against the Person Act 1861 *[see 2.3.1]*; or
(b) an offence under s 47 of that Act *[see 2.1.2]*; or
(c) a common assault *[see 2.1.1]*,
which is **racially or religiously aggravated** for the purposes of this section.

Crime and Disorder Act 1998, s 29(1)

Points to prove

✓ committed offence under ss 20 or 47 of OAPA 1861; or s 39 of CJA 1988
✓ such offence was racially/religiously aggravated

7.10.2 Racially or Religiously Aggravated Assaults

Meaning of racially or religiously aggravated (see 7.10.1)

Explanatory notes

If, on the trial on indictment of a person charged with this offence, the jury find the defendant not guilty of the offence charged, they may find them guilty of the relevant 'basic' offence (eg ss 20 or 47 of the OAPA 1861; or s 39 of CJA 1988).

Related cases

DPP v Woods [2002] EWHC 85 (Admin), QBD On being refused entry to licensed premises, the doorman was called a 'black bastard' and assaulted. Although the words were used out of frustration, and the victim was unconcerned and did not consider the words racially offensive, the offence of racially aggravated common assault was still committed.

DPP v Pal [2000] Crim LR 256, QBD Asian caretaker asked four youths, two Asian and two white, to leave the premises. One Asian youth refused, pushed the caretaker against a bin, accused him of being a white man's lackey and a brown Englishman, then kicked him before leaving. Held: Not racially aggravated common assault as the caretaker was abused because of his job not his race. Therefore, this was **not** hostility based on the victim's membership of a racial group.

Practical considerations

Always charge the defendant with the relevant 'basic' offence, as there is no provision for an alternative verdict at a magistrates' court.

 Either way   None

   Offence under s 29(1)(a) or (b)

Summary: 6 months' imprisonment and/or a fine not exceeding the statutory maximum.

Indictment: 7 years' imprisonment and/or a fine.

Offence under s 29(1)(c)

Summary: 6 months' imprisonment and/or a fine not exceeding the statutory maximum.

Indictment: 2 years' imprisonment and/or a fine.

7.10.3 **Racially or religiously aggravated criminal damage**

Section 30 creates an offence of racially or religiously aggravated criminal damage.

Offence

A person is guilty of an offence under this section if he commits an offence under s 1(1) of the Criminal Damage Act 1971 (destroying/damaging property belonging to another) which is **racially or religiously aggravated** for the purposes of this section.

Crime and Disorder Act 1998, s 30(1)

Points to prove

✓ committed s 1(1) criminal damage offence (see **4.4**)
✓ offence was racially/religiously aggravated

Meaning of racially or religiously aggravated (see **7.10.1**)

Explanatory notes

- For the purposes of this section, s 28(1)(a) (see **7.10.1**) has effect as if the person to whom the property belongs or is treated as belonging for the purposes of that Act was the victim of the offence.
- If, on the trial on indictment of a person charged with this offence, the jury find the defendant not guilty of the offence charged, they may find them guilty of the relevant 'basic' offence.

Practical considerations

- Where this offence is shown to be motivated by racial hostility under s28(1)(b) (see **7.10.1**) there is no need to identify a specific victim (eg painting racist graffiti on a wall would be likely to constitute this offence).
- This offence is triable either way irrespective of the value of the damage caused (unlike the relevant 'basic' offence).

Either way None

 Summary: 6 months' imprisonment and/or a fine not exceeding the statutory maximum.

Indictment: 14 years' imprisonment and/or a fine.

7.10.4 **Racially or religiously aggravated public order offences**

Section 31 relates to racially or religiously aggravated public order offences.

Offences

A person is guilty of an offence under this section if he commits—

(a) an offence under s 4 of the Public Order Act 1986 (fear/provocation of violence) *[see 7.6]*; or

(b) an offence under s 4A of that Act (intentional harassment, alarm, or distress) *[see 7.7]*; or

(c) an offence under s 5 of that Act (harassment, alarm, distress) *[see 7.8]*,

which is racially or religiously aggravated for the purposes of this section.

Crime and Disorder Act 1998, s 31(1)

Points to prove

✓ committed an offence
✓ under ss 4 or 4A or 5 of the Public Order Act 1986
✓ such offence was racially/religiously aggravated

Explanatory notes

- If, on the trial on indictment of a person charged with an offence under s 31(1)(a) or (b), the jury find him not guilty of the offence charged, they may find him guilty of the 'basic' offence.
- For the purposes of s 31(1)(c), s 28(1)(a) *[see 7.10.1]* shall have effect as if the person likely to be caused harassment, alarm, or distress were the victim of the offence.

Related cases

DPP v McFarlane [2002] EWHC 485, QBD During an argument over a disabled parking bay a white person referred to a black person as a 'jungle bunny', a 'black bastard', and a 'wog' and was charged with racially aggravated threatening behaviour. Anger about another's inconsiderate behaviour is not an excuse for racial comments.

Norwood v DPP [2003] EWHC 1564 (Admin), QBD Displaying a racially insulting poster in a window where it could be seen by the public can constitute an offence. Its location and contents were capable of causing harassment, alarm or distress to any right-minded member of society.

DPP v Ramos [2000] Crim LR 768, QBD After a serious bomb attack, threatening letters were sent to an organization offering help and advice to the Asian community. Held that it was the state of mind of the victim, not the likelihood of violence happening. If the wording of the letter suggested immediate violence would occur, it was for the magistrates to decide whether the victim believed, or was likely to believe, that violence could occur at some time. The sender had established an intention to cause the victim to believe that violence could occur at any time.

DPP v Woods [2002] EWHC 85 (Admin), QBD When abuse is racially aggravated, it is important to prove racial hostility towards the victim or racial motivation.

Practical considerations

If the defendant is found not guilty of the offence charged under s 31(1)(a) or (b) at magistrates' court there is no provision for an alternative verdict, therefore it is good practice to include the relevant 'basic' offence as an alternative charge.

s 31(1)(a) or (b) offence

 Either way
 None

 Summary: 6 months' imprisonment and/or a fine not exceeding the statutory maximum.
Indictment: 2 years' imprisonment and/or a fine.

s 31(1)(c) offence

 Summary
 6 months

 A fine not exceeding level 4 on the standard scale.

7.10.5 **Racially or religiously aggravated harassment**

Section 32 creates the offence of racially or religiously aggravated harassment.

Offences

A person is guilty of an offence under this section if he commits—

(a) an offence under s 2 *[see 7.11.1]* of the Protection from Harassment Act 1997; or

(b) an offence under s 4 *[see 7.11.2]* of that Act,

which is racially or religiously aggravated for the purposes of this section.

Crime and Disorder Act 1998, s 32(1)

Points to prove

✓ committed an offence

✓ under s 2 or s 4 of the Protection from Harassment Act 1997

✓ such offence was racially/religiously aggravated

Explanatory notes

- If, on the trial on indictment of a person charged with an offence under s 32(1)(a), the jury find him not guilty of the offence charged, they may find him guilty of the basic offence.
- If, on the trial on indictment of a person charged with an offence under s 32(1)(b), the jury find him not guilty of the offence charged, they may find him guilty of an offence falling within s 32(1)(a).
- Section 5 of the Protection from Harassment Act 1997 (restraining orders) shall have effect in relation to a person convicted of an offence under this section as if the reference in subsection (1) of that section to an offence under section 2 or section 4 included a reference to an offence under this section *[see 7.11]*.

Practical considerations

- If the defendant is found not guilty of the offence charged under s 32(1)(a) at magistrates' court there is no provision for an alternative verdict, therefore it is good practice to include the relevant basic offence as an alternative charge.

- Similarly there is no provision for an alternative verdict under s 32(1)(b) at magistrates' court, therefore it is good practice to include the offence under s 32(1)(a) as an alternative charge.

 Either way None

Offence under s 32(1)(a)

Summary: 6 months' imprisonment and/or a fine not exceeding the statutory maximum.

Indictment: 2 years' imprisonment and/or a fine.

Offence under s 32(1)(b)

Summary: 6 months' imprisonment and/or a fine not exceeding the statutory maximum.

Indictment: 7 years' imprisonment and/or a fine.

Links to alternative subjects and offences

7.11 **Harassment**

The Protection from Harassment Act 1997 provides criminal and civil remedies to restrain conduct amounting to harassment (stalking). Sections 42 and 42A of the Criminal Justice and Police Act 2001 concern prevention of harassment of a person in their own home.

7.11.1 **Harassment—no violence**

Section 1(1) prohibits harassment, while s 2 creates the offence of harassment.

Offences

1(1) A person must not pursue a **course of conduct**—
  (a) which amounts to **harassment** of another, and
  (b) which he knows or ought to know amounts to harassment of the other.
1(1A) A person must not pursue a course of conduct—
  (a) which involves harassment of two or more persons, and
  (b) which he knows or ought to know amounts to harassment of those persons, and
  (c) by which he intends to persuade any person (whether or not one of those mentioned above)—
    (i) not to do something that he is entitled or required to do, or
    (ii) to do something that he is not under any obligation to do.
2(1) A person who pursues a course of conduct in breach of section 1(1) or (1A) is guilty of an offence.
Protection from Harassment Act 1997, ss 1(1), (1A), and 2(1)

Points to prove

✓ pursued a course of conduct
✓ on at least two occasions
✓ amounting to harassment
✓ which you knew/ought to have known amounted to harassment

Meanings

Course of conduct

• Must involve to a single person under s 1(1), conduct on at least two occasions in relation to that person, **or** to two or more persons under s 1(1A), conduct on at least one occasion in relation to each of those persons.
• Conduct includes speech.

Harassment

Includes causing the person(s) alarm or distress.

Explanatory notes

- If a reasonable person in possession of the same information as the defendant would think the course of conduct amounted to harassment, then the offender should have realized this as well.
- A person may be subjected to harassment by writing (eg emails or letters), orally (eg in person or by telephone), or by conduct (eg stalking).
- An offender does not have to act in a malicious, threatening, abusive, or insulting way. It could be that they may be infatuated with the victim and actually intend them no harm.
- In addition to any other punishment, the court can also impose a 'restraining order' (see **7.11.3—'Restraining orders'**) on a defendant convicted of this offence.

Defences

Section 1(1) or (1A) does not apply to a course of conduct if the person who pursued it shows—

(a) that it was pursued for the prevention or detection of crime,

(b) that it was pursued under any enactment or rule of law or to comply with any condition or requirement imposed by any person under any enactment, or

(c) that in the particular circumstances the pursuit of the course of conduct was reasonable.

Protection from Harassment Act 1997, s 1(3)

Defence notes

- These defences would apply to the police, customs, security services, including the private sector (eg private detective or store detective).
- A suspect suffering from some form of obsessive behaviour or schizophrenia cannot use their mental illness as a defence because of the 'reasonable person' test.

Related cases

Buckley, Smith v DPP [2008] EWHC 136 (Admin), QBD Case provides guidance on a continuing course of conduct over a period of time.

Daniels v Metropolitan Police Commissioner [2006] EWHC 1622, QBD In establishing vicarious liability for harassment there must be an established case of harassment by at least one employee who is shown on at least two occasions to have pursued a course of conduct amounting to harassment, or by more than one employee each acting on different occasions in furtherance of some joint design.

7.11.1 Harassment—No Violence

DPP v Baker [2004] EWHC 2782 (Admin), QBD Harassment may occur either continuously or intermittently over a period of time. Providing at least one of the incidents relied on by the prosecution occurred within the six month limitation period.

Kellett v DPP [2001] EWHC 107(Admin), QBD It is harassment if a person telephones the victim's employer alleging that they are pursuing their own activities in work's time. The caller knew, or ought to have known, that this conduct amounted to harassment.

Pratt v DPP [2001] EWHC (Admin) 483, CA The fewer and wider apart the incidents were the more *unlikely* that harassment would be proved. In this case the second incident was sufficiently similar to the first incident to amount to a 'course of conduct'.

Lau v DPP [2000] All ER 224, QBD During an argument Lau hit his girlfriend across her face. Four months later he threatened violence against her new boyfriend. Held: Lau had not 'pursued a course of conduct' because of the time between the two incidents and the conduct was against two different people.

Practical considerations

- Evidence of previous complaints of harassment to prove continuance of the harassment on at least two separate occasions.
- Two isolated incidents do not constitute a course of conduct.
- Have any previous warnings been given to the alleged offender?
- A campaign of collective harassment applies equally to two or more people as it does to one. Namely, conduct by one person shall also be taken, at the time it occurs, to be conduct by another if it is aided, abetted, counselled or procured by that other person.
- Consider the intentional harassment, alarm or distress offence under s 4A of the Public Order Act 1986 (see 7.7).
- If it is racially or religiously aggravated harassment see 7.10.5.
- Obtain CJA witness statements.
- Obtain all available evidence (eg other witnesses, CCTV camera footage, detailed telephone bills, entries in domestic violence registers).
- Could any of the defences apply?
- If a restraining order is required ensure a request is made to the CPS to apply for one.

 RRA

 Summary   6 months

 6 months' imprisonment and/or a fine not exceeding level 5 on the standard scale.

7.11.2 **Harassment (fear of violence)**

Section 4 relates to a course of conduct, which, on at least two occasions, causes another to fear that violence will be used against them.

Offence

A person whose course of conduct causes another to fear, on at least two occasions, that violence will be used against him is guilty of an offence if he knows or ought to know that his course of conduct will cause the other so to fear on each of those occasions.

Protection from Harassment Act 1997, s 4(1)

Points to prove

✓ caused fear of violence
✓ by a course of conduct on at least two occasions
✓ which you knew/ought to have known
✓ would cause fear of violence on each occasion

Meaning of course of conduct (see **7.11.1**)

Explanatory notes

- The person whose course of conduct is in question ought to know that it will cause another to fear that violence will be used against him on any occasion if a reasonable person with the same information would think it would cause the other so to fear on that occasion.
- A defendant found not guilty of this offence may be convicted of the lesser offence of harassment without violence (see **7.11.1**).
- The court can impose a 'restraining order' (see **7.11.3**) on a defendant convicted of this offence.

Defences

It is a defence for a person charged with an offence under this section to show that—
(a) his course of conduct was pursued for the purpose of preventing or detecting crime,
(b) his course of conduct was pursued under any enactment or rule of law or to comply with any condition or requirement imposed by any person under any enactment, or
(c) the pursuit of his course of conduct was reasonable for the protection of himself or another or for the protection of his or another's property.

Protection from Harassment Act 1997, s 4(3)

Defence notes (see **7.11.1**)

Related cases

R v Patel [2004] EWCA Crim 3284, CA Incidents must be so connected in type and context that they amount to a course of conduct.

Howard v DPP [2001] EWHC (Admin) 17, QBD A family suffered continual abuse from the defendant and their neighbours. One of the many threats made by the defendant was to kill their dog. This was sufficient grounds for the family to fear violence being used against them.

Caurti v DPP [2002] Crim LR 131, DC Conduct must be aimed against the same victim on at least two occasions.

Practical considerations (see also **7.11.1**)

- Offence not limited to 'stalking', and could cover long standing disputes where violence is a possibility against one of the parties.
- Consider intentional harassment, alarm or distress offence under s 4A of the Public Order Act 1986 (see 7.7).

 Either way   None

 Summary: 6 months' imprisonment and/or a fine not exceeding the statutory maximum.

Indictment: 5 years' imprisonment and/or a fine.

7.11.3 **Restraining orders**

Section 5 provides for the making of a restraining order against a person convicted under ss 2 or 4.

> **Offence**
> If without reasonable excuse the defendant does anything which he is prohibited from doing by an order under this section, he is guilty of an offence.
>
> Protection from Harassment Act 1997, s 5(5)

Points to prove
- ✓ without reasonable excuse
- ✓ did something prohibited by a restraining order

Explanatory notes

- A court sentencing or otherwise dealing with the defendant convicted of an offence under s 2 or 4 may, as well as sentencing or dealing with the defendant in any other way, make an order under s 5(1).
- The order may prohibit the defendant from doing anything described in the order, for the purpose of protecting the victim(s), or any other person mentioned in the order, from further conduct which amounts to harassment or will cause fear of violence.
- The order may last for a specified period or until a further order is made.
- The prosecutor, defendant, or any person named therein may apply for it to be varied or discharged by a further order.

Related cases

R v Evans [2004] EWCA Crim 3102, CA The terms of a restraining order must be precise and capable of being understood by the offender; there was no need to use a phrase having a specially narrow or wide interpretation in the order.

Practical considerations

- Unlike the previous sections of this Act, one incident is sufficient to breach an order.
- These are criminal matters and should not be confused with civil injunctions.
- When an order is made it must identify the protected parties, so ensure the details are available.
- Include a copy of the original order in the file for CPS attention.
- If you require an order you must request the CPS to apply for one.

E&S

 Either way   None

 Summary: 6 months' imprisonment and/or a fine not exceeding the statutory maximum.

Indictment: 5 years' imprisonment and/or a fine.

7.11.4 **Civil remedies**

Section 3 provides a civil remedy for harassment, allowing the victim to obtain damages and/or an injunction. Section 3A provides for injunctions to protect persons from harassment within s 1(1A).

Offence

Where—
(a) the High Court or a county court grants an injunction for the purpose mentioned in subsection (3)(a), and
(b) without reasonable excuse the defendant does anything which he is prohibited from doing by the injunction,
he is guilty of an offence.

Protection from Harassment Act 1997, s 3(6)

Points to prove

✓ without reasonable excuse
✓ pursued course of conduct prohibited by injunction
✓ granted by High Court/county court

Meanings

Injunction

An order or decree issued by a court for a person to do or not do that which is specified for a specified amount of time.

Subsection (3)(a)

In such proceedings the High Court or a county court grants an injunction for the purpose of restraining the defendant from pursuing any conduct which amounts to harassment

Reasonable excuse (see 'Defence' below)

Explanatory notes

• An actual or perceived breach of s 1 may result in a claim in civil proceedings by the victim of the course of conduct in question.
• On such a claim, damages may be awarded for, among other things, any anxiety caused by, and financial loss resulting from, the harassment.
• Where, in such proceedings, the court grants an injunction restraining the defendant from pursuing any conduct amounting to harassment, and the plaintiff considers that the defendant has done anything prohibited by the injunction, they may apply to have a warrant issued for the arrest of the defendant.
• The warrant application must be made to the court that issued the injunction.
• Section 3A stipulates that where there is an actual or apprehended breach of s 1(1A) (see **7.11.1**) by the relevant person, then any person who is or may be—
  ◆ a victim of the course of conduct in question, or
  ◆ a person falling within section 1(1A)(c),

may apply to the High Court or a county court for an injunction restraining the relevant person from pursuing any conduct which amounts to harassment in relation to any person or persons mentioned or described in the injunction.

Defence

The defence of reasonable excuse was meant for a **life-saving** situation such as a rescue from a burning house or something similar (*Huntingdon Life Sciences v Curtin* [1997] EWCA Civ 2486).

Related cases

Thomas v News Group Newspapers Ltd [2001] EWCA Civ 1233, CA A national newspaper and journalists were sued for harassment under s 3 after publishing an article about police discipline which gave the complainant's name, place of work, and described them as 'a black clerk'. Held: It was not the conduct of the offender that created the offence or civil wrong of harassment, but the effect of that conduct.

DPP v Moseley [1999] All ER (D) 587, QBD A High Court injunction had been granted to prevent harassment of a mink farmer. The defendant took part in a peaceful protest within the area covered by the injunction and claimed this conduct was reasonable. Held: Only in serious circumstances could it be reasonable to flout a High Court injunction.

Practical considerations

If a person is convicted of a breach of an injunction under this section, their conduct is not punishable as a contempt of court, or vice versa.

 Either way   None

 Summary: 6 months' imprisonment and/or a fine not exceeding the statutory maximum.

Indictment: 5 years' imprisonment and/or a fine.

7.11.5 **Harassment of person in their home**

Sections 42 and 42A of the Criminal Justice and Police Act 2001 provide a person in their home with protection from harassment. All references in the following are to the 2001 Act unless otherwise stated.

Offences

42(7) Any person who knowingly fails to comply with a requirement in a **direction** given to him under this section (other than a requirement under subsection (4)(b)) shall be guilty of an offence.

7.11.5 Harassment of Person in their Home

42(7A) Any person to whom a constable has given a direction including a requirement under subsection (4)(b) commits an offence if he—

    (a) returns to the vicinity of the premises in question within the period specified in the direction beginning with the date on which the direction is given; and

    (b) does so for the purpose described in subsection (1)(b).

42A(1) A person commits an offence if—

    (a) that person is outside or in the vicinity of any premises that are used by any individual ('the resident') as his **dwelling**;

    (b) that person is present there for the purpose (by his presence or otherwise) of representing to the resident or other individual (whether or not one who uses the premises as his dwelling), or of persuading the resident or such other individual—

        (i) that he should not do something that he is entitled or required to do; or

        (ii) that he should do something that he is not under any obligation to do;

    (c) that person—

        (i) intends his presence to amount to the **harassment** of, or to cause alarm or distress to, the resident, or

        (ii) knows or ought to know that his presence is likely to result in the harassment of, or to cause alarm or distress to, the resident; and

    (d) the presence of that person—

        (i) amounts to the harassment of, or causes alarm or distress to, any person falling within subsection (2); or

        (ii) is likely to result in the harassment of, or to cause alarm or distress to, any such person.

Criminal Justice and Police Act 2001, ss 42, 42A

Points to prove

s 42(7) offence

✓ outside/in vicinity of premises
✓ knowingly
✓ contravened the direction of a constable

s 42(7A) offence

✓ having been given a direction by a constable
✓ to leave the vicinity of premises
✓ not to return within a specified period
✓ returned there within that period
✓ to persuade the resident/another individual
✓ not to do something they are entitled to do/do something not obliged to do/tl>

---

s 42A(1) offence
- ✓ present outside/in vicinity of a dwelling
- ✓ to persuade resident/other individual
- ✓ not to do something entitled/required to do/to do something not obliged to do
- ✓ intended to harass/cause alarm/distress to the resident
- ✓ knew/ought to have known such presence was likely to do so
- ✓ and their presence amounted to harassment/caused alarm/distress/ likely to do so

---

Meanings

Directions

(1) Subject to the following provisions of this section, a constable who is at the scene may give a direction under this section to any person if—

    (a) that person is present outside or in the vicinity of any premises that are used by any individual ('the resident') as his dwelling;

    (b) that constable believes, on reasonable grounds, that that person is present there for the purpose (by his presence or otherwise) of representing to the resident or another individual (whether or not one who uses the premises as his dwelling), or of persuading the resident or such another individual—

        (i) that he should not do something that he is entitled or required to do; or

        (ii) that he should do something that he is not under any obligation to do; and

    (c) that constable also believes, on reasonable grounds, that the presence of that person (either alone or together with that of any other persons who are also present)—

        (i) amounts to, or is likely to result in, the harassment of the resident; or

        (ii) is likely to cause alarm or distress to the resident.

(2) A direction under this section is a direction requiring the person to whom it is given to do all such things as the constable giving it may specify as the things he considers necessary to prevent one or both of the following—

    (a) the harassment of the resident; or

    (b) the causing of any alarm or distress to the resident.

(3) A direction under this section may be given orally; and where a constable is entitled to give a direction under this section to each of several persons outside, or in the vicinity of, any premises, he may give that direction to those persons by notifying them of his requirements either individually or all together.

(4) The requirements that may be imposed by a direction under this section include—

    (a) a requirement to leave the vicinity of the premises in question, and

(b) a requirement to leave that vicinity and not to return to it within such period as the constable may specify, not being longer than 3 months;

and (in either case) the requirement to leave the vicinity may be to do so immediately or after a specified period of time.

(5) A direction under this section may make exceptions to any requirement imposed by the direction, and may make any such exception subject to such conditions as the constable giving the direction thinks fit; and those conditions may include—

(a) conditions as to the distance from the premises in question at which, or otherwise as to the location where, persons who do not leave their vicinity must remain; and

(b) conditions as to the number or identity of the persons who are authorised by the exception to remain in the vicinity of those premises.

(6) The power of a constable to give a direction under this section shall not include—

(a) any power to give a direction at any time when there is a more **senior ranking** police officer at the scene; or

(b) any power to direct a person to refrain from conduct that is lawful under section 220 of the Trade Union and Labour Relations (Consolidation) Act 1992 (right peacefully to picket a work place);

but it shall include power to vary or withdraw a direction previously given under this section.

Criminal Justice and Police Act 2001, s 42

Dwelling

Means any structure or part of a structure occupied as a person's home or as other living accommodation (whether the occupation is separate or shared with others) but does not include any part not so occupied, and for this purpose 'structure' includes a tent, caravan, vehicle, vessel, or other temporary or movable structure.

Harassment (see **7.11.1**)

Explanatory notes

• A requirement in a direction under s 42(4)(b) means to leave that vicinity immediately or after a specified period of time and not to return within a specified period (no more than 3 months).

• Under the s 42A(1)(d)(i) offence a person falls within s 42A(2) if he is the resident, a person in the resident's dwelling, or a person in another dwelling in the vicinity of the resident's dwelling.

• Under s 42 a constable in attendance may give a direction to any person if that person is outside or in the vicinity of premises used by a resident as their dwelling, having reasonable grounds to believe that the person's presence amounts to harassment of the resident or is likely to cause them alarm or distress.

- Such a direction requires the person to whom it is given to do everything specified by the constable as necessary to prevent the harassment of and/or the causing of alarm or distress to, the resident.
- A direction under s 42 may include a requirement to leave—
  - the vicinity of the premises in question, and
  - not return to it within such period as the constable may specify, not being longer than 3 months.
- The references in s 42A(1)(c) and (d) to a person's presence refer to their presence either alone or together with any other person(s) also present.
- For s 42A(1)(c) a person ought to know that their presence is likely to result in the harassment of, or cause alarm or distress to, a resident if a reasonable person possessing the same information would think that their presence would have that effect.

Practical considerations

- Directions given under this section may be given orally, but it is important that the direction must be both heard and understood by the person concerned.
- If a direction is given to more than one person the constable may give it to them either individually or all together.
- The power of a constable to give a direction under s 42 does not include where there is a more **senior-ranking** officer present. If the senior officers are of the same rank, then the greater length of service in that rank determines who should give the direction.
- Similarly a constable cannot give a direction if the person(s) are exercising their right to peacefully picket a work place.
- A constable may vary or withdraw any direction previously given.

 Summary   6 months

   ### *Offence under s 42(7)*

3 months' imprisonment and/or a fine not exceeding level 4 on the standard scale.

Offence under s 42(7A) or s 42A

6 months' imprisonment and/or a fine not exceeding level 4 on the standard scale.

Links to alternative subjects and offences

7.12 **Offensive/False Messages**

The Malicious Communications Act 1988 concerns the sending and delivery of letters or other articles to cause distress or anxiety; the Communications Act 2003 regulates all types of media, including the sending of grossly offensive material via the public electronic communications network; whilst the offence of giving or causing to be given a false alarm of fire is dealt with by the Fire and Rescue Services Act 2004.

7.12.1 **Send letters, etc intending to cause distress/anxiety**

Section 1 of the Malicious Communications Act 1988 creates offences in relation to the sending of indecent, offensive, or threatening letters, electronic communications, or articles with intent to cause distress or anxiety to the recipient.

Offences

Any person who sends to another person—
(a) a letter, **electronic communication** or article of any description which conveys—
  (i) a message which is indecent or grossly offensive;
  (ii) a threat; or
  (iii) information which is false and known or believed to be false by the sender; or
(b) any article or electronic communication which is, in whole or part, of an indecent or **grossly offensive** nature,
is guilty of an offence if his purpose, or one of his purposes, in sending it is that it should, so far as falling within paragraph (a) or (b) above, cause distress or anxiety to the recipient or to any other person to whom he intends that it or its contents or nature should be communicated.

Malicious Communications Act 1988, s 1(1)

Points to prove

s 1(1)(a) offence
- ✓ sent a letter/an electronic communication/an article
- ✓ which conveys an indecent/grossly offensive message/threat/false information which you knew/believed to be false
- ✓ for the purpose of causing distress/anxiety
- ✓ to the recipient/any other person
- ✓ to whom its contents/nature were intended to be communicated

---

7.12.1 Send Letters, etc Intending to Cause Distress/Anxiety

---

s 1(1)(b) offence

✓ sent to another person
✓ an article/an electronic communication
✓ wholly/partly of an indecent/grossly offensive nature
✓ for the purpose of causing distress/anxiety
✓ to the recipient/any other person
✓ to whom its contents/nature were intended to be communicated

---

Meanings

Electronic communication

Includes any—

• oral or other communication by means of an **electronic communications network**; and
• communication (however sent) that is in electronic form.

Electronic communications network

Means—

• a transmission system for the conveyance, by the use of electrical, magnetic or electro-magnetic energy, of signals of any description; and
• such of the following as are used, by the person providing the system and in association with it, for the conveyance of the signals—
   ♦ apparatus comprised in the system;
   ♦ apparatus used for the switching or routing of the signals; and
   ♦ software and stored data.

Grossly offensive

This has to be judged by the standards of an open and just multi-racial society. Whether a message falls into this category depends not only on its content but on the circumstances in which the message has been sent (*DPP v Collins* [2005] EWHC 1308, HL).

Explanatory notes

• Sending includes delivering or transmitting and causing to be sent, delivered, or transmitted; 'sender' will be construed accordingly.
• Offence only requires that the communication be sent—not that the intended victim actually received it.

Defence

A person is not guilty of an offence by virtue of sub-s (1)(a)(ii) above *[threat]* if he shows—

(a) that the threat was used to reinforce a demand made by him on reasonable grounds; and
(b) that he believed, and had reasonable grounds for believing, that the use of the threat was a proper means of reinforcing the demand.

Malicious Communications Act 1988, s 1(2)

Related cases

Connolly v DPP [2007] EWHC 237, QBD C telephoned chemist shops to ascertain whether they stocked the morning after pill, sending pictures of aborted foetuses to those that did. These pictures were indecent and grossly offensive with the purpose of causing distress or anxiety. Rights of expression under Articles 9 or 10 (see **1.1**) did not excuse the distress, anxiety caused and conviction was necessary in a democratic society. The words 'indecent' and 'grossly offensive' have their ordinary meaning.

Practical considerations

- As well as letters and telephone systems this offence would include emails, fax, or text messages.
- What was the intended purpose of the defendant in sending the communication?
- If the intent is to cause the victim annoyance, inconvenience, or needless anxiety, then consider the offence under s 127 of the Communications Act 2003 (see **7.12.2**).
- If there has been more than one incident an offence under s 2 of the Protection from Harassment Act 1997 may be more appropriate (see **7.11.1**).
- If any threat used includes an unwarranted demand consider the more serious offence of blackmail (see **3.2.3**).
- Preserve the means or item that was used to deliver the message to the victim.
- The original message can be retrieved from phones or computers, the original letter or envelope can be fingerprinted or examined for DNA.

 Summary   6 months

 6 months' imprisonment and/or a fine not exceeding level 5 on the standard scale.

7.12.2 Improper use of electronic public communications network

Section 127 of the Communications Act 2003 creates offences regarding improper use of an electronic public communications network.

Offences

(1) A person is guilty of an offence if he—
    (a) sends by means of a **public electronic communications network** a message or other matter that is **grossly offensive** or of an indecent, obscene or **menacing** character; or
    (b) causes any such message or matter to be so sent.

7.12.2 Improper Use of Electronic Public Communications Network

(2) A person is guilty of an offence if, for the purpose of causing annoyance, inconvenience or needless anxiety to another, he—

(a) sends by means of a public electronic communications network, a message that he knows to be false,

(b) causes such a message to be sent, or

(c) **persistently** makes use of a public electronic communications network.

Communications Act 2003, s 127

Points to prove

s 127(1) offence

✓ sent
✓ by means of a public electronic communications network
✓ a message/other matter
✓ that was grossly offensive/of an indecent/obscene/menacing character

or

✓ caused such a message/matter to be so sent

s 127(2) offence

✓ to cause annoyance/inconvenience/needless anxiety to another
✓ sent
✓ by means of a public electronic communications network
✓ a message known to be false

or

✓ caused such a message to be sent

or

✓ persistently made use
✓ of a public electronic communications network

Meanings

Public electronic communications network

Means an **electronic communications network** provided wholly or mainly for the purpose of making electronic communications services available for use by members of the public.

Electronic communications network (see 7.12.1)

Grossly offensive (see 7.12.1)

Menacing

Means a message which conveys a threat; which seeks to create a fear in or through the recipient that something unpleasant is going to happen. Here the intended or likely effect on the recipient must ordinarily be a central factor (*DPP v Collins* [2005] EWHC 1308, HL).

Persistently

Includes any case in which the misuse is repeated on a sufficient number of occasions for it to be clear that the misuse represents a pattern of behaviour or practice, or recklessness as to whether people suffer annoyance, inconvenience, or anxiety.

Explanatory notes

- 'Electronic communications network' covers current and future developments in communication technologies (eg telephone, computers (internet), satellites, mobile terrestrial networks, emails, text messages, fax, radio, and television broadcasting including cable TV networks).
- These offences do not apply to anything done in the course of providing a broadcasting service, such as a television programme; public teletext; digital television; radio programme; or sound provided by the BBC.
- Sections 128 to 130 empower OFCOM (Office of Communications) to enforce this Act to stop a person persistently misusing a public electronic communications network or services.

Related cases

R v Johnson [1996] 2 Cr App R 434, CA Making numerous obscene/offensive telephone calls can amount to a public nuisance (see **7.13.3**).

R v Ireland [1998] AC 147 HL and **R v Burstow [1997] 4 All ER 225 HL** Silent telephone calls which caused psychiatric injury to a victim was capable of being an AOABH (see **2.1**) or grievous bodily harm (see **2.3**) if they caused the victim to fear imminent violence on themselves. Expert evidence confirmed that the victims had suffered palpitations, breathing difficulties, cold sweats, anxiety, sleeplessness, dizziness, and stress.

Practical considerations

- These offences do not apply to a private/internal network. In these instances consider s 1 of the Malicious Communications Act 1988 (see **7.12.1**).
- Under sub-s (1) there is no requirement to show any specific purpose or intent by the defendant.
- Consider s 1 of the Malicious Communications Act 1988 (see **7.12.1**) if the offence involves intent to cause the victim distress or anxiety.
- Also consider an offence under the Protection from Harassment Act 1997 (see **7.11**).
- If the threats or information relate to bombs, noxious substances, or the placing of dangerous articles, consider the offences under the Anti-terrorism, Crime and Security Act 2001 and the Criminal Law Act 1977 (see **11.4.2**).

7.12.3 Giving/Cause to be Given False Alarm of Fire

- Section 125 creates the offence of dishonestly obtaining an electronic communications service with intent to avoid the applicable payment.
- Possession or control of apparatus which may be used dishonestly to obtain an electronic communications service, or in connection with obtaining such a service is also an offence under s 126.
- A PND may be issued by a police officer, PCSO, or other accredited person for an offence under s 127(2) (see **7.1.1**).

 Summary 6 months

 6 months' imprisonment and/or a fine not exceeding level 5 on the standard scale.

7.12.3 Giving/cause to be given false alarm of fire

Section 49 of the Fire and Rescue Services Act 2004 creates an offence of giving or causing to be given a false alarm of fire.

Offences

A person commits an offence if he **knowingly** gives or causes to be given a false alarm of fire to a person acting on behalf of a **fire and rescue authority.**

Fire and Rescue Services Act 2004, s 49(1)

Points to prove
✓ date and location
✓ knowingly
✓ gave/caused to be given
✓ a false alarm of fire
✓ to a person acting on behalf of a fire and rescue authority

Meanings

Knowingly (see **9.1.3**)

Fire and rescue authority

This can be the fire and rescue authority for the county/county borough/area or the London Fire and Emergency Planning Authority.

Practical considerations

- The prosecutor may apply to the court for an **Anti-social Behaviour Order** (see **7.13.1**), even if a PND has been issued.
- A PND can be issued by a police officer or PCSO for this offence (see **7.1.1**).
- Where the offender is aged 10 to 15 years a PND (see **7.1.1**) can be issued, but this only applies to specific force pilot areas.

 Summary   6 months

 3 months' imprisonment and/or a fine not exceeding level 4 on the standard scale.

Links to alternative subjects and offences

7.13 **Anti-Social Behaviour**

Anti-social behaviour is dealt with in various pieces of legislation including the Crime and Disorder Act 1998, Police Reform Act 2002, Anti-social Behaviour Act 2003, and at common law.

7.13.1 **Anti-social behaviour orders—application/breach**

Section 1 of the Crime and Disorder Act 1998 empowers magistrates to make an ASBO against an individual whose conduct has caused harassment, alarm, or distress, and creates an offence for breaching such an order.

Offence

If without reasonable excuse a person does anything which he is prohibited from doing by an **anti-social behaviour order**, he is guilty of an offence.

Crime and Disorder Act 1998, s 1(10)

Points to prove

✓ without reasonable excuse
✓ did an act
✓ prohibited from doing
✓ by anti-social behaviour order

Meanings

Anti-social behaviour order

(1) An application for an order under this section may be made by a **relevant authority** if it appears to the authority that the following conditions are fulfilled with respect to any person aged 10 or over, namely—

(a) that the person has acted in an anti-social manner, that is to say, in a manner that caused or was likely to cause harassment, alarm or distress to one or more persons not of the same household as himself; and

(b) that such an order is necessary to protect **relevant persons** from further anti-social acts by him.

(3) Such an application shall be made by complaint to a magistrates' court.

(4) If, on such an application, it is proved that the conditions mentioned in subsection (1) above are fulfilled, the magistrates' court may make an order under this section (an 'anti-social behaviour order') which prohibits the defendant from doing anything described in the order.

Crime and Disorder Act 1998, s 1

Relevant authority

- Council for a **local government area** or county council (England);
- Chief constable of any police force maintained for a police area or the BTP;
- Person(s) registered as a social landlord who provides/manages a house/hostel in local government area or Housing Action Trust established by order.

Local government area

Means in England, a district or London borough, City of London, Isle of Wight, and Isles of Scilly. In Wales, a county or county borough.

Relevant persons

Means persons from council/police areas; BTP jurisdiction or residing in/being on or in vicinity of premises provided/managed by landlord/authority/trust.

Explanatory notes

- These are civil proceedings, but be aware that the standard of proof is the criminal standard of 'beyond reasonable doubt' and **not** the civil standard of 'balance of probabilities'. This is a safeguard owing to the serious consequences of the proceedings.
- The Human Rights Act does not prevent hearsay evidence being used in anti-social behaviour proceedings.
- Although the hearing which grants the order is a civil matter, the breaching offence is a criminal matter and is subject to the criminal rules of evidence.
- An application by the police will only be made after consultation with the council in which the subject of the application resides or appears to reside. Similarly an application by a council will only be made after consulting with the police for the police area within which the local authority lies.
- An ASBO prevents the person named in it from doing anything described in it.
- The order is valid for the period of time stated in it (minimum 2 years) or until a further order is made.
- A warning letter will be served on the offender outlining the substance of any allegations and an application for an ASBO will only be made if the offending behaviour continues after the service of the letter.
- Where a person is convicted of an offence under this section the court cannot make an order for a conditional discharge.
- In criminal proceedings, if the offender is convicted of an offence and the court considers that they have acted in an anti-social manner and that an ASBO is necessary to protect other people in the area from further such behaviour, the court may, under s 1C, issue an ASBO against that individual. This order may only be made in addition to the sentence imposed on the offence.

- An interim ASBO may be granted by a court pending the hearing of the main application. This interim order will be for a fixed period, may be varied, renewed, or discharged and will cease to have effect on determination of the main application.
- An ASBO may be varied or discharged on the application of the offender, the DPP, or a relevant authority (see above). If the offender makes such application they must also send written notification of their application to the DPP.

Related cases

N v DPP [2007] EWHC 883 (Admin), QBD A youth convicted of disorderly conduct was given an ASBO that was far too wide and disproportionate. It was redrafted so that they could not congregate in a public place in a group of two or more persons in a manner that might cause someone to fear for their safety.

R v Stevens [2006] EWCA Crim 255, CA If the conduct which forms the breach of the order is also a criminal offence with a maximum sentence threshold, then this should be considered when sentencing for breaching the order in the interests of proportionality. Although the breaching offence carries a maximum penalty of 5 years' imprisonment, this should not be used to circumvent maximum penalties considered too lenient.

R v Nicholson [2006] EWCA Crim 1518 CA Ignorance, forgetfulness or misunderstanding may be capable of giving rise to a defence of reasonable excuse in cases involving the breach of an ASBO; but this is fact specific and the issues of fact and the judgment of those facts was a matter for the court to decide.

R v Wadmore and Foreman [2006] EWCA Crim 686 CA Issued guidelines when applying for an ASBO—
- Proceedings are civil, so hearsay is admissible, but the court must be satisfied to the criminal standard that the behaviour had been anti-social.
- Necessity of order requires exercise of judgement or evaluation.
- The findings of fact giving rise to the making of the order must be recorded.
- The terms of the order must be precise, capable of being understood and must be explained to the offender.
- The conditions must be enforceable, allowing any breach to be readily identified and capable of being proved.
- If an order is suspended until the offender has been released from custody (on licence subject to recall), the circumstances in which the necessity test can be met will be limited.
- An order must deal with the offender and be necessary to protect others from their anti-social behaviour.
- Not all conditions need to run for the full term of the order, provided the necessity test is met and restrictions are proportionate in the circumstances.

- The court should not impose an order prohibiting the commission of criminal offences if the sentence on conviction would be a sufficient deterrent.
- It is unlawful to impose an ASBO if it is a further sentence or punishment and must not be used to increase the sentence of imprisonment.

R (on the application of Chief Constable of West Mercia Police) v Boorman [2005] EWHC 2559 (Admin), QBD Stated that—

- The conduct and complaint must be within the 6 months limitation period, not the evidence. It is wrong to exclude evidence that was outside this period.
- ASBO is about preventive justice and is not part of criminal law, but Art 6 (see **1.1**) requires that reasons should be given about the making of an ASBO.
- Proof of mens rea (intent) is not required, but the court (not the victim) will decide whether the conduct was likely to cause harassment, alarm or distress.

R (Stanley and others) v Metropolitan Police Commissioner [2004] EWHC 2229 (Admin), DC Publicity is needed to inform and reinforce existing ASBOs and to inhibit the behaviour of the offenders, or to deter others. It needed a photograph, name, and partial address so that people knew who the ASBOs referred to, ensuring that there was no possibility of misidentification. No criminal convictions could be disclosed. Publicity may go beyond the excluded area, but it must be necessary and proportionate for protecting the rights of all concerned.

R (on the application of Kenny and M) v Leeds Magistrates Court [2003] EWHC (Admin) 2963, QBD After an area suffered large scale anti-social behaviour problems including drug dealing and associated crime, interim ASBOs without notice were issued against 66 people. It was established that, although Article 6(1) applied to ASBOs, there was nothing unlawful in interim injunctions without notice and such power is only used to urgently protect the interests of other parties or to ensure the order of a court is effective.

Practical considerations

- An ASBO application is made by way of complaint to a magistrates' court, and is subject to the 6 months limitation period.
- The application hearing for an ASBO is civil in nature, but breaching that order is a criminal matter where the burden of proof is 'beyond reasonable doubt' not on the balance of probabilities.
- The onus is on the prosecution to prove, beyond reasonable doubt, that the defendant was subject of and breached the ASBO and that the defendant had no reasonable excuse for breaching the order. In order to prove this the defendant should be interviewed under caution.
- In proceedings for an offence under this section a certified court copy of the original ASBO is admissible as evidence of its issue and content.

- The police or local authority, in consultation with each other, can make an application for an ASBO against an individual or several individuals.

 Either way   None

 Summary: 6 months' imprisonment and/or a fine not exceeding the statutory maximum.

Indictment: 5 years' imprisonment and/or a fine.

7.13.2 Act in anti-social manner—fail to give name/address

Section 50 of the Police Reform Act 2002 empowers a police officer to request the name and address of a person behaving in an anti-social manner, and creates an offence of failing to comply with that request.

Offences

Any person who—

(a) fails to give his name and address when **required to do so** under subsection (1), or

(b) gives a false or inaccurate name or address in response to a requirement under that subsection,

is guilty of an offence.

Police Reform Act 2002, s 50(2)

Points to prove

✓ being a person whom a constable had reason to believe

✓ had been/was acting in anti-social manner

✓ failed or gave false/inaccurate details

✓ when required by the constable to provide their name and address

---

Meanings

Required to do so (by a constable in uniform)

If a constable in uniform has reason to believe that a person has been acting, or is acting, in an **anti-social manner**, he may require that person to give his name and address to the constable.

Anti-social manner

In a manner that caused or was likely to cause harassment, alarm, or distress to one or more persons not of the same household as themselves.

Explanatory notes

- A person who fails to give their name and address or gives a false/inaccurate name or address will commit an offence.
- This power also applies to a PCSO.

Practical considerations

A constable must be in uniform to request under s 50(1).

 Summary 6 months

 A fine not exceeding level 3 on the standard scale.

7.13.3 **Public nuisance**

Types of behaviour which used to be prosecuted as a 'public nuisance' are now covered by statute (eg food, noise, waste disposal, highways, animals, agriculture, medicines). However, 'public nuisance' is still an offence at common law.

Offences

A person is guilty of this offence if he—
(a) does an **act not warranted by law,** or
(b) omits to discharge a **legal duty,**
and the effect of the act or omission is to endanger the life, health, property, morals or comfort of the public, or to obstruct the public in the exercise or enjoyment of rights common to everyone.

Common Law

Points to prove

✓ by doing an act not warranted by law or omitting to discharge a legal duty
✓ caused
✓ a public nuisance

7.13.3 Public Nuisance

Meanings

Act not warranted by law

Means illegal conduct, but does not have to be a specific offence covered by legislation.

Legal duty

Means a duty under any enactment, instrument or rule of law.

Explanatory notes

- This offence is described as 'a nuisance that is so wide spread in its range or so indiscriminate in its effect that it would not be reasonable to expect any one person to take proceedings on their own responsibility to put a stop to it, but that it should be taken on the responsibility of the community at large'.
- The purpose that the defendant has in mind when they commit the act is immaterial if the probable result is to affect the public as described in the offence.
- Where some work is done by an employee in a manner that causes a nuisance it is no defence for the employer to claim that they did not personally supervise the work and had instructed that it be carried out in a different way.

Related cases

R v Kavanagh [2008] EWCA Crim 855, CA Hundreds of sexually explicit telephone calls were made to various women over 2 years. This offence went beyond voyeurism as it involved invasion of privacy and making contact with the victims that put them in fear.

R v Rimmington, R v Goldstein [2005] UKHL 63, HL If a statutory offence was made out, with possible defences, mode of trial, and maximum penalty, then prosecution should be under statute and not common law where the potential penalty was unlimited.

R v Shorrock [1993] 3 All ER 917, CA Defendant leased a field at his farm for a weekend which was used for an acid house party/rave. S was away during the event and denied any knowledge that a public nuisance would be committed on his land. The farmer was held responsible for this nuisance which S knew or ought to have known about; because the means of knowledge were available, so were the consequences of what S did or omitted to do.

R v Johnson [1996] 2 Cr App R 434, CA Over a number of years, J used the public telephone system to cause nuisance annoyance, harassment, alarm, and distress to a number of women by making hundreds of obscene calls. The cumulative effect of all the calls was a public nuisance, as the number of individuals affected was sufficient for his actions to be public.

Practical considerations

- This common law offence is still important because of its flexibility in adapting to those areas not covered by specific legislation.
- For extreme acts of unpleasantness or lewdness consider offences under the Sexual Offences Act 2003 (see **Chapter 6**) or the common law offence of outraging public decency (see **6.9**—'**Indecent exposure**').
- Conspiracy to commit this offence is contrary to s 1(1) of the Criminal Law Act 1977.

 Either way   None

 Summary: 6 months' imprisonment and/or a fine not exceeding the statutory maximum.

Indictment: Imprisonment and/or a fine.

7.13.4 **Premises closure notices/orders (disorder/nuisance)**

Section 11A of the Anti-social Behaviour Act 2003 gives police powers to issue a closure notice in respect of premises associated with persistent disorder or nuisance. The provisions are very similar to closure notices/orders when premises are being used for Class A drugs (see **5.3.2**). Section 4 of this Act creates offences of remaining in or entering property subject to a closure notice or order.

Offences

(1) A person who remains on or enters **premises** in contravention of a **Part 1A closure notice** commits an offence.

(2) A person who—
  (a) obstructs a person acting under section 11A(7) or 11C(2),
  (b) remains on **closed premises**, or
  (c) enters closed premises
commits an offence.

Anti-social Behaviour Act 2003, s 11D

Points to prove

Closure notice

✓ date and location
✓ remained on/entered premises
✓ in contravention of a Part 1A closure notice

7.13.4 **Premises Closure Notices/Orders (Disorder/Nuisance)**

> *Obstruction*
> - ✓ date and location
> - ✓ obstructed
> - ✓ constable/local authority employee
> - ✓ acting under
> - ✓ s 11A(7) (service)/s 11C(2) (enforcement)
>
> *Closure order*
> - ✓ date and location
> - ✓ entered/remained on closed premises
> - ✓ in respect of which a Part 1A closure order is in force

Meanings

Premises (see 5.3.2)

Part 1A closure notice

Means a notice issued under s 11A (see below, procedure).

Closed premises

Means premises in respect of which a **Part 1A closure order** has effect.

Part 1A closure order

Means an order issued by a magistrates court—
- made under s 11B;
- extended under s 11E;
- made or extended under s 11F which has the like effect as an order made or extended under s 11B or 11E (as the case may be).

Defences

A person who has a reasonable excuse for entering or being on the premises does not commit an offence under s 11D(1) or (2)(b) or (c) (as the case may be).

Anti-social Behaviour Act 2003, s 11D(4)

Closure notice procedure

Grounds

(1) This section applies to premises if a police officer not below the rank of superintendent (the authorising officer) or the local authority has reasonable grounds for believing—
  - (a) that at any time during the **relevant period** a person has engaged in **anti-social behaviour** on the premises, and
  - (b) that the use of the premises is associated with significant and persistent disorder or persistent serious nuisance to members of the public.

Authorisation

(2) The authorising officer may authorise the issue of a Part 1A closure notice in respect of the premises if the officer is satisfied—

(a) that the local authority has been consulted; and

(b) that reasonable steps have been taken to establish the identity of any person who lives on the premises or who has control of or responsibility for, or an interest in, the premises.

(3) The local authority may authorise the issue of a Part 1A closure notice in respect of the premises if it is satisfied—

(a) that the appropriate chief officer has been consulted; and

(b) that reasonable steps have been taken to establish the identity of any person who lives on the premises or who has control of or responsibility for, or an interest in, the premises.

Requirements

(4) An authorisation under subsection (2) or (3) may be given orally or in writing, but if it is given orally the authorising officer or local authority (as the case may be) must confirm it in writing as soon as it is practicable.

(5) A Part 1A closure notice must—

(a) give notice that an application will be made under section 11B for the closure of the premises;

(b) state that access to the premises by any person other than a person who habitually resides in the premises or the owner of the premises is prohibited;

(c) specify the date and time when, and the place at which, the application will be heard;

(d) explain the effects of an order made in pursuance of section 11B;

(e) state that failure to comply with the notice amounts to an offence; and

(f) give information about **relevant advice providers**.

Service

(6) A Part 1A closure notice must be served by—

(a) a constable if its issue was authorised by the authorising officer, or

(b) an employee of the local authority if its issue was authorised by the authority.

(7) Service is effected by—

(a) fixing a copy of the notice to at least one prominent place on the premises,

(b) fixing a copy of the notice to each normal means of access to the premises,

(c) fixing a copy of the notice to any outbuildings which appear to the server of the notice to be used with or as part of the premises,

(d) giving a copy of the notice to at least one person who appears to the server of the notice to have control of or responsibility for the premises, and

(e) giving a copy of the notice to the persons identified in pursuance of subsection(2)(b) or (3)(b) (as the case may be) and to any other person appearing to the server of the notice to be a person of a description mentioned in that provision.

7.13.4 **Premises Closure Notices/Orders (Disorder/Nuisance)**

(8) The Part 1A closure notice must also be served on any person who occupies any other part of the building or other structure in which the premises are situated if the server of the notice reasonably believes, at the time of serving the notice under subsection (7), that the person's access to the other part of the building or structure will be impeded if a Part 1A closure order is made under section 11B.

Anti-social Behaviour Act 2003, s 11A

Meanings

Relevant period

Means the period of 3 months ending with the day on which the authorising officer or the local authority (as the case may be) considers whether to authorise the issue of a Part 1A closure notice in respect of the premises.

Anti-social behaviour

Means behaviour by a person which causes or is likely to cause harassment, alarm, or distress to one or more other persons not of the same household as the person.

Relevant advice providers   (see 5.3.2)

Explanatory notes

- Section 11A(1) sets out the grounds which must be satisfied before a superintendent (or above) or local authority can issue a Part 1A closure notice.
- The police or local authority must have reasonable grounds for believing that a person has engaged in anti-social behaviour on the premises in the preceding 3 months and that the premises are associated with significant and persistent disorder or persistent serious nuisance.
- For the purpose of fixing a copy of the notice to at least one prominent place on the premises, a constable or local authority employee may enter any premises to which s 11A applies, using reasonable force if necessary.
- The police and local authority must consult with each other, and ensure that reasonable steps have been taken to identify those living on the premises or with an interest in it before the notice is issued.
- Various steps and consultations must be made before application can be made to the magistrates' court for a Part 1A closure order under s 11B (which must be heard by the magistrates within 48 hours of the Part 1A closure notice being served).

Closure orders procedure

Sections 11B and 11C of the Anti-social Behaviour Act 2003 relate to closure orders.

Court procedure

(1) If a Part 1A closure notice has been issued under section 11A an application must be made under this section to a magistrates' court for the making of a Part 1A closure order.

(2) An application under subsection (1) must be made by—
   (a) a constable if the issue of the Part 1A closure notice was authorised by the authorising officer, or
   (b) the local authority if the issue of the Part 1A closure notice was authorised by the authority.

(3) The application must be heard by the magistrates' court not later than 48 hours after the notice was served in pursuance of section 11A(7)(a).

(4) The magistrates' court may make a Part 1A closure order if and only if it is satisfied that each of the following paragraphs applies—
   (a) a person has engaged in anti-social behaviour on the premises in respect of which the Part 1A closure notice was issued;
   (b) the use of the premises is associated with significant and persistent disorder or persistent serious nuisance to members of the public;
   (c) the making of the order is necessary to prevent the occurrence of such disorder or nuisance for the period specified in the order.

Anti-social Behaviour Act 2003, s 11B

Enforcement

(1) This section applies if a magistrates' court makes an order under section 11B.

(2) A **relevant person** may—
   (a) enter the premises in respect of which the order is made;
   (b) do anything reasonably necessary to secure the premises against entry by any person.

(3) A person acting under subsection (2) may use reasonable force.

(4) But a relevant person seeking to enter the premises for the purposes of subsection (2) must, if required to do so by or on behalf of the **owner**, occupier or other person in charge of the premises, produce evidence of his identity and authority before entering the premises.

(5) A relevant person may also enter the premises at any time while the order has effect for the purpose of carrying out essential maintenance of or repairs to the premises.

Anti-social Behaviour Act 2003, s 11C

Meanings

Relevant person

In relation to premises in respect of which a police Part 1A closure order has effect, means a constable or person authorized by the chief officer. For a local authority Part 1A closure, means a person authorized by the local authority.

7.13.4 Premises Closure Notices/Orders (Disorder/Nuisance)

Owner

Means a person who—
- is for the time being entitled to dispose of the fee simple in the premises, whether in possession or in reversion (apart from a mortgagee not in possession), or
- holds or is entitled to the rents and profits of the premises under a lease which (when granted) was for a term of not less than 3 years.

Explanatory notes

- A Part 1A closure order is an order that the premises in respect of which the order is made are closed to all persons for such period (not exceeding 3 months) as is specified in the order.
- However, the order may include such provision as the court thinks appropriate relating to access to any part of the building or structure of which the premises form part.
- The magistrates' court may adjourn the hearing on the application for a period of not more than 14 days to enable: the occupier; the person who has control of or responsibility for the premises, or any other person with an interest in the premises—to show why a Part 1A closure order should not be made.
- If the magistrates' court adjourns the hearing it may order that the Part 1A closure notice continues in effect until the end of the period of the adjournment.
- A Part 1A closure order may be made in respect of the whole or any part of the premises in respect of which the Part 1A closure notice was issued.

Practical considerations

- Reasonable steps must be taken to establish the identity of any person who lives on the premises or who has control of or responsibility for or an interest in the premises.
- The police or local authority authorized persons may enter the premises at any time to carry out essential maintenance or repairs.
- Where premises are being used in the unlawful production or supply of a Class A controlled drug, and this use is associated with the occurrence of disorder or serious nuisance to members of the public, consider issuing premises closure notices/orders under s 1 (see **5.3.2**).

 Summary   6 months

 6 months' imprisonment and/or a fine not exceeding level 5 on the standard scale.

Links to alternative subjects and offences

7.14 Vehicles Causing Annoyance

Section 59 of the Police Reform Act 2002 empowers police officers to seize motor vehicles used in a way as to cause alarm, distress, or annoyance to members of the public. The Police (Retention and Disposal of Motor Vehicles) Regulations 2002 govern how such seized vehicles should be retained and disposed of.

7.14.1 Vehicles used in a manner causing alarm, distress, or annoyance

Section 59 of the Police Reform Act 2002 concerns the use of vehicles in a manner that causes alarm, distress, or annoyance to members of the public.

Police powers

(1) Where a constable in uniform has reasonable grounds for believing that a **motor vehicle** is being used on any occasion in a manner which—
  (a) contravenes section 3 or 34 of the Road Traffic Act 1988 (careless and inconsiderate **driving** and prohibition of off-road driving), **and**
  (b) is causing, or is likely to cause, alarm, distress or annoyance to members of the public, he shall have the powers set out in subsection (3).
(2) A constable in uniform shall also have the powers set out in subsection (3) where he has reasonable grounds for believing that a motor vehicle has been used on any occasion in a manner falling within subsection (1).
(3) Those powers are—
  (a) power, if the motor vehicle is moving, to order the person driving it to stop the vehicle;
  (b) power to seize and remove the motor vehicle;
  (c) power, for the purposes of exercising a power falling within paragraph (a) or (b), to enter any **premises** on which he has reasonable grounds for believing the motor vehicle to be;
  (d) power to use reasonable force, if necessary, in the exercise of any power conferred by any of paragraphs (a) to (c).
(4) A constable shall not seize a motor vehicle in the exercise of the powers conferred on him by this section unless—
  (a) he has warned the person appearing to him to be the person whose use falls within subsection (1) that he will seize it, if that use continues or is repeated; and
  (b) it appears to him that the use has continued or been repeated after the warning.

---

(5) Subsection (4) does not require a warning to be given by a constable on any occasion on which he would otherwise have the power to seize a motor vehicle under this section if—

(a) the circumstances make it impracticable for him to give the warning;

(b) the constable has already on that occasion given a warning under that subsection in respect of any use of that motor vehicle or of another motor vehicle by that person or any other person;

(c) the constable has reasonable grounds for believing that such a warning has been given on that occasion otherwise than by him; or

(d) the constable has reasonable grounds for believing that the person whose use of that motor vehicle on that occasion would justify the seizure is a person to whom a warning under that subsection has been given (whether or not by that constable or in respect of the same vehicle or the same or a similar use) on a previous occasion in the previous twelve months.

(7) Subsection (3)(c) does not authorise entry into a **private dwelling house**.

Police Reform Act 2002, s 59

Offence

A person who fails to comply with an order under subsection (3)(a) is guilty of an offence.

Police Reform Act 2002, s 59(6)

Points to prove

✓ failed to stop
✓ a moving vehicle
✓ on the order of a police constable in uniform
✓ having reasonable grounds for believing
✓ that the vehicle was being used in a manner given in s 59(1)

Meanings

Motor vehicle

Any mechanically propelled vehicle, whether or not it is intended or adapted for use on roads (see **10.1.3**).

Driving (see **10.1.4**)

Private dwelling house

Does not include any garage or other structure occupied with the dwelling house, or any land appurtenant to the dwelling house.

Explanatory notes

- An offence is committed if the driver of the moving motor vehicle fails to stop the vehicle when ordered to do so by a constable in uniform.
- A constable in uniform has the power to seize the vehicle but only after warning the person. If, after the warning has been given, the driving continues or is repeated then the vehicle can be seized.
- The requirement to give the warning does not apply where it is impracticable to do so or where it has been given on a previous occasion in the previous 12 months.
- The powers under this section cannot be exercised unless the driver is **both** using the vehicle anti-socially **and** is driving contrary to s 3 (careless and inconsiderate driving, see **10.6.1**) or s 34 (prohibition of off-road driving, see **10.23**) of the Road Traffic Act 1988.

Practical considerations

- The warning under s 59(4) **must** be given and ignored before the vehicle can be seized (see **7.14.2**). Therefore it is important that the warning is both heard and understood.
- A warning given within the last 12 months does not have to have been given in respect of the same vehicle.
- Where a motor vehicle is seized a seizure notice must be given to the person who appears to be the owner of the vehicle.
- A previous warning given on the same occasion need not have been given by the same constable nor does it have to have been given to the same person **or** in respect of the same vehicle. It could have been given to the same person using another vehicle or to different person using the same vehicle. This covers situations where people use their vehicles anti-socially and swap them around.
- Consider the powers as to dispersal or directions to leave a public place (see **7.15**) or the public nuisance offence (see **7.13.3**).

 Summary   6 months

 A fine not exceeding level 3 on the standard scale.

7.14.2 **Retention/disposal of seized motor vehicle**

The Police (Retention and Disposal of Motor Vehicles) Regulations 2002 relate to vehicles seized under s 59 of the Police Reform Act 2002 (see **7.14.1**).

Power

A **relevant motor vehicle** shall be passed into and remain in the custody of a constable or other person authorised under this regulation by the chief officer of the police force for the area in which the vehicle was seized ('the authority') until—

(a) **the authority** permit it to be removed from their custody by a person appearing to them to be the owner of the vehicle; or

(b) it has been disposed of under these Regulations.

Police (Retention and Disposal of Motor Vehicles) Regulations 2002, reg 3(1)

Meanings

Relevant motor vehicle

As seized and removed under s 59(3)(b) of the Police Reform Act 2002 (see **7.14.1**).

The authority

Means a constable or other person authorized by the chief officer.

Explanatory notes

• A relevant motor vehicle will pass into and remain in the custody of a constable or other person authorized under this regulation by the chief officer of police in the area in which it was seized, until the authority permit a person appearing to them to be the owner of it to remove it, or it has been disposed of under these regulations.

• While the vehicle is in the custody of the authority, they must take any necessary steps for its safe keeping.

• As soon as reasonably practicable after taking a vehicle into their custody the authority must take reasonable steps to serve a seizure notice on the person who is, or appears to be, the owner, except where the vehicle has been released from their custody.

• If a person satisfies the authority that they are the owner of the vehicle and pays the charges accrued concerning its removal and retention, the authority shall permit them to remove it from custody.

• A person otherwise liable to pay charges concerning the removal and retention of the vehicle will not be liable if they were not the user when it was seized under s 59 and they did not know of its use leading to the seizure, had not consented to such use and could not, by reasonable steps, have prevented such use.

• Where it has not been possible to serve a seizure notice on the relevant person, or such a notice has been served and the vehicle has not been released from their custody under these regulations, they may dispose of the vehicle in accordance with reg 7.

• The authority may not dispose of the vehicle under reg 7—
   (a) during the period of 14 days, starting with the date of seizure;
   (b) if the 14 day period has expired, until after the deadline specified in the seizure notice;

7.14.2 Retention/Disposal of Seized Motor Vehicle

(c) if (a) or (b) does not apply, during the period of 7 working days starting with the date on which the vehicle is claimed.

- Where the authority disposes of the vehicle by way of selling, it must pay the net proceeds of the sale to any person who, within a year of the sale, satisfies them that they were the vehicle owner at the time of the sale.

Practical considerations

- A seizure notice may be served by personal delivery to the person addressed in it, by leaving it at their usual or last known address or by registered delivery to their last known address.
- If the owner is a body corporate (eg a company) the notice must be served or sent to the company secretary or clerk at its registered office.
- The seizure notice must inform the owner that they have 7 working days to collect the vehicle and that charges are payable from when the vehicle is claimed by the owner under reg 5.

Links to alternative subjects and offences

7.15 Powers to Give Directions to Leave Public Place

7.15.1 Dispersal of groups (anti-social behaviour)

Sections 30 to 32 of the Anti-social Behaviour Act 2003 provide, if the proper authority is in place, police powers to disperse groups of two or more people and return young persons under 16 years, who are unsupervised in a public place, to their residence.

Authorisation

(1) This section applies where a **relevant officer** has reasonable grounds for believing—
  (a) that any members of the public have been intimidated, harassed, alarmed or distressed as a result of the presence or behaviour of groups of two or more persons in **public places** in any locality in his police area (the 'relevant locality'), and
  (b) that **anti-social behaviour** is a significant and persistent problem in the relevant locality.

(2) The relevant officer may give an authorisation that the powers conferred on a constable in uniform by subsections (3) to (6) are to be exercisable for a period specified in the authorisation which does not exceed 6 months.

Directions

(3) Subsection (4) applies if a constable in uniform has reasonable grounds for believing that the presence or behaviour of a group of two or more persons in any public place in the relevant locality has resulted, or is likely to result, in any members of the public being intimidated, harassed, alarmed or distressed.

(4) The constable may give one or more of the following directions—
  (a) a direction requiring the persons in the group to disperse (either immediately or by such time as he may specify and in such way as he may specify),
  (b) a direction requiring any of those persons whose place of residence is not within the **relevant locality** to leave the relevant locality or any part of the relevant locality (either immediately or by such time as he may specify and in such way as he may specify), and
  (c) a direction prohibiting any of those persons whose place of residence is not within the relevant locality from returning to the relevant locality or any part of the relevant locality for such period (not exceeding 24 hours) from the giving of the direction as he may specify,
  but this subsection is subject to **subsection (5)**.

7.15.1 Dispersal of Groups (Anti-Social Behaviour)

Removal to place of residence

(6) If, between the hours of 9 pm and 6 am, a constable in uniform finds a person in any public place in the relevant locality who he has reasonable grounds for believing—
  (a) is under the age of 16, and
  (b) is not under the effective control of a parent or a responsible person aged 18 or over,

he may remove the person to the person's place of residence unless he has reasonable grounds for believing that the person would, if removed to that place, be likely to suffer significant harm.

Anti-social Behaviour Act 2003, s 30

Offence

A person who knowingly contravenes a direction given to him under s 30(4) commits an offence.

Anti-social Behaviour Act 2003, s 32(2)

Points to prove

- ✓ knowingly contravened a direction given by a constable/ PCSO
- ✓ under s 30(4) requiring you as part of a group
- ✓ to disperse immediately/by a specified time and in such specified way, **or**
- ✓ requiring you as a person not residing within the relevant locality
- ✓ to leave that locality or any part of it
- ✓ immediately/by a specified time and in such way as specified, **or**
- ✓ prohibiting you as a person not being resident within the locality
- ✓ from returning to the relevant locality or any part of it
- ✓ for such period from giving the direction as specified

Meanings

Relevant locality

Any locality in the **relevant officer's** police area.

Relevant officer

Police officer giving the authorization being superintendent or above.

Public place

Any highway and any place to which at the material time the public or any section of the public has access, on payment or otherwise, as of right or by virtue of express or implied permission.

Anti-social behaviour

Behaviour by a person which causes, or is likely to cause, harassment, alarm, or distress to one or more other persons not of the same household as the person.

Subsection (5)

A direction under s 30 may not be given to any person who is involved in an industrial dispute or a person taking part in a public procession in respect of which the appropriate notice, if required, has been given.

Explanatory notes

- The power to disperse groups **or** to return people under 16 to their place of residence applies where a relevant officer has reasonable grounds for believing that any members of the public have been intimidated, harassed, alarmed, or distressed because of the presence or behaviour of two or more people in **public places** in the relevant locality and that **anti-social behaviour** is a significant and persistent problem in the relevant locality.
- Power to give directions must be for a specified period, as given in the authorization, but cannot exceed 6 months.
- An 'authorization notice' is a notice which states the authorization has been given, specifies the relevant locality, and specifies the period during which the relevant powers are exercisable.
- The officer who gave it or another relevant officer whose police area includes the relevant locality who is of the same or higher rank than the officer who gave it may withdraw an authorization.
- Before withdrawal of an authorization, any local authority whose area includes the whole or part of the relevant locality must be consulted.
- The powers conferred on a constable in uniform by s 30 also apply to a designated PCSO, who is also empowered to require the name and address of any person who commits an offence under s 32(2) and may detain that person for 30 minutes pending the arrival of a police constable.

Related cases

R (on the application of W) v Commissioner of the Metropolitan Police & Another [2006] EWCA Civ 458, CA Children, like adults, have a right to go as they wish in public but if they misbehave within a given dispersal area they are liable to a direction from the police as are adults. However, a child can be removed to a place of residence and should be protected as far as is possible. The removal power allows the use of reasonable force, is an express power which is coercive, but is not one of arrest. Similarly it does not have a curfew effect and is not an arbitrary power to remove any unaccompanied child within a designated dispersal area at night whatever the child is doing. This power can only be used if it is reasonable to do so and must have regard to the age of the child; time of night; whether child is vulnerable or in distress; and reason for being in the area/behaviour.

R (on the application of Singh and another) v Chief Constable of West Midlands Police [2006] EWCA Civ 1118, CA Section 30 applies

7.15.1 Dispersal of Groups (Anti-Social Behaviour)

to protests, otherwise it would have been excluded by way of express provision as given in s 30(5) for industrial disputes or public processions. Furthermore, s 30 does not breach the rights contained in Articles 9, 10 and 11 (see **1.1**) but its use is subject to them.

Bucknell v DPP [2006] EWHC 1888 (Admin), QBD School pupils were simply going home from school by a reasonable route and behaving properly: does not meet requirements. Unless there are exceptional circumstances a reasonable belief must normally depend, in part, on some behaviour by the group that can be construed as being possible of causing harassment, intimidation, alarm, or distress to avoid the illegitimate intrusion into the rights of persons to go about their legitimate business.

Practical considerations

- The removal power allows the use of reasonable force, it is an express power which is coercive, but is not one of arrest.
- If the power to take a person under 16 to their residence is exercised any local authority whose area includes whole or part of the relevant locality must be informed.
- A reference to the presence or behaviour of a group of people includes a reference to the presence or behaviour of any one or more of the people in the group.
- An authorization must be in writing, signed by the relevant officer making it, specify the relevant locality, grounds on which it is given, and the period during which the powers are exercisable.
- An authorization may not be given without the consent of the local authority or each local authority whose area includes the whole or part of the relevant locality.
- Publicity must be given to an authorization by either or both of the following methods—
  - publishing an authorization notice in a newspaper circulating in the relevant locality,
  - posting an authorization notice in some conspicuous place or places within the relevant locality.
- Publicity requirements must be complied with before the period during which the powers conferred by section 30(3)–(6) are exercisable.
- A direction under s 30(4) may be given orally, to an individual or to two or more persons together and may be withdrawn or varied by the person who gave it.

 PCSO

 Summary   6 months

 3 months' imprisonment and/or a fine not exceeding level 4 on the standard scale.

7.15.2 **Directions to leave (alcohol-crime or disorder)**

Section 27 of the Violent Crime Reduction Act 2006 provides police with a power to issue directions to individuals to leave a locality in order to reduce the risk of alcohol-related crime or disorder arising and/or taking place.

Directions

(1) If the test in subsection (2) is satisfied in the case of an individual aged 16 or over who is in a **public place**, a constable in uniform may give a direction to that individual—
   (a) requiring him to leave the locality of that place; and
   (b) prohibiting the individual from returning to that locality for such period (not exceeding 48 hours) from the giving of the direction as the constable may specify.

Direction test

(2) That test is—
   (a) that the presence of the individual in that locality is likely, in all the circumstances, to cause or to contribute to the occurrence of alcohol-related crime or **disorder** in that locality, or to cause or to contribute to a repetition or continuance there of such crime or disorder; and
   (b) that the giving of a direction under this section to that individual is necessary for the purpose of removing or reducing the likelihood of there being such crime or disorder in that locality during the period for which the direction has effect or of there being a repetition or continuance in that locality during that period of such crime or disorder.

Direction requirements

(3) A direction under this section—
   (a) must be given in writing;
   (b) may require the individual to whom it is given to leave the locality in question either immediately or by such time as the constable giving the direction may specify;
   (c) must clearly identify the locality to which it relates;
   (d) must specify the period for which the individual is prohibited from returning to that locality;
   (e) may impose requirements as to the manner in which that individual leaves the locality, including his route; and
   (f) may be withdrawn or varied (but not extended so as to apply for a period of more than 48 hours) by a constable.

Restrictions

(4) A constable may not give a direction under this section that prevents the individual to whom it is given—

   (a) from having access to a place where he resides;
   (b) from attending at any place which he is required to attend for the purposes of any employment of his or of any contract of services to which he is a party;
   (c) from attending at any place which he is expected to attend during the period to which the direction applies for the purposes of education or training or for the purpose of receiving medical treatment; or
   (d) from attending at any place which he is required to attend by any obligation imposed on him by or under an enactment or by the order of a court or tribunal.
(5) A constable who gives a direction under this section must make a record of—
   (a) the terms of the direction and the locality to which it relates;
   (b) the individual to whom it is given;
   (c) the time at which it is given;
   (d) the period during which that individual is required not to return to the locality.

Violent Crime Reduction Act 2006, s 27

Offence

A person who fails to comply with a direction under this section is guilty of an offence.

Violent Crime Reduction Act 2006, s 27(6)

Points to prove
- ✓ date and location
- ✓ being a person aged 16 or over
- ✓ in a public place
- ✓ failed to comply with a direction
- ✓ given by a constable in uniform
- ✓ by failing to leave the locality or
- ✓ returned to that locality within period specified

Meanings

Public place

Highway; or any **place** to which at the material time the public or any section of the public has access, on payment or otherwise, as of right or by virtue of express or implied permission.

Place

This includes a place on a means of transport.

Disorder (see 7.2.1)

No definition is provided. Therefore, it has to be given its ordinary meaning (eg unruly or offensive behaviour).

Explanatory notes

- Section 27 has given the police an early intervention power for dealing with alcohol-related crime and disorder before a potential public order situation develops.
- A constable can issue a direction to leave to any person 16 years or over in a public place where it is believed that the presence of that person is likely to cause or contribute to the occurrence, repetition or continuance of alcohol-related crime and disorder, and that issuing such a direction is necessary to remove or reduce the likelihood in that given locality.
- The direction to leave prohibits the return of that person to that location for a period not exceeding 48 hours and must be issued in writing.
- The meaning of public place includes on a means of transport, for example, a bus or train which members of the public have access to and use.

Practical considerations

- HOC 26/2007 provides details about the s 27 power which should be used proportionately, reasonably and with discretion in circumstances where it is considered necessary to prevent the likelihood of alcohol-related crime or disorder. Detailed guidance is given on the Home Office website (see **Appendix 1**).
- Ensure that the test in s 27(2) is considered before giving a direction, in that—
  - ◆ their continued presence is likely to cause or contribute to the occurrence, repetition or continuance of alcohol-related crime or disorder in that locality; **and**
  - ◆ the giving of a direction is **necessary** for the purpose of removing, reducing or preventing a repetition or continuance in the locality during that period of such crime or disorder.
- Some examples of circumstances where issuing a direction might be appropriate are where an individual or group of individuals—
  - ◆ are in a public place causing a nuisance by being loud or troublesome or drinking alcohol and compliant but likely to continue drinking and will become drunk;
  - ◆ are disorderly on licensed premises or public transport, or to prevent them entering such premises or transport;
  - ◆ have been given a PND for an offence.
- Apart from the restrictions in s 27(4), a constable should also consider not giving a direction when it would prevent the individual from—
  - ◆ taking a child for medical treatment or to school;
  - ◆ attending their normal place of worship;
  - ◆ fulfilling any special dietary requirements.

7.15.2 Directions to Leave (Alcohol-Crime or Disorder)

- The Home Office guidance also advises—
  - implementing the shortest period to achieve the desired aim—the maximum 48 hour period should not be imposed as a matter of course;
  - confirming the age of an individual (whether they are aged 16);
  - enforcement through shift briefings, notice boards or intelligence bulletins;
  - identifying individual(s) via CCTV or other photographic evidence (eg using digital or Polaroid camera), although they must be informed when a photograph is being taken.
- Section 64A(1B)(ca) of PACE provides the power to photograph person(s) who are given a direction by a constable under s 27.

 Summary   6 months

A fine not exceeding level 4 on the standard scale.

Links to alternative subjects and offences

PND Penalty notice for disorder offences   PCSO Police community support officers

7.16 **Litter and Abandoned Vehicles**

Litter is legislated for by the Environmental Protection Act 1990 and the Litter Act 1983, whereas the Refuse Disposal (Amenity) Act 1978 concerns the removal and disposal of abandoned vehicles and other refuse.

7.16.1 **Leaving litter**

Section 87 of the Environmental Protection Act 1990 creates an offence of defacing a place by the leaving of litter.

Offences

A person is guilty of an offence if he throws down, drops or otherwise **deposits** any **litter** in any **place** to which this section applies, and leaves it.

Environmental Protection Act 1990, s 87(1)

Points to prove

✓ threw down/dropped/deposited litter
✓ in a place to which this section applies
✓ and left it there

Meanings

Deposits

Means no more than places or puts (*Felix v DPP* [1998] Crim LR 657).

Litter

Includes the discarded ends of cigarettes, cigars and like products, chewing gum, and the remains of other products designed for chewing.

Place

- Any place in the area of a **principal litter authority** that is open to the air. Land shall be treated as 'open to the air' notwithstanding that it is covered, providing it is open to the air on at least one side.
- This section does not apply to a place which is 'open to the air' if the public does not have access to it, with or without payment.

Principal litter authority

Means a county council; county borough council; district council; London borough council; Common Council of the City of London; and the Council of the Isles of Scilly.

7.16.1 Leaving Litter

Explanatory notes

- It is immaterial whether the litter is deposited on land or in water, so the offence extends to dropping or depositing litter in bodies of water such as rivers and lakes.
- Under s 88 an authorized officer of a litter authority or a suitably designated constable may, if they have reason to believe that a person has committed an offence under s 87, issue a fixed penalty notice to that person.

Defences

No offence is committed under subsection (1) above where the depositing of the litter is—

(a) authorised by law, or

(b) done with the consent of the owner, occupier or other person having control of the place where it is deposited.

Environmental Protection Act 1990, s 87(4A)

Defence notes

A person may only give consent under s 87(4A)(b) in relation to the depositing of litter in a lake or pond or watercourse if they are the owner, occupier, or other person having control of all the land adjoining that lake, pond, or watercourse and all the land through or into which water in that lake, pond, or watercourse directly or indirectly discharges, otherwise than by means of a public sewer.

Practical considerations

- The area of a local authority which is on the coast extends down to the low-water mark (s 72 of the Local Government Act 1972). Therefore, it is an offence to deposit litter on the beach.
- Consider issuing a PND (see **7.1**) for this litter offence (applies to constable only).
- If a **fixed penalty notice** is issued under s 88 by an authorized officer (suitably designated constable or PCSO) a copy of it must be sent to the relevant litter authority within 24 hours.

 Summary   6 months

 A fine not exceeding level 4 on the standard scale.

  Penalty notice for disorder offences   **PCSO** Police community support officers

7.16.2 **Removal/interference with litter bins or waste**

Section 5 of the Litter Act 1983 creates an offence in relation to the removal of, or interference with, litter bins or notice boards.

Offences

Any person who wilfully removes or otherwise interferes with any litter bin or notice board **provided** or erected under this section or section 185 of the Highways Act 1980 commits an offence.

Litter Act 1983, s 5(9)

Points to prove

✓ wilfully
✓ removed/otherwise interfered with
✓ litter bin/notice board
✓ provided under this section **or** s 185 of the Highways Act 1980

Meanings

Provided

The **litter authority** can provide and maintain litter bins for refuse or litter in any street or public place. Similarly s 185 of the Highways Act 1980 gives power to a highway authority or local authority to install/provide/maintain refuse or storage bins in streets.

Litter authority

Means, except where otherwise provided: county council; district council; London borough council; Common Council of the City of London; parish council; community council; **joint body**; Sub-Treasurer of the Inner Temple; or Under Treasurer of the Middle Temple.

Joint body

Means a joint body consisting solely of 2 or more of the above councils.

Explanatory notes

- Duties of the litter authority include emptying and cleaning the bins provided by them as well as the power to empty and clean bins provided in any street or public place by any other person. Emptying must be sufficiently frequent to ensure no litter bin or its contents become a nuisance or gives reasonable cause for complaint.
- Where such litter bins are provided the authority may erect and maintain notices/notice boards about the leaving of refuse or litter.
- A litter authority has no power under this section to place any litter bin or notice board on any land—

♦ forming part of an open space provided by or under the management and control of another litter authority or parish meeting, without the consent of that authority or meeting;

♦ not forming part of a street, without the consent of the owner and of the occupier of that land.

Practical considerations

- In addition to the penalty for this offence, the court may order a defendant to pay compensation to the litter authority concerned.
- This section also applies to receptacles provided under s 76 of the Public Health Act 1936 or s 51 of the Public Health Act 1961.
- If a bin is taken with a view to its never being recovered as opposed to a prank (eg moving round the corner) consider the offence of theft (see **3.1**). Also if appropriate, consider the offence of criminal damage (see **4.4**).
- Section 60 of the Environmental Protection Act 1990 makes it a summary offence for a person to sort over or disturb (rummage) through anything deposited in waste sites or contained in receptacles that hold household waste or commercial/industrial waste, unless they have the relevant consent or right to do so.

 Summary   6 months

 A fine not exceeding level 1 on the standard scale.

7.16.3 Unauthorized dumping/abandoned vehicles

Section 2 of the Refuse Disposal (Amenity) Act 1978 creates an offence of abandoning motor vehicles or any other thing on land in the open air.

Offences

Any person who, without lawful authority—

(a) abandons on any land in the open air, or on any other land forming part of a highway, a **motor vehicle** or any thing which formed part of a motor vehicle and was removed from it in the course of dismantling the vehicle on the land; or

(b) **abandons** on any such land any thing other than a motor vehicle, being a thing which he has brought to the land for the purpose of abandoning it there,

shall be guilty of an offence.

Refuse Disposal (Amenity) Act 1978, s 2(1)

Points to prove

✓ without lawful authority
✓ abandoned on land
✓ in the open air/forming part of a highway
✓ a motor vehicle/part of a motor; **or**
✓ an item brought to the land
✓ for the purpose of abandoning it there

Meanings

Motor vehicle

Means a mechanically propelled vehicle intended or adapted for use on roads, whether or not it is in a fit state for such use, and includes any trailer intended or adapted for use as an attachment to such a vehicle, any chassis or body, with or without wheels, appearing to have formed part of such a vehicle or trailer and anything attached to such a vehicle or trailer.

Abandoned

A person who leaves any thing on any land in such circumstances or for such a period that they may reasonably be assumed to have abandoned it or to have brought it to the land for the purpose of abandoning it there shall be deemed to have abandoned it there or, as the case may be, to have brought it to the land for that purpose unless the contrary is shown.

Explanatory notes

In addition to any penalty, the court may order the defendant to pay any costs involved in the removal and disposal of the offending article.

Practical considerations

- Removal and disposal of items under this section is the responsibility of the local authority.
- Section 2A of the Refuse Disposal (Amenity) Act 1978 gives an authorized officer of a local authority the power to issue a fixed penalty in respect of the offence of abandoning a vehicle.
- Before contacting the local authority, consider checking the motor vehicle for other offences or involvement in crime.

 Summary   6 months

 3 months' imprisonment and/or a fine not exceeding level 4 on the standard scale.

Links to alternative subjects and offences

7.17 Trespassers Residing on Land/Failing to Leave

The Criminal Justice and Public Order Act 1994 empowers police officers to direct trespassers to leave land, seize and remove motor vehicles from land, including common land. All references are to the 1994 Act unless otherwise stated

7.17.1 Power to remove trespassers from land

Section 61 empowers the senior police officer at the scene to direct two or more persons trespassing on land, intending to reside there for a period of time, to leave that land.

Directions

(1) If the senior police officer present at the scene reasonably believes that two or more persons are **trespassing** on **land** and are present there with the common purpose of residing there for any period, that reasonable steps have been taken by or on behalf of the occupier to ask them to leave and—
   (a) that any of those persons has caused **damage** to the land or to **property** on the land or used threatening, abusive or insulting words or behaviour towards the occupier, a member of his family or an employee or agent of his, or
   (b) that those persons have between them six or more **vehicles** on the land,

he may direct those persons, or any of them, to leave the land and to remove any vehicles or other property they have with them on the land.

Offences

(4) If a person knowing that a direction under subsection (1) has been given which applies to him—
   (a) fails to leave the land as soon as is reasonably practicable, or
   (b) having left again enters the land as a trespasser within the period of 3 months beginning with the day on which the direction was given,

he commits an offence.

Criminal Justice and Public Order Act 1994, s 61

Points to prove

✓ knowing a direction to leave land had been given which applied to you
✓ failed to leave the land as soon as reasonably practicable; **or**
✓ returned to the land as a trespasser within 3 months of day the direction was given

7.17.1 Power to Remove Trespassers from Land

Meanings

Land

Does not include—
- land forming part of a highway unless it is a footpath, bridleway, or byway open to all traffic or a road used as a public path, or is a restricted byway or a cycle track; or
- buildings other than agricultural buildings or scheduled monuments.

Trespass

Means (subject to the extensions effected by the references to common land), trespass as against the occupier of the land.

Property

In relation to damage to property on land, means property within the meaning of s 10(1) of the Criminal Damage Act 1971 (see **4.5**).

Damage

Includes the deposit of any substance capable of polluting the land.

Vehicle

Means any vehicle whether or not it is in a fit state for use on roads, and includes any chassis or body, with or without wheels, appearing to have formed part of such a vehicle, and any load carried by, and anything attached to, such a vehicle. It includes a touring caravan, static caravan, or mobile home.

Explanatory notes

- Before giving the direction the senior officer must reasonably believe that two or more people are trespassing on land for the common purpose of residing there AND caused **damage** to the land/property OR used threatening, abusive, or insulting words or behaviour towards the occupier/family/employee/agent, OR that the trespassers have, between them, 6 or more vehicles on the land.
- The senior officer must be satisfied that reasonable steps have been taken by or on behalf of the occupier of the land to ask them to leave and that the above criteria are met before directing the trespassers to leave the land, together with their vehicles and any other property they have with them.
- If the senior police officer believes that the people in question were not originally trespassers but have since become trespassers, they must believe that the other criteria are met after they became trespassers before directions are given.
- This section applies to common land as if references to trespassing and trespassers were references to acts or people doing acts constituting a trespass against the occupier or an infringement of the commoners' rights.

- References to 'the occupier' include any of the commoners or, where the public have access to common land, the local authority as well as a commoner.
- If there is more than one occupier a person will not trespass if they are permitted to be there by any one of the occupiers.
- 'Local authority', in relation to common land, means any local authority which has powers in relation to the land under s 9 of the Commons Registration Act 1965.
- 'Occupier' means the person entitled to possession of the land by virtue of an estate or interest held by them.
- Under s 62 a constable may seize and remove a vehicle if a direction has been given under s 61 and they reasonably suspect that a person to whom it applies has, without reasonable excuse, failed to remove a vehicle which appears to belong to them, or to be in their possession or under their control; or they have entered the land as a trespasser with a vehicle within 3 months of the direction being given.

Defences

In proceedings for an offence under this section it is a defence for the accused to show—

(a) that he was not trespassing on the land, or
(b) that he had a reasonable excuse for failing to leave the land as soon as reasonably practicable or, as the case may be, for again entering the land as a trespasser.

Criminal Justice and Public Order Act 1994, s 61(6)

Practical considerations

- If the senior police officers are of the same rank then the direction must be given by the one who has been in that rank the longest.
- Any constable at the scene, whether in uniform or not, may communicate the direction from the senior officer to the trespassers.
- There is no legal requirement to give the direction in writing, but it may negate arguments later.
- After confirmation that the occupier has asked the trespassers to leave, if the occupier has set a time limit for the offenders to leave, do not give a direction until that time has expired.
- For the purpose of this section a person may be regarded as having a purpose of residing in a place notwithstanding that he has a home elsewhere.
- If an alternative site is available then consider **7.17.2** ('**Power to remove trespassers— alternative site available**').
- The local authority has similar powers under s 77 where persons are for the time being residing in vehicle(s) within that authority's area on: land forming part of a highway; any other unoccupied land; or on any occupied land without the consent of the occupier. The authority may give them directions to leave the land and remove the vehicle(s) and any other property they have with them on the land.

Summary   6 months

 3 months' imprisonment and/or a fine not exceeding level 4 on
the standard scale.

7.17.2 Power to remove trespassers— alternative site available

Section 62A provides for the directing of trespassers to leave land when
there is an alternative site available. Section 62B creates an offence of failing to leave the land as directed or re-entering it as a trespasser within 3
months and s 62C provides a power to seize any vehicle not so removed
or taken back onto the land. Section 62D relates to common land.

Directions

(1) If the senior police officer present at a scene reasonably believes that
the conditions in subsection (2) are satisfied in relation to a person and
land, he may direct the person—
  (a) to leave the **land**;
  (b) to remove any **vehicle** and other property he has with him on the
  land.
(2) The conditions are—
  (a) that the person and one or more others (the trespassers) are
  trespassing on the land;
  (b) that the trespassers have between them at least one vehicle on the
  land;
  (c) that the trespassers are present on the land with the common
  purpose of residing there for any period;
  (d) if it appears to the officer that the person has one or more caravans
  (see subsection (6) below) in his possession or under his control on
  the land, that there is a suitable pitch on a **relevant caravan site**
  (see subsection (6) below) for that caravan or each of those caravans;
  (e) that the **occupier** of the land or a person acting on his behalf has
  asked the police to remove the trespassers from the land.

Criminal Justice and Public Order Act 1994, s 62A

Offences

A person commits an offence if he knows that a direction under s 62A(1)
has been given which applies to him and—
(a) he fails to leave the **relevant land** as soon as reasonably practicable, or
(b) he enters any land in the area of the **relevant local authority** as a
trespasser before the end of the **relevant period** with the intention of
residing there.

Criminal Justice and Public Order Act 1994, s 62B(1)

Points to prove

✓ knowing that a direction under s 62A(1) had been given
✓ which applied to you
✓ failed to leave the land as soon as reasonably practicable, **or**
✓ entered any land
✓ in the area of the relevant local authority
✓ as a trespasser
✓ before the end of the relevant period
✓ with the intention of residing there

Meanings

Relevant period

Three months starting with the day on which the direction is given.

Vehicle (see 7.17.1)

Occupier (see 7.17.1)

Relevant caravan site

Means a caravan site that is situated in the area of a **local authority** within whose area the land is situated, and managed by a **relevant site manager**.

Relevant site manager

Means a local authority within whose area the land is situated or a **registered social landlord**.

Registered social landlord

Means a body registered as a social landlord under the Housing Act 1996.

Land

Does not include buildings other than agricultural buildings or scheduled monuments.

Local authority

Means—
(a) in Greater London, a London borough, or the Common Council of the City of London;
(b) in England outside Greater London, a county council, or the Council of the Isles of Scilly;
(c) in Wales, a county council or a county borough council.

Relevant land

Means the land in respect of which a direction under s 62A(1) is given.

Relevant local authority

Means—
(a) if the relevant land is situated in the area of more than one local authority (but is not in the Isles of Scilly), the district council, or county borough council within whose area the relevant land is situated;
(b) if the relevant land is situated on the Isles of Scilly, the Council of the Isles of Scilly;

7.17.2 Power to Remove Trespassers—Alternative Site Available

(c) in any other case, the local authority within whose area the relevant land is situated.

Explanatory notes

- The senior officer present at the scene may, if they reasonably believe that certain conditions are satisfied concerning a person and land, give a direction to that person to leave the land and/or to remove any vehicle and other property they have with them on the land.
- The conditions that need to be satisfied are that—
  - one or more are trespassing on the land;
  - they have between them at least one vehicle on the land;
  - they have a common purpose of residing there for any period;
  - there is a suitable pitch on a relevant caravan site for each caravan; and
  - the land occupier/representative has asked the police to remove the trespassers from the land.
- Under s 62C a constable may seize and remove a vehicle if a direction has been given under s 62A(1) and they reasonably suspect that a person to whom it applies has, without reasonable excuse, failed to remove a vehicle which appears to belong to them, or to be in their possession or under their control; or they have entered the land of the relevant local authority as a trespasser with a vehicle before the end of the relevant period with the intention of residing there.
- Sections 62A to 62C apply to common land as if references to trespassing and trespassers were references to acts or persons doing acts constituting a trespass against the occupier or an infringement of the commoners' rights.
- References to 'the occupier' where the public has access to the land, include the local authority and any commoner or, in any other case, include the commoners or any of them.
- If there is more than one occupier a person will not trespass if they are permitted to be there by the other occupier.

Defences

In proceedings for an offence under this section it is a defence for the accused to show—

(a) that he was not trespassing on the land in respect of which he is alleged to have committed the offence, or
(b) that he had a reasonable excuse—
  (i) for failing to leave the relevant land as soon as reasonably practicable, or
  (ii) for entering land in the area of the relevant local authority as a trespasser with the intention of residing there, or
(c) that, at the time the direction was given, he was under the age of 18 years and was residing with his parent or guardian.

Criminal Justice and Public Order Act 1994, s 62B(5)

Practical considerations

- In practice liaison is made with the duty inspector and the 'relevant local authority' before any action is taken.
- A direction given by the senior officer may be communicated to the trespassers by any constable (whether in uniform or not) at the scene.
- If it is intended to give a direction under this section and it appears that the person has one or more caravans in their possession or control on the land, every local authority within whose area the land is situated must be consulted about a suitable pitch for each caravan on a relevant caravan site situated in the local authority's area.

 Summary   6 months

 3 months' imprisonment and/or a fine not exceeding level 4 on the standard scale.

Links to alternative subjects and offences

7.18 Violent Entry to Premises/ Squatters

Sections 6 and 7 of the Criminal Law Act 1977 relate to the use or threat of violence to secure entry into premises and unauthorized entry or remaining on premises in certain circumstances.

7.18.1 Violent entry to premises

Section 6 creates the offences of using or threatening violence to secure entry to premises.

Offences

Subject to the following provisions of this section, any person who, without lawful authority, uses or threatens violence for the purpose of securing entry into any **premises** for himself or for any other person is guilty of an offence, provided that—
(a) there is someone present on those premises at the time who is opposed to the entry which the violence is intended to secure; and
(b) the person using or threatening the violence knows that that is the case.

Criminal Law Act 1977, s 6(1)

Points to prove

✓ without lawful authority
✓ used/threatened violence
✓ to secure entry to premises
✓ knowing someone present on the premises opposed entry

Meanings

Premises

Any building, part of a building under separate occupation (eg flat), land ancillary to a building, and the site comprising any building(s) together with any land ancillary thereto.

Subject to the following provisions of this section

Section 6(1) does not apply to a **displaced residential occupier** or a **protected intending occupier** of the relevant premises or a person acting on behalf of such an occupier. If the defendant produces sufficient evidence that they are, or were acting on behalf of, such an occupier they will be presumed to be so unless the prosecution prove the contrary.

Displaced residential occupier

Subject to the following **exception**, any person who was occupying any premises as a residence immediately before being excluded from occupation by anyone who entered those premises, or any **access** to those premises, as a **trespasser** is a displaced residential occupier of the premises so long as they continue to be excluded from occupation of the premises by the original trespasser or by any subsequent trespasser.

Exception

A person who was occupying the relevant premises as a trespasser immediately before being excluded from occupation shall not be a displaced residential occupier of the premises.

Access

Means, in relation to any premises, any part of any site or building within which those premises are situated that constitutes an ordinary means of access to those premises (whether or not that is its sole or primary use).

Trespasser

Someone who wrongfully enters onto someone else's premises.

Protected intending occupier

This is extensively defined in s 12A, but, in brief, means someone who has made a formal declaration to a commissioner of oaths that they were due to move into the affected premises.

Explanatory notes

- Anyone who enters, or is on or in occupation of, any premises under a title derived from a trespasser or by a licence or consent given by a trespasser or by a person deriving title from a trespasser will themselves be treated as a trespasser (whether or not they would be a trespasser apart from this provision).
- The fact that a person has an interest in, or right to possession or occupation of, the premises does not, for s 6(1) constitute lawful authority for the use or threat of violence by them or anyone else to secure entry into those premises.

Practical considerations

- It is immaterial whether the violence is directed against a person or property and whether the violent entry is to acquire possession of the premises.
- A person who, by virtue of the definition of 'displaced residential occupier', is a displaced residential occupier of any premises is also deemed a displaced residential occupier of any access to those premises.
- A person on premises as a trespasser does not cease to be a trespasser under this legislation by being allowed time to leave there, nor does a person cease to be a displaced residential occupier of any premises because of any such allowance of time to a trespasser.

- Proceed with care where squatting appears to have lasted for a long time. It is possible for a squatter (someone who possesses premises without the lawful consent of the owner) to gain legal title if they have held the property for 12 years adversely but without disturbance or legal attempts to repossess it.

 Summary   6 months

 6 months' imprisonment and/or a fine not exceeding level 5 on the standard scale.

7.18.2 **Adverse occupation of residential premises**

Section 7 creates an offence of failing to leave residential premises once the lawful occupiers have gained legitimate entry.

Offences

Subject to the provisions of this section and s 12A(9), any person who is on any **premises** as a **trespasser** after having entered as such is guilty of an offence if he fails to leave those premises on being required to do so by or on behalf of—

(a) a **displaced residential occupier** of the premises; or

(b) an individual who is a **protected intending occupier** of the premises.

Criminal Law Act 1977, s 7(1)

Points to prove

✓ on premises
✓ as a trespasser
✓ having entered as such
✓ failed to leave when required
✓ by/on behalf of a displaced residential occupier/protected intending occupier

Meanings

Premises (see 7.18.1)

Trespasser (see 7.18.1)

Displaced residential occupier (see 7.18.1)

Protected intending occupier (see 7.18.1)

Explanatory notes

A reference to any premises includes a reference to any access to them, whether or not the access itself constitutes premises.

Defences

7(2) It is a defence for the accused to prove that he believed that the person requiring him to leave the premises was not a displaced residential occupier or protected intending occupier of the premises or a person acting on their behalf.

7(3) In proceedings for an offence under this section it is a defence for the accused to prove that—
  (a) the premises in question are, or form part of, premises used mainly for residential purposes; and
  (b) he was not on any part of the premises used wholly or mainly for residential purposes.

12A(9) In proceedings for an offence under s 7 where the accused was requested to leave the premises by a person claiming to be or to act on behalf of a protected intending occupier of the premises—
  (a) it shall be a defence for the accused to prove that, although asked to do so by the accused at the time the accused was requested to leave, that person failed at that time to produce to the accused such a statement as is referred to in s 12A(2)(d) or s 12A(4)(d) or such a certificate as is referred to in s 12A(6)(d); and
  (b) any document purporting to be a document under 12A(6)(d) will be received in evidence and, unless the contrary is proved, will be determined to have been issued by or on behalf of the authority stated in the certificate.

Criminal Law Act 1977, ss 7 and 12A

Practical considerations

- Officers wishing to apply these provisions in an operational situation should make themselves conversant with the terms—displaced residential occupier, squatters and protected intending occupier (see **7.18.1**).
- A displaced residential occupier or a protected intending occupier (once they have completed the formalities) can use force (either personally or by others on their behalf) to break into the premises to regain possession. They can also demand that the premises be vacated and s 7 makes it an offence (subject to any defences) for the trespassers to remain.
- If the squatter is being evicted by a protected intending occupier (this does not apply to an eviction by a displaced residential occupier) then they are entitled to see a copy of the statement or certificate which must be held by the person making the eviction. They have a statutory defence if the certificate is not produced.

7.18.2 Adverse Occupation of Residential Premises

 Summary   6 months

 6 months' imprisonment and/or a fine not exceeding level 5 on the standard scale.

Links to alternative subjects and offences

Chapter 8

Firearms, Fireworks, and Weapons

8.1 'Section 1 Firearms' Offences

The Firearms Act 1968 provides various offences connected with firearms, air weapons, shotguns, and associated ammunition.

8.1.1 Possessing s 1 firearm/ammunition without certificate

This offence involves being in possession of a firearm/ammunition without a valid firearm certificate. Any weapon or ammunition applicable to this section is commonly known as a 'section 1 firearm/ammunition'.

Offences

Subject to any **exemption** under this Act, it is an offence for a person—

(a) to have in his **possession**, or to **purchase** or **acquire**, a **firearm to which this section applies** without holding a **firearm certificate** in force at the time, or otherwise than as authorised by such a certificate;

(b) to have in his possession, or to purchase or acquire, any **ammunition to which this section applies** without holding a firearm certificate in force at the time, or otherwise than as authorised by such a certificate, or in quantities in excess of those so authorised.

Firearms Act 1968, s 1(1)

Points to prove

✓ Date and location
✓ possessed/purchased/acquired
✓ a s 1 firearm/ammunition

8.1.1 Possessing s 1 Firearm/Ammunition without Certificate

> ✓ without/not authorized by/in quantities exceeding those
>   authorized by
> ✓ a firearms certificate

Meanings

Exemptions

This includes: antique firearms; rifles loaned on private land; carriers, auctioneers and warehousemen; crown servants; police; armed forces; athletics and other approved activities; museums; police permits; registered firearms dealers; rifle and pistol clubs; ship and aircraft equipment; licensed slaughterers; theatres and cinemas; Northern Ireland firearms certificate holder; visiting forces; visitors' permits.

Possession

This has a wide meaning. The term has two distinct elements—
- The mental element: whereby the defendant must know of the existence of the firearm, but cannot claim ignorance that it was technically 'a firearm'.
- The practical element: this term is broader than actual physical possession; a person can 'possess' a firearm in a house or premises under their control, even though they are not at the premises. Similarly, the same firearm could be 'possessed' by two people at the same time, such as the firearm's lawful owner and also its custodian who keeps the firearm at his home (see **5.2.1** notes on 'constructive possession' in relation to drugs).

Purchase

This is not defined and should be given its natural meaning.

Acquire

Means hire, accept as a gift or borrow.

Firearm to which s 1 applies

This section applies to every **firearm** except—
- normal shotguns (see **8.2.1** for description);
- normal air weapons (see **8.7.2** for description).

Firearm

Means a **lethal barrelled weapon** of any description from which any **shot, bullet or other missile** can be discharged and includes—
- any **prohibited weapon**, whether it is such a lethal weapon as aforesaid or not; **and**
- any **component part** of such a lethal or prohibited weapon; and
- any **accessory** to any such weapon designed or adapted to diminish the noise or flash caused by firing the weapon;

but excludes component parts of, and accessories for, a shotgun or air weapon (being firearms excluded by s 1).

Lethal barrelled weapon

This is not defined although the courts have determined that the weapon must be capable of causing injury from which death may result. This also includes a weapon not designed to kill or inflict injury but capable of doing so if misused (such as a signal pistol or a flare launcher).

Shot, bullet, or other missile

These terms are not defined and should be given their natural meaning—

- 'Shot' usually means round pellets.
- 'Bullet' is normally discharged from a weapon with a rifled barrel.
- 'Missile' is a more general term—darts and pellets have been held to be missiles.

Prohibited werapons

- Prohibited weapons require an authority from the Secretary of State and are listed under s 5, being weapons such as: machine gun, self-loading or pump-action rifled gun (other than a 0.22 rifle), rocket launcher, CS spray, electric stun gun (applying contacts directly to the body), electroshock weapon (uses Electro-Muscular Disruption technology where an electrical current is sent through probes to achieve incapacitation), air weapon with self-contained gas cartridge system, grenade, any weapon of whatever description designed or adapted for the discharge of any noxious liquid, gas, or other thing.
- This written authority will have conditions imposed so as not to endanger the public safety or the peace.
- A person commits an offence under s 5 if, without an authority from the Secretary of State, they possess, purchase, acquire, manufacture, sell, or transfer any prohibited weapon.
- Failure to comply with any condition imposed by this authority is an offence under s 5(5).
- The Secretary of State may revoke an authority by notice in writing. Failure to return the authority within 21 days is an offence under s 5(6).

Component part

Means any working part of the mechanism of a lethal weapon. This will include the trigger but not the trigger guard, for example.

Accessory

This is given its natural meaning, and includes such accessories as a silencer or flash eliminator.

Firearm certificate

Means a certificate granted by a chief officer of police in respect of any firearm or ammunition to which s 1 applies.

Ammunition to which s 1 applies

This section applies to any ammunition for a firearm, except the following articles, namely—

- cartridges containing 5 or more shot, none of which exceeds 0.36 inch in diameter;

- ammunition for an air gun, air rifle, or air pistol; and
- blank cartridges not more than one inch in diameter.

Ammunition

Means ammunition [*being any shot, bullet, or other missile*] for any firearm and includes grenades, bombs, and other like missiles, whether capable of use with a firearm or not, and also includes prohibited ammunition.

Explanatory notes

- This is an absolute offence so no intent is required, only knowledge of the existence of the item, as opposed to its nature.
- A telescopic laser/night sight is **not** a component part or accessory that requires a firearm certificate.
- Whether a silencer or flash eliminator can be an accessory will be a question of fact to be determined in all the circumstances. For instance, if it could be used with the particular firearm and whether the defendant had it with them for that purpose. It is the accessory that must be 'so designed or adapted' not the weapon.
- Blank cartridges are cases with primer (small explosive charge at the end of the cartridge) and gunpowder; or primed cartridges (as blank but without the gunpowder) both able to be used in a firearm and producing an explosive effect when fired.
- It is a summary offence under s 35 of the Violent Crime Reduction Act 2006 for a person to sell or purchase a cap-type primer designed for use in metallic ammunition for a firearm being either—
  - ◆ a primer to which this section applies,
  - ◆ an empty cartridge case incorporating such a primer unless that person: is a registered firearms dealer; it is their trade or business; produces a certificate authorizing possession; is in Her Majesty's Services entitled to do so; or shows that they are entitled by virtue of any enactment.
- Blank cartridges greater than one inch in diameter are s 1 ammunition.
- The diameter of a cartridge is obtained by measuring immediately in front of the cannelure or rim of its base.

Defence

There is no statutory defence as it is an absolute offence.

Related cases

Flack v Baldry [1988] 1 All ER 673, HL A hand held 'stun gun' with two prongs and designed to discharge 46,000 volts of electricity into a victim's body was held to be a prohibited weapon under s 5(1)(b) being 'a weapon designed or adapted for the discharge of any noxious liquid, gas or other thing'. Emission of electricity from the device to stun a victim was a 'discharge of other thing'.

R v Deyemi and another [2007] All ER 369, CA Defendants were in possession of an electrical stun gun which discharged electricity through electrodes. In it were a lens and a bulb. The defendants believed that it was a torch, but it was in fact a s 5(1)(b) prohibited weapon. Held: that s 5 imposed an absolute offence, the prosecution merely had to prove possession and was a s 5 prohibited firearm.

Moore v Gooderham [1960] 3 All ER 575, QBD A lethal barrelled weapon must be capable of causing injury from which death may result.

Read v Donovan [1947] 1 All ER 37 A lethal barrelled weapon includes a weapon not designed to kill or inflict injury. It also includes one that is capable of doing so if misused (signal pistol).

R v Singh [1989] Crim LR 724 A lethal barrelled weapon can also include a flare launcher.

Grace v DPP The Times, 9 December 1988, QBD Evidence that the firearm can be fired is required from the prosecution to prove that it is a lethal barrelled weapon.

Price v DPP [1996] 7 CL 49 The defendant had someone else's rucksack containing s 1 ammunition. Although unaware of the contents of the rucksack, the offence was still committed.

Sullivan v Earl of Caithness [1976] 1 All ER 844, QBD Possession does not have to be physical possession.

R v Stubbings [1990] Crim LR 811, CA Primer cartridges are ammunition.

Watson v Herman [1952] 2 All ER 70 A telescopic laser/night sight is not a component part or accessory.

R v Buckfield [1998] Crim LR 673 A silencer designed for a different weapon does not prevent it from being an accessory to a firearm if it could be used as such and the defendant had it for that purpose.

Practical considerations

- The prosecution need only prove knowledge of the existence of the item, as opposed to its nature. Similarly, there is no onus to prove that the defendant knew that the article was a firearm.
- In practice, the Forensic Science Laboratory will examine weapons and say whether or not they are lethal. The main characteristic that is measured is the muzzle velocity (the speed at which the projectile leaves the barrel).
- Certain imitation or replica firearms maybe a s 1 firearm (see **8.1.4**).
- A s 1 firearm can only be possessed by a firearms certificate holder or some other lawful authority such as a registered firearms dealer, member of the armed forces, or police officer.

- If someone had a silencer in their possession with no evidence linking it to a suitable weapon, possession alone is unlikely to be an offence.
- All repeating shotguns holding more than two cartridges (eg pump-action and revolver shotguns) are 'section 1 firearms'.

 Either way   None

 Summary: 6 months' imprisonment and/or a fine not exceeding the statutory maximum.

Indictment: 5 years' imprisonment and/or a fine.

8.1.2 **Aggravated section 1 offences/ registered firearms dealers**

The offences of possessing, purchasing, or acquiring a s 1 firearm carry a greater punishment if they are aggravated by the shotgun barrel being less than 24 inches (creating a 'sawn-off' shotgun) or illegally converting anything having the appearance of a firearm into a s 1 firearm.

Offences

(1) Subject to this section [see *'Defence'*], it is an offence to shorten the barrel of a shot gun to a length less than 24 inches.

(3) It is an offence for a person other than **a registered firearms dealer** to convert into a firearm anything, which though having the appearance of being a firearm, is so constructed as to be incapable of discharging any missile through its barrel.

(4) A person who commits an offence under section 1 of this Act by having in his possession, or purchasing or acquiring, a shot gun which has been shortened contrary to subsection (1) above or a firearm which has been converted as mentioned in subsection (3) above (whether by a registered firearms dealer or not), without holding a firearm certificate authorising him to have it in his possession, or to purchase or acquire it, shall be treated for the purposes of provisions of this Act relating to the punishment of offences as committing that offence in an aggravated form.

Firearms Act 1968, s 4

Points to prove

✓ date and location
✓ possessed/purchased/acquired
✓ a shortened shotgun barrel (to length less than 24 inches) or a
  thing converted into a firearm
✓ without holding/not authorized by
✓ a firearm certificate

Meanings

Registered

In relation to a **firearms dealer**, means registered under s 33 of this Act, and references to 'the register', 'registration' and a 'certificate of registration' shall be construed accordingly, except in s 40.

Firearms dealer

Means a person who, by way of trade or business—
• manufactures, sells, transfers, repairs, tests, or proves firearms or ammunition to which s 1 of this Act applies or shotguns; or
• sells or transfers air weapons.

Explanatory notes

• This offence could apply to weapons such as starting pistols or imitation firearms which have been converted to a s 1 firearms.
• A shotgun which has a barrel shortened to less than 24 inches becomes a s 1 firearm. The length of the barrel is determined by measuring from the muzzle to the point at which the charge is exploded on firing the cartridge.

Defence

It is not an offence under subsection (1) above for a **registered firearms dealer** to shorten the barrel of a shotgun for the sole purpose of replacing a defective part of the barrel so as to produce a barrel not less than 24 inches in length.

Firearms Act 1968, s 4(2)

Practical considerations

• Section 3(1) makes it an offence, if by way of trade or business, a person—
  ♦ manufactures, sells, transfers, repairs, tests, or proves any firearm or ammunition to which s 1 of this Act applies, or a shotgun;
  ♦ exposes for sale or transfer, or has in his possession for sale, transfer, repair, test, or proof any such firearm or ammunition, or a shotgun; or

♦ sells or transfers an air weapon, exposes such a weapon for sale or
transfer, or has such a weapon in his possession for sale or transfer;
without being registered under this Act as a firearms dealer.

- The s 3 offence is triable either way and carries the same penalties as
the s 1(1) offence above (see **8.1.1**).
- Section 31 of the Violent Crime Act 2006 added the sale and transfer
of air weapons to s 3(1) and required dealers, under s 40(2), to keep a
register of transactions involving air weapons.
- Consider confiscation of cash and property for the s 3(1) offence of
dealing in firearms or ammunition by way of trade or business without being registered as a firearms dealer. This is given as a 'criminal
lifestyle' offence under Sch 2 of the Proceeds of Crime Act 2002 (see **5.6**
for details).
- Section 32 of the Violent Crime Act 2006 makes it a summary offence
(6 months' imprisonment and/or a fine not exceeding level 5) to sell
air weapons by way of trade or business other than face-to-face to an
individual who is not a registered firearms dealer. This allows an air
weapon to be sent from one registered firearms dealer to another to
make the final transfer in person to the buyer. Guidance is given on ss
31 and 32 in HOC 31/2007.

 Either way   None

 Summary: 6 months' imprisonment and/or a fine not exceeding
the statutory maximum.

Indictment: 7 years' imprisonment and/or a fine.

8.1.3 **Restrictions on s 1 firearms/ ammunition to under 14 years**

Sections 22(2) and 24(2) of the Firearms Act 1968 place tight restrictions
on persons under the age of 14 years from possessing, receiving as gifts or
on loan any s 1 firearm/ammunition.

Offences

Possession by under 14

It is an offence for a person under the age of 14 to have in his **possession** any
firearm or ammunition to which **section 1** of this Act or **section 15** of the
Firearms (Amendment) Act 1988 applies, except where under section 11(1),
(3) or (4) of this Act he is entitled to have possession of it without holding a
firearm certificate.

Firearms Act 1968, s 22(2)

414   Stop, search, and
seize powers   Entry and search
powers

> **Make gift, lend, or part with possession to under 14**
>
> It is an offence—
> (a) to make a gift of or lend any firearm or ammunition to which section 1 of this Act applies to a person under the age of 14; or
> (b) to part with the possession of any such firearm or ammunition to a person under that age, except in circumstances where that person is entitled under section 11(1), (3) or (4) of this Act or section 15 of the Firearms (Amendment) Act 1988 to have possession thereof without holding a firearm certificate.
>
> Firearms Act 1968, s 24(2)

Points to prove

Possess by under 14

- ✓ date and location
- ✓ being a person under the age of 14 years
- ✓ possessed
- ✓ any s 1 firearm or ammunition

Make gift/lend/part possession to under 14

- ✓ date and location
- ✓ make a gift/lend/part with possession
- ✓ a s 1 firearm or ammunition
- ✓ to a person under the age of 14 years

Meanings

Possession

This has a wide meaning (see **8.1.1**)

Section 1 firearm or ammunition (see **8.1.1**)

Section 15 of the Firearms (Amendment) Act 1988

This provides the mechanism for the creation of approved rifle and **muzzle loading pistol** clubs where members can, if they wish, use such weapons without being the holder of a firearm certificate.

Muzzle loading pistol

Means a pistol designed to be loaded at the muzzle end of the barrel or chambered with a loose charge (such as gun powder) and a separate ball (or other missile).

Explanatory notes

- These restrictions are in addition to those imposed on persons under 18, 17, and 15 years of age.

- Both offences can be committed anywhere and not just in a public place.
- The 1968 Act s 11 exceptions, applicable to both offences are—
  - carrying a firearm or ammunition belonging to a certificate holder under instructions from, and for the use of, that person for sporting purposes only;
  - a person conducting or carrying on a miniature rifle range (whether for a rifle club or otherwise) or shooting gallery at which no firearms are used other than air weapons or miniature rifles not exceeding .23 inch calibre, may possess, purchase, or acquire, such miniature rifles and ammunition suitable for that purpose; and
  - any person using such rifles/ammunition at such a range or gallery.
- Any firearm or ammunition found on a person for these offences may be confiscated by the court.

Defences

Both offences— the s 11 exceptions (see 'Explanatory notes' above) may apply.

Section 24(2) offence—under s 24(5) having reasonable grounds to believe that the person was 14 years of age or over (see **8.7.1**).

Related cases

Morton v Chaney [1960] 3 All ER 632 Shooting rats has been held not to be for sporting purposes.

 Summary

 48 months (Consent of DPP required after 6 months)

 6 months' imprisonment and/or a fine not exceeding level 5 on the standard scale.

8.1.4 **Imitation/replica firearm—convertible to s 1 firearm**

Section 1 of the Firearms Act 1982 came into force to control imitation firearms that were readily convertible to become a working s 1 firearm.

Offences

This Act applies to an **imitation** firearm if it—
(a) has the appearance of being a **firearm** to which **section 1** of the 1968 Act (firearms requiring a **certificate**) applies; and
(b) is so constructed or adapted as to be **readily convertible into a firearm** to which that section applies.

Firearms Act 1982, s 1(1)

Points to prove

✓ date and location
✓ possessed/purchased/acquired
✓ an imitation firearm
✓ having the appearance of a section 1 firearm **and**
✓ is constructed/adapted so as to be readily converted into a s 1 firearm
✓ without holding
✓ a firearms certificate

Meanings

Imitation firearm (see **8.3.3**)

Section 1 firearm (see **8.1.1**)

Certificate (see **8.1.1**)

Readily convertible into a firearm

Section 1(6) states that an imitation firearm shall be regarded as readily convertible into a firearm to which section 1 of the 1968 Act applies if—
(a) it can be so converted without any special skill on the part of the person converting it in the construction or adaptation of firearms of any description; and
(b) the work involved in converting it does not require equipment or tools other than such as are in common use by persons carrying out works of construction and maintenance in their own homes.

Explanatory notes

- A readily convertible imitation firearm that can be turned into a s 1 firearm will require a firearms certificate.
- The Firearms Act 1982, s 1 was enacted because some 'replica' weapons could be converted into s 1 working firearms with no specialist skill/tools.
- Excepting s 4(3) and (4), ss 16 to 20 and s 47 of the 1968 Act shall apply in relation to an imitation firearm to which this Act applies as it applies to a 's 1 firearm'.

8.1.5 Failing to Comply with Firearm Certificate Conditions

- Apart from excepted air weapons, component parts, and accessories, any expression given a meaning for the purposes of the 1968 Act has the same meaning in this Act.

Defence

It shall be a defence for the accused to show that he did not know and had no reason to suspect that the imitation firearm was so constructed or adapted as to be readily convertible into a firearm to which s 1 of that Act applies.

Firearms Act 1982, s 1(5)

Related cases

R v Howells [1977] 3 All ER 417, CA The defendant believed he had an antique gun (thereby falling within an agreed Home Office exemption) but it was in fact a replica, a s 1 firearm. The offence was still committed as it is one of strict liability.

Cafferata v Wilson [1936] 3 All ER 149, KBD A solid barrel that can be readily converted/adapted to fire missiles by boring the barrel may be a component part of a firearm.

 Either way   None

 Summary: 6 months' imprisonment and/or a fine not exceeding the statutory maximum.

Indictment: 5 years' imprisonment and/or a fine.

Aggravated offence (see **8.1.2**): 7 years' imprisonment and/or a fine.

8.1.5 **Failing to comply with firearm certificate conditions**

Offence

It is an offence for a person to fail to comply with a condition subject to which a firearm certificate is held by him.

Firearms Act 1968, s 1(2)

Points to prove

- ✓ date and location
- ✓ failed to comply with condition
- ✓ subject to which firearm certificate is held

Meaning of firearm certificate (see 8.1.1)

Explanatory notes

- Section 27(2) of the 1968 Act stipulates that a firearm certificate shall be in the prescribed form and shall specify the conditions subject to which it is held. The general conditions which should be imposed are set out in the Firearms Rules 1998 (SI 1998/1941).
- A statutory condition under the Firearms (Amendment) Act 1988, s 14 also imposes a duty on auctioneers, carriers, or warehousemen to take reasonable care of the custody of firearms and/or ammunition which they have in their possession without holding a certificate; being an offence if they fail to keep them in safe custody or fail to notify any loss or theft forthwith to the police.

Related cases

Hall v Cotton [1976] 3 WLR 681, QBD The owner/certificate holder is 'in possession' of the firearms even though they do not have physical control. Similarly, a custodial keeper of the guns has possession requiring a certificate.

R v Chelmsford Crown Court, ex parte Farrer [2000] 1 WLR 1468, CA Family members had knowledge of where the key to the gun cabinet was kept and so could gain access to the weapons. The Chief Constable was right to refuse certificate renewal on the grounds of a breach of the condition to prevent, so far as is reasonably practicable, access to the guns by an unauthorized person.

 Summary   48 months

 6 months' imprisonment and/or a fine not exceeding level 5 on the standard scale.

Links to alternative subjects and offences

8.1.5 Failing to Comply with Firearm Certificate Conditions

8.2 **Shotgun Offences**

The Firearms Act 1968 provides various offences connected with fire-arms, associated ammunition, air weapons, and shotguns.

8.2.1 **Shotgun without a certificate**

Section 2 of the Firearms Act 1968 creates the offence of possess, purchase, or acquire a shotgun when not being the holder of a relevant certificate.

> **Offences**
>
> Subject to any **exemption** under this Act, it is an offence for a person to have in his **possession** or to **purchase** or **acquire** a **shotgun** without holding a **certificate** under this Act authorising him to possess shotguns.
>
> Firearms Act 1968, s 2(1)

Points to prove
- ✓ date and location
- ✓ possessed/purchased/acquired
- ✓ a shotgun
- ✓ without a certificate

Meanings

Exemptions (see **8.1.1**)

Possession (see **8.1.1**)

Purchase (see **8.1.1**)

Acquire (see **8.1.1**)

Shotgun

Means a smooth-bore gun (not being an air gun), which—

- has a barrel not les s than 24 inches in length and does not have any barrel with a bore exceeding 2 inches in diameter;
- either has no magazine or has a non-detachable magazine incapable of holding more than 2 cartridges; **and**
- is not a **revolver** gun.

Revolver

In relation to a smooth-bore gun, means a gun containing a series of chambers which revolve when the gun is fired.

8.2.1 Shotgun without a Certificate

Shotgun certificate

Means a certificate granted by a chief officer of police under this Act authorizing a person to possess shotguns.

Explanatory notes

- The length of the barrel of a firearm is measured from the muzzle to the point at which the charge is exploded on firing and, in the case of a shotgun that length must not be less than 24 inches, otherwise it becomes a s 1 firearm (see **8.1.2**).
- Some antique shotguns may be classed as an 'antique firearm' and thus be exempt from shotgun offences. However, if 'modern' cartridges can be bought and fired using an antique shotgun it cannot be exempt. This exemption does not cover a modern replica of an antique weapon.
- An auctioneer cannot sell shotguns without either being a registered firearms dealer or obtaining a police permit.
- A person may, without holding a shotgun certificate, borrow a shotgun from the occupier of private premises and use it on that land in the occupier's presence (s 11(5)).
- Similarly, (without holding a shotgun certificate) a person may use a shotgun at a time and place approved for shooting at artificial targets by the chief officer of police for the area in which the place is situated (s 11(6)).

Related cases

Watts v Seymour [1967] 1 All ER 1044, QBD The test as to when a purchase/sale was complete was if the purchaser could validly sell and transfer title to the weapon to another person.

R v Howells [1977] 3 All ER 417 A modern reproduction is not an antique.

Richards v Curwen [1977] 3 All ER 426, QBD Whether a firearm is an 'antique' is a matter of fact for justices to decide in each case.

Hall v Cotton [1976] 3 WLR 681, QBD The owner/certificate holder remained in possession of their shotguns despite having no physical control. Similarly, the custodial keeper of the shotguns also has possession and therefore requires a certificate.

Practical considerations

- All repeating shotguns holding more than two cartridges (eg pump-action and revolver shotguns) are s 1 firearms.
- Offences may be committed in relation to persons under 15 years where they have an assembled shotgun with them or for them to be given a gift of a shotgun/ammunition (see **8.2.2**).

- Any offence involving a shotgun that has an illegally shortened barrel (less than 24 inches), thus creating a 'sawn-off' shotgun, will be an 'aggravated offence' (see **8.1.2**) carrying a greater penalty. It will also make the shotgun a s 1 firearm.
- A shotgun is deemed to be loaded if there is a cartridge in the barrel or approved magazine that can feed the cartridge into the barrel by manual or automatic means.
- A shotgun adapted to have a magazine must bear a mark on the magazine showing approval by the Secretary of State.
- 'Shotgun' includes any component part and any accessory for a shotgun designed or adapted to diminish the noise or flash caused by firing the gun.

 Either way   None

 Summary: 6 months' imprisonment and/or a fine not exceeding the statutory maximum.

Indictment: 5 years' imprisonment and/or a fine.

8.2.2 **Shotgun restrictions to under 15 years**

Sections 22 and 24 of the Firearms Act 1968 impose shotgun restrictions relating to persons under 15.

Offences

Under 15 have with them

It is an offence for a person under the age of 15 to have **with him** an assembled **shot gun**, except while under the supervision of a person of or over the age of 21, or while the shot gun is so covered with a securely fastened gun cover that it cannot be fired.

Firearms Act 1968, s 22(3)

Make gift to under 15

It is an offence to make a gift of a shot gun or ammunition for a shot gun to a person under the age of 15.

Firearms Act 1968, s 24(3)

8.2.2 Shotgun Restrictions to under 15 years

Points to prove

Under 15 have with them

✓ date and location
✓ person under 15
✓ had with them
✓ assembled shotgun

Make gift to under 15

✓ date and location
✓ made a gift of
✓ shotgun/ammunition for a shotgun
✓ to a person under 15

Meanings

With him (see **8.3.6**)

Shotgun (see **8.2.1**)

Defence

A statutory defence is available, but only to the s 24 offence (see **8.7.1**).

Practical considerations

- Unless exempted, or s 11(5) and (6) applies (see **8.2.1**) the person concerned must also be the holder of a shotgun certificate before they can possess, purchase, or acquire a shotgun.
- Offences in relation to air weapons are imposed on persons under 17/18 years (see **8.7.1** and **8.7.2**).
- Both ss 22(3) and 24(3) offences can be committed anywhere and not just in a public place.
- A court can order the destruction of any shotgun and ammunition to which this offence relates.
- Restrictions also apply to persons under 14 years in relation to s 1 firearms (see **8.1.3**).

 Summary   6 months

 A fine not exceeding level 3 on the standard scale.

8.2.3 **Fail to comply with shotgun certificate conditions**

Section 2 of the Firearms Act 1968 creates an offence of failing to comply with a condition imposed by a shotgun certificate.

Offence

It is an offence for a person to fail to comply with a condition subject to which a **shotgun certificate** is held by him.

Firearms Act 1968, s 2(2)

Points to prove
✓ date and location
✓ failed to comply with condition
✓ subject to which shotgun certificate is held

Meaning of shotgun certificate (see **8.2.1**)

Practical considerations

- Regarding public safety, the two main conditions applying to shotgun certificate holders are the failure to keep the shotgun(s) and/or cartridges in safe custody or in failing to notify any loss forthwith to the police.
- A chief officer of police has to be satisfied that the applicant can be permitted to possess a shotgun without danger to the public safety or to the peace.
- Section 28(1A) states that no certificate shall be granted or renewed if the chief officer of police has reason to believe that the applicant is prohibited from possessing a shotgun; **or** does not have a good reason for possessing, purchasing, or acquiring one.
- It is an offence, under s 28A(7), to knowingly or recklessly make a false statement for the purpose of procuring the grant or renewal of a certificate.
- There is a presumption in favour of granting unless the police can prove any of the exemptions.
- The certificate must contain a description of the weapon including any identity numbers.

 Summary   48 months

 6 months' imprisonment and/or a fine not exceeding level 5 on the standard scale.

Links to alternative subjects and offences

8.3 Criminal Use of Firearms

There is a raft of legislation which has been put in place to try and curb possession of firearms by criminals: some of these measures are discussed below.

8.3.1 Ban on possession by convicted person

Section 21 of the Firearms Act 1968 creates an offence for the possession of any firearm or ammunition by convicted criminals. The section first provides three types of ban: total; 5 years from date of release; while under a licence, order, or binding over condition.

Lengths of ban

Total ban—s 21(1)

Anyone sentenced to custody for life or preventive detention or corrective training for a term of 3 years or more or to youth custody or detention in a young offender institution for such a term, shall not **at any time** have a firearm or ammunition in his possession.

5 years—s 21(2)

A person who has been sentenced to imprisonment for a term of 3 months or more but less than 3 years or to youth custody or detention in a young offender institution for such a term, or who has been subject to a secure training order or a detention and training order, shall not at any time before the expiration of the period of 5 years from the **date of release** have a firearm or ammunition in their possession.

Other bans

- s 21(2B) intermittent custody order—during any licence period specified.
- s 21(3) following persons shall not have a firearm or ammunition in their possession—
    (a) whilst discharged on licence, being holder of licence, issued for detention of children and young persons convicted of serious crime;
    (b) whilst subject of recognizance to keep peace or be of good behaviour or community order with a condition not to possess, use, or carry a firearm.

8.3.1 Ban on Possession by Convicted Person

Offences

Possess whilst banned

It is an offence for a person to contravene any of the foregoing provisions of this section *[subject of above bans on having firearm or ammunition in their possession]*.

Firearms Act 1968, s 21(4)

Sell/transfer/repair/test/prove for banned person

It is an offence for a person to sell or transfer a firearm or ammunition to, or to repair, test or prove a firearm or ammunition for, a person whom he knows or has reasonable ground for believing to be prohibited by this section from having a firearm or ammunition in his possession.

Firearms Act 1968, s 21(5)

Points to prove

Possess whilst banned

- ✓ date and location
- ✓ being person sentenced to
- ✓ imprisonment/youth custody/detention in YOI/detention and training order/secure training order
- ✓ for a term of [period]
- ✓ possessed a firearm and/or ammunition namely [description]
- ✓ while banned/before the expiration of ban

Sell/transfer/repair/test/prove for banned person

- ✓ date and location
- ✓ sell/transfer **or** repair/test/prove
- ✓ firearm or ammunition for
- ✓ a person
- ✓ prohibited by s 21 from possessing

Meanings

Date of release

Details vary and are as follows—

- Normal sentence—actual date a prisoner leaves prison.
- Part imprisonment and part suspended sentence—date of release from prison.
- A 'secure training order' or 'detention and training order' whichever is the latest of the following—
  - ◆ actual date of release;
  - ◆ date the person was released from the order because of a breach;

♦ date halfway through the total period of the order.
- Imprisonment under an intermittent custody order—date of final release.

Possession (see **8.1.1**)

Firearm or ammunition (see **8.1.1**)

Related cases

R v Fordham [1969] 3 All ER 532 A suspended sentence is not imprisonment for the purpose of this provision.

Practical considerations

- A suspended sentence is not imprisonment for the purpose of this section.
- Where there are several short sentences, it is the total sentence that counts.
- Anyone who is banned by these provisions can apply to the Crown Court under s 21(6) for removal of the ban.
- Do not confuse the terms firearm or ammunition with s 1 firearms or ammunition. This section includes **all** firearms including air weapons and shotguns.
- An air weapon is not generally looked upon by the courts as a lethal barrelled weapon. Therefore, the prosecution must prove that the air weapon can discharge a shot or missile and that it is capable of causing injury from which death could result.

 Either way

None

 Summary: 6 months' imprisonment and/or a fine not exceeding the statutory maximum.

Indictment: 5 years' imprisonment and/or a fine.

8.3.2 **Possession with intent to endanger life**

Section 16 of the Firearms Act 1968 creates the offence of possession of a firearm or ammunition with intent to endanger life.

8.3.2 Possession with intent to Endanger Life

Offences

It is an offence for a person to have in his **possession** any **firearm or ammunition** with **intent** by means thereof to **endanger life** or to enable another person by means thereof to endanger life, whether any injury has been caused or not.

Firearms Act 1968, s 16

Points to prove

✓ date and location
✓ possessed firearm/ammunition
✓ with intent
✓ to endanger life/enable another to endanger life thereby

Meanings

Possession (see **8.1.1**)

Firearm or ammunition

Includes all firearms and ammunition (see **8.1.1**)

Intent (see 4.1.2)

Endanger life

The key element is the intention that life be endangered, life need not actually be endangered, although if there is danger to life this may assist in proving intent. It is sufficient that life was endangered, there is no need to prove harm or injury to any victim.

Explanatory notes

The intention to endanger life need not be immediate, but it must result from the firearm/ammunition (eg if the defendant possesses the firearm or ammunition but intends to endanger life some other way, say by arson, this offence is **not** committed).

Related cases

R v Salih [2007] EWCA Crim 2750, CA If a person is in fear of an imminent attack and is carrying a firearm or offensive weapon for self -protection against an explicit and specific threat then self-defence may apply; it is a matter for the jury to decide.

R v Bentham [1972] 3 All ER 271, CA Possession is a continuing state and the intention to endanger life might last as long as the possession. The intent may not be limited to an immediate intention.

R v El-hakkaoui [1975] 2 All ER 146, CA It is an offence for a person to have in his possession a firearm/ammunition with intent to endanger the life of people outside the UK.

R v Jones & Others The Times, 14 August 1996 Possession for another to endanger life requires the firearm to be held for that reason, not just for someone involved in crime.

Practical considerations

- Intention to endanger life in another country is also an offence under this section.
- The offence of possession for another to endanger life requires the firearm to be specifically held intending that the other should endanger life with it. If the firearm/ammunition is simply held for someone known to be involved in crime, that will be insufficient for this offence.
- Consider the alternative offences of possession—
  - with intent to cause fear of violence (which covers a wider set of circumstances) (see **8.3.3**).
  - at the time of committing/being arrested for a relevant offence (see **8.3.5**).

 Indictable

 None

 Life imprisonment and/or a fine.

8.3.3 Possession with intent to cause fear of violence

Section 16A of the Firearms Act 1968 creates an offence of possessing a firearm (or imitation firearm) with intent to cause others to fear unlawful violence being used against them.

Offences

It is an offence for a person to have in his **possession** any **firearm** or **imitation firearm** with **intent**—

(a) by means thereof to cause; or

(b) to enable another person by means thereof to cause

any person to believe that **unlawful violence** will be used against him or another person.

Firearms Act 1968, s 16A

8.3.3 Possession with Intent to Cause Fear of Violence

Points to prove

✓ date and location
✓ had in your possession
✓ a firearm/imitation firearm
✓ with intent
✓ to cause/enable another to cause
✓ any person
✓ to believe unlawful violence will be used
✓ against them or another person

Meanings

Possession (see **8.1.1**)

Firearm

Means all firearms, not just s 1 firearms (see **8.1.1**)

Imitation firearm

Means any thing that has the appearance of being a firearm (other than appearance of prohibited weapon under s 5(1)(b) for discharge of any noxious liquid, gas or other thing) whether or not it is capable of discharging any shot, bullet, or other missile.

Intent (see **4.1.2**)

Unlawful violence

Means the unlawful exercise of physical force so as to cause injury or damage to property.

Practical considerations

- The offence can be committed anywhere and does not require an intent to commit any specific criminal offence.
- It does not matter if the weapon is an imitation, inoperative, or unloaded.

 SSS **E&S**

 Indictable None

 10 years' imprisonment and/or a fine.

8.3.4 **Using a firearm to resist or prevent a lawful arrest**

Section 17(1) of the Firearms Act 1968 creates the offence of using a firearm or imitation firearm to resist or prevent a lawful arrest.

Offences

It is an offence for a person to make or attempt to make any use whatsoever of a **firearm** or **imitation firearm** with **intent** to resist or prevent the lawful arrest or detention of himself or another person.

Firearms Act 1968, s 17(1)

Points to prove
- ✓ date and location
- ✓ made/attempted to make use
- ✓ of a firearm/an imitation firearm
- ✓ with intent
- ✓ to resist/prevent lawful arrest/detention
- ✓ of self/another

Meanings

Firearm

Means all firearms, not just s 1 firearms (see **8.1.1**). Although it does not include component parts and accessories designed or adapted to diminish the noise or flash caused by firing the weapon.

Imitation firearm (see **8.3.3**)

Intent (see **4.1.2**)

Explanatory notes
- In this section, 'firearm' means a complete weapon and does not include component parts and such items as silencers and flash eliminators.
- It has to be proved that the firearm was being used intentionally to resist/prevent the lawful arrest of the offender or another person.

  Indictable

  None

  Life imprisonment and/or a fine.

8.3.5 **Possession at time of committing/ being arrested**

Section 17(2) of the Firearms Act 1968 makes it an offence to be in possession of a firearm or imitation firearm at the time of arrest for certain specified offences.

Offences

If a person at the time of his committing or being arrested for an offence specified in **schedule 1** to this Act, has in his **possession** a **firearm** or **imitation firearm** he shall be guilty of an offence under this subsection unless he shows that he had it in his possession for a lawful object.

Firearms Act 1968, s 17(2)

Points to prove

✓ date and location
✓ at the time of
✓ being arrested for/committing
✓ a Sch 1 offence
✓ possessed firearm/imitation firearm

Meanings

Schedule 1 offences

- Criminal Damage Act 1971, s 1—damage; damage with intent endanger life; arson
- Offences Against the Person Act 1861
  - s 20—wounding/GBH
  - s 21—criminal intent choke/strangle
  - s 22—criminal use of stupefying drugs
  - s 30—laying explosive to building etc
  - s 32—endangering persons by tampering with railway
  - s 38—assault with intent to resist lawful arrest
  - s 47—assault occasioning actual bodily harm
- Child Abduction Act 1984, Pt 1—abduction of children
- Theft Act 1968—burglary; blackmail; theft (including robbery); taking of motor vehicles
- Police Act 1996—assaulting a police officer
- Criminal Justice Act 1991—assault prisoner custody officer
- Criminal Justice and Public Order Act 1994—assault secure training centre custody officer

- Sexual Offences Act 2003
  - rape
  - assault by penetration
  - cause person engage in sexual activity involving penetration
  - rape of a child under 13
  - assault of a child under 13 by penetration
  - cause/incite child under 13 to engage in sexual activity involving penetration
  - sexual activity with a mentally disordered person involving penetration
  - cause/incite mental disorder person to engage in penetrative sexual activity
- Aiding and abetting any of the Sch 1 offences
- Attempting to commit any of the Sch 1 offences

Possession (see **8.1.1**)

Firearm (see **8.3.4**)

Imitation firearm (see **8.3.3**)

Defences

Proving possession of the firearm or imitation firearm for a lawful reason or purpose.

Explanatory notes

- In this section, 'firearm' means a complete weapon and does not include component parts and such items as silencers and flash eliminators.
- There is no need to prove any use or intended use of the firearm. Possession of it may be completely unconnected with the other offence committed by the person or for which they are arrested.

Related cases

R v Guy (1991) 93 Cr App R 108, CA Schedule 1 applies to any offence where theft is an element.

R v Nelson [2000] 2 Cr App R 160, CA When the defendant is arrested for a 'relevant' Sch 1 offence there is no need to prove the Sch 1 offence itself.

R v Bentham [2005] UKHL 18, HL The defendant carried out a robbery with his finger in his jacket pocket pointing towards the victim. Held that as the fingers were part of the person, and not separate and distinct, then they could never be possessed as a 'thing' having the appearance of a firearm.

SSS   E&S

 Indictable   🕐 None

🏛 Life imprisonment and/or a fine.

8.3.6 **Carrying firearm—criminal intent/resist arrest**

Section 18 of the Firearms Act 1968 makes it an offence to carry a firearm or imitation firearm with criminal intent or to resist/prevent arrest.

Offences

It is an offence for a person to **have with him** a **firearm** or **imitation firearm** with **intent** to commit an **indictable offence**, or to resist arrest or prevent the arrest of another, in either case while he has the firearm or imitation firearm with him.

Firearms Act 1968, s 18

Points to prove

✓ date and location
✓ had with you
✓ a firearm/imitation firearm
✓ with intent
✓ to commit an indictable offence/resist arrest/prevent the arrest of another

Meanings

Has with him

This is a narrower definition than 'possession' (see **8.1.1**). Here there is a need to prove—

- a knowledge of the existence of the article;
- that the article was 'to hand and ready for use' (it may, for example, be hidden a few feet away: it does not have to be physically on the defendant's person).

Firearm (see **8.3.3**)

Imitation firearm (see **8.3.3**)

Intent (see **4.1.2**)

Indictable offence

This includes either way offences.

Related cases

R v Duhaney, R v Stoddart The Times, 9 December 1997, CA Whether or not the firearm is used, or intended to be used, to further that particular offence, is irrelevant.

R v Pawlicki and Swindell [1992] 3 All ER 903, CA Accessibility, not distance, is the test for 'have with him'.

Practical considerations

- Proof that the defendant had a firearm or imitation firearm with them and intended to commit the offence or to resist or prevent arrest, is evidence that they intended to have it with them while doing so.
- Consider 'possess firearm with intent to cause the fear of unlawful violence' (see **8.3.3**) which has a much wider scope.

  Indictable   None

  Life imprisonment and/or a fine.

8.3.7 **Using person to mind a firearm/ weapon**

Section 28 of the Violent Crime Reduction Act 2006 makes it an offence to use another person to look after, hide, or transport a dangerous weapon, subject to an agreement that it would be available when required for an unlawful purpose.

> **Offences**
>
> (1) A person is guilty of an offence if—
>   (a) he uses another to look after, hide or transport a **dangerous weapon** for him; and
>   (b) he does so under arrangements or in circumstances that facilitate, or are intended to facilitate, the weapon's being **available** to him for an unlawful purpose.
>
> *Violent Crime Reduction Act 2006, s 28*

8.3.7 Using Person to Mind a Firearm/ Weapon

Points to prove

✓ uses another person to
✓ look after/hide/transport
✓ dangerous weapon and
✓ under arrangements made or facilitation agreed/intended
✓ the weapon is made available
✓ for an unlawful purpose

Meanings

Dangerous weapon (s 28(3))

In this section 'dangerous weapon' means—
(a) a firearm [see **8.1.1**] **other than** an air weapon or a component part of, or accessory to, an air weapon [see **8.7.2**]; or
(b) a weapon to which s 141 [see **8.9.2**] or s 141A [see **8.10.2**] of the Criminal Justice Act 1988 applies (specified offensive weapons, knives and bladed weapons).

Available for an unlawful purpose (s 28(2))

For the purposes of this section the cases in which a dangerous weapon is to be regarded as available to a person for an unlawful purpose include any case where—
(a) the weapon is available for him to take possession of it at a time and place; and
(b) his possession of the weapon at that time and place would constitute, or be likely to involve or to lead to, the commission by him of an offence.

 Indictable   None

 Different penalties are provided by s 29—4 to 10 years imprisonment and/or fine.

Links to alternative subjects and offences

8.4 Trespassing with Firearms

The Firearms Act 1968 provides various offences connected with firearms, air weapons, shotguns, and associated ammunition. Some such offences involve trespassing.

8.4.1 Trespass with any firearm in a building

Section 20 of the Firearms Act 1968 creates two offences of trespassing with firearms, one of which is concerned with trespass in buildings.

Offences

A person commits an offence if, while he has a **firearm** or **imitation firearm** **with him**, he enters or is in any building or part of a building as a trespasser and without reasonable excuse (the proof whereof lies on him).

Firearms Act 1968, s 20(1)

Points to prove
- ✓ Date and location
- ✓ had with him/her
- ✓ firearm/imitation firearm
- ✓ entered or was in
- ✓ building/part of building
- ✓ as a trespasser
- ✓ without reasonable excuse

Meanings

Firearm (see 8.3.3)
Imitation firearm (see 8.3.3)
Has with him (see 8.3.6)

Explanatory notes
- A firearm in these circumstances means any firearm—shotgun, air weapon, prohibited weapon, and s 1 firearm.
- The terms 'enters', 'building', 'part of a building', and 'trespasser' should be interpreted as terms used in legislation/case law relating to burglary (see 3.3).

Defence

Reasonable excuse (the burden of proof lies with the defendant). This defence could include saving life/property or self-defence (eg the police carrying out a planned firearms operation). Whether an excuse is reasonable would be for the court to decide having considered all the circumstances.

Practical considerations

- It is important to note that although this is an either way offence; if the weapon is an air weapon or imitation firearm it is triable summarily only.
- The burden of proof lies with the defendant if they claim to have a reasonable excuse.
- Unless it is an imitation, there needs to be some evidence that the weapon is a firearm.
- Consider the offences of aggravated burglary (see **3.4**) or attempt aggravated burglary (see **4.1.1**) (especially if an imitation or air weapon is used—greater penalty).

 Either way   None

 Summary: 6 months' imprisonment and/or a fine not exceeding the statutory maximum.

Indictment: 7 years' imprisonment and/or a fine.

Air weapons/imitation firearms

 Summary   48 months

 6 months' imprisonment and/or a fine not exceeding level 5.

8.4.2 Trespass with firearm on land

Section 20(2) of the Firearms Act 1968 creates an offence of trespass with a firearm on land.

8.4.2 Trespass with Firearm on Land

Offences

A person commits an offence if, while he has a **firearm** or **imitation firearm with him**, he enters or is on any **land** as a **trespasser** and without reasonable excuse (the proof whereof lies on him).

Firearms Act 1968, s 20(2)

Points to prove

✓ date and location
✓ while having with you
✓ firearm/imitation firearm
✓ entered/was on land
✓ as a trespasser
✓ without reasonable excuse

Meanings

Firearm (see **8.3.3**)

Imitation firearm (see **8.3.3**)

Has with him (see **8.3.6**)

Land

This includes land covered with water.

Trespass (see **3.3**)

Explanatory notes

A firearm in these circumstances means any firearm—shotgun, air weapon, prohibited weapon, and s 1 firearm.

Defence

Reasonable excuse (see **8.4.1**)

Practical considerations

- In order to prove a trespass it must be shown that the defendant knew that they were a trespasser or was reckless as to whether the facts existed which made them a trespasser.
- If a defence of reasonable excuse is claimed, the burden of proof lies with the defendant.
- Unless it is an imitation firearm, there needs to be some evidence that the weapon is 'a firearm'.

Summary

 48 months

 3 months' imprisonment and/or a fine not exceeding level 4 on the standard scale.

Links to alternative subjects and offences

8.5 **Possess Firearm or Imitation Firearm in a Public Place**

The Firearms Act 1968 provides various offences connected with firearms, air weapons, shotguns, and associated ammunition. Some of these offences relate specifically to public places.

Section 19 of the Firearms Act 1968 provides various offences relating to the possession of shotguns, air weapons, firearms, and imitation firearms in a public place.

Offences

A person commits an offence if, without lawful authority or reasonable excuse (the proof whereof lies on him) he **has with him** in a **public place**—
(a) a **loaded shot gun**,
(b) an **air weapon** (whether loaded or not),
(c) any **other firearm** (whether loaded or not) together with ammunition suitable for use in that firearm, or
(d) an **imitation firearm**.

Firearms Act 1968, s 19

Points to prove

✓ date and location
✓ without lawful authority/reasonable excuse
✓ had with them in a public place a
✓ firearm (together with suitable ammunition) **or**
✓ loaded shotgun **or**
✓ loaded/unloaded air weapon **or**
✓ an imitation firearm

Meanings

Has with him (see 8.3.6)

Public place

This includes any highway and any other premises or place to which at the material time the public have or are permitted to have access, whether on payment or otherwise.

Loaded

Means if there is a cartridge in the barrel or approved magazine that can feed the cartridge into the barrel by manual or automatic means.

Shotgun (see **8.2.1**)

Air weapon (see **8.7.2**)

Other firearm (see **8.1.1**)

Imitation firearm (see **8.3.3**)

Explanatory notes

In this offence the requirement for the weapons to be loaded or not varies—

* the requirement for a loaded weapon only applies to shotguns;
* for air weapons, there is no need to have ammunition for it;
* for other firearms, the defendant must have ammunition suitable for use with that firearm.

Defences

Having lawful authority or reasonable excuse (the burden of proof lies with the defendant). This defence could include saving life/property or self-defence (eg the police carrying out a planned firearms operation). Whether an excuse is reasonable would be for the court to decide having considered all the circumstances.

Related cases

R v Harrison [1996] Crim LR 200 During a robbery one of the robbers had a loaded sawn-off shotgun which the other knew nothing about. On the arrival of the police the other offender took possession of the gun. Even though he did not know it was loaded he still committed the offence.

Bates v DPP (1993) 157 JP 1004, QBD Inside a vehicle may be a public place.

Anderson v Miller [1976] Crim LR 743 The space behind a counter in a shop was held to be a public place.

Ross v Collins [1982] Crim LR 368, QBD A shotgun certificate gives no lawful authority for a loaded shotgun in a public place.

R v Jones [1995] 2 WLR 64, CA A firearms certificate does not give the holder a defence of 'lawful authority' against a charge under s 19. The certificate is granted for a specific purpose with conditions attached.

8.5 Possess Firearm or Imitation Firearm in a Public Place

R v Morris & King (1984) 149 JP 60, 79 Cr App Rep 104, CA The test for an imitation firearm is whether the 'thing' looked like a firearm at the time when the accused actually had it with him.

Practical considerations

- Section 161 of the Highways Act 1980 deals with the offence of discharging any firearm within 50 feet from the centre of a highway (see **8.8.6**).
- Section 28 of the Town Police Clauses Act 1847 (does not apply to the Metropolitan Police District) states that a person who recklessly discharges a firearm in the street to the annoyance or danger of residents or passengers will commit an offence (see **8.8.6**).
- If a defence of lawful authority or reasonable excuse is claimed, the burden of proof lies with the defendant.
- The 'guilty knowledge' that the prosecution must prove is knowledge of existence of the firearm, not the nature and quality of the weapon.
- The prosecution must prove that the firearm is 'to hand and able to be used'.
- With an imitation firearm, the key word is 'appearance': whether the 'thing' looked like a firearm at the time of the offence. It is ultimately for the jury to decide on the circumstances of the case.
- Offences involving imitation firearms are of having or possessing an imitation firearm not of falsely pretending to have one (*R v Bentham* [2005] UKHL 18—see **8.3.5**).
- Imitation or replica weapons that can be converted into working firearms will be classed as s 1 firearms (see **8.1.4**).
- Unless it is an imitation firearm, there needs to be some evidence that the weapon is a firearm (see **8.1.1**).
- If the weapon is a shotgun, firearm, or imitation firearm then it is an either way offence. However, if the weapon is an air weapon then it is summary trial only.

 Either way   None

 Summary: 6 months' imprisonment and/or a fine not exceeding the statutory maximum.

Indictment: If the weapon is an imitation firearm, 12 months' imprisonment and/or a fine.

In any other case (except air weapons), 7 years' imprisonment and/or a fine.

Air weapons

 Summary   48 months

 6 months' imprisonment and/or a fine not exceeding level 5.

Links to alternative subjects and offences

8.6 **Police Powers—Firearms**

The Firearms Act 1968 provides various offences connected with firearms, air weapons, shotguns, and associated ammunition. Central to the practical effectiveness of that legislation, in policing terms, are the relevant powers that accompany these offences

8.6.1 **Requirement to hand over firearm/ammunition**

Section 47 of the Firearms Act 1968 deals with police powers to stop and search for firearms and provides an offence for failure to do so.

Police stop and search powers

A constable may require any person whom he has **reasonable cause to suspect**—
(a) of having a **firearm**, with or without **ammunition**, **with him** in a **public place**; or
(b) to be committing or about to commit, **elsewhere** than in a public place, an **offence relevant** for the purposes of this section,
to **hand** over the firearm or any ammunition for examination by the constable.

Firearms Act 1968, s 47(1)

Meanings

Reasonable cause to suspect

This concept is used in other legislation and depends very much on the circumstances in each case. There must be objective grounds for the suspicion based on facts, information or intelligence that are relevant to the likelihood of finding the article(s) (see **12.1**).

Firearm/ammunition (see **8.1.1**)

Has with him (see **8.3.6**)

Public place (see **8.5**)

Relevant offence

This refers to s 18 and s 20 offences, being either having a firearm or imitation firearm—

• with intent to commit an indictable offence, or to resist arrest or prevent the arrest of another (see **8.3.6**);

- with them and enters either a building or part of a building **or** land as a trespasser (see **8.4**).

Offences

It is an offence for a person having a firearm or ammunition with him to fail to hand it over when required to do so by a constable under subsection (1) above.

Firearms Act 1968, s 47(2)

Points to prove

✓ date and location
✓ failed to hand over
✓ a firearm/ammunition for a firearm
✓ in your possession
✓ when required to do so
✓ by a constable

Section 47 of the Firearms Act 1968 also provides qualified powers to search for firearms in respect of both people and vehicles and detain them for that purpose.

Police search and detain powers

Person

If a constable has reasonable cause to suspect a person of having a firearm with him in a public place, **or** to be committing or about to commit **elsewhere** than in a public place an offence relevant for the purposes of this section, the constable may search that person and may detain him for the purpose of doing so.

Firearms Act 1968, s 47(3)

Vehicle

If a constable has reasonable cause to suspect that there is a firearm in a vehicle in a public place, **or** that a vehicle is being or is about to be used in connection with the commission of an offence relevant for the purposes of this section elsewhere than in a public place, he may search the vehicle and for that purpose require the person driving or in control of it to stop it.

Firearms Act 1968, s 47(4)

Explanatory notes

- In exercising these powers, s 47(5) also gives a constable power to enter any place.
- The police also have the power to demand the production of shotgun or firearm certificates (see **8.6.2**).

- The power to stop the vehicle is not restricted to a constable in uniform.
- Officers should ensure that the stop and search procedures comply with PACE and the relevant Code of Practice (see **12.1.2**)
- With regard to premises a search warrant will have to be obtained under s 46 (see **8.6.3**).

 Summary   🕐   48 months

🎚️   3 months' imprisonment and/or a fine not exceeding level 4 on the standard scale.

8.6.2 Police powers—firearms/shotgun certificates

Section 48 of the Firearms Act 1968 gives a constable power to demand from a person they believe to be in possession of s 1 firearm/ammunition or shotgun the production of a valid certificate or European pass or to show that they are exempt.

Production of certificate

A constable may **demand**, from any person whom he **believes** to be in possession of a **firearm** or **ammunition** to which **section 1** of this Act applies, or of a **shotgun**, the production of his **firearm certificate** or, as the case may be, his **shotgun certificate**.

Firearms Act 1968, s 48(1)

Meanings

Demand production

Where a person upon whom a demand has been made by a constable under subsection (1) and whom the constable believes to be in possession of a firearm fails—

(a) to produce a firearm certificate or, as the case may be, a shotgun certificate;

(b) to show that he is a person who, by reason of his place of residence or any other circumstances, is not entitled to be issued with a document identifying that firearm under any of the provisions which in the other member States correspond to the provisions of this Act for the issue of European firearms passes; or

(c) to show that he is in possession of the firearm exclusively in connection
with the carrying on of activities in respect of which, he or the person
on whose behalf he has possession of the firearm, is recognised, for the
purposes of the law of another member State relating to firearms, as a collector of firearms or a body concerned in the cultural or historical aspects
of weapons,

the constable may demand from that person the production of a document
which has been issued to that person in another member State under any such
corresponding provisions, identifies that firearm as a firearm to which it relates
and is for the time being valid.

Firearms Act 1968, s 48(1A)

Believes

This is a more stringent requirement than 'suspects' and requires stronger
grounds.

Section 1 firearm/ammunition (see 8.1.1)

Firearm certificate (see 8.1.1)

Shotgun (see 8.2.1)

Shotgun certificate (see 8.2.1)

Offence

It is an offence for a person who is in possession of a firearm to fail to comply
with a demand under subsection (1A) above.

Firearms Act 1968, s 48(4)

Points to prove

✓ date and location
✓ being in possession
✓ of a firearm
✓ failed
✓ to comply with a demand
✓ by constable
✓ to produce a valid certificate/document or show exemption

Seize/detain weapon and require details

If a person upon whom a demand is made fails to produce the certificate
or document, **or** to permit the constable to read it, **or** to show that he is
entitled by virtue of this Act to have the firearm, ammunition or shotgun in his

8.6.3 Premises Search Warrant

possession without holding a certificate, the constable may seize and detain the firearm, ammunition or shotgun and may require the person to declare to him immediately his name and address.

Firearms Act 1968, s 48(2)

Offences

If under this section a person is required to declare to a constable his name and address, it is an offence for him to refuse to declare it or to fail to give his true name and address.

Firearms Act 1968, s 48(3)

Points to prove
✓ date and location
✓ having possession
✓ of a firearm/shotgun
✓ failed/refused
✓ to divulge
✓ when required by a constable
✓ their name and address

Explanatory notes
- A firearm certificate also includes a Northern Ireland Certificate.
- As the requirement is to declare 'immediately' their name and address, it is taken that the demand to produce a valid certificate/document or show exemption and (if applicable) the subsequent seizure of the firearm, ammunition or shotgun will also follow the same immediacy.

 Summary   6 months

 A fine not exceeding level 3 on the standard scale.

8.6.3 **Premises search warrant**

Section 46 of the Firearms Act 1968 deals with the issue of premises search warrants for firearms and authorities attached thereto.

Granting of warrant

If a justice of the peace is satisfied by information on oath that there is reasonable ground for suspecting—

(a) that an **offence relevant** for the purposes of this section has been, is being, or is about to be committed; or

(b) that, in connection with a firearm or ammunition, there is a danger to the public safety or to the peace,

he may grant a warrant for any of the **purposes** mentioned in subsection (2) below.

Firearms Act 1968, s 46(1)

Meanings

Relevant offences

All offences under this Act except an offence under s 22(3) [*unsupervised 15-year-old possess shotgun—see* **8.2.3**] or an offence relating specifically to air weapons.

Purposes of warrant

A warrant under this section may authorise a constable or civilian officer—

(a) to enter at any time any premises or place named in the warrant, if necessary by force, and to search the premises or place and every person found there;

(b) to seize and detain anything which he may find on the premises or place, or on any such person, in respect of which or in connection with which he has reasonable ground for suspecting—

  (i) that an offence **relevant** for the purposes of this section has been, is being or is about to be committed; or

  (ii) that in connection with a firearm, imitation firearm, or ammunition, there is a danger to the public safety or to the peace.

Firearms Act 1968, s 46(2)

Offences

It is an offence for any person intentionally to obstruct a constable or **civilian officer** in the exercise of his powers under this section.

Firearms Act 1968, s 46(5)

Points to prove

✓ date and location
✓ intentionally obstruct
✓ constable/civilian officer
✓ whilst exercising their powers under s 46

8.6.3 Premises Search Warrant

Meaning of civilian officer

Means a person employed by a police authority or the Corporation of the City of London who is under the direction and control of a chief officer of police.

Explanatory notes

• Ensure that the application and execution of the warrant complies with PACE and the COP (see **12.4**).
• In some forces inspections of gun clubs and other routine firearms enquiries are performed by civilian staff rather than police officers.

 Summary   48 months

 6 months' imprisonment and/or a fine not exceeding level 5 on the standard scale.

Links to alternative subjects and offences

8.7 Air Weapons, Imitations, Firearms—Age Restrictions

The Firearms Act 1968 provides various offences connected with firearms, imitation firearms, air weapons, shotguns, and associated ammunition. A number of important offences and restrictions relate to the age of the person involved.

8.7.1 Purchase/hire or supply air weapons, firearms, or ammunition

Sections 22(1) and 24(1) of the Firearms Act 1968 prohibit purchase/hire or supply (sell or let on hire) of any air weapon, firearm and ammunition by or to a person under 17/18 years of age.

Offences

Purchase/hire by under 17/18

It is an offence—
(a) for a person under the age of 18 to purchase or hire an **air weapon** or ammunition for an air weapon;
(b) for a person under the age of 17 to purchase or hire any **firearm** or ammunition of any other description.

Firearms Act 1968, s 22(1)

Supplier (sell/hire) to under 17/18

It is an offence—
(a) to sell or let on hire an air weapon or ammunition for an air weapon to a person under the age of 18;
(b) to sell or let on hire any firearm or ammunition of any other description to a person under the age of 17.

Firearms Act 1968, s 24(1)

Points to prove

Purchase/hire by under 17/18
✓ date and location
✓ purchased/hired, **either**

8.7.1 Purchase/Hire or Supply Air Weapons

✓ by under 18 years—an air weapon/ammunition for an air weapon **OR**
✓ by under 17 years—firearm/ammunition of any other description

Supplier (sell/hire) to under 17/18

✓ date and location
✓ sold/let on hire, **either**
✓ air weapon/ammunition for an air weapon to under 18 **OR**
✓ firearm/ammunition of any other description to under 17

Meanings of firearm/ammunition

• Air weapons and air pellets/darts (see **8.7.2**);
• Shotguns and cartridges (see **8.2.1**);
• Section 1/other firearms or ammunition (see **8.1.1**).

Defence for supplier under s 24

In proceedings for an offence under any provision of this section it is a defence to prove that the person charged with the offence believed the other person to be of or over the age mentioned in that provision and had reasonable ground for the belief.

Firearms Act 1968, s 24(5)

Practical considerations

• Restrictions prevent people under 14 years of age from possessing, receiving as gifts, or on loan any s 1 firearms or ammunition (see **8.1.3**).
• It is an offence under s 24A for a person under 18 to purchase or to be sold an imitation firearm (see **8.7.5**).
• Selling air weapons by way of trade or business is a summary offence, unless sold by a registered firearms dealer (see **8.1.2**).
• Any firearm, air weapon, or ammunition seized by the police as a result of committing these offences may be confiscated by the court.
• Two specific shotgun offences (see **8.2.2**) apply to people under 15 years—
   ♦ having an assembled shotgun without being supervised (by a person aged 21 years or over) or securely fastened in a gun cover;
   ♦ making a gift of a shotgun or cartridges to such person.

 SSS

 Summary   48 months

6 months' imprisonment and/or a fine not exceeding level 5 on the standard scale.

8.7.2 **Further offences/restrictions—air weapons**

The Firearms Act 1968 provides exceptions for young people to possess air weapons, but generally it is an offence for a person under 18 to have with them or be given an air weapon or ammunition for an air weapon. It is also an offence to fire missiles from an air weapon beyond premises, subject to a defence of consent from the other premises occupier.

Offences (by under 18)

Subject to **section 23**, it is an offence for a person under the age of 18 to **have with him** an air weapon or ammunition for an air weapon.

Firearms Act 1968, s 22(4)

Points to prove

✓ date and location
✓ being under 18 years of age
✓ had with you
✓ an air weapon or ammunition for an air weapon

Meanings

Section 23 (see 'Exceptions and offences' below)

Has with him (see 8.3.6)

Air weapon

In reality, most air weapons are firearms, but not s 1 firearms (see **8.1.1**). Part of the definition of a s 1 firearm (s 1(3)(b) of the Firearms Act 1968) relates to every firearm, except air weapons: 'an air weapon that is to say, an air rifle, air gun or air pistol which does not fall within s 5(1) [being a prohibited weapon—having compressed gas cartridge system] and which is not of a type declared by rules [sets the power levels at which an air weapon becomes a s 1 firearm] made by the Secretary of State under s 53 of this Act to be specially dangerous'.

Exceptions and offences

(1) It is **not** an offence under section 22(4) of this Act for a person to have with him an air weapon or ammunition while he is under the supervision of a person of or over the age of 21; **but** where a person has with

him an air weapon on any premises in circumstances where he would be prohibited from having it with him but for this subsection, it is an **offence** for the person under whose supervision he is to allow him to use it for firing any missile beyond those premises.

(2) It is **not** an offence under section 22(4) of this Act for a person to have with him an air weapon or ammunition at the time when:

 (a) being a member of a rifle club or miniature rifle club for the time being approved by the Secretary of State for the purposes of this section or section 15 of the Firearms (Amendment) Act 1988, he is engaged as such a member in or in connection with target shooting; or

 (b) he is using the weapon or ammunition at a shooting gallery where the only firearms used are either air weapons or miniature rifles not exceeding .23 inch calibre.

(3) It is **not** an offence under section 22(4) of this Act for a person of or over the age of fourteen to have with him an air weapon or ammunition on private premises with the consent of the occupier.

Firearms Act 1968, s 23

Points to prove

s 23(1) supervisor

- ✓ date and location
- ✓ being person of/over 21
- ✓ supervising person under 18 who had an air weapon
- ✓ on premises (**specify**)
- ✓ allowed them to fire a missile beyond those premises

Offences (make gift/part with possession to person under 18)

It is an offence—

(a) to make a gift of an air weapon or ammunition for an air weapon to a person under the age of 18; or

(b) to part with the possession of an air weapon or ammunition for an air weapon to a person under the age of 18 except where by virtue of section 23 [*above*] of this Act the person is not prohibited from having it with him.

Firearms Act 1968, s 24(4)

Points to prove

s 24(4)(a) make a gift to under 18

✓ date and location
✓ made a gift
✓ of an air weapon/ammunition for an air weapon
✓ to a person under the age of 18

s 24(4)(b) part possession to under 18 (not s 23 excepted)

✓ Date and location
✓ parted with possession
✓ of an air weapon/ammunition for an air weapon
✓ to a person under the age of 18
✓ being prohibited from having possession

Defences

Section 24 offence (see 8.7.1).

Offences under s 23(1) or s 21A(1)

It shall be a defence for him to show that the only premises into or across which the missile was fired were premises the occupier of which had consented to the firing of the missile (whether specifically or by way of a general consent).

Firearms Act 1968, ss 23(1A) and 21A(2)

Explanatory notes

- Section s 21A(1) makes it a summary offence (level 3 fine) for a person **of any age** to have an air weapon on premises that is used to fire a missile beyond those premises (see above for defence).
- HOC 31/2007 provides guidance in relation to air weapons as to: raising the age limits to 18, firing air weapons beyond premises, sales or transfer to be only through a registered firearms dealer by 'face to face' transactions.
- As 'air gun', 'air rifle' and 'air pistol' are not defined in the Firearms Act 1968, each case will have to be considered on its own facts and the article in question. Whether a weapon falls into these categories, the court will have to be aware of the following—
  - ◆ an 'air gun' is generally a weapon that has an unrifled barrel;
  - ◆ an 'air rifle' is a weapon that does have a rifled barrel; and
  - ◆ an 'air pistol' is a weapon designed to be fired by using one hand and having the appearance of a pistol.

- ◆ air weapons using or designed/adapted for use with a self-contained compressed gas cartridge system will be prohibited weapons (see **8.7.3**).
- An air weapon is deemed to be loaded if there is ammunition in the chamber or barrel.

Related cases

Moore v Gooderham [1960] 3 All ER 575, QBD As an airgun is capable of causing injury from which death could result it is a lethal barrelled weapon.

Grace v DPP The Times, 9 December 1988, QBD Evidence that the weapon in question can be fired is required. The prosecution needs to prove that the rifle was a lethal barrelled weapon capable of discharging a shot or missile.

Practical considerations

- The prosecution have to prove that the air weapon was a lethal barrelled weapon capable of discharging a shot or missile.
- In practice, the Forensic Science Laboratory will examine weapons and say whether or not they are lethal. The main characteristic which is measured is the muzzle velocity (the speed at which the projectile leaves the barrel).
- An air weapon normally fires a projectile by compressed air/gases and is a firearm, namely 'a lethal barrelled weapon of any description from which any shot, bullet or other missile can be discharged' (do not confuse a 'firearm' with the narrower definition of a s 1 firearm).
- Certain air weapons can be subject to the prohibition under rules denoting them as especially dangerous.
- Air weapons using, or designed/adapted for use with, a self-contained compressed gas cartridge system will be prohibited weapons (**8.7.3**).
- Application may be made to the court for a confiscation order in relation to a seized air weapon or ammunition.
- Police powers relating to firearms/ammunition are discussed under **8.6**.
- Normally it is an offence for a person under 18 years to have an air weapon and/or ammunition anywhere. However, a young person may possess one if accompanied by someone of or over 21 years of age.
- On premises the person under 18 years old is allowed to fire the weapon, but the missiles must not go beyond those premises—otherwise an offence is committed by the supervisor (subject to defence). Furthermore, the user (who must be at least 14 years old) may have with them an air weapon or ammunition on private premises with permission of the occupier.
- Consider the offence under s 21A, which is for any person to have an air weapon on premises and it is used to fire a missile beyond those

premises, although it is a defence if the occupier of the premises into or across which the missile was fired had consented.

- Under s 19 it is an offence for a person to have with them in a public place an air weapon (loaded or not) or imitation firearm without lawful authority or reasonable excuse (see **8.5**).

 Summary   6 months

 A fine not exceeding level 3 on the standard scale.

8.7.3 **Air weapons deemed prohibited weapons**

Any person who has with him any air rifle, air gun, or air pistol that uses, or is designed or adapted for use with, a self-contained compressed gas cartridge system (SCGC) will be in possession of a prohibited weapon under s 5(1)(af) of the Firearms Act 1968 (see **8.1.1**).

Explanatory Notes

- Weapons that use a CO_2 bulb system are not affected because CO_2 bulbs do not contain a projectile and are not therefore self-contained.
- A CO_2 bulb system that gives a pressure less than 12 ft/lbs on air rifles or 6 ft/lbs on air pistols is not restricted, but over that pressure they become s 1 firearms.
- If the air weapon contains a brass cartridge system and uses a self-contained gas cartridge system that can be converted to fire conventional ammunition, say, then this would make it a prohibited weapon under s 5(1)(af).
- If the weapon comes under s 5(1)(af), then it cannot be possessed, purchased, acquired, manufactured, sold, or transferred without a written authority from the Secretary of State. Although under special arrangements, a person may have been granted permission to possess such a weapon under the terms of a firearms certificate.
- Further details on this matter are given in HOC 1/2004.

8.7.4 **'BB guns'**

BB guns derived their name from guns that fired ball bearings by different methods such as compressed air or an electrical system, some even fired 4.5 mm lead shot. Such weapons would almost certainly be firearms for the purposes of s 1(3) (see **8.1.1**).

If the method of propulsion is a self-contained compressed gas cartridge, the BB gun may be a prohibited weapon (see **8.7.3**). However, most gas BB guns do not have cartridges: the built-in gas container is recharged by an external aerosol, which is not the same thing.

A more common and readily available BB gun is designed to fire plastic or aluminium pellets which may be too powerful to be officially classed as a toy.

These are unlikely to be lethal barrelled weapons (see **8.1.1**) because they are usually too low powered to be 'lethal'.

This type of BB gun will normally have a power rating of about 0.06 ft/lbs.

Compare this to a BSA Airsporter .22 air rifle that has a power rating of 10.07 ft/lbs (150 times more powerful).

If required, the Forensic Science Laboratory can test the BB gun in order to ascertain its power rating, categorize the gun, and say whether or not it is lethal.

As some BB guns closely resemble other firearms, if one is being used in a public place, consider the offence of possession of an imitation firearm in a public place (see **8.5.1**).

8.7.5 **Under 18—sell/buy an imitation firearm**

Section 24A of the Firearms Act 1968 makes it an offence to sell an imitation firearm to a person under the age of 18, or for a young person under the age of 18 to purchase one.

Offences

(1) It is an offence for a person under the age of eighteen to purchase an imitation firearm.
(2) It is an offence to sell an imitation firearm to a person under the age of eighteen.

Firearms Act 1968, s 24A

Points to prove

s 24A(1) under 18 purchase
- ✓ date and location
- ✓ being a person under 18 years of age
- ✓ purchased an imitation firearm

s 24A(2) sell to under 18
- ✓ date and location
- ✓ sold an imitation firearm
- ✓ to a person under 18 years of age

Meaning of imitation firearm

Means any thing which has the appearance of being a firearm whether or not it is capable of discharging any shot, bullet or other missile.

Explanatory notes

Imitation firearms have been increasingly misused to threaten and intimidate others. Although offences and controls exist relating to imitation firearms, s 24A seeks to tackle the problem at source by restricting the sale of imitation firearms.

Defence for seller

In proceedings for an offence under subsection (2) it is a defence to show that the person charged with the offence—

(a) believed the other person to be aged eighteen or over; and

(b) had reasonable ground for that belief.

Firearms Act 1968, s 24A(3)

Practical considerations

- The onus is on the prosecution to show that the seller did not take sufficient steps (eg producing identity card) to establish that the purchaser was 18 or over.
- Under the Violent Crime Reduction Act 2006—
  - s 36 makes it an offence to manufacture, import or sell a realistic imitation firearm;
  - s 37 provides a defence to s 36 if it is shown that the only purpose of making the imitation firearm was for—
    - a museum or gallery;
    - theatrical performances and rehearsals;
    - production of films or television programmes;
    - an organization for holding historical re-enactments;
    - Crown servants.
  - s 38 defines realistic imitation firearm (for ss 36 and 37) as an imitation firearm which appears so realistic that it can only be distinguished from a real firearm by—
    - an expert or on close examination;
    - attempting to load or fire it; and
    - it is not a de-activated firearm or an antique.
  - The Violent Crime Reduction Act 2006 (Realistic Imitation Firearms) Regulations 2007 (SI 2007/2606) provide defences, burden of proof, details on historical re-enactments, size, and colours of imitation firearms.
- Home Office Circular 31/2007 gives guidance on ss 36–41 (imitation firearms).

8.7.5 Under 18—Sell/buy an imitation Firearm

 Summary 48 months

 6 months' imprisonment and/or a fine not exceeding level 5 on the standard scale.

Links to alternative subjects and offences

8.8 **Fireworks**

The Fireworks Regulations 2004 and Fireworks (Safety) Regulations 1997 introduce firework prohibitions that are enforced by the Fireworks Act 2003 and Consumer Protection Act 1987 respectively. The Highways Act 1980 and Town Police Clauses Act 1847 also deal with offences involving fireworks in a street or highway.

8.8.1 **Categories of fireworks (BS 7114)**

There are four specific categories of fireworks within British Standard 7114, being categories 1, 2, and 3 fireworks which are considered suitable for use by the general public, whereas Category 4 can only be possessed/used by certain people (see **8.8.4**).

Category 1 includes fireworks that are suited to indoor use (Indoor Fireworks). These are pretty innocuous fireworks (eg caps, cracker snaps, novelty matches, party poppers, serpents, sparklers, or throwdowns).

Category 2 fireworks are for outdoor use in relatively confined areas (Garden Fireworks), requiring a minimum spectator distance of 5 metres.

Category 3 fireworks are for use in large outdoor spaces (Display Fireworks), being larger fireworks that require spectator distances of a minimum of 25 metres.

Category 4 fireworks are for specialist use and may only be used by a professionally qualified, trained person (use at an organized public fireworks display, for example). The general public is prohibited from possessing these fireworks.

8.8.2 **Under 18 years—possess 'adult' fireworks**

Offence

Any person who contravenes a prohibition imposed by fireworks regulations is guilty of an offence.

Fireworks Act 2003, s 11(1)

8.8.2 Under 18 Years—Possess 'Adult' Fireworks

Points to prove

✓ date and location
✓ breached a reg 4 prohibition, namely
✓ being a person under the age of 18
✓ possessed in a public place
✓ an adult firework

Prohibition

Subject to **regulation 6** below, no person under the age of eighteen years shall possess an **adult firework** in a **public place**.

Fireworks Regulations 2004, reg 4(1)

Meanings

Regulation 6

- Regulations 4 and 5 shall not prohibit the possession of any firework by any person who is employed by/in trade or business as—
  - professional organizer or operator of firework displays;
  - manufacture of fireworks or assemblies;
  - supply of fireworks or assemblies;
  - local authority/Government department/forces of the Crown for use at a firework display or national public celebration/commemorative event;
  - special effects in the theatre, on film, or on television;
  - acting on behalf of and for purposes of exercising enforcement powers of local authority or enforcement body;
  - Government department use for research or investigations;
  - supplier of goods designed and intended for use in conjunction with fireworks or assemblies for testing and safety purposes.

Adult firework

Means any firework, except Category 1 Indoor Fireworks, namely cap, cracker snap, novelty match, party popper, serpent, sparkler, or throwdown.

Public place

Includes any place to which at the material time the public have or are permitted access, whether on payment or otherwise.

Explanatory notes

- This offence prohibits any person under the age of 18 years, from possessing any firework in a public place (except Category 1 Indoor Fireworks) (see **8.8.1**).
- Those people listed in reg 6 (above) are exempted from liability for this offence and are not prohibited from possession.

Practical considerations

- Any breach of the prohibitions in the Fireworks Regulations 2004 is a criminal offence under the Fireworks Act 2003, s 11(1).
- Consider issuing a penalty notice for disorder (PND) for this offence (see **7.1.1**).
- There are powers to stop, search, and detain people or vehicles and to seize any found fireworks that a person possesses in contravention of a prohibition imposed by these Fireworks Regulations (see **12.1.1**).

 Summary   12 months

 6 months' imprisonment and/or a fine not exceeding level 5 on the standard scale.

8.8.3 **Ban on possession of Category 4 fireworks**

Offence

Any person who contravenes a prohibition imposed by fireworks regulations is guilty of an offence.

Fireworks Act 2003, s 11(1)

Points to prove

- ✓ date and location
- ✓ breached a reg 5 prohibition, namely
- ✓ possessed a Category 4 firework
- ✓ when not exempt from such possession

8.8.4 Use Firework after 11 p.m.

Prohibition

Subject to **regulation 6**, no person shall possess a **Category 4 firework**.

Fireworks Regulations 2004, reg 5

Explanatory notes

- Those people listed in reg 6 (see **8.8.2**) are exempted from liability for this offence and are not prohibited from possession.
- Unless exempted by reg 6, this prohibits a person of any age from possessing **anywhere** a Category 4 firework and an offence will be committed by that person if they breach that regulation.

Practical considerations

- Any breach of the prohibitions in the Fireworks Regulations 2004 is a criminal offence under s 11(1) of the Fireworks Act 2003.
- Consider issuing a PND for disorder for this offence (see **7.1.1**).
- There are powers to stop, search, and detain people or vehicles and to seize any fireworks that a person possesses in contravention of a prohibition imposed by these Fireworks Regulations (see **12.1.1**).
- Category 4 fireworks are for specialist use only under reg 6 (see **8.8.1**).

 Summary 12 months

 6 months' imprisonment and/or a fine not exceeding level 5 on the standard scale.

8.8.4 **Use firework after 11 p.m.**

Offence

Any person who contravenes a prohibition imposed by fireworks regulations is guilty of an offence.

Fireworks Act 2003, s 11(1)

Points to prove

- ✓ date and location
- ✓ breached a reg 7(1) prohibition, namely
- ✓ use an adult firework
- ✓ during night hours

SSS Stop, search, and seize powers   **PND** Penalty notice for disorder offences   **PCSO** Police community support officers

Prohibition

Subject to paragraph (2) *[exception]* below, no person shall use an **adult firework** during **night hours**.

Fireworks Regulations 2004, reg 7(1)

Meanings

Exception—reg 7(2)

Regulation 7(1) above shall not prohibit the use of a firework—
(a) during **a permitted fireworks night**; or
(b) by any person who is employed by a local authority and who uses the firework in question:
  (i)   for the purposes of putting on a firework display by that local authority; or
  (ii) at a national public celebration or a national commemorative event.

Adult Firework (see **8.8.2**)

Night hours

Means the period beginning at 11 p.m. and ending at 7 a.m. the following day.

Permitted fireworks night

Means a period beginning at 11 p.m.—
• on the first day of the Chinese New Year and ending at 1 a.m. the following day;
• and ending at midnight on 5 November;
• on the day of Diwali and ending at 1 a.m. the following day;
• on 31 December and ending at 1 a.m. the following day.

Explanatory notes

• This prohibits the use of a firework (except Category 1 'Indoor Fireworks') (see **8.8.1**) at night and an offence being committed by that person if they breach that regulation.
• Exceptions are New Year's Eve, Diwali, Chinese New Year (extended 11 p.m.–1 a.m.); Bonfire Night (extended 11 p.m.–midnight) or the local authority putting on a firework display.
• This offence is not restricted to a public place and will be committed if a person breaches this prohibition in their own private garden/land.

Practical considerations

• A breach of this prohibition is a criminal offence under s 11(1) of the Fireworks Act 2003, for which a PND can be issued (see **7.1.1**).

- Powers to stop, search, and detain people or vehicles and to seize any fireworks that a person possesses in contravention of a prohibition imposed by the Fireworks Regulations (see **12.1.1**).

 Summary   12 months

 6 months' imprisonment and/or a fine not exceeding level 5 on the standard scale.

8.8.5 **Supply of fireworks to under 18**

Regulation 6 of the Fireworks (Safety) Regulations 1997 prohibits the supply of fireworks to people who are under the age of 18 years, being an offence under s 12(1) of the Consumer Protection Act 1987.

Offences

Where safety regulations prohibit a person from supplying or offering or agreeing to supply any goods or from exposing or possessing any goods for supply, that person shall be guilty of an offence if he contravenes the prohibition.

Consumer Protection Act 1987, s 12(1)

Points to prove

✓ date and location
✓ breached safety regulations prohibition, namely
✓ supply firework/assembly of fireworks
✓ to person apparently under 18 years

Prohibition

(1) Subject to regulation 6(2) below, no person shall **supply** any firework or any assembly to any person under the age of eighteen years.
(2) Regulation 6(1) above shall not prohibit the supply of any cap, cracker snap, novelty match, party popper, serpent or throwdown.

Fireworks (Safety) Regulations 1997, reg 6

SSS Stop, search, and seize powers   **PND** Penalty notice for disorder offences   **PCSO** Police community support officers

Practical considerations

- A breach of this prohibition is a criminal offence under s 12(1) of the Consumer Protection Act 1987.
- Supply includes offering or agreeing to supply, and exposing or possessing for supply: it is not limited to sale.
- Prosecution will be more likely where fireworks have been supplied in the course of a business, rather than a 'casual supply' between friends or family.
- The offence includes all fireworks **except** innocuous 'indoor' ones listed in reg 6(2) of the Fireworks (Safety) Regulations 1997.
- Although supply of Indoor Fireworks (as listed in reg 6(2)) may be an offence under s 31 of the Explosives Act 1875, this states that it is an offence to sell gunpowder to any person under the age of 16 years (eg throwdowns, crackers).
- These offences are not subject to the penalty notices for disorder procedure.

Defence

Section 39(1) of the Consumer Protection Act 1987 states that it shall be a defence for that person to show that he took all reasonable steps and exercised all due diligence to avoid committing the offence under the Act.

 Summary   12 months

 6 months' imprisonment and/or a fine not exceeding level 5 on the standard scale.

8.8.6 Other fireworks/firearms offences (in a highway/street)

Explosives Act

Section 80 of the Explosives Act 1875 creates various offences relating to throw, cast or fire any fireworks in the highway or public place.

Offences

If any person throw, cast, or fire any fireworks in or into any highway, street, thoroughfare, or public place, he shall be guilty of an offence.

Explosives Act 1875, s 80

8.8.6 Other Fireworks/Firearms Offences (in a Highway/Street)

Points to prove
- ✓ date and location
- ✓ throw/cast/fire
- ✓ a firework
- ✓ in/into a highway/street/thoroughfare/public place

Practical considerations

Consider issuing a PND for this offence—'Throwing fireworks in a thoroughfare' (see **7.1.1**).

 Summary   6 months

 A fine not exceeding level 5 on the standard scale.

Highways Act

Section 161 of the Highways Act 1980 creates various offences relating to causing danger on the highway.

Offences

If a person without lawful authority or excuse—

(a) lights any fire on or over a **highway** which consists of or comprises a **carriageway**; or

(b) discharges any firearm or firework within 50 feet of the centre of such a highway,

and in consequence a user of the highway is injured, interrupted or endangered, that person is guilty of an offence.

Highways Act 1980, s 161(2)

Points to prove
- ✓ date and location
- ✓ without lawful authority/excuse
- ✓ discharged
- ✓ a firework or firearm
- ✓ within 50 ft centre of highway
- ✓ comprising a carriageway
- ✓ as a result
- ✓ user injured/interrupted/endangered

 Stop, search, and seize powers   Penalty notice for disorder offences   Police community support officers

Meanings

Highway (see 10.22.2)

Carriageway

Means a way constituting or comprised in a highway, being a way (other than a cycle track) over which the public have a right of way for the passage of vehicles.

 Summary   6 months

 A fine not exceeding level 3 on the standard scale.

Town Police Clauses Act

Section 28 of the Town Police Clauses Act 1847 creates numerous offences.

Offences

Every person who wantonly (without lawful motive and thoughtless as to possible consequences) throws or sets fire to a firework in the street to the obstruction, annoyance, or danger of residents or passengers will commit an offence.

Town Police Clauses Act 1847, s 28

Points to prove
✓ date and location
✓ in street
✓ wantonly
✓ threw/set fire to a firework
✓ to the obstruction/annoyance/danger of residents/passengers

Meaning of street

Street includes any road, square, court, alley, thoroughfare, public passage, carriageway, and footways at the sides.

Explanatory notes

• Section 28 of the Town Police Clauses Act 1847 also states that every person who wantonly (recklessly, without regard for consequences) discharges a firearm in the street to the obstruction, annoyance, or danger of residents or passengers will commit an offence.

8.8.6 Other Fireworks/Firearms Offences (in a Highway/Street)

- None of the Town Police Clauses Act offences are complete unless it can be proved that they would obstruct, annoy, or cause danger to any residents or passengers.
- This Act does not apply to the Metropolitan Police District.

Related cases

Mantle v Jordan [1897] 1 QB 248 The Town Police Clauses Act offences can only be committed in the street, but the annoyance may be to 'residents', meaning the occupiers of houses in the street, although they may not be in the street at the time.

 Summary   6 months

 14 days' imprisonment or a fine not exceeding level 3 on the standard scale.

Links to alternative subjects and offences

8.9 Offensive Weapons and Crossbows

Possession of offensive weapons in a public place, the manufacture and sale of offensive weapons, trespassing with a weapon of offence, and offences involving crossbows form a key part of operational policing and will be dealt with in this section.

8.9.1 Offensive weapons—possession in a public place

The Prevention of Crime Act 1953 prohibits the carrying of offensive weapons in public places without lawful authority or reasonable excuse. This legislation is important in understanding the way in which the courts have approached some cases.

Offences

Any person who without lawful authority or reasonable excuse, the proof whereof shall lie on him, has with him in any public place any offensive weapon shall be guilty of an offence.

Prevention of Crime Act 1953, s 1(1)

Points to prove
✓ date and location
✓ without lawful authority/reasonable excuse
✓ had with you
✓ in a public place
✓ an offensive weapon

Meanings

Has with him (see **8.3.6**)

Public place

Includes any highway and any other premises or place to which at the material time the public have or are permitted to have access, whether on payment or otherwise.

8.9.1 Offensive Weapons—Possession in a Public Place

Offensive weapon

Means any article **made** or **adapted** for use for causing injury to the person, or **intended** by the person having it with them for such use by them, or by some other person.

Explanatory notes

- Within the meaning of offensive weapon particular terms were used and case law has provided meanings to those terms as follows—
  - ◆ 'made' includes articles that have been specifically created for the purpose of causing injury, and includes knuckledusters, flick knives, butterfly knives, sword sticks, truncheons, daggers, bayonets, and rice flails. All of these items are generally classed as offensive weapons per se ('by themselves').
  - ◆ 'adapted' consists of articles that have generally been altered in some way with the intention of causing injury, such as smashing a bottle to make the broken end into a weapon for causing injury.
  - ◆ 'intended' these can be otherwise inoffensive articles that the defendant proposes to use to cause injury to a person, such as a bunch of keys held in the fist with the keys projecting through the fingers (making it an impromptu knuckleduster).
- However, it is important to note that the primary aim of the offence is the **carrying** of such weapons rather than their **use** in the heat of the moment.

Defences

Lawful authority

This extends to people such as an on-duty police officer with a baton.

Reasonable excuse

Whether an excuse is reasonable is for the court to decide having heard all the circumstances. These could include—

- people carrying the tools of their trade (eg hammer/saw by a carpenter or filleting knife by a fishmonger),
- self-defence—if there is an imminent threat, this defence may be available.

Related cases

R v Archbold [2007] EWCA Crim 2137, CA It is for the prosecution to disprove lawful authority or reasonable excuse, but for the defendant to raise it as a defence where appropriate to do so. The issue of lawful authority or reasonable excuse should be left to the jury.

Evans v Hughes [1972] 3 All ER 412, QBD Before a defence of reasonable excuse can be successful, an imminent threat (in this instance self-defence) has to be shown as to why the weapon was carried.

R v Cugullere [1961] 2 All ER 343, CA The defendant must knowingly have article with them in a public place.

Davis v Alexander [1971] Crim LR 595, QBD No need for intention to use if offensive weapon per se.

Ohlson v Hylton [1975] 2 All ER 490, QBD and R v Veasey [1999] Crim LR 158, CA No offence committed if defendant seizes a weapon for 'instant use' on the victim or grabs something innocuous (like a hammer or snooker cue) in the heat of the moment. In these cases the 'weapon' was not carried unlawfully with prior intent. The seizing and use of the weapon were all part of the assault.

R v Allamby and R v Medford [1974] 3 All ER 126, CA Kitchen knives were not offensive weapons per se and so intent to use must be proved.

Practical considerations

- Consider s 1 of PACE where a constable can stop and search persons/ vehicles relating to offensive weapons, bladed/pointed articles and to seize such weapons/articles (see **12.1.1**).
- Where an article is 'made' or 'adapted' to cause injury (offensive per se), the prosecution do not need to prove an intent to cause injury as merely having it with you is sufficient.
- The 'intended' use requires an element of intent to use the article to cause injury, which must be proved. An instant use of an innocent article will need proof of a prior intent otherwise no offence of carrying a weapon is committed.
- Upon conviction the court may make an order for the forfeiture or disposal of any weapon in respect of which the offence was committed.
- If appropriate, consider the offence of possession of a blade/pointed article in a public place (see **8.10**).
- There is a need to prove a knowledge of the existence of the article and that the article is 'to hand and ready for use' (it may, for example, be hidden a few feet away, it does not have to be physically on the defendant's person).
- The burden of proof for lawful authority or reasonable excuse lies with the accused.

 Either way None

 Summary: 6 months' imprisonment and/or a fine not exceeding the statutory maximum.

Indictment: 4 years' imprisonment and/or a fine.

8.9.2 **Offensive weapons—provide/ trade/manufacture**

Transferring ownership, trading in, importing, or manufacturing certain offensive weapons is an offence.

Offences

Any person who manufactures, sells or hires or offers for sale or hire, exposes or has in his possession for the purpose of sale or hire, or lends or gives to any other person, a **weapon to which this section applies** shall be guilty of an offence.

Criminal Justice Act 1988, s 141(1)

Points to prove

✓ date and location
✓ manufactured/sold/hired/lent/gave
✓ an offensive weapon
or
✓ date and location
✓ possess/exposed/offered
✓ for sale/hire
✓ an offensive weapon

Meaning of weapon to which s 141 applies

The Criminal Justice Act 1988 (Offensive Weapons) Order 1988 specifies weapons to which s 141 applies (see **8.9.3**).

Explanatory notes

- The importation of weapons to which s 141 applies is prohibited.
- Some will also fall into the category of being a blade/pointed article (see **8.10**).
- See also a warrant to search for and a power to stop/search/seize these weapons (see **8.11**).
- There are also separate restrictions on make/import/sale/hire of flick and gravity knives (see **8.10.3**).
- This section does not apply to any weapons subject to the Firearms Act 1968 (see **8.1**) or crossbows (see **8.9.5**).
- Consider the offence of using another person to look after, hide or transport a firearm, offensive/bladed weapon or knife, so that it would be available when required for an unlawful purpose (see **8.3.7**).

Defences

This applies to an offence under s 141(1) or s 50(2) or (3) of the Customs and Excise Management Act 1979 (improper importation) if it can be shown that their conduct was only for the purposes of—

- functions carried out on behalf of the Crown or of a visiting force;
- making the weapon available to a museum or gallery;
- making the weapon available for the purposes specified in s 141(11B).

Defence notes

- A person acting on behalf of a museum or gallery can use the above defence if they had reasonable grounds to believe that the person to whom they lent or hired it would use it only for cultural, artistic or educational purposes. The defence will only apply if the **museum or gallery** does not distribute profits.
- **Museum or gallery** includes any institution which has as its purpose, or one of its purposes, the preservation, display and interpretation of material of historical, artistic, or scientific interest and gives the public access to it.
- The purposes under s 141(11B) are for theatrical performances and rehearsals for such performances or for the production of films or television programmes.
- An antique weapon is exempt (more than 100 years old).

 Summary 6 months

 6 months' imprisonment and/or a fine not exceeding level 5 on the standard scale.

8.9.3 The Criminal Justice Act 1988 (Offensive Weapons) Order 1988

This order provides a list of weapons where their sale, hire, offering for sale/hire, exposing, or importation is prohibited. The order excludes antique weapons and provides that a weapon is an antique if it was manufactured more than 100 years before the date of any offence alleged to have been committed in respect of that weapon.

This list only applies to s 141 offences (see **8.9.2**) and is not a list of all offensive weapons per se: knuckleduster; swordstick; butterfly knife; death star; belt buckle knife; hollow kubotan (cylinder holding sharp spikes); push dagger; kusari (rope, cord, wire, or chain with hooked knife, sickle, hard weight or hand grip fastened at one end); foot or hand claw;

blowpipe; telescopic truncheon; disguised knife; baton; stealth knife (non-metallic); disguised knife (blade or sharp point concealed within an everyday object such as a comb, brush, writing instrument, cigarette lighter, key, lipstick, or telephone) and sword with a curved blade.

Explanatory notes

- There are exceptions even if the weapon is on this list.
- The list given above is not an exhaustive or descriptive list, it just gives an idea of the type of weapons included in this order.
- Stealth knives are non-metallic hunting or stiletto knives, made of a range of materials, such as nylon zytel or high impact plastic. Although they look like conventional knives, they are difficult to detect by security apparatus. Their design and construction means that their possession in public may be an offence under—
  - ♦ s 1(1) of the Prevention of Crime Act 1953 (**8.9.1**); or
  - ♦ s 139(1) of the Criminal Justice Act 1988 (**8.10**).
- The 2008 Weapons Amendment Order (SI 2008/973) added a sword with a curved blade of 50 centimetres or over in length to the list, the length of the blade being measured in a straight line from the top of the handle to the tip of the blade. It is a defence if a person can show that—
  - ♦ the sword was made in Japan before 1954 or at any other time using traditional Japanese methods of forging swords, and
  - ♦ an organization requires the use of the weapon for a permitted activity (historical re-enactment or a sporting activity) and that public liability insurance was in force which indemnified those taking part in the activity.

8.9.4 **Trespassing with weapon of offence**

Section 8 of the Criminal Law Act 1977 creates the offence of 'trespassing with a weapon of offence'.

Offence

A person who is on any **premises** as a **trespasser**, after having entered as such, is guilty of an offence if, without lawful authority or reasonable excuse, he **has with him** on the premises any **weapon of offence**.

Criminal Law Act 1977, s 8(1)

Points to prove

- ✓ date and location
- ✓ on premises as trespasser
- ✓ having entered as such
- ✓ had weapon of offence
- ✓ without lawful authority or reasonable excuse

Meanings

Premises

This consists of any—

- building/part of a building (under separate occupation);
- land adjacent to and used/intended for use in connection with a building;
- site comprising any building(s) together with ancillary land;
- fixed structure; and
- moveable structure, vehicle, or vessel designed or adapted for residential purposes.

Trespasser (see 3.3)

Has with him (see 3.4)

Weapon of offence (see 3.4)

Practical considerations

- This offence is worth bearing in mind if the carrying of offensive weapons in a public place/school premises or aggravated burglary does not apply.
- Consider s 1 of the PACE where a constable can stop and search persons/vehicles relating to offensive weapons, bladed/pointed articles and seize such weapons/articles (see 12.1.1).
- Entry must have been as a trespasser— it does not extend to a person who has entered lawfully and later becomes a trespasser (eg being asked to leave by the occupier).

 Summary   6 months

 3 months' imprisonment and/or a fine not exceeding level 5 on the standard scale.

8.9.5 Crossbows

Crossbows are extremely accurate weapons and potentially as lethal as a firearm. This legislation creates offences in relation to persons under 18 years preventing them from possessing, hiring, or purchasing crossbows.

Sell or hire to under 18

Section 1 of the Crossbows Act 1987 creates the offence of selling or letting on hire such a weapon.

8.9.5 Crossbows

Offences

A person who sells or lets on hire a crossbow or part of a crossbow to a person under the age of 18 is guilty of an offence unless he believes him to be 18 years of age or older and has reasonable grounds for that belief.

Crossbows Act 1987, s 1

Points to prove

✓ date and location
✓ sold/let on hire or sold/let on hire part(s) of
✓ a crossbow
✓ to person under 18 years of age

Meaning of crossbow

The Act does not apply to crossbows with a draw weight of less than 1.4 kilograms.

Defences

- Crossbows with a draw weight of less than 1.4 kilograms.
- Reasonable grounds to believe that the person is 18 years or older

Practical considerations

- Proof required of actual age (eg by means of birth certificate).
- The Violent Crime Reduction Act 2006, s 44 raised the age from 17 to 18 years.

 Summary   6 months

 6 months' imprisonment and/or a fine not exceeding level 5 on the standard scale.

Under 18—purchase/hire a crossbow

Offences

A person under the age of 18 who buys or hires a crossbow or a part of a crossbow is guilty of an offence.

Crossbows Act 1987, s 2

Points to prove

✓ date and location
✓ person under 18 years of age
✓ hired/purchased or purchased/hired part(s) of
✓ a crossbow

Practical considerations

- Evidential proof required of the age of the person (eg ID card or birth certificate).
- This Act only applies to crossbows that are of a certain strength (called the draw weight).
- The draw weight limit is very low and can be determined by the Forensic Science Laboratory; only toys will be excluded by this definition.

 Summary　　　　　 6 months

 A fine not exceeding level 3 on the standard scale.

Under 18—possess a crossbow

Offences

A person under the age of 18 who **has with him**—

(a) a crossbow which is capable of discharging a missile, or
(b) parts of a crossbow which together (and without any other parts) can be assembled to form a crossbow capable of discharging a missile,

is guilty of an offence, unless he is under the supervision of a person who is 21 years of age or older.

Crossbows Act 1987, s 3

Points to prove

✓ date and location
✓ being under the age of 18
✓ had with you
✓ a crossbow/crossbow parts (able to form a crossbow)
✓ capable of discharging a missile

8.9.5 Crossbows

Meanings

Has with him (see **8.3.6**)

Crossbow

The Act only applies to crossbows with a draw weight of more than 1.4 kilograms.

Explanatory notes

- This offence can be committed anywhere and not just in public.
- No offence will be committed if (under 18 years old) is under supervision of person age 21 or over.

Practical considerations

- Ages require actual proof (eg ID card or birth certificate).
- This Act only applies to crossbows that are of a certain strength (called the draw weight).
- The draw weight limit is very low and can be determined by the Forensic Science Laboratory; only toys will be excluded by this definition.
- Although the Act may allow a person of 18 or over to possess a crossbow in public, it may be an offence under s 139 of the Criminal Justice Act 1988 (pointed article/blades) due to the crossbow bolts (**8.10**).

 Summary   6 months

 A fine not exceeding level 3 on the standard scale.

Crossbows—search and seizure powers

Section 4 of the Crossbows Act 1987 gives police officers quite wide powers of search, detain, seizure, and entry onto land if a person under 18 years is unsupervised and is in possession of a crossbow/parts.

Powers

(1) If a constable suspects with reasonable cause that a person is committing or has committed an offence under section 3, the constable may—
   (a) search that person for a crossbow or part of a crossbow;
   (b) search any vehicle, or anything in or on a vehicle, in or on which the constable suspects with reasonable cause there is a crossbow, or part of a crossbow, connected with the offence.
(2) A constable may detain a person or vehicle for the purpose of a search under subsection (1).

---

(3) A constable may seize and retain for the purpose of proceedings for an offence under this Act anything discovered by him in the course of a search under subsection (1) which appears to him to be a crossbow or part of a crossbow.

(4) For the purpose of exercising the powers conferred by this section a constable may enter any land other than a dwelling-house.

Crossbows Act 1987, s 4

Explanatory notes

- A constable may detain a person or vehicle for the purpose of this search.
- A constable may seize and retain anything found in the course of this search which appears to be a crossbow or part of a crossbow.
- In exercising this power a constable may enter on any land **other than** a dwelling house.

Practical considerations

- Consider powers under s 1 PACE that could apply. Ensure compliance with the PACE COP procedures relating to stop and searches (see **12.1**).
- This Act only applies to crossbows that are of a certain strength (called the draw weight).
- The draw weight limit is very low and can be determined by the Forensic Science Laboratory; only toys will be excluded by this definition.
- Although the Act may allow a person of 18 or over to possess a crossbow in public, the person may commit an offence under s 139 of the Criminal Justice Act 1988 (pointed article/blades) due to the crossbow bolts (**8.10**).

Links to alternative subjects and offences

8.9.5 Crossbows

8.10 Bladed Articles/Knives Offences

The Criminal Justice Act 1988 deals with offences of having knives/bladed articles in a public place or on school premises, and sale to persons under 18 years. Whereas the Restriction of Offensive Weapons Act 1959, deals with making, importing, selling, or hiring a flick or gravity knife.

8.10.1 Possession of bladed/pointed article in public place

Section 139 of the Criminal Justice Act 1988 creates an offence of having a bladed or pointed article in a public place.

Offence

Subject to subsections (4) and (5) [*defences*] below, any person who has an **article** to which this section applies **with him** in a **public place** shall be guilty of an offence.

Criminal Justice Act 1988, s 139(1)

Points to prove
✓ Date and location
✓ had with them
✓ without good reason/lawful authority
✓ an article being bladed/sharply pointed
✓ in a public place

Meanings

Article
Applies to any article that has a **blade** or is sharply pointed, except a folding pocket knife where the cutting edge of the blade is 7.62 cm (three inches) long or less.

Blade
Examples of this will be the blade of a knife, sword.

Has with him (see **8.3.6**)

8.10.1 Possession of Bladed/Pointed Article in Public Place

Public place

Includes any place to which at the material time the public have or are permitted access, whether on payment or otherwise.

Explanatory notes

- A folding pocket knife does not include a lock knife, regardless of the blade length.
- Possession of a multi-tool incorporating a prohibited blade/pointed article is capable of being an offence under this section, even if there are other tools on the instrument that may be of practical use (such as a bottle-opener).
- The burden of proof is with the defendant to show good reason or lawful authority for having the blade/pointed article with them.
- Consider s 1 of PACE where a constable can stop and search persons/ vehicles relating to offensive weapons, bladed/pointed articles and to seize such weapons/articles (see **12.1.1**).
- Be aware of specific offences relating to possession of blade/pointed article and offensive weapons on school premises (see **8.10.4**).

Defences

(4) It shall be a defence for a person charged with an offence under this section to prove that he had good reason or lawful authority for having the article with him in a public place.

(5) Without prejudice to the generality of subsection (4) above, it shall be a defence for a person charged with an offence under this section to prove that he had the article with him—
   (a) for use at work;
   (b) for religious reasons; or
   (c) as part of any national costume.

Criminal Justice Act 1988, s 139

Defence notes

Examples of having the article with them could be—

- **for use at work**—fishmonger, carpet fitter, chef;
- **for religious reasons**—members of the Sikh religion having a *kirpan*;
- **as part of a national costume**—the *skean dhu* in Highland dress.

Related cases

Harriott v DPP [2005] EWHC 965 (Admin), QBD The forecourt area of a Bail Hostel was part of private premises. Unless it is shown that the general public have a right of access, a place will not come within the meaning of a 'public place'.

R v Davis [1998] Crim LR 564, CA Ruled that a screwdriver was not a 'bladed article'. A blade needs to fall within the same category as a sharply pointed item or the blade on a folding pocket knife having a cutting edge.

Brooker v DPP [2005] EWHC 1132, QBD Stated that a butter knife was a bladed article—there is no rule that it only applies to sharp blades.

Harris v DPP [1993] 1 WLR 82, QBD A lock knife is not a folding pocket knife, regardless of the blade length.

R v Daubney (2000) 164 JP 519, CA The prosecution must prove that the defendant had the article with them and their actual knowledge of the article.

R v Cheong Wang [2003] EWCA Crim 3228, CA A Buddhist practising the martial art of Shaolin had a sword and Gurkha-type knife with him in public, but had failed to provide sufficient religious reason for possession.

 Either way   6 months

 Summary: 6 months' imprisonment and/or a fine not exceeding the statutory maximum.

Indictment: 4 years' imprisonment and/or a fine.

8.10.2 **Sale of knives/blades to persons under 18**

Section 141A of the Criminal Justice Act 1988 creates the offence of selling knives or certain articles with a blade or point to people under the age of 18.

Offence

Any person who sells to a person under the age of 18 years an **article** to which **this section applies** shall be guilty of an offence.

Criminal Justice Act 1988, s 141A(1)

Points to prove
- ✓ date and location
- ✓ sold
- ✓ knife/axe/knife blade/razor blade or
- ✓ blade/sharply pointed article being made/adapted for use for causing injury
- ✓ to person under 18 years

8.10.2 Sale of Knives/Blades to Persons Under 18

Meanings

Article to which this section applies

Subject to **subsection (3)** below, this section applies to—

(a) any knife, knife blade or razor blade,

(b) any axe, and

(c) any other article which has a blade or which is sharply pointed and which is made or adapted for use for causing injury to the person.

Subsection (3)

This section does not apply to any article described in—

(a) section 1 of the Restriction of Offensive Weapons Act 1959,

(b) an order made under section 141(2) of this Act, or

(c) an order made by the Secretary of State under this section.

Explanatory notes

- Section 1 of the Restriction of Offensive Weapons Act 1959 deals with offences of trading in flick knives, flick guns or gravity knives (see **8.10.3**).
- An order made under s 141(2) of this Act (see **8.9.2**) relates to weapons given in the Criminal Justice Act 1988 (Offensive Weapons) Order 1988 such as knuckledusters, swordsticks, belt daggers (see **8.9.3**).
- The Criminal Justice Act 1988 (Offensive Weapons) (Exemption) Order 1996, states that this section does not apply to—
  - folding pocket-knives if the cutting edge of the blade does not exceed 7.62 centimetres (3 inches);
  - razor blades permanently enclosed in a cartridge or housing where less than 2 millimetres of any blade is protruding.

Defence

It shall be a defence for a person charged with an offence under s 141A(1) to prove that they took all reasonable precautions and exercised all due diligence to avoid the commission of the offence.

Practical Considerations

- The above defence goes beyond appearance or enquiring about the age of the purchaser, such as proving age by identity card.
- Consider the offence of using another person to look after, hide, or transport a firearm, offensive/bladed weapon or knife, so that it would be available when required for an unlawful purpose (see **8.3.7**).

Summary 6 months

6 months' imprisonment and/or a fine not exceeding level 5 on the standard scale.

8.10.3 **Make/import/sell/hire a flick or gravity knife**

The Restriction of Offensive Weapons Act 1959 creates offences of trading in flick or gravity knives.

Offences

Any person who manufactures, sells or hires, or offers for sale or exposes or has in his possession for the purpose of sale or hire, or lends or gives to any other person—

(a) any knife which has a blade which opens automatically by hand pressure applied to a button, spring or other device in or attached to the handle of the knife, sometimes known as a 'flick knife' or 'flick gun'; or

(b) any knife which has a blade which is released from the handle or sheath thereof by the force of gravity or the application of centrifugal force and which, when released, is locked in place by means of a button, spring, lever, or other device, sometimes known as a 'gravity knife',

shall be guilty of an offence.

Restriction of Offensive Weapons Act 1959, s 1(1)

Points to prove

✓ date and location
✓ manufactured/sold/hired/offered for sale **or**
✓ exposed **or**
✓ possessed for the purpose of sale/hire **or**
✓ lent or gave
✓ to a person
✓ any flick knife/flick gun/gravity knife

Expanatory notes

- The importation of any flick knife, flick gun, or gravity knife is an offence under s 170 of the Customs and Excise Management Act 1979.
- A lock knife is not a gravity knife.

 Summary 6 months

6 months' imprisonment and/or a fine not exceeding level 5 on the standard scale.

8.10.4 Possess weapon/blade/sharp point on school premises

Section 139A of the Criminal Justice Act 1988 creates the offence of possessing an article with a blade or sharp point or an offensive weapon on school premises.

Offences

(1) Any person who has an article to which section 139 of this Act applies **with him** on **school premises** shall be guilty of an offence.
(2) Any person who has an offensive weapon within the meaning of section 1 of the Prevention of Crime Act 1953 with him on school premises shall be guilty of an offence.

Criminal Justice Act 1988, s 139A

Points to prove

✓ date and location
✓ without good reason/lawful authority
✓ had with you
✓ on school premises
✓ an offensive weapon/article being a blade/sharply pointed

Meanings

Has with him (see 8.3.6)

School premises

Means land used for the purposes of a **school**, excluding any land occupied solely as a dwelling by a person employed at the school.

School (Education Act 1996, s 4)

Means an educational institution which is outside the further or higher education sector and is an institution for providing—

(a) primary education,

(b) secondary education, or

(c) both primary and secondary education

whether or not the institution also provides further education.

Article (see **8.10.1**)

Offensive weapon (see **8.9.1**)

Explanatory notes

- School premises can include open land, such as playing fields or schoolyards. However, dwellings occupied within the premises by employees, such as caretakers' or wardens' houses, are outside the scope of this section.
- The offence applies to both publicly maintained and independent schools.
- An offence can be committed at any time of the day or night, during term time or holidays; it does not have to be during school hours;
- Many schools do not allow access to the general public outside or even during school hours, so these offences cover the situation where such weapons are carried on school premises that are not public places.

Defences

(3) It shall be a defence for a person charged with an offence under subsection (1) or (2) above to prove that he had good reason or lawful authority for having the article or weapon with him on the premises in question.

(4) Without prejudice to the generality of subsection (3) above, it shall be a defence for a person charged with an offence under subsection (1) or (2) above to prove that he had the article or weapon in question with him—

  (a) for use at work,

  (b) for educational purposes,

  (c) for religious reasons, or

  (d) as part of any national costume.

Criminal Justice Act 1988, s 139A

Practical considerations

- Section 93 of the Education and Inspections Act 2006 gives members of staff powers to restrain pupils to prevent the pupil from: committing a specific offence, causing personal injury/damage to property, or engaging in any behaviour prejudicial to the maintenance of good order and discipline at the school.
- Section 550AA of the Education Act 1996 gives authorized members of staff (England only), powers to use reasonable force to search

pupils for weapons, namely a bladed article/knife (see **8.10.1**) or an offensive weapon (see **8.9.1**). It also gives power to seize and retain any such weapons found.

- Similar powers exist under the **Further and Higher Education Act 1992**—
  - ◆ Under s 85A a person who is causing a nuisance or disturbance on higher educational premises will commit an offence. This section also gives a constable or authorized person power to remove such a person from those premises.
  - ◆ Section 85B gives the principal or authorized member of staff in a further education institution (England only) power to use reasonable force to search further education students and their possessions for a bladed article/knife (see **8.10.1**) or offensive weapon (see **8.9.1**). It also gives power to seize and retain any such weapons found.
- Consider the offence of causing/permitting a nuisance/disturbance on school premises (see **8.10.5**).
- There is a specific police power to enter and search school premises in connection with this offence (see **8.11.2**).
- Consider s 1 of PACE where a constable can stop and search persons/vehicles relating to offensive weapons, bladed/pointed articles and to seize such weapons/articles (see **12.1.1**).

 Either way

 None

 Summary: 6 months' imprisonment and/or a fine not exceeding the statutory maximum.

Indictment: 4 years' imprisonment and/or a fine.

8.10.5 **Nuisance/disturbance on school premises**

Section 547 of the Education Act 1996 creates the offence of causing a nuisance or disturbance on school premises and gives the police power to remove people committing such an offence.

Offences

Any person who without lawful authority is present on premises to which this section applies and causes or permits nuisance or disturbance to the annoyance of persons who lawfully use those premises (whether or not any such persons are present at the time) is guilty of an offence.

Education Act 1996, s 547(1)

SSS Stop, search, and seize powers   **E&S** Entry and search powers

Points to prove

✓ date and location
✓ without lawful authority
✓ was present on
✓ premises of local authority maintained/grant-maintained school
✓ and permitted/caused
✓ a nuisance/disturbance
✓ to the annoyance of persons lawfully using those premises

Power to remove offenders

If a police constable, or an authorised person (of appropriate authority) has reasonable cause to suspect that any person is committing or has committed an offence under this section, he may remove him from the premises in question.

Education Act 1996, s 547(3)

Explanatory notes

• A power also exists to enter school premises and search persons on those premises on reasonable grounds for believing that offences are being or have been committed in relation to articles and weapons (see **8.10.4** and **8.11.2**).

• Similar powers exist for teachers at schools, and members of staff at higher education establishments (see **8.10.4**).

• **Premises** includes playgrounds, playing fields, and other premises for outdoor recreation of any—
  ◆ school maintained by a local education authority,
  ◆ special school not so maintained, and
  ◆ independent school.

• **Premises** also applies to those provided by the local education authority for recreation, social, and physical training and used wholly or mainly in connection with instruction or leadership in sporting, recreational, or outdoor activities.

 Summary   6 months

 A fine not exceeding level 2 on the standard scale.

Links to alternative subjects and offences

8.11 Stop and Search Powers—Knives and Weapons

The Criminal Justice Act 1988 deals with premises search warrants and stop and search powers for school premises.

8.11.1 Search warrant for premises

Section 142 of the Criminal Justice Act 1988 creates a search power in respect of premises.

Grounds for issue of warrant

If on an application made by a constable a justice of the peace is satisfied that there are reasonable grounds for believing—

(a) that there are on premises specified in the application—
   (i) knives such as are mentioned in section 1(1) of the Restriction of Offensive Weapons Act 1959; or
   (ii) weapons to which section 141 applies; and
(b) that an offence under section 1 of the Restriction of Offensive Weapons Act 1959 or section 141 above has been or is being committed in relation to them; and
(c) that any of the **conditions** specified in subsection (3) below applies, he may issue a warrant authorising a constable to enter and search the premises.

Criminal Justice Act 1988, s 142(1)

Meaning of conditions

The conditions relate to any of the following, in that—

* it is not practicable to communicate with any person entitled to grant entry to the premises or grant access to the knives or weapons to which the application relates;
* entry to the premises will not be granted unless a warrant is produced;
* the purpose of a search may be frustrated or seriously prejudiced unless a constable arriving at the premises can secure immediate entry to them.

Explanatory notes

* Restriction of Offensive Weapons Act 1959 refers to any flick knife, flick gun, or gravity knife (see **8.10.3**).

- Weapons under s 141 are listed in The Offensive Weapons Order 1988 (see **8.9.2** and **8.9.3**).
- A constable may seize and retain anything for which a search has been authorized under s 142(1) above.

8.11.2 **Powers for article/weapon on school premises**

Section 139B of the Criminal Justice Act 1988 provides a power of entry to school premises to search for offensive weapons or articles with a blade or sharp point, and to seize/retain any weapon/article found.

Enter and search

A constable may enter school premises and search those premises and any person on those premises for—

(a) any article to which section 139 of the Criminal Justice Act 1988 applies, **or**

(b) any offensive weapon within the meaning of section 1 of the Prevention of Crime Act 1953,

if he has reasonable grounds for suspecting that an offence under section 139A of this Act is being, or has been, committed.

Criminal Justice Act 1988, s 139B(1)

Seize and retain

If, in the course of a search under this section, a constable discovers an article or weapon which he has reasonable grounds for suspecting to be an article or weapon of a kind described in subsection (1) above, he may seize and retain it.

Criminal Justice Act 1988, s 139B(2)

Explanatory notes

- A constable may use reasonable force, if necessary, in the exercise of the power of entry conferred by this section.
- For the offence under s 139A of the CJA 1988 see **8.10.4**.
- An article under s 139 is a bladed/sharply pointed article (see **8.10.1**).
- For offensive weapon under the Prevention of Crime Act 1953, s 1 see **8.9.1**.

Practical considerations

- Consider s 1 of PACE where a constable can stop and search persons/vehicles relating to offensive weapons, bladed/pointed articles and seize such weapons/articles (see **12.1.1**).
- Powers under s 139B are additional to and overlap the powers of entry and search under s 17 of PACE (see **12.3.2**).

- If a large number of people are involved, causing fear of a serious public order situation, then stop and search powers under the Criminal Justice and Public Order Act 1994, s 60, should be considered (see **8.11.3**).
- Consider the offence and power to remove a person who causes or permits a nuisance or disturbance on school premises (see **8.10.5**).

8.11.3 **Stop and search—serious violence/ offensive weapon**

Section 60 of the Criminal Justice and Public Order Act 1994 allows senior police officers to authorize constables to stop and search people or vehicles in a specific area, either where a serious public order problem is likely to arise, has taken place or people are carrying offensive weapons or sharp pointed blades. An offence will be committed if that person fails to comply with constable's requirements.

Authorisation

If a police officer of or above the rank of inspector reasonably believes—

(a) that incidents involving serious violence may take place in any locality in his police area, and that it is expedient to give an authorisation under this section to prevent their occurrence,

(aa) that—

   (i) an incident involving serious violence has taken place in England and Wales in his police area;

   (ii) a dangerous instrument or offensive weapon used in the incident is being carried in any locality in his police area by a person; and

   (iii) it is expedient to give an authorisation under this section to find the instrument or weapon; or

(b) that persons are carrying dangerous instruments or offensive weapons in any locality in his police area without good reason,

he may give an authorisation that the powers conferred by this section are to be exercisable at **any place** within that locality for a specified period not exceeding 24 hours.

Criminal Justice and Public Order Act 1994, s 60(1)

Explanatory notes

- Where a serious violent incident has occurred, and it is believed that the weapon used in the incident is still being carried in the locality, this power assists in locating the weapon used, and in apprehending the offender before they leave the area or disperse.
- If an authorization has been given orally under s 60(1)(aa) it needs to be in writing as soon as is practicable. Authorizations made under s 60(1)(a) or (b) will still need to be made in writing.

8.11.3 Stop and Search—Serious Violence/Offensive Weapon

- The inspector giving an authorization must, as soon as practicable, inform an officer of or above the rank of superintendent.
- If it appears to an officer of or above the rank of superintendent that it is expedient to do so, they may direct that the authorization shall continue being in force for a further 24 hours. This shall be recorded in writing as soon as practicable.
- Any authorization shall be in writing signed by the officer giving it, and shall specify the grounds, locality, and the period during which the powers are exercisable.

Power to stop and search pedestrian/vehicle

(4) This section confers on any constable in uniform power—
  (a) to stop any pedestrian and search him or anything carried by him for **offensive weapons** or **dangerous instruments**;
  (b) to stop any **vehicle** and search the vehicle, its driver and any passenger for offensive weapons or dangerous instruments.
(5) A constable may, in the exercise of the powers conferred by subsection (4) above, stop any person or vehicle and make any search he thinks fit whether or not he has any grounds for suspecting that the person or vehicle is carrying weapons or articles of that kind.

Criminal Justice and Public Order Act 1994, s 60

Power to seize

If in the course of such a search under this section a constable discovers a dangerous instrument or an article which he has reasonable grounds for suspecting to be an offensive weapon, he may seize it.

Criminal Justice and Public Order Act 1994, s 60(6)

Offences

A person who fails to stop, or to stop a vehicle, when required to do so by a constable in the exercise of his powers under this section commits an offence.

Criminal Justice and Public Order Act 1994, s 60(8)

Points to prove

- ✓ date and location
- ✓ failed to stop (person) or vehicle
- ✓ when required to do so
- ✓ by a constable in uniform
- ✓ in exercising powers of stop/search

Meanings

Offensive weapon

Means any article made or adapted for use for causing injury to persons; or intended by the person having it with them for such use by them or by some other person. In the case of an incident that has taken place under 60(1)(aa)(i) above—means any article used in the incident to cause or threaten injury to any person or otherwise to intimidate.

Dangerous instrument

Means instruments which have a blade or are sharply pointed.

Vehicle

This is the natural meaning of vehicle (see **12.1.1**) and includes a caravan.

Explanatory notes

- Once a written authority has been given for searches, under s 60(5) a constable can stop any person/vehicle or make any search that they think fit. There is **no requirement** to have 'reasonable grounds for suspicion' before the constable can do any stop searches.
- Any driver or persons stopped and/or searched under this section are entitled to a written statement stating that they were stopped and/or searched under these powers if they apply within 12 months.
- A person carries a dangerous instrument or an offensive weapon if they have it in their physical possession.

Related cases

R (on the application of Laporte) v Chief Constable of Gloucestershire [2006] UKHL 55, HL This case involved 3 coaches stopped and searched under a s 60 authority (see **'Related cases'** under **7.3** for further details).

Practical considerations

- Apart from BT police, only Inspectors and Superintendents from Home Office forces may authorize these powers to be exercised, although officers from other police forces (RMP, Civil Nuclear Constabulary) may be involved in such searches.
- With the necessary modifications, s 60 also applies to ships, aircraft, and hovercraft as it applies to vehicles.
- Powers conferred by s 60 are in addition to and do not derogate from any other statutory powers.
- Where a s 60 authority exists, a power under s 60AA can be utilized, whereby any items, masks or disguises which are used in order to conceal identity can be removed and seized. An offence will be committed if a person fails to remove an item worn by them when required to do so by a constable in exercising this power.

8.11.3 Stop and Search—Serious Violence/Offensive Weapon

 Summary

 6 months

1 months' imprisonment and/or a fine not exceeding level 3 on the standard scale.

Links to alternative subjects and offences

Chapter 9

Alcohol and Licensing

9.1 Alcohol Restrictions on Persons under 16/18

The sale and supply of alcohol is regulated by the Licensing Act 2003 and creates a number of offences relating to children, young people, alcohol, drunkenness, and disorderly conduct.

The following offences will protect children both **on and off licensed premises**; some of them apply anywhere and are not restricted to licensed premises.

9.1.1 Unaccompanied children prohibited from certain premises

It is an offence to admit children under 16 to certain categories of relevant premises if they are not accompanied by an adult or allow them to be on these premises between midnight and 5 a.m., and those premises are open for the supply of alcohol for consumption therein.

Offences

A person to whom **subsection (3) applies** commits an offence if—
(a) knowing that **relevant premises** are **within subsection (4),** he allows an unaccompanied **child** to be on the premises at a time when they are open for the purposes of being used for the supply of **alcohol** for consumption there, **or**
(b) he allows an **unaccompanied** child to be on relevant premises at a time between the hours of midnight and 5 a.m. when the premises are open for the purposes of being used for the **supply of alcohol** for consumption there.

Licensing Act 2003, s 145(1)

9.1.1 Unaccompanied Children Prohibited from Certain Premises

> **Points to prove**
> - ✓ date and location
> - ✓ being a person to whom sub-s (3) applies
> - ✓ knowing they were relevant premises
> - ✓ allowed an unaccompanied child
> - ✓ to be on premises at a time/between midnight and 5 a.m.
> - ✓ when open for supplying alcohol for consumption therein

Meanings

Person to whom subsection (3) applies

Any person who—

- Works at the premises in a capacity, whether paid or unpaid, which authorizes him to request the unaccompanied child to leave the premises.
- In the case of licensed premises, to the holder of a premises licence in respect of the premises, and the designated premises supervisor (if any) under such a licence.
- In the case of premises in respect of which a club premises certificate has effect, to any member or officer of the club which holds the certificate who is present on the premises in a capacity which enables him to make such a request.
- In the case of premises which may be used for a permitted temporary activity by virtue of Pt 5 of the Licensing Act 2003, to the premises user in relation to the temporary event notice in question.

Relevant premises

Means premises—
- that are licensed, or
- which has a club premises certificate in force, or
- that may be used for a permitted temporary activity (under Pt 5 of the Act).

Relevant premises within subsection 4

Relevant premises are within this subsection if they are—
- exclusively or primarily used for the supply of alcohol for consumption on the premises, **or**
- open for the purposes of the supply of alcohol for consumption on the premises by virtue of Part 5 (permitted temporary activities) and, at the time the temporary event notice has effect, they are exclusively or primarily used for such supplies.

Child

Means an individual aged under 16.

Alcohol—s 191

Means spirits, wine, beer, cider or any other fermented, distilled or spirituous liquor, but does **not** include—

- alcohol which is of a strength not exceeding 0.5 per cent at the time of the sale or supply in question;
- perfume;
- flavouring essences recognised by HMRC as not being intended for consumption as or with dutiable alcoholic liquor;
- the aromatic flavouring essence commonly known as Angostura bitters;
- alcohol which is, or is included in, a medicinal product, or a veterinary medicinal product;
- denatured alcohol;
- methyl alcohol;
- naphtha; or
- alcohol contained in liqueur confectionery.

Unaccompanied

Means not in the company of an individual aged 18 or over.

Supply of alcohol

Means the sale by retail of alcohol, or the supply of alcohol by or on behalf of a club to, or to the order of, a member of the club.

Explanatory notes

No offence is committed if the unaccompanied child is on the premises solely for the purpose of passing to or from some other place to or from which there is no other convenient means of access or exit.

Defences—s 145(6)–(8)

- That the conduct was by act or default of some other person and that the defendant exercised all **due diligence** to avoid committing it.
- Where the defendant by reason of their own conduct—
  - **believed** that the unaccompanied child was aged **16 or over** or that an individual accompanying the child was aged 18 or over, and
  - either—
    - had taken **all reasonable steps** to establish the individual's age, or
    - nobody could reasonably have suspected from the individual's appearance that they were aged under 16 or, as the case may be, under 18.

Defence notes

- A person is treated as having taken all reasonable steps to establish an individual's age if—
  - they asked the individual for evidence of their age, and
  - the evidence would have convinced a reasonable person.

9.1.2 Sale of Alcohol to Person Under 18

- This defence will fail if it is proved by the prosecution that the evidence of age was such that no reasonable person would have been convinced by it—for example, if the proof of age was either an obvious forgery or clearly belonged to another person.
- The defence also applies in situations where the child looks exceptionally old for his or her age.

Practical considerations

Age to be identified by ID card, driving licence, or similar document.

 Summary 12 months

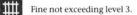 Fine not exceeding level 3.

9.1.2 Sale of alcohol to person under 18

The sale of alcohol to a person under 18 anywhere is an offence.

> **Offence**
> A person commits an offence if he sells **alcohol** to an individual aged under 18.
>
> Licensing Act 2003, s 146(1)

Points to prove
- ✓ date and location
- ✓ sold alcohol
- ✓ to person under the age of 18

Meaning of alcohol (see **9.1.1**)

Explanatory notes

- Similar offences apply where a club supplies alcohol to under 18 by it or on its behalf (s 146(2)) or where a person supplies to under 18 on behalf of the club (s 146(3)).
- The sale of alcohol to children is not only an offence if it occurs on relevant licensed premises, but **anywhere**.

Defences—s 146(4)–(6)

- Where a defendant by reason of their own conduct—
    - ♦ believed that the individual was aged 18 or over, and
    - ♦ either—
        - they had taken all reasonable steps to establish the individual's age, or
        - nobody could reasonably have suspected from the individual's appearance that they were aged under 18.
- That the offence was committed by act or default of some other person and that the defendant exercised all **due diligence** to avoid committing it.

Defence notes

- For the meaning of 'having taken all reasonable steps' (see **9.1.1** '**Defence notes**').
- The statutory defence could apply, for example, where the actual sale was made by a barman and the manager had exercised all due diligence to avoid the offence being committed.

Practical considerations

- Age to be identified by ID card, driving licence, or similar document.
- This offence can be dealt with by way of a penalty notice for disorder (see **7.1.1**).

PND Issue for s 146(1), (3) offences only (not s 146(2) club offences).

PCSO Applies to s 146(1) offences only (no powers in relation to clubs).

Summary   12 months

A fine not exceeding level 5.

9.1.3 Allowing the sale of alcohol to person under 18

It is also an offence to allow alcohol to be sold to a person under 18.

Offence

A person to whom **subsection (2)** applies commits an offence if he **knowingly** allows the sale of **alcohol** on **relevant premises** to an individual aged under 18.

Licensing Act 2003, s 147(1)

9.1.3 Allowing the Sale of Alcohol to Person Under 18

Points to prove

✓ date and location
✓ being person to whom sub-s (2) applies
✓ on relevant premises
✓ knowingly allowed the sale of alcohol
✓ to a person under the age of 18

Meanings

Person to whom subsection (2) applies

Any person who works at the premises in a capacity, whether paid or unpaid, which authorizes them to prevent the sale.

Knowingly

Means having knowledge (see '**Related cases**'), an awareness, informed, consciously, intentionally, or an understanding.

Alcohol   (see **9.1.1**)

Relevant premises   (see **9.1.1**)

Explanatory notes

- There are no statutory defences to this offence. The mental element 'knowingly' applies only to allowing the sale; it does not require knowledge that the individual was under 18. The prosecution need only prove that the individual was under 18.
- Similar offences apply under s 147(3) where an employee or member/officer of a club fail to prevent supply on relevant premises by or on behalf of the club to a member/individual who is aged under 18.

Related cases

Ross v Moss and Others [1965] 3 All ER 145, QBD If the licensee or other appropriate person is on the premises and looks the other way to a particular unlawful practice they cannot then say that they had no personal knowledge. 'Knowledge' not only means actual knowledge, but it also includes 'shutting one's eyes' to what is going on and the intention that what is happening should happen but deliberately looking the other way.

Practical considerations

- Age to be identified by ID card, driving licence, or similar document.
- An offence of **persistently selling alcohol to children (under 18)** will be committed under s 147A if on three or more different occasions, within a period of three consecutive months, alcohol is unlawfully sold on the same premises to an individual aged under 18.

- The following procedural requirements under s 147A also apply—
  - The premises must be either licensed premises or authorized premises for a permitted temporary activity by virtue of Pt 5, and the offender must hold the premises licence or be the named premises user for a temporary event notice.
  - The same sale may not be counted as different offences for this purpose.
  - The following shall be admissible as evidence that there has been an unlawful sale of alcohol to an individual aged under 18 on any premises on any occasion—
    - a conviction for a s 146 offence in respect of a sale to that individual on those premises on that occasion;
    - a caution in respect of such an offence; or
    - payment of a penalty notice for disorder in respect of such a sale.
  - A sale of alcohol is not to count as an occasion if it took place before the commencement of s 147A (6 April 2007).
- Section 147B provides that if the holder of a premises licence is convicted of an offence under s 147A for sales on those premises, the court may order that the premises licence is suspended for a period not exceeding three months.
- A closure notice for persistently selling alcohol to children under 18 can be issued (see **9.3.4**).

 Summary   12 months

 A fine not exceeding level 5.

9.1.4 Purchase of alcohol by or on behalf of person under 18

Offences are committed by a person under 18, or person on behalf of the under 18, who purchases or attempts to purchase alcohol anywhere. Similarly it is an offence for a person to buy or attempt to buy alcohol for consumption by a person who is under 18 on licensed premises.

Offences

(1)(a) An individual aged under 18 commits an offence if he buys or attempts to buy **alcohol**.

(3)(a) A person commits an offence if he buys or attempts to buy **alcohol** on behalf of an individual aged under 18.

(4)(a) A person commits an offence if he buys or attempts to buy **alcohol** for consumption on **relevant premises** by an individual aged under 18.

Licensing Act 2003, s 149

9.1.4 Purchase of Alcohol by or on Behalf of Person Under 18

Points to prove

s 149(1)(a) offence
- ✓ date and location
- ✓ being a person under the age of 18
- ✓ bought alcohol or attempted to buy alcohol

s 149(3)(a) offence
- ✓ date and location
- ✓ bought alcohol **or** attempted to buy alcohol
- ✓ on behalf of individual under the age of 18

s 149(4)(a) offence
- ✓ date and location
- ✓ bought alcohol **or** attempted to buy alcohol
- ✓ for consumption on relevant premises
- ✓ by an individual under the age of 18

Meanings

Alcohol (see **9.1.1**)

Relevant premises (see **9.1.1**)

Explanatory notes

- Offences in s 149(1)(a) and s 149(3)(a) may be committed **anywhere**.
- 'On behalf of' does not mean that the purchase must be instigated by the child; the alcohol need only be bought for a child.
- An example of an offence under this section would be where a person under 18 gives money to an adult to buy alcohol in an off-licence for consumption by that child/young person.
- Section 149(2) states that the s 149(1) offence does not apply to an individual aged under 18 who buys or attempts to buy the alcohol at the request of a constable, or a weights and measures inspector who are acting in the course of their duty. This exception allows test-purchasing operations to take place (see **9.3.1**).
- Similarly s 149(5) states that a s 149(4) offence does not apply if—
  - ◆ the relevant person is aged 18 or over,
  - ◆ the individual is aged 16 or 17,
  - ◆ the alcohol is beer, wine or cider,
  - ◆ its purchase or supply is for consumption at a **table meal** on relevant premises, and
  - ◆ the individual is accompanied at the meal by an individual aged 18 or over.
- **Table meal** means a meal eaten by a person seated at a table, or at a counter or other structure which serves the purpose of a table and is not used for the service of refreshments for consumption by persons not seated at a table or structure serving the purpose of a table.

- Bar snacks do not amount to a table meal.
- Similar offences apply to clubs, under s 149(1)(b); (3)(b) and (4)(b) respectively, where a member of a club is supplied with alcohol by or on behalf of that club for—
  - that member (being under 18), as a result of his act, default or attempts to do so;
  - an individual aged under 18 as a result of his making, attempting to make such arrangements; and
  - consumption on relevant premises by an individual aged under 18, by his act, default or attempts to do so.

Defences

Section 149(3) and (4) offences only

The defendant had no reason to suspect that the individual was aged under 18 (s 149(6)).

Related cases (on test purchases see **9.3.1**)

Practical considerations

All the s 149 offences can be dealt with by way of PND (see **7.1.1**).

  (Except clubs)

 Summary 12 months

 s 149(1) offence
A fine not exceeding level 3.

s 149(3) and s 149(4) offences
A fine not exceeding level 5.

9.1.5 **Consumption of alcohol by person under 18**

Persons aged under 18 are not allowed to consume alcohol on relevant premises.

Offences

(1) A person under 18 commits an offence if he **knowingly** consumes **alcohol** on **relevant premises**.
(2) A **person to whom subsection (3) applies** commits an offence if he knowingly allows the consumption of alcohol on relevant premises by an individual aged under 18.

Licensing Act 2003, s 150

9.1.5 Consumption of Alcohol by Person Under 18

Points to prove

s 150(1) offence
- ✓ date and location
- ✓ being a person under the age of 18
- ✓ knowingly consumed alcohol on relevant premises

s 150(2) offence
- ✓ date and location
- ✓ being a person to whom sub-s (3) applies
- ✓ knowingly allowed
- ✓ an individual under the age of 18
- ✓ to consume alcohol on those premises

Meanings

Knowingly (see **9.1.3**)

Alcohol (see **9.1.1**)

Relevant premises (see **9.1.1**)

Person to whom subsection (3) applies

This subsection applies—
(a) to a person who works at the premises in a capacity, whether paid or unpaid, which authorizes him to prevent the consumption, and
(b) where the alcohol was supplied by a club to or to the order of a member of the club, to any member or officer of the club who is present at the premises at the time of the consumption in a capacity which enables him to prevent it.

Explanatory notes

- The s 150(1) knowingly consumed offence will not be committed if the individual inadvertently consumes alcohol, for example if the drink is spiked.
- Section 150(4) states the s 150(1) and (2) offences do not apply if—
  - ◆ the individual is aged 16 or 17,
  - ◆ the alcohol is beer, wine or cider,
  - ◆ its consumption is at a **table meal** on relevant premises, and
  - ◆ the individual is accompanied at the meal by an individual aged 18 or over.
- **Table meal** meaning is given in '**Explanatory notes**' under **9.1.4**.
- Both offences under s 150(1) and (2) also apply to clubs.

Practical considerations

- Knowledge has to be proved for both offences, either to 'knowingly' consume or to 'knowingly' allow consumption of the alcohol.
- Age to be proved by ID card, driving licence, or similar documentation.
- Consider issuing a PND for the s 150(1) and (2) offences (see **7.1.1**).

  (Except clubs)

 Summary 12 months

 s 150(1) offence
    A fine not exceeding level 3.
    s 150(2) offence
    A fine not exceeding level 5.

9.1.6 **Delivering alcohol to person under 18**

It is an offence for certain people to deliver or allow delivery of alcohol to a person under 18.

Offences

(1) A person who works on **relevant premises** in any capacity, whether paid or unpaid, commits an offence if he **knowingly** delivers to an individual aged under 18—
   (a) **alcohol** sold on the premises, or
   (b) alcohol supplied on the premises by or on behalf of a club to or to the order of a member of the club.
(2) A **person to whom subsection (3) applies** commits an offence if he knowingly allows anybody else to deliver to a person under 18 **alcohol** sold on **relevant premises**.

Licensing Act 2003, s 151

Points to prove

s 151(1) offence

✓ date and location
✓ being a person who worked in a capacity, whether unpaid or paid
✓ on relevant premises
✓ knowingly delivered to an individual under the age of 18
✓ alcohol sold on those premises **or**
✓ supplied on those premises (by or on behalf of a club/order of member)

9.1.6 Delivering Alcohol to Person Under 18

---

s 151(2) offence
- ✓ date and location
- ✓ being a person to whom subsection (3) applies
- ✓ on relevant premises
- ✓ knowingly allowed another person to deliver
- ✓ to an individual under the age of 18
- ✓ alcohol sold on those premises

Meanings

Relevant premises (see **9.1.1**)

Knowingly (see **9.1.3**)

Alcohol (see **9.1.1**)

Person to whom subsection (3) applies

Any person who works on the premises in a capacity, whether paid or unpaid, which authorizes him to prevent the delivery of the alcohol.

Explanatory notes

- Offences in this section cover various situations, for example, under s 151(1)(a) a child takes delivery of a consignment of alcohol bought by a parent from an off-licence (unless the defence applies); or a person authorizes a delivery of that sort, under s 151(2).
- A similar offence to s 151(2), is to knowingly allow somebody else to deliver alcohol supplied by a club under s 151(4).

Defences—s 151(6)

Subsections (1), (2) and (4) do not apply where—
- (a) the alcohol is delivered at a place where the buyer or, as the case may be, person supplied lives or works, or
- (b) the individual aged under 18 works on the relevant premises in a capacity, whether paid or unpaid, which involves the delivery of alcohol, or
- (c) the alcohol is sold or supplied for consumption on the relevant premises.

Defence notes

This covers cases where, for example, a child answers the door and signs for the delivery of an order for the house, or where a 16-year-old office worker is sent to collect an order for their employer.

Practical considerations

- Knowledge has to be proved for all the offences, either to 'knowingly' (see **9.1.3**) deliver or to 'knowingly' allow anybody else to deliver the alcohol.

- Age to be proved by ID card, driving licence, or similar document.
- Consider issuing a PND for these offences (see **7.1.1**).

 Summary 12 months

A fine not exceeding level 5.

9.1.7 **Sending person under 18 to obtain alcohol**

A person under 18 must not be sent to obtain alcohol.

Offences

A person commits an offence if he **knowingly** sends an individual aged under 18 to obtain—

(a) **alcohol** sold or to be sold on **relevant premises** for consumption off the premises, or

(b) alcohol supplied or to be supplied by or on behalf of a club to or to the order of a member of the club for such consumption.

Licensing Act 2003, s 152(1)

Points to prove

✓ date and location
✓ knowingly sent an individual under the age of 18
✓ to obtain alcohol
✓ sold/to be sold on relevant premises **or**
✓ supplied/to be supplied (by/on behalf of club/order of member)
✓ for consumption off those premises

Meanings

Knowingly (see **9.1.3**)

Alcohol (see **9.1.1**)

Relevant premises (see **9.1.1**)

Explanatory notes

- It is immaterial whether the individual aged under 18 is sent to obtain the alcohol from the relevant premises or from other premises from which it is delivered in pursuance of the sale or supply.

9.1.7 Sending Person Under 18 to Obtain Alcohol

* Section 152(3) allows an individual under 18 who works on the relevant premises in a capacity (whether paid or unpaid) that involves delivery of alcohol.
* Similarly s 152(4) states that no offence will be committed if an individual aged under 18 is sent by a constable, or a weights and measures inspector, who are acting in the course of their duty. This exception allows test-purchasing operations to take place (see **9.3.1**).

Related cases (on test purchases see **9.3.1**)

Practical considerations

* This offence covers, for example, circumstances where a parent sends their child (being under 18) to an off-licence to buy and collect alcohol for them.
* Knowledge has to be proved as to 'knowingly' send an individual aged under 18 to obtain alcohol sold or supplied from the relevant premises.
* Further offences concerning alcohol and children are—
  * sale of liqueur confectionery to children under 16 (s 148);
  * prohibition of unsupervised sales by children (s 153)

 Summary   12 months

 A fine not exceeding level 5.

Links to alternative subjects and offences

9.2 Drunkenness on Licensed Premises

The sale and supply of alcohol is regulated by the Licensing Act 2003. This Act creates a number of offences relating to alcohol and offences concerning drunkenness and disorderly conduct.

9.2.1 Sale of alcohol to person who is drunk

It is an offence to sell or attempt to sell alcohol to a person who is drunk, or to allow alcohol to be sold to such a person, on relevant premises.

Offences

A **person to whom subsection (2) applies** commits an offence if, on **relevant premises**, he **knowingly**—
(a) sells or attempts to sell **alcohol** to a person who is **drunk**, or
(b) allows alcohol to be sold to such a person.

Licensing Act 2003, s 141(1)

Points to prove

✓ date and location
✓ person to whom sub-s (2) applies
✓ knowingly sold/attempted to sell/allowed sale of alcohol
✓ on those premises to a person who was drunk

Meanings

Person to whom subsection (2) applies
- Any person who works at the premises in a capacity, whether paid or unpaid, which gives him authority to sell the alcohol concerned.
- In licensed premises, clubs or permitted temporary activity premises, the same persons as given in s 145(3) (see **9.1.1**).

Relevant premises (see **9.1.1**)

Knowingly (see **9.1.3**)

Alcohol (see **9.1.1**)

Drunk (see **7.2.1**)

9.2.2 Failure to Leave Licensed Premises

Explanatory notes

- In each case, drunkenness will be a question of fact for the court to decide.
- It is also an offence, under s 141(3), to supply alcohol by or on behalf of a club or to the order of a member of the club to a person who is drunk.

Practical considerations

- If the person is under 18 consider offences under s 145 (see **9.1.1**).
- Knowledge has to be proved as to 'knowingly' sell, attempt to sell or allows to be sold alcohol to a person who is drunk.
- The licence gives details of the holder and/or the designated premises supervisor, this should be clearly displayed in the premises.
- Under s 142 it is also an offence to knowingly obtain or attempt to obtain alcohol on relevant premises for consumption on relevant premises by a person who is drunk.

  (Except clubs)

 Summary　　　　　　　 12 months

A fine not exceeding level 3 on the standard scale.

9.2.2 **Failure to leave licensed premises**

People who are drunk or disorderly may be requested to leave certain premises and commit an offence if they fail to do so.

Offences

A person who is **drunk** or **disorderly** commits an offence if, without reasonable excuse—

(a) he fails to leave **relevant premises** when requested to do so by a constable or by a **person to whom subsection (2) applies,** or

(b) he enters or attempts to enter relevant premises after a constable or a person to whom subsection (2) applies has requested him not to enter.

Licensing Act 2003, s 143(1)

Points to prove

✓ date and location
✓ without reasonable excuse while drunk or disorderly
✓ failed to comply with request to leave **or not to** enter/attempt to enter relevant premises
✓ by a constable **or** a person to whom sub-s (2) applies

Meanings

Drunk (see **7.2.1**)

Disorderly (see **7.2.1**)

Relevant premises (see **9.1.1**)

Person to whom subsection (2) applies

- Any person who works at the premises in a capacity, whether paid or unpaid, which authorizes them to make such a request.
- In licensed premises, clubs, or permitted temporary activity, the same persons as given in s 145(3) (see **9.1.1**).

Explanatory notes

- An offence may not be committed if the person has a reasonable excuse, for example, if they are physically prevented by serious disability or injury from leaving the premises.
- Apart from licensed premises, this offence also applies to clubs and premises being used for a permitted temporary activity.
- Whether a person is drunk and/or disorderly will be a question of fact for the court to decide.

Practical considerations

- On being requested to do so by the appropriate person, a constable must help to expel from relevant premises a person who is drunk/disorderly or help to prevent such a person from entering relevant premises.
- Consider the offence of being drunk on licensed premises (see **7.2.2**), for which a PND (see **7.1.1**) can be issued.

 Summary   12 months

 A fine not exceeding level 1.

9.2.3 **Allowing disorderly conduct on licensed premises**

It is also an offence to knowingly allow disorderly conduct on relevant premises.

Offence

A **person to whom subsection (2) applies** commits an offence if he **knowingly** allows **disorderly** conduct on **relevant premises**.

Licensing Act 2003, s 140(1)

9.2.3 Allowing Disorderly Conduct on Licensed Premises

Points to prove

- ✓ date and location
- ✓ **being a person to whom sub-s (2) applies**
- ✓ knowingly allowed disorderly conduct to take place on relevant premises

Meanings

Person to whom subsection (2) applies

- Any person who works at the premises in a capacity, whether paid or unpaid, which authorizes them to prevent the conduct.
- In licensed premises, clubs or permitted temporary activity, the same persons as given in s 145(3) (see **9.1.1**).

Knowingly (see **9.1.3**)

Disorderly (see **7.2.1**)

Relevant premises (see **9.1.1**)

Explanatory notes

- Knowledge has to be proved as to 'knowingly' allow disorderly conduct on the relevant premises.
- Apart from licensed premises, this offence also applies to clubs and premises which may be used for a permitted temporary activity.

 Summary   12 months

A fine not exceeding level 3 on the standard scale.

Links to alternative subjects and offences

9.3 Powers to Enter/Close Licensed Premises and Test Purchases

The sale and supply of alcohol is regulated by the Licensing Act 2003. Apart from the Act creating a variety of offences relating to alcohol, it also contains powers to enter/close licensed premises/clubs and allows test purchases.

9.3.1 Test purchases

Sections 149 and 152 allow the police and trading standards officers to use individuals under 18 to make test purchases to ascertain if such individuals can buy or be supplied with alcohol from on/off licensed premises, certified club premises, or premises used for a permitted temporary activity without any offences being committed.

Authorities

149(2) But subsection (1) [see **9.1.4**] does not apply where the individual buys or attempts to buy the alcohol at the request of—
(a) a constable, or
(b) a weights and measures inspector,
who is acting in the course of his duty.
152(4) Subsection (1) [see **9.1.7**] also does not apply where the individual aged under 18 is sent by—
(a) a constable, or
(b) a weights and measures inspector,
who is acting in the course of his duty.

Licensing Act 2003, ss 149(2) and 152(4)

Explanatory notes

This statutory authority allows test-purchasing operations to establish whether licensees and staff working in relevant licensed premises are complying with the prohibition on the sale/supply of alcohol to individuals aged under 18.

Related cases

DPP v Marshall [1988] 3 All ER 683, QBD Police in plain clothes bought alcohol from a shop; it was argued that evidence should be excluded under s 78 of PACE, as the officers had not revealed the fact that they were policemen at the time of the purchase and this was unfair. On appeal it was held that evidence of police officers had been wrongly excluded; it had not been shown that the evidence would have had an adverse effect on the proceedings.

R v Loosely/Attorney-General's Reference No 3 of 2000 [2001] UKHL 53, HL This was a case on entrapment; police officers must not instigate the commission of an offence. But if police do what an ordinary customer would do, whether lawful or unlawful, this will not normally be regarded as objectionable.

Practical considerations
- Consider the protection of children engaged in such operations.
- Assess the reliability of their evidence.

9.3.2 **Powers to enter licensed premises and clubs**

The Licensing Act 2003 contains provisions dealing with powers of entry to investigate licensable activities and offences, namely:

- Section 179(1) gives power to a constable or an authorized person to enter premises, if they have reason to believe that they are being, or are about to be used for a licensable activity, in order to see whether the activity is being carried on in accordance with the authorization. However, this does not apply to clubs, unless there is other authorization apart from a club premises licence.
- Similarly under s 180(1) a constable may enter and search any premises in respect of which they have reason to believe that an offence under the Licensing Act has been, is being or is about to be committed.
- PCSOs can enter and search premises (other than clubs), in relevant police area, providing they are in the company and under the supervision of a constable, unless they are 'off-licence' premises (see **11.1.2**).
- Section 97(1) allows a constable to enter and search club premises if they have reasonable cause to believe that certain offences relating to the supply of drugs have been, are being or are about to be committed or that there is likely to be a breach of the peace.

Explanatory notes
- In exercising these powers a constable may, if necessary, use reasonable force.
- It is not necessary to obtain a warrant.

- Police have lawful authority to require production of a premises licence, club premises certificate, or temporary event notice.
- The police may lawfully enter premises in order to inspect them before a licence or certificate is granted.

9.3.3 **Police powers—closure orders**

A police officer of or above the rank of inspector may close specific premises for up to 24 hours, if there is actual or imminent disorder on, or in the vicinity of and related to the premises or if it is necessary to prevent a public nuisance caused by noise coming from the premises.

Offences

A person commits an offence if, without reasonable excuse, he permits **relevant premises** to be open in contravention of a closure order or any extension of it.

Licensing Act 2003, s 161(6)

Points to prove

✓ date and location
✓ without reasonable excuse
✓ permitted relevant premises
✓ to be open in contravention of a closure order/extension to a closure order

Meanings

Relevant premises

Premises in respect of which a **premises licence** and/or a **temporary event notice** have effect.

Premises licence

Means a licence granted under the Licensing Act 2003, in respect of any premises, which authorizes the premises to be used for one or more licensable activities, namely—

- sale and/or supply of alcohol;
- provision of regulated entertainment;
- late night refreshments.

Temporary event notice

Used on premises where licensable activities are allowed to take place for not more than 96 hours.

Explanatory notes

- An inspector (or above) can make a closure order on reasonable belief that—
  - there is actual or likely imminent disorder and the closure of the premises is required in the interests of public safety; **or**
  - closure is necessary to prevent a public nuisance caused by excessive noise coming from the premises.
- This closure order cannot exceed 24 hours, after coming into force.
- If required the order can be extended (by inspector or above) for a further 24 hours if it is apparent that a magistrates' court will not have had the opportunity to determine the matter.

Practical considerations

- A superintendent or above can make an application to a magistrates' court for an order to close all licensed premises in an area experiencing disorder. If granted, it is an offence (under s 160) to knowingly allow/keep such premises open during the period of the order.
- Should a review of the licence be sought instead?
- Have other premises been closed/licence holders warned in the area?
- Has the licence holder been given any early reminders or warnings or the opportunity to close the premises voluntarily?
- The police have powers to close down premises, if there are reasonable grounds for believing that they are being used in connection with the production, supply or use of Class A controlled drugs (see **5.3**).

 Summary   12 months

 3 months' imprisonment and/or a fine not exceeding £20,000.

9.3.4 **Police powers—closure notice**

Where an offence of persistently selling alcohol to children (under 18) has been committed under s 147A (see **9.1.3**) then a closure notice can be issued by a superintendent (or above) to close the premises for up to 48 hours.

> **Closure notice**
>
> A **relevant officer** may give a notice under this section (a 'closure notice') applying to any premises if—
> (a) there is evidence that a person ('the offender') has committed an offence under section 147A in relation to those premises;

(b) the relevant officer considers that the evidence is such that, if the offender were prosecuted for the offence, there would be a realistic prospect of his being convicted; and

(c) the offender is still, at the time when the notice is given, the holder of a premises licence in respect of those premises, or one of the holders of such a licence.

Licensing Act 2003, s 169A(1)

Meaning of relevant officer

Means a police officer of the rank of superintendent or above; or an appointed inspector of weights and measures.

Explanatory notes

- The closure notice will—
  - propose to prohibit sales of alcohol on the premises, not exceeding 48 hours; and
  - if accepted will discharge all criminal liability in respect of the s 147A offence (see **9.1.3**).
- A closure notice must—
  - be in the form as prescribed by regulations;
  - specify the premises and circumstances surrounding the offence;
  - specify the period when sales of alcohol are prohibited;
  - explain the consequences/penalties of any sale of alcohol on the premises during that period; the rights of that person; and how those rights may be exercised.

Practical considerations

- The period specified must be not more than 48 hours; and the time specifying when that period begins must be not less than 14 days after the date of the service of the closure notice.
- Service of the closure notice may be served on the premises by a constable, PCSO or trading standards officer to a person having control/responsibility for the premises; and only when licensable activities are being carried on there. A copy must be served on the licence holder of the premises.
- Section 169 gives a constable power to use such force as may be necessary for the purposes of closing premises in compliance with a closure order.
- A closure notice must not be given more than 3 months after the s 147A offence.
- No more that one closure notice may be given in respect of offences relating to the same sales; nor may such a notice be given in respect of an offence in respect of which a prosecution has already been brought.

9.3.4 Police Powers—Closure Notice

• Section 169B prescribes other matters when a closure notice has been issued:
  ♦ No proceedings may be brought for the s 147A offence or any related offence at any time before the time when the prohibition proposed by the notice would take effect.
  ♦ If the premises' licence holder accepts the proposed prohibition in the manner specified in the notice then that prohibition takes effect (as specified) and no proceedings may be brought against that person for the alleged offence or any related offence.
  ♦ 'Related offence' means an offence under s 146 (see **9.1.2**) or s 147 (see **9.1.3**) in respect of any of the sales to which the alleged offence relates.

PCSO

Links to alternative subjects and offences

9.4 **Alcohol in Designated Places**

Section 12 of the Criminal Justice and Police Act 2001 is intended to reduce the incidence of disorder and public nuisance arising from alcohol consumption in designated public places. A police officer or PCSO can require a person to cease drinking alcohol in the designated public place, with powers to confiscate and dispose, and failure to comply is an offence.

9.4.1 **Power to require to cease drinking alcohol**

Powers

(1) Subsection (2) applies if a constable reasonably believes that a person is, or has been, consuming **alcohol** in a **designated public place** or intends to consume alcohol in such a place.

(2) The constable may require the person concerned—
   (a) not to consume in that place anything which is, or which the constable reasonably believes to be, alcohol;
   (b) to surrender anything in his possession which is, or which the constable reasonably believes to be, alcohol or a container for alcohol.

Criminal Justice and Police Act 2001, s 12

Meanings

Alcohol (see **9.1.1**)

Designated public place
Is a public place in the area of a local authority; and identified in an order made by that authority under s 13.

Explanatory notes

- Local authorities designate areas as public places for the purposes of s 12. Police powers under s 12 automatically become available, once an order has been made.
- The person must be informed that failure to comply with the police officer's request, without reasonable excuse, is an offence (see **9.4.2**).
- Section 14 denotes those areas that are not public places for the purposes of consuming alcohol in public places (eg consumption of alcohol in these places is allowed subject to regulation by other legislation).

- A place is not a designated public place or a part of such a place if it is—
  - premises which have a premises licence or club premises certificate;
  - a place within the curtilage of any premises which have a premises licence or club premises certificate;
  - a place where the sale of alcohol is for the time being authorized by a temporary event notice or was so authorized within the last 30 minutes;
  - a place where facilities/activities relating to the sale/consumption of alcohol are permitted by a permission granted under s 115E of the Highways Act 1980.
- A constable/PCSO may dispose of anything surrendered to them under s 12(2) in such manner as they consider appropriate.
- Consider using the power to confiscate alcohol from people under 18 years of age (see **9.5**).

9.4.2 **Failure to comply with alcohol requirements**

Offence

A person who fails without reasonable excuse to comply with a **requirement** imposed on him under subsection 12(2) [**see 9.4.1**] commits an offence.

Criminal Justice and Police Act, s 12(4)

Points to prove

Surrender alcohol

- ✓ date and location
- ✓ without reasonable excuse
- ✓ failed to surrender
- ✓ something that was or reasonably believed to be
- ✓ alcohol or container for such
- ✓ in their possession
- ✓ in a designated public place
- ✓ when required by a constable

Consume alcohol

- ✓ date and location
- ✓ without reasonable excuse
- ✓ failed to comply with requirement
- ✓ imposed by constable
- ✓ not to consume in a designated public place
- ✓ something that was or reasonably believed to be
- ✓ alcohol

Example of constable's requirement

'This is a designated public place in which I have reason to believe that
you are/have been drinking alcohol. I require you to stop drinking and
give me the container from which you are/have been drinking and any
other containers (sealed or unsealed). I must inform you that failure to
comply with my request, without reasonable excuse, is an offence for
which you can be arrested.'

Practical considerations

- A constable who imposes the requirement shall inform the person
  concerned that failing without reasonable excuse to comply with the
  requirement is an offence.
- The seizure and disposal of alcohol in both sealed and unsealed
  containers is allowed, although officers should follow their own force
  orders in relation to disposal.
- Consider issuing a PND (see **7.1**).

 Summary 6 months

A fine not exceeding level 2 on the standard scale.

Links to alternative subjects and offences

9.5 Alcohol Confiscation/Fail to Surrender Offence

The Confiscation of Alcohol (Young Persons) Act 1997 addresses the problem of young people drinking alcohol on the streets and allows the police to confiscate alcohol from people under 18 years in certain public places.

9.5.1 Power to confiscate alcohol

Power

Where a constable reasonably suspects that a person in a **relevant place** is in **possession** of **alcohol** and that either—

(a) he is under the age of 18; or

(b) he intends that any of the alcohol should be consumed by a person under the age of 18 in that or any other relevant place; or

(c) a person under the age of 18 who is, or has **recently** been, with him has recently consumed alcohol in that or any other relevant place,

the constable may require him to surrender anything in his possession which is, or which the constable reasonably believes to be, alcohol or a container for alcohol, and to state his name and address.

Confiscation of Alcohol (Young Persons) Act 1997, s 1(1)

Meanings

Relevant place

Means any **public place**, other than licensed premises; or any place, other than a public place, to which the person has unlawfully gained access; and for this purpose a place is a public place if at the material time the public or any section of the public has access to it, on payment or otherwise, as of right or by virtue of express or implied permission.

Possession

At common law possession is defined as: **actual** or **potential** physical control and an intention to possess. In practice visible or external signs of possession, which can be demonstrated to a court, must support the two conditions above (*Jowetts Dictionary of English Law*).

Alcohol   (see **9.1.1**)

Recently

Defined by The *Oxford English Dictionary* as 'lately' or 'comparatively near to the present time'.

Explanatory notes

- Officers can seize sealed and open containers, as well as the alcohol they hold, and dispose of both in an appropriate manner. However, a constable may not under s 1(1) require a person to surrender any sealed containers unless he reasonably believes that the person is, or has been, consuming, or intends to consume alcohol in any relevant place. Where a young person has, for example, a sealed six-pack under his arm, officers should still consider who sold it, and whether there are any child welfare issues, and take action as appropriate.
- A constable may dispose of anything surrendered to him under s 1(1) in such manner as he considers appropriate.
- When imposing a requirement to surrender a constable must inform the person of the suspicion and that failing without reasonable excuse to comply with a requirement imposed under that subsection is an offence.

Example of officer's requirement:

'I have reason to suspect that you are under 18 years of age. You are/have been drinking alcohol/beer/cider (or whatever). You must stop drinking immediately (if applicable). I require you to give me that can/bottle/plastic cup etc. and to give me your name and address. I must warn you that failure to comply with my requests is an offence for which you can be arrested.'

Practical considerations

- Officers should follow their own force orders in relation to disposal.
- A PCSO has the same powers as a police constable under this section (other than the arrest power) (see **11.1.2**).

9.5.2 **Failing to surrender alcohol**

Offence

A person who fails without reasonable excuse to comply with a require-ment imposed on him under subsection (1) *[see **9.5.1**]* commits an offence.
Confiscation of Alcohol (Young Persons) Act 1997, s 1(3)

Points to prove

- ✓ date and location
- ✓ without reasonable excuse
- ✓ failed to comply with requirement
- ✓ imposed by constable
- ✓ to surrender
- ✓ alcohol/suspected alcohol **or** a container for such
- ✓ in their possession
- ✓ and/or state their name and address

9.5.2 Failing to Surrender Alcohol

 Summary 6 months

 A fine not exceeding level 2 on the standard scale.

Links to alternative subjects and offences

Chapter 10
Road Traffic

10.1 Meanings: Roads, Public Places, Vehicles, and Drives

10.1.1 Roads

The term 'road' has many meanings within various pieces of legislation.

Meaning of road

'Road' is defined in several Acts. The two most commonly used meanings of a road are—

- any highway and any other road to which the public has access, and includes bridges over which a road passes (Road Traffic Act 1988, s 192(1));
- any length of highway and any other road to which the public has access, and includes bridges over which a road passes (Road Traffic Regulation Act 1984, s 142(1)).

Explanatory notes

- 'Road' includes obvious public highways, footpaths, and bridleways maintained by government agencies or local authorities.
- The term 'public road' in the Vehicle Excise and Registration Act 1994 means a road repairable at public expense.
- The physical nature of a road provides a defined or definable route or way to which the general public has legal access, being a route allowing travel between two places.
- A field used for parking at an agricultural show was held not to be a road, as it had no definable way.
- Where there is no physical point at which a road ends reasonable judgment will need to be used to determine the road's end.
- A privately owned hotel forecourt used as a shortcut between two streets is a road.

10.1.1 Roads

- Walking or driving must take place on the road and such walking or driving must be lawful.
- Case decisions regarding roads need to be considered very carefully. As questions of 'fact', usually taken by lower courts, these decisions are heavily dependent on the individual circumstances of the case.

Related cases

Adams v Metropolitan Police [1980] RTR 289, QBD If the owner of a private road tolerates its use by the general public it may be a 'road to which the public have access'.

Cutter v Eagle Star Insurance Company Ltd [1998] 4 All ER 417, HL and Clarke v Kato and others [1998] 4 All ER 417, HL A part of a car park may be a road but the whole of the car park will not necessarily be (ie properly designated parking bays will not be a road, but a definable route (direction arrows, lane markings, etc) may make the rest of the car park a road under the Act).

Sadiku v DPP [2000] RTR 155, QBD A paved area used as a thoroughfare by pedestrians can be a road.

Griffin v Squires [1958] 2 All ER 468, QBD Where the public used a car park, but only a certain sector of the public used it to gain access to private property, it was held not to have been a road.

Brewer v DPP The Times, 5 March 2004, QBD A railway station car park where the only people going through it are employees crossing to the staff car park is not a road.

McGurk and Another v Coster [1995] CLY 2912, Southport County Court Access to a temporary car park on a beach by driving over part of the beach between the sea and sand dunes was held not to be a road.

Practical considerations

- What are the physical characteristics, function, and public access of the place involved?
- Public access alone is not sufficient to make a place a road; similarly, some form of private use will not necessarily prevent it from being a road.
- Most important road traffic legislation relates to 'public places' as well—this is a wider and different definition that should be considered in each case (see **10.1.2**).
- The footway, lay-by, or verge is normally part of the road.
- The mode of transport is not relevant and such travellers may be on foot, riding on animals, or in a vehicle.
- In instances of real doubt the courts have to decide on a case-by-case basis.

10.1.2 **Public place**

Meaning of public place

The term 'public place' has, for the purposes of the Road Traffic Act 1988, been defined as: 'Any place to which the public have open access is a public place, even if payment must be made to gain entry.'

Explanatory notes

- Whether a place to which the public have limited or restricted access is a public place is a question of fact and degree in each case.
- The time at which the place was being used is important in dealing with 'public place' considerations. A car park of a public house may be a public place during licensing hours but may not be so outside those hours.
- An off-road parking bay adjacent to a highway with no physical impediment between the bay and the road is a public place.
- Lanes at a ferry port could be a public place or road as the public have access to them.

Related cases

DPP v Coulman [1993] Crim LR 399, QBD When deciding if a lane from a ferry through the immigration and docking terminal was a 'public road' it should be considered whether people were there for reasons personal to themselves which were not available to the general public. If so, it is unlikely to be a public road; otherwise it was a public road. Disembarking in this case determined that the land was a public road.

R v Spence [1999] Crim LR 975, CA A company car park in an industrial estate, used by employees, customers, and visitors on business was held not to be a public place.

Practical considerations

- The test for whether or not it is a public place is to consider: 'Do the people gaining access there have a special characteristic or personal reason which is not possessed by the general public?'
- Public use of the area must be shown evidentially.

10.1.3 **Vehicles/motor vehicles/mechanically propelled vehicles**

Meaning of vehicles

General

The *Oxford English Dictionary* defines a 'vehicle' as a conveyance, usually with wheels, for transporting people, goods, etc; a car, cart, truck, carriage, sledge, etc; any means of carriage or transport; a receptacle in which something is placed in order to be moved.

For vehicle excise duty purposes

In the following provisions of this Act 'vehicle' means:
(a) a mechanically propelled vehicle, or
(b) any thing (whether or not it is a vehicle) that has been, but has ceased to be, a mechanically propelled vehicle.

> Vehicle Excise and Registration Act 1994, s 1(1B)

Explanatory notes

- The above definitions of 'vehicle' should not be confused with the meaning of 'motor vehicle' or 'mechanically propelled vehicle'.
- **Motor vehicle**
  Means as follows—
  - (subject to s 20 of the Chronically Sick and Disabled Persons Act 1970 which makes special provision about invalid carriages, within the meaning of that Act), a **mechanically propelled vehicle** intended or adapted for use on roads (Road Traffic Act 1988, s 185);
  - any mechanically propelled vehicle, whether or not it is intended or **adapted for use on a road** (Police Reform Act 2002, s 59);
  - any vehicle whose function is or was to be used on roads as a mechanically propelled vehicle (Vehicles (Crime) Act 2001, s 16).
- **Mechanically propelled vehicle**
  This is not legally defined but, it has a wider meaning than 'motor vehicle' as a mechanically propelled vehicle does not have to be 'intended or adapted for use on a road'. It means a vehicle which can be propelled by mechanical means and would include electric or steam powered vehicles.
  Whether it is a mechanically propelled vehicle will have to be determined by the court.
- **Adapted for use on a road**
  Means fit and apt for use on a road.
- A sidecar is part of a motor vehicle when attached to a motorbike and is not a trailer (Road Traffic Act 1988, s 186(1)).
- Conversely, a semi-trailer of an articulated vehicle is a trailer and not part of the towing vehicle (Road Traffic Act 1988, s 187(1)).

- An articulated bus ('bendy bus') should be treated as one vehicle (Road Traffic Act 1988, s 187(2)).
- A hovercraft is a motor vehicle (Road Traffic Act 1988, s 188).
- Certain specialized vehicles may be used as invalid carriages on pavements without being classified as motor vehicles.

Related cases

DPP v King [2008] EWHC 447 (Admin), QBD A 'City Mantis' electric scooter which looked like a bicycle, except that it did not have any pedals or other means of manual propulsion and was capable of speeds up to 10 miles per hour, was held to be a motor vehicle.

Chief Constable of North Yorkshire Police v Saddington [2001] Crim LR 41, QBD A 'Go-Ped' (which resembles a child's scooter with an engine) has been held to be a motor vehicle. Despite a warning on it that it was not intended for use on a road, the correct test would be whether a reasonable person would say that one of its uses would be some general use on a road.

Thomas v Hooper [1986] RTR 1, QBD A vehicle may no longer be a motor vehicle if it has none of the normal vehicular controls operative.

Reader v Bunyard [1987] RTR 406, QBD A motor vehicle remains a mechanically propelled vehicle unless there was evidence that there was no likelihood of it being so used again. The onus is on the prosecution to prove that the vehicle is capable of being repaired or used.

Burns v Currell [1963] 2 All ER 297, QBD When deciding whether one of the uses of a vehicle would be on a road a 'reasonable person' test should be applied to the vehicle and not the intentions of the specific user at the time it was stopped.

Practical considerations

- What was the vehicle intended for and what use is it currently being put to?
- The onus of proving that a motor vehicle remained a mechanically propelled vehicle lies with the prosecution.
- Pedestrian controlled mowing machines, other pedestrian controlled vehicles and electrically assisted pedal cycles approved by the Secretary of State are **not** motor vehicles (Road Traffic Act 1988, s 189).
- It is a matter of fact and degree for the court to decide whether or not a vehicle is a motor vehicle/mechanically propelled vehicle at the time of a specific incident.
- In such cases, include evidence of the characteristics of the vehicle, which may be a photograph if appropriate.

10.1.4 **Drives/driving**

Meaning of drives/driving

- The statutory definition of a 'driver' is—
  Where a separate person acts as a steersman of a motor vehicle, includes (except for the purposes of s 1 of this Act) that person as well as any other person engaged in the driving of the vehicle, and 'drive' is to be interpreted accordingly (Road Traffic Act 1988, s 192(1)).
- This means that a driver is any person who is engaged in the driving of the vehicle including, where a separate person acts as a steersman of a motor vehicle, that person.
- Case law has laid down a number of helpful considerations but the principal test is—
  - ◆ 'the essence of driving is the use of the driver's controls for the purpose of directing the movement of the car however the movement is produced' (*R v McDonagh* [1974] 2 All ER 257, CA).
- Whether or not a person was driving is ultimately a matter of fact and degree. It is for the court or jury to decide on the facts in each case (*Edkins v Knowles* [1973] 2 All ER 503, QBD).

Explanatory notes

- The vehicle does not have to be moving. A driver is still driving until he has completed the normal operations, such as applying the handbrake, that occur at the end of a journey.
- A vehicle may halt temporarily such as at traffic lights. Each case will have to be looked at using three questions—
  - ◆ What was the purpose of the stop?
  - ◆ How long was the vehicle stopped?
  - ◆ Did the driver get out of the vehicle?
- It is also possible for two people to be driving the same vehicle.

Related cases

Cawthorn v DPP [2000] RTR 45, QBD Driver left vehicle for a few minutes. C set the handbrake and switched on the hazard warning lights, but passenger released handbrake, the vehicle rolled down a hill and hit a brick wall. This intervening act did not make that person the driver, as the passenger did not have sufficient control to fulfil the definition of driving. C still remained the driver until the journey was complete or someone else had taken over the driving. Whether someone was a driver at any particular time was a question of fact for the court or jury to decide.

DPP v Hastings (1993) 158 JP 118, QBD A passenger snatching the wheel momentarily is not a 'driver' because this action does not constitute the act of driving. H had interfered with the driving of the car, but was not the driver.

Burgoyne v Phillips [1982] RTR 49, QBD Since B had set the car in motion, was sitting in the driving seat and was trying to control the car, the fact that the steering was momentarily locked did not prevent B from 'driving' the car.

McQuaid v Anderton [1980] 3 All ER 540, QBD Steering a car being towed can be 'driving'. The essence of 'driving' was the use of the driver's controls in order to direct the movement of the car, the method of propulsion being irrelevant.

Tyler v Whatmore [1975] RTR 83, QBD Two people can be driving a vehicle at the same time. T was sitting in the front passenger seat and was leaning across steering the car, whilst the other driver manipulated the controls. In this case neither person had full control of both the brakes and the steering and although T could not control the propulsion, there was some control over the handbrake and ignition system. T was therefore driving the vehicle.

Practical considerations

- If there is some doubt as to whether a person is driving or not, the circumstances must be looked at individually.
- As a general rule there are three elements to driving—
  - ◆ control of the steering; **and**
  - ◆ control of the propulsion; **and**
  - ◆ the actions of the person must fall within the everyday meaning of driving.

Links to alternative subjects and offences

10.1.4 Drives/Driving

10.2 Powers to Stop/Direct Vehicles and Pedestrians

The Road Traffic Act 1988 provides various powers to stop vehicles for different circumstances. These powers are given, in varying degrees, to police officers, traffic wardens, authorized vehicle examiners, and PCSOs.

10.2.1 Drivers to comply with traffic directions

Section 35 of the Road Traffic Act 1988 provides for drivers who refuse or neglect to comply with traffic directions given by a police constable.

Offences

(1) Where a constable or **traffic officer** is for the time being engaged in the regulation of traffic in a **road**, a person **driving** or propelling a **vehicle** who neglects or refuses—

    (a) to stop the vehicle; or

    (b) to make it proceed in, or keep to, a particular line of traffic,

when directed to do so by the constable in the exercise of his duty or the traffic officer (as the case may be) is guilty of an offence.

(2) Where—

    (a) a traffic survey of any description is being carried out on or in the vicinity of a road, and

    (b) a constable or traffic officer gives a person driving or propelling a vehicle a direction—

        (i) to stop the vehicle,

        (ii) to make it proceed in, or keep to, a particular line of traffic, or

        (iii) to proceed to a particular point on or near the road on which the vehicle is being driven or propelled,

being a direction given for the purposes of the survey (but not a direction requiring any person to provide any information for the purposes of a traffic survey),

the person is guilty of an offence if he refuses or neglects to comply with the direction.

Road Traffic Act 1988, s 35

Points to prove

s 35(1) offence

✓ constable/traffic warden/PCSO/traffic officer
✓ engaged in the regulation of traffic in a road
✓ driver/rider of vehicle neglected/refused
✓ to stop vehicle/proceed/keep to particular line of traffic
✓ as directed

s 35(2) offence

✓ traffic survey on/in vicinity of a road
✓ driver/rider of vehicle
✓ refused/failed/neglected to comply
✓ with directions given by constable/TW/PCSO/traffic officer
✓ for purposes of the survey

Meanings

Traffic officer

Person designated under the Traffic Management Act 2004, s 2.

Road (see **10.1.1**)

Driving (see **10.1.4**)

Vehicle (see **10.1.3**)

Explanatory notes

- The constable/traffic officer must be engaged in the regulation of traffic and acting in the execution of their duty.
- A constable may direct a person to disobey a traffic sign if it is reasonably necessary for the protection of life.
- A suitably designated PCSO has the same powers as a constable under s 35 in any police area in England and Wales.
- Reference to a constable includes a traffic warden.
- The prosecution needs to show that the given signal was obvious and should have been evident to the motorist, not that the motorist saw it.
- Although a constable/traffic officer can direct a driver/rider to a specific point for a traffic survey, they cannot direct any person to supply information for the survey.
- Any direction in connection with a traffic survey must not cause undue delay to a person who indicates that they are unwilling to give information for the survey.

Practical considerations

- Offences under s 35 are not confined to mechanically propelled vehicles.
- Stop does not automatically mean the driver must remain stationary until signalled to proceed, unless the direction was to remain stationary.
- Notice of intended prosecution (NIP) to be issued (see **10.5**).
- Consider using a traffic fixed penalty notice (see **10.4**).

 Summary   6 months

 A fine not exceeding level 3 on the standard scale.
Discretionary disqualification and obligatory endorsement of 3 penalty points—if committed in a motor vehicle

10.2.2 **Directions to pedestrians**

Section 37 of the Road Traffic Act 1988 empowers a constable in uniform or traffic officer engaged in the direction of vehicular traffic on a road, to also direct a pedestrian walking along or across the carriageway, to stop.

Offences

Where a constable in uniform or **traffic officer** is for the time being engaged in the regulation of vehicular traffic in a **road**, a person on foot who proceeds across or along the carriageway in contravention of a direction to stop given by the constable in the execution of his duty or traffic officer (as the case may be), either to persons on foot or to persons on foot and other traffic, is guilty of an offence.

Road Traffic Act 1988, s 37

Points to prove

- ✓ being a pedestrian proceeded along/across carriageway
- ✓ contravened direction of constable/traffic officer/PCSO/TW
- ✓ engaged in direction of vehicular traffic on a road

10.2.3 Testing the Condition of Vehicles on a Road

Meanings

Traffic officer (see 10.2.1)

Road (see 10.1)

Explanatory notes
- Reference to a constable includes reference to a traffic warden.
- A suitably designated PCSO has same powers as a constable under s 37 in any police area in England and Wales.

Practical considerations
- A pedestrian breaching s 37 may be required to give their name and address.
- The constable must be in uniform—include details in evidence.

 Summary   6 months

A fine not exceeding level 3 on the standard scale.

10.2.3 **Testing the condition of vehicles on a road**

Section 67 of the Road Traffic Act 1988 empowers authorized vehicle examiners to test motor vehicles on the road, but any vehicle stopped for a test must be stopped by a constable in uniform, traffic warden, or suitably designated PCSO.

> **Offences**
>
> If a person obstructs an **authorised examiner** acting under this section, or fails to comply with a requirement of this section or Schedule 2 (deferred **tests** of conditions of **vehicles**) to this Act, he is guilty of an offence.
>
> Road Traffic Act 1988, s 67(9)

Meanings

Authorized vehicle examiner

Includes a constable authorized by or on behalf of the chief officer of police.

Test

Includes inspect or inspection.

Vehicle (see **10.1.3**)

Includes a trailer drawn by it.

Explanatory notes

- Vehicle examiners may test all motor vehicles that are on the road.
- A vehicle shall not be required to stop for a test except by a constable in uniform or a suitably designated PCSO.

Related cases

Sadiku v DPP [2000] RTR 155, QBD A constable requiring the test to be carried out may ask for the keys while awaiting the arrival of the examiner.

Practical considerations

- An authorized examiner may test a motor vehicle on a road to ascertain whether it meets construction and use requirements, and its condition does not involve a danger of injury to any person.
- For the purpose of testing a vehicle the examiner may require the driver to comply with reasonable instructions, and to drive the vehicle.
- The driver may elect for the test to be deferred to a time and place in accordance with Sch 2. However, if the vehicle has been involved in an accident on a road or is so defective that it ought not to be allowed to proceed, the constable may require that the vehicle shall not be taken away until the test has been carried out.
- A constable who is not an authorized examiner cannot use s 67 to carry out this test. However, a constable can still enforce regulations concerning construction and use where the driver is cooperative.
- This section applies to vehicles registered outside Great Britain.

 Summary   6 months

 A fine not exceeding level 3 on the standard scale.

10.2.4 **Police powers to stop a vehicle on a road**

Section 163 of the Road Traffic Act 1988 empowers a police constable in uniform or a traffic officer to stop a mechanically propelled vehicle on a road.

Offences

(1) A person **driving** a **mechanically propelled vehicle** on a road must stop the vehicle on being required to do so by a constable in uniform or a **traffic officer**.

(2) A person riding a cycle on a road must stop the cycle on being required to do so by a constable in uniform or a traffic officer.

(3) If a person fails to comply with this section he is guilty of an offence.

Road Traffic Act 1988, s 163

Points to prove

✓ drove mechanically propelled vehicle/rode cycle
✓ on a road
✓ required by constable/TW/traffic officer/PCSO
✓ to stop the vehicle/cycle
✓ failed to do so

Meanings

Driving (see 10.1.4)

Mechanically propelled vehicle (see 10.1.3)

Road (see 10.1.1)

Traffic officer (see 10.2.1)

Explanatory notes

• 'Mechanically propelled vehicle' is not defined in the Act and is a matter of fact and degree to be decided by the court; for further details see 10.1.3.

• Reference to a constable includes traffic warden.

• A suitably designated PCSO has powers to stop a cycle, but only for an offence under the Highways Act 1835, s 72 (riding on footway—see 10.12.4).

Practical considerations

Consider issuing a traffic fixed penalty notice (see 10.4.1).

Summary 6 months

 A fine not exceeding level 3 on the standard scale.

Links to alternative subjects and offences

10.3 **Fail to Comply with Traffic Signs**

Section 36 of the Road Traffic Act 1988 creates an offence of failing to comply with certain traffic signs.

Offences

Where a **traffic sign**, being a sign—
(a) of the prescribed size, colour and type, or
(b) of another character authorised by the Secretary of State under the provisions in that behalf of the Road Traffic Regulation Act 1984,
has been **lawfully placed** on or near a **road**, a person **driving** or propelling a **vehicle** who fails to comply with the indication given by the sign is guilty of an offence.

Road Traffic Act 1988, s 36(1)

Points to prove

✓ traffic sign lawfully placed
✓ on or near a road
✓ driver/rider of vehicle on that road
✓ failed to comply with the direction of that sign

Meanings

Traffic sign

As given in the Traffic Signs and General Directions Regulations 2002.

Lawfully placed

A sign will not be lawfully placed unless it indicates a statutory prohibition, restriction, or requirement, or a provision of the Traffic Acts specifically states that it is a sign to which this section applies.

Road (see 10.1.1)

Driving (see 10.1.4)

Vehicle (see 10.1.3)

Explanatory notes

• Some of the traffic signs to which this section applies are: double white line markings, box junction markings, traffic lights (including temporary traffic lights at roadworks), 'stop' sign (including manually operated at roadworks), flashing red 'stop' lights on motorways or automatic tram/railway crossing, no entry sign, give way sign, directional arrow, keep left/right sign, bus/cycle/tramcar route sign, no U turn sign, weight/height restriction sign.

- This section applies to traffic survey signs and emergency traffic signs put out by police (eg football matches, processions).
- A single dotted white line in the centre of the road separating two carriageways does not fall into this section.
- For contravention of a 'stop' sign or red traffic light signal it is necessary to prove that the vehicle did not stop at the stop line or, if the stop line is not visible, before entering the major road or beyond the mounting of the primary signal respectively.
- Emergency vehicles may be exempted from the requirement to conform to a red traffic light, but must proceed so as not to cause danger to the driver of another vehicle or to cause such driver to change their speed or direction to avoid an accident, or cause danger to non-vehicular traffic.
- Failure by the driver to see the traffic sign is not a defence, except in very limited situations (see *Coombes v DPP* (2006)—below), and will generally be evidence to support an offence of driving without due care and attention (see **10.6**).

Defences

This section creates absolute offences except for the possible defences of mechanical defect, automatism or not seen due to badly located signage.

Defence notes

- 'Automatism' has been defined as 'the involuntary movement of a person's body or limbs'.
- The source or cause of the automatism must be something of which the driver was unaware or something that they could not reasonably be expected to foresee.
- Falling asleep whilst driving a vehicle does not amount to automatism.
- In very limited situations where a driver fails to see the sign (see *Coombes v DPP*, 2006).

Related cases

McKenzie v DPP The Times, 14 May 1996, QBD A vehicle can stop on a road where double white lines are present to drop/pick up passengers, load/unload goods, to carry out road/building work or to remove obstructions.

10.3 Fail to Comply with Traffic Signs

Coombes v DPP [2006] EWHC 3263, QBD Signs must indicate the relevant speed limit. This requires, at the very least, that at the geographical point where the motorist exceeds the speed limit the signs could reasonably be expected to have conveyed the limit to an approaching motorist in sufficient time for the motorist to reduce from the previous lawful limit to a speed within the new limit.

O'Halloran v DPP (1989) 154 JP 837, QBD Arrows warning drivers to pull back in as they are approaching solid white lines in the road are mandatory before every stretch of solid lines and not only at the beginning of a complete set of markings. If the arrow is missing it is not a legal traffic sign for this section.

Watmore v Jenkins [1961] 2 All ER 868, QBD A driver took the correct dosage of insulin prior to driving and drove normally most of the day, but drove erratically for 5 miles before being stopped. The driver was dazed when stopped, but recovered after treatment. The defence of automatism was not accepted as there had been an element of conscious control in the driving.

Attorney-General's Reference (No 2 of 1992) [1993] 4 All ER 683, CA Driving without awareness (such as falling asleep) is not a case where automatism could be used as a defence.

Practical considerations

- Traffic signs placed on or near a road are deemed to be of the correct specification and to have been lawfully placed unless the contrary is proved.
- A stop sign at a junction indicates that a vehicle must at least momentarily stop at the stop line and not merely slow down.
- Consider issuing a traffic fixed penalty notice (see **10.4**).
- Is the traffic sign one that is specified for this section?
- Is the contravention evidence of a more serious offence (eg dangerous driving, driving without due care and attention)?
- An NIP must be served for offences of failing to comply with some types of traffic signs (see **10.5**).

 Summary 6 months

 A fine not exceeding level 3 on the standard scale.

Discretionary disqualification, obligatory endorsement—3 penalty points.

TFPN Traffic Fixed Penalty Notices   **PCSO** Police community support officers   **NIP** Notice of intended prosecution

Links to alternative subjects and offences

10.4 **Traffic Fixed Penalty Notices**

Traffic Fixed Penalty Notices (TFPNs) and procedures with regard to road traffic offences are covered by s 51 to s 90 of the Road Traffic Offenders Act 1988.

10.4.1 **Traffic fixed penalty notices**

Section 54 of the Act allows a constable in uniform who has reason to believe that a person is committing or has committed a traffic penalty offence to then issue a TFPN in respect of that offence.

Offences

A person is guilty of an offence if he removes or interferes with any notice fixed to a vehicle under this section, unless he does so by or under the authority of the driver or person in charge of the vehicle or the person liable for the fixed penalty offence in question.

Road Traffic Offenders Act 1988, s 62(2)

A person who, in a response to a notice to owner, provides a statement which is false in a material particular and does so recklessly or knowing it to be false in that particular is guilty of that offence.

Road Traffic Offenders Act 1988, s 67

Points to prove

s 62(2) offence
- ✓ without authority of driver/person in charge or liable for TFPN
- ✓ removed/interfered with TFPN fixed to vehicle

s 67 offence
- ✓ in response to notice to owner
- ✓ provided false statement
- ✓ recklessly/knowing it to be false

Meaning of 'Traffic Fixed Penalty Notice'

Means a notice offering the opportunity of the discharge of any liability to conviction of the offence to which the notice relates by payment of a fixed penalty in accordance with Pt 3 of this Act.

Explanatory notes

- TFPNs apply where a constable in uniform believes that a person is committing or has committed a **relevant offence** (see below), and may be issued either at the time of the offence or at a police station.
- If the offence involves obligatory endorsement the constable may only issue a TFPN if the offender produces and surrenders their driving licence and counterpart to the constable and is not liable to disqualification under the 'totting up' procedure.
- Where the offender has no licence and counterpart with them, the constable may issue a notice requiring their production within 7 days at a specified police station and, if certain requirements are met, can then be issued with a TFPN.
- References to constable include a traffic warden.
- A suitably designated PCSO may issue a TFPN for cycling on a footway.
- A TFPN must give details of the offence, suspended enforcement period, penalty payable, and how it should be paid.
- 'Suspended enforcement period' means the period following the date of the offence during which no proceedings will be brought against the offender.
- Where the penalty has not been paid or a hearing elected during the suspended enforcement period, the penalty plus 50 per cent may be registered against them.
- If the offence involves obligatory endorsement the surrendered licence and counterpart must be forwarded to the fixed-penalty clerk, who must endorse details on the counterpart then return both to the licence holder.
- The person receiving a surrendered licence and counterpart must issue a receipt, which will be valid for 1 month after issue. The fixed-penalty clerk, on application by the licence holder, may issue a new receipt expiring on a date specified therein.
- If the licence holder is liable to disqualification under the 'totting up' (see **10.13**) system, the fixed-penalty clerk must not endorse the counterpart but forward it and the licence to the chief officer of police who may commence proceedings. Where such proceedings are commenced any action already taken (eg registration as a fine) is void.
- At the end of the suspended enforcement period, if the penalty has not been paid or a hearing requested by the driver at the relevant time, a notice to owner may be served on the owner.
- A notice to owner must include particulars as to the offence, TFPN issued, response time allowed (minimum 21 days), penalty if it is not paid, requesting a hearing.
- If the person on whom the notice to owner was served was not the owner of the vehicle at the time of the offence and provides a statutory statement of ownership to that effect, they are not liable for the fine registered against them.

10.4.1 Traffic Fixed Penalty Notices

- If a notice to owner has been served, proceedings may not be brought against anybody else in relation to that offence unless they are identified as the driver at the relevant time in a statutory statement of facts.

Relevant offences

Schedule 3 of this Act lists the TFPN offences—

Highways Act 1835

s 72—driving/cycling on footway.

Transport Act 1968

s 96(11)—contravened drivers' hours

s 96(11A)—contravened periods of driving

s 97(1)—contravened recording equipment regs

s 98(4)—contravened drivers' hours written records regs

s 99(4)—fail to produce records/obstruction

s 99ZD(1)—fail to comply with requirements/obstruction

s 99C—fail to comply with prohibition/direction

Road Traffic (Foreign Vehicles) Act 1972

s 3(1)—drive foreign GV or PSV in contravention of prohibition

Greater London Council (General Powers) Act 1974

s 15—parking vehicles on footways, verges, other related offences.

Highways Act 1980

s 137—obstruction of highway committed in respect of a vehicle.

Public Passenger Vehicles Act 1981

s 12(5)—use PSV on road without PSV operator's licence.

Road Traffic Regulation Act 1984

s 5(1)—traffic regulation order outside Greater London.

s 8(1)—traffic regulation order in Greater London.

s 11—experimental traffic order.

s 13—breach of experimental traffic scheme.

s 16(1)—temporary prohibition or restriction.

s 17(4)—wrongful use of special road.

s 18(3)—one-way traffic order on trunk road.

s 20(5)—prohibition/restriction of driving on certain classes of road.

s 25(5)—breach of pedestrian crossing regulations, except offence in respect of moving motor vehicle, other than contravention of regs 23, 24, 25, and 26 of the Zebra, Pelican and Puffin Pedestrian Crossings Regulations and General Directions 1997.

s 29(3)—street playground order.

s 35A(1)—local authority parking place on a road.

s 47(1)—parking place designation order.

s 53(5)—parking place designation order under s 53(1)(a).

s 53(6)—designation order authorized parking on road without charge.

s 88(7)—minimum speed limit.

s 89(1)—speeding.

Road Transport (International Passenger Services) Regulations 1984

reg 19(1)—use vehicle for carriage of passengers without authorisation/certificate.

reg 19(2)—use vehicle for carriage of passengers without passenger waybill.

Road Traffic Act 1988

s 14—seat belt regulations.

s 15(2)—restriction re children in front of vehicles.

s 15(4)—restriction re children in rear of vehicles.

s 16—crash helmet regulations re motorcycle rider/passenger.

s 18(3)—breach use of eye protector regulations on motorcycles.

s 19—parking heavy commercial vehicle on verge/footway.

s 22—leave vehicle in dangerous position.

s 23—unlawfully carry passenger on motorcycle.

s 24—carry more than one person on pedal cycle.

s 34—drive mechanically propelled vehicle elsewhere than on road.

s 35—fail to comply with traffic directions.

s 36—fail to comply with prescribed traffic signs (see **10.3**).

s 40A—use vehicle where condition; purpose used; passengers carried; load involves danger of injury.

s 41A—breach of requirements re brakes, steering-gear or tyres.

s 41B—breach of weight requirement re goods and passenger vehicles.

s 41D—breach of requirements re control, view of road or use hand-held device.

s 42—breach of other construction and use regulations.

s 47—using vehicle without a test certificate.

s 71(1)—contravened prohibition order or fail comply order

s 87(1)—drive vehicle otherwise than in accordance with licence.

s 143—using a motor vehicle without insurance.

s 163—fail to stop vehicle when required by officer in uniform.

s 172—failed to give information re driver of motor vehicle.

Road Traffic Offenders Act 1988

s 90D(6)—drive in contravention of prohibition or fail comply direction

10.4.1 Traffic Fixed Penalty Notices

Goods Vehicles (Community Authorisations) Regulations 1992

reg 3—use goods vehicle without community authorisation.

reg 7—use vehicle contravening regs under community authorisation

Vehicle Excise and Registration Act 1994

s 33—use vehicle on road not displaying VEL, trade licence or nil licence.

s 34—use trade licence for unauthorised purposes/circumstances.

s 42—driving/keeping vehicle without required registration mark.

s 43—drive/keep vehicle with registration mark obscured.

s 43C—offence of using an incorrectly registered vehicle.

s 59—fail to affix prescribed registration mark to vehicle.

Goods Vehicles (Licensing of Operators) Act 1995

s 2(5)—use GV on road for carriage of goods—no operator's licence.

Public Service Vehicles (Community Licences) Regulations 1999

reg 3—use PSV on road without community licence.

reg 7—use PSV under community licence—contravened licence conditions.

Road Transport (Passenger Vehicles Sabotage) Regulations 1999

reg 3—using vehicle on road for UK sabotage operations—no EC licence.

reg 4—using vehicle on road for UK sabotage operations—no control document.

reg 7(1)—fail to produce EC licence when requested.

reg 7(3)—failed to produce control document when requested.

Vehicle Drivers (Certificates of Professional Competence) Regulations 2007

reg 11(7)—driver of relevant vehicle failed to produce evidence/ document.

Practical considerations

- Consider the seriousness of the offence. There is no obligation to issue a TFPN—it is at the discretion of the constable, TW or PCSO.
- Is the fixed penalty scheme appropriate? Are there other reasons (eg National Intelligence Model) for conventional proceedings?
- Is the offence endorsable—if so, is the offender with the vehicle?
- Only a non-endorsable TFPN may be attached to a vehicle.
- Is the offender liable to disqualification under the totting up system?

 Summary

s 62 offence

A fine not exceeding level 2 on the standard scale.

s 67 Offence

A fine not exceeding level 5 on the standard scale.
If statutory declaration is made, 6 months from date of declaration, up to a maximum of 12 months from the original offence.
In all other cases—6 months.

10.4.2 Control of vehicle and use of hand-held device

Offences

A person who contravenes or fails to comply with a **construction and use requirement**—

(a) as to not driving a motor vehicle in a position which does not give proper control or a full view of the road and traffic ahead, or not causing or permitting the driving of a motor vehicle by another person in such a position, or

(b) as to not driving or supervising the driving of a motor vehicle while using a hand-held mobile telephone or other hand-held interactive communication device, or not causing or permitting the driving of a motor vehicle by another person using such a telephone or other device

is guilty of an offence.

Road Traffic Act 1988, s 41D

Points to prove

s 41D(a) offence

✓ contravened/failed to comply with requirement
✓ by driving a motor vehicle on a road
✓ without proper control of vehicle or full view **or**
✓ caused/permitted the above offences

s 41D(b) offence

✓ contravened/failed to comply with requirement
✓ being the driver/driving supervisor
✓ of a motor vehicle on a road
✓ driver used hand-held mobile/similar device **or**
✓ caused/permitted above offence

10.4.2 Control of Vehicle and Use of Hand-Held Device

Meaning of 'construction and use requirement'

Means requirement imposed by regulations made under s 41 of the Road Traffic Act 1988, being mainly the Road Vehicles (Construction and Use) Regulations 1986.

Explanatory notes

- Not being in a position to have proper control of the vehicle or a full view of the road and traffic ahead comes under reg 104 of the Road Vehicles (Construction and Use) Regulations 1986.
- Using a hand-held mobile telephone or similar device comes under reg 110 of the Road Vehicles (Construction and Use) Regulations 1986.

Practical considerations

- These offences provide for obligatory endorsement and disqualification (at the court's discretion).
- A two-way radio, which performs an interactive communication function by transmitting and receiving data is not a device under reg 110.
- Regulation 110(5) states that a person does not contravene reg 110 if—
  - ◆ they are using the telephone or device to call the police, fire, ambulance, or other emergency service on 112 or 999;
  - ◆ they are acting in response to a genuine emergency; and
  - ◆ it is unsafe or impracticable for them to cease driving in order to make the call.
- A mobile telephone or other device is to be treated as hand-held if it is, or must be, held at some point during the course of making or receiving a call or performing any other interactive communication function.
- A person supervises the holder of a provisional licence if they do so pursuant to a condition imposed on that licence holder.

TFPN

 Summary   6 months

 Fine not exceeding level 4 on the standard scale for goods vehicle or vehicle carrying more than eight passengers.
Fine not exceeding level 3 on the standard scale in any other case.
Discretionary disqualification. Obligatory endorsement—3 penalty points.

10.4.3 **Graduated fixed penalties, penalty deposits, and immobilization**

The Road Safety Act 2006 has introduced the graduated fixed penalty scheme, roadside deposits, and vehicle immobilization.

Schedule 2 of the Fixed Penalty Order 2000 lists the graduated fixed penalties and graduates the level of specified fixed penalties based on the seriousness of the offending. It increases the level of fine for some offences to above the default amount (£60 endorsable and £30 non-endorsable). Initially these graduated fixed penalties only apply to specific offences relating to commercial and PSV vehicles.

Any officer appointed by their force or a VOSA officer will have responsibility for dealing with graduated fixed penalties.

Roadside deposits

The Road Traffic Offenders Act 1988, ss 90A to 90D provide enforcement powers under what is termed the 'roadside deposit scheme'.

Offences

A person who—
(a) drives a vehicle in contravention of a prohibition under this section,
(b) causes or permits a vehicle to be driven in contravention of such a prohibition, or
(c) fails to comply within a reasonable time with a direction under subsection (5) above,
is guilty of an offence.

Road Traffic Offenders Act 1988, s 90D(6)

Points to prove

✓ drives a vehicle or causes/permits vehicle to be driven
✓ in contravention of a prohibition **or**
✓ fails to comply within a reasonable time a direction under s 90D(5)

Meanings

Prohibition

(1) This section applies where a person on whom a financial penalty deposit requirement is imposed does not make an immediate payment of the appropriate amount in accordance with section 90B(1) of this Act (and any order made under it).

10.4.3 Graduated Fixed Penalties, Penalty Deposits

(2) The constable or vehicle examiner by whom the requirement was imposed may prohibit the driving on a road of any vehicle of which the person was in charge at the time of the offence by giving to the person notice in writing of the prohibition.

(3) The prohibition—

   (a) shall come into force as soon as the notice is given, and

   (b) shall continue in force until the happening of whichever of the events in subsection (4) below occurs first.

(4) Those events are—

   (a) the person making a payment of the appropriate amount in accordance with section 90B(1) of this Act (and any order made under it) at any time during the relevant period,

   (b) (where a fixed penalty notice was given, or a conditional offer handed, to the person in respect of the offence) payment of the fixed penalty,

   (c) the person being convicted or acquitted of the offence,

   (d) the person being informed that he is not to be prosecuted for the offence, and

   (e) the coming to an end of the prosecution period.

Direction

(5) A constable or vehicle examiner may by direction in writing require the person to remove the vehicle to which the prohibition relates (and, if it is a motor vehicle drawing a trailer, also to remove the trailer) to such place and subject to such conditions as are specified in the direction; and the prohibition does not apply to the removal of the vehicle (or trailer) in accordance with the direction.

                                        Road Traffic Offenders Act 1988, s 90D

Explanatory notes

- Section 90A gives a constable in uniform or vehicle examiner power to require the payment of a deposit from a person, whom they believe is committing or has committed an offence in relation to a motor vehicle and is unable to provide a satisfactory address in the UK at which they can be found. Furthermore, the police officer or vehicle examiner must also believe that the person, the offence, and the circumstances in which the offence is committed are of a description specified by order made by the Secretary of State.

- Under s 90B a financial penalty deposit, of an amount specified by order, can be paid to the constable or examiner. That person must then be given either a fixed penalty notice or written notice as to proposed court proceedings for the offence.

- The specified amounts are—

   ◆ When it is a TFPN—the amount of that fixed penalty.

   ◆ In other cases it is a maximum of £300 per offence—to a maximum of £900 per vehicle stoppage.

- Once payment is made, s 90C stipulates that the person must be issued with a written receipt and notice outlining the process that applies through the various provisions of s 90C.
- If the driver does not contest the roadside deposit within 28 days, then the deposit is paid into court and that is the end of the matter. Alternatively should the driver contest and the court decide in their favour or if the case did not go to court within a year (or less than this if a shorter prosecution period applies), then the deposit would be refunded with the relevant interest. Similarly, if the court decided against them, the deposit would be retained to be offset against all, or part, of the fine imposed.
- Under s 90D, if a person does not make an immediate roadside deposit payment of the appropriate amount, the constable or vehicle examiner may then give the person a prohibition notice which prohibits the moving of the vehicle, though the vehicle/trailer may be moved to a specified place by way of a written direction.
- This prohibition will remain in force until one of the following occurs—
  - ◆ payment of the appropriate amount, during the relevant period,
  - ◆ payment of the fixed penalty notice,
  - ◆ conviction or acquittal of the offence,
  - ◆ driver informed that they will not be prosecuted, or
  - ◆ the prosecution period has expired.

Practical considerations

- This legislation provides enforcement powers against both UK and non-UK drivers who do not have a satisfactory UK address and were previously able to avoid payment of fixed penalties and prosecution as a result. It applies to both fixed penalty offences and other traffic offences.
- Enforcement of this scheme is through prohibition notices and vehicle immobilization, removal, and disposal powers.
- Under the Road Safety (Immobilisation, Removal and Disposal of Vehicles) Regulations 2009 a vehicle may be immobilized when the vehicle was being driven—
  - ◆ whilst unfit for service or overloaded;
  - ◆ in contravention of the drivers' hours rules;
  - ◆ in contravention of international transport requirements;
  - ◆ by a person who has failed to pay the financial penalty deposit.
- Immobilization will physically prevent a prohibition being disregarded, but the vehicle cannot be immobilized simply because it appears that the driver is likely to abscond.
- Therefore, where a driver does not make a payment under the roadside deposit scheme, the prohibition and immobilization powers can be applied by the enforcement officer until such time as the prohibition requirements are satisfied or, in cases of offenders who do not

10.4.3 Graduated Fixed Penalties, Penalty Deposits

have a reliable UK address, until such time as a deposit is paid or the case is settled in court.

- Prior to this scheme, prohibitions were usually imposed for breaches of drivers' hours or when the vehicle was not roadworthy.
- It is believed payment will be by cash or switch/debit cards; it is doubtful if credit cards will be accepted as payment can be cancelled prior to the transfer taking place (unlike switch which is immediate).

 (including graduated TFPN)

 Summary: Fine not exceeding level 5 on the standard scale. Time limit: 6 months
Discretionary disqualification

Links to alternative subjects and offences

10.5 **Notice of Intended Prosecution**

Section 1 of the Road Traffic Offenders Act 1988 requires a notice of intended prosecution to be given to a defendant for certain offences.

Requirement

Subject to **section 2** of this Act, a person shall not be convicted of an offence to which this section applies unless—

(a) he was warned at this time the offence was committed that the question of prosecuting him for one or other of the offences to which this section applies would be taken into consideration, or

(b) within 14 days of the commission of the offence a summons for the offence was served on him, or

(c) within 14 days of the commission of the offence a notice of the intended prosecution specifying the nature of the alleged offence and the time and place where it is alleged to have been committed, was—

   (i) in the case of an offence under section 28 or 29 of the Road Traffic Act 1988 *[see* **10.12***]*, served on him,

   (ii) in the case of any other offence, served on him or on the person, if any, registered as the keeper of the vehicle at the time of the commission of the offence.

Road Traffic Offenders Act 1988, s 1(1)

Meanings

Subject to s 2

This section will not apply if—

- At the time of the offence or immediately after it, the vehicle concerned was involved in an accident.
- A fixed penalty notice or a notice under the fixed penalty scheme requiring production of the defendant's licence and counterpart at a police station is issued (see **10.4**).

Within 14 days

Means the notice must be posted to reach the defendant within 14 days of the offence.

Explanatory notes

- NIPs may be served personally, or by registered post, recorded delivery, or first class post to their last known address.

- A notice of intended prosecution sent by registered post or recorded delivery is deemed served if addressed to them at their last known address even if it is returned undelivered or not received by them for some other reason.
- Requirements of s 1 are met unless the contrary is proved or if the defendant is charged and given a copy of the charge within 14 days of the commission of the offence.
- A notice of intended prosecution posted the day after the offence, which failed to arrive within the 14 days, was good service; whereas one sent by recorded delivery on the 14th day was deemed not 'served'.
- Failure to comply with s 1 is not a bar to conviction if the name and address of the defendant or the registered keeper could not be ascertained with due diligence in time to comply, or that the accused's conduct contributed to the failure.
- If an alternative verdict is returned by the court and the alternative offence requires NIP this is not a bar to conviction, providing the original offence did not require NIP.

Related cases

Shield v Crighton [1974] Crim LR 605, DC 'At the time the offence was committed' is not limited to the exact time of the offence. It has to be construed sensibly, not literally.

R v Myers [2007] EWCA, CA There has to be a causal link between a traffic offence and the accident, otherwise the driver requires serving with NIP.

Relevant offences

Schedule 1 of the Road Traffic Offenders Act 1988 lists the offences for which NIP is required under s 1, being—

Road Traffic Regulation Act 1984

s 16—contravene speed restriction at road works.

s 17(4)—contravene motorway speed limit.

s 88(7)—contravene minimum speed limit.

s 89(1)—exceeding speed limit.

Road Traffic Act 1988

s 2—dangerous driving.

s 3—careless, and inconsiderate, driving.

s 22—leaving vehicles in dangerous position.

s 28—dangerous cycling.

s 29—careless, and inconsiderate, cycling.

s 35—failing to comply with traffic directions.

s 36—failing to comply with traffic signs prescribed under s 36 [see **10.3**].

Practical considerations

- If the offence arises out of an accident of which the driver may not be aware NIP required (*Bentley v Dickinson* [1983] RTR 356).
- No NIP required if a TFPN (see **10.4**) is issued, or notice that one will be issued on production and surrender of driving licence and counterpart at a police station is issued.
- There is no need to quote exact Act and section of the offence—keep it simple.

Links to alternative subjects and offences

10.6 **Driving Without Due Care and Attention**

Section 3 of the Road Traffic Act 1988 relates to the offence of driving without due care and attention or without reasonable consideration for other users of the road or public place. Section 168 requires a person alleged to have committed this offence to give their details to any person having reasonable grounds for obtaining them.

10.6.1 **Driving without due care and attention**

Offences

If a person drives a **mechanically propelled vehicle** on a **road** or other **public place without due care and attention, or** without **reasonable consideration** for other persons using the road or public place, he is guilty of an offence.

Road Traffic Act 1988, s 3

Points to prove

✓ drove mechanically propelled vehicle
✓ on road/other public place
✓ without due care and attention/reasonable consideration for other road users

Meanings

Drives (see 10.1.4)

Mechanically propelled vehicle (see 10.1.3)

Road—s 192 (see 10.1.1)

Public place (see 10.1.2)

Driving without due care and attention or reasonable consideration

(1) This section has effect for the purposes of sections 2B, 3 and 3A.
(2) A person is to be regarded as driving without due care and attention if (and only if) the way he drives falls below what would be expected of a competent and careful driver.

(3) In determining for the purposes of subsection (2) above what would be expected of a careful and competent driver in a particular case, regard shall be had not only to the circumstances of which he could be expected to be aware but also to any circumstances shown to have been within the knowledge of the accused.

(4) A person is to be regarded as driving without reasonable consideration for other persons only if those persons are inconvenienced by his driving.

Road Traffic Act 1988, s 3ZA

Explanatory notes

- Breaching certain road traffic regulations (eg crossing central white lines without explanation) can be enough to prove this offence.
- Section 168 of the Road Traffic Act 1988 empowers the obtaining of the defendant's name and address (see **10.6.2**).
- Riding a pedal cycle without due care and attention is an offence under s 29 (see **10.12.2**).

Defences

The defences of automatism, unconsciousness and sudden illness, duress, sudden mechanical defect, assisting in the arrest of offenders and taking part in an authorized motoring event may be used.

Defence notes

- 'Automatism' means an affliction which overcomes the driver and causes them to lose control of the vehicle. It must be sudden and something that they were unaware of and could not reasonably be expected to foresee.
- 'Unconsciousness and sudden illness' applies if a driver is rendered unconscious and unable to control the vehicle. For example a blow to the head or sudden and unforeseen epileptic fit may cause this.
- The defence of duress may be split into two parts—duress by threat or duress of necessity (of circumstances).
- For duress by threat to apply a person cannot deliberately put themselves in a position where they are likely to be subject to threats and, if they can escape the duress by escaping the threats, they must do so.
- Sudden mechanical defect applies if a sudden and unexpected defect in the motor vehicle causes the driver to totally lose control. It does not apply to a defect which is already known to the driver or which could have been easily discovered with reasonable prudence.
- The defence of assisting in the arrest of offenders may be available to a driver if their driving, though careless or inconsiderate, amounted to reasonable force assisting in the arrest of an offender (see **1.2.1**).

10.6.1 Driving Without due Care and Attention

- Section 13A(1) states that a person shall not be guilty of an offence under sections 1, 2 or 3 of this Act by virtue of driving a vehicle in a public place other than a road if they show that they were driving in accordance with an authorization for a motoring event given under regulations made by the Secretary of State (currently the Motor Vehicles (Off Road Events) Regulations 1992).

Related cases

Agnew v DPP [1991] RTR 144, QBD A police officer driving an unmarked surveillance vehicle in a training exercise on a public road crossed a red traffic signal and collided with another vehicle. The court did not agree to 'special reasons' for not endorsing his licence, stating that public safety was paramount and must always take priority over police training.

DPP v Harris [1994] 158 JP 896, QBD A detective constable driving an unmarked police car was covertly following a vehicle carrying suspects planning to commit an armed robbery when H went through a red traffic light and collided with another vehicle. Care due in these circumstances would involve edging slowly forwards, being prepared to stop if required. In order to justify a defence of 'necessity' it would be necessary to show that any actions were reasonable and proportionate in the light of a threat of death or serious injury.

McCrone v Riding [1938] 1 All ER 157, KBD The standard of driving required from a driver is an objective one, fixed in relation to the safety of other users of the highway. It does not relate to the degree of proficiency or experience attained by the individual driver.

Kay v Butterworth (1945) 110 JP 75, CA If a driver falls asleep whilst driving, they are guilty of at least driving without due care and attention.

Watts v Carter The Times, 22 October 1959, QBD A car leaving the road and mounting the footpath can be driving without due care and attention.

Practical considerations

- This offence requires a notice of intended prosecution to be served (see **10.5**).
- Although there is no special standard for emergency vehicles, the courts have made it clear that public safety must be paramount (see '**Related cases**').
- This section creates two offences and it is bad for duplicity to charge both of them as alternatives.
- Other persons using the road includes other drivers, passengers, pedestrians, or cyclists.
- Ensure compliance of the CPS charging standards for this offence.
- The s 3ZA statutory meaning of driving without due or reasonable consideration for others also applies to s 3A (death by careless driving when under influence) (see **10.8.2**) and s 2B (death by careless driving) (see **10.8.3**).

Summary 6 months

 A fine not exceeding level 4 on the standard scale.
Discretionary disqualification. Obligatory endorsement—3 to 9
penalty points.

10.6.2 **Request details after reckless, careless, or inconsiderate driving or cycling**

Offences

Any of the following persons—

(a) the **driver** of a **mechanically propelled vehicle** who is alleged to
    have committed an offence under section 2 or 3 of this Act, or

(b) the rider of a cycle who is alleged to have committed an offence under
    section 28 or 29 of this Act,

who refuses, on being so required by any person having reasonable ground
for so requiring, to give his name and address, or gives a false name and
address, is guilty of an offence.

Road Traffic Act 1988, s 168

Points to prove

✓ driver of mechanically propelled vehicle/rider of cycle
✓ commits offence under ss 2/3 or 28/29 of RTA 1988
✓ when required by person having reasonable grounds
✓ refused to give name and address/gave false details

Meanings

Mechanically propelled vehicle (see **10.1.3**)

Driver (see **10.1.4**)

Explanatory notes

Above offences committed under this Act are—

• Dangerous driving, s 2 (see **10.7**).
• Driving without due care and attention/without reasonable consideration, s 3 (see **10.6.1**).
• Sections 28 and 29 involve similar offences to above, but riding pedal
  cycles (see **10.12**).

10.6.2 Request Details

 Summary   6 months

 A fine not exceeding level 4 on the standard scale.

Links to alternative subjects and offences

10.7 **Dangerous Driving**

10.7.1 **Dangerous driving**

Section 2 of the Road Traffic Act 1988 relates to dangerous driving.

Offences

A person who drives a mechanically propelled vehicle dangerously on a road or other public place is guilty of an offence.

Road Traffic Act 1988, s 2

Points to prove

✓ being driver of a mechanically propelled vehicle
✓ drove dangerously
✓ on a road/other public place

Meanings

Drives (see 10.1.4)

Mechanically propelled vehicle (see 10.1.3)

Driving dangerously

Where the driving falls far below what would be expected of a competent and careful driver, **and** it would be obvious to a competent and careful driver that driving in that way and/or driving the vehicle in its current state would be dangerous.

Road—s 192 (see 10.1.1)

Public place (see 10.1.2)

Explanatory notes

- In considering the state of the vehicle, anything attached to or carried in or on it, and the manner of it being so attached or carried is also relevant.
- Dangerous refers to either danger of injury to any person or serious damage to property.
- Consideration will be taken not only of the circumstances which a competent and careful driver could be expected to be aware of, but also any circumstances shown to be within the defendant's knowledge.

- There is an offence of dangerous cycling under s 28
  (see **10.12.1**).
- Section 168 empowers obtaining of driver's name and address (see
  10.6.2).

Defences (see **10.6.1**)

Defence notes (see **10.6.1**)

Related cases

R v Spurge [1961] 2 All ER 688, CA A driver aware of a mechanical defect, which caused the vehicle to be dangerous, could not use this defence.

R v Strong [1995] Crim LR 428, CA The danger is 'obvious' only if it can be seen or realized at first glance, or is evident to the competent or careful driver, or the defendant knew of it.

R v Roberts and George [1997] RTR 462, CA Where the driver was an employee it was important to consider the instructions he had from his employer concerning checks to be made on the vehicle. If they were reasonable it would be wrong to expect the driver to do more than instructed.

R v Woodward [1995] 3 All ER 79, CA Evidence of consumption of alcohol is admissible only where it is to the effect that the defendant had drunk so much of it as would adversely affect a driver.

R v Pleydell [2005] EWCA Crim 1447, CA Evidence that a driver had taken cocaine was, by itself, admissible as P had driven dangerously as a result of being adversely affected by drugs.

DPP v Milton [2006] EWHC 242 (Admin) QBD Excessive speed alone is insufficient for dangerous driving; the driving has to be considered with all the circumstances.

Practical considerations

- This offence requires NIP to be served (see **10.5**).
- Consider CPS charging standards advice and specific guidance.
- A court may convict of an alternative offence under s 3
  (see **10.6.1**).
- Consider any CCTV evidence that may be available.
- Forfeiture of the vehicle used may also be ordered.

 Either way   None

 Summary: 6 months' imprisonment and/or a fine not exceeding the statutory maximum.

Indictment: 2 years' imprisonment and/or a fine. Obligatory disqualification until test passed.

Obligatory endorsement—3 to 11 penalty points (unless special reasons apply).

10.7.2 **Wanton or furious driving**

Section 35 of the Offences Against the Person Act 1861 provides for the offence of wanton or furious driving.

Offences

Whosoever, having the charge of any carriage or vehicle, shall by wanton or furious driving or racing, or other wilful misconduct, or by wilful neglect, do or cause to be done any bodily harm to any person whatsoever, shall be guilty of an offence.

Offences Against the Person Act 1861, s 35

Points to prove
- ✓ **in** charge of a carriage/vehicle
- ✓ by wanton/furious driving/racing or other wilful misconduct/ neglect
- ✓ did/caused bodily harm to be done to another

Meanings

Vehicle (see **10.1.3**)

Wanton

Means without any lawful motive and being thoughtless as to the possible consequences.

Driving (see **10.1.4**)

Bodily harm (see **2.1.2**)

Explanatory notes

A person riding a pedal cycle in a wanton or furious manner resulting in injuries to another person may be convicted under this section.

Practical considerations

This offence can be committed anywhere.

10.7.2 Wanton or Furious Driving

 Indictment None

 2 years' imprisonment.

If a mechanically propelled vehicle—discretionary disqualification and obligatory endorsement of 3 to 9 penalty points.

Links to alternative subjects and offences

10.8 **Fatal Road Traffic Collision Incidents**

A driver involved in a fatal road traffic incident has the same obligations as a driver involved in any other reportable road traffic collisions (see **10.9**). Offences connected with deaths caused by road traffic incidents are found in s 1 (dangerous driving), s 2B (due care), s 3A (careless driving when under influence of drink or drugs), and s 3ZB (no licence/insurance or disqualified).

10.8.1 **Causing death by dangerous driving**

Causing death by dangerous driving is an offence created by s 1 of the Road Traffic Act 1988.

Offences

A person who causes the death of **another person** by **driving** a mechanically propelled **vehicle dangerously** on a **road** or other **public place** is guilty of an offence.

Road Traffic Act 1988, s 1

Points to prove

✓ caused the death of another person
✓ by driving a mechanically propelled vehicle dangerously
✓ on a road/public place

Meanings

Another person

Means anybody, other than the defendant. It has been held to include a foetus in utero (still in the uterus) and subsequently born alive, but who later dies of their injuries.

Driving (see **10.1.4**)

Mechanically propelled vehicle (see **10.1.3**)

Driven dangerously (see **10.7**)

Road—s 192 (see **10.1.1**)

Public place (see **10.1.2**)

Explanatory notes

- The death of the person concerned must be shown to have been caused in some way by the incident to which the charge relates.
- The cause of death does not need to be a substantial cause, but neither should it be a slight or trifling link. It will suffice if the driving was a cause of the death even though it was not the sole or even a substantial cause.
- A person charged with this offence may be convicted of the alternative offences of dangerous driving (see **10.7**), death by driving without due care (see **10.8.3**), or careless, and inconsiderate, driving (see **10.6**).

Defences (see 10.6.1)

Defence notes (see 10.6.1)

Related cases (see also '**Dangerous driving**' cases **10.7.1**)

R v Hennigan [1971] 3 All ER 133, CA A vehicle on the main road was travelling at an excessive speed, and collided with a vehicle emerging from the side road, killing the driver. The other driver was convicted of s 1, even though the deceased was mainly to blame, the excessive speed and dangerous driving of the defendant was partly to blame.

R v Ash [1999] RTR 347, QBD Where only one blood sample is taken the result of the analysis can still be used under this section. The requirement to take two samples under s 15 of the Road Traffic Offenders Act 1988 does not apply to this section.

R v Buono [2005] EWCA Crim 1313, CA A fatal collision had been caused by the defendant taking a bend in the middle of the road at excessive speed. Similar fact evidence was admitted to show the manner in which the car had been driven earlier—swerving across the road and driving at excessive speed. Such evidence had considerable probative force, which undoubtedly outweighed any prejudice to the defendant.

Practical considerations

- This section applies to tramcars and trolley vehicles operating under a statutory power.
- If appropriate consider manslaughter (see **2.7**) for this offence.
- Theoretically, two different drivers could cause the same death.
- *R v Beckford* (1994) 159 JP 305, CA (see **10.8.2**) also applies to this offence.
- Consideration must be given to the CPS driving offences charging standards.
- When dealing with the incident follow Force Policy, preserve the scene, involve supervision, scenes of crime, CID and other agencies.
- Consider CCTV evidence that may be available.
- The vehicle may be forfeited.

Indictment   None

 14 years' imprisonment.
Obligatory disqualification until extended test passed.

Obligatory endorsement—3 to 11 penalty points (only if special reasons apply).

10.8.2 Causing death by careless driving when under influence

Section 3A of the Road Traffic Act 1988 provides an offence of causing the death of another by careless driving when under the influence of drink or drugs, or failing to provide or give permission for a specimen.

Offences

If a person causes the death of **another person** by **driving a mechanically propelled vehicle** on a **road** or other **public place without due care and attention**, or without **reasonable consideration** for other persons using the road or public place, and—

(a) he is, at the time when he is driving, **unfit to drive through drink or drugs**, or

(b) he has consumed so much alcohol that the proportion of it in his breath, blood or urine at that time **exceeds the prescribed limit**, or

(c) he is, within 18 hours after that time, required to provide a specimen in pursuance of section 7 of this Act *[see 10.11.2]*, but without reasonable excuse fails to provide it, or

(d) he is required by a constable to give his permission for a laboratory test of a specimen of blood taken from him under section 7A of this Act *[see 10.11.2]*,

but without reasonable excuse fails to do so he is guilty of an offence.

Road Traffic Act 1988, s 3A(1)

Points to prove

✓ caused the death of another person
✓ by driving a motor vehicle
✓ on a road/public place
✓ without due care or reasonable consideration for other road users **and**
✓ at the time of driving was unfit through drink/drugs **or**
✓ was over the prescribed limit **or**
✓ within 18 hours of incident failed to provide specimen **or**
✓ on being required failed to give permission to take specimen of blood

---

Meanings

Another person (see **10.8.1**)

Driving (see **10.1.4**)

Mechanically propelled vehicle (see **10.1.3**)

Road—s 192 (see **10.1.1**)

Public place (see **10.1.2**)

Without due care and attention or reasonable consideration
(see **10.6.1**)

Unfit to drive
When his ability to drive properly is impaired.

Through drink or drugs (see **10.10**)

Exceeds the prescribed limit (see **10.11**)

Explanatory notes

- The careless or inconsiderate driving (see **10.6**) must be a cause of
  the death of another person, as must being under the influence of
  drink/drugs, or failing to provide or give permission for a specimen.
- Section 3A(3) states that s 3A(1)(b), (c) and (d) do not apply to a
  mechanically propelled vehicle. They only apply to a motor vehicle.
- It is not necessary for the intoxication to be a direct cause of the care-
  less/inconsiderate driving.
- A person charged with this offence may be convicted of the alternative driving offences of careless, and inconsiderate (see **10.6**), unfit
  through drink/drugs (see **10.10**), excess alcohol in breath/blood/urine,
  or failing to provide a specimen (see **10.11**).

Defences (see **10.6.1**)

Defence notes (see 10.6)

Related cases

R v Beckford (1994) 159 JP 305, CA Following a road traffic accident
in which a passenger was killed, the vehicle was scrapped after a few
weeks. Defendant relied upon defence of 'mechanical defect' where the
steering had locked. Court stated that 'procedures' should be in place
which ensure that cars are not scrapped before express permission has
been given by the police. Permission will never be given where serious
criminal charges are to be brought which may involve the possibility of
some mechanical defect in a car.

Practical considerations

- Consideration must be given to the CPS driving offences charging standards.
- Cases where the actual standard of driving itself would not normally attract a prosecution, may merit proceedings for this offence.
- As with all fatal road traffic collisions protect and prevent contamination of the scene.
- Ensure that cars are not scrapped, as serious criminal charges may be brought and the defence of a mechanical defect in the car maybe alleged. Consider seizing the vehicle as it may be forfeited.
- Consider CCTV evidence, if available, of both the collision and the manner of driving prior to the collision.

 Indictment None

14 years' imprisonment.

Obligatory disqualification until extended test passed.

Obligatory endorsement—3 to 11 penalty points (only if special reasons apply).

10.8.3 Causing death by driving without due care

Section 2B of the Road Traffic Act 1988 provides for the offence of causing death by driving without due care and attention or reasonable consideration for others.

Offences

A person who causes the death of **another person** by **driving** a **mechanically propelled vehicle** on a **road** or other **public place without due care and attention**, or without **reasonable consideration** for other persons using the road or place is guilty of an offence.

Road Traffic Act 1988, s 2B

Points to prove

✓ caused the death of another person
✓ by driving a mechanically propelled vehicle
✓ on a road/public place
✓ without due care and attention/reasonable consideration for others

Meanings

Another person (see 10.8.1)

Driving (see 10.1.4)

Mechanically propelled vehicle (see 10.1.3)

Road—s 192 (see 10.1.1)

Public place (see 10.1.2)

Without due care and attention or reasonable consideration
(see 10.6.1)

Explanatory Notes (see 10.6.1)

Defences (see 10.6.1)

Practical considerations (see also **10.6.1** and **10.8.2**)

- This section may be an alternative verdict to an offence under—
  - ◆ s 1 (causing death by dangerous driving—see **10.8.1**);
  - ◆ s 3A (causing death by driving without due care when under the influence—see **10.8.2**).
- Ensure compliance with the law in relation to reporting road traffic collisions (see **10.9**).

 Either way   None

 Summary: 12 months' imprisonment and/or a fine not exceeding the statutory maximum.
Indictment: 5   years'   imprisonment   and/or   a   fine. Obligatory disqualification and obligatory endorsement with 3 to 11 penalty points.

10.8.4 **Causing death by driving when disqualified or no insurance or licence**

Section 3ZB of the Road Traffic Act 1988 provides for the offence of causing the death of another person by driving a motor vehicle on a road and at the time was disqualified, or otherwise than in accordance with a licence, or without insurance.

Offences

A person is guilty of an offence under this section if he causes the death of **another person** by **driving** a **motor vehicle** on a **road** and, at the time when he is driving, the circumstances are such that he is committing an offence under—

- (a) section 87(1) of this Act (driving otherwise than in accordance with a licence),
- (b) section 103(1)(b) of this Act (driving while disqualified), or
- (c) section 143 of this Act (using motor vehicle while uninsured or unsecured against third party risks).

Road Traffic Act 1988, s 3ZB

Points to prove

- ✓ caused the death of another person
- ✓ by driving a motor vehicle
- ✓ on a road
- ✓ without driving licence/insurance **or** whilst disqualified

Meanings

Another person (see **10.8.1**)

Driving (see **10.1.4**)

Motor vehicle (see **10.1.3**)

Road—s 192 (see **10.1.1**)

Explanatory notes

This offence is subject to a fatal road traffic collision and committing an offence of—

- driving otherwise than in accordance with a licence under s 87(1) (see **10.14.1**);
- driving whilst disqualified under s 103(1)(b) (see **10.13**), or
- using motor vehicle without insurance under s 143 (see **10.16.1**).

Practical considerations

- Consideration must be given to the CPS driving offences charging standards.
- As with all fatal road traffic collisions protect and prevent contamination of the scene.

10.8.4 Causing Death by Driving when Disqualified

- Consider using the powers of seizing and removing vehicles being used without insurance or driving licence for that class under s 165A (see **10.16.5**). As serious criminal charges may be brought this will also ensure that the vehicle can be examined for any mechanical defect defences before eventual disposal.
- CCTV evidence, if available, for both the collision and the manner of driving prior to the collision.

 Either way   None

 Summary: 12 months' imprisonment and/or a fine not exceeding the statutory maximum.
Indictment: 2 years' imprisonment and/or a fine. Obligatory disqualification and obligatory endorsement with 3 to 11 penalty points

Links to alternative subjects and offences

10.9 Road Traffic Collisions

Section 170 of the Road Traffic Act 1988 imposes duties on the driver of a mechanically propelled vehicle involved in certain road traffic collisions on a road or other public place.

10.9.1 Incidents to which applicable

Collisions which apply

If owing to the presence of a **mechanically propelled vehicle** on a **road** or other **public place**, an **accident** occurs whereby—

(a) personal **injury** is caused to a person other than the **driver** of that mechanically propelled vehicle, or

(b) damage is caused—

    (i) to a vehicle other than that mechanically propelled vehicle or a trailer drawn by that mechanically propelled vehicle, or

    (ii) to an **animal** other than an animal in or on that mechanically propelled vehicle or a trailer drawn by that mechanically propelled vehicle, or

    (iii) to any other property constructed on, fixed to, growing in or otherwise forming part of the land on which the road or place in question is situated or land adjacent to such land.

Road Traffic Act 1988, s 170(1)

Meanings

Mechanically propelled vehicle (see **10.1.3**)

Road (see **10.6.1**)

Public place (see **10.1.2**)

Accident

This is an unintended occurrence having an adverse physical result.

Injury

Includes any actual bodily harm and may well include nervous shock.

Driver (see **10.1.4**)

Animal

Means horse, cattle, ass, mule, sheep, pig, goat, or dog.

Practical considerations

• There must be some link between the presence of the vehicle and the occurrence of the accident.

- 'Vehicle', in respect of the other vehicle damaged, may include a pedal cycle.
- If attending a potential fatal collision preserve the scene and request assistance from specialist traffic officers, Scenes of Crime and CID (see **10.8**).

10.9.2 **Duties of driver after accident**

Offences

(2) The **driver** of the **mechanically propelled vehicle** must stop and, if required to do so by any person having reasonable grounds for so requiring, give his name and address and also the name and address of the owner and the identification marks of the vehicle.

(3) If for any reason the driver of the mechanically propelled vehicle does not give his name and address under subsection (2) above, he must report the **accident**.

(4) A person who fails to comply with subsection (2) or (3) above is guilty of an offence.

Road Traffic Act 1988, s 170

Points to prove

✓ being the driver of a mechanically propelled vehicle
✓ involved in a road traffic accident
✓ failed to stop **and**
✓ on being requested by a person having grounds to do so
✓ failed to provide details, as required

Meanings

Driver (see **10.1.4**)

Mechanically propelled vehicle (see **10.1.3**)

Accident (see **10.9.1**)

Explanatory notes

- If the driver does not stop immediately they must do so as soon as it is safe and convenient to do so.
- The fact that the person requiring details from the driver knows them does not negate the obligation imposed on the driver.
- If personal injury is involved and the vehicle is a motor vehicle, and the driver does not, at the time of the collision, produce evidence of insurance to a constable or some person having reasonable grounds for

requiring them to do so, they must report the collision and produce such evidence (see **10.9.3**).

- After stopping the driver must remain there long enough to enable them, if required, to furnish the relevant information.

Related cases

DPP v Hay [2005] EWHC 1395 (Admin), QBD H was driving a vehicle involved in an accident and was taken to hospital without exchanging details or reporting the accident to the police, and subsequently failed to report the accident after being discharged from hospital. Held: that H had failed to comply with s 170, even though the police observed the accident and had made no request for information.

DPP v McCarthy [1999] RTR 323, DC The requirement to give a name and address has a wider meaning than just the driver's home address. An address needs to be somewhere where a person can be contacted.

McDermott v DPP [1997] RTR 474, QBD The driver of a horsebox collided with the side of a car causing damage, and drove on to some stables 80 yards away. Although returning, the driver had left the scene, and could have stopped at the time of the accident.

Practical considerations

- The driver does not commit this offence if they are unaware that an accident has happened.
- These two subsections create two separate offences (failing to stop and give information **and** failing to report). Therefore the driver may be charged with either one or both of them. A further offence maybe committed in a s 170(1)(a) injury accident and the driver fails to comply with s 170(5) (see **10.9.3**).
- The scene of the accident is the place in the road or public place where the collision occurs. Remember the vehicles themselves may also be 'scenes'.

 Summary   6 months

 6 months' imprisonment and/or a fine not exceeding level 5 on the standard scale.
Discretionary disqualification.

Obligatory endorsement—5 to 10 penalty points.

10.9.3 **Duty of driver to report the incident**

Section 170 provides for the obligation and a subsequent offence where a reportable accident occurs.

10.9.3 Duty of Driver to Report the Incident

Offences

(5) If, in a case where this section applies by virtue of subsection (1)(a) above *[injury, see* **10.9.1***]*, the driver of a motor vehicle does not at the time of the accident produce such a certificate of insurance or security, or other evidence, as is mentioned in section 165(2)(a) of this Act—

   (a) to a constable, or

   (b) to some person who, having reasonable grounds for so doing, has required him to produce it,

the driver must report the accident and produce such a certificate or other evidence.

(7) A person who fails to comply with a duty under subsection (5) above is guilty of an offence.

Road Traffic Act 1988, s 170

Points to prove

- ✓ being driver of a motor vehicle
- ✓ involved in a relevant road traffic accident
- ✓ did not at the time of the accident
- ✓ produce to a constable/person with grounds for requiring
- ✓ relevant evidence of insurance **or**
- ✓ failed to report the accident and produce relevant insurance

---

Meanings

Driver (see 10.1.4)

Motor vehicle (see 10.1.3)

Accident (see 10.9.1)

Explanatory notes

- To comply with the requirement to produce the relevant proof of insurance, s 170(6) states that the driver must do so at a police station or to a constable, which must be done as soon as is reasonably practicable and, in any case, within 24 hours of it occurring.
- A person will not be convicted of this offence only because they failed to produce the relevant insurance document if, within 7 days following the accident it is produced at a police station specified by them at the time they reported the accident.
- The obligation to report the accident includes where there is nobody else about to whom the driver can give the details (eg damage to street furnishings).

Practical considerations

- Note that whereas s 170(2) and s 170(3) create offences in relation to a mechanically propelled vehicle, this offence is in relation to the use of a motor vehicle.
- This requirement does not apply to an invalid carriage.
- 'At a police station' means the motorist should report it in person at a police station or to a constable; a report by telephone will not suffice.

 Summary   6 months

 6 months' imprisonment and/or a fine not exceeding level 5 on the standard scale.
Discretionary disqualification.

Obligatory endorsement—5 to 10 penalty points.

Links to alternative subjects and offences

10.10 Drive/Attempt to Drive/in Charge of Vehicle Whilst Unfit Through Drink/Drugs

10.10.1 Drive whilst unfit drink/drugs

Section 4 of the Road Traffic Act 1988 provides for the offences of driving, attempting to drive, and being in charge of a mechanically propelled vehicle on a road or public place while unfit through drink or drugs.

Offences

(1) A person who, when **driving** or attempting to drive a **mechanically propelled vehicle** on a **road** or other **public place**, is unfit to drive through drink or drugs is guilty of an offence.

(2) Without prejudice to subsection (1) above, a person who, when **in charge** of a mechanically propelled vehicle which is on a road or other public place, is unfit to drive through drink or drugs is guilty of an offence.

Road Traffic Act 1988, s 4

Points to prove

s 4(1) offence

✓ drove/attempted to drive
✓ a mechanically propelled vehicle
✓ on a road/other public place
✓ when unfit to drive through drink/drugs

s 4(2) offence

✓ in charge of a mechanically propelled vehicle
✓ on a road/public place
✓ being unfit to drive through drink/drugs

Meanings

Driving (see 10.1.4)

Mechanically propelled vehicle (see 10.1.3)

Road (see 10.6.1)

Public place (see 10.1.2)

In charge

There is no legislation or test for what constitutes 'in charge' for the purposes of being in charge of a vehicle under s 4 or s 5 (see **10.11.1**), but a close connection between the defendant and control of the vehicle is required.

Explanatory notes

- A person is unfit to drive properly if their ability is for the time being impaired. The prosecution must give evidence of unfitness.
- It needs to be ascertained whether the person is in charge of the vehicle by virtue of being the owner, lawful possessor or recent driver. Are they still in charge or have they relinquished charge at the relevant time; have they assumed charge?
- Factors that need to be considered in establishing whether the person was in charge include—
  - Who is the registered keeper of the vehicle; who is insured to drive it; where were the other insured drivers (if any)?
  - What were their immediate and future intended movements?
  - If away from their home/accommodation, how did they propose to return without driving?
  - How had the vehicle got to where it was; when did they last drive it; are they in possession of a key which fits the ignition?
  - What was their position in relation to the car; were they in the vehicle; if not how far from it were they?
  - Was anyone else in or around the vehicle; what were they doing at the relevant time?
  - Is there evidence of an intention to take control of the vehicle?
  - When and where had they been drinking; time of last drink; what had they been doing since then?
- The evidence of a doctor who examines the defendant at the request of the police is admissible even if they had to persuade the defendant to allow the examination.

Defence

For the purposes of subsection (2) above, a person shall be deemed not to have been in charge of a mechanically propelled vehicle if he proves that at the material time the circumstances were such that there was no likelihood of his driving it so long as he remained unfit to drive through drink or drugs.

Road Traffic Act 1988, s 4(3)

Defence notes

- In the case of *Sheldrake v DPP (Attorney-General's Reference No 4 of 2002)* [2005] 1 Cr App R 28 it was held that the burden of proof should remain on the defendant, to be decided on the balance of probabilities. This imposition did not contravene the presumption of innocence and was compatible with ECHR.

- The court, in determining whether there was a likelihood of a person driving whilst still unfit through drink or drugs, should disregard any injury to them and any damage to the vehicle (ie it is not the practical possibility of the person being able to drive the vehicle that is relevant here, but rather the possibility of that person driving at all while still impaired).

Related cases

R v Ealing ex parte Woodman (1994) 158 JP 997, QBD If there was sufficient proof that they had taken more than their normal dose of insulin and failed to counterbalance it with food intake, insulin would be treated by the court as a drug under this section.

Smith v Mellors & Another [1987] RTR 210, QBD If the driver cannot be identified and each occupant of the car is over the prescribed limit, each one can be charged with the relevant drink driving offence and alternatively with aiding and abetting the other(s) to commit the drink driving offence. However, evidence of the aiding must be put to the court.

Practical considerations

- A charge under this section, which uses both the alternatives of 'drink or drugs', is not bad for duplicity.
- The CPS are unlikely to take the case forward unless there is evidence that the suspect was likely to drive whilst under the influence of drink/drugs. Similarly if in charge, ensure that the s 4(3) defence can be countered if raised.
- This section applies to trolley vehicles operated under statutory powers, but not to tramcars.
- An indictment containing a charge under s 1 of the Road Traffic Act 1988 (see **10.8**) should not include a charge under this section, as this section is triable summarily only.
- A non-expert witness may give evidence of the defendant's condition, but not of their fitness to drive.

 Summary   6 months

 s 4(1) offence

> 6 months' imprisonment and/or a fine not exceeding level 5 on the standard scale.

> Obligatory disqualification for a minimum of 12 months.

> Obligatory endorsement—3 to 11 penalty points.

s 4(2) offence

> 3 months' imprisonment and/or a fine not exceeding level 4 on the standard scale.

> Discretionary disqualification.
> Obligatory endorsement—10 penalty points.

10.10.2 **Preliminary Test Powers**

Section 6 of the Road Traffic Act 1988 provides for the requiring of preliminary tests for alcohol, impairment, or drugs to drivers of motor vehicles. Sections 6A to 6C relate to the specific tests, whilst s 6D provides a power of arrest and s 6E a power of entry.

Offence

A person commits an offence if without reasonable excuse he **fails** to co-operate with a **preliminary test** in pursuance of a **requirement** imposed under this section.

Road Traffic Act 1988, s 6(6)

Points to prove

✓ without reasonable excuse
✓ failed to cooperate with a preliminary test
✓ when required under this section

Meanings

Fails

Fail includes refuse.

Preliminary test

Reference to a preliminary test is to any of the tests described in sections 6A to 6C and means a preliminary test—of breath/impairment or for drugs.

Requirements

Under s 6(1)–(5) a constable may require a person to co-operate with any one or more preliminary tests administered to them by that constable or another constable, if the constable reasonably suspects that—

• they are driving, attempting to drive, or are in charge of a motor vehicle on a road or other public place, and have alcohol or a drug in their body or are under the influence of a drug; **or**
• they had been driving, attempting to drive, or in charge of a motor vehicle on a road or other public place while having alcohol or a drug in their body or while unfit to drive because of a drug, and still have alcohol or a drug in their body or are still under the influence of a drug; **or**
• they are or have been driving, attempting to drive, or in charge of a motor vehicle on a road or other public place, and have committed a **traffic offence** while the vehicle was in motion; or

- an accident has occurred owing to the presence of a motor vehicle on a road or other public place, and a constable reasonably believes that they were driving, attempting to drive, or in charge of the vehicle at the time of the accident.

Explanatory notes

- Only a constable in uniform may administer a preliminary test.
- **Traffic offence** means an offence under the Public Passenger Vehicles Act 1981, Pt 2 (s 6 to s 29), Road Traffic Regulation Act 1984, Road Traffic Offenders Act 1988 (except Pt 3—fixed penalties), or Road Traffic Act 1988 (except Pt 5—driving instruction).
- A preliminary breath test (s 6A) is a procedure by which the person taking the test provides a specimen of breath to ascertain, using a device approved by the Secretary of State, whether the proportion of alcohol in their breath or blood is likely to exceed the prescribed limit.
- For a preliminary impairment test (s 6B) the constable requesting it observes the person taking it performing tasks specified by the constable and makes any observations of the person's physical state as they think is expedient. The constable shall have regard to the code of practice issued by the Secretary of State which governs preliminary impairment tests.
- For a preliminary drug test (s 6C) a specimen of sweat or saliva is obtained (using a device approved by the Secretary of State) to ascertain whether the person tested has a drug in their body.
- A person will not be required at random to provide a specimen of breath for a breath test.
- An asthma sufferer who is incapable of providing a sample has a duty to inform the officer requiring it.
- A person who refuses (without good cause) to take a test is deemed to have failed to take it.
- Whilst in hospital, no person will be requested to supply a breath sample or laboratory specimen without the knowledge and permission of the doctor in charge of their case.

Power of arrest

(1) A constable may arrest a person without warrant if as a result of a preliminary breath test the constable reasonably suspects that the proportion of alcohol in that person's breath or blood exceeds the prescribed limit.

(2) A constable may arrest a person without warrant if—
    (a) the person fails to co-operate with a preliminary test in pursuance of a requirement imposed under s 6, and
    (b) the constable reasonably suspects that the person has alcohol or a drug in his body or is under the influence of a drug.

Road Traffic Act 1988, s 6D

Power of entry (after injury accident)

A constable may enter any place (using reasonable force if necessary) for the purpose of—

    (a) imposing a requirement by virtue of section 6(5) following an accident in a case where the constable reasonably suspects that the accident involved injury of any person, or

    (b) arresting a person under section 6D following an accident in a case where the constable reasonably suspects that the accident involved injury of any person.

Road Traffic Act 1988, s 6E(1)

Related cases

Whelehan v DPP [1995] RTR 177, QBD A constable does not need to administer a caution prior to asking a person who had obviously been drinking whether they had driven the motor car in which they were sitting because the constable would have no grounds for suspecting an offence under s 5 until after they had obtained a positive breath test.

R v Beckford [1995] RTR 251, CA A constable questioned, without a caution, a driver who had been involved in a fatal accident as to how much drink he had consumed. The man replied '3 pints' which then gave rise to a requirement that a caution be given before any further questions were put.

Practical considerations

- A constable can arrest a person under s 6D(1A) if specimens of breath have been provided under s 7 (see **10.11.2**) and the constable imposing the requirement has reasonable cause to believe that the approved device used for analysis did not produce a reliable result.
- A preliminary breath test requested because a constable suspects that a person has alcohol or a drug in their body or is under the influence of a drug may only be given at or near the place where it is requested.
- Following an accident a preliminary impairment test or preliminary drugs test may be given at or near the place where it is requested or, if the constable requesting it thinks it expedient, at a police station specified by them.
- Only a constable approved by their chief officer may give a preliminary impairment test, which must satisfy the COP.
- A person arrested under the above powers may, instead of being taken to a police station, be detained at or near the place where the preliminary test was, or would have been, administered, to impose a requirement there under s 7 on them (see **10.11.2**).
- A person may not be arrested under s 6D while at a hospital as a patient.

10.10.2 Preliminary Test Powers

- A constable may enter (by reasonable force if necessary) to impose a requirement by virtue of an accident having occurred, or to arrest a person under s 6D following an accident, where they reasonably suspect that such accident involved injury to a person.
- If a motorist supplies enough breath for the device to give a reading they cannot be said to have failed to co-operate.
- Evidential specimens can be obtained at the roadside.

 Summary   6 months

 A fine not exceeding level 3 on the standard scale. Discretionary disqualification.

Obligatory endorsement—4 penalty points.

Links to alternative subjects and offences

10.11 Drive/Attempt to Drive/in Charge Whilst over the Prescribed Limit

Section 5 of the Road Traffic Act 1988 provides the offences of driving, attempting to drive and being in charge of a motor vehicle on a road or public place while over the prescribed limit of alcohol in blood, breath or urine. Section 7 of the Act relates to the offences of failing to provide specimens for analysis and s 7A the offence of failing to give permission to submit the blood sample for a laboratory test.

10.11.1 Drive motor vehicle while over the prescribed limit

Offences

If a person—
(a) **drives** or attempts to drive a **motor vehicle** on a **road** or other **public place**, or
(b) is **in charge** of a motor vehicle on a road or other public place,
after **consuming** so much alcohol that the proportion of it in his breath, blood or urine exceeds the **prescribed limit** he is guilty of an offence.

Road Traffic Act 1988, s 5(1)

Points to prove

✓ drove/attempted to drive/in charge of motor vehicle
✓ on a road/public place
✓ proportion of alcohol in blood/breath/urine exceeded prescribed limit

Meanings

Drive (see **10.1.4**)

Motor vehicle (see **10.1.3**)

Road (see **10.6.1**)

Public place (see **10.1.2**)

In charge (see **10.10.1**)

10.11.1 Drive Motor Vehicle While Over the Prescribed Limit

Consuming

With regard to alcohol primarily means by mouth, but can include other means of ingesting it into the blood, breath or urine.

Prescribed limit

For driving offences the limits are—

- 35 microgrammes of alcohol in 100 millilitres of breath,
- 80 milligrammes of alcohol in 100 millilitres of blood,
- 107 milligrammes of alcohol in 100 millilitres of urine.

Explanatory notes

- Be aware of the powers to administer a preliminary breath test (see **10.10.2**).
- Being so hopelessly drunk that they are incapable of driving a motor vehicle is not a defence to this offence.
- If the offence is under s 5(1)(b) then it needs to be ascertained whether the person is in charge of the vehicle (see '**Explanatory notes**' 10.10.1).
- Evidence of the proportion of alcohol at the time of driving other than that provided by the specimen is admissible.
- Where it is established that the defendant was driving and has given a positive sample, it is assumed that the amount of alcohol at the time of the alleged offence is not less than the specimen provided.

Power of arrest (see 10.10.2)

Defence—being in charge

It is a defence for a person charged with an offence under subsection (1)(b) above to prove that at the time he is alleged to have committed the offence the circumstances were such that there was no likelihood of his driving the vehicle whilst the proportion of alcohol in his breath, blood or urine remained likely to exceed the prescribed limit.

Road Traffic Act 1988, s 5(2)

Defence notes (see also **10.10.1**)

- The burden of proof is on the defendant.
- In determining whether there was any likelihood of them driving, the court may ignore any injury to them or damage to the vehicle.

Related cases

CPS v Thompson [2007] EWHC 1841 (Admin), QBD The court should consider whether the defendant has shown that there is no likelihood of their driving the vehicle whilst the alcohol in their body remains likely to be above the prescribed limit.

DPP v Wilson [1991] Crim LR 441, QBD An officer is entitled to form an opinion that a driver has been drinking from information from an anonymous caller.

DPP v Johnson (1994) 158 JP 891, QBD The 'consumption' of alcohol may be by injection.

Sharpe v DPP (1994) JP 595, QBD If the officer is a trespasser at the time of the screening test it may invalidate the procedure but will not always do so.

Drake v DPP [1994] Crim LR 855, QBD A clamped vehicle may allow the 'being in charge' defence to be used, but each case must be considered on its merits.

DPP v Jones and DPP v McKeown [1997] 2 Cr App R 155, HL If the Lion Intoximeter had an inaccurate clock this alone would not invalidate the accuracy of the relevant information on the printout. Similarly, this would not be a 'reasonable excuse' for failing to provide a specimen for analysis.

DPP v H [1997] 1 WLR 1406, QBD Insanity cannot be used as a defence against a charge under this section as there is no requirement for any intent; the offence is one of strict liability.

Lafferty v DPP [1995] Crim LR 430, QBD In considering a claim by the defence that the intoximeter reading was inaccurate the court may consider evidence of the roadside breath test.

Practical considerations

- The CPS are unlikely to take the case forward unless there is evidence of a likelihood of driving whilst under the influence of drink or drugs. Similarly if in charge, ensure that the s 5(2) defence can be countered if raised.
- A person acting as a supervisor of a provisional licence holder is 'in charge' of the vehicle and can commit that offence under this section.
- 'Lacing' a person's drink without their knowledge may constitute an offence of aiding and abetting the commission of an offence under this section, if there is proof that the intent was to bring about the offence.
- Be aware of the 'Hip Flask Defence' (where the suspect claims to have had an alcoholic drink since driving but before providing a specimen). Ascertain amount drunk and inform the laboratory so the appropriate calculations can be made.
- A power of entry is available for the provision of a preliminary test in cases which involve an injury accident. Reasonable force may be used to effect entry under s 6E, or carry out a preliminary test and arrest a person under s 6D (see **10.10.2**).

Summary 6 months

 s 5(1)(a) offence

6 months' imprisonment and/or a fine not exceeding level 5 on the standard scale.
Obligatory disqualification.

Obligatory endorsement—3 to 11 penalty points (if special reasons apply).

s 5(1)(b) offence

3 months' imprisonment and/or a fine not exceeding level 4 on the standard scale.
Discretionary disqualification.

Obligatory endorsement—10 penalty points.

10.11.2 **Provision of specimens for analysis**

Section 7 of the Road Traffic Act 1988 addresses the provision of specimens for analysis.

Offence

A person who, without reasonable excuse, **fails** to provide a **specimen** when required to do so in pursuance of this section is guilty of an offence.

Road Traffic Act 1988, s 7(6)

Points to prove
✓ without reasonable excuse
✓ failed/refused to provide specimen
✓ when lawfully required to do so

Meanings

Fails (see **10.10.2**)

Specimen

Specimens taken under s 7(1) may consist of two specimens of breath for analysis by an approved device or a specimen of blood or urine for laboratory analysis.

Explanatory notes

Specimens may be required from a person suspected of having committed an offence under—

- s 3A causing death by careless driving when under influence of drink or drugs (see **10.8.2**);
- s 4 driving, or being in charge, when under influence of drink or drugs (see **10.10.1**);
- s 5 driving or being in charge of a motor vehicle with alcohol concentration above prescribed limit (see **10.11.1**).

Related cases

DPP v Smith (Alan) The Times, 1 June 1994, QBD The accused cannot insist that blood should be taken by their own GP.

Wade v DPP [1996] RTR 177, QBD A defendant on medication may have a medical reason for not providing a specimen of blood under this section.

DPP v Nesbitt and Duffy [1995] 1 Cr App R 38, QBD Where a request for blood or urine is made at a hospital the required warnings must explain the procedures in full, with reasons, and state the consequences of failing to comply.

DPP v Coyle [1996] RTR 287, CA It is not necessary to wait for the intoximeter machine to 'time out' before a suspect's refusal or failure to give a sample of breath will be complete.

DPP v Garrett [1995] RTR 302, QBD Where the blood sample procedure was flawed, but the sample was not taken and used, it did not affect the request for a urine sample.

Hague v DPP [1997] RTR 146, QBD Breath samples were taken on an intoximeter machine. The officer believed the machine to be faulty and requested blood or urine, which was refused. The machine was examined and found to be working correctly so the readings were still admissible.

Francis v DPP The Times, 2 May 1996, QBD A request can be legitimately made of a mentally unstable person if they understand what is happening.

DPP v Wythe [1996] RTR 137, QBD If a medical reason is put forward by the suspect, the final decision as to whether or not blood can or should be taken is the doctor's.

DPP v Furby [2000] RTR 181, QBD A medical condition of which they are unaware cannot later be used as an excuse for failing to provide the required sample.

Causey v DPP [2004] EWHC 3164 (Admin), QBD There is no general duty on the police to delay taking a specimen at the police station until the detainee has obtained legal advice.

10.11.2 Provision of Specimens for Analysis

DPP v Baldwin [2000] RTR 314, QBD The purpose of the requirement to provide a specimen of urine one hour after the first specimen is to give the motorist a finite time. If this period is extended, that extension does not make any findings inadmissible.

Practical considerations

- On requiring a person to provide a specimen under this section, a constable **must** warn them that failure to provide it may render them liable to prosecution.
- A requirement for a specimen of breath can only be made at a police station, a hospital, or at or near a place where a relevant breath test has been given to the person concerned or would have been so given but for their failure to co-operate.
- The constable requiring the breath sample must be in uniform, or have imposed a requirement on the defendant to co-operate with a breath test as a result of an accident.
- Where a requirement has been imposed for a person to cooperate with a relevant breath test at any place, the constable may remain at or near there to impose a requirement under this section.
- If a requirement is made for two samples of breath for analysis by an approved device at a place other than a police station, it may revert to being made at a police station if a device or reliable device is not available there or it is not practicable to use one there, or the constable making the previous requirement believes that the device has not produced a reliable result.
- Under this section, a requirement for a specimen of blood or urine can only be made at a police station or a hospital.
- A requirement for a sample of blood or urine can be made at a police station unless the constable requiring it believes that for medical reasons it cannot or should not be made, specimens of breath have not been provided elsewhere and an approved device is not available there, an approved device has been used but the constable believes the result to be unreliable, the constable believes, following a preliminary drugs test, that the defendant has a drug in their body or, if the offence is under s 3 or s 4 of the Act, the constable has been informed by a medical practitioner that the person's condition may be because of a drug.
- The above requirement may be made even if the defendant has been required to supply two specimens of breath.
- If a specimen other than breath is required, the question as to whether it is blood or urine (and, if it is blood, who will take it) will be decided by the constable making the requirement.
- If a medical practitioner or registered health care professional thinks that, for medical reasons, blood cannot or should not be taken the requirement will not be made. A urine sample may then be required instead.
- A specimen of urine must be provided within an hour of its being required and after the provision of a previous such specimen.

- In cases involving a failure to provide breath, consider retaining the mouthpiece as a possible exhibit.
- If a person is involved in a traffic accident and their medical condition prevents them from giving consent, then s 7A(1) allows taking a blood specimen from that person—providing blood could have been requested under s 7.
- If blood has been taken by a 'police medical practitioner' under s 7A(1), then under s 7A(5) a constable must require the person to give permission for a laboratory test of the blood specimen taken, and warn that failure to give this permission may render them liable to prosecution under s 7A(6).
- **Section 7A(6) offence**—A person who, without reasonable excuse, fails to give his permission for a laboratory test of a specimen of blood taken from him under this section is guilty of a summary offence.

 Summary　　　　　 6 months

　Driving or attempting to drive

6 months' imprisonment and/or a fine not exceeding level 5 on the standard scale.

Obligatory disqualification for 12 months. Obligatory endorsement—3 to 11 penalty points (if special conditions apply).

In all other cases

3 months' imprisonment and/or a fine not exceeding level 4 on the standard scale.
Discretionary disqualification.

Obligatory endorsement—10 penalty points.

Links to alternative subjects and offences

10.11.2 Provision of Specimens for Analysis

10.12 **Pedal Cycle Offences**

Sections 28, 29, and 30 of the Road Traffic Act 1988 provide similar offences for cyclists to those contained in ss 1, 2, and 3 for motorists. Additionally, there is the offence of driving/cycling on a footpath under s 72 of the Highways Act 1835.

10.12.1 **Dangerous cycling**

Section 28 creates an offence of dangerous cycling on a road.

Offence

A person who rides a **cycle** on a **road dangerously** is guilty of an offence.

Road Traffic Act 1988, s 28(1)

Points to prove
- ✓ rode a cycle
- ✓ on a road
- ✓ dangerously

Meanings

Cycle
Means a bicycle, a tricycle, or a cycle having four or more wheels, not being in any case a motor vehicle.

Road (see **10.6.1**)

Dangerously
A person is to be regarded as riding dangerously if and only if—
- the way that they ride falls far below what would be expected of a competent and careful cyclist; **and**
- it would be obvious to a competent and careful cyclist that riding in that way would be dangerous.

Explanatory notes
- The term 'danger' refers to danger either of injury to any person or of serious damage to property.
- To determine what would be obvious to a competent and careful cyclist in a particular case consideration must be given

603

to circumstances of which they could be expected to be aware and any shown to have been within their knowledge.
• A person may be convicted of the alternative offence of careless, and inconsiderate, cycling (see **10.12.2**).

Practical considerations

• NIP to be issued (see **10.5**).
• This offence must be on a road—it does not extend to a public place.

 Summary   6 months

 A fine not exceeding level 4 on the standard scale.

10.12.2 **Careless, and inconsiderate, cycling**

Section 29 creates an offence of cycling on a road without due care and attention or without reasonable consideration for other road users.

Offences

If a person rides a **cycle** on a **road** without **due care and attention**, or without **reasonable consideration** for other persons using the road, he is guilty of an offence.

Road Traffic Act 1988, s 29

Points to prove
✓ rode a cycle
✓ on a road
✓ without due care and attention/reasonable consideration for other road users

Meanings

Cycle (see **10.12.1**)

Road (see **10.6.1**)

Without due care and attention
Means that their cycling falls below the level of care, skill, and attention that would have been exercised by a competent and careful cyclist.

Without reasonable consideration
This only requires other persons to be inconvenienced by the defendant's driving.

Explanatory notes

- Cycling on a road without due care and attention is a question of fact for the court to decide on the evidence as to whether or not the cycling is careless. The standard of care and attention is an objective one.
- Cycling on a road without reasonable consideration for other road users is a subjective test that has to be decided by the court on the evidence before it. The other persons using the road can include drivers or passengers in vehicles, pedestrians or other cyclists. It can include giving a misleading signal, cutting across a car or causing a pedestrian to stop.

Practical considerations

- NIP to be issued (see **10.5**).
- This offence must be on a road—it does not extend to a public place.

 Summary   6 months

 A fine not exceeding level 3 on the standard scale.

10.12.3 Cycling when under the influence of drink or drugs

Section 30 creates an offence of cycling on a road or public place while unfit through drink or drugs.

Offences

A person who, when riding a cycle on a **road** or other **public place**, is unfit to ride through drink or drugs (that is to say, is under the influence of drink or a drug to such an extent as to be incapable of having proper control of the cycle) is guilty of an offence.

Road Traffic Act 1988, s 30(1)

Points to prove

✓ rode a cycle
✓ on a road/other public place
✓ while unfit to ride through drink/drugs

Meanings

Road (see 10.6.1)

Public place (see 10.1.2)

Practical considerations

- As there is no power to require a specimen of breath, blood, or urine, other methods of calculating the extent to which the defendant is under the influence of drink or drugs need to be used.
- This offence does not extend to being in charge of a cycle as it would with other forms of transport.
- A bicycle or tricycle is a carriage under the Licensing Act 1872. Therefore consider the offence of being drunk in charge of a carriage on any highway or other public place under s 12 of that Act (see 7.2.2).

 Summary   6 months

A fine not exceeding level 3 on the standard scale.

10.12.4 **Riding/driving on the footpath**

Section 72 of the Highways Act 1835 creates an offence of wilfully riding or driving on the footpath.

Offences

If any person shall **wilfully** ride upon any **footpath** or causeway by the side of any road, made or set apart for the use or accommodation of foot passengers; or shall wilfully lead or drive any horse, ass, sheep, mule, swine, cattle or **carriage of any description**, or any truck or sledge, upon any such footpath or causeway or tether any horse, ass, mule, swine or cattle on any highway so as to suffer or permit the tethered animal to be thereon, he shall be guilty of an offence.

Highways Act 1835, s 72

Points to prove
- ✓ wilfully rode/drove/led/tethered
- ✓ carriage of any description, truck, sledge or animal (as described)
- ✓ upon a footpath/causeway
- ✓ by the side of a road
- ✓ made/set apart
- ✓ for the use/accommodation of foot passengers

Meanings

Wilfully

'Wilful' under this section means 'purposely'.

Footpath

A footpath is part of a highway, if it is beside a road.

Carriage of any description

This includes bicycles, tricycles, motor vehicles and trailers.

Explanatory notes

- Section 72 applies not only to the riding of bicycles or tricycles on the footpath/causeway, but also to the riding/driving of motor vehicles/trailers/truck/sledge and leading/tethering any animals as described.
- This offence requires proof of wilfully riding, driving a carriage or leading/tethering animals as specified.
- Proceedings may be instituted by anyone.
- Consider issuing a TFPN for driving or cycling on the footway (see **10.4**).

 Summary 6 months

 A fine not exceeding level 2 on the standard scale. Discretionary disqualification. Not endorsable.

Links to alternative subjects and offences

10.13 **Driving While Disqualified**

Section 103 of the Road Traffic Act 1988 creates the offences of obtaining a driving licence while disqualified from driving and driving a motor vehicle on a road while so disqualified.

Offences

A person is guilty of an offence if, while **disqualified** for holding or obtaining a **licence**, he—
(a) obtains a licence, or
(b) drives a motor vehicle on a road.

Road Traffic Act 1988, s 103(1)

Points to prove

✓ while disqualified for holding/obtaining a licence
✓ obtained a licence/drove a motor vehicle on a road

Meanings

Disqualified

Means disqualified for holding or obtaining a licence and, where the disqualification relates only to vehicles of a particular class, a licence to drive vehicles of that particular class.

Licence (see 10.14.1)

Drives (see 10.1.4)

Motor vehicle

This is defined by s 185 (see 10.1.3).

Road (see 10.6.1)

Explanatory notes

- An underage driver (unless disqualified by the court) should be charged with the offence of 'driving otherwise than in accordance with a licence' (see 10.14.1).
- Subsection (1)(b) does not apply to a person disqualified for obtaining a licence authorizing them to drive a motor vehicle of a specific class while they hold another licence to drive that class of vehicle.
- Such a person is disqualified for obtaining such a licence, even if the licence held is suspended (s 102).
- Disqualification given in England and Wales applies to all of Great Britain, even if they hold a foreign or international driving licence or permit or service driving licence.

- A driver disqualified in a foreign country would not be guilty of this offence, but may be guilty of driving without a licence.
- Disqualification by a court is usually for a specified period as punishment for a road traffic offence.
- If penalty points imposed by the court, together with any to be taken into account on that occasion, total 12 or more (the 'totting up' system) the court must, other than in exceptional circumstances, disqualify the defendant for at least a **minimum period** (Road Traffic Offenders Act 1988, s 35).
- **Minimum period** is 6 months if no previous disqualification, one year if one such period is to be taken into account and 2 years if two or more such periods are taken into account.
- All penalty points imposed will be endorsed on the counterpart of the defendant's licence.
- The court may order a driver to be disqualified until they pass a driving test. Such driver may not drive during the disqualification period; after this period they can only drive on a provisional licence. Thereafter, if they fail to comply with the provisional licence conditions they may be guilty of driving whilst disqualified. Disqualification will only come to an end after they have passed the driving test.

Related cases (see also **10.1.4** cases)

Pattison v DPP [2005] EWHC (Admin) 2938, QBD The prosecution must prove beyond reasonable doubt that the defendant was the disqualified driver. Identification of the defendant as the person convicted in court may be established by admission, fingerprints, or by a person in court at the time of the conviction.

DPP v Barker [2004] EWHC 2502 (Admin), QBD If a person was disqualified until they had passed a driving test, the burden of proof was on the driver to show that they had a provisional licence and were driving in accordance with the licence conditions.

Practical considerations

- This offence is committed only if the defendant drives a motor vehicle of a class that is subject of the disqualification, although a disqualification by order of the court will not normally be limited to a particular class of vehicle.
- A licence obtained by a disqualified person is not valid.
- Proving beyond reasonable doubt that the person named on the certified court extract is the accused is an essential element of the prosecution case, although there is no prescribed way in which identity must be proved.
- Proof that the defendant knew of the disqualification is not necessary.

10.13 Driving While Disqualified

- A person is disqualified for holding or obtaining a licence to drive a certain class of motor vehicle if they are under the age stipulated for that class (s 101), but the offence would be contrary to s 87(1) (see **10.14.1**).
- Minimum ages for driving specified classes of motor vehicles are shown in **10.14.2**.

 Summary

Normally 6 months but no more than 3 years after the offence.

 s 103(1)(a) offence

A fine not exceeding level 3 on the standard scale.

s 103(1)(b) offence

6 months' imprisonment and/or a fine not exceeding level 5 on the standard scale.

Discretionary disqualification.

Obligatory endorsement—6 penalty points.

Links to alternative subjects and offences

10.14 Driving not in Accordance with a Driving Licence

Section 87 of the Road Traffic Act 1988 requires all people driving a motor vehicle on a road to hold a driving licence for that class of vehicle and to comply with any conditions attached to it.

10.14.1 Drive motor vehicle of a class not authorized

Offences

(1) It is an offence for a person to **drive** on a **road** a **motor vehicle** of any class otherwise than in accordance with a licence authorising him to drive a motor vehicle of that **class**.

(2) It is an offence for a person to **cause** or **permit** another person to drive on a road a motor vehicle of any class otherwise than in accordance with a **licence** authorising that other person to drive a motor vehicle of that class.

Road Traffic Act 1988, s 87

Points to prove

s 87(1) offence

✓ drove motor vehicle
✓ on a road
✓ otherwise than in accordance with licence
✓ authorizing driving of that class of vehicle

s 87(2) offence

✓ caused/permitted
✓ another person to commit s 87(1) offence

Meanings

Drive (see **10.1.4**)

Road (see **10.6.1**)

Motor vehicle (see **10.13**)

Class (see **10.14.2** and Appendix 2)

Cause

Means involving some degree of control or dominance by or some express mandate from the causer. It also requires some positive action and knowledge by the defendant (*Price v Cromack* [1975] 1 WLR 988).

10.14.1 Drive Motor Vehicle of a Class not Authorized

Permit

Is less direct or explicit than causing and involves leave or licence to do something. Permission can be express or inferred. A person cannot permit a vehicle to be used unless they are in a position to forbid and no one can permit what he cannot control.

Licence

Means a licence to drive a motor vehicle under pt 3 of the Road Traffic Act 1988 or a **community licence**.

Community licence

Means a document issued by an EEA state (other than the UK) by authority of the EEA State authorizing the holder to drive a motor vehicle.

Full licence

Means a licence other than a **provisional licence**.

Provisional licence

Means a licence issued to enable an applicant to drive motor vehicles with a view to passing a test of competence to drive.

Explanatory notes

- The holder of a convention driving permit, a domestic driving licence/permit issued by a country outside the UK, or a British Forces driving permit who is resident outside the UK may drive any class of vehicle specified in the permit or licence for 12 months.
- A person who is an EU citizen and holds a driving licence or permit issued in another EU country may drive on that licence or permit in this country in accordance with that licence or permit. They would not need to exchange the licence or permit for a UK licence no matter how long they stayed here.
- Under s 88 a person who has held a driver's licence, a community licence, a Northern Ireland licence, a British external licence, a British Forces licence, or an exchangeable licence may, in certain circumstances, still drive a relevant vehicle even if the licence and its counterpart have been surrendered or revoked. This includes where a qualifying application has been received at DVLA or their licence to drive that class of vehicle and its counterpart has been revoked or surrendered for renewal, it was granted in or contains an error, or for amendment of a requirement or the holder's name and address.

Practical considerations

- Where a person is charged with driving without a licence, the burden of proving that they have a licence is with that person (*John v Humphreys* [1955] 1 All ER 793, QBD).
- The police have powers to seize and remove a motor vehicle if the driver has no driving licence **or** there is no insurance in force for the vehicle (see **10.16.5**).

- It is an offence for a person not to produce their driving licence (see **10.16.3**).
- A TFPN can be issued for the s 87(1) offence (see **10.4**).
- This offence includes circumstances where the driver is driving under age.
- The classes of vehicles which a licence holder is authorized by it to drive are stated on the licence itself.
- A licence is valid only when it is used in accordance with its conditions of use.

 Summary   6 months

  s 87(1) offence

A fine not exceeding level 3 on the standard scale. Discretionary disqualification.
Obligatory endorsement—3 to 8 penalty points.

s 87(2) offence

A fine not exceeding level 3 on the standard scale.
Obligatory endorsement—minimum 3 penalty points.

10.14.2 Minimum ages for holding/ obtaining driving licences

Section 101 of the Road Traffic Act 1988 provides that persons are prohibited from holding or obtaining a licence to drive a certain class of vehicle if they are under a specified age for that class. The class of motor vehicle and minimum ages are as follows—

- Invalid carriage—16 years.
- Moped—16 years.
- Motor bicycle—17 years.
  - Where the motor bicycle is a large motor bicycle that age becomes 21 years (see **Appendix 2**), unless it is used for military purposes.
- Agricultural or forestry tractor—17 years.
  - However, that age will be 16 years, if it is a wheeled tractor (not tracked) and is not more than 2.45 metres wide or has a trailer which is either 2-wheeled or close-coupled 4-wheeled (maximum 840mm gap) and both have a maximum width of 2.45 metres **and** the person has passed, is going to, taking or returning from a test for a category F vehicle.
- Small vehicles (cars)—17 years.
  - This age may become 16 years if driven by a person in receipt of the higher rate component of the disability living allowance without a trailer.

- Medium-sized goods vehicles—18 years, except—
  - where vehicle is towing a trailer and the maximum authorized mass of the combination exceeds 7.5 tonnes that age will be 21 years; or
  - if the vehicle is being used for military purposes the minimum age will be 17 years.
- Other motor vehicles—21 years.
  This age will be 18 years for—
  - a vehicle which carries over 8 passengers if the driver holds a full licence for that category **and** is carrying passengers on a regular 50 kilometre route **or** driving a vehicle in category D1;
  - a passenger-carrying vehicle if the driver has a provisional licence for that category and there are no passengers;
  - a vehicle which is a category D1 vehicle AND is an ambulance;
  - a vehicle in category $C1 + E$ with a maximum mass not exceeding 7.5 tonnes;
  - a person who is part of a training scheme for large goods vehicle drivers either with their employer or an authorized school.
  This age will be 17 years if—
  - the vehicle is being used for military purposes or the vehicle is a road roller propelled otherwise than by steam, has no wheel fitted with pneumatic, soft, or elastic tyres, does not exceed 11.69 tonnes unladen and only carries tools and equipment for its own use.

Explanatory notes

- If a person under the minimum age for driving a particular class of motor vehicle drives that vehicle without such a licence he commits the offence of driving without a licence for that class under s 87(1) (see **10.14.1**).
- **Appendix 2** contains two tables and provides further information on—
  - comparing old groups/class with new categories;
  - vehicle categories and minimum driving age.

Links to alternative subjects and offences

10.15 Drive with Defective Eyesight

Section 96 of the Road Traffic Act 1988 creates an offence of driving with defective eyesight.

Offences

Drive with uncorrected defective eyesight

(1) If a person **drives** a **motor vehicle** on a **road** while his eyesight is such (whether through a defect which cannot be or one which is not for the time being sufficiently corrected) that he cannot comply with any requirement as to eyesight prescribed under this Part of this Act for the purposes of tests of competence to drive, he is guilty of an offence.

Refuse to submit to eyesight test

(2) A constable having reason to suspect that a person driving a motor vehicle may be guilty of an offence under subsection (1) above may require him to submit to a test for the purpose of ascertaining whether, using no other means of correction than he used at the time of driving, he can comply with the requirement concerned.

(3) If that person refuses to submit to the test he is guilty of an offence.

Road Traffic Act 1988, s 96

Points to prove

s 96(1) offence

✓ drove a motor vehicle
✓ on a road
✓ while unable to meet eyesight requirements

s 96(3) offence

✓ being the driver of a motor vehicle
✓ on a road
✓ and being required to take eyesight test
✓ by a constable under s 96(2)
✓ refused to take such test

Meanings

Drives (see 10.1.4)

Motor vehicle (see 10.1.3)

Road (see 10.6.1)

10.15 Drive with Defective Eyesight

Explanatory notes

- This section creates two offences—
  - driving with defective eyesight;
  - refusing to submit to an eyesight test.
- The prescribed 'requirement as to eyesight' can be found in the Motor Vehicles (Driving Licences) Regulations 1999.
- The prescribed requirement is for a person to be able to read, in good light (with visual aids if used) a number plate on a vehicle containing characters of the **prescribed size**.
- **Prescribed size** means characters which are 79.4 mm high and either 57 or 50 mm wide.
- The distance from which the number plate should be read is, for category K vehicles (eg mowing machines and pedestrian controlled vehicles), 12.3 metres or 12 metres respectively and, in any other case, 20.5 or 20 metres.
- Spectacles or contact lenses may be used for the test if they were wearing them while driving.
- For the purposes of this offence it does not matter whether the defect is one that can be corrected or not. The important matter is the state of their eyesight at the time they were driving.
- Knowledge of the defect by the defendant is not necessary, although this may be used in mitigation if the defendant has suffered a gradual and unnoticed deterioration in their eyesight.
- However, under s 92(1) any person holding or applying for a licence has a duty to inform the DVLA of any prescribed disability likely to cause the driving of a vehicle by them in accordance with the licence to be a source of danger to the public. This includes a 'prospective' disability such as a condition that does not at the time amount to a relevant disability, but which is likely to deteriorate to that level in the course of time.

Practical considerations

- The degree by which the defendant's eyesight fails to meet the requirement is particularly relevant as this will reflect the degree of risk taken or danger created by them.
- The more severe the defect the more difficult it will be for the defendant to mitigate the offence.
- An inability to read the characters in the test will amount to a prescribed disability and the person will have to inform the DVLA under s 92(1).

 Summary   6 months

 A fine not exceeding level 3 on the standard scale.
Discretionary disqualification.

Obligatory endorsement—3 penalty points.

Links to alternative subjects and offences

10.16 Vehicle Document Offences and Seizure of Vehicles

The requirement for a vehicle to be covered by third party insurance before it can be used on a road is provided by the Road Traffic Act 1988.

10.16.1 No insurance

Section 143 requires the user of a motor vehicle to be insured or secured against third party risks.

Offences

(1) Subject to the provisions of this Part of this Act—

(a) a person must not **use** a **motor vehicle** on a **road** or other **public place** unless there is in force in relation to the use of the vehicle by that person such a **policy of insurance** or such a **security** in respect of third party risks as complies with the requirements of this Part of this Act, and

(b) a person must not **cause** or **permit** any other person to use a motor vehicle on a road or other public place unless there is in force in relation to the use of the vehicle by that other person such a policy of insurance or such a security in respect of third party risks as complies with the requirements of this Part of this Act.

(2) If a person acts in contravention of subsection (1) above he is guilty of an offence.

Road Traffic Act 1988, s 143

Points to prove
✓ used/caused/permitted another to use
✓ motor vehicle
✓ on a road/public place
✓ without insurance/security for third party risks

Meanings

Use

Means the driver of a vehicle, the driver's employer while it is being used for their business, the vehicle owner if they are in it while somebody else is driving it, or the steersman of a broken down vehicle which is being towed.

Motor vehicle (see **10.1.3**)

Road (see **10.6.1**)

Public place (see **10.1.2**)

Policy of insurance

This includes a cover note.

Security

This section does not apply to a vehicle owned by a person who has deposited and keeps deposited with the Accountant General of the Supreme Court (Senior Courts) the sum of £500,000, at a time when the vehicle is being driven under the owner's control.

Cause (see **10.14.1**)

Permit (see **10.14.1**)

Explanatory notes

- This section does not apply to invalid carriages.
- Section 144 states that s 143 does not apply to—
  - a vehicle owned by: a county or county district council, Broads Authority, City of London Common/Borough Council, National Park Authority, Inner London Education Authority, London Fire and Emergency Planning Authority, joint (local government) waste authorities, or a joint authority (except a police authority) or a joint board or committee which includes member representatives of such council—at a time when the vehicle is being driven under the owner's control;
  - a police authority owned vehicle when it is being driven under the owner's control or a vehicle being driven for police purposes by or under the direction of a constable or a police authority employee;
  - a vehicle being driven to or from a place for the purposes of salvage under the Merchant Shipping Act 1995;
  - to the use of a vehicle as directed under the Army and Air Force Acts of 1955;
  - a vehicle owned by a health service body, Primary Care Trust, or Local Health Board—at a time when the vehicle is being driven under the owner's control;
  - an ambulance owned by an NHS Trust or Foundation Trust at a time when the vehicle is being driven under the owner's control;
  - a vehicle made available to a person, body or local authority under ss 12 or 80 of the National Heath Service Act 2006 (ss 10 or 38 of the National Health Service (Wales) Act 2006) while being used in accordance with the terms under which it was made available;
  - a vehicle owned by the Commission for Social Care Inspection, at a time when the vehicle is being driven under the owner's control.
- Section 144(2)(b), on its plain and ordinary meaning, exempts a police officer on duty using his own vehicle for police purposes, from the requirement for third party insurance (*Jones v Chief Constable of Bedfordshire* [1987] RTR 332).

Defences

A person charged with using a motor vehicle in contravention of this section shall not be convicted if he proves—
- (a) that the vehicle did not belong to him and was not in his possession under a contract of hiring or of loan,
- (b) that he was using the vehicle in the course of his employment, and
- (c) that he neither knew nor had reason to believe that there was not in force in relation to the vehicle such a policy of insurance or security as is mentioned in subsection (1) above.

Road Traffic Act 1988, s 143(3)

Related cases

Plumbien v Vines [1996] Crim LR 124, QBD A vehicle left on a road for several months such that it could not be moved, is still at the disposal of the owner and so requires insurance.

Dodson v Peter H Dodson Insurance Services [2001] 1 WLR 1012, CA In the absence of a condition in the policy of insurance making it clear that the policyholder would only be covered while they were the owner of the relevant vehicle, the policy is valid until expiry.

DPP v Hay [2005] EWHC 1395 (Admin), QBD It is for the defendant to show that there was in force a policy of insurance, once it has been proved that they used the motor vehicle on a road or public place.

Practical considerations

- Read the conditions on the insurance very carefully, as it may, for example cover a person who is not a current driving licence holder. Similarly, a valid insurance certificate may not cover that person for the vehicle being used or for that particular purpose.
- A TFPN for the s 143(1)(a) 'using' offence can be issued (see **10.4**).
- The policy must be issued by an authorized insurer (eg a member of the Motor Insurers Bureau).
- It is an offence to fail to produce insurance (see **10.16.4**).
- The motor vehicle can be seized if no insurance is in force for the vehicle (see **10.16.5**).

 Summary

Normally 6 months, but depending on knowledge of the offence can be up to 3 years.

 A fine not exceeding level 5 on the standard scale.

Discretionary disqualification.

Obligatory endorsement—6 to 8 penalty points.

10.16.2 **No test certificate**

Section 47 creates an offence relating to motor vehicles over 3 years old being on a road without a valid test certificate in force, and s 53 creates a similar offence for goods vehicles over 12 months old.

Offences
Motor vehicle
A person who **uses** on a **road** at any time, or **causes** or **permits** to be so used, a **motor vehicle** to which **this section applies**, and as respects which no test certificate has been issued within the **appropriate period** before that time, is guilty of an offence.

Road Traffic Act 1988, s 47(1)

Goods vehicle
If any person at any time on or after the relevant date—
(a) uses on a road a goods vehicle of a class required by regulations under s 49 to have been submitted for a goods vehicle test, or
(b) causes or permits to be used on a road a goods vehicle of such a class, and at the time there is no goods vehicle test certificate in force for the vehicle, he is guilty of an offence.

Road Traffic Act 1988, s 53(2)

Points to prove
s 47(1) offence
- ✓ used/caused to use/permitted to use
- ✓ a motor vehicle to which s 47 applies
- ✓ on a road
- ✓ without a valid test certificate

s 53(2) offence
- ✓ used/caused to use/permitted to use
- ✓ a goods vehicle as specified by regs under s 49
- ✓ on a road
- ✓ without a valid goods vehicle test certificate

Meanings

Uses (see **10.16.1**)

Road (see **10.1.1**)

Causes (see **10.14.1**)

Permits (see **10.14.1**)

Motor vehicles to which s 47 applies

Motor vehicles (see **10.1.3**) (not being goods vehicles) which have been registered under the Vehicles Excise and Registration Act 1994 for not less than three years or were manufactured at least three years ago and have been used on roads (whether in Great Britain or elsewhere) before being so registered.

Appropriate period

Means a period of 12 months or shorter as may be prescribed.

Related cases

Plumbien v Vines [1996] Crim LR 124, QBD A vehicle left on a road for several months in such condition that it could not be moved, is still at the disposal of the owner and still requires a test certificate for its use.

Explanatory notes

Motor vehicles

- Types of motor vehicles to which s 47 applies are—
  - ◆ passenger vehicles with not more 8 seats (excluding the driver's seat);
  - ◆ rigid goods motor cars—unladen weight does not exceed 1525 kg;
  - ◆ dual-purpose vehicles, motor cycles (including 3 wheelers, mopeds), and motor caravans.

  These vehicles (unless exempt) must obtain a test certificate annually, after the first test certificate.
- Similarly a motor vehicle used to carry passengers and having more than 8 seats excluding the driver's seat, a taxi licensed to ply for hire or an **ambulance**, is required to be submitted for an annual test from the first anniversary of its registration or manufacture.
- 'Ambulance' means a motor vehicle that is constructed or adapted, and primarily used, for the carriage of persons to a place where they will receive, or from a place where they have received, medical or dental treatment, and which, by reason of design, marking, or equipment is readily identifiable as a vehicle so constructed or adapted.

Goods vehicles

- Heavy motor cars, motor cars constructed or adapted to form part of an articulated vehicle, other heavy motor cars that exceed 3500 kg design weight, semi-trailers, converter dollies manufactured on or after 1.1.1979 and trailers exceeding 1020 kg unladen weight **all require a goods vehicle test certificate**.
- All vehicles requiring a goods vehicle test certificate must be submitted for their first test, in the case of a motor vehicle, before the last day of the calendar month in which falls the first anniversary of its date of registration, and in relation to trailers, before the last day of the calendar month in which falls the first anniversary of the date on which it was first sold or supplied by retail.

Practical considerations

- **Vehicles exempted** from a s 47 test certificate are vehicles—
  - ◆ being driven to a pre-arranged test;

- being tested by an authorized examiner;
- where a test certificate is refused, vehicles—
  - being driven from the test,
  - being delivered by pre-arranged delivery to or from a place where work is to be or has been done to remedy the defects,
  - delivering or towing to a place to be scrapped;
- being removed under a statutory power;
- being tested by a motor trader under a trade licence;
- that are imported and which are being driven from entry port to the owner's residence;
- detained/seized by police and HMRC;
- exempt from testing by order under s 44 (see below).
- Vehicles exempted by s 44 are described in reg 6(1) of the Motor Vehicles (Tests) Regulations 1981, being vehicles that are: temporarily in Great Britain (not exceeding 12 months); proceeding to a port for export; used on a public road only to travel between land in occupation of the vehicle keeper n/e aggregate of six miles per calendar week; provided for police purposes by a police authority and maintained in approved workshops; provided for SOCA; heavy locomotive; light locomotive; motor tractor; track laying vehicle; goods vehicle exceeding 3500 kg design gross weight (subject to goods vehicle testing); articulated vehicle not being an articulated bus; works truck; pedestrian controlled vehicle; invalid carriage n/e 306 kg u/w (510kg u/w if supplied by NHS), visiting forces' or imported Armed forces' vehicles; current Northern Ireland test certificate; electrically propelled goods vehicle n/e 3500 kg design gross weight; licensed hackney carriage or private hire car which undergo testing by the local authority; agricultural motor vehicle; street cleansing, refuse and gully cleaning vehicle constructed and not merely adapted being either—3 wheeled vehicle, or maximum design speed of 20mph or inside track width less than 810 mm; tramcar and trolley vehicles.
- Vehicles exempt from goods vehicle testing are given in Sch 2 of the Goods Vehicle (Plating and Testing) Regulations 1988. Nearly 40 categories of vehicles are listed and in some instances they are similar to those given in s 44 exemptions list—above.
- It is an offence to fail to produce (if required) the test certificate, plating certificate, or goods vehicle test certificate (see **10.16.4**).
- The date of manufacture is taken to be the last day of the year in which its final assembly is completed.
- Consider issuing a TFPN for a motor vehicle s 47 offence (see **10.4**).
- A TFPN **cannot** be issued for a goods vehicle s 53 offence.
- Authorized examiners may carry out roadside tests on vehicles under s 67 (see **10.2.3**).
- Under s 68(4) a vehicle examiner or police officer in uniform, may direct a goods vehicle or PSV to proceed to a suitable place for inspection, provided it is within 5 miles from where the requirement has been made. It is a summary offence to obstruct the examiner under s 68(3) or refuse/fail to comply with request under s 68(5) (both level 3 fine).

Summary 6 months

 s 47(1) offence

A fine not exceeding level 3 on the standard scale. Level 4 if vehicle adapted to carry more than 8 passengers.

s 53(2) offence

A fine not exceeding level 4 on the standard scale.

10.16.3 **Fail to produce driving licence**

Section 164 empowers a constable or vehicle examiner to require production of a driving licence and its counterpart and a certificate of completion of a motorcycle course.

Offences

If a person **required** under the preceding provisions of this section **to produce** a licence and its counterpart or **state his date of birth** or to produce his certificate of completion of a training course for motorcyclists fails to do so he is, subject to subsections (7) to (8A) *[defences]*, guilty of an offence.

Road Traffic Act 1988, s 164(6)

Points to prove

✓ when required by a constable/vehicle examiner
✓ failed to state date of birth or produce driving licence, counterpart, motorcycle training certificate

Meanings

Required to produce—s 164(1)

Any of the following persons—

(a) driving a motor vehicle on a road,

(b) whom a police constable or vehicle examiner has reasonable cause to believe to have been the driver of a motor vehicle at a time when an accident occurred owing to its presence on a road,

(c) whom a constable or vehicle examiner has reasonable cause to believe to have committed an offence in relation to the use of a motor vehicle on a road, or

(d) a person—

(i) who supervises the holder of a **provisional licence** while the holder is driving a motor vehicle on a road, or

(ii) whom a constable or vehicle examiner has reasonable cause to believe was supervising the holder of a provisional licence while driving, at a time when an accident occurred owing to the presence of the vehicle on a road or at a time when an offence is suspected of having been committed by the holder of the provisional licence in relation to the use of the vehicle on a road,

must, on being so required by a constable or vehicle examiner, produce his licence and its counterpart for examination, so as to enable the constable or vehicle examiner to ascertain the name and address of the holder of the licence, the date of issue, and the authority by which they were issued.

State date of birth—s 164(2)

A person required by a constable under s 164(1) to produce their licence must in **prescribed circumstances**, on being required by the constable, state his date of birth.

Prescribed circumstances

The circumstances in which a constable may require a person's date of birth are given in reg 83(1) of the Motor Vehicles (Driving Licences) Regulations 1999. Where the person—

- fails to produce their licence and counterpart for immediate examination;
- produces a licence which the constable suspects was not granted to that person, was granted to them in error or contains an alteration in particulars entered on the licence made with intent to deceive or where the driver number has been altered, removed, or defaced; or
- is a supervisor under s 164(1)(d) and the constable suspects they are under 21 years of age.

Provisional licence (see **10.14**)

Explanatory notes

Other preceding provisions for fail to produce offences under s 164(6) are—

- 164(3): Where a licence has been revoked by the Secretary of State, a constable may require its production, together with its counterpart, and, if they are produced, may seize them and deliver them to the Secretary of State.
- 164(4): If a constable reasonably believes that a licence holder, or any other person, has knowingly made a false statement to obtain a licence he may require the holder to produce it and its counterpart to them.
- 164(4A): Where a provisional licence is produced by a motor-cyclist and a constable reasonably believes that the holder was not riding it as part of an approved training course, the constable may require production of his certificate of completion of a training course for motorcyclists.
- 164(5): If a person has been required to produce his licence and its counterpart to a court and fails to do so, a constable may require him

10.16.3 Fail to Produce Driving Licence

to produce them and, when they are produced, may seize them and deliver to the court.

Defences

(7) Subsection (6) *[offences]* above does not apply where a person required on any occasion under the proceeding provisions of this section to produce a licence and its counterpart—

   (a) produces on that occasion a current receipt for the licence and its counterpart issued under section 56 of the Road Traffic Offenders Act 1988 and, if required to do so, produces the licence and its counterpart in person immediately on their return at a police station that was specified on that occasion, or

   (b) within 7 days after that occasion produces such a receipt in person at a police station that was specified by him on that occasion and, if required to do so, produces the licence and its counterpart in person immediately on their return at a police station.

(8) In proceedings against any person for the offence of failing to produce a licence and its counterpart it shall be a defence for him to show that—

   (a) within 7 days after the production of his licence and its counterpart was required he produced them in person at a police station that was specified by him at the time their production was required, or

   (b) he produced them in person there as soon as was reasonably practicable, or

   (c) it was not reasonably practicable for him to produce them there before the day on which the proceedings were commenced.

(8A) Subsection (8) above shall apply in relation to a certificate of completion of a training course for motorcyclists as it applies in relation to a licence.

Road Traffic Act 1988, s 164

Practical considerations

- A Photocard Driving Licence consists of a credit card style licence showing an image of the holder and their signature; issued with this licence is a paper Counterpart Driving Licence which gives details of the categories of vehicles a person can drive, their entitlement history and any endorsements together with name and address and image of signature. **Both** parts **must** be produced. It will be an offence under s 164(6) if only one part is produced.
- In certain circumstances reference to a constable includes reference to a TW.

 Summary 6 months

 A fine not exceeding level 3 on the standard scale.

10.16.4 Fail to provide details or produce insurance, test certificate, plating certificate, or goods vehicle test certificate

Section 165 empowers a constable or vehicle examiner to require production of insurance and vehicle test documents.

Requirements

Any of the following persons—

(a) driving a motor vehicle (other than an invalid carriage) on a road, or

(b) whom a constable or vehicle examiner has reasonable cause to believe to have been the driver of a motor vehicle (other than an invalid carriage) at a time when an accident occurred owing to its presence on a road or other public place, or

(c) whom a constable or vehicle examiner has reasonable cause to believe to have committed an offence in relation to the use on a road of a motor vehicle (other than an invalid carriage),

must, on being so required by a constable or vehicle examiner, give his name and address and the name and address of the **owner** of the vehicle and produce the following **documents** for examination.

Road Traffic Act 1988, s 165(1)

Offence

Subject to subsection (4) *[defence]*, a person who fails to comply with a requirement under subsection (1) is guilty of an offence.

Road Traffic Act 1988, s 165(3)

Points to prove

✓ being a person falling under s 165(1)

✓ failed when required by a constable/vehicle examiner

✓ to give name and address or name and address of vehicle owner AND/OR

✓ produce for inspection a test certificate **or** goods vehicle test certificate **or** certificate of insurance **or** certificate of security

Meanings

Owner

In relation to a vehicle which is the subject of a hiring agreement this includes each party to the agreement.

627

10.16.4 Fail to Provide Details or Produce Insurance

Documents—s 165(2)

The documents specified in subsection (1) are—

- a relevant certificate of insurance or certificate of security;
- a test certificate required by s 47; and
- a plating certificate or goods vehicle test certificate required by s 53.

Explanatory notes

- Under s 165(5) a supervisor of a provisional licence holder must, on being required by a constable/vehicle examiner, give their name and address and the name and address of the owner of the vehicle.
- This supervisor's requirement applies when the provisional driver was driving a motor vehicle (except invalid carriage) on a road; or whom a constable/vehicle examiner believes was supervising when an accident occurred owing to presence of that vehicle on a road or suspecting that the provisional licence holder committed an offence by using the vehicle on a road.
- If the supervisor fails to comply with the name and address requirements, then under s 165(6) they will commit an offence.

Defences

A person shall not be convicted of an offence under subsection (3) by reason only of failure to produce any certificate or other evidence in proceedings against him for the offence if he shows that—

(a) within 7 days after the date on which the production of the certificate or other evidence was required it was produced at a police station that was specified by him at the time when its production was required, or

(b) it was produced there as soon as was reasonably practicable, or

(c) it was not reasonably practicable for it to be produced there before the day on which the proceedings were commenced,

and for the purposes of this subsection the laying of the information shall be treated as the commencement of the proceedings.

Road Traffic Act 1988, s 165(4)

Practical considerations

- In the above defence, the question of whether a defendant produced documents 'as soon as was reasonably practicable' will be a question of fact for the court to decide in each case.
- In this section reference to a constable includes, in certain circumstances, a TW.

 Summary   6 months

 A fine not exceeding level 3 on the standard scale.

10.16.5 **Seize and remove motor vehicle (no insurance/driving licence)**

Section 165A empowers a constable to seize and remove a motor vehicle, which they believe is being used without a driving licence or insurance.

Powers

Seizure conditions

Under s 165A a constable may seize a motor vehicle under this section if any of the following sections apply—
- s 164, by a constable in uniform to produce their licence and counterpart for examination (see **10.16.3**), a person fails to do so, and the constable reasonably believes that they are or were driving without a licence (see **10.14**);
- s 165, by a constable in uniform to produce evidence of insurance, a person fails to do so (see **10.16.4**), and the constable reasonably believes that the vehicle was being driven without such insurance (see **10.16.1**);
- s 163, by a constable in uniform to stop a vehicle, the driver fails to do so (see **10.2.4**), or fails to do so long enough for the constable to make appropriate enquiries, and the constable reasonably believes that they are or were driving without a licence or insurance.

Removal

The Road Traffic Act 1988 (Retention and Disposal of Seized Motor Vehicles) Regulations 2005, made under s 165B, specifically provide for the retention, safe keeping, and disposal by the police or persons authorized by them, of vehicles seized under s 165A.

Explanatory notes

- Before seizing the motor vehicle the driver or person appearing to be the driver must be warned of the consequences of failure to immediately produce their driving licence and its counterpart or provide evidence of insurance, unless circumstances make it impracticable to give the warning.
- If the vehicle fails to stop or drives off and cannot be seized immediately, it may be seized at any time within 24 hours of the original incident.
- In order to seize the vehicle a constable may enter any premises (except a private **dwelling house**) on which they reasonably believe the vehicle to be. If necessary, reasonable force may be used in the exercise of this power.
- A **dwelling house** does not include a garage or other structure occupied with the dwelling house or land belonging to it.

Practical considerations

- In this section motor vehicle does not include an invalid carriage.
- A constable must be in uniform and may use reasonable force, if necessary, to exercise these powers.
- The police are under a duty to ensure the retention and safekeeping of a seized vehicle until it is released to the owner or otherwise disposed of under the 2005 Regulations (see '**Removal**' above).
- Regulation 4 of the 2005 Regulations states that when the vehicle is seized, a seizure notice shall be given to the driver of the seized vehicle, unless the circumstances make it impracticable to do so. It also gives the procedure to follow in respect of seized vehicles.
- Where practicable a seizure notice must be given to the registered keeper and the owner.

Links to alternative subjects and offences

10.17 **Seat Belts**

Section 14 of the Road Traffic Act 1988 relates to the wearing of seat belts in motor vehicles by adults and s 15 by children.

10.17.1 **Seat belts—adults**

Section 14 empowers the Secretary of State to make regulations concerning the wearing of seat belts in motor vehicles by adults, and creates an offence of failing to comply with such regulations.

> ### Offences
>
> A person who **drives** or rides in a **motor vehicle** in contravention of **regulations** under this section is guilty of an offence; but notwithstanding any enactment or rule of law, no person other than the person actually committing the contravention is guilty of an offence by reason of the contravention.
>
> Road Traffic Act 1988, s 14(3)

Points to prove

✓ drove/rode in a motor vehicle
✓ contravened regulations made under s 14

Meanings

Drives (see **10.1.4**)

Motor vehicle

Defined by s 185 (see **10.1.3**), **but** for s 14 **does not include** a motorcycle (with or without a sidecar).

Regulations

(1) Subject to the following provisions of these regulations, every person—
    (a) driving a motor vehicle; or
    (b) riding in a front or rear seat of a motor vehicle;
    shall wear an adult belt.

(2) Paragraph (1) does not apply to a person under the age of 14 years.
    Motor Vehicles (Wearing of Seat Belts) Regulations

1993, reg 5

Exemptions

Regulation 6 of the above regs gives exemptions to reg 5 requirements—

• person holding a medical certificate;

10.17.1 Seat Belts—Adults

- driver/passenger in a motor vehicle constructed or adapted for carrying goods, being on a journey which does not exceed 50 metres used for delivery or collection;
- driver of a vehicle performing a manoeuvre including reversing;
- qualified driver supervising provisional licence holder who is performing a manoeuvre including reversing;
- driving test examiner conducting a test of competence to drive and wearing a seat belt would endanger the examiner or any other person;
- person driving or riding in a vehicle being used for fire and rescue authority, police, or SOCA purposes or for carrying a person in lawful custody;
- driver of a licensed taxi used for seeking hire, or answering a call for hire, or carrying a passenger for hire, or driver of a private hire vehicle used to carry a passenger for hire;
- person riding in a vehicle, used on trade plates to investigate or remedy a fault in the vehicle;
- disabled person wearing a disabled person's belt;
- person riding in a vehicle taking part in a procession organized by or on behalf of the Crown;
- person driving a vehicle if the driver's seat is not provided with an adult belt;
- person riding in the front/rear of a vehicle if no adult belt is available for them;
- person riding in a small or large bus which is—
  - ◆ being used to provide a local service in a built-up area, or
  - ◆ constructed or adapted for the carriage of standing passengers and on which the operator permits standing.

Explanatory notes

- Regulation 47(1) of the Road Vehicles (Construction and Use) Regulations 1986 stipulates that seatbelts are required to be fitted to a motor vehicle to which reg 46 applies—seat belt anchorage points to be fitted to motor vehicles.
- Regulation 46 applies to a motor vehicle, which is not an **excepted vehicle** and is a—
  - ◆ bus first used on or after 1st April 1982;
  - ◆ wheeled motor car first used on or after 1st January 1965;
  - ◆ 3-wheeled motorcycle having an u/w exceeding 255 kg, first used on or after 1st September 1970; or
  - ◆ heavy motor car first used on or after 1st October 1988.
- **Excepted vehicles** are listed in reg 46(2) being a: goods vehicle (except a dual-purpose vehicle) being first used before 1/4/67 or 1/4/80–1/10/88 (exceeding 3500 kg max gross wt) or u/w exceeding 1525 kg before 1/4/80 (but if manufactured before 1/10/79 then first used before 1/4/82); motor tractor; works truck; goods vehicle (electrically propelled—first used before 1/10/88); pedestrian controlled vehicle; vehicle used on roads outside GB (being driven

from port of entry place of residence of owner or driver, or to pre-arranged place for fitting of anchorage points and seat belts as required by regs 46 and 47); vehicle having max speed n/e 16 mph; locomotive or agricultural motor vehicle.

• The holder of a medical certificate cannot rely on the reg 5 exception unless they produce the certificate to the constable at the time of being reported for summons, or produce it within 7 days or as soon as practicable after being reported at a police station specified by them, or where it is not so produced it is not reasonably practicable to produce it there before the commencement of proceedings.

Practical considerations

• Consider issuing a TFPN for this offence (see **10.4**).
• Each passenger is responsible for wearing a seatbelt and liable for the s 14(3) offence, except passengers under the age of 14 years (see **10.17.2**) where the responsibility is then with the driver.
• Regulation 5 above does not apply where there is no adult seat belt available in that part of the vehicle.

 Summary   6 months

 A fine not exceeding level 2 on the standard scale.

10.17.2 **Seat belts—children**

Section 15 creates offences concerning the wearing of seat belts by children in motor vehicles.

Offences

Seated in front

(1) Except as provided by **regulations**, where a child under the age of 14 years is in the front of a **motor vehicle**, a person must not without reasonable excuse drive the vehicle on a **road** unless the child is wearing a **seat belt** in conformity with regulations.

(1A) Where—
   (a) a **child** is in the front of a motor vehicle other than a **bus**,
   (b) the child is in a rear-facing child restraining device, and
   (c) the passenger seat where the child is placed is protected by a front air bag,

   a person must not without reasonable excuse drive the vehicle on a road unless the air bag is deactivated.

(2) It is an offence for a person to drive a motor vehicle in contravention of subsection (1) or (1A) above.

Seated in rear

(3) Except as provided by regulations, where—
  (a) a child under the age of three years is in the rear of a motor vehicle, or
  (b) a child of or over that age but under the age of fourteen years is in the rear of a motor vehicle and any seat belt is fitted in the rear of that vehicle,

  a person must not without reasonable excuse drive the vehicle on a road unless the child is wearing a seat belt in conformity with regulations.

(3A) Except as provided by **regulations**, where—
  (a) a child who is under the age of 12 years and less than 150 cms in height is in the rear of a passenger car,
  (b) no seat belt is fitted in the rear of the **passenger car**, and
  (c) a seat in the front of the passenger car is provided with a seat belt but is not occupied by any person,

  a person must not without reasonable excuse drive the passenger car on a road.

(4) It is an offence for a person to drive a motor vehicle in contravention of subsection (3) or (3A) above.

Road Traffic Act 1988, s 15

Points to prove

s 15(2) offence (front seated)

✓ without reasonable excuse
✓ drove a motor vehicle
✓ on a road
✓ child under 14 years
✓ in the front of the vehicle
✓ not wearing a seat belt **or**
✓ in a rear-facing restraining device and front air bag not deactivated

s 15(4) offence (rear seated)

✓ per first four points of s 15(2)
✓ in the rear of the vehicle
✓ a child under the age of 3 years **or** aged 3 years to 13 years
✓ not wearing a fitted seat belt

or

✓ motor vehicle was a passenger car
✓ child under 12 years and less than 150 cms tall
✓ with no rear seat belt fitted and
✓ a front seat (with belt) was available

Seat Belts—Children 10.17.2

Meanings

Motor vehicle

As defined by s 185 (see **10.1.3**), **but** for the purposes of s 15(1) does not include a motorcycle (with or without a sidecar).

Road (see **10.1.1**)

Seat belt

This includes any description of restraining device for a child.

Bus

Means a motor vehicle that—
- has at least four wheels,
- is constructed or adapted for the carriage of passengers,
- has more than 8 seats in addition to the driver's seat, and
- has a maximum design speed exceeding 25 kilometres per hour.

Passenger car

Means a motor vehicle which—
- is constructed or adapted for use for the carriage of passengers and is not a goods vehicle,
- has no more than 8 seats in addition to the driver's seat,
- has four or more wheels,
- has a maximum design speed exceeding 25 kilometres per hour, and
- has a **maximum laden weight** not exceeding 3.5 tonnes.

Maximum laden weight

In relation to a vehicle or combination of vehicles means—
- in respect of which a gross weight not to be exceeded in Great Britain is specified in construction and use requirements, **that weight**;
- in respect of which **no such weight is specified** in construction and use requirements, the weight which the vehicle, or combination of vehicles, is designed or adapted not to exceed when in normal use and travelling on a road laden.

Regulations (seated in front)

Motor Vehicles (Wearing of Seat Belts by Children in Front Seats) Regulations 1993. Regulation 5 describes the belt or restraint to be worn.

Regulations (seated in rear)

Motor Vehicles (Wearing of Seat Belts) Regulations 1993.

Small child

Is a child under the age of 12 years and under 135cm in height.

Large child

Is a child who is not a small child.

10.17.2 Seat Belts—Children

Explanatory notes

- The concept of a small child and a large child has been added by the above regulations, this has resulted in the lowering of the height from 150cms down to 135cms for a small child. This only affects the type of restraint that a small child should wear.
- Section 15(3) and 15(3A) rear seat prohibitions do not apply to a—
  - ◆ child for whom there is a medical certificate;
  - ◆ small child aged under 3 years who is riding in a licensed taxi or licensed hire car, if no appropriate seat belt is available for them in the front or rear of the vehicle;
  - ◆ small child aged 3 years or more who is riding in a licensed taxi, a licensed hire car, or a small bus and wearing an adult belt if an appropriate seat belt is not available for them in the front or rear of the vehicle;
  - ◆ small child aged 3 years or more who is wearing an adult belt and riding in a passenger car or light goods vehicle where the use of child restraints by the child occupants of two seats in the rear of the vehicle prevents the use of an appropriate seat belt for that child and no appropriate seat belt is available for them in the front of the vehicle;
  - ◆ small child riding in a vehicle being used for the purposes of the police, security, or emergency services to enable the proper performance of their duty;
  - ◆ small child aged 3 years or more who is wearing an adult belt and who, because of an unexpected necessity, is travelling a short distance in a passenger car or light goods vehicle in which no appropriate seat belt is available for him; or
  - ◆ disabled child who is wearing a disabled person's belt or whose disability makes it impracticable to wear a seat belt where a disabled person's belt is unavailable to him.
- Prohibitions in s 15(1) do not apply to a—
  - ◆ small child aged 3 years or more who is riding in a bus and is wearing an adult belt if an appropriate seat belt is not available for him in the front or rear of the vehicle;
  - ◆ child for whom there is a medical certificate;
  - ◆ disabled child who is wearing a disabled person's belt;
  - ◆ child riding in a bus which is being used to provide a local service in a built-up area, or which is constructed/adapted for the carriage of standing passengers and on which the operator permits standing; or
  - ◆ large child if no appropriate seat belt is available for him in the front of the vehicle.
- The driver of a motor vehicle has the same opportunity to produce a medical certificate for a child not wearing a seat belt as an adult (see **10.17.1**).

Practical considerations

- Consider issuing a TFPN for this offence (see **10.4**).
- The seat belt must be appropriate for a child of a particular weight and height travelling in a particular vehicle.

- A seat is regarded as provided with child restraint if the child restraint is—
  - fixed in such a position that it can be worn by an occupier of that seat, or
  - elsewhere in or on the vehicle but—could readily be fixed in such a position without the aid of tools, and is not being worn by a child for whom it is appropriate and who is occupying another seat.
- A seat belt is considered appropriate in relation to a—
  - **small child**, if it is a child restraint of a description prescribed for their height and weight by reg 5;
  - **large child**, if it is a child restraint of a description prescribed for their height and weight by reg 5 or an adult belt; or
  - person aged 14 years or more, if it is an adult belt.
- In relation to ages and height, subject to exceptions/requirements—
  - under 3 must travel in front or rear in an appropriate baby/child seat;
    - EU approved and selected according to weight;
    - where a rear facing baby seat is in the front seat, the air bag has to be de-activated.
  - Aged 3–11 and under 135 cms in rear using appropriate child seat, booster seat, or booster cushion.
  - Aged 12–13 or under 12 but over 135cm, front or rear using adult seat belt, if no suitable child restraint is available.
  - Aged 14 and over adult regulations apply (see **10.17.1**).

Summary

 6 months

s 15(2) offence

A fine not exceeding level 2 on the standard scale.

s 15(4) offence

A fine not exceeding level 1 on the standard scale.

Links to alternative subjects and offences

10.18 Motorcycle—No Crash Helmet/Eye Protectors

Section 16 of the Road Traffic Act 1988 empowers the Secretary of State to make regulations concerning the wearing of crash helmets by motorcyclists and an offence of breaching such regulations.

Offences

A person who **drives** or rides on a **motor cycle** in contravention of **regulations** under this section is guilty of an offence; but not withstanding any enactment or rule of law no person other than the person actually committing the contravention is guilty of an offence by reason of the contravention unless the person actually committing the contravention is a child under the age of 16 years.

Road Traffic Act 1988, s 16(4)

Points to prove
✓ drove/rode on motorcycle
✓ contravened regulations under s 16

Meanings

Drives (see 10.1.4)

Motorcycle

Means a **mechanically propelled vehicle**, not being an invalid carriage, having less than 4 wheels and the unladen weight does not exceed 410 kg.

Mechanically propelled vehicle (see 10.1.3)

Regulations

Every person driving or riding (otherwise than in a sidecar) on a motor bicycle when on a **road** shall wear protective headgear (Motor Cycles (Protective Helmets) Regulations 1998, reg 4).

Road (see 10.1.1)

Explanatory notes
- This section does not include people riding in a sidecar or of the Sikh religion while wearing a turban.
- A British/EU standards mark must be on the helmet.
- Regulation 4 does not apply to a mowing machine or if propelled by a person on foot.
- If the vehicle is being propelled by 'scooter' style (eg the rider sat astride the machine and propelling it by pushing on the ground with their foot/feet) then a helmet should be worn.

- 'Motor bicycle' means a 2-wheeled motorcycle, whether or not having a sidecar attached, although where the distance measured between the centre of the area of contact with the road surface of any 2 wheels of a motorcycle is less than 460 millimetres, those wheels are counted as one wheel.
- *Eye Protectors offence*—Motor Cycles (Eye Protectors) Regulations 1999, reg 4 creates an offence under s 18(3) of not wearing approved eye protectors. Each person driving or riding (otherwise than in a sidecar) on a motor bicycle is required to wear eye protectors of a prescribed type.

Related cases

DPP v Parker [2005] RTR 1616, QBD A motorcycle fitted with enhanced safety features (eg a roof) does not negate the requirement to wear protective headgear.

Practical considerations

- Consider issuing a TFPN for these offences (see **10.4**).
- Any helmet worn must be securely fastened using straps or other means of fastening provided.
- If the helmet has a chin cup it must have an additional strap to fit under the jaw.
- Eye protectors/ visors marked 'Daytime Use' or bearing a symbol of the same meaning should only be used in daytime.
- Visors that transmit less than 50% of visible light cannot be legally used on the road.

 Summary   6 months

 A fine not exceeding level 2 on the standard scale.

Links to alternative subjects and offences

10.19 Improper Use of Trade Plates

The Vehicle Excise and Registration Act 1994 provides for the registration
and excise duty payable in respect of motor vehicles. Section 34 relates to
offences committed in relation to trade licences.

Offences

A person holding a **trade licence** or trade licences is guilty of an offence
if he—

(a) **uses** at any one time on a **public road** a greater number of vehicles
    (not being vehicles for which vehicle licences are for the time being
    in force) than he is authorised to use by virtue of the trade licence or
    licences,
(b) uses a **vehicle** (not being a vehicle for which a vehicle licence is for the
    time being in force) on a public road other than for a purpose which
    has been prescribed under **section 12(2)(b)**,
(c) uses the trade licence, or any of the trade licences, for the purposes of
    keeping on a public road in any circumstances other than circumstanc-
    es which have been prescribed under **section 12(1)(c)** a vehicle which
    is not being used on that road.

Vehicle Excise and Registration Act 1994, s 34(1)

Points to prove

s 34(1)(a) offence

✓ being the holder of trade licence(s)
✓ used on a public road
✓ by virtue of that licence
✓ more vehicles than authorized by the licence

s 34(1)(b) offence

✓ being the holder of trade licence(s)
✓ used a vehicle on a public road
✓ by virtue of that licence
✓ for purposes other than as prescribed in the licence

s 34(1)(c) offence

✓ being the holder of trade licence(s)
✓ kept a vehicle on a public road
✓ by virtue of that licence
✓ when the vehicle was not being used on that road

Meanings

Trade licence

Is a licence issued under s 11.

Uses (see **10.16.1**)

Public road—s 62

Means a **road** repairable at public expense.

Road

Defined by s 192 of the Road Traffic Act 1988 (see **10.1.1**).

Vehicle—s 1(1B)

Means a mechanically propelled vehicle, or anything (whether or not it is a vehicle) that has been, but has ceased to be, a mechanically propelled vehicle.

Section 12(2)(b)

Allows the Secretary of State to make regulations prescribing purposes for which the holder of a trade licence may use a vehicle under that licence.

Section 12(1)(c)

The holder of a trade licence is not entitled to keep any vehicle on a road if it is not being used for the purposes prescribed.

Explanatory notes

- A trade licence will only be issued to a motor trader (including a vehicle manufacturer), vehicle tester, or person intending to start a business as a motor trader or vehicle tester.
- Where the conviction is for a continuing offence the offence will be taken as committed on the latest date to which the conviction relates.
- The trade licence holder who changes their name or the name and/or address of their business must notify the Secretary of State and submit the licence for amendment.
- It is an offence under s 44 for a person to forge, fraudulently alter or use or fraudulently lend or allow to be used by another person any trade licence or plate.
- Nothing that can be mistaken for a trade plate should be displayed on a vehicle.
- The trade licence must be displayed on the front of the vehicle so as to be clearly visible at all times in daylight and fixed to it by means of the trade plate containing the licence holder.

Practical considerations

- Consider issuing a TFPN (see **10.4.1**) for offences under s 34.
- A trade licence is valid only for vehicles temporarily in the possession of a motor trader (including a vehicle manufacturer) or vehicle tester in the course of their business.
- A trade licence only authorizes the use of one vehicle at any one time under s 12(1)(a), but a person may hold more than one licence.
- A vehicle and semi-trailer superimposed thereon counts as only one vehicle.

10.19 Improper Use of Trade Plates

- A trade licence will be issued for a year or 6 months, but where a person intends to start a relevant business it can be for a period of 7 to 11 months.
- One of a set of trade plates includes a trade licence holder to facilitate the displaying of the trade licence.
- If a question arises as to the number of vehicles used, their character, weight, or cc rating, the seating capacity or the purpose for which they were being used, s 53 places the burden of proof on the defendant.
- Section 29 creates the offence of using/keeping an unlicensed vehicle on a public road (see **10.20.2**).

 Summary 36 months

 A fine not exceeding level 3 on the standard scale or 5 times the amount of vehicle excise duty payable in respect of the vehicle.

Links to alternative subjects and offences

10.20 Vehicle Excise Licences and Registration Marks/Documents

The Vehicle Excise and Registration Act 1994 governs the registration of, and excise duty payable in respect of, motor vehicles.

The Act creates several offences including failing to produce a registration document, using or keeping an unlicensed vehicle on a road, failing to exhibit a licence, failing to fix a registration mark to a vehicle, and using or keeping a vehicle bearing an obscured registration mark.

10.20.1 Production of registration document

Section 28A provides for a constable to require production of a registration document.

Offence

(1) A person **using** a **vehicle** in respect of which a **registration document** has been issued must produce the document for inspection on being so required by—
  (a) a constable, or
  (b) a person authorised by the Secretary of State for the purposes of this section (an '**authorised person**').
(3) A person is guilty of an offence if he fails to comply with subsection (1).

Vehicle Excise and Registration Act 1994, s 28A

Points to prove
✓ used a vehicle
✓ for which a registration document had been issued
✓ requested by constable/authorized person
✓ to produce the registration document
✓ failed to do so

Meanings

Using (see **10.16.1**)

Vehicle (see **10.19**)

Registration document
Issued under s 22(1)(e).

Authorised person

Authorised by the Secretary of State.

Explanatory notes

- An authorized person exercising power under s 28A must, if requested, produce evidence of their authority to do so.
- A person authorized by the Secretary of State may conduct and appear in any proceedings under this Act at a magistrates' court or before a district judge of a county court.
- This section does not apply if the defendant produces the required document at a police station specified by them within 7 days of the request or as soon as reasonably practicable.
- If an authorized person imposes the requirement then production may be made at a goods vehicle testing station instead of a police station.

 Summary   6 months

 A fine not exceeding level 2 on the standard scale.

10.20.2 **Using/keeping unlicensed vehicle**

Section 29 creates the offence of using or keeping an unlicensed vehicle on a public road.

> **Offences**
>
> If a person uses, or keeps, a **vehicle** which is **unlicensed** he is guilty of an offence.
>
> Vehicle Excise and Registration Act 1994, s 29(1)

Points to prove

✓ used/kept a vehicle
✓ without VEL or trade licence being in force

Meanings

Uses (see 10.16.1)

Vehicle (see 10.19)

Unlicensed

If there is no vehicle licence or trade licence in force for vehicle.

Exempt vehicles (*exempt from vehicle excise duty*)

Applies to the following vehicles listed under Sch 2—
- certain vehicles first constructed before 1 January 1973,
- electrically assisted pedal cycles,
- vehicles not used or adapted for carrying a driver or passenger,
- emergency vehicles,
- disabled persons' vehicles,
- a vehicle on test,
- a vehicle travelling between parts of private land,
- a vehicle for export or imported by members of foreign armed forces,
- a vehicle which is off-road after notifying the DVLA,
- tractor, light agricultural vehicle, agricultural engine,
- mowing machine,
- steam powered vehicles,
- electrically propelled vehicle, trams, and snow ploughs.

Explanatory notes

- Various people can 'use' a vehicle being the driver, employer if the vehicle is being used for the employer's business, owner being driven by another person while owner is in the vehicle, or steersman where a broken down vehicle is being towed.
- If the holder of a vehicle licence surrenders it under s 10(2) they must deliver a Statutory Off Road Notification (SORN) to the Secretary of State unless they no longer own the relevant vehicle or are a relevant vehicle trader.
- Where a vehicle licence or nil licence has expired and a new licence is not taken out to run from the expiration of that licence the vehicle keeper must send a SORN to the Secretary of State.

Related cases

Plumbien v Vines [1996] Crim LR 124, QBD If a motor vehicle's moving parts are seized and it is no longer driveable, the owner still has use of the vehicle.

Practical considerations

- All exempt vehicles require a nil licence except trams, electrically assisted pedal cycles, vehicles that do not carry a driver or passenger, vehicles going to, from, or taking a test of road worthiness or pollution or vehicles which are zero rated whilst awaiting export.
- Under s 43A it is an offence to use/keep a vehicle that requires a nil licence without such licence.
- Where a vehicle changes ownership the VEL is no longer valid unless it is passed to the new keeper with the vehicle.
- The burden of proof that the defendant was the keeper of the vehicle on the relevant day is on the prosecutor, but it is on the defendant to prove that a VEL was in force for the vehicle.

- The burden of proof is on the defendant if a question arises as to the character, weight, cubic capacity (cc) rating, or seating capacity of the vehicle; or the purpose for which it was being used.
- If offences involve misuse of trade plates under s 34 see **10.19**.

 Summary 6 months

 A fine not exceeding level 3 on the standard scale or 5 times the amount of vehicle excise duty payable, whichever is the greater. A greater penalty can be imposed if the keeper commits the offence or if a SORN declaration has been made.

10.20.3 **Fail to display a vehicle excise licence**

Section 33 provides for the offence of failing to display a VEL on a vehicle being used or kept on a public road.

> **Offences**
>
> (1) A person is guilty of an offence if—
>
>   (a) he **uses**, or keeps, on a **public road** a **vehicle** in respect of which **vehicle excise duty** is chargeable, and
>
>   (b) there is not fixed to and exhibited on the vehicle in the manner prescribed by regulations made by the Secretary of State a **licence** for, or in respect of, the vehicle which is for the time being in force.
>
> (1A) A person is guilty of an offence if—
>
>   (a) he uses, or keeps, on a public road an **exempt vehicle**,
>
>   (b) that vehicle is one in respect of which regulations under this Act require a nil licence to be in force, and
>
>   (c) there is not fixed to, and exhibited on the licence in the manner prescribed by regulations made by the Secretary of State a nil licence for that vehicle which is for the time being in force.
>
> Vehicle Excise and Registration Act 1994, s 33

Points to prove

✓ used/kept
✓ on a public road
✓ vehicle
✓ valid VEL or nil licence not displayed

Meanings

Uses (see **10.16.1**)

Public road (see **10.19**)

Road (see **10.1.1**)

Vehicle (see **10.19**)

Vehicle excise duty

To be construed in accordance with s 1(1).

Licence

To be construed in accordance with s 1(2).

Exempt vehicle (see **10.20.2**)

Explanatory notes

- The offence under s 33(1) includes both vehicle licences and trade licences (see **10.19**).
- Under s 33(1B), a person is not guilty of an offence under section 33(1) or (1A) if during any of the 5 **working days** following when a licence or nil licence for the vehicle ceases to be in force, an application for a licence or nil licence has been received.
- **Working day** means any day other than a Saturday or Sunday, or Christmas Eve, Christmas Day, Good Friday, or a bank holiday.

Practical considerations

- Consider issuing a TFPN (see **10.4**).
- Charge in addition to use/keep a vehicle on a public road without a valid vehicle licence (see **10.20.2**).
- Under s 43A it is an offence to use/keep a vehicle that requires a nil licence without such licence. Exempt vehicles requiring a nil licence are listed in **10.20.2** under 'Practical considerations'.

 Summary 6 months

 A fine not exceeding level 1 on the standard scale.

10.20.4 **Fail to fix registration mark to vehicle**

Section 42 relates to the fixing of the registration mark to a vehicle and creates an offence of failure to do so.

Offence

If a **registration mark** is not fixed on a **vehicle** as required by virtue of **section 23**, the **relevant person** is guilty of an offence.

Vehicle Excise and Registration Act 1994, s 42(1)

10.20.4 Fail to Fix Registration Mark to Vehicle

Points to prove

✓ drove/kept a vehicle
✓ on a road
✓ no registration mark fixed to front/rear of vehicle

Meanings

Registration mark—s 23(1)

A vehicle registered under s 21(1) shall be assigned a registration mark indicating the registered number of that vehicle.

Vehicle (see 10.19)

Relevant person

Driver of vehicle or, if not being driven, the keeper.

Explanatory notes

- The Road Vehicles (Display of Registration Marks) Regulations 2001 govern how such marks must be displayed on vehicles first registered on or after 1 October 1938; such as the size, shape and character of the lettering and the manner by which the registration marks are to be displayed and rendered easily distinguishable (whether by day or by night).
- The above regs apply to all vehicles except works trucks, road rollers, and agricultural machines.
- A registration plate must be fixed to the rear of the vehicle or, if towing a trailer or trailers, the rear of the rearmost trailer, in a vertical position or, if that is not practicable, as close to vertical as possible, and in such position that, in normal daylight, the characters are easily distinguishable.
- Similarly, except a motorcycle, a registration plate must be fixed to the front of the vehicle in a vertical position or, if that is not practicable, as close to vertical as possible, and in such position that, in normal daylight, the characters are easily distinguishable.

Defences

(4) It is a defence for a person charged with an offence under subsection (1) to prove that—

    (a) he had no reasonable opportunity to register the vehicle under this Act, and

    (b) the vehicle was being driven for the purpose of being so registered.

(5) It is a defence for a person charged with an offence under subsection (1) in relation to a vehicle to which s 47 of the Road Traffic Act 1988 applies by virtue of subsection (2)(b) of that section (vehicles manufactured before the prescribed period and used before registration) to prove that he had no reasonable opportunity to register the vehicle under this Act and that the vehicle was being driven in accordance with subsection (6).

Vehicle Excise and Registration Act 1994, s 42

Defence notes

A vehicle is driven under s 42(6) if it is being driven for, or in connection with, examination under s 45 of the Road Traffic Act 1988 (MOT tests) in circumstances in which its use is exempted from s 47(1) of that Act by regulations.

Practical considerations

- The Regulations concerning the displaying of registration marks do not apply to invalid vehicles or pedestrian controlled vehicles.
- A motorcycle first registered on or after 1 September 2001 **must not** have a registration plate fixed to the front, and one first registered before 1 September 2001 does not need to have a front registration plate fixed to it.
- If an agricultural machine is towing a trailer the registration plate on the rear of the trailer may show the registration mark of any similar machine owned by the keeper.

 Summary 6 months

 A fine not exceeding level 3 on the standard scale.

10.20.5 **Obscured registration mark**

Section 43 requires a registration plate fixed to a vehicle to be unobscured and easily distinguishable.

Offences

If a **registration mark** fixed on a **vehicle** as **required by** virtue of **section 23** is in any way—

(a) obscured, or
(b) rendered, or allowed to become, not easily distinguishable,
the **relevant person** is guilty of an offence.

Vehicle Excise and Registration Act 1994, s 43(1)

Points to prove

- ✓ drove/kept
- ✓ vehicle on a road
- ✓ registration mark obscured/rendered/allowed to become indistinguishable

10.20.5 Obscured Registration Mark

Meanings

Registration mark (see 10.20.4)

Vehicle (see 10.19)

Relevant person (see 10.20.4)

Required by section 23

The Road Vehicles (Display of Registration Marks) Regulations 2001 have been made under s 23 (see **10.20.4**).

> **Defence**
>
> It is a defence for a person charged with an offence under this section to prove that he took all steps which it was reasonably practicable to take to prevent the mark being obscured or rendered not easily distinguishable.
>
> **Vehicle Excise and Registration Act 1994, s 43(4)**

Practical considerations

- Examples of this offence could be where the registration plate is obscured by the tow bar/ball, or covered by a pedal cycle rack, or is covered by dirt/mud and is allowed to remain there.
- Officers should use their discretion when dealing with this type of offence.
- Using fixing screws of the wrong colour to change the appearance of letters/numbers can also be an offence under this section.
- Consider issuing a TFPN for this s 43 offence (see **10.4**).
- The Vehicles (Crime) Act 2001 concerns the control of registration plate suppliers. Section 28 of that Act makes it an offence to sell a defective plate or one where the registration mark is misrepresented. The onus is on the prosecution to show that the supplier knew of the defect or was reckless with regard to the nature of the plate.

 Summary 6 months

A fine not exceeding level 3 on the standard scale.

Links to alternative subjects and offences

10.21 Using Vehicle Without an Operator's Licence

The Goods Vehicles (Licensing of Operators) Act 1995 provides for the licensing of certain goods vehicles. Section 2 requires that a person who uses a goods vehicle on a road to carry goods for hire or reward or in connection with their business must be covered by a goods vehicle operator's licence.

Offences

(1) Subject to **subsection (2)** and **section 4**, no person shall use a **goods vehicle** on a **road** for the carriage of **goods**—
    (a) for **hire** or **reward**, or
    (b) for or in connection with any trade or business carried on by him,
    except under a licence issued under this Act; and in this Act such a licence is referred to as an 'operator's licence'.
(5) A person who uses a vehicle in contravention of this section is guilty of an offence.

Goods Vehicles (Licensing of Operators) Act 1995, s 2

Points to prove
✓ used a goods vehicle for the carriage of goods
✓ for hire/reward/in connection with a business
✓ on a road
✓ without an operator's licence

Meanings

Subsection (2)

Subsection (1) does not apply to—
(a) the use of a small goods vehicle within the meaning given in Schedule 1;
(b) the use of a goods vehicle for international carriage by a haulier established in a member State other than the UK and not established in the UK;
(c) the use of a goods vehicle for international carriage by a haulier established in Northern Ireland and not established in Great Britain; or
(d) the use of a vehicle of any class specified in regulations.

Section 4

Allows for the Traffic Commissioners to issue a temporary exemption (for standard licence) in an emergency, or some other special need.

Goods vehicle

Means a motor vehicle constructed or adapted for use for the carriage/haulage of goods, or a trailer so constructed or adapted, but does not include a tramcar or trolley vehicle.

Road

Means any highway or any other road to which the public has access, and includes bridges over which a road passes.

Goods

This includes goods or burden of any description.

Hire or reward

Means a systematic carrying of passengers for reward that went beyond the bounds of mere social kindness (*Albert v Motor Insurance Bureau* [1972] AC 301).

Explanatory notes

- The performance by a local or public authority of their functions constitutes the carrying on of a business.
- Different types of Operator's licence are denoted by the colour of the identity disc—
  - Restricted (orange)—own goods nationally and internationally;
  - Standard National (blue)—hire and reward transportation nationally only;
  - Standard International (green)—as blue, plus international as well;
  - Interim/temporary (yellow).
- The licence may specify the maximum number of vehicles that may be used under it, or may specify the maximum number of vehicles exceeding a certain weight (specified therein), for which it authorizes the use.
- The Traffic Commissioner for an area issues an Operator's licence.
- An Operator may hold a licence in more than one area, but cannot hold more than one licence in the same area.

Related cases

Rout v Swallow Hotels Ltd [1993] RTR 80, QBD Swallow Hotels group operated courtesy coaches. No fares were charged but the coaches were driven by company employees and were exclusively for use of hotel guests. Held to be for hire or reward. No binding contract was necessary and the customers obviously paid for this service in their hotel bills.

VOSA v Greenfarms Ltd [2005] EWHC 3156 (Admin), CA An articulated tractor unit had been adapted to allow it to draw a trailer tank carrying liquid fertilizer. G had borne the burden of proof and failed to show purpose and evidence of reinstatement. Despite the modification the vehicle remained a heavy goods vehicle and not an agricultural tractor and so required an operator's licence.

Practical considerations

- If the defendant has previously held an Operator's licence specify the date on which it expired.
- Vehicles must only be used from a centre specified in the licence as the operating centre.
- This section extends to foreign vehicles by virtue of the Road Traffic (Foreign Vehicles) Act 1972.
- A standard licence may authorize transport operations both nationally and internationally.
- An Operator's licence authorizes the use of any vehicle in the lawful possession of the licence holder and any trailer so possessed.
- An authorized person, believing that an offence under s 2 is being or has been committed, may detain the vehicle and its contents.
- Where a vehicle is seized, the authorized person may immobilize that vehicle there or may remove it, or cause it to be removed, to a move convenient place for it to be immobilized.
- A power of entry exists under s 40 where an **officer**/constable may, at any reasonable time having regard to the circumstances of the case, enter any premises of the applicant or holder of an Operator's licence and inspect any facilities there for the maintenance of vehicles used under that licence. An offence will be committed if that officer/constable is obstructed.
- **Officer** means an examiner appointed under s 66A of the Road Traffic Act 1988 or person authorized by the Traffic Commissioner.
- A power of seizure also exists under s 42 where if an officer/constable has reason to believe that a document or article carried on or by the driver of a vehicle, or a document produced may be subject to s 38 (forge/alter with intent to deceive) or s 39 (false statement to obtain a licence) offences, then they may seize that document or article.
- Consider issuing a TFPN for this s 2(5) offence (see **10.4.1**).

 Summary 6 months

 A fine not exceeding level 5 on the standard scale.

Links to alternative subjects and offences

TFPN Traffic Fixed
Penalty Notices

10.22 **Obstruction of the Road/Footpath**

Obstruction of a road is catered for in various legislation, including the Highways Act 1980, the Road Vehicles (Construction and Use) Regulations 1986 and the Town Police Clauses Act 1847.

10.22.1 **Obstruct the footpath**

Section 28 of the Town Police Clauses Act 1847 provides numerous offences. The following list contains only those which relate to obstruction of the footpath.

> **Offence**
>
> Every **person** who in any **street** to the obstruction, annoyance or danger, of the residents or **passengers**, commits any of the following (**relevant offences**) is guilty of an offence.
>
> Town Police Clauses Act 1847, s 28

Points to prove
- ✓ in a street
- ✓ to the obstruction, annoyance or danger of residents/passengers
- ✓ committed one of the relevant offences

Meanings

Person

Includes a corporation, whether aggregate or sole.

Street

Includes any road, square, court, alley and thoroughfare, or public passage.

Passenger

Means pedestrian or passer-by.

Relevant offences

Means every person who—
- being in charge of a wagon, cart, or **carriage**, by obstructing the street, wilfully prevents any person or carriage from passing him, or any wagon, cart, or carriage, in his charge;
- causes any public carriage, sledge, truck, or barrow, with or without horses, or any beast of burden, to stand longer than is necessary

for loading and unloading goods, or for taking up or setting down passengers (except hackney carriages and horses and other animals standing for hire in a lawfully authorized place);

- by using a cart, carriage, sledge, truck, or barrow, or any animal, or **other means**, wilfully interrupts a public crossing, or wilfully causes an obstruction in any public footpath or thoroughfare;
- leads, rides, or fastens any horse or other animal across or upon any footway;
- places or leaves any furniture, goods, wares, or merchandise, or any cask, tub, basket, pail, or bucket on a footway;
- places or uses any standing place, stool, bench, stall, or show-board on any footway;
- places any blind, shade, covering, awning, or other projection, over or along a footway unless it is at least 8 feet above the ground;
- exposes to sale any goods, wares, merchandise, matter, or other thing, so that it projects into or over any footway, or beyond the line of any house, shop, or building where it is exposed, thereby obstructing and hindering the passage over or along that footway;
- rolls or carries any cask, tub, hoop, or wheel, or any ladder, plank, pole, timber, or log of wood upon any footway, except for loading or unloading any cart or carriage, or to cross the footway;
- places any line, cord, or pole across any street, or hangs or places any clothes thereon.

Carriage

Includes a bicycle (*Taylor v Goodwin* (1879) 43 JP 653, QBD), but a pram may not be (*R v Mathias* [1861]).

Other means

This does not include a person not using a carriage, or other conveyance to obstruct (*R v Long* (1888) 52 JP 630).

Related cases

Torbay Borough Council v Cross (1995) 159 JP 882, QBD A shopkeeper who put a display outside his shop was guilty of this offence irrespective of how little the display projected onto the footpath. The public should have free access to the whole of the highway.

Practical considerations

- None of these offences are complete unless it can be proved that obstruction, annoyance, or danger was caused to any resident or passenger.
- **Note:** This Act does not apply to the Metropolitan Police District.
- Consider offences under s 72 of the Highways Act 1835 (see **10.12.4**) of **wilfully** riding a bicycle/tricycle or riding/driving of motor vehicle, trailer, truck, sledge or leading, tethering any animals (as described) on the footpath/causeway.

Summary 6 months

14 days' imprisonment or a fine not exceeding level 3 on the standard scale.

10.22.2 **Wilful obstruction of the highway**

Section 137 of the Highways Act 1980 provides an offence of wilful obstruction of the highway.

> **Offence**
>
> If a **person**, without lawful authority or excuse, in any way **wilfully** obstructs the free passage along a **highway** he is guilty of an offence.
>
> Highways Act 1980, s 137(1)

Points to prove
- ✓ without lawful authority/excuse
- ✓ wilfully obstructed
- ✓ free passage of the highway

Meanings

Person

Includes a body corporate.

Wilfully

Means purposefully, delberately.

Highway

Means the whole or part of a highway other than a ferry or waterway. Where a highway passes over a bridge or through a tunnel, that bridge or tunnel is taken to be part of the highway.

Explanatory notes

- Causing someone to stop them from using the highway by fear alone is insufficient to commit obstruction: there should be some physical obstruction.
- The highway does not need to be completely blocked, only made less convenient or roomy.

- If a person is convicted under s 137 and the obstruction is continuing, the court may, instead of or in addition to imposing any punishment, order them to remove it within a fixed period under s 137ZA. Failure to comply with this order, without reasonable excuse, will be an offence.

Related cases

Birch v DPP [2000] Crim LR 301, QBD People at a demonstration sat in the road blocking traffic. The defendant admitted obstructing the traffic, but claimed to have a lawful excuse. Held: Lawful excuse included activities that were lawful in themselves. Only the evidence of the purpose of this action (obstruct the traffic) was relevant.

Torbay Borough Council v Cross (1995) 159 JP 882, QBD Although the de minimis principle (eg court is not concerned with trifles) applies to obstruction cases, it is reserved for cases of fractional obstructions.

Nagy v Weston [1965] 1 All ER 78, QBD The test for determining whether a particular use of the highway amounts to an obstruction is if in the particular circumstances, such use is unreasonable. Circumstances would include duration, position of the obstruction, its purpose, and whether it caused an actual or potential obstruction.

Practical considerations

- Consider whether the obstruction is—
  - ♦ Wilful or deliberate (as opposed to accidental)?
  - ♦ Without lawful excuse?
- If a motor vehicle is involved consider issuing a TFPN (see **10.4**).
- Where the offence is committed by a body corporate, if it can be proved it was with the consent or connivance of an officer of that body corporate, then they as well as the body corporate may be guilty of the offence.
- Duration and extent of the obstruction are important considerations.

 Summary 6 months

 A fine not exceeding level 3 on the standard scale.

10.22.3 **Builders' skips on the highway**

Section 139 of the Highways Act 1980 controls the use of builders' skips deposited on the highway.

Offences

(3) If a **builder's skip** is deposited on a **highway** without a permission granted under this section, the **owner** of the skip is, subject to subsection (6) below, guilty of an offence.

(4) Where a builder's skip has been deposited on a highway in accordance with a permission granted under this section, the owner of the skip shall secure—

(a) that the skip is properly lighted during the **hours of darkness** and, where regulations made by the Secretary of State under this section require it to be marked in accordance with the regulations (whether with reflecting or fluorescent material or otherwise), that it is so marked;

(b) that the skip is clearly and indelibly marked with the owner's name and with his telephone number or address;

(c) that the skip is moved as soon as practicable after it has been filled;

(d) that each of the conditions subject to which that permission was granted is complied with;

and, if he fails to do so, he is, subject to subsection (6) below, guilty of an offence.

Highways Act 1980, s 139

Points to prove

s 139(3) offence

✓ deposited builder's skip on a highway
✓ without permission under s 139

s 139(4) offence

✓ owner of a builder's skip
✓ deposited skip on a highway
✓ with a permission granted under s 139
✓ failed to secure that the skip was
✓ properly lighted during the hours of darkness; **or**
✓ clearly and indelibly marked with owner's details; **or**
✓ removed as soon as practicable after being filled; **or**
✓ not complying with each of the conditions

Meanings

Builder's skip

Means a container designed to be carried on a road vehicle and to be placed on a highway or other land for the storage of builders' materials, or for the removal and disposal of builders' rubble, waste household and other rubbish or earth.

Highway (see 10.22.2)

Owner

In relation to a builder's skip, subject of a hiring agreement, being an agreement for a hiring of not less than one month, or a hire purchase agreement, means the person in possession of the skip under that agreement.

Hours of darkness

Half an hour after sunset and half an hour before sunrise.

Power to move skip

Under s 140, the highways authority or a constable in uniform may require the owner of a skip to remove or reposition it; or cause it to be so removed or repositioned themselves. This applies even though it has been deposited with a permission granted under s 139.

Explanatory notes

- A permission under s 139 authorizes a person to whom it is granted to deposit, or cause to be deposited, a skip on a highway specified therein.
- Such permission may be granted unconditionally or with specified conditions such as: siting of skip, its dimensions, manner in which it must be marked to be visible to oncoming traffic, care and disposal of contents, way in which it must be lighted or guarded, and its removal at the expiry of the permission.
- Permission must be in writing and blanket permission is not allowed (*York City Council v Poller* [1976] RTR 37).
- Nothing in this section authorizes the creation of a nuisance or a danger to users of the highway or imposes on a highway authority granting permission any liability for any injury caused, damage, or loss resulting from the presence on a highway of a skip to which the permission relates.

Defences

(6) In any proceedings for an offence under this section it is a defence, subject to subsection (7) below, for the person charged to prove that the commission of the offence was due to the act or default of another person and that he took all reasonable precautions and exercised all due diligence to avoid the commission of such an offence by himself or any person under his control.

(7) A person charged with an offence under this section is not, without leave of the court, entitled to rely on the defence provided by subsection (6) above unless, within a period ending 7 clear days before the hearing, he has served on the prosecutor a notice in writing giving such information identifying or assisting in the identification of that other person as was then in his possession.

(8) Where any person is charged with an offence under any other enactment of failing to secure that a builder's skip which has been deposited on a highway in accordance with a permission granted under this section was properly lighted during the hours of darkness, it is a defence for the person charged to prove that the commission of the offence was due to the act or default of another person and that he took all reasonable precautions and exercised all due diligence to avoid the commission of such an offence by himself or any person under his control.

(9) Where a person is charged with obstructing, or interrupting any user of, a highway by depositing a builder's skip on it, it is a defence for the person charged to prove that the skip was deposited on it in accordance with a permission granted under this section and either—

(a) that each of the requirements of subsection (4) above had been complied with; or

(b) that the commission of any offence under that subsection was due to the act or default of another person and that he took all reasonable precautions and exercised all due diligence to avoid the commission of such an offence by himself or any person under his control.

Highways Act 1980, s 139

Practical considerations

- If a person commits an offence under s 139 because of an act or default of another person, that other person is guilty of the offence, and may be charged with and convicted of the offence whether or not proceedings are taken against the first-mentioned person.

- Requirement for a skip to be moved must be made face to face (*R v Worthing Justices, ex parte Waste Management Ltd* (1988) 152 JP 362, DC).

PCSO

 Summary 6 months

 A fine not exceeding level 3 on the standard scale.

10.22.4 **Cause injury/danger/annoyance on the highway**

Section 161 of the Highways Act 1980 creates various offences that relate to causing danger on a highway, including annoyance by playing games on the highway.

Offences

(1) If a person, without lawful authority or excuse, deposits any thing whatsoever on a **highway** in consequence of which a user of the highway is injured or endangered, that person is guilty of an offence.
(2) *[See* **8.8.6***]*
(3) If a person plays at football or any other game on a highway to the annoyance of a user of the highway he is guilty of an offence.
(4) If a person, without lawful authority or excuse, allows any filth, dirt, lime or other offensive matter or thing to run or flow on to a highway from any adjoining premises, he is guilty of an offence.

Highways Act 1980, s 161

Points to prove

s 161 (1) offence

✓ without lawful authority/excuse
✓ deposits any thing whatsoever on a highway
✓ thus injuring/endangering user of the highway

s 161 (3) offence

✓ played football/a game on a highway
✓ thus annoying a user of the highway

s 161 (4) offence

✓ without lawful authority/excuse
✓ allowed any filth, dirt, lime or other offensive matter or thing
✓ to run or flow on to a highway
✓ from any adjoining premises

Meaning of highway (see 10.22.2)

Explanatory notes

- The s 161(2) offences relate to lighting any fire on/over a highway or discharging any firearm or firework within 50 feet of the centre of a highway and are dealt with in **8.5** and **8.8.6**.
- Section 161A creates another offence of lighting a fire on any land (not part of a highway/carriageway) and as a result the user of any highway is injured, interrupted or endangered by smoke from that fire.
- Any rope, wire, or other apparatus placed across a highway so as to cause danger to users of the highway is an offence under s 162, unless adequate warning has been given of this danger.
- The s 161(3) offence is very wide and covers all types of 'game'. For example, a mock hunt with a man dressed as a stag being chased by people in fancy dress and with trumpets has been held to be a game (*Pappin v Maynard* (1863) 27 JP 745).

10.22.5 Unnecessary Obstruction

 Summary   6 months

 s 161(1) offence
A fine not exceeding level 3 on the standard scale.

s 161(3) & (4) offences
A fine not exceeding level 1 on the standard scale.

10.22.5 **Unnecessary obstruction**

Regulation 103 of the Road Vehicles (Construction and Use) Regulations 1986 creates an offence of causing an unnecessary obstruction.

Offences

No person in charge of a **motor vehicle** or **trailer** shall cause or permit the vehicle to stand on a **road** so as to cause any unnecessary obstruction of the road.

Road Vehicles (Construction and Use) Regulations 1986, reg 103

Points to prove

✓ in charge of a motor vehicle/trailer
✓ caused/permitted vehicle
✓ to stand on a road
✓ so causing an unnecessary obstruction on road

Meanings

Motor vehicle (see 10.1.3)

Mechanically propelled vehicle intended or adapted for use on roads.

Trailer

Vehicle drawn by a motor vehicle, but does not apply to any part of an articulated bus.

Road

Includes the footpath.

Explanatory notes

- A motor vehicle left on a road for an unreasonable time may be unreasonable obstruction.
- Consider the use to which the highway was being put by the vehicle causing the obstruction. The highway is intended as a means of transit, not a store (*Nelmes v Rhys Howells Transport Ltd* [1977] RTR 266).

- Where a motorist parks their vehicle on one side of the road and the subsequent parking of vehicles on the opposite side of the road causes an obstruction, no offence under this regulation was committed by the parking of the original vehicle (*Langham v Crisp* [1975] Crim LR 652).

Related cases

Carey v Chief Constable of Avon and Somerset [1995] RTR 405, CA The purpose of the Removal and Disposal of Vehicles Regulations 1986 is to clear the road of an 'obstruction' as a matter of urgency even if no one is really at fault. They do not apply to s 137 of the Highways Act 1980 and reg 107 of the Road Vehicles (Construction and Use) Regulations 1986 which relates to obstruction of the highway without a lawful excuse and constitutes an unreasonable use of the highway.

Practical considerations

- Consider the offence of wilfully obstructing the free passage of the highway, without lawful authority or excuse, under s 137(1) of the Highways Act 1980 (see **10.22.2**). A TFPN can be issued for this offence (see **10.4.1**).

 Summary   6 months

 A fine not exceeding level 4 on the standard scale if goods vehicle or a vehicle adapted to carry more than 8 passengers. A fine not exceeding level 3 on the standard scale in any other case.

Links to alternative subjects and offences

10.23 **Off-Road Driving**

Section 34 of the Road Traffic Act 1988 prohibits the driving of motor vehicles elsewhere than on a road. All references are to the Road Traffic Act 1988 unless otherwise stated.

Offences

Subject to the provisions of this section, if without lawful authority a person **drives** a **mechanically propelled vehicle**—

(a) on to or upon any **common land**, moorland or land of any other description, not being land forming part of a **road,** or

(b) on any road being a footpath, bridleway or restricted byway, he is guilty of an offence.

Road Traffic Act 1988, s 34(1)

Points to prove

✓ without lawful authority
✓ drove a mechanically propelled vehicle
✓ on to/upon common land/moorland/land
✓ not being land forming part of a road **or**
✓ on a road being a footpath/bridleway/restricted byway

Meanings

Drives (see 10.1.4)

Mechanically propelled vehicle (see 10.1.3)

Excluding a pedestrian controlled vehicle, a pedestrian controlled mowing machine or an electrically assisted pedal cycle.

Common land

Land that is—

• subject to '**rights of common**' whether those rights are exercisable at all times or only during limited periods; and
• waste land of a manor not subject to 'rights of common'.

Rights of common

This includes—

• rights of sole or several vesture or herbage (rights to take vegetation or flowers from the land);
• rights of sole or several pasture (allowing animals to be put out to pasture on the land);
• cattlegates and beastgates (a particular right, mainly existing in northern England, to graze an animal on common land).

They do not include rights held for a term of years or from year to year.

Road (see **10.1.1**)

Footpath

Means a highway over which the public have a right of way on foot only, not being a footway.

Bridleway

A way over which the public have the following, but no other, rights of way: a right of way on foot and a right of way on horseback or leading a horse, with or without a right to drive animals of any description along the way.

Restricted byway

A way over which the public have restricted byway rights within the meaning of pt 2 of the Countryside and Rights of Way Act 2000, with or without a right to drive animals of any description along the way, but no other rights of way.

Explanatory notes

- A way shown in a definitive map and statement as a footpath, bridleway, or restricted byway is to be taken to be a way of the kind shown, unless the contrary is shown.
- Nothing in s 34 prejudices the rights of the public over: commons and waste lands, or any byelaws applying to any land, or affects the law of trespass to land or any right or remedy to which a person may by law be entitled in respect of any such trespass or in particular confers a right to park a vehicle on any land.
- Police powers concerning the stopping, seizure, and removal of a motor vehicle that is used in contravention of s 34, which is causing, or likely to cause, alarm, distress, or annoyance to members of the public can be used under s 59 of the Police Reform Act 2002 (see **7.14**).

Defences

(2A) It is not an offence under this section for a person with an **interest in land**, or a visitor to any land, to drive a mechanically propelled vehicle on a road if, immediately before the commencement of section 47(2) of the Countryside and Rights of Way Act 2000, the road was—

    (a) shown in a definitive map and statement as a road used as a public path, and

    (b) in use for obtaining access to the land by the driving of mechanically propelled vehicles by a person with an interest in the land or by visitors to the land.

(3) It is not an offence under this section to drive a mechanically propelled vehicle on land within 15 yards of a road, being a road on which a motor vehicle may legally be driven, for the purpose only of parking the vehicle on that land.

(4) A person shall not be convicted of an offence under this section with respect to a vehicle if he proves to the satisfaction of the court that it was driven in contravention of this section for the purpose of saving life or extinguishing fire or meeting any other like emergency.

Road Traffic Act 1988, s 34

Practical considerations

- Interest in land—includes any estate in land and any right over land (whether exercisable by virtue of the ownership of an estate or interest in the land or by virtue of a licence or agreement) and, in particular, includes rights of common and sporting rights.
- Consider issuing a TFPN (see **10.4**).
- A power of entry to premises to exercise the powers of seizure and removal of the motor vehicle is granted by s 59 of the Police Reform Act 2002 (see **7.14**).
- Reasonable force may be used, if necessary, to stop, seize, or remove the motor vehicle, or of the power of entry under s 59 of the Police Reform Act 2002 (see **7.14**).

TFPN

 Summary   6 months

A fine not exceeding level 3 on the standard scale.

Links to alternative subjects and offences

Chapter 11
General: Patrol

11.1 Police Community Support Officers (PCSOs)

Many police forces now refer to Community Support Officers (CSOs) as Police Community Support Officers (PCSOs), in compliance with ACPO guidelines.

Section 38 of the Police Reform Act 2002 enables the chief officer of police to designate suitably skilled and trained police staff under their direction and control as PCSOs in order to exercise powers and undertake duties as described in Sch 4 to the Police Reform Act 2002.

Under s 38A the Secretary of State has designated a number of discretionary powers within Sch 4 as standard powers, thus ensuring that PCSOs have sufficient powers to support Neighbourhood Policing Teams and deal with low level anti-social behaviour and disorder.

These powers are listed in the Police Reform Act 2002 (Standard Powers and Duties of Community Support Officers) Order 2007 and apply to every PCSO designated under s 38.

HOC 33/2007 provides guidance on the standard powers, duties, and training of PCSOs and lists: standard powers that apply to all PCSOs; discretionary powers and issuing of PNDs that can be designated by chief officers.

Although they may be given the *powers* of a constable under certain circumstances, PCSOs do not have the common law *duties* of a constable.

11.1.1 General powers

Enter premises
- Where a power allows for the use of reasonable force when exercised by a constable, a PCSO has the same entitlement to use reasonable force when exercising a designated power.

11.1.1 General Powers

- If a PCSO has been granted the power to force entry to premises, **it will be limited** to when they are both under the direct supervision of a constable and accompanied by them. The only exception to this is when the purpose of forcing entry is to save life or limb or to prevent serious damage to premises.

Entry to save life or limb or prevent serious damage to property

Standard power

Powers of a constable under s 17 PACE (see **12.3**), to enter and search any premises in the relevant police area for the purpose of saving life or limb or preventing serious damage to property.

Reasonable force

Where a PCSO has a power to detain they can use reasonable force in respect of—

- relevant penalty notice offences;
- relevant licensing offences; (note conditions—see **11.1.2**)
- anti-social behaviour;
- searches for alcohol/tobacco;
- dispersal of groups;
- removal of child to their place of residence under Crime and Disorder Act 1998, s 15(3) (contravention of a curfew notice);
- preventing the person making off when subject to the requirement to provide details or accompany the PCSO to the police station;
- power to remove truants or excluded pupils and return them to school or designated premises;
- offences connected with begging or a relevant byelaw.

Issue penalty notices

Fixed penalty notices

Standard power

Issue **fixed penalty notices** for cycle riding on a footway, litter offences, and offences under dog control orders.

Discretionary power

Issue **fixed penalty notices** for failure to attend school, an excluded pupil found in a public place, graffiti, fly-posting, and dog fouling (land designated under the Dogs (Fouling of Land) Act 1996).

Penalty notices for disorder—Discretionary power

In addition, PND can be issued in respect of a range of anti-social behaviour and disorder offences under the Criminal Justice and Police Act 2001 (except the **theft and litter** listed offences). These offences are shown in the 'Penalty Notices for Disorder' part of this book (see **7.1**).

Require name and address

Standard power

- Can be given this power without also being given the power to detain.
- Can require the name and address of a person who has committed the following offence—
  - **relevant offence** in the relevant police area; or
  - relevant licensing offence within or outside of the relevant police area;
  - failure to provide name and address is in itself an offence.

Discretionary power

- May enforce a relevant by-law only within the place to which the by-law relates. Where a PCSO has this power they also have the power of a constable under a relevant by-law to remove a person from a place.

Detain a person—Discretionary power

- Can only be given the power to detain a person if they have also been given the power to request the person's name and address (but note the licensing exceptions to detention— see **11.1.2**).
- Where there is non-compliance with the request, or the PCSO has reason to believe the information is false or inaccurate, they can require the other person to wait with them for up to 30 minutes, pending the arrival of a constable.
- The individual may choose, if asked, to accompany the PCSO to a police station rather than wait.
- A refusal of the requirement to wait or making off while subject to a requirement pending the arrival of a constable; or making off while accompanying the PCSO to the police station, is an offence.
- See also '**Reasonable force**' (above).

Search, seize, and retain—Discretionary power

- They have a limited power to search a detained person for any item that could be used to injure themselves or others if the PCSO believes the person could be dangerous.
- A PCSO also has a power to search a detained person for anything that could be used to assist escape.
- They must comply with the instructions of a constable about what to do with any seized item and inform the person from whom it has been seized about where they can make inquiries about it.

Meanings

Relevant offence

This means—
- a relevant fixed penalty offence (see above and **7.1**);
- contravention of a dispersal direction under the Anti-social Behaviour Act 2003;

- an offence that appears to have caused alarm, injury, or distress to any other person or loss of or damage to any other person's property;
- an offence under the Parks Regulation Act 1872 (contravention of park regulations/assaulting park-keeper);
- begging (Vagrancy Act 1824, s 3);
- where a person has been convicted of begging and sleeps in certain unoccupied premises or in the open air without being able to give a valid reason for doing so;
- showing wounds or deformities to aid begging and to collect money for charitable purposes under false pretence (Vagrancy Act 1824, s 4);
- an offence under a relevant by-law.

Relevant licensing offences (see licensing **11.1.2**)

Relevant police area (see licensing **11.1.2**)

11.1.2 **Powers relating to licensing/alcohol**

Entry to investigate licensing offences—Discretionary powers

- Limited powers to enter and search licensed premises, other than clubs, under s 180 of the Licensing Act 2003 if they believe that one of the **relevant licensing offences** (see below) has been, or is being committed in relation to alcohol.
- These licensing offences are all connected with the sale and consumption of alcohol by and to young people or persons who are drunk.
- Can enter any premises, other than clubs, for the purposes of investigating a relevant licensing offence with a constable.
- Can only enter premises alone where they reasonably believe that a premises licence authorizes the sale of alcohol for consumption off the premises.
- This limited power of entry and search adds to a PCSO's powers to deal with alcohol related anti-social behaviour and those who supply alcohol to young people.

Power to require name and address—Standard power

- Can require the name and address of a person who has committed a **relevant licensing offence** within or outside of the **relevant police area**. Failure to provide details is an offence.
- Although they have the power to require name and address, the power to detain does **not** apply to licensing offences in relation to the sale of alcohol to a drunk, to under 18 (or knowingly allow such sale), if the offence is believed to have been committed on relevant licensed premises in any police area.

- Powers to enter and search premises other than clubs in relation to a relevant licensing offence are restricted to the relevant police area in the company and under the supervision of a constable, **unless** the PCSO has reason to believe the premises are off-licence premises.

Meanings

Relevant licensing offences

These offences relate to alcohol and are as follows—
- sale (or attempt) to a person who is drunk (see **9.2**);
- allow sale to drunken person (see **9.2**);
- obtaining for a person who is drunk (see **9.2**);
- sale to children under 18 (see **9.1**);
- purchase (or attempt) by a child under 18 (see **9.1**);
- purchase (or attempt) on behalf of person under 18 (see **9.1**);
- purchase (or attempt) for consumption on relevant premises by person under 18 (see **9.1**);
- knowingly consume on relevant premises by person under 18 (see **9.1**);
- knowingly allow consumption on relevant premises by person under 18 (see **9.1**);
- knowingly send person under 18 to obtain alcohol on relevant premises (see **9.1**).

Relevant police area

This is the police area in which a PCSO's powers apply.

Power to serve closure notice—Discretionary powers

Where the offence of persistently selling alcohol to children under 18 has been committed on licensed premises (see **9.1.3**) then a PCSO can enter those premises to serve a closure notice on a responsible person during licensing hours (see **9.3.4**).

Alcohol consumption in designated public places— standard powers

- Powers of a constable under s 12 of the Criminal Justice and Police Act 2001 (see **9.4**) to—
  - require a person to cease drinking alcohol (or anything reasonably believed to be alcohol) in a designated public place, and
  - to confiscate and dispose of the alcohol and its container.
- Seizure can apply to both sealed and unsealed containers.
- The person **must** be informed that failure to comply with the PCSO's request, without reasonable excuse, is an offence.

Confiscation of alcohol from young persons—Standard power

- Same powers (except for the arrest power) as a constable under s 1 of the Confiscation of Alcohol (Young Persons) Act 1997 (see **9.5**).

- Confiscate and dispose of the alcohol and its container.
- Seizure can apply to both sealed and unsealed containers.
- Person **must** be informed that failure to comply with the PCSO's request, without reasonable excuse, is an offence.

Search and seizure powers
(alcohol)—Discretionary power

- In association with the power to confiscate alcohol, PCSOs have the power to search the person if they reasonably believe the person has either alcohol or its container in their possession.
- Search is limited to what is reasonably required for the purpose and does not authorize the PCSO to require a person to remove any of their clothing in public other than an outer coat, jacket, or gloves.
- A person who refuses to be searched can be required to give their name and address.
- If a person refuses to give their name and address, or gives an answer that a PCSO has reasonable grounds for suspecting to be false or inaccurate, PCSOs can then invoke their detention powers.
- If on searching the person the PCSO discovers what they are searching for, they may seize and dispose of it.

11.1.3 **Powers relating to tobacco**

Confiscation of tobacco—Standard power

- Power of a constable or a uniformed park-keeper under s 7(3) of the Children and Young Persons Act 1933 to 'seize tobacco or cigarette papers from any person who appears to be under 16 years old who they find smoking in any street or public place'.
- May then dispose of any seized material in such manner as the relevant police authority provides.

Search and seizure powers: tobacco—Discretionary power

- In addition the power to search the person if they reasonably believe the person has either tobacco or cigarette papers in their possession.
- Search is limited to what is reasonably required for the purpose and does not authorize the PCSO to require a person to remove any of their clothing in public other than an outer coat, jacket, or gloves.
- A person who refuses to be searched can be required to give their name and address.
- If a person refuses to give their name and address, or gives an answer that a PCSO has reasonable grounds for suspecting to be false or inaccurate, PCSOs can then invoke their detention powers.

11.1.4 **Powers relating to drugs**

Seize and detain controlled drugs—Standard power

- Can seize and retain controlled drugs when found in a person's unlawful possession.
- Must comply with a constable's instructions about what to do with any controlled drugs seized. If a person maintains that they are lawfully in possession of the drug then the PCSO must inform the person about where inquiries can be made about recovery.
- If a PCSO finds a controlled drug in a person's unlawful possession or reasonably believes that a person is in unlawful possession of a controlled drug then the PCSO may require the person's name and address.
- If a person refuses to give their name and address, or gives an answer that a PCSO has reasonable grounds for suspecting to be false or inaccurate, the PCSO can then invoke their detention powers.

11.1.5 **Powers relating to truancy and curfews**

Curfew notices—Discretionary powers

- Power of a constable where they have reasonable cause to believe that a child (under 16) is in contravention of a ban imposed by a curfew notice and they should, as soon as reasonably practicable, inform the local authority for the area that the child has contravened the ban.
- May remove the child to the child's place of residence unless they have reasonable cause to believe that the child would, if removed to that place, be likely to suffer significant harm.

Truancy—Discretionary powers'

- Power of a constable, to remove a child or young person to **designated premises**, or to the school from which they are absent, if they have reasonable cause to believe that the child or young person found by the PCSO in a public place in a **specified area** during a **specified period**—
  - is of compulsory school age; AND
  - is absent from a school without lawful authority.

Note: In England only this power also applies to excluded pupils.

- **Designated premises** are those premises notified to the police by the relevant Local Authority
- **Specified area** and 'specified time' are to be determined by a police officer of at least the rank of superintendent.

11.1.6 **Powers relating to traffic matters**

Power to require name and address—Standard powers

- Powers to direct traffic and to require the name and address of a person who fails to comply with these directions. This is based on those of constables under ss 35 and 37 of the Road Traffic Act 1988 (see **10.2**) and allow PCSOs to direct a person driving a vehicle to stop or follow a line of traffic and to direct pedestrians and traffic for the purposes of conducting a traffic survey.
- Can require a driver or pedestrian to give their name and address for failure to follow the directions of a PCSO or a police officer.
- If a person refuses to give their name and address, or gives an answer that a PCSO has reasonable grounds for suspecting to be false or inaccurate, then PCSOs can invoke their detention powers.
- Can only exercise these traffic powers within their own police force area.

Vehicles causing obstruction/danger—Standard powers

Same powers as a constable in uniform, within the relevant police area, under s 99 of the Road Traffic Regulation Act 1984— to require the removal of vehicles that are causing an obstruction or likely to cause a danger to other road users or are parked in contravention of a prohibition or restriction.

Power to stop vehicles for testing—Discretionary powers

- Powers of a constable in uniform, within the relevant police area, to stop a vehicle under s 67(3) of the Road Traffic Act 1988 (see **10.2**), for the purposes of a test under s 67(1).
- These powers would enable PCSOs to help agencies such as the Vehicle Inspectorate, the Vehicle and Operator Services Agency (VOSA), and local authorities to conduct roadworthiness and emissions tests and also to facilitate the escorting of abnormal loads.

Power to control traffic—Standard powers

- Power to control traffic for the purposes of escorting a load other than of exceptional dimensions (either to or from the relevant police area). **Discretionary power** if it is an exceptional dimension load.
- Can also direct traffic in other situations, based on the powers constables have under ss 35 and 37 of the Road Traffic Act 1988 (see **10.2**). This will allow PCSOs to direct a person driving a vehicle to stop or follow a line of traffic and to direct pedestrians.
- HOC 2/2009 dealt with the uniform to be worn by traffic wardens who are also designated PCSOs under s 38, Police Reform Act 2002.

It determined that such traffic wardens should wear the local PCSO uniform without differentiation.

- PCSOs have the power to direct traffic for the purposes of conducting a traffic survey.
- A PCSO can require a driver or pedestrian to give their name and address for failure to follow the directions of a PCSO or a police officer.
- If a person refuses to give their name and address, or gives an answer that a PCSO has reasonable grounds for suspecting to be false or inaccurate, then the PCSOs can invoke their detention powers.
- Can only exercise these traffic powers within their own police force area (except for escorting a load of exceptional dimensions).
- These powers will enable PCSOs to assist with traffic management at public events, road traffic accidents, and other incidents where traffic diversions are necessary.

Power to stop cycles—Standard powers

Power to stop cyclists riding on the pavement and to issue a fixed penalty notice. The power to issue a fixed penalty notice also applies where the PCSO believes that the offence of riding on the pavement has been committed.

Carrying out of road checks—Standard powers

- Power of a police officer to carry out an authorized road check under s 4 of PACE 1984 (see **10.2** for details). This enables a road check (authorized by a Police Superintendent or above) to be established for the purposes of ascertaining—
  - whether a vehicle is carrying a person who has committed an offence (other than a road traffic offence or a vehicle excise offence);
  - a person who is witness to such an offence;
  - a person intending to commit such an offence;
  - or a person who is unlawfully at large.
- It also includes the powers of a constable conferred under s 163 of the Road Traffic Act 1984 (see **10.2**) to enable him to require a vehicle to stop for the purpose of a road check.

Power to place traffic signs—Standard powers

- Power as a constable (under s 67 of the Road Traffic Regulation Act 1984) (see **10.3** for details) to place temporary traffic signs on a road in extraordinary circumstances.
- A driver who fails to comply with a traffic sign placed by a PCSO commits an offence.
- This power helps PCSO provide assistance with road traffic accidents and other road incidents.

Seizure of vehicles used to cause alarm—Standard powers

- Powers of a constable under s 59 of the Police Reform Act 2002 (see **7.14**) regarding vehicles used in a manner causing alarm, distress, or annoyance.
- These include powers to stop and to seize and to remove motor vehicles where they are being driven—
  - off-road, contrary to s 34 of the Road Traffic Act 1988 (see **10.23**); or
  - on the public road or other public place without due care and attention or reasonable consideration for other road users, contrary to s 3 of the 1988 Act (see **10.6**).
- A police officer may enter premises, other than a private dwelling house, for the purpose of exercising these powers. However, the powers, in so far as they include power to enter premises, **are only exercisable by a PCSO** when in the company of and under the supervision of a constable.
- It is an offence for a person to fail to stop a vehicle when required to do so by a police officer (or a PCSO) acting in accordance with this section.
- The officer (or PCSO) must warn the person before seizing the vehicle, to enable its anti-social use to be stopped. But the requirement to give prior warning does not apply where it is impracticable to do so or where a warning has previously been given.

11.1.7 **Power relating to anti-social behaviour**

Require name and address—Standard powers

- Powers of a constable under s 50 of the Police Reform Act 2002 to require the name and address of a person who is, or is believed to have been, acting in an anti-social manner (as defined in s 1 of the Crime and Disorder Act 1998), namely: 'in a manner that caused or was likely to cause harassment, alarm or distress to one or more persons not of the same household as himself'.
- Can then invoke the power of detention in relation to a person who fails to comply with the requirement or appears to have given a false or inaccurate name or address.

11.1.8 **Power relating to terrorism**

Cordon areas—Standard powers

- Powers of a constable in uniform under s 36 of the Terrorism Act 2000, in respect of cordoned areas established under the Act.

- This includes the power to give orders, make arrangements, or impose prohibitions or restrictions.

Stop and search vehicles in authorized areas—Standard powers

- Powers of a constable under ss 44 and 45 of the Terrorism Act 2000 to—
  - stop and search vehicles;
  - search anything in or on a vehicle or carried by the driver or by any passenger in that vehicle;
  - search anything carried by a pedestrian;
  - seize and retain any article discovered in the course of a search by them or a constable under these provisions.
- **However**, the powers cannot be exercised by PCSOs unless they are in the company of and under the supervision of a constable.

11.1.9 Power relating to illegal trading

Park trading offences—Discretionary powers

- Where a PCSO reasonably suspects a person to have committed illegal trading in a Royal Park (or other specified place) and has required a person to await the arrival of a constable, the PCSO may take possession of anything of a non-perishable nature that the person has under their control and the PCSO reasonably believes to have been used in the commission of the offence.
- A PCSO can retain the thing for a period not exceeding 30 minutes until able to transfer control of it to a constable.

11.1.10 Power relating to photographing persons

Persons arrested, detained, or given fixed penalty notices—Standard powers

A PCSO has the power to photograph a person who has been arrested, detained, or given fixed penalty notices elsewhere than at a police station.

Links to alternative subjects and offences

11.2 Mentally Disordered People in Public Places

The Mental Health Act 1983 makes provisions in relation to people with a suspected mental disorder found in public places, in order to ensure their safety and that of the public.

Powers

(1) If a constable finds in a **place** to which the **public** have access a person who appears to him to be suffering from **mental disorder** and to be in immediate need of care or control, the constable may, if he thinks it necessary to do so in the interests of that person or for the protection of other persons, remove that person to a **place of safety** within the meaning of s 135.

(2) A person removed to a place of safety under this section may be detained there for a period not exceeding 72 hours for the purpose of enabling him to be examined by a registered medical practitioner and to be interviewed by an **approved mental health professional** and of making any necessary arrangements for his treatment or care.

(3) A constable, an approved mental health professional or a person authorised by either of them for the purposes of this subsection may, before the end of the period of 72 hours mentioned in subsection (2) above, take a person detained in a place of safety under that subsection to one or more other places of safety.

(4) A person taken to a place of a safety under subsection (3) above may be detained there for a purpose mentioned in subsection (2) above for a period ending no later than the end of the period of 72 hours mentioned in that subsection.

Mental Health Act 1983, s 136

Meanings

Public place

This does not include a place adjacent to areas to which the public have access (*R v Roberts* [2003] EWCA Crim 2753, CA).

Mental disorder

Means any disorder or disability of the mind and mentally disordered shall be construed accordingly.

Place of safety

Means residential accommodation provided by a local social services authority, a hospital as defined by this Act, a police station, an **independent hospital** or **care home** for mentally disordered persons or any other suitable place the occupier of which is willing temporarily to receive the patient.

Approved mental health professional

Means a person approved under s 114(1) by any local social services authority.

Care home/independent hospital

These have the same meaning as in the Care Standards Act 2000.

Related cases

Francis v DPP [1997] RTR 113, QBD Police officers were not precluded from administering a breath test to a drink-drive suspect detained under s 136. Although they had formed an opinion about the suspect's mental state justifying detention under s 136, they could still conclude that the suspect understood both the request and knew what was happening. On that basis they had the right to breath test that person.

Practical considerations

- A suspected mentally ill person removed under s 136(1) can only be taken from a place to which the public have access.
- Section 135 deals with an application for a warrant on suspicion that a person is suffering from a mental disorder and has been, or is being, ill-treated, neglected or kept otherwise than under proper control, in any place or being unable to care for him/her self, is living alone in any such place. The warrant may authorize any constable to enter the place, if need be by force in order to take that person to a place of safety.
- A person cannot be deemed to be suffering from mental disorder by reason only of their promiscuity, immoral conduct, sexual deviancy, dependence on alcohol or drugs.
- If an offence has also been committed, the appropriate power of arrest could be considered.
- The power under s 136 is a **power of removal** for the purposes of getting the person out of a public place until they can be examined by an approved mental health professional.
- As the Mental Health Act 2007 has simplified the meaning of mental disorder and allowed transfer between different places of safety within the 72 hour period, it has removed conflict between the police, medical practitioners, psychiatrists, and mental health professionals as to: the meaning of 'mental disorder', how long the police could 'hold' a person detained under s 136 and whether a police station was an appropriate place for detaining such a person for 72 hours.
- Problems may arise where a person although 'confused' is assessed as not suitable for further compulsory detention under the Act and is released without any treatment or care.

- Forming inter-agency agreements with NHS agencies is encouraged by HOC 66/1990 and 12/1995. Similarly HOC 17/2004 provides guidance and best practice regarding local protocols between the police and health services on handling potentially violent individuals detained under s 136.
- A revised Mental Health COP issued by the Department of Health came into force on 3rd November 2008 and provides guidance to NHS staff and approved mental health professionals when undertaking duties under the Act. Paragraph 10.21 of that code states that a police station should only be used as a place of safety in exceptional circumstances; although it may be necessary to do so if the person's behaviour poses an unmanageably high risk to other patients, staff, or users in a healthcare setting.
- Where possible, the detainee's general medical practitioner should be involved, their role will be important in deciding whether or not there is to be a medical admission.
- Legality of detention issues—
  - People removed from public places under s 136 should be assessed as soon as possible. If that assessment is to take place in a police station, an approved mental health professional and registered medical practitioner **must** be called to carry out the interview and examination (PACE Code C 3.16). Once interviewed, examined, and suitable arrangements made for their treatment or care they can no longer be lawfully detained under s 136.
  - The person should not be released until they have been assessed by an approved mental health professional and the registered medical practitioner.
  - If the decision has been made that the person is not 'mentally disordered', admittance for treatment can only be given by that person's consent.

Links to alternative subjects and offences

11.3 **Illegal Entry into the United Kingdom**

The legislation relating to immigration is vast. However, there are three major aspects that potentially affect everyday policing; these are dealt with below and include: illegal entry into the UK, illegal entry by deception, and assisting and harbouring an illegal immigrant.

11.3.1 **Illegal entry into the UK**

Section 24 of the Immigration Act 1971 creates offences in relation to illegal entry.

Offences

A person who is not a British citizen shall be guilty of an offence in any of the following cases—

(a) if contrary to this Act he knowingly enters the UK in breach of a deportation order or without leave;

(b) if, having only a limited leave to enter or remain in the UK, he knowingly either—

    (i) remains beyond the time limited by the leave; or

    (ii) fails to observe a condition of the leave;

(c) if, having lawfully entered the UK without leave by virtue of section 8(1), he remains without leave beyond the time allowed by section 8(1);

(d) if, without reasonable excuse, he fails to comply with any requirement imposed on him under Schedule 2 to this Act to report to a medical officer of health, or to attend, or submit to a test or examination, as required by such an officer;

(e) if, without reasonable excuse, he fails to observe any restriction imposed on him under Schedule 2 or 3 to this Act as to residence, as to his employment or occupation or as to reporting to the police to an immigration officer or to the Secretary of State;

(f) if he disembarks in the UK from a ship or aircraft after being placed on board under Schedule 2 or 3 to this Act with a view to his removal from the UK;

(g) if he embarks in contravention of a restriction imposed by or under an Order in Council under section 3(7) of this Act.

Immigration Act 1971, s 24(1)

Points to prove

✓ date and location
✓ not being a British Citizen
✓ committed one or more of the acts in s 24(1)

Explanatory notes

- European Union nationals and those exercising EU rights do not need leave to enter or remain in the UK.
- A person commits an offence under s 24(1)(b)(i) on the day when they first knew that the time limited by the leave had expired and continues to commit it throughout any period during which they remain in the UK; but that person shall not be prosecuted more than once in respect of the same limited leave.

Related cases

R v Uxbridge Magistrates' Court ex parte Sorani, Adimi and Kaziu [1999] 4 All ER 529, QBD Provides guidance on the prosecution of asylum seekers as illegal immigrants (see below).

Practical considerations

- Illegal entrants should not be prosecuted for offences of illegal entry or travelling on false documents if they are claiming political asylum, arriving directly from a place where they were in danger, present themselves immediately and show good reason for their entry. This is in line with the UN Convention relating to refugee status and was followed in the case of *R v Uxbridge Magistrates' Court* ex *parte Sorani, Adimi and Kaziu* [1999] 4 All ER 529. This only applies to offences relating to asylum seekers who face charges relating to illegal entry and the use of false travel documents; they are still subject to prosecution for other offences in the usual way.
- Section 25D provides that where a person has been arrested for assisting in illegal entry (see **11.3.3**) or any of the following offences—
  - ◆ s 25 Assist in unlawful immigration to member State/does act in breach of immigration law;
  - ◆ s 25A For gain—help asylum seeker gain entry into UK;
  - ◆ s 25B Assist arrival/entry/remain in UK in breach of deportation/ exclusion order;

  then any vehicle, ship or aircraft used when committing these offences may be seized and detained by a police constable or senior immigration officer, pending a court order for their forfeiture.
- Consider confiscation of cash and property for the s 25, 25A, or 25B Immigration Act 1971 (assisting unlawful immigration) offences.

These and other people trafficking offences are given as 'criminal lifestyle' offences under Sch 2 of the Proceeds of Crime Act 2002 (see 5.6 for details).

 Summary   36 months

6 months' imprisonment and/or a fine not exceeding level 5 on the standard scale.

11.3.2 Illegal entry by deception

Offences

A person who is not a British citizen is guilty of an offence if, by means which include deception by him—

(a) he obtains or seeks to obtain leave to enter or remain in the United Kingdom; or
(b) he secures or seeks to secure the avoidance, postponement or revocation of enforcement action against him.

Immigration Act 1971, s 24A(1)

Points to prove

✓ date and location
✓ not being a British citizen
✓ by any means including deception
✓ obtained/sought to obtain leave to enter/ remain in UK

or

✓ secured/sought to secure the avoidance/postponement/revocation of enforcement action

Meaning of enforcement action

Enforcement action in relation to a person means—

• giving of directions for removal from the UK;
• making of a deportation order under s 5; or
• removal from UK from directions or deportation order.

Either way None

 Summary: 6 months' imprisonment and/or a fine not exceeding the statutory maximum.

Indictment: 2 years' imprisonment and/or a fine.

11.3.3 **Assisting illegal entry**

Section 25 of the Immigration Act 1971 deals with assisting unlawful immigration to a Member State.

Offences

A person commits an offence if he—

(a) does an act which facilitates the commission of a breach of **immigration law** by an individual who is not a citizen of the EU,

(b) knows or has reasonable cause for believing that the act facilitates the commission of a breach of immigration law by the individual, and

(c) knows or has reasonable cause for believing that the individual is not a **citizen of the European Union.**   Immigration Act 1971, s 25(1)

Points to prove

✓ date and location
✓ did an act
✓ which facilitated breach of immigration law
✓ by a person
✓ who was not a citizen of the EU
✓ knowing/having reasonable cause for believing
✓ that the act facilitated breach of immigration law
✓ by that person
✓ knowing/having reasonable cause for believing
✓ that person was not a citizen of the EU

Meanings

Immigration law—s 25(2)

Means a law which has effect in a **Member State** and which controls, in respect of some or all persons who are not nationals of the State, entitlement to enter, transit across, or be in the State.

11.3.3 Assisting Illegal Entry

Member State

Apart from an EC member State, it also includes a state named on a list known as the 'Section 25 List of Schengen Acquis States'.

Citizen of the European Union

Includes reference to a national of a state on the s 25 list.

Practical considerations

- Section 25(4), states that s 25(1) applies to things done whether inside or outside the UK.
- The 'Section 25 List of Schengen Acquis States' refers to Norway, Iceland, and Switzerland; although they are not members of the EC they are signatories to the Schengen agreement.
- Section 25A of the Immigration Act 1971 creates an offence of knowingly and for gain facilitating the arrival into the UK of an individual, and knowing/having reasonable cause to believe that the individual is an asylum seeker.
- Section 25D gives a power to seize the means of transport used for this offence and s 25C provides power of court to order forfeiture of this transport (see **11.3.1**).
- Consider confiscation of cash and property for the s 25 offences of assisting unlawful immigration/entry. This and other people trafficking offences are given as 'criminal lifestyle' offences under Sch 2 of the Proceeds of Crime Act 2002 (see **5.6** for details).

E&S

 Either way

 None

 Summary: 6 months' imprisonment and/or a fine not exceeding the statutory maximum.

Indictment: 14 years' imprisonment and/or a fine.

Links to alternative subjects and offences

11.4 Wasting Police Time

This section considers two aspects of taking up police resources on false pretences, that of wasting police time and of carrying out a bomb hoax.

11.4.1 Wasting police time

Section 5(2) of the Criminal Law Act 1967 creates the offence of the wasteful employment of the police by making false reports.

Offences

Where a person causes any wasteful employment of the police by knowingly making to any person a false report tending to show that an offence has been committed or to give rise to apprehension for the safety of any persons or property, or tending to show that he has information material to any police inquiry, he commits an offence.

Criminal Law Act 1967, s 5(2)

Points to prove

✓ date and location
✓ knowingly caused
✓ wasteful employment of police
✓ by false report
✓ that offence committed **or**
✓ gives apprehension for safety of persons/property **or**
✓ had information material to police enquiry

Explanatory notes

Giving rise to apprehension for safety of any persons or property could apply where a person falsely reports a house fire in order to commit a robbery or a mother falsely reports that her child is missing in an attempt to get her estranged husband back.

Practical considerations

- Consent of DPP is required before commencing a prosecution.
- If suitable, consider issuing a PND (see **7.1.1**).
- Decisions to prosecute are often inconsistent and may bear no relation to the number of hours wasted on the investigation.

11.4.2 Bomb and Terrorist Type Hoaxes

- Consider other similar offences such as hoax bomb calls (see **11.4.2**) or false messages (see **7.12**).

 Summary   6 Months

 Summary: 6 months' imprisonment and/or a fine not exceeding level 4 on the standard scale.

11.4.2 **Bomb and terrorist type hoaxes**

Bomb hoaxes

Section 51 of the Criminal Law Act 1977 concerns bomb hoaxes.

Offences

(1) A person who—
   (a) places any **article** in any place whatever; or
   (b) dispatches any article by post, rail or any other means whatever of sending things from one place to another,
   with the **intention** (in either case) of inducing in some other person a belief that it is likely to explode or ignite and thereby cause personal injury or damage to property is guilty of an offence.
(2) A person who communicates any information which he knows or believes to be false to another person with the intention of inducing in him or any other person a false belief that a bomb or other thing liable to explode or ignite is present in any place or location whatever is guilty of an offence.   Criminal Law Act 1977, s 51

Points to prove

s 51(1) offence

- ✓ date and location
- ✓ placed in any place **or** dispatched by post/rail/other means of sending things
- ✓ an article
- ✓ with intent
- ✓ to induce in another the belief
- ✓ that the article
- ✓ was likely to explode/ignite
- ✓ and cause personal injury/damage to property

> **s 51(2) offence**
> ✓ date and location
> ✓ communicated
> ✓ information to another person
> ✓ knew/believed to be false
> ✓ with intent
> ✓ of inducing a false belief in that person/any other person
> ✓ that bomb/thing was in place or location and
> ✓ was liable to explode/ignite at that place/location

Meanings

Article

This includes substance.

Intention (see **4.1.2**)

Person

It is not necessary to have any particular person in mind as the person in whom they intend to induce the belief in question.

Explanatory notes

- Section 51(1) concerns the placing or dispatching of articles with the intention that people believe that they are bombs or explosive devices; whereas s 51(2) concerns people who communicate false information intending others to believe there is a bomb or explosive device likely to explode.
- This section does not require a specific place or location to be given.

Related cases

R v Webb [1995] 27 LS Gaz R 31, CA The hoax message does not have to give a specific place or location.

Terrorist-type hoaxes

Section 114 of the Anti-terrorism, Crime and Security Act 2001 has created a similar offence for biological, chemical, and nuclear hoaxes. These include actions such as sending powders or liquids through the post and claiming that they are harmful.

> **Offences**
> (1) A person is guilty of an offence if he—
>   (a) places any substance or other thing in any place; or

11.4.2 Bomb and Terrorist Type Hoaxes

(b) sends any substance or other thing from one place to another (by post, rail or any other means whatever);

with the intention of inducing in a person anywhere in the world a belief that it is likely to be (or contain) a noxious substance or other noxious thing and thereby endanger human life or create a serious risk to human health.

(2) A person is guilty of an offence if he communicates any information which he knows or believes to be false with the intention of inducing in a person anywhere in the world a belief that a noxious substance or other noxious thing is likely to be present (whether at the time the information is communicated or later) in any place and thereby endanger human life or create a serious risk to human health.

Anti-terrorism, Crime and Security Act 2001, s 114

Points to prove

s 114(1) offence
✓ date and location
✓ placed **or** sent
✓ a substance/thing
✓ intending
✓ to induce in a person
✓ a belief that it is likely to be/contain a noxious substance/thing
✓ and thereby endanger human life/create a serious risk to human health

s 114(2) offence
✓ date and location
✓ communicated information
✓ knew/believed to be false
✓ intending
✓ to induce in a person
✓ anywhere in the world
✓ a belief that a noxious substance/thing
✓ was likely to be present in any place
✓ thereby endanger human life/create a serious risk to human health

Meanings

Substance
Includes any biological agent and any other natural or artificial substance (whatever its form, origin, or method of production).

Intention (see 4.1.2)

Person (see 'Bomb hoaxes' above)

Practical considerations

- A related offence is food contamination contrary to s 38 of the Public Order Act 1986. It is an offence under s 38(1) to intend to cause alarm, injury, or loss by contamination or interference with **goods** or by making it appear that goods have been contaminated or interfered with in a place where goods of that description are consumed, used, sold, or otherwise supplied. It is also an offence under s 38(2) to make threats or claims relating to s 38(1) or to possess materials under s 38(3) with a view to committing a s 38(1) offence.

- Section 38 concerns 'consumer terrorism' which could involve animal rights activists or an individual trying to blackmail a manufacturer or supermarket chain. **Goods** includes substances whether natural or manufactured and whether or not incorporated in or mixed with other goods.

- The court should be made aware of the disruptions and anxiety caused by the hoax

- How much time and expense were wasted by the hoax?

 SSS   E&S

 Either way   None

 Summary: 6 months' imprisonment and/or a fine not exceeding the statutory maximum.

Indictment: 7 years' imprisonment

Links to alternative subjects and offences

SSS Stop, search, and seize powers   E&S Entry and search powers   **691**

11.5 **Supplying Intoxicating Substances**

This subject is presented in two parts: first, the supplying of intoxicating substances and second, the supplying of butane lighter refills.

11.5.1 **Supplying intoxicating substances**

Section 1 of the Intoxicating Substances (Supply) Act 1985 creates offences, and a defence, in relation to the supply of 'inhalants' other than controlled drugs to people under 18 years of age.

Offences

It is an offence for a person to supply or offer to supply a substance other than a controlled drug—

(a) to a person under the age of 18 whom he knows or has reasonable cause to believe, to be under that age; or

(b) to a person—

    (i) who is acting on behalf of a person under that age; and

    (ii) whom he knows or has reasonable cause to believe, to be so acting,

if he knows or has reasonable cause to believe that the substance is, or its fumes are, likely to be inhaled by the person under the age of 18 for the purpose of causing intoxication.

Intoxicating Substances (Supply) Act 1985, s 1(1)

Points to prove

✓ date and location
✓ supplied/offered to supply a substance other than a controlled drug

s 1(1)(a) offence

✓ to a person under 18
✓ that you knew/had reasonable cause to believe was under that age

s 1(1)(b) offence

✓ person acting on behalf of person under 18 and
✓ whom you knew/had reasonable cause to believe was so acting

---

✓ knowing/having reasonable cause to believe substance/fumes
were likely to be inhaled
✓ by person under 18 to cause intoxication

Meanings

Supply
Provide or make available (something needed or wanted); furnish for use
or consumption.

Controlled drug (see 5.1.1)

Explanatory notes

- This legislation was introduced to try and curb 'glue sniffing' or getting high on the fumes from solvents.
- The offence does not require that the substance must actually cause
intoxication or even have the potential to do so; just that the person
under 18 is likely to inhale it for that purpose.
- There may be a case against a shopkeeper who has the appropriate
intentions and beliefs about the substance, believing that the person
under 18 was going to be intoxicated on the substance supplied.

Defence
In proceedings against any person for an offence under subsection 1(1) it is a
defence for them to show that at the time they made the supply or offer they
were under the age of 18 and were acting otherwise than in the course or
furtherance of business.

Intoxicating Substances (Supply) Act 1985, s 1(2)

Practical considerations

- If you are unsure about a substance's likely effect, it may be possible to
contact the manufacturers who may be willing to give expert advice.
- There is no definitive list of substances and more or less any chemical
substance could be involved.
- The substance could even include products considered harmful such as
aerosols for air fresheners, pain relief and anti-perspirants/ deodorants.
This is because it is the propellant and not the liquid in aerosols, which
is inhaled, and the majority of aerosol products use butane as the main
propellant.

 Summary   6 months

 6 months' imprisonment and/or a fine not exceeding level 5 on
the standard scale.

11.5.2 **Supplying butane lighter refills and tobacco**

The Cigarette Lighter Refill (Safety) Regulations 1999 (SI 1999/1844) make it an offence to supply butane lighter refills to people under 18. It is also an offence to sell tobacco or cigarette papers to a person under 18, with a power to search and seize from people under 16 found smoking in a street or public place.

Offences

No person shall supply any cigarette lighter refill canister containing butane or a substance with butane as a constituent part to any person under the age of 18 years.

Cigarette Lighter Refill (Safety) Regulations 1999, reg 2

Points to prove
✓ date and location
✓ supplied
✓ cigarette lighter refill canister containing butane
✓ to person aged under 18 years

Meaning of Supply (see **11.5.1**).

Explanatory notes
- These Regulations prohibit the supply of cigarette lighter refill canisters containing butane to persons under the age of 18.
- Contravention of these Regulations is an offence under s 12 of the Consumer Protection Act 1987.

Defence

Under s 39 of the Consumer Protection Act 1987, it is a defence for a person to show that they took all reasonable steps and exercised all due diligence to avoid committing the offence.

Practical considerations
- Section 7(1) of the Children and Young Persons Act 1933 makes it an offence to sell to a person under the age of 18 any tobacco or cigarette papers, whether for their own use or not. It is a defence for the seller

---

to prove that they took all reasonable precautions and exercised all due diligence to avoid committing the offence.

- A power of seizure exists, but there is an anomaly in that it only applies to a person who appears to be under 16. A constable in uniform can seize any tobacco or cigarette papers from a person who appears to be under 16, whom they find smoking in any street or public place, and can dispose of any seized tobacco or cigarette papers as directed by the police authority.
- A PCSO has the same powers as a constable to seize tobacco or cigarette papers from any person, who appears to be under 16, whom they find smoking in any street or public place (see **11.1.3**).

 Summary 6 months

Butane refills: 6 months' imprisonment and/or a fine not exceeding level 5 on the standard scale.

Tobacco: Fine not exceeding level 4 on the standard scale.

Links to alternative subjects and offences

11.6 **Animal Welfare and Control of Dogs**

The Animal Welfare Act 2006 is discussed in the first subject area, and the remaining topics deal with dogs that worry livestock; orders for their control; dangerous dogs; and guard dogs.

11.6.1 **Animal welfare offences**

The Animal Welfare Act 2006 has introduced a large number of offences that are intended to prevent harm and distress to animals. The offence of unnecessary suffering under s 4 is dealt with, but other offences within the Act are given in a bullet point/precis form so that the reader is at least aware of them.

Unnecessary suffering

Offences

(1) A person commits an offence if—
   (a) an act of his, or a failure of his to act, causes an animal to suffer,
   (b) he knew, or ought reasonably to have known, that the act, or failure to act, would have that effect or be likely to do so,
   (c) the animal is a protected animal, and
   (d) the suffering is unnecessary.
(2) A person commits an offence if—
   (a) he is responsible for an animal,
   (b) an act, or failure to act, of another person causes the animal to suffer,
   (c) he permitted that to happen or failed to take such steps (whether by way of supervising the other person or otherwise) as were reasonable in all the circumstances to prevent that happening, and
   (d) the suffering is unnecessary.   Animal Welfare Act 2006, s 4

Points to prove

s 4(1) offence
✓ did an act/failed to act
✓ that caused a protected animal to suffer
✓ knowing/ought to have known by this act/failure to act

> ✓ caused/was likely to cause this suffering and
> ✓ the suffering is unnecessary
>
> **s 4(2) offence**
>
> ✓ being responsible for an animal where
> ✓ another person did an act/failed to act
> ✓ that caused the animal to suffer
> ✓ permitted/failed to prevent this suffering happening
> ✓ it caused/was likely to cause this suffering and
> ✓ the suffering is unnecessary

Meanings

Animal

Means a vertebrate other than man. It does not apply to an animal while in a foetal or embryonic form.

Protected animal

Means that it is—
- of a kind which is commonly domesticated in the British Islands,
- under the control of man whether on a permanent or temporary basis, or
- not living in a wild state.

Responsible

A person is responsible for an animal—
- whether on a permanent or temporary basis
- when they are in charge of it
- when they own it
- when they have actual care and control of a person under the age of 16 who is responsible for it.

Explanatory notes

- Matters to consider whether suffering is unnecessary include—
  - Could it have been avoided or reduced?
  - Complying with legislation/licence/code of practice.
  - Was it for a legitimate purpose, such as benefiting the animal, or protecting a person, property or another animal?
  - Was it proportionate to the purpose of the conduct concerned?
  - Was the conduct that of a reasonably competent and humane person?
- This section does not apply to the destruction of an animal in an appropriate and humane manner.
- Summary offence; for Icons/Penalty details—see below

Other animal welfare offences

Section 5—Mutilation

- It is an offence if a person carries out/causes to be carried out a prohibited procedure on a protected animal.
- Similarly the person responsible for the animal will commit an offence if they carry out the procedure or permit/fail to prevent this happening.
- The procedure involves interference with the sensitive tissues or bone structure of the animal, otherwise than for the purpose of its medical treatment.

Section 6—Docking of dogs' tails

- With certain exceptions it is an offence if a person removes/causes to be removed all/part of a dog's tail.
- Similarly the person responsible for the dog is liable if the dog's tail is docked or permits/fails to prevent this happening.

Section 7—Administration of poisons or injurious drug/substance

- It is an offence if a person, without lawful authority or reasonable excuse administers or causes to be taken any poisonous or injurious drug or substance to/by a protected animal, knowing it to be poisonous or injurious.
- Similarly a person responsible for an animal, commits an offence if—
  - without lawful authority or reasonable excuse, another person administers a poisonous or injurious drug or substance to the animal or causes the animal to take such a drug or substance, **and**
  - they permitted that to happen or, knowing the drug or substance to be poisonous or injurious, they failed to take such steps (whether by way of supervising the other person or otherwise) as were reasonable in all the circumstances to prevent that happening.
- A poisonous or injurious drug or substance includes a drug or substance which, by virtue of the quantity or manner in which it is administered or taken, has the effect of a poisonous or injurious drug or substance.

Section 8—Offences involving animals fighting

- A person commits an offence if they—
  - cause an animal fight to take place, or attempts to do so;
  - knowingly receive money for admission to an animal fight;
  - knowingly publicize a proposed animal fight;
  - provide information about an animal fight to another with the intention of enabling or encouraging attendance at the fight;
  - make or accept a bet on the outcome of an animal fight or on the likelihood of anything occurring or not occurring in the course of an animal fight;
  - take part in an animal fight;
  - have in their possession anything designed or adapted for use in connection with an animal fight with the intention of its being so used;

* ♦ keep or train an animal for use for in connection with an animal fight;
  ♦ keep any premises for use for an animal fight.
* A person commits an offence if, without lawful authority or reasonable excuse, they are present at an animal fight.
* A person commits an offence if, without lawful authority or reasonable excuse, they—
  ♦ knowingly supply a video recording of an animal fight,
  ♦ knowingly publish a video recording of an animal fight,
  ♦ knowingly show a video recording of an animal fight to another, or
  ♦ possess a video recording of an animal fight, knowing it to be such a recording, with the intention of supplying it.
* There are exceptions to the video recording offences involving an animal fight and they are that—
  ♦ it took place outside Great Britain, or
  ♦ it took place before 6 April 2007, or
  ♦ it is for inclusion in a programme service.
* Interpretation of terms used in this section are given as—
  ♦ *Animal fight*—means an occasion on which a protected animal is placed with an animal, or with a human, for the purpose of fighting, wrestling or baiting.
  ♦ *Video recording*—means a recording, in any form, from which a moving image may by any means be reproduced and includes data stored on a computer disc or by other electronic means which is capable of conversion into a moving image.
  ♦ *Supplying/publishing a video recording*—means supplying or publishing a video recording in any manner, including, in relation to a video recording in the form of data stored electronically, by means of transmitting such data.
  ♦ *Showing a video recording*—includes showing a moving image reproduced from a video recording by any means.
* Section 22(1) gives a constable power to seize any animal that appears to have been involved in fighting, where the offences under s 8 (except video recording offences) have been committed.

Section 11—Transfer animals by sale/transaction/prize to under 16

* A person commits an offence if they sell an animal to a person having reasonable cause to believe to be under the age of 16 years.
  ♦ Selling includes transferring ownership in consideration of entering into another transaction.
* It is an offence to enter into an arrangement with a person having reasonable cause to believe to be under the age of 16 years, where the 16-year-old has the chance to win an animal as a prize, unless it is—
  ♦ in the presence of and they are accompanied by a person over 16 years; or
  ♦ in the belief that the person who has care and control has consented; or
  ♦ arranged in a family environment.

Practical considerations

- Section 18 gives a constable powers to take such steps as appear to be immediately necessary to alleviate a protected animal's suffering. It is an offence to intentionally obstruct a person exercising the s 18 powers.
- Section 19 allows a constable to enter premises (or part) used as a private dwelling to search for a protected animal in order to exercise their s 18 power, having reasonable belief that the animal is on the premises, and is suffering or likely to suffer. A constable may use reasonable force to gain entry, but only if it appears that entry is required before a warrant can be obtained and executed.
- Section 54 states that a constable in uniform may stop and detain a vehicle for the purpose of entering and searching it in the exercise of a search power conferred under—
  - ◆ s 19 for a protected animal believed to be suffering; or
  - ◆ s 22 for an animal, believed involved in fighting under s 8.
- A vehicle may be detained for as long as is reasonably required to permit a search or inspection to be carried out (including the exercise of any related power under this Act) either at the place where the vehicle was first detained or nearby.
- Section 17 of PACE (see **12.3.2**) gives further power to a constable in order to enter and search premises for the purpose of arresting a person for offences under ss 4, 5, 6(1) and (2), 7, and 8(1) and (2) of this Act.

 Summary

 Maximum of three years from date of offence, **but** six months from date of having sufficient evidence to justify proceedings.

 6 months' imprisonment and/or a fine not exceeding £20,000 or level 4/5 on standard scale.

11.6.2 **Dangerous dogs not under control**

The Dangerous Dogs Act 1991 imposes restrictions on keeping dogs which are a danger to the public and creates offences relating to a dog being dangerously out of control.

Offences

(1) If a dog is **dangerously out of control** in a **public place**—
  (a) the **owner**; **and**
  (b) if different, the person for the time being in charge of the dog,
  is guilty of an offence, or, if the dog while so out of control injures any person, an aggravated offence, under this subsection.

(3) If the owner or, if different, the person for the time being in charge of a dog allows it to enter a place which is not a public place but where it is not permitted to be and while it is there—
(a) it injures any person; **or**
(b) there are grounds for reasonable apprehension that it will do so,
he is guilty of an offence, or, if the dog injures any person, an aggravated offence, under this subsection.   **Dangerous Dogs Act 1991, s 3**

Points to prove

s 3(1) offence
✓ date and location
✓ owner/person in charge of dog
✓ dangerously out of control
✓ in a public place

s 3(1) aggravated offence
✓ while out of control caused injury

s 3(3) offence
✓ date and location
✓ owner/person in charge of a dog
✓ allowed it to enter a place not being a public place
✓ where it was not permitted to be
✓ whilst there—grounds for reasonable apprehension
✓ that the dog would injure a person

s 3(3) aggravated offence
✓ whilst there caused injury to person(s)

Meanings

Dangerously out of control

Means when there are grounds for reasonable apprehension that the dog will injure any person, whether or not it actually does so.

Public place

Means any street, road, or other place (whether or not it is enclosed) to which the public have or are permitted to have access, whether for payment or otherwise, including the common parts of a building containing two or more dwellings.

Owner

Where a dog is owned by a person who is under 16, any reference to its owner shall include a reference to the head of the household, if any, of which that person is a member.

11.6.2 Dangerous Dogs not Under Control

Explanatory notes

The purpose of s 3 is to extend the powers of the courts in relation to dog attacks. Officers are reminded that this Act is not intended to replace other statutes concerning the control of dogs (eg Dogs Act 1871 see **11.6.3**).

Defences

In proceedings for an offence under subsection (1) above against a person who is the owner of a dog, but was not at the material time in charge of it, it shall be a defence for the accused to prove that the dog was, at the material time, in the charge of a person whom he reasonably believed to be a fit and proper person to be in charge of it.

Dangerous Dogs Act 1991, s 3(2)

Destruction and disqualification orders

(1) Where a person is convicted of an offence under section 1 or 3(1) or (3) above the court—

(a) may order the destruction of any dog in respect of which the offence was committed and, subject to subsection (1A) below, shall do so in the case of an offence under section 1 or an aggravated offence under section 3(1) or (3) above; and

(b) may order the offender to be disqualified, for such period as the court thinks fit, for having custody of a dog.

(1A)Nothing in subsection (1)(a) above shall require the court to order the destruction of a dog if the court is satisfied that the dog would not constitute a danger to public safety.

Dangerous Dogs Act 1991, s 4

Related cases (see **11.6.4** for further cases)

R v Bogdal [2008] EWCA Crim 1, CA A driveway shared by neighbouring private properties, in this case a care home and a residential house, was not a public place simply because the public were only able to use it if they were visitors to either B's house or the care home.

Fellowes v DPP [1993] 157 JP 936, QBD A front garden is **not** a public place. Tradesmen are not members of the public but lawful visitors.

Practical considerations

- An order under s 2 of the Dogs Act 1871 (order on complaint that dog is dangerous and not kept under proper control) (see **11.6.3**) may be made whether or not the dog is shown to have injured any person; and may specify measures for keeping the dog under proper control, whether by muzzling, keeping on a lead, excluding it from specified places, or otherwise.

- If it appears to a court on a complaint under s 2 of the 1871 Act that the dog to which the complaint relates is a male and would be less dangerous if neutered, the court may make an order requiring it to be neutered.
- If animals are injured consider using powers under s 2 of the 1871 Act (see **11.6.3**).
- Section 1 of the Dogs (Protection of Livestock) Act 1953 provides an offence for the owner (person in charge) of a dog that has worried livestock on agricultural land. This could be attacking or chasing livestock or being at large in a field or enclosure in which there are sheep. Any dog found under such circumstances (without an owner/person in charge on any land) may be seized and detained by a police officer under s 2 of that Act.

Standard offence

 Summary   6 months

 6 months' imprisonment and/or a fine not exceeding level 5 on the standard scale.

Aggravated offence

 Either way   None

Summary: 6 months' imprisonment and/or a fine not exceeding the statutory maximum.

Indictment: 2 years' imprisonment and/or a fine not exceeding the statutory maximum

11.6.3 **Dog control orders**

Section 2 of the Dogs Act 1871 allows magistrates' courts to make orders in respect of dangerous dogs.

> **Complaint**
>
> Any magistrates' court may hear a complaint that a dog is dangerous and not kept under proper control, and if satisfied that it is dangerous, may order that it be kept under proper control by the owner, or destroyed.
>
> Dogs Act 1871, s 2

Meanings

Dangerous

Is not limited to meaning dangerous to people. It could include other animals.

Proper control

Is also a question of fact for the court. If a dog is kept under proper control, an order cannot be made in respect of it.

Explanatory notes

The expression '**dangerous**' will be a question of fact for the courts to determine, it includes—

- Being dangerous to livestock, birds and other dogs (*Briscoe v Shattock* The Times, 12 October 1998, QBD).
- However, a dog that killed two pet rabbits on only one occasion was held not to be dangerous, as it was in the nature of dogs to chase and kill other small animals.
- A dog could be dangerous on private property to which people have a right of access.

Practical considerations

- Where a court orders a dog to be destroyed, it may appoint a person to undertake the seizure and destruction, and require any person with custody to deliver it up, and in addition may disqualify the owner from having custody of a dog, under s 1 of the Dangerous Dogs Act 1989, or under s 4(1)(b) of the 1991 Act (see **11.6.2**).
- In a statement of complaint, the victim must identify the dog. It is usually necessary for the victim to then identify the dog in the presence of the owner and the investigating officer. Any injuries should be examined by the officer and described in both their statement and that of the victim. This is a complaint rather than an offence, but it is advisable to interview the owner under the provisions of PACE.
- If there has been a genuine transfer of ownership of the dog, an order could only be made against the new owner.

11.6.4 Restrictions on dangerous dog breeds

The Dangerous Dogs Act 1991 imposed restrictions on keeping dogs that are a danger to the public. Section 1 created offences relating to dogs bred for fighting.

Offences

(2) No person shall—

    (a) breed, or breed from, a dog to which this section applies;

    (b) sell or exchange such a dog or offer, or expose such a dog for sale or exchange;

    (c) make or offer to make a gift of such a dog or expose such a dog as a gift;

    (d) allow such a dog of which he is the owner or for the time being in charge, to be in a public place without being muzzled and kept on a lead; or

    (e) abandon such a dog of which he is the owner or, being the owner or for the time being in charge of such a dog, allow it to stray.

(3) No person shall have any dog to which this section applies in his possession or custody except—

    (a) in pursuance of the power of seizure; or

    (b) in accordance with an order for its destruction under the subsequent provisions of this Act.

(7) Any person who contravenes this section is guilty of an offence.

Dangerous Dogs Act 1991, s 1

Points to prove

s 1(2) offence

✓ date and location

✓ breed from/sell/exchange/make a gift of/allow in a public place without a muzzle and kept on a lead/abandon/allow to stray

✓ a fighting dog (as defined in s 1(1))

s 1(3) offence

✓ date and location

✓ had in possession/custody

✓ a fighting dog (as defined in s 1(1))

Meanings

Dog

- This section applies to any dog of—

    (a) the type known as the **Pit Bull Terrier**;

    (b) the type known as the **Japanese Tosa**; and

    (c) any dog of any type designated for the purposes of this section by an order of the Secretary of State, being a type appearing to him to be bred for fighting or to have the characteristics of a type bred for that purpose.

Dangerous Dogs Act, s 1(1)

11.6.4 Restrictions on Dangerous Dog Breeds

- An order (SI 1991/1743) has added another two dogs deemed dangerous—
  - ♦ the type known as the **Dogo Argentino**; and
  - ♦ the type known as the **Fila Braziliero**.

Public place (see **11.6.2**)

> **Defences**
>
> The above does not apply to dogs being used for lawful purposes by a constable or any other person in the service of the Crown, such as dogs being used by the Police, Prison Service, Military Police, and Customs & Excise.

Related cases (see **11.6.2** for further cases)

R v Haringey Magistrates' Court & Another ex parte Cragg The Times, 8 November 1996, QBD, and R v Trafford Magistrates' Court ex parte Riley (1996) 160 JP 418, QBD The offender may not be the owner, in which case the owner must be identified and be made party to, or informed of, a destruction hearing.

DPP v Kellet (1994) 158 JP 1138, Divisional Court A dangerous dog wandered into a public place because the defendant was drunk and had left their front door open. Held: that voluntary intoxication is not a defence.

Bates v DPP (1993) 157 JP 1004, QBD An unmuzzled pit bull terrier was found loose in the back of a car and B was convicted under s 1(2)(d). Held: that a dog in a vehicle may be deemed to be in a public place, if the vehicle itself is in a public place.

Cummings v DPP The Times, 26 March 1999, QBD Common areas located around council housing held to be a public place.

Practical considerations

- For further guidance on this Act see HOC 29/1997.
- The word **'type'** has a wider meaning than **'breed'** in that behavioural characteristics can also be taken into account: *Brock v DPP* [1993] 4 All ER 491, QBD.
- If it is alleged that a dog is of a type to which this section applies, it is presumed to be so until the owner proves to the contrary. If there is any doubt, the dog may be seized and taken to kennels where the owner may have it examined at his own expense.
- DEFRA have published guidance to help the police and local authorities enforce dangerous dog laws more effectively and crack down on irresponsible dog ownership, it provides—
  - ♦ an outline and explanation of current law;
  - ♦ best practice for the main enforcement authorities;

- guidance on identifying pit bull terrier-type dogs; and
- examples of existing local initiatives.

Full details can be found on the DEFRA website (see **Appendix 1**).

 Summary

 6 months

 6 months' imprisonment and/or a fine not exceeding level 5 on the standard scale.

11.6.5 **Guard dogs**

The Guard Dogs Act 1975 was introduced to regulate the use of guard dogs.

Offences

1(1) A person shall not use or permit the use of a guard dog at any premises unless a person ('the handler') who is capable of controlling the dog is present on the premises, and the dog is under the control of the handler at all times while being so used, except while it is secured so that it is not at liberty to go freely about the premises.

1(2) The handler of a guard dog shall keep the dog under his control at all times while it is being used as a guard dog at any premises, except—
   (a) while another handler has control over the dog; or
   (b) while the dog is secured so that it is not at liberty to go freely about the premises.

1(3) A person shall not use or permit the use of a guard dog at any premises unless a notice containing a warning that a guard dog is present is clearly exhibited at each entrance to the premises.

5(1) A person who contravenes section 1 or 2 of this Act shall be guilty of an offence.   Guard Dogs Act 1975, ss 1 and 5

Points to prove

s 1(1) offence

✓ date and location
✓ use/permit the use of
✓ a guard dog(s)
✓ on premises without a capable controller present
✓ and not under control
✓ of handler at all times

11.6.5 Guard Dogs

---

s 1(2) offence

- ✓ date and location
- ✓ handler of guard dogs(s)
- ✓ fail
- ✓ to keep dogs
- ✓ under control at all times
- ✓ on premises

s 1(3) offence

- ✓ date and location
- ✓ use/permit the use of
- ✓ a guard dog(s)
- ✓ on premises
- ✓ when warning notice(s) that a guard dog was present
- ✓ was/were not clearly exhibited at each entrance

Meanings

Guard dog

Means a dog which is being used to protect: premises; or property kept on the premises; or a person guarding the premises or such property.

Premises

Means land **other than agricultural land** and land within the curtilage of a dwelling house; and buildings, including parts of buildings, other than dwelling houses.

Agricultural land (see 11.6.2)

Related cases

Hobson v Gledhill [1978] 1 WLR 215 The handler is not required to be on the premises whilst the dog is properly secured.

 Summary   6 months

 A fine not exceeding level 5 on the standard scale.

Links to alternative subjects and offences

Chapter 12

Powers and Procedures

12.1 Stop and Search Powers

The Police and Criminal Evidence Act 1984 (PACE) creates the generic stop and search powers for a constable in places to which the public has access.

12.1.1 Search and detain

Section 1 of PACE creates the power for a constable to stop and search people and vehicles for stolen property, offensive weapons, bladed/pointed articles, or prohibited fireworks.

Power—search and detain

(1) A constable may exercise any power conferred by this section—
   (a) in any place to which at the time when he proposes to exercise the power the public or any section of the public has access, on payment or otherwise, as of right or by virtue of express or implied permission; **or**
   (b) in any other place to which people have ready access at the time when he proposes to exercise the power but which is **not** a dwelling.
(2) Subject to **subsection (3)** to (5) below, a constable—
   (a) may **search**—
      (i) any person or **vehicle**;
      (ii) anything which is in or on a vehicle;
   for **stolen** or **prohibited** articles, any article to which subsection **(8A)** below applies or any firework to which subsection **(8B)** below applies; **and**
   (b) may **detain** a person or vehicle for the purpose of such a search.

Police and Criminal Evidence Act 1984, s 1

12.1.1 Search and Detain

Meanings

Vehicle

This is not defined. In the *Oxford English Dictionary* it means 'a convey-ance, usually with wheels, for transporting people, animals, goods or other objects and includes (amongst others) a car, cart, truck, bus, train carriage or sledge'. Although, the Act states that vessels (including any ship, boat, raft, or other apparatus constructed or adapted for floating on water), aircraft, and hovercraft, also fall within the meaning of vehicles.

Stolen article (see **3.1**)

Prohibited articles

Prohibited articles given under s 1(7) and (8) means—

- an offensive weapon (see **8.9.1**) being any article—
  - ♦ made or adapted for use for causing injury to persons; or
  - ♦ intended by the person having it with them for such use by them or by some other person;
- an article made or adapted for use in the course of or in connection with the following offences **or** intended by the person having it with them for such use by them or by some other person—
  - ♦ burglary (see **3.3**);
  - ♦ theft (see **3.1**);
  - ♦ taking a conveyance without consent (see **4.3**);
  - ♦ fraud (see **3.9**);
  - ♦ criminal damage (see **4.5**);

Article—s 1(8A) applies

Any pointed or bladed article, in which a person has committed, or is committing or is going to commit, an offence under s 139 of the Criminal Justice Act 1988 (see **8.10.1**).

Firework—s 1(8B) applies

Any firework possessed in breach of prohibition imposed by fireworks regulations (see **8.8**).

Reasonable grounds for suspicion (sub-section (3))

This section **does not** give a constable power to search a person or vehicle or anything in or on a vehicle **unless** he has **reasonable grounds for sus-pecting** that he will find stolen or prohibited articles, any article to which subsection (8A) applies or any firework to which subsection (8B) applies.

Meaning of reasonable grounds

PACE COP A governs the exercise by police officers of statutory powers of stop and search. Paragraphs 2.2 to 2.11 provide an explanation of what are considered to be reasonable grounds for suspicion when conducting a search.

PACE Code of practice A

Reasonable grounds for suspicion depend on the circumstances in each case—

- There must be an objective basis for that suspicion based on facts, information, and/or intelligence that are relevant to the likelihood of finding an article of a certain kind, or that the person is a terrorist (for a s 43 Terrorism Act 2000 search).
- It can never be supported on the basis of personal factors alone without reliable supporting intelligence or information or specific behaviour by the person concerned. For example, a person's race, religion, age, appearance, or the fact that they have a previous conviction, cannot be used as the reason for searching that person.
- It cannot be based on generalizations or stereotyping certain groups or categories of people as more likely to be involved in criminal activity.

Further points contained within this code are—

- Reasonable suspicion can be on the basis of behaviour of a person (eg an officer encountering someone on the street at night who is obviously trying to hide something).
- On reliable information or intelligence that members of a group or gang habitually carry knives unlawfully or weapons or controlled drugs, and they wear a distinctive item of clothing or denote their membership by other means, if that distinctive means of identification is displayed that may provide the reasonable grounds to stop and search a person.
- An officer who has reasonable grounds for suspicion may detain that person in order to carry out a search.
- Before carrying out a search the officer may ask questions relating to the circumstances giving rise to the suspicion; as a result the grounds for suspicion may be confirmed or, because of a satisfactory explanation, be eliminated.
- Reasonable grounds for suspicion cannot be provided retrospectively by such questioning during a person's detention or by refusal to answer any questions put.
- Once reasonable grounds to suspect that an article is being carried cease to exist, no search may take place. In the absence of any other lawful power to detain, the person is free to leave and must be so informed.
- There is no power to stop or detain a person in order to find grounds for a search.
- A brief introductory conversation or exchange is desirable to: avoid unsuccessful searches, explain the grounds for the stop/search, gain cooperation, and so reduce any possible tension.
- If a person is lawfully detained for the purpose of a search, but no search takes place, the detention will not subsequently be rendered unlawful.

Restrictions in a garden/yard (sub-sections (4) and (5))

If a person or vehicle is in a garden or yard occupied with and used for the purposes of a dwelling or on other land so occupied and used, a constable may not search that person or vehicle, in exercising the power under s 1, unless the constable has reasonable grounds for believing that the suspect or—

- person in charge of the vehicle does not reside in the dwelling; **and**
- the vehicle is not in the place in question with the express or implied permission of a person who resides in the dwelling.

Power to seize

If in the course of such a search a constable discovers an article which he has reasonable grounds for suspecting to be a stolen or prohibited article, an article to which subsection (8A) applies or a firework to which subsection (8B) applies, he may seize it.

Police and Criminal Evidence Act 1984, s 1(6)

12.1.2 **Conduct of a search**

Section 2 of PACE provides safeguards for when a constable detains a person or **vehicle** under s 1 or in the exercise of **any search powers prior to arrest**, they are—

- A search can be abandoned if it is no longer required or it is impracticable to conduct one.
- The time for which a person or vehicle may be detained for a search is as reasonably required to permit the search to be carried out, either at the place detained or nearby.
- A search and detain power does not authorize a constable to—
  - require a person to remove any of his clothing in public other than an outer coat, jacket, or gloves; or
  - stop a vehicle, if not in uniform.
- Before commencing a search (excepting an unattended vehicle), a constable shall take reasonable steps to bring to the attention of the detainee or person in charge of the vehicle the following matters and provide the following details—
  - name of constable and police station (where based), plus identification if the constable is not in uniform;
  - object of the proposed search;
  - grounds for proposing the search;
  - entitlement to a copy of the written stop and search record, unless it appears to the constable that it will not be practicable to make/provide the record at the time of the search (see **12.1.3**).

- Where an unattended vehicle is searched, a constable shall leave a notice inside the vehicle (unless it would damage the vehicle) stating: they have searched it; name of police station where based; that an application for compensation for any damage caused by the search may be made to that police station; the procedure as to the entitlement of a copy of the written stop and search record (see **12.1.3**).

Meaning of vehicle (see 12.1.1)

12.1.3 **Written records of stop and search**

Section 3 of PACE details the following procedures to be adhered to when making written records of stop searches carried out by a constable, while exercising **any of their stop and search powers**, relating to a person or **vehicle**—

- A record shall be made in writing of the stop and search, unless it is not practicable to do so.
- If it is not practicable to make a record 'on the spot', then it shall be made as soon as practicable after the completion of the search.
- This search record shall include their name (if known or ascertained), but a person may not be detained to find out these details. Otherwise their description shall be entered in the record.
- Similarly the search record for a vehicle shall include details describing that vehicle.
- A record of the search of a person or vehicle shall include—
  - ♦ object of the search;
  - ♦ grounds for making it;
  - ♦ date and time made;
  - ♦ place where it was made;
  - ♦ whether anything found, and if so what;
  - ♦ whether any injury to a person or damage to property was received as a result of the search, if so, details to be entered on the record;
  - ♦ details to identify the constable making it.
- A person searched, or the owner/person in charge of a searched vehicle, are entitled to a copy of the record, if they ask for one. This can be up to 12 months from the date when the search was made.

Meaning of vehicle (see **12.1.1**)

Explanatory notes

- Fireworks possessed in breach of prohibitions imposed by the Fireworks Regulations 2004 would give grounds for invoking the 'stop and search' powers (see **8.8** for details).
- Articles that are made, adapted, or intended for use for one of the listed offences could include—
  - ♦ crowbar/screwdriver (burglary),

♦ car keys (for taking a vehicle without owner's consent),
♦ stolen credit card (fraud), or
♦ spray paint can/pens intending to cause graffiti (damage).
• This section does not give a constable power to search a person or vehicle or anything in or on a vehicle unless they have reasonable grounds for suspecting that they will find stolen property, prohibited articles or fireworks.

Related cases

B v DPP [2008] EWHC 1655 (Admin), QBD Failure by a constable in plain clothes to produce their warrant card was a breach of s 2(2) PACE and paragraph 3.9 of Code A. As a result the drugs search was deemed unlawful.

R v Bristol [2007] EWCA Crim 3214, CA If a person is searched for drugs under s 23 of the Misuse of Drugs Act 1971 (see **5.5**) then s 2 of PACE applies. As the officer had failed to state his name and police station, then s 2 was breached, the search was unlawful and the conviction was set aside (following *Osman v DPP* (1999) 163 JP 725, QBD).

R v Park (1994) 158 JP 144, CA Procedures laid down in PACE and the COP have to be followed as far as practicable. Any breach of these procedures could justify exclusion of evidence and render the search unlawful.

R v Fennelley [1989] Crim LR 142, CC F had not been properly informed of the reasons for a street search. Held that the evidence obtained was unfair and so was excluded under s 78 of PACE.

O'Hara v Chief Constable of the RUC [1997] 1 All ER 129, HL Reasonable grounds for suspicion can arise from information/intelligence passed to an officer by a colleague, an informant, or anonymously.

Practical considerations

• If a person is stopped to account for themselves, but not searched, they should be provided with a record of the encounter. This can be an electronic receipt and need only contain the ethnicity of that person. A 'stop and account' incident should comply with paragraphs 4.11 to 4.20 of Code A. Further details are given in HOC 32/2008.
• All COP are legally binding; failure to comply with them could result in the CPS declining to institute or continue proceedings. A court case may be lost through evidence being disallowed and the police officer could be subject to severe penalties. Indeed, s 67(8) of PACE provides that failure to comply with these codes will make an officer liable to disciplinary proceedings.
• The COP are not confined to police officers, they apply to all people involved in criminal investigations: HMRC, DSS, private investigators, and security staff in industry.

- Code of Practice A provides assistance and guidance to police officers in the exercise of their powers to stop and search people and vehicles. It should always be read in conjunction with the law in this area.
- Searches based on up-to-date and accurate intelligence are likely to be effective and lawful, thus securing public confidence. Ensure that all stop and search powers are used objectively, fairly, and without any bias against ethnic or other groups within the community.
- Officers must be fully aware and ready to take account of the special needs of juveniles and other vulnerable groups.

Links to alternative subjects and offences

12.2 **Powers of Arrest**

Sections 24, 24A, and 28 to 31 (inclusive) of the Police and Criminal Evidence Act 1984 deal with arrests made by a constable or other people and other related matters.

12.2.1 **Arrest without warrant: constables**

Arrest without warrant

Section 24 of PACE provides the power of arrest for a constable without a warrant and the conditions that must apply before the arrest power can be used.

Powers of arrest

Arrest

(1) A constable may arrest without a warrant—
  (a) anyone who is about to commit an offence;
  (b) anyone who is in the act of committing an offence;
  (c) anyone whom he has reasonable grounds for suspecting to be about to commit an offence;
  (d) anyone whom he has reasonable grounds for suspecting to be committing an offence.
(2) If a constable has reasonable grounds for suspecting that an offence has been committed, he may arrest without a warrant anyone whom he has reasonable grounds to suspect of being guilty of it.
(3) If an offence has been committed, a constable may arrest without a warrant—
  (a) anyone who is guilty of the offence;
  (b) anyone whom he has reasonable grounds for suspecting to be guilty of it.

Necessity criteria

(4) But the power of summary arrest conferred by subsection (1), (2) or (3) is exercisable only if the constable has reasonable grounds for believing that for any of the **reasons** mentioned in subsection (5) it is **necessary** to arrest the person in question.

Reasons

(5) The **reasons** are—
   (a) to enable the name of the person in question to be ascertained (in the case where the constable does not know, and cannot readily ascertain, the person's name, or has reasonable grounds for doubting whether a name given by the person as his name is his real name);
   (b) correspondingly as regards the person's address;
   (c) to prevent the person in question—
       (i) causing physical injury to himself or any other person;
       (ii) suffering physical injury;
       (iii) causing loss of or damage to property;
       (iv) committing an offence against public decency (subject to subsection (6)); or
       (v) causing an unlawful obstruction of the highway;
   (d) to protect a child or other vulnerable person from the person in question;
   (e) to allow the prompt and effective investigation of the offence or of the conduct of the person in question;
   (f) to prevent any prosecution for the offence from being hindered by the disappearance of the person in question.
(6) Subsection (5)(c)(iv) applies only where members of the public going about their normal business cannot reasonably be expected to avoid the person in question.

Police and Criminal Evidence Act 1984, s 24

Explanatory notes

- The use of this arrest power is governed by Code G under the PACE COP.
- An exception to using Code G would be when a person is arrested on suspicion of being a terrorist, in which case Code H would apply in connection with the detention, treatment and questioning by police officers of persons arrested under s 41 and Sch 8 of the Terrorism Act 2000.
- The Director General of SOCA may confer some or all of the s 24 powers on SOCA staff, and nominate them as 'designated persons' (role of constable, officer of Revenue and Customs or immigration officer).
- The above legislation means that a constable/designated person may only arrest a person without a warrant under this general power where—
  - they are about to commit/in the act of committing an offence;
  - there are reasonable grounds to suspect they are about to commit/ to be committing an offence;
  - there are reasonable grounds to suspect that an offence has been committed, has reasonable grounds to suspect they are guilty of it;

12.2.1 Arrest without Warrant: Constables

> ♦ an offence has been committed: they are guilty of the offence; reasonable grounds to suspect they are guilty of it;
>
> **and** the constable has reasonable grounds to believe (more than 'suspect') that it is **necessary** to arrest that person for any of the reasons listed.

- A lawful arrest requires both elements of—
    - ♦ a person's involvement or suspected involvement or attempted involvement in the commission of a criminal offence; **and**
    - ♦ reasonable grounds to believe that the arrest is necessary.
- The requirement for reasonable grounds makes this an **objective test**—that is, it requires some verifiable material fact other than the belief of the arresting officer.
- The exercise of these arrest powers will be subject to a test of necessity, based on the nature and circumstances of the offence and the interests of the criminal justice system.
- An arrest will only be justified if the constable believes it is necessary for any of the reasons set out, **and** they had reasonable grounds on which that belief was based.
- Criteria for what may constitute necessity remains an operational decision at the discretion of the arresting officer.
- Paragraph 4 of Code G deals with 'Records of Arrest' in that—
    - ♦ The arresting officer is required to record in his pocketbook or other methods used for recording information—
        - ■ the nature and circumstances of the offence leading to arrest;
        - ■ the reason or reasons why arrest was necessary;
        - ■ the giving of the caution;
        - ■ anything said by the person at the time of arrest.
    - ♦ Such record should be made at the time of arrest unless impracticable to do so, in which case to be completed as soon as possible thereafter.
- Some of the reasons to consider under s 24(5)(e) may be where there are reasonable grounds to believe that the person—
    - ♦ has made false statements;
    - ♦ has made statements which cannot be readily verified;
    - ♦ has presented false evidence;
    - ♦ may steal or destroy evidence;
    - ♦ may make contact with co-suspects or conspirators;
    - ♦ may intimidate or threaten or make contact with witnesses; or
    - ♦ where it is necessary to obtain evidence by questioning.
- If an arrest is an indictable offence, there could be other reasons under s 24(5)(e) to consider such as a need to—
    - ♦ enter and search any premises occupied or controlled by a person;
    - ♦ search the person;
    - ♦ prevent contact with others;
    - ♦ take fingerprints, footwear impressions, samples or photographs; or
    - ♦ ensure compliance with statutory drug testing requirements.
- Apart from arrest, other options such as—
    - ♦ report for summons;
    - ♦ grant street bail;

♦ issue a fixed penalty notice, PND; or
♦ other methods of disposal
will have to be considered and excluded before arrest is decided upon.

- This statutory power of arrest for a constable applies to all offences except offences under s 4(1) (assisting offenders) and s 5(1) (concealing information on relevant offences of the Criminal Law Act 1967), which require that the offences to which they relate carry a sentenced fixed by law or one in which a first-time offender aged 18 or over could be sentenced to 5 years' or more imprisonment.
- Also some preserved powers of arrest under Sch 2 have been retained.
- Arrest (without warrant) by other people is subject to s 24A of the Police and Criminal Evidence Act 1984 (see **12.2.4**).
- Use of reasonable force – see '**Use of force resolution**' subject at **1.2**.

12.2.2 **Information to be given on arrest**

Cautions

Code of Practice C deals with when a caution must be given.

Code of Practice C

Police officers and other persons subject to observing PACE should be aware of the following paragraphs in this code of practice—

- A person whom there are grounds to suspect of an offence must be cautioned before any questions about an offence, or further questions (if the answers provide the grounds for suspicion) are put to them; if either the suspect's answers or silence, may be given in evidence to a court in a prosecution (para 10.1).
- A person need not be cautioned if questioned in order to—
  ♦ solely establish identity or ownership of vehicle;
  ♦ obtain information to comply with a statutory requirement;
  ♦ conduct a proper and effective search;
  ♦ seek clarification for a written record;
- A person who is arrested or further arrested, must also be cautioned unless—
  ♦ it is impracticable to do so by reason of their condition or behaviour at the time;
  ♦ they have already been cautioned immediately prior to arrest (para 10.4).
- The **caution** that must be given on—
  ♦ arrest;
  ♦ before a person is charged or informed they may be prosecuted,

should (unless the restriction on drawing adverse inferences from silence applies) **be in the following terms**:

'You do not have to say anything. But it may harm your defence if you do not mention when questioned something which you later rely on in Court. Anything you do say may be given in evidence.' (Code C para 10.5; for terrorism Code H para 10.4.)

Explanatory notes

- Whenever a person not under arrest is initially cautioned, or reminded they are under caution, that person must at the same time be told that they are not under arrest and are free to leave if they want to.
- Minor deviations from the words of any caution given in accordance with this Code do not constitute a breach of this Code, provided the sense of the relevant caution is preserved.
- After any break in questioning under caution the person being questioned must be made aware they remain under caution. If there is any doubt, the relevant caution shall be given again in full when the interview resumes.
- Failure to comply with cautioning procedures will allow the accused to claim a breach of this code at any subsequent court proceedings. By virtue of ss 76 or 78 of PACE, the court may then exclude the evidence of confession so obtained.

Statutory requirements

Section 28 of PACE determines the information that must be given to a person when arrested.

Information to be given on arrest

(1) Subject to subsection (5) below, where a person is arrested, otherwise than by being informed that he is under arrest, the arrest is not lawful unless the person arrested is informed that he is under arrest as soon as is practicable after his arrest.

(2) Where a person is arrested by a constable, subsection (1) above applies regardless of whether the fact of the arrest is obvious.

(3) Subject to subsection (5) below, no arrest is lawful unless the person arrested is informed of the ground for the arrest at the time of, or as soon as practicable after, the arrest.

(4) Where a person is arrested by a constable, subsection (3) above applies regardless of whether the ground for the arrest is obvious.

(5) Nothing in this section is to be taken to require a person to be informed—

    (a) that he is under arrest; or

    (b) of the ground for the arrest,

if it was not reasonably practicable for him to be so informed by reason of his having escaped from arrest before the information could be given.

Police and Criminal Evidence Act 1984, s 28

Explanatory notes

- A person who is arrested, or further arrested, must be informed at the time, or as soon as practicable thereafter, in a language they understand (see COP and ECHR), that they are under arrest and the grounds for their arrest.
- When arresting using the power under s 24, the officer must tell the person, not only the offence/suspected offence involved, but also the reason why the officer believes that arrest is necessary. The necessity criteria must also be recorded by the officer.
- If it becomes apparent that a more serious offence may have been committed the suspect must be made aware of these facts immediately (eg originally arrested and interviewed for sexual assault, which now transpires is rape).
- It would be manifestly unfair if defendant did not know the true extent of the situation they were in and any interviews could be excluded at trial.

Related cases

Sneyd v DPP [2006] EWHC 560 (Admin), QBD S was driving a car and as the officer suspected S had alcohol in his body requested a specimen of breath for testing under s 6(1) of the Road Traffic Act 1988. Held: It was only after a positive test had been provided that the officer had grounds to suspect that an offence had been committed and was only then required to caution S.

Edwards v DPP (1993) 97 Cr App R 301, QBD When an arrest is made, reasonable grounds for suspicion and reason for the arrest must exist in the mind of the arresting officer at the time of arrest and be supported by objective evidence. The arresting officer should cite the offence and reasons for making the arrest.

Dhesi v CC West Midlands Police The Times, 9 May 2000, CA The officer informing the offender that they were under arrest and giving the grounds does **not** have to be the same officer as the one who is physically detaining that person.

R v Kirk [1999] 4 All ER 698, CA A suspect is entitled to know the nature of the offence for which they are being arrested/interviewed, especially if it is more serious than the offence for which they were originally arrested.

12.2.3 **Arrest procedures**

Arrest at police station—voluntary attendance

Where for the purpose of assisting with an investigation a person attends voluntarily at a police station or at any other place where a constable is present or accompanies a constable to a police station or any such other place without having been arrested—

(a) he shall be entitled to leave at will unless he is placed under arrest;

(b) he shall be informed at once that he is under arrest if a decision is taken by a constable to prevent him from leaving at will.

Police and Criminal Evidence Act, s 29

Explanatory notes

Confusion sometimes arises about the status of a suspect who has attended at a police station voluntarily. If the investigating officer concludes that the suspect should not be allowed to leave and an arrest is necessary, then the officer should caution the suspect (unless recently cautioned) and inform the suspect that they are under arrest and take them before the custody officer. However, the officer must ensure that the necessity test is satisfied (see **12.2.1**). Simply giving the grounds for the arrest as 'for the prompt and effective investigation' is unlikely to be a good enough reason.

Arrest—not at a police station

Section 30 of the Police and Criminal Evidence Act 1984 provides the procedure to be applied when a constable either makes an arrest or takes a person into custody after arrest by a person other than a constable (at any place other than a police station). the relevant points are—

• The arrested person must be taken to a police station as soon as practicable after arrest.

• This must be a police station designated for dealing with 'PACE' prisoners, unless—
   ◆ it is anticipated that the arrested person will be dealt with in less than six hours, but the location must be a police station maintained by the police authority;
   ◆ the arrest/taken into custody is without the assistance of any other constable(s) and none were available to assist;
   ◆ it is considered that the arrested person cannot be conveyed to a designated police station without the arrested person injuring himself, the constable, or some other person.

• If the first police station to which an arrested person is taken after their arrest is not a designated police station, they shall be taken to a designated police station not more than six hours after their arrival at the first police station unless they are released previously.

• Prior to arrival at the police station, the arrested person must be released without bail if the constable is satisfied that there are no longer grounds for keeping them under arrest or releasing them on bail; if this occurs the constable shall record the fact that they have done so and shall make the record as soon as practicable after release. This requirement should be read in conjunction with the necessity criteria as, once the relevant criterion making the arrest necessary has ceased, arguably the person should be released.

• A constable can delay taking a person to a police station or releasing them on bail, if the presence of the arrested person at a place (other than a police station) is necessary in order to carry out such investigations as it is reasonable to carry out immediately; if such delay occurs the reason(s) for the delay must be recorded when the person first arrives at a police station or (as the case may be) is released on bail.

Explanatory notes

• There is no requirement that a person must be taken to the nearest police station: s 30(1A) states 'The person must be taken by a constable to a police station as soon as practicable after the arrest'—there is no mention of the word 'nearest'.

• The type of record that has to be made, if the arrested person is 'de-arrested' prior to arrival at the police station, is not specified, but could for example include completing a formal custody record, but is dependent on individual Force policies.

Arrest—for further offences

Where—
(a) a person—
   (i)   has been arrested for an offence; and
   (ii) is at a police station in consequence of that arrest; and
(b) it appears to a constable that, if he were released from that arrest, he would be liable to arrest for some other offence,
he shall be arrested for that other offence.

Police and Criminal Evidence Act 1984, s 31

Explanatory notes

The 'liability' to arrest referred to will have to take into account the necessity criteria under s 24(4) (see **12.2.1**).

12.2.4 Arrest without warrant: other persons

Section 24A of the Police and Criminal Evidence Act 1984 details the power of arrest (without warrant) which is available to other people.

Arrest power (other persons)

(1) A person **other than a constable** may arrest without a warrant—
   (a) anyone who is in the act of committing an **indictable offence**;
   (b) anyone whom he has reasonable grounds for suspecting to be committing an indictable offence.
(2) Where an indictable offence has been committed, a person other than a constable may arrest without a warrant—
   (a) anyone who is guilty of the offence;
   (b) anyone whom he has reasonable grounds for suspecting to be guilty of it.
(3) But the power of summary arrest conferred by subsection (1) or (2) is exercisable only if—
   (a) the person making the arrest has reasonable grounds for believing that for any of the **reasons** mentioned in subsection (4) it is necessary to arrest the person in question; and
   (b) it appears to the person making the arrest that it is not reasonably practicable for a constable to make it instead.
(4) The **reasons** are to prevent the person in question—
   (a) causing physical injury to himself or any other person;
   (b) suffering physical injury;
   (c) causing loss of or damage to property; or
   (d) making off before a constable can assume responsibility for him.
(5) This section does not apply in relation to an offence under Part 3 or 3A of the Public Order Act 1986.

Police and Criminal Evidence Act 1984, s 24A

Meaning of indictable offence

An indictable offence also includes triable 'either way offences'.

Explanatory notes

- An exception to the power of arrest by other persons is given in s 24A(5) above; this refers to ss 17 to 29 and ss 29A to 29N of the Public Order Act 1986 (see **7.9**).
- A person (other than a constable) may only arrest a person without a warrant where—
  ◆ they are in the act of committing an indictable offence; there are reasonable grounds to suspect that they are committing an indictable offence;
  ◆ an indictable offence has been committed and—
    ▪ they are guilty of the offence; **or**
    ▪ there are reasonable grounds to suspect they are guilty of it.

- However, this arrest power is only exercisable if the person making the arrest—
  - has reasonable grounds to believe that it is **necessary** to arrest that person for any of the reasons listed in s24A(4); **and**
  - decides that it is not reasonably practicable for a constable to make the arrest instead.

Practical considerations

- Searches, arrests, and any other statutory duties, including taking fingerprints and samples, are all subject to the use of reasonable force.
- Consideration should be given to lawful authorities for using reasonable force and use of force resolution (see **1.2**).
- All the COP are legally binding, failure to comply with them could result in evidence being disallowed and the police officer could be subject to disciplinary proceedings.
- Code C deals with the detention, treatment, and questioning of persons.
- Code G deals with the statutory power of arrest by police officers.
- Search upon arrest is subject to s 32 PACE (see **12.3.1**).
- Section 110(4) of the Serious Organised Crime and Police Act 2005 stipulates that ss 24 and 24A of PACE are to have effect in relation to any offence whenever committed.

Links to alternative offences or subjects

12.3 Entry, Search, and Seizure Powers

Sections 32 and 17 to 22 (inclusive) of the Police and Criminal Evidence Act 1984 deal with matters relating to searching people/premises, seizure and retention of property plus entry and access for copying of seized items. These powers, without warrant, apply either upon or after arrest.

12.3.1 Search upon arrest

Section 32 of the Police and Criminal Evidence Act 1984 creates powers of search relating to arrested persons before they are conveyed to a police station. **The relevant points are—**

Person

A constable may search any person arrested at a place other than at a police station on reasonable grounds to believe that—

- the person may present a danger to themselves or others;
- concealed on the arrested person is anything which might be:
  - used to assist escape from lawful custody;
  - evidence relating to an offence.

Premises

- If a person is arrested for an **indictable offence**, at a place other than at a police station, a constable can enter and search any **premises** in which that person was—
  - when arrested;
  - immediately before they were arrested;

  for evidence relating to the indictable offence for which arrested, providing reasonable grounds exist to believe that the evidence is on the premises.
- If the premises consist of two or more separate dwellings, the power to search is limited to any—
  - dwelling in which the arrest took place or in which the person arrested was immediately before their arrest; **and**
  - parts of the premises which the occupier of any such dwelling uses in common with the occupiers of any other dwellings comprised in the premises.

Seizure from person

A constable searching a person in the exercise of this power may seize and retain anything found on that person on reasonable grounds to believe that—

- the person might use it to cause physical injury to that person or to any other person;
- the person might use it to assist him/her to escape from lawful custody (other than an item subject to **legal privilege**);
- it is evidence of an offence or has been obtained in consequence of the commission of an offence (other than an item subject to legal privilege).

Seizure from premises

Section 19 of PACE applies (see **12.3.4**).

Meanings

Indictable offence (see **12.2.4**)

Premises

Premises includes any place, and in particular, includes—

- any vehicle, vessel, aircraft or hovercraft;
- any offshore installation;
- any renewable energy installation; and
- a tent or movable structure.

Legal privilege

- Items subject to legal privilege relate to communications between the client and—
    - a professional legal adviser;
    - any person representing them;
    - between such adviser/representative and any other person.
- This communication was made in connection with the—
    - giving of legal advice;
    - contemplation of legal proceedings for such purpose.
- It also includes items enclosed with or referred to in such communications, when they are in the possession of a person who is entitled to them.
- Items held with the intention of furthering a criminal purpose are not items subject to legal privilege.

Explanatory notes

- This power to search a person does not authorize a constable to require a person to remove any items of clothing in public other than an outer coat, jacket, or gloves.
- It does authorize a search of a person's mouth.

- The power to search premises is only to the extent that is reasonably required for the purpose of discovering any such thing or any such evidence.
- Any search of premises must comply with COP B.
- This power does not apply to an arrest which takes place at a police station.
- Unless an item is for furthering a criminal purpose, items held subject to legal privilege cannot be seized when discovered during a premises search or executing a search warrant for an indictable offence.
- Legal privilege does not extend to a conveyancing document, solicitor's time sheets, fee records, appointment books, and other similar documents.
- Generally, an expert working for the defence is covered by the same legal privilege as the rest of a defence team.
- If it is suspected that the person is a terrorist then stop and search powers given under the Terrorism Act 2000, s 43 will apply.
- For power to search other premises after arrest see **12.3.3** for details.
- For search warrants see **12.4** for details.

12.3.2 **Power of entry to arrest, save life, or prevent damage**

Section 17 of the Police and Criminal Evidence Act 1984 creates a power to enter and search premises to effect an arrest or to save life/prevent damage.

Power to enter premises

(1) Subject to the following provisions of this section, and without prejudice to any other enactment, a constable may enter and search any premises for the purpose—
    (a) of executing—
        (i) a warrant of arrest issued in connection with or arising out of criminal proceedings; or
        (ii) a warrant of commitment issued under s 76 of the Magistrates' Courts Act 1980;
    (b) of arresting a person for an **indictable offence**;
    (c) of arresting a person for an offence under—
        (i) section 1 (prohibition of uniforms in connection with political objects) of the Public Order Act 1936;
        (ii) any enactment contained in sections 6 to 8 or 10 of the Criminal Law Act 1977 (offences relating to entering and remaining on property);

     (iii) section 4 of the Public Order Act 1986 (fear or provocation of violence);

    (iiia) section 4 (driving etc when under influence of drink or drugs) or 163 (failure to stop when required to do so by constable in uniform) of the Road Traffic Act 1988;

    (iiib) section 27 of the Transport and Works Act 1992 (which relates to offences involving drink or drugs);

    (iv) section 76 of the Criminal Justice and Public Order Act 1994 (failure to comply with interim possession order);

    (v) any of sections 4, 5, 6(1) and (2), 7 and 8(1) and (2) of the Animal Welfare Act 2006 (offences relating to the prevention of harm to animals);

(ca) of arresting, in pursuance of s 32(1A) of the Children and Young Persons Act 1969, any child or young person who has been remanded or committed to local authority accommodation under s 23(1) of that Act;

(caa) of arresting a person for an offence to which s 61 of the Animal Health Act 1981 applies;

(cb) of recapturing any person who is, or is deemed for any purpose to be, unlawfully at large while liable to be detained—

    (i) in a prison, remand centre, young offender institution or secure training centre, or

    (ii) in pursuance of s 92 of the Powers of Criminal Courts (Sentencing) Act 2000 (dealing with children and young persons guilty of grave crimes), in any other place;

(d) of recapturing any person whatever who is unlawfully at large and whom he is pursuing; or

(e) of saving life or limb or preventing serious damage to property.

(2) Except for the purpose specified in paragraph (e) of subsection (1) above, the powers of entry and search conferred by this section—

    (a) are only exercisable if the constable has reasonable grounds for believing that the person whom he is seeking is on the premises; and

    (b) are limited, in relation to premises consisting of two or more separate dwellings, to powers to enter and search—

       (i) any parts of the premises which the occupiers of any dwelling comprised in the premises use in common with the occupiers of any other such dwelling; and

       (ii) any such dwelling in which the constable has reasonable grounds for believing that the person whom he is seeking may be.

(3) The powers of entry and search conferred by this section are only exercisable for the purposes specified in subsection (1)(c)(ii) or (iv) above by a constable in uniform.

(4) The power of search conferred by this section is only a power to search to the extent that is reasonably required for the purpose for which the power of entry is exercised.

(5) Subject to subsection (6) below, all the rules of common law under which a constable has power to enter premises without a warrant are hereby abolished.

(6) Nothing in subsection (5) above affects any power of entry to deal with or prevent a breach of the peace.

Police and Criminal Evidence Act 1984, s 17

Conditions

- Except for the purpose of saving life or limb (human) or preventing serious damage to property, these powers are only exercisable if the constable has reasonable grounds for believing that the person whom they are seeking is on the premises.
- In relation to premises consisting of two or more separate dwellings, these powers are limited to—
  ◆ any parts of the premises which the occupiers of any dwelling comprised in the premises use in common with the occupiers of any other such dwelling; **and**
  ◆ any such dwelling in which the constable has reasonable grounds for believing that the person whom they are seeking may be.
- The power to search is only given to the extent that is reasonably required for the purpose for which the power of entry is exercised.

Explanatory notes

- COP B must be complied with when this power is exercised.
- A 'warrant of commitment' is a commitment warrant to prison issued under the Magistrates' Courts Act 1980, s 76 for failing to pay fines. It does not include 'default warrants' where an offender has defaulted on their payment of a fine.
- An **indictable offence** includes triable 'either way offences'.
- Saving animals could be preventing serious damage to property.
- A designated PCSO has the same powers of a police constable to enter and search premises for the purpose of saving life or limb or preventing serious damage to property (see **11.1**).
- Nothing in this section affects any power of entry to deal with or prevent a breach of the peace, at common law (see **7.3**).

Related cases

Blench v DPP [2004] EWHC 2717, QBD A call was received from a female that a drunken man was taking her baby; she then told the police not to attend. Held: Police were allowed to enter the property as they had reason to believe that a child was at risk and there had been and was likely to be another breach of the peace. Therefore, their presence was lawful and they were not trespassers.

O'Loughlin v Chief Constable of Essex [1998] 1 WLR 374, CA When entry to premises is made in order to arrest a person for an offence, any occupier present should be informed of the reason for the entry, unless circumstances make it impossible, impracticable, or undesirable; otherwise the constable would acting unlawfully.

D'Souza v DPP [1992] 4 All ER 545, HL Entry was forced to a dwelling by police officers to recapture a person unlawfully at large from a secure hospital (under the Mental Health Act). As the officers were not in 'immediate pursuit' they were acting unlawfully. **Note:** This 'immediate pursuit' requirement does not apply to people unlawfully at large from prison/custody/remand/serving a sentence.

12.3.3 **Searching of premises after arrest**

Section 18 of the Police and Criminal Evidence Act 1984, creates a power to enter and search premises after someone has been arrested for **an indictable offence** and provides a power to seize relevant items.

Power to enter/search after arrest

(1) Subject to the following provisions of this section, a constable may enter and search any premises **occupied** or **controlled** by a person who is under arrest for an **indictable** offence, if he has reasonable grounds for suspecting that there is on the premises evidence other than items subject to **legal privilege**, that relates—

    (a) to that offence; **or**

    (b) to some other indictable offence which is connected with or similar to that offence.

(2) A constable may seize and retain anything for which he may search under subsection (1) above.

(3) The power to search conferred by subsection (1) above is only a power to search to the extent that is reasonably required for the purpose of discovering such evidence.

(4) Subject to subsection (5) below, the powers conferred by this section may not be exercised unless an officer of the rank of inspector or above has authorised them in writing.

(5) A constable may conduct a search under subsection (1)—

    (a) before the person is taken to police station or released on bail under section 30A; **and**

    (b) without obtaining an authorisation under subsection (4), if the condition in subsection (5A) is satisfied.

12.3.3 Searching of Premises After Arrest

(5A) The condition is that the presence of the person at a place (other than a police station) is necessary for the effective investigation of the offence.

(6) If a constable conducts a search by virtue of subsection (5) above, he shall inform an officer of the rank of inspector or above that he has made the search as soon as practicable after he has made it.

(7) An officer who—

    (a) authorises a search; **or**

    (b) is informed of a search under subsection (6) above, shall make a record in writing—

        (i) of the grounds for the search; **and**

        (ii) of the nature of the evidence that was sought.

(8) If the person who was in occupation or control of the premises at the time of the search is in police detention at the time the record is to be made, the officer shall make the record as part of his custody record.

Police and Criminal Evidence Act 1984, s 18

Meanings

Occupied

This refers to premises where the arrested person resides or works and may include occupancy as an owner, tenant, or 'squatter'.

Controlled

This includes premises in which the arrested person holds some interest, such as owning, renting, leasing, or has use of the premises.

Indictable (see 12.2.4)

Legal privilege (see 12.3.1)

Explanatory notes

- A search should only be conducted if the officer has reasonable grounds for suspecting that evidence of that or another connected or similar indictable offence is on the premises.
- The search must be conducted in accordance with COP B.
- In addition to making the written authority, it is a matter of good practice for the inspector (or above), who authorizes the search, to endorse the custody record as well.
- Another power to search premises immediately after arrest is created by s 32 (see **12.3.1**).
- A designated PCSO has the same powers as a police constable to enter and search premises after arrest under this power.

Related cases

R v Commissioner of the Metropolitan Police and the Home Secretary ex parte Rottman [2002] UKHL 20, HL Common law powers of seizure still exist.

Cowan v Commissioner of the Metropolitan Police [2000] 1 WLR 254, CA Where a constable may seize 'anything' which is on premises, there is no reason why 'anything' could not mean 'everything' that was moveable and it was practicable to remove. It does not matter that property itself could be considered to be premises, so the removal of a vehicle (being premises) is lawful and can be seized if necessary.

12.3.4 **Powers of seizure from premises**

Section 19 of the Police and Criminal Evidence Act 1984 provides a constable who is lawfully on premises with a general power to seize property.

Power to seize

(1) The powers conferred by subsections (2), (3) and (4) below are exercisable by a constable who is lawfully on any premises.

(2) The constable may seize anything which is on the premises if he has reasonable grounds for believing—

    (a) that it has been obtained in consequence of the commission of an offence; **and**

    (b) that it is necessary to seize it in order to prevent it being concealed, lost, damaged, altered or destroyed.

(3) The constable may seize anything which is on the premises if he has reasonable grounds for believing—

    (a) that it is evidence in relation to an offence which he is investigating or any other offence; **and**

    (b) that it is necessary to seize it in order to prevent the evidence being concealed, lost, altered or destroyed.

(4) The constable may require any information which is stored in electronic form and is accessible from the premises to be produced in a form in which it can be taken away and in which it is visible and legible or from which it can readily be produced in a visible and legible form, if he has reasonable grounds for believing—

    (a) that—

        (i) it is evidence in relation to an offence which he is investigating or any other offence; **or**

        (ii) it has been obtained in consequence of the commission of an offence; **and**

    (b) that it is necessary to do so in order to prevent it being concealed, lost, tampered with or destroyed.

---

(5) The powers conferred by this section are in addition to any power otherwise conferred.

(6) No power of seizure conferred on a constable under any enactment (including an enactment contained in an Act passed after this Act) is to be taken to authorise the seizure of an item which the constable exercising the power has reasonable grounds for believing to be subject to **legal privilege**.

Police and Criminal Evidence Act 1984, s 19

Explanatory notes

- Officers using this power can (at all times they are on the premises lawfully) seize any evidence whether it is owned by the defendant or by someone else, provided the seizure of it is necessary for the purpose(s) described. However, this Act does not provide a specific power for seizure of an innocent person's property when it is in a public place.
- As vehicles are deemed to be 'premises' for the purposes of this Act, they can be seized under the same power (*Cowan v MPC* [2000] 1 WLR 254, CA).
- Motor vehicles, if owned by an innocent party and in a public place, may also be searched under authority of a s 8 warrant (see **12.4**) to search premises for evidence.
- A designated civilian investigating officer has the same seizure powers as a police constable.

Seizure of computerized information

Section 20 of the Police and Criminal Evidence Act 1984 relates to the seizure of computerized information from premises.

(1) Every power of seizure which is conferred by an enactment to which this section applies on a constable who has entered premises in the exercise of a power conferred by an enactment shall be construed as including a power to require any information stored in any electronic form and accessible from the premises to be produced in a form in which it can be taken away and in which it is visible and legible or from which it can readily be produced in a visible and legible form.

(2) This section applies—
   (a) to any enactment contained in an Act passed before this Act;
   (b) to sections 8 and 18 above;
   (c) to paragraph 13 of Schedule 1 to this Act; **and**
   (d) to any enactment contained in an Act passed after this Act.

Police and Criminal Evidence Act 1984, s 20

Seizure of bulk material

The Criminal Justice and Police Act 2001 allows seizure of bulk material in order to examine it elsewhere ('seize and sift').

Premises

Section 50 of the 2001 Act allows a person who is lawfully on premises to seize bulk material when using existing seizure powers, providing—

- there are reasonable grounds to believe that it is material which can be searched for and seized;
- in all the circumstances, it is not reasonably practicable for this to be ascertained whilst on the premises;
- it is necessary to remove it from the premises to enable this to be determined and the material to be separated;
- the existing seizure powers are listed in Pt 1 of Sch 1 to the Act—
  - ♦ PACE, ss 8 to 33 (inclusive);
  - ♦ any of the other 65 listed Acts with their named sections.

Person

Section 51 of the 2001 Act gives the police additional powers of seizure of bulk material from the person, where there is an existing power to search as shown in Pt 2 of Sch 1 of the Act—

- PACE, ss 24 to 33 (inclusive);
- any of the 7 named Acts and sections listed in the 2001 Act.

Explanatory notes

- Powers given under s 50 also includes any other authorized people such as HMRC or designated investigating officers.
- What is reasonably practicable will differ in each case. Factors to consider include the time to examine and separate the material, and the type and number of people involved. In addition, the need to reduce the risk of accidentally altering or damaging any of the material may be relevant.
- Where legally privileged material forms part of the 'whole thing' then this can be seized in order to separate from the bulk of the material.
- Section 51 (seizure from person) could apply for example where the person has a hand-held computer or computer disk which holds relevant electronic data; or a briefcase containing bulk correspondence which could not be examined in the street.
- Section 52 requires the occupier and/or some other person or persons from whom material has been seized to be given a notice specifying what has been seized and why, that they can apply to a judge for the return of the material or for access to and copying of the seized material.

12.3.4 Powers of Seizure from Premises

- Section 21 of PACE provides a person, from whom material has been lawfully seized by the police, with certain rights to access to and/or copies of it.
- Section 22 of PACE provides directions and powers in relation to items that have been seized by the police.

Links to alternative subjects and offences

12.4 **Enter and Search Warrants**

Procedures for premises search warrants, the application and execution process for warrants and applying for access to excluded or special procedure materials are all controlled by PACE.

There are several warrants provided under other legislation such as s 23 of the Misuse of Drugs Act 1971 and s 46 of the Firearms Act 1968. When executed they should be conducted in accordance with PACE and the COP, although they do retain individual powers peculiar to themselves.

12.4.1 **Premises search warrant**

Section 8 of the Police and Criminal Evidence Act 1984 provides the grounds and procedure to be followed when applying for a search warrant relating to an indictable offence. It also provides a power to seize certain incriminating items

(1) If on an application made by a constable a justice of the peace is satisfied that there are reasonable grounds for believing—
  (a) that an indictable offence has been committed; and
  (b) that there is material on premises mentioned in subsection (1A) below which is likely to be of substantial value (whether by itself or together with other material) to the investigation of the offence; and
  (c) that the material is likely to be relevant evidence; and
  (d) that it does not consist of or include items subject to legal privilege, excluded material or special procedure material; and
  (e) that any of the following conditions specified in subsection (3) below applies in relation to each set of premises specified in the application,
  he may issue a warrant authorising a constable to enter and search the premises.

(1A) The premises referred to in subsection (1)(b) above are—
  (a) one or more sets of premises specified in the application (in which case the application is for a 'specific premises warrant'); or
  (b) any premises occupied or controlled by a person specified in the application, including such sets of premises as are so specified (in which case the application is for an 'all premises warrant').

(1B) If the application is for an all premises warrant, the justice of the peace must also be satisfied—
  (a) that because of the particulars of the offence referred to in paragraph (a) of subsection (1) above, there are reasonable grounds for believing that it is necessary to search premises occupied or controlled by the person in question which are not specified in the application in order to find the material referred to in paragraph (b) of that subsection; and

> (b) that it is not reasonably practicable to specify in the application all the premises, which he occupies or controls and which might need to be searched.
>
> (1C) The warrant may authorise entry to and search of premises on more than one occasion if, on the application, the justice of the peace is satisfied that it is necessary to authorise multiple entries in order to achieve the purpose for which he issues the warrant.
>
> (1D) If it authorises multiple entries, the number of entries authorised may be unlimited, or limited to a maximum.
>
> (2) A constable may seize and retain anything for which a search has been authorised under subsection (1) above.
>
> (3) The conditions mentioned in subsection (1)(e) above are—
>
> > (a) that it is not practicable to communicate with any person entitled to grant entry to the premises;
> >
> > (b) that it is practicable to communicate with a person entitled to grant entry to the premises but it is not practicable to communicate with any person entitled to grant access to the evidence;
> >
> > (c) that entry to the premises will not be granted unless a warrant is produced;
> >
> > (d) that the purpose of a search may be frustrated or seriously prejudiced unless a constable arriving at the premises can secure immediate entry to them.
>
> Police and Criminal Evidence Act 1984, s 8

Meanings

Indictable offence (see 12.2.4)

This section also applies to a relevant offence as given in s 28D(4) of the Immigration Act 1971 (defines various immigration offences) as it applies in relation to an indictable offence.

Premises (see 12.3.1)

Relevant evidence

In relation to an offence, means anything that would be admissible in evidence at a trial for the offence.

Legal privilege (see 12.3.1)

Excluded material (see 12.4.4)

Special procedure material (see 12.4.4)

Specific premises warrant

This consists of one or more sets of premises named/specified in the application.

All premises warrant

Being all premises occupied or controlled by an individual.

Explanatory notes

- Section 8(5) and HOC 88/1985 states that the power to issue a warrant under this section is in addition to any other powers to issue warrants.
- The Serious Organised Crime and Police Act 2005 amended s 8 so that warrants only apply to indictable offences, and can be for entry to—
  - named/specific premises—Specific premises warrant; or
  - premises 'occupied or controlled by' an individual—All premises warrant.
- An 'all premises' warrant will apply when it is necessary to search all premises occupied or controlled by an individual, but it is not reasonably practicable to specify all such premises at the time of application. The warrant will allow access to all premises occupied or controlled by that person, both those which are specified on the application, and those which are not.
- Section 16(3) states that a warrant for entry and search must be executed within three months from the date of its issue (see **12.4.3**).
- Where items falling outside those which may be seized under s 8(2) are found on the premises, consider the seizure provided by s 19 PACE (see **12.3.4**).
- When applying for and executing warrants then s 15 (see **12.4.2**) and s 16 (see **12.4.3**) together with Code B must be complied with in relation to application, safeguards, and execution.
- In any application also consider the procedures for access to excluded material/special procedure material, if relevant, provided by s 9 PACE (see **12.4.4**).
- Failure to comply with statutory requirements will make the entry and subsequent seizure of property unlawful (*R v Chief Constable of Lancashire* ex *parte Parker* [1993] Crim LR 204 QBD).
- Officers should be aware of the extensive powers to search without a warrant on arrest under s 32 (see **12.3.1**) or after arrest under s 18 (see **12.3.3**).
- Warrants issued under the provision of s 8 do not normally authorize a constable to search people who are on the premises.
- Such people may only be searched if arrested, but there may be a specific power to search in the warrant (eg warrants issued under s 23(2) Misuse of Drugs Act 1971 (see **5.5**) and s 46(2) Firearms Act 1968 (see **8.6.3**)).
- These persons should be moved to 'sterile' areas in the premises during the course of a search (eg drugs search) in order to facilitate the proper execution of the warrant and complete the search of the person out of public view.
- A designated investigating officer, can apply for this warrant for any premises in the relevant police area, as if they were a constable. Similarly they have the powers of seizure under s 8(2) above.
- In relation to seizure and examination of bulk material see **12.3.4** for details.

12.4.2 **Application procedures for a search warrant**

Section 15 of the Police and Criminal Evidence Act 1984 sets out the procedure to be followed when applying for a search warrant. For quick reference s 15 is given in bulleted form as follows—

Application procedure

- This section (and s 16) relates to the issue of warrants (**under any enactment**) for constables to enter and search premises.
- Entering or searching of premises under a warrant is unlawful unless it complies with this section and s 16 (see **12.4.3**).
- Where a constable applies for such warrant the following details must be given—
  - ◆ grounds on which application made;
  - ◆ enactment under which the warrant would be issued;
  - ◆ identify (as far as practicable) the articles or persons sought.
- Furthermore, if the application is for—
  - ◆ a warrant authorizing entry and search on more than one occasion—
    - ■ ground on which application made;
    - ■ whether unlimited number of entries is sought;
    - ■ otherwise the maximum number of entries desired.
  - ◆ a specific premises warrant (see **12.4.1**)—
    - ■ each set of premises to be entered and searched.
  - ◆ an all premises warrant (see **12.4.1**)—
    - ■ specify (as far as reasonably practicable) the sets of premises to be entered and searched;
    - ■ the person who is in occupation or control of those premises and any others which requires entering and searching;
    - ■ why it is necessary to search more premises than those specified and why it is not reasonably practicable to specify all the premises to be entered and searched.
- Such a warrant shall specify—
  - ◆ the name of the person who applied for it;
  - ◆ the date on which it is issued;
  - ◆ the enactment under which it is issued;
  - ◆ the articles or persons to be sought (identified as far as is practicable);
  - ◆ each set of premises to be searched;
  - ◆ in the case of an all premises warrant—
    - ■ the person who is in occupation or control of premises to be searched, together with any premises under his occupation or control which can be specified and which are to be searched.

- The following points also have to be complied with—
    - Applications shall be supported by an information in writing and made ex parte (subject does not have to be present).
    - The constable shall answer on oath any question that the justice of the peace or judge hearing the application puts to them.
    - A warrant shall authorize an entry on one occasion only—unless multiple entries are authorized, in which case it must specify whether the number of entries is unlimited, or limited to a specified maximum.
    - Two copies shall be made of a specific premises warrant that specifies only one set of premises and does not authorize multiple entries. Otherwise, as many copies as are reasonably required may be made of any other kind of warrant.
    - Copies shall be clearly certified as copies.

Explanatory notes

- Advice and guidance are given in the COP B, under search warrants.
- Where premises are multiple occupancy (eg a single house converted into flats) the warrant must specify all the rooms required to be searched (including the common living areas), and not just give the main address.

Related cases

R v CC of Lancashire ex parte Parker and McGrath [1993] Crim LR 204, QBD The magistrate or judge who issues the warrant should make copies of the warrant and certify them with their signature.

12.4.3 **Execution of search warrants**

Section 16 of the Police and Criminal Evidence Act 1984 sets out the procedure to be followed when executing a search warrant. For quick reference s 16 is given in bulleted form as follows—

Execution procedure

A warrant to enter and search **premises**—
- may be executed by any constable;
- it may authorize persons to accompany any constable who is executing it;
    - such a person has the same powers as the constable, but only whilst in the company and under the supervision of a constable;
        - such a person will then be able to execute the warrant, and seize anything to which the warrant relates;
- must be executed within three months from the date of its issue;

12.4.3 Execution of Search Warrants

- must be executed at a reasonable hour unless it appears that the purpose of a search may be frustrated on an entry at a reasonable hour;
- will only authorize a search to the extent required for the purpose for which the warrant was issued.

Specifically, no premises may be entered or searched unless an inspector (or above) authorizes, in writing, entry for—

- an all premises warrant—
  - ◆ premises which are not specified;
- a multiple entries warrant—
  - ◆ for the second or subsequent entry and search;

Notification requirements exist: when a constable is seeking to execute a warrant to enter and search premises, the constable shall—

- where the occupier is present—
  - ◆ identify themselves to the occupier. If not in uniform documentary evidence produced to show that they are a constable;
  - ◆ produce the warrant and supply a copy of the warrant to the occupier;
- if the occupier is not present, but some other person is present who appears to the constable to be in charge of the premises—
  - ◆ the constable shall deal with that person as if they were the occupier and comply with the above requirements;
- if there is no person present (occupier or in charge)—
  - ◆ the constable shall leave a copy of the warrant in a prominent place on the premises.

Where a constable has executed a warrant they shall—

- endorse the warrant stating whether—
  - ◆ the articles or persons sought were found;
  - ◆ any articles were seized, other than articles which were sought.
- unless the warrant is for one set of premises only—
  - ◆ separately endorse each set of premises entered and searched providing the above details.

A warrant shall be returned to the **appropriate person**—

- when it has been executed;
- in the case of—
  - ◆ a **specific premises warrant** (not been executed);
  - ◆ an all premises warrant;
  - ◆ any warrant authorizing multiple entries;

upon the expiry of the three month period or sooner.

Meanings

Premises (see **12.3.1**)

All premises warrant (see **12.4.1**)

Multiple entries warrant (see **12.4.1**)

Appropriate person

If the warrant was issued by—

- a justice of the peace, it will be the designated officer for the local justice area in which the justice was acting when the warrant was issued;
- a judge, it will be the appropriate officer of the court from which the judge issued it.

Specific premises warrant (see **12.4.1**)

Explanatory notes

- A warrant returned to the appropriate person shall be retained by that person for 12 months from its return.
- An occupier of premises to which the warrant relates can inspect the warrant (and should be allowed to do so) during the 12 month retaining period.
- When executing a search warrant, advice and guidance should be obtained from the COP B, under search warrants.
- A person authorized in the warrant to accompany the constable may be an expert in computing or financial matters. Such an expert will then be able to take a more active role in the search and in seizing material, rather than merely being present in an advisory or clerical capacity.
- In practical terms the supervising constable must identify any accompanying persons to the occupier of premises prior to the start of any search and explain that person's role in the process. The constable in charge will have overall supervisory responsibility and will be accountable for any action taken.

12.4.4 Access to excluded and special procedure material

Section 9 of the Police and Criminal Evidence Act 1984 provides the procedures to be adopted in order to gain access to excluded material and special procedure material.

Access procedure

(1) A constable may obtain access to **excluded material** or **special procedure material** for the purposes of a criminal investigation by making an application under **Schedule 1** and in accordance with that Schedule.

(2) Any Act (including a local Act) passed before this Act under which a search of **premises** for the purposes of a criminal investigation could be authorised by the issue of a warrant to a constable shall cease to have effect so far as it relates to the authorisation of searches—

12.4.4 Access to Excluded and Special Procedure Material

    (a) for items subject to legal privilege; or
    (b) for excluded material; or
    (c) for special procedure material consisting of documents or records other than documents.

                            Police and Criminal Evidence Act 1984, s 9

Meanings

Excluded material

Means—

- **personal records** acquired or created in the course of any trade, business, profession, or other occupation or for the purposes of any paid or unpaid office;
- human tissue or tissue fluid taken for the purposes of diagnosis or medical treatment held in confidence;
- both sets of material held in confidence subject to—
  - ♦ an express or implied undertaking to do so;
  - ♦ a disclosure restriction or an obligation of secrecy contained in any legislation;

or

- **journalistic material** which consists of documents or records other than documents, being held or continuously held in confidence (by one or more persons), subject to an undertaking, restriction or obligation of confidence since it was first acquired or created for the purposes of journalism.

Personal records

Means documentary and other records concerning an individual (whether living or dead) who can be identified from them and relates to—

- their physical or mental health;
- spiritual counselling or assistance given/to be given to them; or
- counselling or assistance given/to be given for their personal welfare, by any voluntary organization or individual who by reason of—
  - ♦ their office or occupation has responsibilities for this; or
  - ♦ an order a court has responsibilities for his supervision.

Journalistic material

- Is material acquired or created for the purposes of journalism?
- Providing it is in the possession of a person who acquired or created it for this purpose.
- It will be acquired if a person receives the material from someone who intends that the recipient uses it for that purpose.

Special procedure material

- Includes journalistic material, other than excluded material.
- Includes material, other than items subject to legal privilege and excluded material, in the possession of a person who acquired or created it in the course of any trade, business, profession, or for the purpose of any paid or unpaid office; and holds it in confidence subject to—
  - ◆ an express or implied undertaking to do so;
  - ◆ a disclosure restriction or an obligation of secrecy contained in any legislation.
- Where material is acquired by—
  - ◆ an employee from their employer in their course of employment;
  - ◆ a company from an associated company;
  it is only special procedure material if it was special procedure material immediately before the acquisition.
- Where material is created by—
  - ◆ an employee in the course of their employment;
  - ◆ a company on behalf of an associated company;
  it is only special procedure material if it would have been special procedure material had the employer/associated company created it.

Schedule 1

This gives full details of the procedure to be followed when making an application to a judge in order to gain access to excluded material or special procedure material.

Premises (see **12.3.1**)

Legal privilege (see **12.3.1**)

Explanatory notes

- COP B provides guidance regarding the conduct of searches and advice on Sch 1 searches.
- The CPS makes Sch 1 applications and advice should be sought from them in any application.
- A designated investigation officer can obtain the same access to excluded and special procedure material as a police constable.
- Case law has established that—
  - ◆ police cannot routinely examine hospital records;
  - ◆ search warrant not lawful without the proper paperwork;
  - ◆ a Sch 1 notice should specify the documents being sought.
- In relation to seizure and examination of bulk material see **12.3.4** for details.
- Officers should be mindful of the powers to search (without a warrant) on arrest (see **12.3.1**) or after arrest (see **12.3.3**).
- Special procedure and excluded material can be searched for and seized under PACE, ss 18 and 32, provided—
  - ◆ lawful arrest is made, in good faith; **and**
  - ◆ the search is carried out strictly within the terms of those sections.

12.4.4 Access to Excluded and Special Procedure Material

Related cases

R (on application Faisaltex Ltd) v Preston CC [2008] EWHC (Admin) 2832, QBD A computer and hard drive counted as a single item within 'material' under s 8(1) PACE. This power was sufficient without using s 51 of the Criminal Justice and Police Act 2001 as well.

R v Leaf [2005] EWCA Crim 2152, CA Special procedure and excluded material can be searched for and seized under ss 18 and 32 provided a proper, good faith arrest is made; and that the search is within the terms of those sections.

R v Cardiff CC ex parte Kellam The Times, 3 May 1993 QBD Hospital records relate to the health of an identifiable person; this means that they are 'excluded material' for which there was no power to gain access prior to PACE, so there is no power to gain access now.

R v Manchester CC ex parte Taylor [1988] 2 All ER 769, QBD It is sufficient to give verbal details of documents required to the recipient of a Sch 1 notice.

R v Maidstone CC ex parte Waitt [1988] Crim LR 384, QBD A hearing under Sch 1 should be with the knowledge and in the presence of both parties.

R v Leicester CC ex parte DPP [1987] 3 All ER 654, QBD Normally parties to an application are the police and those with custody of the documents being sought.

R v Bristol CC ex parte Bristol Press and Picture Agency (1986) 85 Cr App R 190, QBD Press photographs showing criminal acts. Access to them could identify the suspects. It was in the public interest to grant the order. Conditions were met.

Links to alternative subjects and offences

Chapter 13

Patrol Matters and Guidance

13.1 Missing Persons

Guidelines are based on established 'best practice' and are intended to provide guidance and assistance to police officers when taking a 'missing from home' report. However, individual force policies must always be complied with and acted upon.

A missing person can be defined as anyone whose whereabouts are unknown, whatever the circumstances of disappearance, who will be considered missing until located and their well-being or otherwise established.

This is a wide definition and there will be times when a person is missing, but police intervention is not always appropriate (eg tracing a long lost relative).

It is important to note that the reason a person has gone missing may be related to their involvement/planned involvement in an offence, for example terrorism. This should be borne in mind when dealing with initial reports.

Initial report

- An officer from the area from where the person has gone missing must attend the report.
- The officer must be aware that a missing person report could turn into the investigation of a serious crime. The officer must **investigate** why the person is missing, where they may have gone, and gather and preserve evidence. Remember it is not a 'paper exercise', just a matter of filling in a form: it should be treated with the seriousness that it deserves.
- The initiating officer taking the report must obtain the following—
  - ◆ name, address, date of birth, sex, skin and hair colour, details of any marks, scars, tattoos, or peculiarities (eg walks with a limp, stutters);
  - ◆ description of height, build, hair style/length, clothing (including shoes and outer clothing);
  - ◆ establish the circumstances of the disappearance—what was said, any clues as to where the missing person may be/may intend to go (keep accurate records of what is said and by whom);

- ◆ time and date last seen, where and by whom (obtain full details of the people who had last seen/spoken to the missing person—including contact details);
- ◆ a recent photograph (obtain permission to release this photograph, if required, to the press/television);
- ◆ has the missing person left a note, taken any spare clothing, got a mobile phone (obtain number), passport, money, transport, access to savings/bank accounts, holder of credit/debit cards?
- ◆ full details (including contact numbers) of friends, relatives, work/school;
- ◆ if this person has gone missing before—details/circumstances, where were they found?
- ◆ suicidal, medical conditions, medication to be taken, details of doctor.
- Take details of the person reporting, relationship and contact details. Assess what, if any, level of support is required for the family/person reporting.
- Make a risk assessment (see below) concerning the missing person and record the reasons for your decision.
- Gather relevant evidence for the investigation to continue. The higher the risk the more detailed the information required.
- In a high-risk case notify a supervisor immediately. In a medium-risk case, notify a supervisor without undue delay and in a low-risk case notify a supervisor by the end of the tour of duty.
- Search the home and immediate vicinity. If appropriate, seize any items of investigatory/evidential value—diary, notes, correspondence, details of any medical treatment, and obtain a recent photograph.
- Carry out all relevant enquiries and make further searches to locate missing person.
- Circulate the person on PNC and any other relevant systems.

Making a risk assessment

When making such a risk assessment, all factors that lead to the decision must be fully recorded by the officer attending the report.

High risk

- Is in danger due to their own vulnerability.
- May have been the victim of a serious crime.
- May have been planning a serious crime.
- There are substantial grounds for believing that the public is in danger.

Action

- Immediate deployment of appropriate resources.
- Notify supervision immediately for involvement in the investigation.
- Notify a member of the senior management team.
- If the victim of/suspected in planning a serious crime an SIO should be appointed.
- A press/media strategy should be implemented.
- Establish and maintain close contact with other relevant agencies.

Medium risk

- The person is likely to be subject to danger and/or is a risk to themselves or others.

Action

- Notify supervision regarding the circumstances and concerns.
- Deployment of appropriate resources.
- Continue an active and measured response by police and other agencies.
- Involve the press/media.

Low risk

- No apparent threat of danger to themselves or the public.

Action

- Carry out appropriate enquiries to locate the missing person.
- Notify supervision by the end of the tour of duty.
- Keep the report under regular review.

Risk assessment factors

- Is the person vulnerable, due to age or infirmity or any other factor?
- Is this type of behaviour out of character?
- Is the person suspected of being the victim of a serious crime in progress (eg abduction)?
- Are there any indications that the person is likely to commit suicide?
- Is there a reason for the person to go missing?
- Are there any indications that the person made preparations for their absence?
- What was the person intending to do when they were last seen (ie go out to the shops, see a friend), and did they carry out that intention?
- Are there family and/or relationship problems or recent history of family conflict?
- Is the person a victim or perpetrator of domestic violence?
- Does the missing person have any physical illness, disability, or mental health problems?
- Are they on the Child Protection Register?
- Do they need essential medical treatment that is not likely to be available to them?
- Is there a belief that the person may not have the physical ability to interact safely with others or in an unknown environment?
- Are there any ongoing bullying or harassment, sexual, racial, or homophobic or any other cultural or community concerns?
- Were they involved in a violent and/or racist incident immediately prior to their disappearance?
- Are they (or a relative) a witness to an offence or otherwise involved in proceedings (eg a juror)?
- Have they previously been missing and been exposed to or suffered harm?

- Any problems with work, school, college, university, or money?
- Are they drug or alcohol dependent?
- Any other problem which may affect the risk assessment not mentioned here?

Subsequent investigation

- A detailed record must be kept of all enquiries carried out.
- Supervision must review the risk assessment and it should be reconsidered at every hand over.
- The report must be regularly reviewed.
- The point of contact for the police must be kept up to date with all the progress.
- The Police National Missing Persons Bureau should be notified within 14 days.
- Could the person be in hospital, prison or custody?
- Consider CCTV, taxi records, details of bank and phone records.
- There are different categories of missing persons, which could have an effect on the subsequent investigation:
  - lost person—a person who is temporarily disorientated such as a young child or elderly person;
  - missing person who has gone voluntarily—a person who has made a conscious decision to take this particular course of action;
  - missing person who is under the influence of a third party—a person who has gone missing against their will (eg abduction or kidnap).
- **It is always advisable to think the worst until the contrary is proved.**

Persons in care

People in care are mostly, by their very nature, vulnerable and special consideration should be given to any person who goes missing from care.

Children in care

- Children in local authority care account for the largest number of missing person's reports.
- The categories of high, medium, and low risk still apply here but there is an additional category—unauthorized absence.
- Unauthorized absence is where the child has failed to return to the care home on time, is staying with a friend at a known location, or running away after a dispute with a member of staff.
- A risk assessment should be carried out as normal. The situation should be kept under review and if the child has not returned within a few hours, then the child should be reported missing.
- The children's home and foster carers are expected to act as any reasonable parent would and make the necessary enquiries into the whereabouts of the child, before making a report to the police.

Found safe and well

- When the missing person is located, if they are over 16 there is no obligation to inform the families of their whereabouts (only that they are safe and well), if it is against the person's wishes.
- If the missing person is under 16, then there **is** an obligation to return the child to their home or a **safe** location, if there are any doubts about the child's safety.
- The report must be completed with as much detail as possible as to the circumstances in which the person was found.
- All computer systems must be updated and relevant agencies informed of the return of the missing person.

Links to alternative subjects and offences

13.2 **Child Abuse**

Specialist departments will carry out most of the investigations into child abuse cases. However, patrol officers may well be the first point of contact with the victim and their families/carers and it is important to recognize child abuse and what action to take.

The following information is based on guidelines established as 'best practice'. However, Force policy must be adhered to and this section is intended as a guide to assist in following that policy.

Child abuse is—

- abuse involving any person under the age of 18;
- the abuse can be physical, emotional, or sexual;
- the abuse can also take the form of neglect, a persistent failure to meet a child's basic physical or psychological needs which is likely to result in serious impairment of the child's development or health.

Taking the initial report

The following is a suggested checklist regarding the relevant information to obtain when taking the initial report. All reports should be treated as serious no matter how minor they appear to be.

Checklist

- Details of the reporting person and relationship to the child.
- Nature and location of the incident or concern.
- Details of the child.
- Current location and identity of any suspect including relationship to child.
- If name not known, then a detailed description of the suspect.
- Whether there are any injuries. If so, details of injuries and whether any medical assistance is required.
- Details of any other children present and whether they are safe.
- Details and locations of any witnesses.
- Whether weapons were used.
- Whether any person present has taken alcohol or drugs.
- Whether there is any history of involvement by social services. If so, details of the social worker.
- Whether there are any relevant court orders in place.
- Whether there are any details of any special needs.
- Details of the behaviour of all parties, reporting person, victim, and suspect.
- A verbatim account of the caller's story.
- Details of the child's school and doctor, if known.

- The Child Protection/Child Abuse Unit and a supervisor must be notified as soon as possible.
- Check all computer systems both national (PNC) and local, including the Child Protection Register. This can be done through the Child Protection Unit or through Social Services.

Welfare of the child

In child abuse cases, the welfare of the child is paramount. As patrol officers you have a responsibility to check the welfare of the child.

- There is no legal requirement for a parent or guardian to be present for an officer to speak to a child.
- If that person is suspected of being involved in the abuse then **every** attempt should be made to speak to the child separately.
- Care should be taken when speaking to the child, to limit the conversation to the welfare of the child and obtaining the minimum amount of information about the incident (offence, suspect, and location), for fear of prejudicing any subsequent prosecutions.
- Officers should take into account the physical appearance, condition, and behaviour of the child.
- Officers should be mindful of the reasons behind a parent/guardian's decision not to allow the police to assess the welfare of a child.
- Further enquiries should be made to establish the welfare of the child, if cooperation with the police is refused.
- Officers should make a record of reasons for refusal of cooperation.

Police powers

- Powers of entry (see **12.3** for details)—
  - Under **s 17 PACE** a constable may enter premises for the purpose of arresting a person for an indictable offence.
  - Under **s 17 PACE** a constable may enter and search premises for the purpose of saving life or limb or preventing serious damage to property.
  - Under **common law** a constable has the power of entry to deal with or prevent a breach of the peace.
  - A warrant may be issued under **Children Act 1989, s 48** to search for children who may be in need of emergency protection.
- For offences involving child cruelty see **2.4.1** for further details.
- Taking a child into police protection (see **2.4.2** for further details)—
  - The **Children Act 1989, s 46**, allows a constable to remove a child if they have reasonable cause to believe is at risk of **significant harm** or to keep the child at place of safety such as a hospital.
  - 'Harm' is defined as 'ill treatment or the impairment of health or development' and could include 'impairment suffered from seeing or hearing ill treatment of another'.

13.2 Child Abuse

- ‘**Significant**’ may be a traumatic event such as suffocating, poisoning, or other violence or a series of events, which together would constitute significant harm.
- Before exercising this power advice should be sought from the Child Protection Unit where possible.
- If this power is used the duty inspector must be informed as soon as possible.
- The child can only be removed under this section for a maximum of 72 hours (although it is unlikely to be for this length of time).
- This power should only be used in emergency situations. Wherever possible child protection orders should be granted by the courts.
- Where the power is exercised there will be an **investigating** officer (the officer who initially took the child into police protection) and a **designated** officer (an officer of at least the rank of inspector who is responsible for safeguarding and/or promoting the child's welfare).
- The child should **not** be taken to a police station (only in exceptional circumstances). Where possible, early liaison with the local authority should be undertaken to find the child suitable accommodation.
- Suitable accommodation would be a registered children's home, certified foster care, or where necessary with relatives or other suitable carers (appropriate checks must be carried out, PNC, sex offenders register, child protection register, and any relevant local systems). The investigating officer must ensure that placement with relatives does not place the child at further risk.
- If the local authority is not already aware of the situation, the investigating officer should inform them as soon as possible of the circumstances.
- The investigating officer should also keep the child informed, at all stages, of what has and is going to happen. If appropriate take into account and act upon their views and wishes.

Links to alternative subjects and offences

13.3 **Domestic Violence**

The information below is based on guidelines established as 'best practice'. However, Force policy must be adhered to and this section is intended as a guide to assist when acting in accordance with that policy.

Domestic violence can be defined as: 'Any incident of threatening behaviour, violence or abuse (psychological, physical, sexual, financial, or emotional) between persons who are or have been intimate partners or family members regardless of gender.'

Parties involved

- It includes same sex partners and ex-partners irrespective of how long ago the relationship ended.
- Family members includes immediate family members (whether directly related or not), in-laws, and step relations.

Attending at the scene

- Prior to arrival at the scene, the officers must be in possession of any previous history of domestic violence.
- Officers must also be aware of any other relevant information, such as outstanding warrants, wanted markers, violence markers, child protection issues, and injunctions.
- The despatch/communications centre must ensure that all this information is passed to the officers prior to their arrival.
- The main duty of a police officer at a report of domestic violence is to protect the victims and children.

Initial report

- A further risk assessment should be carried out in line with force policy, paying particular attention to weapons.
- Check details of suspect.
- Check if the suspect is still present at the scene and if not where they are.
- Circulate full description if suspect has left the scene.
- **Always separate** the parties involved if suspect still at the scene.
- Check the welfare of any person in the house, especially children and assess any needs they may have, ie medical assistance.
- **Do not** ask the victim in front of the defendant for details of the incident, and particularly not if they want to pursue a complaint.
- **Positive action** must always be taken when dealing with cases of domestic violence.
- It is advisable to take the decision about arresting the suspect away from the victim and tell both parties that it is **your** decision to arrest.

- Be prepared to justify your decision where you decide not to arrest, just as much as when you arrest.
- Record everything said by everyone at the scene and their behaviour.
- Evidence should be gathered at the scene of domestic violence as it would at the scene of any other incident.
- A victim statement should be taken in **all** cases even if it looks like the victim will not support any prosecution.

Responsibilities with regards to children

- A child is any person under 18.
- Police officers have a duty to protect a child from harm (see **2.4.2**).
- If no children are present, establish whether any children reside there and their current whereabouts.
- Check the premises to establish the presence of children.
- Obtain details of all children at the scene—
  - name (all names presently or previously used);
  - date of birth;
  - sex;
  - address;
  - doctor;
  - details of school;
  - details of child's circumstances, clothing, behaviour, injuries, cleanliness;
  - details of all children normally resident at the address.

Subsequent investigation

- Always bear in mind the safety of the victim and any children.
- When considering bail and bail conditions keep the victim informed at all times.
- Inform the victim about bail and what the conditions are prior to the release of the suspect.
- Give details of local and national support groups to the victim.
- Follow force policy with regard to notifying the Domestic Violence Unit.

Police powers of entry

- PACE, s 17—enter premises for the purpose of arresting a person for an indictable offence (see **12.3**).
- PACE, s 17—enter premises for the purpose of saving life or limb or preventing serious damage to property (see **12.3**).
- Breach of the peace—enter premises to prevent or deal with a breach of the peace (see **7.3**).

Counter allegations

- These are often made in domestic violence cases, some in self-defence and some false allegations.

- The primary aggressor needs to be identified, note this is not necessarily the first person to use violence.
- Officers should establish the following when investigating counter allegations—
  - injuries of both parties need to be examined;
  - examine the version provided by both parties, to see if self-defence is a genuine issue for either party;
  - any previous reports of domestic violence and counter allegations;
  - any previous convictions/arrests for violence for either party.

Parental responsibility

- If the parents are married, both parents have parental responsibility.
- If the parents are not married the mother has parental responsibility but the father will only have it if he is named on the birth certificate or has obtained it through court proceedings.
- The police do not normally get involved in child custody disagreements unless there is a welfare concern for the child or the action constitutes a criminal offence (eg abduction).
- Any breach of a custody agreement is not a police matter and should be dealt with before a court.

Property

- The police will not get involved in the sharing of property between partners. If the parties involved cannot settle it between themselves then legal advice should be sought from a solicitor.
- If the parties are married all property is classed as joint regardless of whose name it is in or who bought it.
- Where the parties are unmarried it is more complicated and depends on who bought it and what contributions each party made.
- Each party has a right to collect property that belongs to them. The police will only get involved if there is a threat of violence to either party or a breach of the peace. The police will not get involved in resolving the property issues.

Civil action

- The victim should be made aware that they have certain rights enforceable in a civil court but should be advised of the consequences of pursuing these instead of involving police.
- Victims should be informed that civil action can be costly.
- Victims should be told that if they do obtain a civil injunction **with a power of arrest** details would be recorded on police computer systems.

Links to alternative subjects and offences

13.4 **Vulnerable Victim/Witness**

Police duties to all victims

All victims are entitled to services under the COP for Victims of Crime. Services under this Code must be given to anybody who has made an allegation to the police, or on whose behalf an allegation has been made, that they have been directly subjected to criminal conduct under the National Crime Recording Standard. This includes allegations of religious, racial or homophobic insults.

Referrals to Victim Support

The police must ensure that all victims are provided with information and contact details of the appropriate local Victim Support Group.

- The information about support services must be provided as soon as possible after the allegation is made of the criminal conduct and no later than 5 working days. This may be done by handing the victim a current local copy of the 'Victims of Crime' leaflet. It should be explained to the victim that Victim Support is independent, offers support, practical help and information by trained volunteers (eg about compensation and insurance), it is free and confidential, and can provide help in dealing with other organizations.
- It must be explained to the victim that the victim's contact details will be passed on to local support services unless the police are asked not to do so.
- These requirements could be met by officers using a standard form of words when recording details of the crime from the victim: 'Victim Support is an independent charity which can offer you help. We recommend their services, and it is our (force) policy to refer your details to them unless you ask us not to do so.'
- Notification of the victim should be recorded in order to demonstrate that any relevant details were only passed on to Victim Support with their knowledge.
- Contact details of **all** victims must be given to the local Victim Support Group within 2 days of the allegation of criminal conduct being made (or consent being given). Exceptions—
  - certain minor offences (theft of or from a motor vehicle, minor criminal damage, and tampering with motor vehicles, unless there are aggravating factors);
  - sexual offences or domestic violence/relatives of homicide victims: only with the explicit consent of the victim/relative;
  - where victims state they do not wish to be referred (this should be formally recorded); it should be explained that victim support can still be contacted at a later stage.
- The initial needs assessment of the victim on the reverse of the MG11 statement form must always be filled in.

- Similarly inform the victim/witness about victim support's witness service.
- Where the offender is under the age of 18 the victim's contact details must be passed on to the Youth Offending Team unless the victim asks the police not to do so.
- For further information see—
  - HOC 44/2001: Referral of victims' details to victim support, revised version of the 'Victims of Crime' leaflet;
  - ACPO—Victim Support: Victim Referral Agreement (2003).
- A Family Liaison Officer must be assigned to relatives where a victim has died as result of (suspected) criminal conduct.

Information for victims

- During the investigation the police must notify the victim at least monthly of the progress of the case and its conclusion. In cases of serious crime, where no person has been charged, information must be given about the review procedure.
- Certain information and reasons for decisions, court dates etc. must be given to the victim as soon as possible (generally within 5 working days at the latest, within 1 working day in the case of vulnerable and intimidated witnesses) if—
  - the police decide that there will be no investigation into that crime;
  - a suspect is arrested/released with no further action taken/released on police bail/bail altered/bail conditions;
  - a suspect is interviewed/reported for offence (within 3 working days);
  - summons issued by the court;
  - a decision to charge/not to prosecute/insufficient evidence to charge has been made;
  - a suspect is cautioned/reprimanded/given final warning/issued PND etc.
- For details and general advice on dealing with witnesses see: Criminal Justice System, COP for Victims of Crime, October 2005.
- Complainants in respect of sexual offences or domestic abuse and relatives of those who have died are also entitled to an enhanced service.

Vulnerable and intimidated victims

The identification of a vulnerable or intimidated witness at an early stage is of paramount importance. It will assist the witness to give information to the investigating officer and later to the court, and also to the investigation, thus improving the process of evidence gathering. This process will lead to the likelihood of a more efficient and equitable trial. It will also help to ensure that the witness has been adequately supported throughout in order to give the best evidence.

Vulnerable victims

- Children under the age of 17 at the time of the offence (in all cases);
- If the quality of the evidence given by the victim is likely to be diminished because the victim—
  - suffers from mental disorder within the meaning of the Mental Health Act 1983 (see **11.2**);
  - otherwise has a significant impairment of intelligence and social functioning; or
  - has a physical disability or is suffering from a physical disorder (Youth Justice and Criminal Evidence Act 1999, s 16).

Intimidated victims

- Are those where the police/court are satisfied that the quality of evidence given by the victim is likely to be diminished by reason of fear or distress on the part of the victim in connection with testifying in the proceedings. The following must be taken into account—
  - the nature and alleged circumstances of the offence;
  - the age of the victim;
  - where relevant: social and cultural background and ethnic origins of the victim; the domestic and employment circumstances of the victim; any religious beliefs or political opinions of the victim;
  - any behaviour towards the victim on the part of the accused, members of the family, or associates of the accused, or any other person who is likely to be an accused or a witness in the proceedings.
- Any views expressed by the victim should be taken into account when assessing whether a victim is intimidated (Youth Justice and Criminal Evidence Act 1999, s 17).
- Victims may feel intimidated for of a variety of reasons such as fears of threats or reprisals, no confidence in the police, bad experience with the CJS, feeling vulnerable and at risk.
- Intimidated victims have three key needs: safety, information and support. For advice on dealing with intimidated witnesses see: Office for Criminal Justice Reform, Working with intimidated witnesses, November 2006.
- All reasonable steps must be taken to identify vulnerable or intimidated victims using the above criteria. Where such a victim may be called as a witness in criminal proceedings, special measures under the Youth Justice and Criminal Evidence Act 1999 must be considered (see below). (See also **13.2** on **'Child Abuse'**, and **13.6** on **'Hate Incidents' 13.7** on **'Dealing with People with Disabilities'**).
  - The police should consult the vulnerable victim/witness and those who know them best to seek advice on communicating with them.
  - A 'supporter' should be present while a vulnerable witness is being interviewed.
  - When deciding where interviews should take place, account should be taken of the needs and the wishes of the vulnerable witness.

Special measures for vulnerable/intimidated witnesses in court proceedings

Some witnesses are eligible for **special assistance** in criminal proceedings. The measures of the Youth Justice and Criminal Evidence Act 1999 are available to vulnerable and intimidated witnesses (see above for meanings).

Special assistance

- The **special measures** include screening the witness from the accused, evidence by live-link, evidence given in private, removal of wigs and gowns, video-recorded evidence in chief and cross-/re-examination, examination through an intermediary, and aids to communication (Youth Justice and Criminal Evidence Act 1999, ss 23–30). Not all of these measures are currently available in both the Crown Court and the magistrates' court. For further information see HOC 39/2005).
- A video interview will not be needed in all cases. When dealing with a victim/witness who is a child or a vulnerable adult advice should be sought from the appropriate department regarding children and from a supervisory officer for vulnerable adults.

Video interview of evidence

To decide if video recording their evidence may benefit a vulnerable witness the following steps should be taken—
- identify vulnerable witness;
- decide on video interview or written statement;
- obtain authorization to video interview;
- witnesses under 17: record reasons for obtaining or for **not** obtaining video interview on the appropriate form;
- decide if any other special measures are applicable;
- on the appropriate forms: provide explanation on how the quality of the evidence (coherence, completeness, accuracy) would be improved by video interview. Include views of victim/witness;
- arrange for trained video interviewer to conduct interview;
- ensure that room is booked and witness is attending;
- complete short descriptive note of video interview on the appropriate forms.

Explanatory notes

- For each vulnerable or intimidated witness an MG2 form must be filled in.
- Further comprehensive information is included in 'Achieving Best Evidence in Criminal Proceedings: Guidance for Vulnerable or Intimidated Witnesses, including Children', Home Office, July 2006; and in 'Guidance for District Judges (Magistrates' Courts), Magistrates and Legal Advisers on Child and Vulnerable Witnesses', Judicial Studies Board, April 2008.

Links to alternative subjects and offences

13.5 **Forced Marriages**

It is important that the difference between an arranged marriage and a forced marriage is recognized and understood.

An **arranged** marriage is **an agreement** between both parties (usually prompted by the parents) entered into freely and is a practice that has worked successfully in several cultures for many centuries.

A **forced** marriage is where one or both of the parties has **not agreed** to marry and has been forced to do so **against their own free will**. Although it is mostly women who are affected by this, there are cases of men who are also forced to marry and they should be treated in exactly the same way as a woman making the report.

The Forced Marriage (Civil Protection) Act 2007 makes provision for protecting individuals against being forced to enter into marriage without their free and full consent and for protecting individuals who have been forced to enter into marriage without such consent. This legislation inserts ss 63A to 63S into the Family Law Act, which provides powers for the courts to issue protection orders, attach arrest powers and the power for a police officer to arrest a person having reasonable cause to suspect to be breaching such order.

The inserted sections and subject are as follows—

- 63A Forced marriage protection orders;
- 63B Contents of forced marriage protection orders;
- 63C Applications and other occasions for making orders;
- 63D Ex parte orders;
- 63E Undertakings instead of orders;
- 63F Duration of orders;
- 63G Variation of orders and their discharge;
- 63H Attachment of powers of arrest to orders;
- 63I Arrest under attached powers:
  - ◆ Under s 63I(1) a power of arrest can be attached to a forced marriage protection order under section 63H.
  - ◆ Under s 63I(2) A constable may arrest without warrant a person whom the constable has reasonable cause for suspecting to be in breach of any such provision or otherwise in contempt of court in relation to the order.
  - ◆ Section 63I(3) states that a person arrested under s 63I(2) must be brought before the relevant judge within the period of 24 hours beginning at the time of the person's arrest.
- 63J Arrest under warrant;
- 63K Remand: General;
- 63L Remand: medical examination and report;
- 63M Jurisdiction of courts;
- 63O Contempt proceedings;
- 63P Appeals;

- 63Q Guidance;
- 63R Other protection or assistance against forced marriage;
- 63S Interpretation of sections 63A to 63R.

Apart from the above powers, there are criminal offences that can be committed by the family and (potential) husband/wife of the person when forcing someone into marriage such as assaults (see **2.1**), false imprisonment or kidnapping (see **2.6**) and sexual offences (see Chapter 6).

Information contained within this chapter is based on official guidelines. However, any force policy must be adhered to and the information below is intended as a guide to be read in conjunction with any such policy.

The initial report

The most important factors when dealing with cases of forced marriage are the safety of the person, assurance and confidentiality.

- The victim must be seen in a secure place and **on their own**.
- The nominated officer who has responsibility for such matters must be contacted as soon as possible, otherwise duty supervision must be notified.
- Reassure the victim about the confidentiality of police involvement.
- It is important to establish a safe and discreet means of contact with the victim in the future.
- Obtain full details to pass on to the nominated officer.
- Treat the victim in a respectful and sensitive manner and take into account their feelings and concerns.
- If the victim is under 18 then contact the Child Protection department.

If the nominated officer is not available to deal with the incident, then there are additional steps to take to ensure that information is gathered and the safety of the victim is ensured as far as possible.

- Ask the victim if they would prefer an officer of a certain gender, race, nationality or religion to deal with the report.
- Obtain **full** details of the victim, including National Insurance number and a copy of their passport.
- Make a record of any birthmarks, distinguishing features.
- Obtain a recent photograph or take a photograph of the victim (with the victim's consent).
- Create a restricted entry on the local intelligence system.
- Make sure that the victim has the contact details for the nominated officer.
- Perform a risk assessment in every case.
- Identify any possible criminal offences and if appropriate submit a crime report.
- Secure any evidence in case of any future prosecutions.
- Keep a full record of all decisions made and the explanations for those decisions (including decisions not to take action).

13.5 Forced Marriages

- With the victim's consent refer them to local and national support groups (eg Honour Network—see **Appendix 1**).
- Tell them of their right to seek legal advice and representation.

Apart from taking the above actions: **Do not**—

- Send the person away saying it is not a police matter.
- Send them back to the family home against their wishes.
- Approach the family without express consent of the victim.
- Inform anyone of the situation without express consent of the individual.
- Attempt to mediate and reconcile the family.

There are different types of situations where the issue of forced marriage can arise—

- Fear of being forced to marry in the UK or abroad.
- Already in a forced marriage.
- A third party report.
- A spouse brought from abroad.

It is likely that the nominated officer will take over enquiries, however, it is advisable to be aware of the action to be taken in these situations.

Fear of being forced to marry in the UK or abroad

Additional steps to be taken as well as those listed above are—

- Obtain as much detail as possible about the victim's family both here and abroad including the intended spouse's details.
- Discuss with the person if there is any way of avoiding going abroad and if they did not go what difficulties that could cause.
- Obtain exact details of where the victim would be staying abroad.
- Ascertain if there is a family history of forced marriage.
- Report details of the case to the Forced Marriage Unit (FMU) at the Foreign and Commonwealth Office and pass on contact details (see **Appendix 1**) to the victim. The FMU provides advice and assistance to potential and actual victims of forced marriage. It works with partnership agencies both in the UK and abroad to assist those affected by forced marriage.

If the victim does travel abroad ensure the following—

- That they have details of their passport in a safe place.
- That they can learn at least one telephone number and email address of a trusted person.
- Ensure that they contact you on their return **without fail** and ask for an approximate return date.
- Decide on a code word so that if contact is made, verification of identity can be made.
- Advise they take emergency cash and details of a trusted person in that country.
- Ask the victim for details of a trusted person in the UK whom they will be keeping in touch with and whom you can contact in case of problems, ie if they do not return on specified date. Contact that

person prior to the departure of the victim and pass on yours or the nominated officer's contact details.
- Ensure they have the details of the nearest Embassy/British High Commission in the country they are visiting.

Already in a forced marriage

Additional steps to be taken as well as those listed above are—

- Obtain details of the marriage, where, when, who, etc.
- Ascertain if any other family members are at risk.
- Take a statement about adverse behaviour towards the victim, such as threats and harassment (if appropriate).
- Explain different courses of action to the victim.
- Refer the victim with their consent to local and national support groups.
- Establish a safe way to contact the victim and maintain contact with them.
- Refer the matter to the FMU (see **Appendix 1** for contact details) who not only provide advice and assistance to victims of forced marriage, but also assist with concerns about visa issues for parties who are overseas.
- Make a referral to social services and Child Protection Department if the victim is, or has children under, 18.

A third party report

Additional steps to be taken as well as those listed above are—

- Obtain contact details of the informant and stay in contact with them and advise them against making their own enquiries as this may jeopardize the official investigation.
- Ascertain the relationship between the informant and the potential victim.
- Find out as many details as possible such as where the victim is being held and in what circumstances and if there is any evidence available to corroborate the story.
- Check missing persons reports to see if the victim is reported missing.
- Obtain as much information as possible about the victim's family and the intended spouse's family and extended family in the UK and overseas.
- Obtain a recent photograph of the victim.
- Obtain some details (about the victim) that only the victim would know (an aid for verification of identity).
- Prior to contacting the police overseas it is essential to establish if any reliable links exist within that police force (this can be done through other police forces, Interpol and the Foreign and Commonwealth Office). **Do not** contact the force directly without making these enquiries.

A spouse brought from abroad

Additional steps to be taken as well as those listed above—

- Ensure that an independent authorized interpreter is available if required.
- Ensure the victim is put at ease as they may be very frightened, vulnerable, and isolated.
- Refer the victim with their consent to the relevant agencies and support groups, such as solicitors, immigration, and counselling.
- Notify domestic violence vulnerable witness coordinator if applicable.
- Refer to social services and Child Protection Department if the victim is, or has children under, 18.

Support and assistance

A national charity called Karma Nirvana has launched a confidential helpline called the 'Honour Network' which provides support to victims of 'Honour' based violence and forced marriages. The helpline number is 0800 5999 247.

All operators on the helpline are survivors of honour based violence and/ or forced marriages and give both practical and emotional support as well as advocating for callers if they wish.

This helpline is endorsed by the Home Office, FMU (see **Appendix 1** for contact details) and ACPO.

Links to alternative subjects and offences

13.6 **Hate Incidents**

The information in this chapter is based on guidelines established as 'best practice'. However, Force policies and procedure must be adhered to and this section is intended to assist when these policies are being acted upon.

Hate crime/incidents

- A **hate incident** is any incident, which may or may not constitute a criminal offence, which is perceived by the victim or any other person, as being motivated by prejudice or hate.
- A **hate crime** is any hate incident, which constitutes a criminal offence, perceived by the victim or any other person, as being motivated by prejudice or hate.
- Hate crimes and hate incidents have to be distinguished. All hate crimes are hate incidents, but some hate incidents may not constitute a criminal offence and will not be recorded as hate crime. The police are responsible for data collection in relation to hate incidents and hate crimes.
- A hate crime/incident is determined by the **perception of the victim or any other person**. It is not relevant if there is no apparent motivation as the cause of an incident.
- The prejudice or hate perceived can be based on a number of factors: disability, age, religion, faith, sexual orientation, gender identity, race, etc. A victim of a hate incident does not have to be a member of a minority group or someone who is generally considered to be vulnerable. Anyone can be a victim of hate crime.
- For data recording purposes, the police have to specifically record hate incidents where the prejudice is based upon race, religion, sexual orientation, or disability.
- Romany Gypsies and Irish Travellers are specific ethnic groups. They are entitled to the full protection of the Race Relations Act 1976 and associated legislation outlawing racially aggravated conduct.
- Hate incidents may be related to **race, homophobia**, **faith/religion** or **disability. Homophobia** is an irrational fear and dislike of people who identify themselves as lesbian, gay, or bisexual.
- An incident where the effectiveness of the police response is likely to have a significant impact on the confidence of the victim, their family and/or their community is defined as a **critical incident**.
- The aim of a hate crime investigation is to identify and prosecute offenders to the satisfaction of the victim and the community and seek to reduce repeat victimization.

Legislation

- A witness statement may be admitted in evidence instead of the witness having to give oral evidence in certain circumstances, if the witness has made a written statement to a police officer (or similar investigator) and is prevented from testifying either in person or through fear (CJA 2003, s 116).
- The Crime and Disorder Act 1998 creates **racially or religiously aggravated** provisions of the following offences: assault, criminal damage, public order offence, harassment (see **7.10**).
- Similarly ss 17 to 29N of the Public Order Act 1986 relate to racial or religious hatred offences (see **7.9**).
- With other offences, the courts are required to consider racial or religious hostility as an aggravating factor when sentencing (CJA 2003, s 145).
- Hostility based on disability or sexual orientation must also be taken into account as an aggravating factor in sentencing (CJA 2003, s 146).

Reporting and recording of hate crime

- Ignorance, prejudice, and hostility are largely the basis for hate crime rather than personal gain.
- It is important that all police personnel, when dealing with hate crime victims, are aware of their unique needs and vulnerability.
- Hate crime is significantly under-reported. The reasons include negative perception of and experience with the police (including with police abroad) and the sense that reporting will not change anything.
- One should consider issues such as language, religion, and cultural/lifestyle backgrounds and should do the utmost to meet the diverse needs of each victim; consider also specialist officers.
- Understanding and respect must be shown to the victim. See also **13.4** on 'Vulnerable victim/witness'.
- It is essential to be aware that hate crime may escalate into a critical incident. Failure to provide an appropriate and professional response to such reports could cause irreparable damage to future community and confidence in the police service.
- An officer should attend the scene in response to any hate crime incident reported to provide reassurance and immediate support to the victim. It is vital that the level of support offered to the victim or witness is appropriate to their needs.
- Hate crime victims face the added trauma of knowing that the perpetrator's motivation may be an impersonal group hatred, relating to some feature that they will share with others.
- A crime that may normally have a minor impact becomes, with the hate element, a very intimate and hurtful attack that is likely to undermine the victim's quality of life.

13.6 Hate Incidents

- It should be explained to the victim that the details of the incident are likely to be shared with other agencies.
- The report of a hate crime should not be taken over the phone unless the victim expresses the wish to report it that way.
- A supervising officer has to be informed and should attend the scene.
- An officer of at least the rank of inspector has to be informed of any hate crime incident that may develop into a critical incident.
- Victims of possible homophobia should not be questioned regarding their sexuality. If they want to volunteer this information this should be recorded in the report. Where such information is provided it is vital that it remains confidential, otherwise disclosure could seriously erode their confidence in the police.
- Friends/family of the victim or witness may not have been told of their sexuality. (Inadvertent) disclosure could seriously erode their confidence in the police and that of the community they represent.
- Evidence of an offence is **not** required when **recording a hate incident**. There is no evidential test as to what is or is not a hate incident. All that is required is that the incident is perceived by the victim or another person as being motivated by prejudice or hate.
- If it is not immediately apparent that there is a hate element the person reporting should be asked the reasons for their belief. This should be recorded in order to assist identifying possible lines of enquiry. Incidents may be recorded as hate incidents at a later stage, if the victim discloses such a perception or the original perception changes.
- Even where the victim does not regard the incident as a hate incident police officers may identify it as such. This should be recorded in the appropriate manner. Victims may be unwilling to reveal that they are being targeted because of skin colour, religion, or lifestyle or may not be aware that they are a victim of hate crime even if this is apparent to other people.
- Where a hate incident is reported it **must be recorded** regardless of who reported it, whether a crime has been committed, and whether there is any evidence to identify the hate element.
- Individual forces use different hate incident report forms and the computerized Crime Reporting System.
- For further information see Home Office Police Standards Unit/ ACPO, Hate Crime: Delivering a Quality Service, Good Practice and Tactical Guidance (2005).

Religious dates and events

Appendix 4 contains a list of the dates of religious events and celebrations of the main religions. There are other religions that have not been included in this list.

Links to alternative subjects and offences

13.7 **People with Disabilities**

Definition of disabled person

A person with 'a **physical** or **mental impairment** which has a **substantial** and **long-term adverse effect** on his ability to carry out normal day-to-day activities' Disability Discrimination Act 1995, s 1.

Meanings

Physical impairment

Means any impairment affecting the senses such as sight, hearing, or a weakening of part of the body, through illness, by accident or congenitally, such as paralysis of a leg or heart disease. The effect, not the cause, of the impairment needs to be considered.

Mental impairment

Covers a wide range of impairments relating to mental functioning, including what are often known as learning disabilities.

Substantial adverse effect

Means that the effect of the physical or mental impairment on the ability to carry out normal day-to-day activities must be more than minor or trivial. This reflects the general understanding of disability as a limitation going beyond the normal differences in ability which might exist amongst people.

Normal day-to-day activities

The person must be affected in at least one of the following respects: mobility, manual dexterity, physical coordination, continence, ability to lift, carry or otherwise move everyday objects, speech, hearing, eyesight, memory or the ability to concentrate, learn or understand, or perception of risk or physical danger.

Long-term

Means that the effect has to have lasted, or be likely to last, overall for at least 12 months or for the rest of the life of the person affected.

Explanatory notes

- Under the Disability Discrimination Act 1995 it is unlawful for employers and providers of certain services (viz. public and transport authorities—including the police) to discriminate against people on the grounds of their disability.
- Many people have disabilities that are not visible. Many may not refer to themselves as disabled, but as having 'difficulty in hearing/walking', having 'sight problems'. It is essential to screen callers in order to establish if the caller has any special requirements. This ensures that the officer can meet the caller prepared.

- If the person cannot read an ID card, a password may be agreed or simply the names of the officers provided.
- When dealing with disabled people certain words and phrases should be avoided as they may cause offence. Preferences vary and one should be prepared to ask the person. Terms such as 'the disabled' or 'the blind' should be avoided, and expressions like 'disabled people' or 'people with disabilities' used instead. Other terms to be used include 'mental health problems', 'learning difficulties', 'partially sighted', 'visually impaired', 'deaf and without speech', 'hard of hearing', 'a deaf person', 'short stature/restricted growth', 'a wheelchair user/physical disability'.
- One should not make assumptions about disabilities and never assume to know what assistance is required—one should always ask the individual and wait for any offer of assistance to be accepted before attempting to help.
- People with disabilities should be treated in the same manner and with the same respect and courtesy as anyone else, and appropriate physical contact should be used, such as a handshake.
- You should always speak directly to the disabled person, not through any companion, however severe the impairment may seem.

Visual impairments

- A white cane is often used by visually impaired people, a red and white one by deaf and blind people.
- When meeting visually impaired people you should introduce yourself clearly as well as other people present and indicate where they are located. The use of people's names makes clear who is being addressed.
- If you are using a personal radio tell the person about it as the noise may startle them.
- Use format as preferred by the disabled person, eg large print, Braille, audio cassettes. Typed or printed text is easier to read than handwritten.
- In unfamiliar areas you should describe the layout as well as any hazards. People should be guided to their seat and be told if one wants to offer assistance. Also, they should be told if someone leaves a room, or if they will be left on their own.
- During the search of premises the person should be told what is being done. All items should be returned to their original position.

Deaf or hard of hearing

There are various degrees of impairment of hearing. Therefore, communication has to be adapted to the wishes of the individual:

- Hearing loops or qualified British Sign Language interpreters may be used for interviews or meetings.
- Finger-spelling may be used as an alternative to sign-language.
- Many people use lip-reading to reinforce what they hear, some, who have no hearing at all, use this alone. This is a demanding and tiring

skill. To assist keep background noise low; make sure the deaf person is looking at the speaker before they begin to speak; the speaker should look directly at the person and make sure the speaker's face is clearly visible; the speaker should stop talking if they must turn away, and not speak with their back to the light source. You should speak clearly and at an even pace, but not exaggerate lip movement or gestures or block the mouth with hands, food or cigarettes. Written notes can help to present complicated information. Check regularly that everything has been understood.

- Also consider using RNID (Royal National Institute for Deaf People) Typetalk, a national telephone service that enables deaf, deaf-blind, hard of hearing, or speech-impaired people to communicate with hearing people anywhere by telephone.

Speech impairment

- You should not assume that speech and language defects are caused by alcohol or drugs. Slow or impaired speech does not reflect a person's intelligence.
  - ◆ You should not correct or speak for other persons, but wait while they speak and let them finish their sentence.
  - ◆ It might help to break down questions, to deal with individual points, rather than with complex matters, so that short answers can be given.

Learning difficulties and disabilities

- People with such difficulties should be treated in a manner appropriate for their age.
  - ◆ You should make sure that everything has been understood.
  - ◆ It is helpful to repeat questions in plain, clear language if there are doubts.
  - ◆ PACE COP must be complied with when dealing with people who have a learning difficulty or mental illness. For example COP C, s 3, paras 3.12 to 3.20 deal with special groups such as the deaf, juveniles, mentally disordered or otherwise mentally vulnerable when brought to a police station under arrest or if arrested at the police station (see **12.2.2**).

Wheelchair users

- You should use the term 'wheelchair user', not 'wheelchair bound'.
- When communicating with a wheelchair user, it is best to stand back far enough to maintain eye contact comfortably.
- Help with doors, steps and kerbs should be offered, but you should not attempt to push the wheelchair without asking if help is required.
- Leaning on a wheelchair is regarded as a major personal intrusion for most.

Links to alternative subjects and offences

13.8 Contamination of Officers/ Police Staff

The information in this chapter is based on guidelines established as 'best practice'. However, force policies and procedure must be adhered to and this section is intended as a guide to be acted on in accordance with that policy.

Contamination is when any body fluid (blood, saliva, urine, vomit, etc) from a person or a dead body comes into contact with someone's mouth, eyes, ears, nose, or any open wound or if someone is bitten or someone's skin is broken.

Immediate action is necessary.

Eyes and **mouth** should be rinsed thoroughly with water only.

Ears, nose, open wounds or broken skin should be rinsed with cold running water. Where the injury is caused by a sharp pointed instruments (eg needle), the wound should be encouraged to bleed and be washed with soap and running water immediately.

A healthcare professional or police surgeon needs to take a **blood sample** from the contaminated person and (where possible) from the other person.

Appropriate forms must be used for samples. Blood samples are to be stored away from heat at room temperature, but not in a fridge or freezer.

The Occupational Health, Safety and Welfare Unit will require—

- name/rank/collar number;
- date of birth;
- division/department;
- extension number and home phone number;
- date of previous Hepatitis B vaccination;
- detainee's/donor's name;
- detainee's/donor's date of birth;
- (if known) drug user.

If the blood test suggests that extra protection is needed, Hepatitis B immunoglobin can be given to provide immediate protection.

Dealing with people suspected of contamination

When dealing with a person who is suspected of carrying HIV or Hepatitis B or any other contagious infection, a healthcare professional may be contacted for advice.

If staff have been in contact with a (suspected) contaminated person a note should be made, including—

- name, collar number, date of birth, date of Hepatitis B vaccination and Hepatitis B immunity status (if known);
- whether they have any cuts, grazes, or other broken skin;

- how the contamination occurred;
- name and date of birth of contaminated person, whether drug user;
- what the contamination was suspected of being.

Dealing with property

Dealing with property presents a risk of infection. It can conceal items such as needles, knives. Contaminated property must be packaged appropriately and safely.

Cleaning of contamination

When dealing with a contaminated person or spillage appropriate protective equipment must be used.

All police vehicles contain first aid kits, resuscitation aids, vinyl gloves, antiseptic sprays/wipes, and sharps bins. If surfaces like table tops or the interior of vehicles have been in contact with body substances, they should be cleaned with antiseptic wipes. Antiseptic wipes or sprays are effective against the HIV virus and the Hepatitis B virus. When cleaning spillage of blood, vomit etc appropriate protective equipment must be worn and antiseptic used. Contaminated items must be disposed of appropriately.

Forensic evidence

Items stained with body substances (blood, saliva, semen, urine, faeces, tissue) are potential sources of infection and must be handled with caution.

Items for scientific examination must be handled in accordance with Force policy.

- The handling of contaminated items or hypodermic needles should be restricted to a minimum. A high level of personal hygiene must be exercised.
- Samples from people known to be HIV or Hepatitis B positive must be handled with extreme care and advice should be sought from a healthcare professional, doctor or pathologist.
- Nobody who has a cut or open sore should handle samples of body substances (whether they are contaminated or not).
- Accidental injuries can always happen. Needles, staples, and other sharp objects must be avoided. Specimens should be carried in trays or boxes, not in hands. Specimen containers should be touched as little as possible.
- Everyone who is dealing with forensic samples (packaging, labelling, transport) must cover any cuts or grazes on hands with waterproof dressing. Gloves should be worn and hands washed immediately afterwards. Hands should be washed often, especially before meals and after dealing with samples.
- No smoking, drinking, or eating when carrying specimens or in laboratories.

- If specimens are transported, antiseptics should be carried in case of spillage/leaks.
- If specimens leak the laboratory must be contacted.
- Exhibits labelled 'Health Hazard' should only be opened in exceptional circumstances. If it is necessary to open such a bag the laboratory should be consulted about hazards and precautions for handling the item. Where possible the items should be destroyed by incineration in the sealed bag.
- In case of a cut or accident, however small, the supervisor must be informed and the facts recorded.
- If necessary ask for advice from the Occupational Health, Safety and Welfare Unit.

General advice

Advice about vaccinations can be obtained from the NHS, a GP, or the Occupational Health, Safety and Welfare Unit.

AIDS is caused by the Human Immunodeficiency Virus (HIV).

HIV is mainly acquired:

- by unprotected sex with an infected person;
- by inoculation of infected blood, eg by sharing drug injecting equipment;
- during pregnancy, childbirth, or breastfeeding by the baby of an infected mother.

HIV is **not** transmitted by touching, coughing, or sneezing; sharing toilets, cutlery, or crockery; contact with saliva, tears, urine, or faeces; being bitten by insects or humans; being a blood donor.

Hepatitis is an inflammation of the liver. It has a number of causes: one is the Hepatitis B virus. Vaccination can effectively prevent Hepatitis B. Where a person has not been vaccinated, effective treatment can be given if administered within 72 hours.

Hepatitis B is spread by blood-to-blood contact with an infected person's blood or certain body fluids. Hepatitis B is **much more infectious and easily transmitted** than HIV and has been found in virtually all body secretions and excretions in significant quantities).

The main danger of becoming infected with contagious diseases are where blood or body fluids from an infected person come into contact with an open wound, rash, or sore, or if the skin is punctured by a contaminated needle or other sharp object or from a bite by a person. Such risk situations are searching, road traffic accidents, recovering a body, or handling a violent or disorderly person. All incidents involving spillage of blood and body fluids must be treated with special care.

While working in **risk situations**:

- **broken skin** must be properly dressed with waterproof dressing;
- **spillage** on the skin should be washed with soap and running water as soon as possible;
- **antiseptics** are active against HIV and the Hepatitis B virus;

- during **resuscitation** there is a very small risk of transmission of Hepatitis B, especially if there is blood present. A resuscitation aid should always be used, where possible;
- where an incident has occurred where infectious diseases could be present, **protective equipment** must be used.

If someone is ill, they should tell their doctor about the type of work done. It might be necessary to also contact and inform the laboratory.

Links to alternative subjects and offences

13.9 **First Aid**

This chapter covers some basic first aid skills. If, in any of the situations described below you are not sure or the injury ailment is serious, then you should **always** get professional help.

Treatment priorities

The first priority with any casualty is to make sure the airway is open, then to check that they are breathing normally. Once this has been established, the next priority is to treat any major bleeding or burns injuries. After this, the next stage, is to deal with any broken bones.

CPR (Cardiopulmonary Resuscitation)

The first issue to consider is safety. Always wear your gloves and use the resuscitation aid you have been issued with.

Prior to commencing this procedure you should check the following:

Response—Is the casualty conscious or unconscious? Are they responding to you? If they are not, then try to gently shake them to see if you can get some kind of response from them.

Airway—Are there any signs of breathing? Watch the chest to see if it rises and falls, can you hear them breathing?

Breathing—If the person is breathing, them put them on their side into the recovery position. If there is any danger of an injury to the spine, then do not move the person.

If the person is not breathing, or you are not sure, then, before starting CPR, call for an ambulance.

CPR

Prior to commencing CPR official guidelines state that rescue breaths should be administered if the person is not breathing on their own or is making only the occasional gasp.

If **rescue breaths** are required—

- Get medical assistance prior to commencing this procedure.
- Place the victim on his back.
- Ensure there is no obstruction in the mouth.
- Tilt the head gently back to open the airway.
- Hold the nose and, using the resuscitation aid breathe into the person's mouth with two slow long breaths.
- Each breath should last about 2 seconds.
- Remove your mouth from the victim's and wait for the chest to fall.
- Repeat the procedure.

- Check for signs of normal breathing, coughing, or other signs of movement by the person, do not take longer than 10 seconds to carry out these checks.

If there are signs of circulation, continue rescue breathing until the person starts to breathe on their own. If there are no signs or you are not certain then start CPR procedure.

The CPR procedure is in two parts chest compressions and breaths.

Chest compressions

- Ensure the person is lying on their back.
- Using your index and middle fingers find the lower edge of the rib nearest to you and slide them upwards to the point where the sternum joins the rib.
- Place your index finger on this point. Slide your other hand down the sternum until it reaches your fingers.
- Place your other hand on top and lace your fingers together to ensure a firm position.
- Place your self directly above the victim with your arms straight.
- Press the breastbone down and then release. Do this 30 times. You should do this at more than one depression per second.
- After 30 compressions give 2 rescue breaths as described below.

Breaths

- Ensure there is no obstruction in the mouth. Tilt the head gently back to open the airway. Hold the nose and, using the resuscitation aid breathe into the person's mouth with two long breaths.
- Repeat the whole procedure and continue until help arrives.
- Only stop to check for signs of circulation if the person moves or takes an independent breath.

Chest compression only resuscitation

If you are unable (*or unwilling*) to give rescue breaths, then give 'chest compressions only' resuscitation, this will at least circulate any residual oxygen in the blood stream, and will be better than no CPR at all, also—

- If chest compressions only, give at a continual rate of 100 per minute.
- If breathing starts normally, stop to reassess the casualty— otherwise do not interrupt resuscitation.
- To prevent fatigue, change with another rescuer (if available) every two minutes, ensuring change over delay is kept to a minimum.

Small children (1–8 years)

- Give 5 initial rescue breaths.
- If on your own perform CPR for about one minute before requesting help.
- Compress the chest by approximately one-third of its depth, to achieve an adequate depth of compression.
- Use one or two hands for compressions.
- 30 chest compressions and 2 rescue breaths.

Babies (under 12 months)
- Two fingers.
- A puff of air.
- Five compressions and one breath.

ABC procedure

Airway—establish an open airway by tipping the forehead gently back.

Breathing—check that the person is breathing, look for movement of the chest, listen for breath sounds, and feel if there is any air being expelled from nose/mouth.

Circulation—check for heartbeat/pulse. Look for signs of improved colour, eye movement, and coughing. Adverse signs are blueness around lips, cold and pale skin.

Bleeding

- Stop the bleeding straightaway using your hand (ensuring you **always** wear gloves) or the injured person's to apply pressure.
- Lay the person down (injuries permitting).
- If stabbed in arm or leg then attempt to raise the limb.
- If the person has been stabbed with an object and that object is still *in situ*, **do not** remove it but apply pressure around the object.
- If possible apply dressing making sure it is dressed firmly.

Broken bones

- Try and support the injured limb and prevent it from moving.
- **Do not** move the casualty unless they are in danger.

Burns

- Use cold water to try and relieve the pain, this should take at least 10 minutes (in the case of a chemical burn—20 minutes).
- Cover the area in sterile clean material (not cotton wool or similar, as it will stick to the skin). A polythene bag can be used if the burn is adequately cooled.
- If the burn is on the hand/arm if possible remove any jewellery they are wearing before swelling occurs.

Choking

- Assess severity
  - Severe airway obstruction (ineffective cough)
    - Unconscious—start CPR
    - Conscious—5 back blows then 5 abdominal thrusts

♦ Mild airway obstruction (Effective cough)
  ■ Encourage cough
  ■ Continue to check for deterioration to ineffective cough or relief of obstruction.
- Encourage the person to cough.
- Lower the head, so that if the item is dislodged it will come out of the mouth and not go further down the airway.
- If the object is still stuck slap the person hard between the shoulder blades (up to five times), check whether the object has become dislodged between each slap.
- If the object is still lodged then stand behind the person, place your fist into the upper abdomen and hold onto your fist with your other hand. Pull sharply upward to expel the air. Repeat as necessary.
- If the person becomes unconscious, use the ABC procedure as above.

Diabetic emergency

These fall into two types, high blood sugar and low blood sugar.

- *High blood sugar*—this condition brings a slow change to the person; dry skin, possible unconsciousness, possible chemical smell on breath. This is **very similar to drunk and incapable. Action:** requires hospital treatment—insulin and monitoring.

- *Low blood sugar*—this condition brings on a quick change in the person; slurred speech, feeling weak and faint, shaking and trembling, being hungry, skin clammy and cold. Person can also become confused and angry. This is very **similar to drunk and disorderly**. **Action:** requires glucose—chocolate or sugary drink.

Drug/alcohol overdose

- **Alcohol**—the symptoms are: strong smell of alcohol; unconsciousness; the person will be flushed and their face damp; deep loud breathing.
  Action: protect from cold, as may develop hypothermia. Prevent from choking or inhaling vomit. See if casualty responds to calling their name and shaking shoulders. Call ambulance if necessary.
- **Drugs**—the symptoms are; unconsciousness; drug paraphernalia around the person; dilated pupils.
  Action: Get professional help and place in the recovery position (if safe to do so).

Fits

- Do not attempt to restrain the person as this could cause injury.
- Cushion the head to prevent injury.
- Only move if the person is in danger.

- Remove objects around the person to prevent injury.
- When the fit has stopped place the person in the recovery position.
- Check for medic-alert/indicators of epilepsy.

Heart attack

- Described as crushing pain in the chest (sometimes mistaken for indigestion).
- Can also spread to the rest of the body (or just affect throat, back, stomach, jaw).
- The person may also be weak, dizzy, breathless, pale, sweaty and feel cold.

Action: Get professional help, tell the operator it is suspected heart attack. Sit the person up with knees bent up towards them, reassure the person. If the person becomes unconscious, follow ABC above.

Stroke

Symptoms are described as a sudden—

- numbness or weakness of the face, arm or leg, especially on one side of the body;
- confusion, trouble speaking or understanding;
- trouble seeing in one or both eyes;
- trouble walking, dizziness, loss of balance or coordination
- severe headache with no known cause.

Action: Stroke is a medical emergency, every second counts. It is imperative they reach hospital quickly and receive prompt treatment to prevent further brain damage. A '*FAST*' test is used by paramedics to diagnose stroke prior to reaching hospital—

Facial weakness—can the person smile? Has their mouth or eye drooped?

Arm weakness—can the person raise both arms?

Speech problems—can the person speak clearly and understand what you say?

Test all three symptoms.

Vomiting

- Ensure that the person does not choke or inhale any vomit.
- Keep the person warm (if necessary).

Links to alternative subjects and offences

Useful Contacts

Ask the police FAQ (see PNLD)

ACPO (Association of Chief Police Officers)
<http://www.acpo.police.uk> accessed 10 August 2009
Telephone: 020 7084 8950

ASBOs (Provides Home Office guidance and related links)
<http://www.crimereduction.gov.uk/asbos/asbos9.htm> accessed 10
August 2009

British Association of Women Police
<http://www.bawp.org> accessed 10 August 2009
Telephone: 07790 505204

CEHR (Commission for Equality and Human Rights)
<http://www.aboutus.org/Cehr.org.uk> accessed 12 August 2009
Telephone: 020 7215 8415

Child Exploitation and Online Protection Centre (CEOP)
<http://www.ceop.gov.uk> accessed 10 August 2009
Telephone: 0870 000 3344

Citizens Advice Bureau (Provides local links)
<http://www.citizensadvice.org.uk> accessed 10 August 2009
Telephone: 020 7833 2181 (Admin office only)

Commission for Racial Equality (see CEHR)

Consumer Advice (Provides local contact details)
<http://www.tradingstandards.gov.uk> accessed 10 August 2009

Copyright Protection (see **UK Intellectual Property Office**)

Courts Service (see **HMCS**—Her Majesty's Courts Service)

CPS (The Crown Prosecution Service)
<http://www.cps.gov.uk> accessed 10 August 2009
Telephone: 020 7796 8000

Crime Stoppers
<http://www.crimestoppers-uk.org> accessed 10 August 2009
Telephone: 0800 555 111

Criminal Justice System
<http://www.cjsonline.gov.uk> accessed 10 August 2009
email: <cjsonline@cjit.gsi.gov.uk>

DEFRA (Department for Environment, Food and Rural Affairs)
<http://www.defra.gov.uk> accessed 10 August 2009
Telephone: 08459 33 55 77

Design Protection (see **UK Intellectual Property Office**)

Directgov (UK Government Official Information)
<http://www.direct.gov.uk> accessed 10 August 2009

Disability Rights Commission (see **CEHR**)

Drugs (Government Drugs site)
<http://www.drugs.gov.uk> accessed 10 August 2009
Telephone: 0207 035 4848

DSA (Driving Standards Agency)
<http://www.dsa.gov.uk> accessed 10 August 2009
Telephone: 0300 200 1122
email: <driver@dsa.gsi.gov.uk>

DVLA (Driver and Vehicle Licensing Agency)
<http://www.dvla.gov.uk> accessed 10 August 2009
Provides links to service required

Equal Opportunities Commission (see **CEHR**)

Equality and Human Rights Commission (also **CEHR**)
<http://www.equalityhuman rights.com> accessed 10 August 2009
Telephone: 0845 604 6610 (England)
Telephone: 0845 604 8810 (Wales)

European Commission
<http://europa.eu.int/comm> accessed 10 August 2009
Telephone: 00800 67891011

Forced Marriage Unit (see **Honour Network** for victim support)
email: <fmu@fco.gov.uk>
Telephone: 020 7008 0151 Outside office hours: 020 7008 1500

Foreign & Commonwealth Office
<http://www.fco.gov.uk> accessed 10 August 2009
Telephone: 020 7008 1500

Forensic Science Service
<http://www.forensic.gov.uk> accessed 10 August 2009
Telephone: 0121 607 6985

Appendix 1: Useful Contacts

Gay Police Association
<http://www.gay.police.uk> accessed 12 August 2009
Telephone: 07092 700 000

GMB (Union)
<http://www.gmb.org.uk> accessed 10 August 2009
Telephone: 020 8947 3131

Health and Safety Executive
<http://www.hse.gov.uk> accessed 10 August 2009
Incident Contact Centre: 0845 300 9923
Information line: 0845 345 0055

Highways Agency
<http://www.highways.gov.uk> accessed 10 August 2009
email: <ha_info@highways.gsi.gov.uk>
Telephone: 0121 335 8300 or 08457 50 40 30.

HMCS (Her Majesty's Courts Service)
<http://www.hmcourts-service.gov.uk> accessed 10 August 2009
Telephone: 020 7189 2000 or 0845 456 8770

HMIC (HM Inspectorate of Constabulary)
<http://inspectorates.homeoffice.gov.uk/hmic> accessed
10 August 2009
Telephone: 020 7035 2004

HMRC (HM Revenue & Customs)
<http://www.hmrc.gov.uk> accessed 10 August 2009
Telephone: 0800 59 5000

Home Office (Police)
<http://www.police.homeoffice.gov.uk> accessed 10 August 2009
Telephone: 0207 035 4848

Honour Network (Honour violence and forced marriages)
Telephone: 0800 5999 247

Identity and Passport Service
<http://www.ips.gov.uk> accessed 12 August 2009
Telephone: 0870 521 0410

Immigration (Immigration and Nationality Directorate)
<http://www.ind.homeoffice.gov.uk> accessed 10 August 2009

Information Commissioner (Oversees and enforces compliance with the Data
Protection Act 1998 and the Freedom of Information Act 2000)
<http://www.ico.gov.uk> accessed 10 August 2009
Telephone: Helpline 01625 545 745

International Police Association
<http://www.ipa-uk.org> accessed 10 August 2009
Telephone: 0115 981 3638

International Association of Women Police
<http://www.iawp.org> accessed 10 August 2009

IPCC (Independent Police Complaints Commission)
<http://www.ipcc.gov.uk> accessed 10 August 2009

Law Society
<http://www.lawsociety.org.uk> accessed 10 August 2009
Telephone: 020 7242 1222

Legislation (Office of Public Sector Information)
<http://www.opsi.gov.uk/legislation> accessed 10 August 2009

Mental Illness Advice (SANELINE)
<http://www.sane.org.uk> accessed 10 August 2009
Telephone: 0845 767 8000

MIB (Motor Insurers' Bureau)
<http://www.mib.org.uk> accessed 10 August 2009

Ministry of Justice
<http://www.justice.gov.uk> accessed 10 August 2009
Telephone: 020 7210 8500

Missing Persons (National Missing Persons Helpline)
<http://www.missingpeople.org.uk> accessed 10 August 2009
Telephone: 0500 700 700

National Black Police Association
<http://www.nationalbpa.com> accessed 10 August 2009
Telephone: 020 7259 1280

NPIA (National Policing Improvement Agency)
<http://www.npia.police.uk> accessed 10 August 2009
Telephone: 020 8358 5555

NSPCC (National Society for Prevention of Cruelty to Children)
<http://www.nspcc.org.uk> accessed 10 August 2009
Telephone: 0808 800 5000

OPSI (Office of Public Sector Information)
<http://www.opsi.gov.uk> accessed 10 August 2009

Parliament
<http://www.parliament.uk> accessed 10 August 2009

Patent Protection (see UK Intellectual Property Office)

PNLD (Police National Legal Database)
<http://www.pnld.co.uk> accessed 10 August 2009
email: <pnld@westyorkshire.pnn.police.uk>
Telephone: 01924 208229

Appendix 1: Useful Contacts

PNLD (Ask the police FAQ database)
<https://www.askthe.police.uk> accessed 10 August 2009

Police Federation
<http://www.polfed.org> accessed 10 August 2009
Telephone: 020 8335 1000

Prison (HM Prison Office)
<http://www.hmprisonservice.gov.uk> accessed 10 August 2009
email: <public.enquiries@hmps.gsi.gov.uk>

Probation (National Probation Service)
<http://www.probation.homeoffice.gov.uk> accessed 10 August 2009
Telephone: 020 7217 0659

Public Services (Directgov— provides links)
<http://www.direct.gov.uk> accessed 10 August 2009

Rape (Rape counselling and advice service)
<http://www.rapecrisis.org.uk> accessed 10 August 2009
Provides local contact details

Revenue & Customs (see **HMRC**)

RSPB (Royal Society for the Protection of Birds)
<http://www.rspb.org.uk> accessed 10 August 2009
Telephone: 01767 693 690

RSPCA (Royal Society for the Prevention of Cruelty to Animals)
<http://www.rspca.org.uk> accessed 10 August 2009
Telephone: 0870 55 55 999

Samaritans (Organization)
<http://www.samaritans.org> accessed 10 August 2009
Telephone: 08457 90 90 90

Sentencing (Sentencing Guidelines Council/Sentencing Advisory Panel)
<http://www.sentencing-guidelines.gov.uk> accessed 10 August 2009
Telephone: 020 7084 8130

Superintendents' Association
<http://www.policesupers.com> accessed 10 August 2009
Telephone: 0118 984 4005

Trade Marks (see **UK Intellectual Property Office**)

Trading Standards (Provides local contact details)
<http://www.tradingstandards.gov.uk> accessed 10 August 2009

UK Intellectual Property Office
<http://www.ipo.gov.uk> accessed 10 August 2009
Telephone: 0845 9 500 505

Unison (Union)
<http://www.unison.org.uk> accessed 10 August 2009
Telephone: 0845 355 0845

Youth Justice Board
<http://www.yjb.gov.uk> accessed 10 August 2009
Telephone: 020 7271 3033

Traffic Data—Vehicle Categories and Groups

More information or exemptions could apply than are given in this Appendix. Therefore, this table is for guidance only. There will be some instances when a road traffic/policing officer should be consulted to confirm matters.

Descriptions of Vehicle Categories and Minimum Ages

Vehicle description	Category	Minimum age
Mopeds[1]	P	16
Light motorcycles[2]	A1	17
Motorcycles[3]	A	17
Any sized motorcycle with or without sidecar	A	21[a]
3- or 4-wheeled Light vehicles[4]	B1	17[b]
Cars[5]	B	17[c]
Automatic cars (with automatic transmission)	B Automatic	17[c]
Cars with trailers exceeding 750 kg[6]	B + E	17
Medium-sized Goods vehicles[7]	C1	18[d]
Medium-sized Goods vehicles combination[8]	C1 + E	21[d]

[1] Mopeds with an engine capacity not exceeding 50 cc and a maximum design speed not exceeding 50 km/hr.

[2] Light motorcycles not exceeding 125 cc and power output not exceeding 11 kW (14.6 bhp).

[3] Motorcycles up to 25 kW (33 bhp) with power to weight ratio not exceeding 0.16 kW/kg.

[4] Motor tricycles or quadricycles with design speed exceeding 50 km/hr and up to 550 kg unladen.

[5] Motor vehicles up to 3500 kg/not more than 8 passenger seats/trailer up to 750 kg; or vehicle and trailer up to 3500 kg **and** the trailer does not exceed unladen weight of towing vehicle.

[6] Where the combination does not come within category B.

[7] Lorries 3500 kg—7500 kg, with a trailer **up to** 750 kg.

[8] Trailer exceeds 750 kg. Total weight up to 12000 kg and trailer is less than weight of towing lorry.

Note: If category B test was prior to 1.1.1997 then restricted to a total weight not more than 8250 kg.

[a] Or 2 years after passing test on a standard motorcycle.[3] If owned or driven by armed forces—17 years.

[b] 16 if receiving disability living allowance at higher rate, providing no trailer is drawn.

[c] 16 if receiving disability living allowance at higher rate.

[d] 18 if combination weight is under 7500 kg.

Appendix 2: Traffic Data—Vehicle Categories and Groups

Vehicle description	Category	Minimum age
Large Goods vehicles[9] Large Goods vehicles[10]	C C + E	21[e] 21[e]
Minibuses[11] Minibuses[12]	D1 D1 + E	21[f] 21[f]
Buses[13] Buses[14]	D D + E	21[f] 21
Agricultural tractors	F	17[g]
Road rollers	G	21[h]
Tracked vehicles	H	21[i]
Mowing machines or pedestrian controlled vehicles	K	16

[9] Vehicles over 3500 kg, with trailer **up to** 750 kg.
[10] Vehicles over 3500 kg, with trailer **over** 750 kg.
[11] With 9–16 passenger seats, and trailer **up to** 750 kg.
[12] With 9–16 passenger seats, and trailer **over** 750 kg. Provided total weight does not exceed 12000 kg and trailer does not exceed weight of towing lorry.
[13] More than 8 passenger seats, with trailer **up to** 750 kg.
[14] More than 8 passenger seats, with trailer **over** 750 kg.

[e] 17 if member of armed forces or 18 if member of young drivers scheme.
[f] 17 if member of armed forces or 18 while learning to drive or taking PCV test or CPC initial qualification.

Notes: Other conditions may apply. Consult with a road traffic/policing officer or the DSA (see **Appendix 1**) for further details.

[g] 16 if tractor less than 2.45 m wide. Trailer less than 2.45 m (2 wheel) or 4 wheels if close coupled.
[h] 17 for small road rollers with metal or hard rollers. Must not be steam powered, weigh more than 11.69 tonnes, or be made for carrying loads.
[i] 17 if the total weight of the tracked vehicle does not exceed 3500 kg.

Exception

If the driver has held a car driving licence (category/group B) before 1 January 1997, then that person can (without taking separate tests) drive:

- a car and trailer exceeding 750 kg (B + E);
- motor vehicles 3500 kg–7500 kg, with trailers up to a combined weight of 8250 kg (C1 + E);
- passenger vehicles with 9–16 passenger seats, not used for hire or reward (D1 and D1 + E).

These entitlements last for the duration of the licence, without being required to undergo a medical.

Appendix 2: Traffic Data—Vehicle Categories and Groups

However, when the licence expires or is no longer in force, then that person will be required to pass the relevant test and medical examination (as required by new licence holders).

Comparison Guide—Original Groups to Current Categories

More information or exemptions could apply than are given in this Appendix. Therefore, this table is for guidance only. There will be some instances when a road traffic/policing officer should be consulted to confirm matters.

Vehicle description	Current category	Original group/class
Moped	P	E
Motorcycles[15]	A	D
3-or 4-light wheeled vehicles[16]	B1	C
Invalid carriages	B1 Limited	J
Cars[17]	B	A
Cars—with trailers over 750 kg	B + E	A
Automatic cars	B Automatic	B
Medium-sized Goods vehicles[18]	C1	A
Medium-sized Goods vehicles[19]	C1 + E	A
Large Goods vehicles[20]	C	HGV 2/3
Large Goods vehicles[21]	C + E	HGV 2/3
Buses[22]	D1	A
Buses[23]	D	PSV 3
Buses[24]	D Limited	PSV 3
Buses[25]	D Limited	PSV 4

[15] With or without sidecar.

[16] Motor tricycles or quadricycles with design speed exceeding 50 km/hr and up to 550 kg unladen weight. If they exceed 550 kg they fall into a car category—B category.

[17] Includes cars or light vans up to 8 passenger seats and up to 3500 kg.

[18] Gross vehicle weight between 3500 kg–7500 kg, with trailer **up to** 750 kg. The combined weight not to exceed 8250 kg.

[19] Gross vehicle weight between 3500 kg–7500 kg, with trailer **over** 750 kg. The combined weight not to exceed 8250 kg.

[20] Gross weight of vehicle being over 3500 kg, with trailer **up to** 750 kg.

[21] Gross weight of vehicle being over 3500 kg, with trailer **over** 750 kg.

[22] Capacity between 9 and 16 passengers—**not** used for hire reward.

[23] Any bus with more than 8 passenger seats, with trailer up to 750 kg.

[24] Vehicles limited to 16 passenger seats.

[25] Vehicles with more than 8 passenger seats, but no longer than 5.5 m.

Firearms Offences Relating to Age

Under 18 offence

- Using a firearm for a purpose not authorized by the European weapons directive (despite lawful entitlement to possess—being the holder of a firearms/shotgun certificate).
- Purchase or hire an air weapon or ammunition for an air weapon (see **8.7.1**)
- Part with possession of an air weapon or ammunition for an air weapon **subject to exceptions below** (see **8.7.2**).
- Make a gift of an air weapon or ammunition for an air weapon (see **8.7.2**).
- Sell or let on hire or hire an air weapon or ammunition for an air weapon (see **8.7.1**)
- Purchase an imitation firearm (see **8.7.5**)
- Sell an imitation firearm (see **8.7.5**)
- Have an air weapon or ammunition for an air weapon (see **8.7.2**), except if:
  - that person is under the supervision of a person of or over the age of 21;
  - member of approved rifle clubs;
  - using at authorized shooting galleries (not exceeding .23 inch calibre);
  - that person has attained the age of 14 and is on private premises with the consent of the occupier, and is under the supervision of a person of or over the age of 21, but it is an offence for the superviser to allow him to fire any missiles beyond those premises (subject to defence—below).

Notes:

As from 1 October 2007, s 34 of the Violent Crime Reduction Act 2006 inserted s 21 A into the Firearms Act 1968 which makes it an offence for anyone to fire a missile beyond premises—

(1) A person commits an offence if—
   (a) he has with him an air weapon on any premises; and
   (b) he uses it for firing a missile beyond those premises.
(2) In proceedings against a person for an offence under this section it shall be a defence for him to show that the only premises into or across which the missile was fired were premises the occupier of which had consented to the firing of the missile (whether specifically or by way of a general consent).

Under 17 offences

- Purchase or hire **any** firearm or ammunition of any other description (see **8.7.1**).
- Sell or let on hire any firearm or ammunition of any other description (see **8.7.1**).

Under 15 offences

In addition to offences applicable to under 17 and 18—

- Have an assembled shotgun **except** while under the supervision of a person of or over the age of 21, or while the shotgun is so covered with a securely fastened gun cover that it cannot be fired (see **8.2.3**).
- Make a gift of a shotgun or ammunition for a shotgun to a person under the age of 15 (see **8.2.2**).

Under 14 offences

In addition to offences applicable to under 15, 17, and 18—

- Possess s 1 firearm or ammunition (see **8.1.3**), except for—
  - use of a certificate holder, being under their instructions and for sporting purposes only;
  - a member of an approved cadet corps when engaged as a member of the corps in or in connection with drill or target shooting;
  - a person conducting or carrying on a miniature rifle or shooting gallery for air weapons or miniature rifles not exceeding .23 inch calibre;
  - using such rifles/ammunition at such a range or gallery.
- Part with possession of a s 1 firearm or ammunition to a person under 14, **subject to above exceptions** (see **8.1.3**).
- Make a gift of or lend s 1 firearm or ammunition to a person under 14 (see **8.1.3**).

Religious Dates/Events

Advisory notes: These dates are provided for guidance purposes only. Some dates may vary as the festivals are guided by the lunar calendar and some local customs may also vary the date. The religions are listed alphabetically.

	2009	2010
Baha'I		
World Religion Day	18 January 2009	17 January 2010
Naw-Rúz (New Year)	21 March 2009	21 March 2010
First Day of Ridvan	21 April 2009	21 April 2010
Last Day of Ridvan	2 May 2009	2 May 2010
Declaration of the Báb	23 May 2009	23 May 2010
Ascension of Baha'u'llah	29 May 2009	29 May 2010
Martyrdom of the Báb	9 July 2009	9 July 2010
Birth of the Báb	20 October 2009	20 October 2010
Birth of Baha'u'llah	12 November 2009	12 November 2010
Day of the Covenant	26 November 2009	26 November 2010
Ascension of `Abdu' l-Baha	28 November 2009	28 November 2010
Buddhist		
Mahayana Buddhist New Year	10–13 January 2009	30 January–1 Feb 2010
Paranirvana Day	8 February 2009	8 February 2010
Nirvana Day (alternative date)	15 February 2009	15 February 2010
Magha Puja Day	11 March 2009	30 March 2010
Therevadin Buddhist New Year	8–11 April 2009	28 April–1 May 2010
Wesak (Buddha Day)	9 May 2009 ·	27 May 2010
Asalha Puja Day	7 July 2009	26 July 2010
Obon (Ulambana)	13–15 July 2009	13–15 July 2010
Bodhi Day (Rohatsu)	8 December 2009	8 December 2010
Catholic		
Mary Mother of God	1 January 2009	1 January 2010
Blessing of the Animals (Hispanic)	17 January 2009	17 January 2010
Corpus Christi	14 June 2009	3 June 2010
Sacred Heart of Jesus	19 June 2009	11 June 2010
St Benedict Day	11 July 2009	11 July 2010
Assumption of Blessed Virgin Mary	15 August 2009	15 August 2010
St Francis' Day	4 October 2009	4 October 2010
All Souls' Day	2 November 2009	2 November 2010
Immaculate Conception of Mary	8 December 2009	8 December 2010

Appendix 4: Religious Dates/Events

Feast Day—Our Lady of Guadalupe	12 December 2009	12 December 2010
Feast of the Holy Family	27 December 2009	26 December 2010

Chinese

Lunar New Year	26 January 2009	14 February 2010

Christian

Twelfth Night	5 January 2009	5 January 2010
Epiphany	6 January 2009	6 January 2010
Shrove Tuesday	24 February 2009	16 February 2010
Ash Wednesday (Lent begins)	25 February 2009	17 February 2010
St David's Day	1 March 2009	1 March 2010
St Patrick's Day	17 March 2009	17 March 2010
Palm Sunday	5 April 2009	28 March 2010
Maundy Thursday	9 April 2009	1 April 2010
Good Friday	10 April 2009	2 April 2010
Easter Day	12 April 2009	4 April 2010
St George's Day	23 April 2009	23 April 2010
Ascension Day	21 May 2009	13 May 2010
Whit Sunday (Pentecost)	31 May 2009	23 May 2010
Trinity Sunday	7 June 2009	30 May 2010
Lammas	1 August 2009	1 August 2010
All Hallows Eve	31 October 2009	31 October 2010
Advent Sunday	29 November 2009	28 November 2010
St Andrew's Day	30 November 2009	30 November 2010
Christmas Day	25 December 2009	25 December 2010

Hindu

Vasant Panchami (Saraswati's Day)	3 January 2009	20 January 2010
Maha Shivaratri	23 February 2009	12 February 2010
Holi	11 March 2009	1 March 2010
New Year	27 March 2009	16 March 2010
Ramayana Begins	27 March 2009	16 March 2010
Ramanavami	3 April 2009	24 March 2010
Hanuman Jayanti	9 April 2009	30 March 2010
Guru Purnima	7 July 2009	25 July 2010
Raksha Bandhan	5 August 2009	24 August 2010
Krishna Janmashtami	14 August 2009	2 September 2010
Ganesa Chaturthi	23 August 2009	11 September 2010
Navaratri first Day	19 September 2009	8 October 2010
Navaratri Ends	27 September 2009	16 October 2010
Dasera	28 September 2009	17 October 2010
Diwali (Deepavali)	17 October 2009	5 November 2010

Islam

Day of Ashura	7 January 2009	16 December 2010
Mawlid-al-Nabi (Birth of Prophet)	9 March 2009	26 February 2010

Lailat Al-Isra wa Al-Miraj (Ascension to Heaven)	19 July 2009	10 July 2010
Lailat al Bara'ah (Night of Emancipation)	5 August 2009	26 July 2010
Commencement of Ramadhan (Fasting)	21 August 2009	11 August 2010
Laylat al-Qadr	15 September 2009	6 September 2010
Eid Al-Fitr (Completion of Fasting)	20 September 2009	10 September 2010
Waqf al Arafa (Hajj—Pilgrimage Day)	26 November 2009	15 November 2010
Eid-al-Addha (Day of Sacrifice)	27 November 2009	16 November 2010
Muharram (Islamic New Year)	18 December 2009	7 December 2010

Jehovah's Witness

Lord's Evening Meal	8 April 2009	30 March 2010

Jewish

Notes: All Jewish holidays commence/start on the evening before the actual date specified, as the Jewish day actually begins at sunset on the previous night.

Rosh Chodesh Sh'vat	25 January 2009	16 January 2010
Tu B'Shvat	9 February 2009	30 January 2010
Shabbat Shekalim	21 February 2009	13 February 2010
Rosh Chodesh Adar	24 February 2009	14 February 2010
Shabbat Zachor	7 March 2009	27 February 2010
Ta'anit Esther	9 March 2009	26 February 2010
Purim	10 March 2009	28 February 2010
Shushan Purim	11 March 2009	29 February 2010
Shabbat Parah	14 March 2009	6 March 2010
Shabbat HaChodesh	21 March 2009	13 March 2010
Rosh Chodesh Nisan	26 March 2009	16 March 2010
Shabbat HaGadol	3 April 2009	27 March 2010
Ta'anit Bechorot	8 April 2009	30 March 2010
Pesach	9 April 2009	30 March 2010
Yom HaShoah	21 April 2009	11 April 2010
Rosh Chodesh Iyyar	23 April 2009	14 April 2010
Yom HaAtzma'ut	29 April 2009	20 April 2010
Yom HaZikaron	28 April 2009	19 April 2010
Lag B'Omer	12 May 2009	2 May 2010
Yom Yerushalayim	21 May 2009	12 May 2010
Rosh Chodesh Sivan	23 May 2009	14 May 2010
Shavuot	29 May 2009	19 May 2010
Rosh Chodesh Tamuz	21 June 2009	12 June 2010
Tzom Tammuz	9 July 2009	29 June 2010
Rosh Chodesh Av	21 July 2009	12 July 2010
Shabbat Hazon	24 July 2009	17 July 2010
Tish'a B'Av	30 July 2009	20 July 2010
Shabbat Nachamu	31 July 2009	24 July 2010

Appendix 4: Religious Dates/Events

Rosh Chodesh Elul	19 August 2009	10 August 2010
Rosh Hashana	19 September 2009	9 September 2010
Tzom Gedaliah	21 September 2009	12 September 2010
Shabbat Shuva	26 September 2009	11 September 2010
Yom Kippur	28 September 2009	18 September 2010
Sukkot	3–9 October 2009	23–29 September 2010
Shmini Atzeret	10 October 2009	30 September 2010
Simchat Torah	11 October 2009	1 October 2010
Rosh Chodesh Cheshvan	17 October 2009	8 October 2010
Rosh Chodesh Kislev	16 November 2009	7 November 2010
Chanukah	12 December 2009	2–9 December 2010

Sikh

Birthday of Guru Gobind Singh Ji	5 January 2009	5 January 2010
Maghi	13 January 2009	14 January 2010
Hola Mohalla	11 March 2009	1 March 2010
Baisakhi (Vaisakhi)	13 April 2009	13 April 2010
Martyrdom of Guru Arjan Dev Ji	16 June 2009	16 June 2010
Diwali (Deepavali)	17 October 2009	5 November 2010
Installation of Scriptures as Guru Granth	20 October 2009	20 October 2010
Birthday of Guru Nanak Dev Ji	2 November 2009	21 November 2010
Martyrdom of Guru Tegh Bahadur Ji	24 November 2009	24 November 2010

Index

Index

Index

Index

Index

Index

Index

Index

Index

Index

Index

Index

Index

Index

Index

Index

Index

Index

Index

Index

Index

Index

Index

Index